Consumer

2001 CARS

All rights reserved under International and Pan American copyright conventions. Copyright © 2001 Publications International, Ltd. This book may not be reproduced or quoted in whole or in part by any means whatsoever without written permission from Louis Weber, CEO of Publications International, Ltd., 7373 North Cicero Avenue, Lincolnwood, Illinois 60712. Permission is never granted for commercial purposes. Printed in U.S.A.

PUBLICATIONS INTERNATIONAL, LTD.

CONTENTS

Introduction	5
Shopper's Guide	6

Buying Guide

Acura CL	10
Acura Integra	12
Acura MDX	15
Acura RL	18
Acura TL	20
Audi A4	22
Audi A6/allroad quattro	25
BMW 3-Series	29
BMW 5-Series	34
BMW 7-Series	38
BMW X5	41
BMW Z3 Series	45
Buick Century	48
Buick LeSabre	51
Buick Park Avenue	55
Buick Regal	58
Cadillac Catera	62
Cadillac DeVille	64
Cadillac Eldorado	68
2002 Cadillac Escalade	70
Cadillac Seville	72
Chevrolet Astro	75
Chevrolet Blazer	78
Chevrolet Camaro	83
Chevrolet Cavalier	87
Chevrolet Corvette	90
Chevrolet Impala	94
Chevrolet Malibu	98
Chevrolet Monte Carlo	100
Chevrolet Prizm	104
Chevrolet Tahoe and Suburban	106
Chevrolet Tracker	111
Chevrolet Venture	114
Chrysler Concorde	118
Chrysler LHS and 300M	120
Chrysler PT Cruiser	123
Chrysler Sebring	127
Chrysler Town & Country and Voyager	131
Dodge Caravan	138
Dodge Durango	145
Dodge Intrepid	148
Dodge/Plymouth Neon	151
Dodge Stratus	155
Ford Crown Victoria	160
Ford Escape	163
Ford Excursion	167
Ford Expedition	170
Ford Explorer	175
2002 Ford Explorer	181
Ford Focus	182
Ford Mustang	186
Ford Taurus	189
Ford Windstar	193
Ford ZX2	198
2002 GMC Envoy	200
GMC Safari	201

GMC Yukon/Denali	204
Honda Accord	209
Honda Civic	212
Honda CR-V	216
Honda Insight	218
Honda Odyssey	220
Honda Passport	223
Honda Prelude	225
Hyundai Accent	226
Hyundai Elantra	229
Hyundai Santa Fe	232
Hyundai Sonata	235
Hyundai Tiburon	238
Hyundai XG300	240
Infiniti G20	243
Infiniti I30	245
Infiniti QX4	248
Isuzu Rodeo	250
Isuzu Rodeo Sport	254
Isuzu Trooper	256
Jaguar S-Type	259
Jaguar XJ Sedan	261
Jaguar XK8	264
Jeep Cherokee	266
Jeep Grand Cherokee	270
Jeep Wrangler	274
Kia Rio	278
Kia Sephia/Spectra	280
Kia Sportage	283
Land Rover Discovery	286
Land Rover Range Rover	289
Lexus ES 300	291
Lexus GS 300/430	294
Lexus IS 300	297
Lexus LS 430	300
Lexus LX 470	303
Lexus RX 300	305
Lincoln Continental	308
Lincoln LS	311
Lincoln Navigator	314
Lincoln Town Car	317
Mazda 626	320
Mazda Miata	323
Mazda Millenia	325
Mazda MPV	327
Mazda Protege	330
Mazda Tribute	333
Mercedes-Benz C-Class	335
Mercedes-Benz CLK	339
Mercedes-Benz E-Class	342
Mercedes-Benz M-Class	345
Mercedes-Benz S-Class/CL-Class	349
Mercury Cougar	353
Mercury Grand Marquis	356
Mercury Mountaineer	359
2002 Mercury Mountaineer	362
Mercury Sable	363
Mercury Villager	366

CONSUMER GUIDE

Mitsubishi Diamante 370
Mitsubishi Eclipse 371
Mitsubishi Galant 375
Mitsubishi Montero 377
Mitsubishi Montero Sport 379
Nissan Altima 382
Nissan Maxima 386
Nissan Pathfinder 389
Nissan Quest 393
Nissan Sentra 395
Nissan Xterra 399
Oldsmobile Alero 402
Oldsmobile Aurora 405
2002 Oldsmobile Bravada 408
Oldsmobile Intrigue 410
Oldsmobile Silhouette 413
Pontiac Aztek 415
Pontiac Bonneville 419
Pontiac Firebird 423
Pontiac Grand Am 426
Pontiac Grand Prix 429
Pontiac Montana 433
Pontiac Sunfire 437
Saab 9-3 440
Saab 9-5 442
Saturn L-Series 445
Saturn S-Series 448
Subaru Forester 452

Subaru Impreza 455
Subaru Legacy 458
Subaru Outback 461
Suzuki Esteem/ Swift 465
Suzuki Vitara 468
Toyota 4Runner 471
Toyota Avalon 474
Toyota Camry/ Solara 478
Toyota Celica 483
Toyota Corolla 486
Toyota Echo 489
Toyota Highlander 492
Toyota Land Cruiser 493
Toyota Prius 496
Toyota RAV4 499
Toyota Sequoia 501
Toyota Sienna 503
Volkswagen Cabrio 507
Volkswagen Jetta/ Golf 509
Volkswagen New Beetle 513
Volkswagen Passat 517
Volvo 40 Series 520
Volvo C70 523
Volvo S60 526
Volvo S80 527
Volvo V70 530

Specifications 535

INTRODUCTION

2001 Cars reports on more than 175 passenger cars, minivans, and sport-utility vehicles that are on sale or will be in the next few months. Major changes for this year, key features, and latest available prices are included for each model. To help readers compare direct competitors, we divide vehicles into 13 model groups based on their size, price, and market position. Each report lists the model group that vehicle belongs to, notes similar vehicles built from the same design, and suggests alternative choices from within the model group. Specifications for each vehicle are arranged by model group in charts that begin on **page 535**.

Best Buy and Recommended Choices

The Auto Editors of Consumer Guide have selected Best Buys as the best overall values in their respective model categories. This is our highest rating. Other models labeled Recommended also merit serious consideration. This is our second-highest rating.

Specifications

Engine specifications are included along with the vehicle report. Here's an explanation of our abbreviations:

All available engines, standard **(S)** or optional **(O)**. **Size, liters/cu. in.:** engine displacement in liters and cubic inches. **ohv:** overhead valve. **ohc:** overhead camshaft. **dohc:** dual overhead camshafts. **I:** inline arrangement of cylinders. **V:** cylinders in a V configuration. **H:** horizontally opposed cylinders. **I4/electric:** "hybrid" with both a gas engine and an electric motor. **rpm:** revolutions per minute. **CVT:** continuously variable (automatic) transmission. **NA** = not available. *This information is supplied by the manufacturers.*

Other specifications, such as wheelbase, overall length, and interior dimensions are in charts that begin on page 535. All dimensions and capacities are supplied by the vehicle manufacturers and represent the base model in the line. Optional equipment usually increases curb weight, and such items as larger tires or a roof rack may increase overall height.

Price Information

• Retail price: the manufacturer's suggested retail price as set by the factory. "Suggested" is the key word here. The actual selling price is dictated by supply, demand, and competition.

• Invoice price: what the dealer pays to buy the car from the factory—the wholesale price.

INTRODUCTION

• Destination charge: the cost of shipping the car to the dealership from the factory or port of entry.

• Note that the optional equipment section of some price lists includes a *Manufacturer's discount price*. This is the price of the option after the manufacturer's discount is calculated.

When a manufacturer offers such a discount, the vehicle's window sticker typically will show the full retail price of the option. The discounted amount typically will be displayed within a separate section on the window sticker. Regardless of how the discounted amount is represented on the window sticker, the *Manufacturer's discount price* is the actual price being charged for the option.

Car companies are free to change their prices at any time, and may have done so after this issue was published. If a dealer claims our prices are incorrect, or the information in this book doesn't match what you see in showrooms, contact us and we'll do our best to help. Good luck in shopping for your next new vehicle!

Consumer Guide
7373 N. Cicero Ave.
Lincolnwood, IL 60712

SHOPPER'S GUIDE

Before you venture out to test drive and compare the new models, here are some suggestions to get you started on the right road:

• Determine how much you are willing to pay—or can afford to pay. If you plan to buy (instead of lease) shop for a loan at a bank or other lending institution before you shop for a car. It's better to figure out how much you can afford at a bank than in a dealer's showroom, where they can juggle numbers faster than you can count.

• Decide which vehicle or type of vehicle best suits your needs and pocketbook. Narrow the field to three or four choices.

Showroom Strategies

If you intend to buy a new vehicle instead of lease, remember:

• There are no formulas for calculating a "good deal." You can't just "knock 10 percent off the sticker." It depends on supply and demand for a particular model in your area and on competition among dealers.

• Don't tell a car salesperson how much you're willing to pay. Your price might be higher than what others are paying, and you may be forfeiting your chance to get a lower price. Remember, it's the dealer's job to price the products they sell. It's your privilege to reject their price.

SHOPPER'S GUIDE

- Once you've settled on which vehicle you want to buy, shop at least three dealers to compare prices on the same model with the same equipment. Let each dealer know you're comparison shopping and that you'll buy from the dealer with the lowest price and best service.
- Get written price quotes that are good next week, not just today. A dealer won't give you a price in writing? Shop elsewhere. A salesperson who offers you a verbal quote "good for today only" is not being honest.
- Take your time and think about the deal at home. Don't be pressured into making a snap decision in the showroom.
- Don't put a deposit on a car just to get a price quote or a test drive. Dealers want a deposit because then you've made a commitment to them, and you're less likely to keep shopping.
- Don't shop for a monthly payment. Dealers will try to convince you to buy a car you can't afford by stretching the payments from 48 months to 60 months. That lowers your monthly payment, but it means you'll pay more interest and be in debt longer. For example, if you borrow $15,000 for 48 months at 8 percent interest, you'll pay $366 per month, or $17,568 in total. If you borrow $15,000 for 60 months you'll likely pay a higher interest rate, say, 8.5 percent. Your monthly payment drops to $308.25, but you'll pay $18,495 over the 5-year life of the loan. That's $927 more in interest than you'll pay on a 4-year loan.
- Keep your trade-in out of the new-car price. If you're thinking about trading in your old vehicle, get a written trade-in value after you settle on a price for the new car. When the dealer asks if you're trading in your old car, respond that you haven't decided yet. Some dealers try to tempt you with the offer of a high trade-in allowance, then inflate the price of the new vehicle. Concentrate on the price of the new car before you talk trade-in value.

Window Stickers

All cars sold in the U.S. must have posted on a side window what is called a "Monroney sticker" (named for the Congressman who introduced the legislation). This law does not apply to light trucks, including passenger vans and most sport-utility vehicles, but most car companies and dealers voluntarily put the price sticker on trucks. You decide if you want to do business with one that doesn't.

The Monroney sticker must show:
- The manufacturer's suggested retail price (MSRP) for the vehicle and all factory-installed options.
- A destination charge for shipping from final assembly point or port of importation to the dealer.
- EPA fuel economy estimates.

SHOPPER'S GUIDE
Dealer Price Stickers
Many dealers add a second window sticker that lists accessories installed at the dealership, and/or other charges. Everything on this added sticker should be considered "optional"—and probably overpriced. If you don't want a particular item—say, pinstriping or rustproofing—don't pay for it, even if it's already on the car.

Such add-on stickers typically include:
- Rustproofing: Most manufacturers advise against extra-cost rustproofing.
- Protection packages: These usually consist of dealer-applied paint sealers and fabric protectors, often in addition to rustproofing. They are of little or no value or duplicate the substances applied at the factory or those you can apply yourself for far less cost.
- M.V.A., A.D.P., or another abbreviation or code: These are smoke screens for dealer-invented profit-generators. M.V.A. stands for "Market Value Adjustment," and A.D.P. is "Additional Dealer Profit." Both sound official but are created by dealers to squeeze more money out of you. Some dealers dream up dandy new names for old add-on charges, such as "Currency Valuation Fee" and "Import Tariff." Those that do are best avoided.

Rather than arguing over individual charges like dealer prep, take the "bottom line" approach. Simply ask for a final price—the total amount you'll have to pay—and compare it to the price offered by competing dealers.

Lease Instead of Buy?
Leasing has become a popular alternative to buying, accounting for an estimated 30 percent of new-car sales and more than 50 percent of transaction on vehicles costing $30,000 or more.

Here are some guidelines to help you decide whether to lease or buy:
• When you buy a car, banks typically want a down payment of at least 20 percent. That requires $4000 in cash or trade-in value on a $20,000 vehicle. If you don't have that much, leasing might be a good deal because a large down payment isn't needed to lease. However, most leases require a substantial initial payment (usually called a "capital cost reduction"). Another plus is that monthly lease payments are generally lower than the monthly loan payment for an equivalent car.

• The major disadvantage to leasing is that unless you eventually buy a car, you'll always be making a monthly payment. At the end of a lease you have the option of returning the vehicle to the leasing company or buying it. Either way, you're going to have to dig into your pocket again to have a car. Think ahead two or three years. Will your financial situation allow you to lease another new car or to take out a loan to buy one?

SHOPPER'S GUIDE

• While the monthly payments may be lower on a lease, in the long run it is usually cheaper to buy if you keep cars five years or longer. For example, if you pay off a car loan in four years and keep the car another three years, your only expenses once the car is paid for will be for maintenance, repairs, and insurance.

• On the other hand, would you rather drive a 7-year-old car or a much newer one? A 2- or 3-year lease gives you the option of having a new car more often. The car you lease will probably always be under warranty and you don't have the hassle of selling or trading in an old car. After two or three years, you simply turn it in to the leasing agent.

• Leasing generally is less expensive than buying for those who claim their car as a business expense. You can write off more of the expense of a leased vehicle than one that is purchased and tie up less capital.

How do you find out if leasing is for you? Talk to your accountant or financial adviser—not the guy next door. Because everyone has a different situation, leasing can be a great deal for your next-door neighbor but of no real benefit to you.

Read the Fine Print on Leases

Here's where leasing gets tricky. If you're enticed by leasing ads that tout "No money down, $299 a month" for a $25,000 car, read the fine print. It should explain some of the following:

• Most leases allow you to put 10,000 to 12,000 miles per year on the vehicle. Exceed the mileage limit and you'll pay a penalty of 10 to 15 cents a mile. A higher mileage limit can usually be negotiated.

• On most leases, you have to pay up front the first month's payment and a refundable security deposit.

• Some states require that the lessee—that's you—pay sales tax on the full suggested retail price of the car. If the sales tax is 8 percent in your area and you're leasing a $30,000 car, that's $2400 you have to pay. You usually have the option of rolling the sales tax into your monthly payment. In addition, if you purchase the car at the end of the lease, you may have to pay sales tax on that amount. Check your local tax laws.

• You'll also probably have to pay an "acquisition fee" when you sign the lease and may be hit with a "disposition fee" when you return it at the end. The amount is usually $250 to $500.

• Early termination and purchase options: Before signing, learn whether you can terminate the lease early and how much of a penalty you must pay. It might cost hundreds of dollars to terminate early.

• End-of-lease costs: You'll be liable for "excessive wear" or may be charged for having the car prepped for resale. It pays to take good care of a leased car so it passes inspection when you turn it in.

ACURA

ACURA CL

Acura CL S-Type

Front-wheel-drive near-luxury car; similar to Acura TL and Honda Accord

Base price range: $27,980-$30,330. Built in USA. **Also consider:** BMW 3-Series, Toyota Solara, Volvo C70

FOR • Acceleration • Steering/handling • Build quality **AGAINST** • Navigation system controls • Rear-seat entry/exit • Rear-seat head room

Arriving in spring 2000 as an early '01 model, this near-luxury coupe continues the general look and 4-seat format of its 1997-99 predecessor in a slightly larger, heavier package based on the platform of Acura's near-luxury TL sedan and parent Honda's family Accord. The base CL uses the TL's 225-horsepower 3.2-liter V6; a 260-hp version is exclusive to a new performance-oriented CL Type S model. Like the TL, the only transmission for both coupes is a 5-speed automatic with manual-shift gate. The previous CL offered manual shift with a 4-cylinder engine, plus a 200-hp 3.0 V6 and 4-speed automatic.

Against that earlier CL, the new one is a half-inch longer in wheelbase and 2 inches longer overall, has 2 inches more rear leg room, and is about 200 pounds heavier. Front side airbags and antilock 4-wheel disc brakes are standard. So are alloy wheels, but the Type S comes with 17-inchers instead of 16s, plus handling-oriented suspension tuning. Traction control is standard; the Type S adds an antiskid system.

Like the TL, CLs have numerous other standard features, including heated power front seats, leather upholstery, Xenon headlamps, power sunroof, automatic climate control, heated mirrors, and 6-disc in-dash CD changer. The only factory option is a satellite navigation system with in-dash touch screen. Also shared with the TL and Acura's luxury RL sedan is a sensor system designed to disable the front passenger's airbags if it detects a child or out-of-position occupant.

PERFORMANCE CL means "contemporary luxury," and while the '01

Specifications begin on page 535.

ACURA

maintains solid near-luxury credentials, it's noticeably sportier than previous models. We haven't clocked a base CL, but our Type S ran 0-60 mph in just 6.7 seconds and showed equally strong highway passing power. Add quick steering, fine grip and cornering balance, and a stable high-speed ride, and the Type S rivals most any competitor for dynamic ability, including the vaunted BMW 3-Series. The base model, expected to account for about 60 percent of sales, is a shade tamer overall, but still boasts sure acceleration and confident road manners. The automatic transmission in either model can be slightly indecisive in mountain driving and light-throttle cruising, though it shifts promptly and without jolting. Both CLs require premium gas. Our Type S test cars averaged 19.5-23 mpg. The base model may do a bit better.

Either CL is taut but comfortable over broken surfaces, though lower-profile tires and firmer suspension make the S jiggle a bit on washboards and expansion joints. Tire noise intrudes only on really coarse pavement. There's little wind noise, and engines make a pleasant muted snarl under hard throttle. Braking is swift, straight, and easy to modulate; our simulated panic stops showed little nosedive.

ACCOMMODATIONS Carefully assembled from classy materials, the CL cabin is rare among coupes for being airy and, at least in front, roomy. Thin roof pillars and Honda's typical low-cowl dashboard provide terrific visibility. The front bucket seats are comfortable, and there's plenty of leg and shoulder space; only the very tall will lack for head room. In back is bucket-type seating for two only, and only preteens will want to ride there for long. Front entry/exit is no problem, but rear access is typical coupe crouch-and-crawl despite front seats that power forward on tipping the backrests.

The CL uses the well-designed TL dashboard, which means standard climate controls are a stretch for those with shorter arms. The optional navigation system absorbs some climate and audio functions, which complicates their operation, and its touch screen doesn't always respond right away if the car's been sitting in very hot weather. Some functions can also be controlled by a joystick that we found fiddly to use. Lack of height-adjustable outboard shoulder-belt anchorages is surprising at the price, and we'd exchange the foot-pedal parking brake for the pull-up lever expected in sporty cars.

Interior storage is good, but the dual front and rear cupholders aren't deep enough to secure anything larger than a 12-ounce soda can. The roomy trunk features a knee-high liftover and a pass-through portal, but fold-down seatbacks are not available and sickle-shaped hinges steal cargo space.

VALUE The previous CL seemed little more than a restyled 2-door Honda Accord, but the new one has a sportier personality that should satisfy demanding drivers. Being an Acura, it's also very well-equipped, and makes few concessions to pricier European coupes in performance,

Prices are accurate at time of publication; subject to manufacturer's change.

ACURA

comfort, and quality.

ENGINES

	ohc V6	ohc V6
Size, liters/cu. in.	3.2/196	3.2/196
Horsepower @ rpm	225 @ 5600	260 @ 6100
Torque (lb-ft) @ rpm	217 @ 4700	232 @ 3500
Availability	S[1]	S[2]
EPA city/highway mpg		
5-speed OD automatic	19/29	19/29

1. Base model. 2. Type S.

PRICES

Acura CL	Retail Price	Dealer Invoice
3.2CL 2-door coupe	$27980	$25508
Type S 2-door coupe	30330	27648
Destination charge	480	480

STANDARD EQUIPMENT:

3.2CL: 3.2-liter V6 225-horsepower engine, 5-speed automatic transmission w/manual-shift capability, traction control, dual front airbags, front side-impact airbags, antilock 4-wheel disc brakes, air conditioning w/automatic climate control, interior air filter, variable-assist power steering, leather-wrapped tilt steering wheel, cruise control, leather upholstery, heated front bucket seats, 8-way power driver seat w/lumbar adjustment, 4-way power passenger seat, center console, cupholders, rear bucket seats w/trunk pass-through, memory driver seat and mirrors, heated power mirrors w/passenger-side tilt-down back-up aid, power windows, power door locks, remote keyless entry, Bose AM/FM/cassette w/6-disc CD changer, steering wheel radio controls, automatic day/night rearview mirror, rear defogger, power sunroof, variable intermittent wipers, illuminated visor mirrors, universal garage door opener, map lights, auxiliary power outlets, automatic-off headlights, floormats, theft-deterrent system, Xenon headlights, fog lights, 205/60VR16 tires, alloy wheels.

Type S adds: 3.2-liter V6 260-horsepower engine, antiskid system, sport suspension, 215/50VR17 tires.

OPTIONAL EQUIPMENT:
Comfort and Convenience

Navigation system	2000	1822

ACURA INTEGRA

Front-wheel-drive sports coupe

Base price range: NA. Built in Japan. **Also consider:** Honda Prelude, Mitsubishi Eclipse, Toyota Celica

Specifications begin on page 535.

ACURA

Acura Integra 2-door coupe

FOR • Fuel economy • Steering/handling • Acceleration (manual transmission) • Exterior finish **AGAINST** • Rear-seat room • Road noise • Acceleration (automatic transmission)

An emergency in-trunk opener and standard carpeted floormats are the only changes for Acura's entry-level 2001 models. The current Integra is derived from the previous Honda Civic, but the redesigned '01 Civic platform will support new 2002 Integras that may be badged Acura RS. Meantime, the vintage-1994 design puts in a final appearance with LS, GS, and sporty GS-R hatchback coupes and 4-door sedans, plus a limited-edition high-performance Type R coupe. All use 1.8-liter 4-cylinder engines. LS and GS models have 140 horsepower, GS-Rs 170, the Type R 195. Manual transmission is standard, with automatic optional only for LS and GS.

EVALUATION Integras are great fun to drive, but engine and tire noise intrude at highway speeds, and there's not enough low-speed torque to pull the automatic transmission with much gusto. Manual-shift models are quick and frugal. Our test LS did 0-60 mph in 8.3 seconds and averaged 25 mpg; a GS-R did 7.6 and 28.3 mpg. Automatic models are slower and a bit thirstier. The sedan's ride is controlled and comfortable, but the shorter, lighter coupes react abruptly to some bumps, especially the GS-Rs and the even stiffer Type R. Front-seat room is fine, but rear-seat space is tight, especially in coupes. Sedans have small but useable trunks. The coupes' hatchback layout is a plus for versatility, but brings an awkwardly high liftover. The driving position is low but comfortable, the dashboard simple and handy. Outward visibility is good, despite being slightly restricted aft in coupes. Build quality is first-rate, though some interior plastics aren't that classy. Though Integra is overdue for a redesign, it remains an appealing premium small car that offsets relatively high prices with fine reliability and resale value. Coupes far outsell the sedans and rate as solid, if aging, choices among today's sporty compacts.

Prices are accurate at time of publication; subject to manufacturer's change.

ACURA

ENGINES

	dohc I4	dohc I4	dohc I4
Size, liters/cu. in.	1.8/112	1.8/110	1.8/110
Horsepower @ rpm	140 @ 6300	170 @ 7600	195 @ 8000
Torque (lb-ft) @ rpm	124 @ 5200	128 @ 6200	130 @ 7500
Availability	S[1]	S[2]	S[3]
EPA city/highway mpg			
5-speed OD manual	25/31	25/31	25/31
4-speed OD automatic	24/31		

1. LS, GS. 2. GS-R. 3. Type R.

2001 prices unavailable at time of publication.

PRICES

2000 Acura Integra	Retail Price	Dealer Invoice
LS 2-door hatchback, 5-speed	$19300	$17403
LS 2-door hatchback, automatic	20100	18123
LS 4-door sedan, 5-speed	20100	18123
LS 4-door sedan, automatic	20900	18843
GS 2-door hatchback, 5-speed	20950	18888
GS 2-door hatchback, automatic	21750	19608
GS 4-door sedan, 5-speed	21500	19384
GS 4-door sedan, automatic	22300	20104
GS-R 2-door hatchback, 5-speed	22200	20014
GS-R 4-door sedan, 5-speed	22500	20284
Type R 2-door hatchback, 5-speed	24350	21950
Destination charge	480	480

STANDARD EQUIPMENT:

LS: 1.8-liter dohc 140-horsepower 4-cylinder engine, 5-speed manual or 4-speed automatic transmission, driver- and passenger-side airbags, antilock 4-wheel disc brakes, air conditioning, variable-assist power steering, tilt steering wheel, leather-wrapped steering wheel and shift knob, cruise control, cloth upholstery, front bucket seats w/driver-side height and lumbar adjustment, center console w/armrest, split folding rear seat (hatchback), one-piece folding rear seat (sedan), cupholders, power sunroof, map lights, power mirrors, power windows, power door locks, tachometer, AM/FM/CD player w/six speakers, power antenna (hatchback), digital clock, remote fuel-door and decklid/hatch releases, rear defogger, rear wiper/washer (hatchback), intermittent wipers, visor mirrors, cargo cover (hatchback), theft-deterrent system, 195/55VR15 tires, alloy wheels.

GS adds: leather upholstery, rear spoiler (hatchback).

GS-R adds: 1.8-liter dohc VTEC 170-horsepower engine, wood-grain console (sedan).

Type R adds: 1.8-liter dohc VTEC 195-horsepower engine, limited-slip dif-

Specifications begin on page 535.

ACURA

ferential, upgraded brakes, sport seats, titanium shift knob, dashboard serial number plate, bodyside cladding, sport suspension.

Options are available as dealer-installed accessories.

ACURA MDX

Acura MDX

4-wheel-drive midsize sport-utility vehicle
Base price: $34,370-$38,970. Built in Canada. **Also consider:** BMW X5, Lexus RX 300, Mercedes-Benz M-Class

FOR • Passenger and cargo room **AGAINST** • Climate controls • Fuel economy • Navigation system controls

The first sport-utility designed and built by Honda's upscale division takes aim at the popular Lexus RX 300 and other car-based SUVs. Based on the Honda Odyssey minivan platform, the MDX ("Multi Dimensional Luxury") is about 5 inches longer than a BMW X5 and 8.5 inches longer than a Lexus RX, both of which seat five passengers. MDX seats seven and includes among its standard features leather upholstery, heated power front buckets, power sunroof, and 17-inch alloy wheels.

The sole engine is a more powerful version of Odyssey's 3.5-liter V6 linked to a 5-speed automatic transmission instead of a 4-speed. Standard is Acura's Variable Torque Management or "VTM-4" 4-wheel drive, which normally powers the front wheels but is designed to sense impending wheel slip and direct up to 52 percent of the power to the rear wheels. A rear-wheel locking device kicks in for maximum traction below 6 mph. Towing ratings are 3500 pounds for trailers and 4500 pounds for boats.

MDX has standard 7-passenger seating with second- and third-row bench seats. Both benches fold flat with the rear cargo floor, and both are split so the sections can stow individually to suit passenger/cargo loads. Other standard features include front side airbags, antilock 4-wheel disc brakes, rear air conditioning, heated mirrors, and CD play-

Prices are accurate at time of publication; subject to manufacturer's change.
CONSUMER GUIDE

ACURA

er. The Touring model includes driver's seat/mirror memory and a 6-disc in-dash CD changer. Also available is a navigation system with dashboard screen.

PERFORMANCE MDX presents a highly competent and pleasing compromise, feeling lighter on its feet than a Mercedes ML, if not quite as athletic as a V8 X5. Road manners are carlike and even sporty at reasonable cornering speeds. The suspension is quite firm and though it's not jolting over most bumps, you'll feel most every surface imperfection. Body lean isn't excessive, particularly by SUV standards.

Acura's 3.5 V6 is pulling a lot of weight here, which makes it feel weaker than its power rating implies. Even so, acceleration is lively enough for most situations, aided by the transmission's smooth, prompt downshifts. In our brief preview drives, we did not have an opportunity to measure fuel economy, but Acura estimates 17 mpg city, 23 mpg highway.

The brakes have good stopping power, with easy pedal modulation. The engine is hushed at idle, refined under hard acceleration. Tire noise is noticeable on all but smooth pavement, however, and there's considerable wind rush at highway speed.

ACCOMMODATIONS MDX's cabin eschews opulence for a comfortably upscale, contemporary feel. All but the very tallest front passengers have good head and leg room in comfortable, supportive seats. Side bolstering is adequate even for spirited performance work. It complements an efficient driving position whose only significant fault is an awkwardly shaped left-foot dead pedal.

Passengers in the second-row seat have similarly generous head room, with knee room enough for six-footers. It's also comfortable and is wide enough for 3-across adult seating, although shoulders will likely rub. MDX's third-row seat is too small and hard to get into and out of for anything but children and emergency adult use. It is nonetheless a value-enhancing standard feature that's optional on most rivals.

Step-in isn't carlike, but it's lower than many midsize SUVs. However, the rear side door bottoms are narrow—as on most wagons—and getting to the third-row seat means a tight squeeze between the second-row seat and the doorjamb. Helping matters is the handy one-lever tip-slide for the second-row seat's left-side portion. Unfortunately, the driver's side section lacks this feature, thus limiting entry/exit options. The flush-folding second- and third-row seats have simple one-lever latches and are easy to stow for cargo hauling. Headrests have to be removed before folding the third row, which adds a step to the process, but at least there's a handy covered bin with mounting holes to prevent the headrests from flopping about the cabin.

The dashboard layout is mostly clear, logical, and handy. The automatic climate system's controls are high in the center of the dashboard

Specifications begin on page 535.

ACURA

and don't require an attention-diverting downward look, but they're a far reach for some drivers and their indicator lights and temperature display wash out in bright sunlight. MDX's optional navigation system is more complicated and distracting than we like. Headrests intrude into some sightlines to the rear but outward visibility is otherwise good.

Typical of Acuras, MDXs we tested had consistent panel gaps inside and out, glossy paint, and rich interior materials. A minor rattle from one test model's driver's door was the only assembly flaw we noticed.

VALUE Although a late-comer to the SUV market, Acura has clearly done its homework. MDX is competent, comfortable, and convenient—a must-see for near-luxury SUV shoppers. Even at near-$35,000 to start, overall refinement and generous standard equipment make MDX a fine value. Expect to pay every penny of sticker price until supply catches up with demand.

ENGINES

	ohc V6
Size, liters/cu. in.	3.5/212
Horsepower @ rpm	240 @ 5300
Torque (lb-ft) @ rpm	245 @ 3000
Availability	S

EPA city/highway mpg

5-speed OD automatic	17/23

PRICES

Acura MDX	Retail Price	Dealer Invoice
Base 4-door wagon	$34370	$30621
Base w/navigation system 4-door wagon	36370	32401
Touring 4-door wagon	36970	32935
Touring w/navigation system 4-door wagon	38970	34715
Destination charge:	480	480

STANDARD EQUIPMENT:

Base: 3.5-liter V6 engine, 5-speed automatic transmission, full-time 4-wheel drive, dual front airbags, front side-impact airbags, antilock 4-wheel disc brakes, air conditioning w/front and rear automatic climate controls, variable-assist power steering, tilt leather-wrapped steering w/radio controls, cruise control, leather upholstery, 7-passenger seating, heated front bucket seats, 8-way power driver seat, center console, cupholders, second and third row split-folding bench seats, heated power mirrors, power windows, power door locks, remote keyless entry, AM/FM/cassette/CD player, digital clock, power sunroof, illuminated visor mirrors, universal garage door opener, automatic day/night rearview mirror, trip computer, map lights, rear defogger, rear wiper/washer, auxiliary power outlet, auto-

Prices are accurate at time of publication; subject to manufacturer's change.

ACURA

matic-off headlights, floormats, theft-deterrent system, rear privacy glass, fog lights, 235/65R17 tires, alloy wheels.

Touring adds: 8-way power passenger seat, memory system for driver seat and mirrors, tilt-down passenger-side mirror back-up aid, Bose AM/FM/cassette w/in-dash 6-disc CD changer, roof rack.

Options available as dealer-installed accessories.

ACURA RL

Acura RL

Front-wheel-drive luxury car

Base price range: NA. Built in Japan. **Also consider:** BMW 5-Series, Lexus GS 300/430, Mercedes-Benz E-Class

FOR • Acceleration • Steering/handling • Ride • Build quality
AGAINST • Navigation system controls • Steering feel

Honda's luxury-brand flagship sedan gets an in-trunk emergency opener and standard carpeted floormats as its only changes for 2001. The 3.5RL continues with a 3.5-liter V6, automatic transmission, side airbags, antilock 4-wheel-disc brakes, Acura's antiskid Vehicle Stability Assist (VSA) with traction control, heated front seats, and high-intensity headlamps. The only major factory option is a satellite-linked navigation system with in-dash touch screen and a digital video disc (DVD) database covering the entire continental U.S. Also standard is a sensor system that deactivates the passenger-side airbags if a child or out-of-position occupant is detected and triggers the dashboard airbag at normal or reduced force as needed.

EVALUATION Though it lacks the punch of most V8 rivals, the RL is no slouch at 8.0 seconds 0-60 mph by our stopwatch. It also gets slightly better fuel economy than the class norm—17.3 mpg in our tests on the required premium gas—despite having a 4-speed automatic to many competitors' 5-speed. The RL otherwise behaves as a luxury car should, exhibiting a firm yet supple ride, shudder-free

Specifications begin on page 535.

ACURA

solidity, and low noise levels. It's also one of the more agile big sedans, though that's spoiled a bit by slightly numb steering. The standard VSA/traction control is a safety plus, especially in foul weather, as is the "smart" right front airbag system. RL offers plenty of room for four adults, comfortable seats, and an easily tailored driving position. Controls are simple and intuitive, although the navigation system requires a little practice. RL is a solid Best Buy, and you should be able to work a good deal on a car that's often overlooked despite its many virtues.

ENGINES

	ohc V6
Size, liters/cu. in.	3.5/212
Horsepower @ rpm	210 @ 5200
Torque (lb-ft) @ rpm	224 @ 2800
Availability	S

EPA city/highway mpg

4-speed OD automatic	18/24

2001 prices unavailable at time of publication.

PRICES

2000 Acura RL	Retail Price	Dealer Invoice
Base 4-door sedan	$42000	$36972
Base w/Navigation System 4-door sedan	44000	38732
Destination charge	480	480

STANDARD EQUIPMENT:

Base: 3.5-liter V6 engine, 4-speed automatic transmission, traction control, dual front airbags, front side-impact airbags, antilock 4-wheel disc brakes, antiskid system, air conditioning w/front and rear automatic climate controls, interior air filter, variable-assist power steering, power tilt/telescopic steering wheel w/memory, leather-wrapped steering wheel and shifter, cruise control, leather upholstery, heated front seats, 8-way power driver seat w/memory and lumbar support, 4-way power passenger seat, center console, cupholders, rear-seat trunk pass-through, wood interior trim, power sunroof, heated power mirrors w/memory, power windows, power door locks, remote keyless entry, Bose AM/FM/cassette, 6-disc CD changer, digital clock, tachometer, rear defogger, automatic day/night rearview mirror, remote fuel-door and decklid releases, variable intermittent wipers, illuminated visor mirrors, map lights, auxiliary power outlets, universal garage door opener, theft-deterrent system, Xenon headlights, fog lights, 215/60VR16 tires, alloy wheels.

Base w/Navigation System adds: Global Positioning/Navigation System.

Options are available as dealer-installed accessories.

Prices are accurate at time of publication; subject to manufacturer's change.

ACURA

ACURA TL

Acura TL

Front-wheel-drive near-luxury car; similar to Acura CL and Honda Accord

Base price range: $28,550-$30,550. Built in USA. **Also consider:** Audi A4, BMW 3-Series, Infiniti I30, Lexus ES 300

FOR • Acceleration • Build quality • Exterior finish • Interior materials • Steering/handling **AGAINST** • Navigation system controls

The best-seller of Honda's upscale division stands pat for 2001, adding only an in-trunk emergency opener and standard carpeted floormats. The TL shares its platform with Honda Accord models and Acura's redesigned CL coupe; all are built in America. This sedan again comes in one well equipped model featuring a 225-horsepower V6, 5-speed automatic transmission with Acura's Sportshift manual shift gate, antilock 4-wheel disc brakes, traction control, side air bags, leather upholstery, heated front seats, power moonroof, and high-intensity headlamps. The sole factory option is an in-dash navigation system with nationwide DVD database. Like the CL and Acura's premium RL sedan, the TL also includes "smart" right front airbags that deactivate when a sensor system detects a child or out-of-position occupant; this data also determines whether the dashboard airbag deploys with normal or reduced force.

PERFORMANCE Quick, quiet, and composed, the TL is a very polished performer. The 5-speed automatic transmission makes for more relaxed cruising than many rivals' 4-speed and also subtly improves acceleration. We haven't tested the latest TL, but it should run 0-60 mph in about 7 seconds flat based on our 1999-model tests. Fuel economy should also improve slightly from the 19.3-24.5 mpg we averaged before. Premium fuel again is required.

Complementing the smooth powertrain, the TL offers unerring high-speed stability allied to grippy, athletic cornering. The downside is a firmer ride than that of less dynamic rivals like the Lexus ES 300 and

Specifications begin on page 535.

ACURA

Infiniti I30. Tire rumble and slap are also above the class norm, but not irksome. Engine and wind noise are low. Simulated panic stops are swift and stable, but nosedive is heavier than expected with a sporty sedan.

ACCOMMODATIONS The TL shares its basic architecture with the Accord sedan, so it offers the same ample adult-size room up front, plus good foot and head clearance behind. Leg space in back is only adequate, though, and the bench seat provides unexceptional thigh support. Luggage space is generous, though intrusive trunklid hinges steal some of it.

Like most Honda designs, the TL's driving position is low and sporty but accommodating, gauges large and legible, outward vision unhindered. Climate controls are a fair reach away for the driver and, with the optional navigation system, too small and dimly lit. The navigator itself can be useful, but like most of its kind it can also be a driver distraction.

VALUE Solidly built and impeccably finished, the TL equals or exceeds anything in the near-luxury class for quality and refinement. It also has a sporty nature that will please demanding drivers, but may turn off buyers who expect Lexus-level isolation. That's why the impressive, high-value TL shares Best Buy honors with the ES 300.

ENGINES

	ohc V6
Size, liters/cu. in.	3.2/196
Horsepower @ rpm	225 @ 5500
Torque (lb-ft) @ rpm	216 @ 4700
Availability	S

EPA city/highway mpg

5-speed OD automatic	19/29

PRICES

Acura TL	Retail Price	Dealer Invoice
Base 4-door sedan	$28550	$25738
Base 4-door sedan w/Navigation System	30550	27537
Destination charge	480	480

STANDARD EQUIPMENT:

Base: 3.2-liter V6 engine, 5-speed automatic transmission w/manual-shift capability, traction control, dual front airbags, front side-impact airbags, antilock 4-wheel disc brakes, emergency inside trunk release, air conditioning w/automatic climate control, interior air filter, variable-assist power steering, leather-wrapped tilt steering wheel, cruise control, leather upholstery, heated front bucket seats, 8-way power driver seat w/manual lumbar adjustment, 4-way power passenger seat, center console, cupholders, trunk passthrough, heated power mirrors, power windows, power door locks, remote

Prices are accurate at time of publication; subject to manufacturer's change.

ACURA • AUDI

keyless entry, power sunroof, Bose AM/FM/cassette/CD player, steering wheel mounted radio controls, rear defogger, automatic day/night rearview mirror, variable intermittent wipers, universal garage door opener, auxiliary power outlets, illuminated visor mirrors, automatic-off headlights, floormats, theft-deterrent system, 205/60VR16 tires, alloy wheels.

Base w/Navigation System adds: navigation system with global positioning system, LCD screen, emergency inside trunk release, digital clock, outside temperature indicator, Xenon headlights, map lights, remote fuel door/decklid release, floormats.

Options are available as dealer-installed accessories.

AUDI A4

Audi A4 2.8 4-door sedan

Front- or all-wheel-drive near-luxury car

Base price range: $24,540-$38,900. Built in Germany. **Also consider:** BMW 3-Series, Infiniti I30, Lexus IS 300, Mercedes-Benz C-Class

FOR • Acceleration (S4) • Ride • Handling • Build quality
AGAINST • Rear-seat room • Ride (S4 or with Sport Pkg.)

Though they're being redesigned for 2002, the entry-level Audis get several key changes for '01, including standard curtain side airbags, longer warranties, and a newly available antiskid system. The A4 returns as a 1.8T sedan and Avant wagon with a turbocharged 4-cylinder engine revised to make 170 horsepower versus 150. A4 2.8 models continue with a 190-hp V6. Come late 2000, the sporty S4 sedan gets a companion Avant wagon with the same 250-hp, twin-turbo 2.7-liter V6. Audi's Quattro all-wheel drive is standard on S4s and all Avants, and is available on other sedans in lieu of front-wheel drive with traction control. S4s and 2.8s have standard 5-speed automatic transmission with manual-shift gate; S4s offer 6-speed manual as a no-cost option. The automatic is optional for 1.8Ts in lieu of 5-speed manual, which is no longer offered on the front-drive 2.8 sedan. All automatic-transmission A4s now

Specifications begin on page 535.

AUDI

include a 3-spoke sport steering wheel with buttons for manual shifting. The high-performance S4s feature a sport suspension, 17-inch wheels, performance tires, and unique grille, bumpers, and leather interior.

Audi's Sideguard airbags are now standard instead of optional; they deploy along the side windows as a head-protecting curtain against side impacts. Lower-body front side airbags are standard. The antiskid system is standard on the S4 models and optional on other A4s. A navigation system is no longer available for 1.8Ts and S4s. Finally, the A4's basic warranty coverage, including scheduled maintenance and free roadside assistance, extend to 4 years/50,000 miles from 3/50,000.

PERFORMANCE S4s have outstanding acceleration—our test sedan clocked 6.3 seconds 0-60 mph—but other A4s are not impressively quick. An automatic 2.8 Quattro sedan needed 9.3 seconds 0-60. The lighter front-drive sedans are a tad faster than comparable Quattros, but still trail most class rivals. The 1.8Ts are adequate with automatic but have better scoot with manual shift. Fuel economy is good but not stellar. In recent tests, V6 Quattro sedans averaged 17.5-21.5 mpg, 1.8T Quattros around 23 mpg; S4s 20.3. All require premium fuel.

Quattro provides great traction in any situation, and any A4 is fun to drive, especially the potent S4. Steering is linear and communicative, and a well-designed suspension checks undue cornering lean while smothering most bumps with ease. There's more impact harshness with the available Sport package, which is comparable to the S4 chassis. Stops are short and straight. Wind noise is moderate, but the high-performance tires on some models thrum a little on rough pavement. Both V6s are smooth and quiet, but the turbo-4 becomes a tad growly at high rpm.

ACCOMMODATIONS A4s have good passenger room in front but not in back, where rear leg space all but vanishes without the front seats moved well forward. All-around head room is only adequate with the optional sunroof. Cargo space in sedans is generous, though the Avant is more casual hauler than big-load wagon.

These Audis cater nicely to drivers of all sizes. Gauges and most switchgear are clear and well placed, though controls for the standard automatic climate system are too low and complex, and the optional navigation system isn't easy to operate even when you're stopped. A solid driving feel, exemplary detail finish, and attractive interior materials are typical of Audi and appropriate for the price.

VALUE Tight rear seat aside, the A4 compares well with near-luxury rivals and is one of the few cars in its class offering wagons and all-wheel drive. The antiskid system, curtain airbags, and longer warranty with free maintenance, bolster its appeal.

Prices are accurate at time of publication; subject to manufacturer's change.

AUDI

ENGINES

	Turbocharged dohc I4	dohc V6	Turbocharged dohc V6
Size, liters/cu. in.	1.8/107	2.8/169	2.7/163
Horsepower @ rpm	170 @ 5900	190 @ 6000	250 @ 5800
Torque (lb-ft) @ rpm	166 @ 1950	207 @ 3200	258 @ 1850
Availability	S[1]	S[2]	S[3]
EPA city/highway mpg			
5-speed OD manual	24/32[4]	20/29[6]	
6-speed OD manual			17/24
5-speed OD automatic	21/30[5]	18/26[6]	17/24

1. 1.8T models. 2. 2.8 models. 3. S4 models. 4. 22/29 w/Quattro. 5. 19/28 w/Quattro. 6. 18/26 w/Quattro.

PRICES
Audi A4

	Retail Price	Dealer Invoice
A4 1.8T 4-door sedan	$24540	$21840
A4 1.8T Avant 4-door wagon	27290	24470
A4 2.8 4-door sedan	30340	27048
A4 2.8 Avant 4-door sedan	30990	27726
A4 2.8 Avant 4-door wagon	31990	28660
S4 4-door sedan	38900	34791
Destination charge	550	550

STANDARD EQUIPMENT:

A4 1.8T: 1.8-liter dohc turbocharged 4-cylinder engine, 5-speed manual transmission, electronic limited-slip differential, dual front airbags, front side-impact airbags, front and rear side head-protection system, antilock 4-wheel disc brakes, air conditioning w/automatic climate control, interior air filter, variable-assist power steering, tilt/telescoping steering wheel, leather-wrapped steering wheel and shifter, cruise control, cloth upholstery, front bucket seats with height and lumbar adjustment, center console, cupholders, split folding rear seat, heated power mirrors, power windows, power door locks, remote keyless entry, AM/FM/cassette/CD player, digital clock, tachometer, trip computer, outside temperature indicator, rear defogger, remote decklid and fuel-door releases, variable intermittent wipers, illuminated visor mirrors, map lights, auxiliary power outlets, floormats, theft-deterrent system, tool kit, headlight washers, front and rear fog lights, 205/60R15 tires, alloy wheels.

A4 1.8T Avant adds: permanent all-wheel drive, electronic limited-slip front and rear differentials, ski sack, rear wiper/washer, roof rails.

A4 2.8 adds to A4 1.8T: 2.8-liter dohc V6 engine, 5-speed automatic transmission w/manual-shift capability, traction control, 10-way power front seats, wood interior trim, 205/55HR16 tires.

A4 2.8 Avant adds: permanent all-wheel drive, 5-speed manual transmission, electronic limited-slip front and rear differentials, ski sack, rear wiper/washer (wagon), roof rails (wagon), deletes traction control.

Specifications begin on page 535.

AUDI

S4 adds to A4 1.8T: 2.7-liter dohc turbocharged V6 engine, 5-speed automatic w/manual-shift capability, permanent all-wheel drive, electronic limited-slip front and rear differentials, antiskid system, leather upholstery, 10-way power front sport seats, ski sack, Xenon headlights, sport suspension, full-size spare tire, 225/45R17 tires.

OPTIONAL EQUIPMENT:
Major Packages

	Retail Price	Dealer Invoice
Premium Pkg.	$1200	$1056
Power sunroof, automatic day/night outside and rearview mirrors, universal garage door opener.		
Cold Weather Pkg., A4 sedans, S4	600	528
wagons	450	396
Heated front seats, ski sack (sedans).		
Sport Pkg., 1.8T, 1.8T Avant	750	660
2.8, 2.8 Avant	500	440
S4	400	352
Sport suspension, 205/55WR16 tires, special alloy wheels.		

Powertrains

5-speed automatic trans. w/manual-shift capability, A4	1100	1072
Std. 2.8, S4.		
6-speed manual transmission, S4	NC	NC
Quattro IV all-wheel-drive system, 1.8T sedan, 2.8 sedan	1750	1750

Safety Features

Antiskid system, A4	550	484

Comfort and Convenience

Navigation System, 2.8, 2.8 Avant, S4	1280	1138
Bose sound system	650	572
6-disc CD changer	550	484
Front sport seats, A4	500	440
Leather upholstery, 2.8, 2.8 Avant	1320	1162
Integrated mobile telephone	495	431

Appearance and Miscellaneous

Xenon headlights, A4	500	440

AUDI A6/ ALLROAD QUATTRO

Front- or all-wheel-drive near-luxury car; similar to Volkswagen Passat

Base price range: $34,400-$49,400. Built in Germany. **Also consider:** Acura TL, BMW 5-Series, Infiniti I30, Mercedes-Benz E-Class, Volvo V70

Prices are accurate at time of publication; subject to manufacturer's change.

AUDI

Audi A6 2.8 4-door sedan

FOR • Acceleration (exc. 2.8) • Steering/handling • Passenger and cargo room • Build quality   **AGAINST** • Climate controls

Audi's midrange line gains an SUV-flavored wagon and standard curtain side airbags for 2001. A6s come as a 2.8 sedan and Avant wagon with a 200-horsepower V6, a 2.7T sedan with a twin-turbo 250-hp V6, and a 300-hp V8 4.2 sedan. All have Audi's quattro all-wheel drive except the 2.8 sedan, which offers it optionally in lieu of front drive with traction control. The new allroad quattro is essentially an A6 Avant with the 250-hp V6 and a special air-spring suspension that adjusts for up to 8 inches of ground clearance. A6s offer a 5-speed automatic transmission with manual shifting via a separate gate or—new for '01—steering-wheel buttons. The 2.7T, allroad, and 2.8 sedan also offer manual transmission—a 5-speed on the 2.8, a 6-speed otherwise. Head-protecting window-curtain airbags are newly standard for 2.8s as well as other A6s. Front lower-body side airbags are standard for all, with rear side airbags optional. Audi's anti-skid Electronic Stabilization Program is newly optional for 2.8s and standard for other models. A new steering wheel with controls for audio and optional cell phone is standard on the 4.2. An optional satellite-linked navigation system displays visual prompts within the instrument cluster. A6's basic warranty is now 4 years/50,000 miles instead of 3/50,000, and still includes free scheduled maintenance.

EVALUATION A6s 2.8s go well enough with liberal use of the automatic's manual shift feature and a heavy throttle foot. Our test cars have averaged a decent 19.2-22.4 mpg on the premium gas required for all models. The 2.7T and 4.2 are among the fastest near-luxury contenders. We clocked 0-60 mph at 6.6 seconds with a test V8, about 7 with a 2.7T, and just under 8 with a near-new allroad. All A6s offer no-sweat braking, agile handling, and a quiet, mostly supple ride, though tire thump and roar occur on rough, coarse pavement and the allroad floats a bit over large

AUDI

humps and dips. These Audis boast more rear passenger room than the rival BMW 5-Series, plus ample, easily accessed cargo space, sophisticated interior decor, and intelligent switchgear—save fiddly, low-mounted climate controls. A6s cost less than some rivals, yet deliver Teutonic solidity, high driving satisfaction, and top-drawer workmanship, plus free scheduled maintenance for 4 years/50,000 miles. We recommend them.

ENGINES

	dohc V6	Turbocharged dohc V6	dohc V8
Size, liters/cu. in.	2.8/169	2.7/163	4.2/255
Horsepower @ rpm	200 @ 6200	250 @ 5800	300 @ 6200
Torque (lb-ft) @ rpm	207 @ 3200	258 @ 1850	295 @ 3000
Availability	S[1]	S[2]	S[3]
EPA city/highway mpg			
5-speed OD manual	18/24		
6-speed OD manual		17/24	
5-speed OD automatic	17/26[4]	17/24	17/26

1. 2.8 models. 2. 2.7T, allroad quattro. 3. 4.2. 4. 17/24 w/Quattro.

PRICES

Audi A6/allroad quattro

	Retail Price	Dealer Invoice
2.8 4-door sedan	$34400	$30621
2.8 Avant 4-door wagon	37350	33427
2.7T 4-door sedan	39500	35319
allroad quattro 4-door wagon	41900	37327
4.2 4-door sedan	49400	44031
Destination charge	550	550

STANDARD EQUIPMENT:

2.8: 2.8-liter dohc V6 engine, 5-speed automatic transmission w/manual-shift capability, traction control, dual front airbags, front side-impact airbags, front and rear side head-protection system, antilock 4-wheel disc brakes, air conditioning w/dual-zone automatic climate controls, interior air filter, variable-assist power steering, tilt/telescoping steering wheel, leather-wrapped steering wheel, cruise control, cloth upholstery, 12-way power front bucket seats w/power lumbar adjustment, center console, cupholders, split folding rear seat, wood interior trim, heated power mirrors, power windows, power door locks, remote keyless entry, AM/FM/cassette/CD player, digital clock, tachometer, trip computer, outside-temperature indicator, map lights, illuminated visor mirrors, rear defogger, variable intermittent wipers, auxiliary power outlets, remote fuel-door and decklid release, floormats, theft-deterrent system, tool kit, headlight washers, front and rear fog lights, full-size spare tire, 205/55R16 tires, alloy wheels.

2.8 Avant adds: Quattro permanent all-wheel drive, electronic limited-slip

Prices are accurate at time of publication; subject to manufacturer's change.

AUDI

front and rear differentials, rear wiper/washer, ski sack, remote tailgate release, manual rear window sunshade, cargo cover, roof rails, deletes traction control.

2.7T adds to 2.8: 2.7-liter dohc turbocharged V6 engine, Quattro permanent all-wheel drive, electronic limited-slip front and rear differentials, antiskid system, 215/55R16 tires, deletes traction control.

allroad quattro adds: 6-speed manual transmission, leather upholstery, ski sack, cargo cover, manual rear sunshade, rear wiper/washer, roof rails, height-adjustable suspension, 225/55WR17 tires.

4.2 adds: 4.2-liter dohc V8 engine, power sunroof, power tilt/telescoping steering wheel, leather upholstery, driver seat and mirror memory, ski sack, Bose sound system, steering wheel radio controls, automatic day/night outside and rearview mirrors, universal garage door opener, 235/50R16 tires.

OPTIONAL EQUIPMENT:
Major Packages

	Retail Price	Dealer Invoice
Celebration Luxury Pkg., 2.8, 2.8 Avant	$1975	$1738
Leather upholstery, power sunroof, universal garage door opener.		
Convenience Pkg., allroad quattro	800	704
Heated front and rear seats, heated steering wheel w/radio controls, universal garage door opener.		
Luxury Preferred Pkg., 2.7T	2925	2574
Leather upholstery, driver seat and mirror memory, power sunroof, universal garage door opener.		
Premium Pkg., 4.2	1475	1298
Heated front and rear seats, heated steering wheel, power rear sunshade, manual rear side window sunshades, Xenon headlights.		
Premium Pkg., allroad	900	792
Driver seat and mirror memory, power folding mirrors, automatic day/night rearview and outside mirrors, Xenon headlights.		
Sport Pkg., 2.7T	1000	880
Sport steering wheel, front sport seats, sport suspension, 215/55R16 performance tires, special alloy wheels.		
Sport Pkg., 4.2	1500	1320
Front sport seats, sport suspension, 255/40R17 performance tires.		
Guidance Pkg.	1630	1276
Navigation system, rear acoustic parking aid.		
Warm Weather Pkg., allroad quattro	1750	1540
Solar sunroof, rear side window sunshades.		
Cold Weather Pkg., 2.8, 2.7T	625	550
2.8 Avant	475	418
Heated front and rear seats, ski sack (sedan).		

Specifications begin on page 535.

AUDI • BMW

Powertrains

	Retail Price	Dealer Invoice
5-speed automatic transmission w/manual shift capability, allroad quattro	$1000	$972
6-speed manual transmission, 2.7T	NC	NC
Quattro IV permanent all-wheel-drive system, 2.8 sedan	1750	1750

Safety Features

Rear side-impact airbags	350	308
Antiskid system, 2.8, 2.8 Avant	550	484

Comfort and Convenience

Power sunroof, 2.8, 2.8 Avant	1200	1058
allroad	1000	880
2.8, 2.8 Avant include universal garage door opener.		
Leather upholstery, 2.8, 2.8 Avant, 2.7T	1550	1364
Rear-facing seat, 2.8 Avant, allroad	750	660
6-disc CD changer	550	484
Bose sound system	750	660
Std. 4.2.		
Integrated mobile telephone	495	431

Appearance and Miscellaneous

Polished alloy wheels, 4.2	750	660
Dual spoke alloy wheels, allroad	950	836

BMW 3-SERIES

BMW 330i 4-door sedan

Rear-wheel-drive near-luxury car

Base price range: $26,990-$42,400. Built in Germany. **Also consider:** Audi A4, Lexus IS 300, Mercedes-Benz C-Class and CLK

FOR • Acceleration • Steering/handling • Build quality • Exterior finish **AGAINST** • Cargo room (convertible) • Rear-seat entry/exit (coupe)

Prices are accurate at time of publication; subject to manufacturer's change.

BMW

BMW's best-selling line began 2001 last summer by adding available all-wheel drive, new-design engines with more power, and a new edition of the hot M3 coupe. Styling is not changed, but most model names are.

The previous 323i sedan, 323Ci coupe and convertible, and 323i sport wagon get 325i/325Ci badges to signal a new 2.5-liter inline 6-cylinder engine with 14 more horsepower than last year's 2.5, though torque declines 6 pound-feet. Similarly, the 328i sedan and 328Ci coupe and convertible become 330 models via a 3.0-liter six with an extra 32 hp and 8 lb-ft over the 2.8 liter it replaces. In addition, permanent all-wheel-drive, similar to the system of BMW's X5 sport-utility vehicle, is a new option for the wagon and both sedans, badging them 325xi and 330xi—BMW's first AWD cars in 10 years.

All 330s have standard 17-inch wheels and tires, versus 16s on 328s, plus larger brakes. Finally, the M3 returns after a 2-year absence with the latest 3-Series coupe styling, a revised 3.2-liter six making 330 hp—up 90 from the previous model—plus unique front and rear spoilers, 18-inch wheels, sport front seats and steering wheel, and mandatory 6-speed manual transmission. Other 3s offer a 5-speed manual or extra-cost 5-speed automatic with "Steptronic" manual shift gate.

Linewide standards again include traction control, an antiskid system, front side airbags and, convertibles excepted, BMW's front Head Protection System tubular airbags. Rear side airbags are optional for sedans and wagons. Coupes and convertibles seat four instead of five. Convertibles have roll bars behind the rear seat designed to deploy automatically if the car is about to flip over. A power folding top with glass rear window is standard for the 330Ci convertible, optional for the 325Ci model; an aluminum hard top is available for both. The 325i wagon features a one-piece tailgate with separate opening window.

PERFORMANCE As ever, the 3-Series appeals for its silky engines, solid driving feel, modest noise levels, and athletic road manners. The Sport suspension, standard on coupes and available elsewhere, sharpens cornering grip and steering response in exchange for some unwanted ride jiggle on rough pavement, plus mediocre grip in snow despite the standard traction and antiskid systems. The convertible suffers mild body shake on rough broken pavement, but is impressively solid for a droptop. Other models feel reassuringly all-of-a-piece on most any surface.

Acceleration is another plus. We haven't yet driven this year's 325 models, but their new six should perform at least as well as last year's 323 engine in coupes, sedans, and wagons, though it's likely to be no more impressive in the heavier ragtop. BMW says rear-drive 330s do 0-60 mph in 6.4 seconds with manual shift, a big improvement over the 7.5 we clocked with last year's 328i sedan. Automatic 330s take a claimed 7.0 seconds. The M3 should reach 60 in well under 6 seconds. All engines still require premium fuel, but economy should be little changed despite the higher horsepower. Our last 328i sedan averaged 23.5 mpg. BMW's auto-

Specifications begin on page 535.

BMW

matic transmission provides quick, velvety gear changes in normal mode, with ratios well matched to engine power and torque curves. The Steptronic mode enhances driver control, but is no substitute for a true manual gearbox.

As for the new AWD, BMW says the 330xi sedan does 0-60 in 6.9 seconds with manual shift, and our near-new test car bettered that at 6.8 while averaging 20.8 mpg despite hard driving. The automatic 330xi sedan does 0-60 in a claimed 7.5 seconds. The AWD hardware adds about 200 pounds to curb weight, but only 0.7-inch to ride height and 1.3 feet to the turning circle. In other words, xi models perform almost exactly like comparable rear-drive 3-Series.

ACCOMMODATIONS All 3-Series models are a bit cozy inside, with a rather narrow cabin feel. Head room is plentiful in front and adequate in back. There's no shortage of front leg space, but rear knee and foot room are tight with the front seats moved fully aft, especially in the convertible.

Interior materials are sturdy and attractive, but leather and wood are optional on most models, which seems rather stingy at these prices. You do get a manual tilt/telescopic steering wheel, but a CD player and power driver's seat cost extra too. A well arranged dashboard is complemented by steering-wheel audio and cruise controls as standard on 330s and optional for 325s. Outward vision is good except top-up in the convertible, which suffers the usual rear-quarter blind spot. Rear access is tricky in 2-doors despite front seats that automatically power forward. The convertible has handy switches near the front head rests for adjusting the seat before entering.

Trunk space is sufficient in sedans, a bit less so in coupes, but what's there is usable and easily accessed. The wagon has little more volume than the sedan unless you load it up to the ceiling and employ the split-fold back seat, which is also standard for coupes but optional for sedans. The convertible is least capacious of all, but a clever fold-up tray restores trunk space that would otherwise be lost with the top up. Soft tops seal nicely, but you shouldn't have to shell out some $1500 to get a power roof on the 325 convertible.

VALUE The true "driver's cars" of the near-luxury class, these BMWs offered spirited performance, great handling, high refinement, and terrific workmanship. As such, they're also good value, trailing some rivals in expected standard features but making up for it with resale values.

ENGINES

	dohc I6	dohc I6	dohc I6
Size, liters/cu. in.	2.5/152	3.0/182	3.2/192
Horsepower @ rpm	184 @ 5550	225 @ 5900	330 @ 7900
Torque (lb-ft) @ rpm	175 @ 3500	214 @ 3500	255 @ 4900
Availability	S[1]	S[2]	S[3]
EPA city/highway mpg			
5-speed manual	20/29	21/30	

Prices are accurate at time of publication; subject to manufacturer's change.

BMW

	dohc I6	dohc I6	dohc I6
6-speed OD manual............			16/27
5-speed OD automatic.......	19/27	19/27	

1. 325i, 325Ci. 2. 330i, 330Ci. 3. M3 (preliminary hp and torque).

PRICES

BMW 3-Series	Retail Price	Dealer Invoice
325i 4-door sedan	$26990	$24450
325i 4-door wagon	29400	26620
325Ci 2-door coupe	28990	26250
325Ci 2-door convertible	35990	32550
330i 4-door sedan	33990	30750
330Ci 2-door coupe	34990	31650
330Ci 2-door convertible	42400	33320
Destination charge	570	570

M3 prices and equipment not available at time of publication.

STANDARD EQUIPMENT:

325i: 2.5-liter dohc 6-cylinder engine, 5-speed manual transmission, traction control, dual front airbags, front side-impact airbags, front side head-protection, antiskid system, antilock 4-wheel disc brakes, daytime running lights, air conditioning, variable-assist power steering, tilt/telescoping steering wheel, vinyl upholstery, front bucket seats, cupholders, split folding rear seat (wagon), power mirrors, power windows, power door locks, power decklid release, remote keyless entry, AM/FM/cassette, digital clock, tachometer, variable intermittent wipers, rear defogger, rear wiper/washer (wagon), theft-deterrent system, roof rails (wagon), full-size spare tire (sedan), 205/55R16 tires, alloy wheels.

325Ci coupe adds: cruise control, leather-wrapped steering wheel w/radio controls, split folding rear seat, heated power mirrors, trip computer, illuminated visor mirrors, fog lights, sport suspension.

325Ci convertible adds: rollover protection system, 8-way power front seats, passenger-side mirror tilt-down back-up aid, memory system for driver seat and power mirrors, Deletes: side head-protection, split folding rear seat, full-size spare tire, sport suspension.

330i adds to 325i: 3.0-liter dohc 6-cylinder engine, automatic climate control, interior air filter, leather-wrapped steering w/radio controls, cruise control, center console, heated power mirrors, illuminated visor mirrors, map lights, fog lights, full-size spare tire, 205/50R17 tires.

330Ci coupe adds: power front seats, split folding rear seat, sport suspension.

330Ci convertible adds to 330i: rollover protection system, leather upholstery, driver seat and mirror memory, power convertible top, deletes front side head-protection system, full-size spare tire.

Specifications begin on page 535.

BMW

OPTIONAL EQUIPMENT:	Retail Price	Dealer Invoice

Major Packages

Premium Pkg., 325i $3500 $2975
Automatic climate control, cruise control, leather-wrapped steering wheel w/radio and cruise controls, 6-way power front seats, driver seat and mirror memory, passenger-side mirror tilt-down back-up aid, center armrest, power sunroof, automatic day/night rearview mirror, map and footwell lights, trip computer, illuminated visor mirrors, wood interior trim.

Premium Pkg., 325Ci coupe 2100 1785
6-way power front seats, driver seat and mirror memory, automatic climate control, power sunroof, automatic day/night rearview mirror, wood interior trim.

Premium Pkg., 325Ci convertible 1900 1615
Power convertible top, wood interior trim, automatic day/night rearview mirror, universal garage door opener.

Premium Pkg., 330i 3850 3275
330Ci coupe 2900 2465
Leather upholstery, 6-way power front seats (330i), front seat power lumbar support, wood interior trim, power sunroof, automatic day/night rearview mirror, rain-sensing wipers.

Premium Pkg., 330 Ci convertible 800 680
Wood interior trim, front seat power lumbar support, automatic day/night rearview mirror, universal garage door opener, rain-sensing wipers.

Sport Pkg., 325i 1500 1275
Leather-wrapped steering wheel w/radio controls, 10-way adjustable sport bucket seats, heated mirrors and washer jets, fog lights, sport suspension, 225/45R17 tires, special alloy wheels. NA w/all-wheel drive.

Sport Pkg., 325Ci coupe 1000 850
10-way adjustable front sport seats, 225/45WR17 tires, special alloy wheels.

Sport Pkg., 325Ci convertible 1200 1020
10-way power/2-way manual sport bucket seats w/adjustable thigh support, sport suspension, 225/45WR17 tires, special alloy wheels. Requires leather upholstery.

Sport Pkg., 330i 1200 1020
Sport steering wheel, 8-way power front sport seats, driver seat and mirror memory, aerodynamic pkg., sport suspension, 225/45R17 front tires, 245/40R17 rear tires. NA w/all-wheel drive.

Sport Pkg., 330Ci coupe 600 510
330Ci convertible 800 680
Front sport seats, aerodynamic pkg., sport suspension (330Ci convertible), 225/45R17 front tires, 245/40R17 rear tires. NA w/330xi all-wheel drive.

All Wheel Drive Sport Pkg., 325i 1200 1020
Leather-wrapped steering wheel w/radio controls, 10-way adjustable front sport seats, aerodynamic package, 205/50R17 tires. Requires all-wheel drive.

All Wheel Drive Sport Pkg., 330i 900 765
Sport steering wheel, front sport bucket seats, aerodynamic pkg. special wheels. Requires all-wheel drive.

Prices are accurate at time of publication; subject to manufacturer's change.

CONSUMER GUIDE

BMW

	Retail Price	Dealer Invoice
Cold Weather Pkg., 325i sedan, 330i	$1000	$850
325i wagon, 325Ci, 330Ci	700	595

Heated front seats, split folding rear seat w/armrest (325i sedan, 330i), ski bag, headlight washers.

Powertrains
5-speed automatic trans. w/manual-shift capability	1275	1210
All-wheel drive, 325i, 330i	1750	1490

Includes unique antiskid system, xi badging.

Safety Features
Rear side-impact airbags, sedans, wagon	385	325

Comfort and Convenience
Onboard navigation system	1800	1675

Includes trip computer. NA with AM/FM/CD player. 325 requires Premium Pkg.

Cruise control, 325i	475	405

Includes leather-wrapped steering wheel w/radio and cruise controls.

Leather upholstery	1450	1235

Std. 330Ci convertible.

Power front seats, 325i, 325Ci coupe, 330i	945	805

Includes driver seat memory.

Heated front seats	500	425
Harman/Kardon audio system	675	575
AM/FM/CD player	200	170
Power sunroof	1050	895

NA convertible.

Parking distance control, 325i wagon, 330	350	300

Appearance and Miscellaneous
Removable hardtop, 325Ci/330Ci convertible	2295	1950
Fog lights, 325i	260	220

Includes heated mirrors and washer jets.

Xenon headlights	500	425

325i requires fog lights.

BMW 5-SERIES

CG RECOMMENDED AUTO

Rear-wheel-drive luxury car

Base price range: $35,400-$53,900. Built in Germany. **Also consider:** Acura RL, Lexus GS 300/430, Mercedes-Benz E-Class

FOR • Acceleration (540i, M5) • Steering/handling • Ride • Cargo room (wagon) • Quietness • Build quality **AGAINST** • Fuel economy (540i, M5)

New engines, a minor facelift, and two new entry-level models update BMW's midrange series for 2001. Now anchoring this line are a 525i

Specifications begin on page 535.

BMW

BMW 530i 4-door sedan

sedan and wagon powered by BMW's new-design 184-horsepower 2.5-liter inline 6-cylinder engine (shared with the Z3 sports cars and 3-Series models). The 528i wagon is gone, but the 528i sedan becomes a 530i by switching to a new 3.0-liter six making 32 more hp than the 2.8-liter it replaces. The V8 540i sedan and wagon are mechanical carryovers, as is the high-performance 4.9-liter V8 M5 sedan. The standard manual transmission is a 6-speed for M5 and 540i, a 5-speed elsewhere, and all models except M5 offer a 5-speed automatic option with separate manual shift feature. All 5s have an antiskid system, front side airbags, and head-protecting tubular airbags. The M5's lower-body rear side airbags are optional for other models and, for 2001, include rear Head Protection. Among minor styling changes are lighted rings around the headlamps, reshaped lower fascias, revised taillamps, and body-color instead of black side moldings. An in-dash CD player is newly available, and the optional navigation system comes with a wider dashboard display screen.

PERFORMANCE The 5-series sets the class standard for dynamic ability and driving satisfaction. All models are surefooted in corners, aided by quick, precise steering. A stout structure helps the standard suspension deliver a quiet, absorbent ride; the firmer sport setups allow a bit more jiggle and thump. Though no 5-Series is Lexus LS hushed, these cars are well isolated. Tire thrum is audible on only the coarsest surfaces, while engines rise to a subdued but expensive growl in hard acceleration.

We haven't yet tested the latest 6-cylinder models, but they should be decently quick with a firm throttle foot and manual shift. They should also be at least as economical as the previous 528s, which in our tests averaged 20.9 mpg with manual and 18.8 with automatic. Any 540 has plenty of muscle for quick launches and effortless passing, plus acceptable fuel economy: Our test automatic sedan did 0-60 mph in just 6.3 seconds and averaged 15.9 mpg. A test 6-speed manual sedan logged 19.3 mpg, but suffered a balky shifter and heavy clutch action. The M5 has a heavy clutch, too, but, says BMW, does 0-60 mph in about 5 seconds. Our test examples felt that quick, but averaged just 13.4 mpg.

ACCOMMODATIONS These BMWs are somewhat smaller inside than most rivals, so four adults is the practical passenger limit, though all seats are firm and supportive. All-around entry/exit is good, the driving

Prices are accurate at time of publication; subject to manufacturer's change.
CONSUMER GUIDE

BMW

position sound and easily tailored, and visibility no strain, except directly astern in sedans. Some minor controls annoy, especially the complex audio/climate/trip computer display. The sedan's trunk isn't wide, but has a long, flat floor. Split-fold rear seatbacks, optional on sedans and standard on wagons, enhance cargo space. Workmanship and interior materials are first-class, as they ought to be at these prices.

VALUE The 5-Series is aimed at enthusiasts who demand premium engineering and superior road manners. We recommend any version that fits your budget.

ENGINES

	dohc I6	dohc I6	dohc V8	dohc V8
Size, liters/cu. in.	2.5/152	3.0/182	4.4/268	4.9/303
Horsepower @ rpm	184 @ 6000	225 @ 5900	282 @ 5400	394 @ 6600
Torque (lb-ft) @ rpm	175 @ 3500	214 @ 3500	324 @ 3600	368 @ 3800
Availability	S[1]	S[2]	S[3]	S[4]
EPA city/highway mpg				
5-speed manual	20/29	21/30		
6-speed OD manual			15/23	15/23
5-speed OD automatic	19/27	18/26	18/24	

1. 525i. 2. 530i. 3. 540i. 4. M5.

PRICES

BMW 5-Series	Retail Price	Dealer Invoice
525i 4-door sedan, manual	$35400	$32020
525iT 4-door wagon, manual	37200	33640
530i 4-door sedan, manual	39400	35620
540i 4-door sedan, automatic	51100	46150
540i 4-door sedan, manual	53900	48670
540iT 4-door wagon, automatic	53480	48290
Destination charge	570	570

M5 prices and equipment not available at time of publication. 540i w/6-speed manual transmission and 540i with automatic transmission and Sport Pkg. add $1300 Gas Guzzler Tax.

STANDARD EQUIPMENT:

525: 2.5-liter dohc 6-cylinder engine, 5-speed manual transmission, traction control, dual front airbags, front side-impact airbags, front side head-protection system, antilock 4-wheel disc brakes, antiskid system, daytime running lights, variable-assist power steering, power tilt/telescopic steering wheel, leather-wrapped steering w/radio controls, cruise control, air conditioning, vinyl upholstery, 10-way power driver seat, power front head restraints, cupholders, memory system (driver seat, steering wheel, power mirrors),

Specifications begin on page 535.

BMW

heated power mirrors w/passenger-side tilt-down parking aid, power windows, power door locks, remote keyless entry, AM/FM/cassette, tachometer, outside temperature display, trip computer, map lights, variable intermittent wipers, remote decklid release, rear defogger, illuminated visor mirrors, cargo cover (wagon), theft-deterrent system, fog lights, tool kit, roof rails (wagon), full-size spare tire, 225/55HR16 tires, alloy wheels.

530i adds: 3.0-liter dohc 6-cylinder engine, dual-zone automatic climate controls.

540i automatic models add: 4.4-liter dohc V8 engine, 5-speed automatic transmission (sedan), 5-speed automatic transmission w/manual-shift capability (wagon), 10-way power passenger seat, leather upholstery, wood interior trim, power sunroof, automatic day/night rearview mirror, universal garage door opener, rain-sensing wipers, split folding rear seat (wagon), rain-sensing intermittent wipers, Xenon headlights, self-leveling suspension (wagon).

540i manual adds: 6-speed manual transmission, 12-way power front sport seats, sport suspension, 235/45WR17 front tires, 255/40R17 rear tires.

OPTIONAL EQUIPMENT:
Major Packages

	Retail Price	Dealer Invoice
Premium Pkg., 525	$2950	$2510
530i	3100	2635

Leather upholstery, wood interior trim, power sunroof, automatic day/night rearview mirror (530), rain-sensing wipers (530).

Sport Pkg., 525 sedan	1500	1275
525 wagon	1975	1680
530i	1970	1675

Sport steering wheel (530), sport suspension, self-leveling suspension (wagon), cross-spoke alloy wheels, 235/45WR17 tires.

Sport Premium Pkg., 525 sedan	3900	3315
525 wagon	4550	3870
530i	4300	3655

Includes Premium Pkg. and Sport Pkg.

Convenience Pkg., 525, 530i	1300	1105

Automatic climate control, power passenger seat, universal garage door opener. Requires Premium Pkg. or Sport Premium Pkg.

540i Sport Pkg., 540i sedan automatic, 540i wagon	2800	2380

Automatic transmission w/manual-shift capability (sedan), performance axle ratio, 12-way power front sport seats, Sport steering wheel, sport suspension, 235/45WR17 front tires (sedan), 255/40WR17 rear tires (sedan), 235/45WR17 tires (wagon).

Cold Weather Pkg.	600	510

Heated front seats, heated headlight washers.

Powertrains

5-speed automatic trans. w/manual-shift capability, 525, 530i	1275	1210

Prices are accurate at time of publication; subject to manufacturer's change.

BMW

Safety Features

	Retail Price	Dealer Invoice
Rear side-impact airbags	$550	$470

Includes rear side-head-protection system.

Comfort and Convenience

Power sunroof, 525, 530i	1050	895
Navigation system, 525, 530i	1990	1690
540i	1800	1530

NA w/AM/FM/CD player.

Leather upholstery, 525, 530i	1450	1235
Comfort 16-way power front seats, 530i	1800	1530
540i automatic	1200	1020

Includes power lumbar support. 530i includes Convenience Pkg. 530i requires Sport Pkg. and leather upholstery or Premium Pkg. NA with 540i Sport Pkg.

Power lumbar support, 530i, 540i automatic	400	340

NA with 540i Sport Pkg. or 12-way power sport seats.

12-way power sport seats, 530i	475	405

Requires Sport Pkg. and leather upholstery or Premium Pkg.

Split folding rear seat, sedans	475	405

Includes ski sack. 530i requires Premium Pkg.

Heated steering wheel	150	130

Requires Cold Weather Pkg.

AM/FM/CD player	200	170
Premium sound system	1200	1020
Power rear and manual rear-door sunshades, sedans	575	490
Manual rear-door sunshades, wagons	180	155
Front and rear park distance control	700	595

Appearance and Miscellaneous

Xenon headlights, 525, 530i	500	425
Self-leveling suspension, 525 wagon	760	645
Mixed parallel spoke alloy wheels, 540i	300	255

540i automatic requires Sport Pkg.

BMW 7-SERIES

Rear-wheel-drive luxury car

Base price range: $62,900-$92,100. Built in Germany. **Also consider:** Audi A8, Lexus LS 430, Mercedes-Benz S-Class

FOR • Acceleration • Ride • Steering/handling • Passenger room/comfort • Build quality • Exterior finish • Interior materials
AGAINST • Fuel economy • Navigation system controls

Slight appearance changes and wider availability of the Sport Package option marked the springtime debut of BMW's 2001

Specifications begin on page 535.

BMW

BMW 740iL

flagship sedans, the V8 740i and longer-wheelbase 740iL and the V12 750iL. All get body-colored lower body panels and white turn-signal lenses. Returning linewide standards include 5-speed automatic transmission, onboard navigation system, Xenon headlights, antiskid system, front side airbags, and BMW's front Head Protection System with side-window tubular airbags. Rear head-protection airbags are included with the optional lower-body rear sidebags. Standard on the 750iL and optional on 740 models is an Active Ride Package with electronic shock-absorber damping and self-leveling rear suspension. Returning for the 740i and newly available for iL models is the available Sport Package with black exterior trim, special wood interior trim, firm-ride suspension, and 18-inch wheels; the last two are no longer sold as stand-alone options. The 740i package includes BMW's Steptronic manual shift feature, while the 740iL version includes the Active Ride Package with a sport setting.

EVALUATION All 7s are quiet, comfortable, and enjoyable to drive. The V8 is so strong and silky that we see little need to pay so much more for the V12. BMW says half of 740i models are ordered with the Sport Package, which sharpens handling without harming the 7-Series' world-class ride. The 740i doesn't lack for interior or cargo space, but few cars of any size have more rear seat room than the longer iL models. All 7s boast supportive and comfortable seats, clear gauges, strategically placed major controls, and a multitude of standard amenities. Unfortunately, lots of gizmos means lots of controls, not all of which are easy to use, the available in-dash navigation system in particular. A new-generation 7 is due in the U.S. by summer 2002 for the 2003 campaign, leaving the current models facing the newer Mercedes S-Class and Lexus' redesigned LS. The big BMWs remain hard to fault, however, and should carry deeper discounts than those competitors.

ENGINES

	dohc V8	ohc V12
Size, liters/cu. in.	4.4/268	5.4/328
Horsepower @ rpm	282 @ 5400	326 @ 5000
Torque (lb-ft) @ rpm	324 @ 3700	361 @ 3900
Availability	S[1]	S[2]

Prices are accurate at time of publication; subject to manufacturer's change.

BMW

EPA city/highway mpg	dohc V8	ohc V12
5-speed OD automatic	17/23	13/20

1. 740i, 740iL. 2. 750iL.

PRICES

BMW 7-Series	Retail Price	Dealer Invoice
740i 4-door sedan	$62900	$56770
740iL 4-door sedan	66900	60370
750iL 4-door sedan	92100	83050
Destination charge	570	570

750iL adds $2600 Gas Guzzler Tax. 740i w/Sport Pkg. adds $1700 Gas Guzzler Tax.

STANDARD EQUIPMENT:

740i: 4.4-liter dohc V8 engine, 5-speed automatic transmission, traction control, driver- and passenger-side airbags, front side-impact airbags, front side head-protection system, antilock 4-wheel disc brakes, antiskid system, daytime running lights, variable-assist power steering, power tilt/telescopic leather-wrapped steering wheel, cruise control, air conditioning w/dual automatic climate control, interior air filter, navigation system, memory system (steering wheel, driver seat, outside mirrors), leather upholstery, 14-way power front seats w/lumbar adjustment, center console, cupholders, trunk pass-through, wood interior trim, heated power mirrors w/passenger-side tilt-down parking aid, power windows, power door locks, remote keyless entry, power sunroof, rain-sensing variable intermittent wipers and heated windshield-washer jets, automatic day/night rearview mirror, reading lights, illuminated visor mirrors, universal garage door opener, AM/FM/cassette w/6-disc CD changer, steering-wheel radio controls, tachometer, trip computer, rear defogger, remote decklid release, floormats, theft-deterrent system, Xenon headlights, headlight washers, fog lights, tool kit, 235/60R16 tires, alloy wheels.

740iL adds: 6-inch longer wheelbase.

750iL adds: 5.4-liter V12 engine, 5-speed automatic transmission w/manual-shift capability, automatic day/night outside mirrors, Active Comfort Seats, heated front and rear seats, heated steering wheel, power rear seats with power lumbar adjustment, power rear headrests, cellular telephone, power rear sunshade, manual rear side sunshades, parking distance control, ski sack, Electronic Damping Control, self-leveling rear suspension.

OPTIONAL EQUIPMENT:
Major Packages

Convenience Pkg., 740i, 740iL	915	780

Automatic day/night rearview rearview mirrors, power rear sunshade.

BMW

	Retail Price	Dealer Invoice
Cold Weather Pkg., 740iL	$1100	$935
740i	950	810

Heated front and rear seats, heated steering wheel (740iL), ski sack.

Sport Pkg., 740i	2800	2380

Automatic transmission w/manual-shift capability, performance axle and torque converter, 18-way power contour sport seats, sport steering wheel, special wood interior trim, Shadowline exterior trim, sport suspension, 235/50ZR18 front tires, 255/45ZR18 tires, M-parallel spoke alloy wheels. NA w/Active Ride Pkg.

Sport Pkg., 740iL	3100	2635

Shadowline exterior trim, special wood interior trim, electronic damping control w/sport mode, 235/50ZR18 front tires, 255/45ZR18 rear tires, M-parallel spoke alloy wheels. NA w/Active Ride Pkg.

Sport Pkg., 750iL	1800	1530

Special wood interior trim Shadowline exterior trim, M-parallel spoke alloy wheels.

Safety Features

Rear side-impact airbags and rear side head-protection system	550	470
Break-resistant security glass	2600	2210

Comfort and Convenience

Active Comfort Seats, 740i	1700	1445
740iL	500	425

Includes 2-way power upper backrest adjustment, power lumbar support.

Parking distance control, 740i, 740iL	900	765

Appearance and Miscellaneous

Active Ride Pkg., 740i, 740iL	1900	1615

Electronic Damping Control, self-leveling rear suspension.

Ellipsoid style alloy wheels, 740i, 740iL	NC	NC

Includes run-flat tires.

17-inch alloy wheels, 750iL	NC	NC

Includes run-flat tires.

BMW X5

4-wheel-drive midsize sport-utility vehicle

Base price range: $38,900-$49,400. Built in USA. **Also consider:** Acura MDX, Lexus RX 300, Mercedes-Benz M-Class

FOR • Acceleration • Build quality • Cargo room • Exterior finish • Interior materials **AGAINST** • Navigation system controls • Fuel economy

Prices are accurate at time of publication; subject to manufacturer's change.

BMW

BMW X5 3.0i

BMW's first sport-utility vehicle emphasizes the carlike attributes and styling of the Lexus RX 300 instead of the off-road-wagon character of the Mercedes-Benz M-Class. Built in South Carolina on an exclusive unibody platform, the X5 has permanently engaged 4WD, all-independent suspension, and a tailgate with separate liftglass. In exterior size, it's close to the Mercedes and larger than the Lexus, but is smaller inside than both.

The X5 4.4i has a V8 and standard 5-speed automatic transmission featuring BMW's Steptronic manual shift gate. The lower-priced 6-cylinder 3.0i offers a 5-speed manual or the automatic transmission. Both models have standard traction control, an antiskid system, and antilock 4-wheel disc brakes. X5s are not intended for severe off-road use. Their 4WD lacks low-range gearing; instead, it automatically brakes individual wheels to limit slip in low-grip conditions. A standard Hill Descent Control feature limits speed to 6 mph down steep slopes.

Other standard features include power tilt/telescopic steering wheel, 70/30 split-fold rear seat, front side airbags and BMW's head-protecting tubular airbags that deploy from above the front door windows in a side impact. Rear lower-body side airbags are optional. Included on the 4.4i and optional for the 3.0i are load-leveling suspension, 18-inch wheels and tires, and leather upholstery with wood interior trim. An available Sport package delivers black exterior trim, sport suspension and, for the 4.4i, 19-inch wheels and tires. A navigation system with dashboard screen is optional for both.

PERFORMANCE Blend the station-wagon manners of the RX 300 with the robust performance of the V8 ML430, and you have the X5 4.4i. We haven't yet tested a 3.0i, but the V8 version has ready acceleration from any speed (we clocked 0-60 mph at just 7 seconds); outstanding open-road stability; and strong, progressive brakes. Fuel economy is less impressive: just 14.1 mpg in our tests, and both engines require premium fuel. In handling, the X5 never feels sloppy, but it does have a high center of gravity and 7.1 inches of ground clearance. That prompts

BMW

noticeable body lean and some plowing in tight, fast turns. The Sport suspension sharpens steering response and reduces cornering lean, but not to the level of BMW's own 5-Series wagon. Some of our testers find the X5's steering effort too high at parking-lot speeds.

This BMW has a tauter ride than the car-based Lexus but is more absorbent than the Mercedes. The Sport package lets tar strips and the like register through seats and steering wheel, but copes comfortably enough with deep ruts and sharp bumps. Blissfully absent are the bounding motions over wavy or broken surfaces characteristic of truck-type SUVs. The 4WD and Hill Descent worked well during our brief forays off-pavement, but the 19-inch tires offer poor grip in snow. Few SUVs better isolate wind rush, although those 19-inch tires roar over coarse surfaces. The V8 is never loud or unpleasant, but toeing the gas prompts a "sporty" exhaust note that some of us found tiresome.

ACCOMMODATIONS Top-grade materials and solid assembly create a sporty, elegant interior appropriate to the X5's mission—and price. Step-in height is no lower than most midsize SUVs', but wide doorways provide unimpeded ingress and egress. The elevated view is SUV-typical, though shorter drivers must peer over an unusually tall instrument housing. Visibility aft is interrupted by the rear headrests and the tall body build. BMW's Park Distance Control is optional to warn of "hidden" objects both front and rear.

Most switchgear is precise and obvious. There's automatic up/down for all side glass, but the power window controls are awkwardly placed on the driver's armrest. The optional navigation system can be confounding to program and operate, and direct sunlight and fingerprints obscure its screen. Despite its power tilt/telescopic adjustment, the steering-wheel rim can interfer with the driver's view of the speedometer and tachometer.

Front seating is spacious and supportive. In back there's generous head clearance but limited foot room with the front seats more than halfway back. The middle-rear position is tighter and less comfortable than in the M-Class and RX 300, and the BMW's rear wheel housings intrude slightly into outboard hip room. Cargo-bay access is easy except for a lofty liftover. The rear seatbacks fold smoothly, though a ski pass-through costs extra and the accordion-like cargo cover is flimsy and finicky. With a maximum 55-cubic-feet of cargo volume, the X5 trails the M-Class (85 cubic feet), the RX (75), and even BMW's 5-Series wagon (65).

VALUE A 4WD RX 300 is a better value than the X5 4.4i in a station-wagon-type SUV, while the M-Class remains a satisfying Best Buy among luxury truck-type alternatives. But this BMW's overall mix of performance, comfort, and character is unique among SUVs.

Prices are accurate at time of publication; subject to manufacturer's change.

CONSUMER GUIDE

BMW

ENGINES

	dohc I6	dohc V8
Size, liters/cu. in.	3.0/181	4.4/268
Horsepower @ rpm	225 @ 5900	282 @ 5400
Torque (lb-ft) @ rpm	214 @ 3500	324 @ 3600
Availability	S[1]	S[2]
EPA city/highway mpg		
5-speed manual	15/20	
5-speed OD automatic	15/20	13/17

1. 3.0i. 2. 4.4i.

PRICES

BMW X5	Retail Price	Dealer Invoice
3.0i 4-door wagon	$38900	$35170
4.4i 4-door wagon	49400	44620
Destination charge	570	570

STANDARD EQUIPMENT:

3.0i: 3.0-liter dohc 6-cylinder engine, 5-speed manual transmission, permanent 4-wheel drive, traction control, dual front airbags, front side-impact airbags, front side-head-protection system, antilock 4-wheel disc brakes, antiskid system, air conditioning, interior air filter, variable-assist power steering, power tilt/telescoping leather-wrapped steering wheel, cruise control, vinyl upholstery, front bucket seats, 8-way power driver seat, memory system (driver seat, mirrors, steering wheel), center console, cupholders, split folding rear seat, heated power mirrors w/passenger-side tilt-down parking aid, power windows, power door locks, remote keyless entry, AM/FM/cassette, steering wheel radio controls, map lights, variable intermittent wipers, trip computer, outside temperature indicator, illuminated visor mirrors, universal garage door opener, rear defogger, intermittent rear wiper/washer, power tailgate release, cargo cover, theft-deterrent system, fog lights, roof rails, full-size spare, 235/65R17 tires, alloy wheels.

4.4i adds: 4.4-liter dohc V8 engine, 5-speed automatic transmission w/manual-shift capability, dual-zone automatic climate control, rear climate controls, leather upholstery, 6-way-power passenger seat, wood interior trim, rear automatic-leveling suspension, 255/55R18 tires.

OPTIONAL EQUIPMENT:
Major Packages

Premium Pkg., 3.0i	2950	2510

Leather upholstery, 6-way power passenger seat, wood interior trim, power sunroof.

Climate Pkg., 3.0i	850	725

Dual-zone automatic climate control, rear climate controls, rear side shades, privacy glass.

Specifications begin on page 535.

BMW

	Retail Price	Dealer Invoice
Sport Pkg.	$2470	$2100

Sport seats, sport steering wheel, black headliner, titanium-colored grille insert, Shadowline trim, black chrome exhaust pipes, rear automatic-leveling suspension (3.0i), sport suspension, 255/55R18 tires (3.0i), 255/50R19 front and 285/45R19 rear tires (4.4i).

Activity Pkg.	850	725

Heated front seats, ski sack, rain-sensing wipers, headlight washers.

Safety Features

Rear side-impact airbags	385	325

Comfort and Convenience

Navigation system	1990	1690
Includes upgraded trip computer.		
Power sunroof	1050	895
CD player	200	170
NA w/navigation system.		
Premium sound system	1200	1020
Upgraded trip computer, 4.4i	300	255
Park distance control	350	300
Comfort seats, 4.4i	1200	1020
Heated rear seats, 4.4i	350	300
Requires Activity Pkg.		
Front lumbar support	400	340
NA w/Sport Pkg. or sport seats.		
Inside and outside automatic day/night mirrors	300	255
Retractable load floor	380	325

Appearance and Miscellaneous

Xenon headlights	500	425

BMW Z3 SERIES

Rear-wheel-drive sports and GT car

Base price range: NA. Built in USA. **Also consider:** Honda S2000, Mazda Miata, Mercedes-Benz SLK-Class, Porsche Boxster

FOR • Steering/handling • Acceleration • Exterior finish **AGAINST** • Noise • Cargo space • Rear visibility (convertible)

New engines make 2001 news for BMW's American-built 2-seaters. Last year's base 2.5-liter Z3 2.3 Roadster gives way to a 2.5i with a new-design 2.5 inline-6 making 14 more horsepower but 6 pound-feet less torque. Similarly, the 2.8-liter Z3 2.8 Roadster and hatchback Coupe become 3.0i models via a 3.0-liter six with 32 more hp and 8 more lb-ft. The high-performance 3.2-liter M Roadster and M Coupe switch to the

Prices are accurate at time of publication; subject to manufacturer's change.

BMW

BMW Z3 3.0i 2-door convertible

same newly uprated engine as the 2001 M3 coupe, gaining 90 hp and 30 lb-ft. In addition, BMW's 5-speed automatic with Steptronic manual shift gate replaces the previous 4-speed option. Five-speed manual remains standard across the board and mandatory for M models. Redesigned wheels and a little extra interior chrome feature on all models, which also get BMW's Dynamic Brake Control as standard; DSC helps maintain braking stability in turns together with standard traction control and BMW's antiskid Dynamic Stability Control. All Zs retain standard side airbags, with M models adding a new tire-pressure warning system. Convertibles feature fixed rollover bars, and the M Roadster includes a power top that's available on other convertibles.

EVALUATION These BMWs encourage exuberant driving. We haven't yet tested the '01s, but all models should be quicker without using much more fuel. M models will be even more scorching than before, while the 2.5i should remain brisk, at least with manual shift. The 3.0i models aren't M-hot, but are usefully stronger than the base Roadster. Noise levels are high, especially in convertibles, and ride can be choppy, especially in the stiffly sprung M models, but all Z3s are comfortable enough for sports cars. Handling is uniformly great, braking terrific. Though wet-weather grip is the best, the standard electronic chassis controls are proven assets. Large drivers can feel cramped at the wheel, luggage space is meager (coupes have more than convertibles, but still not much), and Roadsters suffer some unwanted body shake. Despite those flaws and an aging design, the Z3s are capable "classic" sports cars at competitive prices, with the base convertible being the best dollar value.

ENGINES

	dohc I6	dohc I6	dohc I6
Size, liters/cu. in.	2.5/152	3.0/182	3.2/192
Horsepower @ rpm	184 @ 5500	225 @ 5900	330 @ 7900
Torque (lb-ft) @ rpm	175 @ 3500	214 @ 3500	255 @ 4900

Specifications begin on page 535.

BMW

	dohc I6 S[1]	dohc I6 S[2]	dohc I6 S[3]
Availability			
EPA city/highway mpg			
5-speed manual	20/27	21/28	19/26
5-speed OD automatic	19/26	19/25	NA

1. Z3 2.5i. 2. Z3 3.0i. 3. M Roadster, M coupe.

2001 prices unavailable at time of publication.

PRICES

2000 BMW Z3 Series	Retail Price	Dealer Invoice
2.3 2-door convertible	$31300	$28330
2.8 2-door convertible	36900	33370
2.8 2-door hatchback	36550	33055
M-Series 2-door convertible	42700	38590
M-Series 2-door hatchback	41800	37780
Destination charge	570	570

STANDARD EQUIPMENT:

2.3: 2.5-liter dohc 6-cylinder engine, 5-speed manual transmission, limited-slip differential, traction control, dual front airbags, side-impact airbags, antilock 4-wheel disc brakes, antiskid system, roll bars (convertible), air conditioning, variable-assist power steering, leather-wrapped steering wheel/shifter/handbrake, vinyl upholstery, 4-way power driver seat, 2-way power passenger seat, center storage console, cupholders, 6-speaker AM/FM/weatherband/cassette, analog clock, power mirrors, power door locks, power windows, tachometer, visor mirrors, intermittent wipers, tool kit, 225/50ZR16 tires, alloy wheels.

2.8 adds: 2.8-liter dohc 6-cylinder engine, leather upholstery, sport seats (hatchback), wood interior trim (hatchback), cruise control, Harman/Kardon sound system, fog lights.

M-Series add: 3.2-liter dohc 6-cylinder engine, power convertible top (convertible), upgraded leather upholstery, heated sport seats, heated mirrors and washer jets, heated driver door lock, chrome interior trim, metallic paint, 225/50ZR17 front tires, 245/40ZR17 rear tires, deletes antiskid system, wood interior trim, fog lights.

OPTIONAL EQUIPMENT:

Major Packages

Premium Pkg., 2.3	2000	1700
2.8	950	810

Power convertible top, leather upholstery (2.3), wood interior trim.

Powertrains

4-speed automatic transmission, 2.3, 2.8	975	925

Prices are accurate at time of publication; subject to manufacturer's change.

BMW • BUICK

Comfort and Convenience

	Retail Price	Dealer Invoice
Cruise control, 2.3	$475	$405
Leather upholstery, 2.3	1150	980
Extended leather upholstery, 2.8	1200	1020

Includes color-keyed leather steering wheel, instrument cluster hood, console sides, door upper ledges and pulls.

Chrome interior trim, 2.3, 2.8	150	130
Aluminum interior trim, 2.8 hatchback	150	130
Heated seats, 2.3, 2.8	500	425

Includes heated mirrors.

Sport seats, 2.3/2.8 convertible	400	340

Requires heated seats.

AM/FM/CD player	200	170
Harman/Kardon sound system, 2.3	675	575
Trip computer, 2.3, 2.8	300	255
Power convertible top, 2.3, 2.8 convertible	750	640
Power tilt-up roof panel, hatchback	300	255

Appearance and Miscellaneous

Fog lights, 2.3	260	220
Hardtop, convertibles	1900	1615
17-inch alloy wheels, 2.8	1125	955

Includes 225/45ZR17 front tires, 245/40ZR17 rear tires.

BUICK CENTURY

Buick Century

Front-wheel-drive midsize car; similar to Buick Regal, Chevrolet Impala, Oldsmobile Intrigue, and Pontiac Grand Prix

Base price range: $19,840-$22,871. Built in Canada. **Also consider:** Honda Accord, Mercury Sable, Toyota Camry

FOR • Ride   **AGAINST** • Handling • Steering

Specifications begin on page 535.

BUICK

Buick's lowest-priced car for 2001 gets new Special Edition option packages, and GM's OnStar assistance system is standard instead of optional on the top Century model. Century shares its basic platform with the sportier Regal, but targets mainstream midsize-sedan buyers over Regal's younger audience.

A 175-horsepower 3.1-liter V6 continues as Century's sole engine. Automatic transmission, traction control, and antilock brakes are standard. Custom and up-trim Limited models are offered. Both have a standard front bench seat for 6-passenger capacity; bucket seats aren't offered. Exclusive to the Limited are standard leather upholstery and a side airbag for the driver.

The Custom's new Special Edition option package adds the Limited's cruise control, OnStar system, power driver seat, and AM/FM cassette. Limited's Special Edition packages include dual-zone climate control, power front passenger seat, split-folding rear seat, and alloy wheels.

PERFORMANCE Century isn't exciting, but it's a quiet, comfortable, sedan at an affordable price. The soft suspension absorbs most bumps easily, and although body lean in turns is pronounced, overall control is good. The low-effort steering furnishes little road feel, but makes for easy low-speed maneuverability. Wind and road noise are minimal. The V6 growls when furnishing passing power, but is otherwise a peaceful runner and nicely suited to this duty. Acceleration and passing power are adequate, aided by smooth gear changes and rapid downshifts. Our test 2000 Century averaged 19.4 mpg, about what we expect from '01s.

ACCOMMODATIONS Four adults get plenty of room, but the softly padded standard cloth seats have subpar thigh and lower-back support. The optional leather seats are firmer and more comfortable. As for why there is a side airbag for the driver only, Buick plans to offer one eventually, but says Century's body design makes it difficult to develop a system safe enough for children. Instrumentation is confined to a speedometer and fuel and coolant gauges, but they're easy to read, and a dashboard light that warns of low tire pressure is a thoughtful touch. No control is obstructed or complex, although those for the climate system are mounted low in the center of the dashboard where they interfere with a center passenger's knees. Generous doorways make for easy entry and exit. Centurys are solidly built with interior materials that feel substantial for this price class. The trunk has a wide, flat floor, but loading and unloading requires stretching over a wide bumper-level shelf.

VALUE Century is a well-thought-out sedan with a no-surprises formula that's proved appealing to conservative buyers. It's worth a look.

ENGINES

	ohv V6
Size, liters/cu. in.	3.1/191

Prices are accurate at time of publication; subject to manufacturer's change.

CONSUMER GUIDE

BUICK

	ohv V6
Horsepower @ rpm	175 @ 5200
Torque (lb-ft) @ rpm	195 @ 4000
Availability	S

EPA city/highway mpg
4-speed OD automatic 20/30

PRICES

Buick Century	Retail Price	Dealer Invoice
Custom 4-door sedan	$19840	$18154
Limited 4-door sedan	22871	20927
Destination charge	600	600

STANDARD EQUIPMENT:

Custom: 3.1-liter V6 engine, 4-speed automatic transmission, traction control, dual front airbags, antilock brakes, daytime running lights, emergency inside trunk release, air conditioning w/dual-zone manual climate control, interior air filter, power steering, tilt steering wheel, cloth reclining front split bench seat, front storage armrest, cupholders, power mirrors, power windows, power door locks, remote keyless entry, AM/FM radio, digital clock, rear defogger, variable intermittent wipers, visor mirrors, map lights, remote decklid release, automatic headlights, theft-deterrent system, cornering lights, tire-pressure monitor, 205/70R15 tires, wheel covers.

Limited adds: driver-side side-impact airbag, variable-assist power steering, leather-wrapped steering wheel, cruise control, OnStar System w/one year service (roadside assistance, emergency services; other services available), leather upholstery, 6-way power driver seat, AM/FM/cassette, heated power mirrors, illuminated visor mirrors, rear courtesy/reading lights, floormats.

OPTIONAL EQUIPMENT:
Major Packages

Premium Pkg. 1SB, Custom	605	520

Cruise control, AM/FM/cassette, heated power mirrors, rear window antenna, cargo net, floormats.

Special Edition Pkg. 1SC, Custom	1986	1708
Manufacturer's discount price	1486	1278

Premium Pkg. 1SB plus OnStar System w/one year service (roadside assistance, emergency services; other services available), 6-way power driver seat, AM/FM/cassette w/automatic tone control, steering-wheel radio controls, illuminated visor mirrors, chrome wheel covers.

Special Edition Pkg. 1SD, Custom	2286	1966
Manufacturer's discount price	1786	1536

Special Edition Pkg. 1SC plus alloy wheels.

Specifications begin on page 535.

BUICK

	Retail Price	Dealer Invoice
Luxury Pkg. 1SF, Limited	$645	$555

Dual-zone automatic climate control, 6-way power passenger seat, automatic day/night rearview and driver side mirrors.

| Special Edition Pkg. 1SG, Limited | 2180 | 1875 |
| Manufacturer's discount price | 1680 | 1445 |

Luxury Pkg. 1SF plus AM/FM/cassette/CD player, upgraded speakers, steering-wheel radio controls, split folding rear seat, alloy wheels.

Comfort and Convenience

Split folding rear seat	275	237

Includes armrest, cupholders. Custom requires option pkg.

6-way power passenger seat, Limited	330	283
Power sunroof, Limited	695	598
AM/FM/cassette, Custom	195	168
AM/FM/cassette/CD player,		
Custom w/Pkg. 1SB	225	194
Custom w/Pkg. 1SC/D, Limited	200	172

Includes steering-wheel radio controls.

| Concert Sound III speakers, Limited | 210 | 181 |

Requires option pkg., AM/FM/cassette/CD player.

| Steering-wheel radio controls, Custom | 125 | 108 |

Appearance and Miscellaneous

Alloy wheels, Limited	375	323
205/70R15 whitewall tires	150	129

BUICK LeSABRE

Buick LeSabre Limited

Front-wheel-drive full-size car; similar to Oldsmobile Aurora and Pontiac Bonneville

Base price range: $24,107-$28,796. Built in USA. **Also consider:** Chrysler Concorde, Mercury Grand Marquis, Toyota Avalon

FOR • Acceleration • Automatic transmission performance

Prices are accurate at time of publication; subject to manufacturer's change.

BUICK

• Instruments/controls • Ride **AGAINST** • Fuel economy • Rear-seat comfort

LeSabre is America's best-selling full-size car and confines its 2001 changes to shuffled equipment. Custom and Limited models continue, both with a 3.8-liter V6 and automatic transmission as the sole powertrain. Traction control is standard on Limited, optional on the Custom. Firmer suspension and 16-inch wheels in place of 15s are available as part of the optional Gran Touring package for both models. Antilock 4-wheel-disc brakes and front side airbags are standard. A standard split front bench seat allows six-passenger seating; bucket front seats with a console are optional.

General Motor's OnStar assistance system is standard on the Limited, and for '01 it's also offered on the Custom as part of the Prestige option package, which includes a CD player and a power front passenger seat. The Custom also gains a standard power driver's seat. The optional Driver Confidence package is no longer available on the Custom but continues on the Limited. It adds GM's StabiliTrak antiskid system, which is designed to sense an impending skid in a turn and brake an individual wheel to keep the car on its intended course. Also included are self-sealing tires and a head-up instrument display. LeSabre shares its structure with the Cadillac Seville, Pontiac Bonneville, and Oldsmobile Aurora.

PERFORMANCE LeSabre is a generally capable performer that makes few demands on its driver. It takes off smartly, has ample passing power, and furnishes smooth, fairly responsive gear changes. We averaged 17.9 mpg in our test of 2000 LeSabres and expect similar results from '01s. Handling is quite competent for a large family 4-door, with moderate lean in turns and good grip in steady-state cornering.

The base suspension's smooth ride is marred by some body float over big humps and dips. The Gran Touring suspension does a poor job of absorbing most sharp bumps and ridges, but worse, it compromises control by feeling jittery over all but blemish-free pavement. There's good directional stability with either suspension, but the steering feels artificially heavy. We know StabiliTrak works well based on experience with recent Cadillacs, so we applaud its availability in the LeSabre.

The brakes are easy to modulate, but stopping power isn't particularly impressive. Wind and road noise are well-muffled, but tires whine on grooved or pebbled surfaces. The engine is quiet at cruise and emits a muted growl in hard acceleration.

ACCOMMODATIONS LeSabre's cabin has a slightly closed-in feel and can't fit three adults across without squeezing. Buckets or bench, the front seats are roomy for two, and the cushions are pillowy but not uncomfortable. Rear-seat comfort is disappointing for a full-size family car. The cushion is low to the floor and its soft foam provides little thigh

Specifications begin on page 535.

BUICK

or back support. Legs and feet are pinched without the front seats moved well up. Oddly, Custom models don't come with a rear center armrest.

Gauges and controls are large, simple, and mostly well-placed, but the headlamp controls use an inconvenient pushbutton design. Also, highly reflective plastic faceplates make it hard to read the transmission-position indicator, trip odometer, and audio and climate panels. And the Limited's automatic climate controls are difficult to adjust while driving.

A large glovebox and an optional bucket-seat center console provide plenty of interior storage, though the console's cupholder is awkward to deploy. Rear seatbacks don't fold but the Limited's rear-seat passthrough is a thoughtful addition, and the roomy trunk has a large opening. Our test cars were tight and rattle free, but LeSabre's interior suffers an abundance of hard plastic and budget-grade upholstery.

VALUE LeSabre imparts a feeling of size and substance, and the standard-equipment list is well-thought-out. Subpar rear-seat accommodations and indifferent interior furnishings are letdowns, but overall, this Buick should satisfy its conservative core audience. Base prices are competitive, too, though options add up quickly and loaded Limiteds nudge $30,000.

ENGINES

	ohv V6
Size, liters/cu. in.	3.8/231
Horsepower @ rpm	205 @ 5200
Torque (lb-ft) @ rpm	230 @ 4000
Availability	S
EPA city/highway mpg	
4-speed OD automatic	19/30

PRICES

Buick LeSabre	Retail Price	Dealer Invoice
Custom 4-door sedan	$24107	$22058
Limited 4-door sedan	28796	26348
Destination charge	655	655

STANDARD EQUIPMENT:

Custom: 3.8-liter V6 engine, 4-speed automatic transmission, dual front airbags, front side-impact airbags, antilock 4-wheel disc brakes, daytime running lights, air conditioning, power steering, tilt steering wheel, cruise control, cloth front split bench seat, 6-way power driver seat, cupholders, power mirrors, power windows, power door locks, remote keyless entry, overhead console, map lights, auxiliary power outlets, AM/FM/cassette, digital clock, variable intermittent wipers, rear defogger, visor mirrors, power decklid release, automatic headlights, floormats, theft-deterrent system, automatic level con-

Prices are accurate at time of publication; subject to manufacturer's change.

BUICK

trol, 215/70R15 tires, wheel covers.

Limited adds: traction control, OnStar System w/one year service (roadside assistance, emergency services; other services available), front dual-zone automatic climate control and rear climate control, interior air filter, heated 10-way power front seats w/power recliners, trunk pass-through, AM/FM/cassette/CD player, steering wheel radio controls, tachometer, tire pressure monitor, heated power mirrors, automatic day/night driver-side and rearview mirrors, compass, universal garage door opener, illuminated visor mirrors, rain-sensing variable intermittent wipers, cornering lights, alloy wheels.

OPTIONAL EQUIPMENT:
Major Packages

	Retail Price	Dealer Invoice
Luxury Pkg. 1SD, Custom	$1105	$950

Illuminated visor mirrors, AM/FM/cassette w/automatic tone control, steering wheel radio controls, upgraded speakers, 6-way power passenger seat, automatic day/night rearview mirror, analog gauge cluster, interior air filter, cargo net, bodyside stripes, alloy wheels.

Prestige Pkg. 1SE, Custom	2314	1990

Luxury Pkg. 1SD plus OnStar System w/one year service (roadside assistance, emergency services; other services available), AM/FM/cassette/CD player, 6-way power passenger seat, rain-sensing wipers, universal garage door opener, compass, theft-deterrent system w/alarm.

Driver Confidence Pkg.,		
Limited w/cross lace alloy wheels	880	757
Limited w/Gran Touring Pkg.	730	628

Antiskid system, head-up instrument display, self-sealing tires (deleted when ordered w/Gran Touring Pkg.).

Gran Touring Pkg.	235	202

Leather-wrapped steering wheel, sport suspension, rear stabilizer bar, 225/60R16 tires, polished alloy wheels. Custom requires Luxury Pkg. or Prestige Pkg.

Seating/Convenience Console Pkg.	70	60

Bucket seats, convenience console w/writing surface, additional cupholders and power outlets, provisions for cellular telephone and fax.

Powertrains

Traction control, Custom	175	151

Includes 225/60R16 tires. Requires Luxury or Prestige Pkg.

Comfort and Convenience

Power sunroof, Limited	1045	899
Leather upholstery	780	671

Custom requires Luxury or Prestige Pkg.

Heated front seats, Custom	260	224

Includes heated power mirrors. Requires Luxury or Prestige Pkg., power passenger seat.

Specifications begin on page 535.

BUICK

	Retail Price	Dealer Invoice
Power passenger seat, Custom	$330	$284
Requires Luxury Pkg.		
Driver seat memory, Limited	190	163
Includes memory mirrors and climate control.		
AM/FM/cassette/CD player, Custom	200	172
Includes automatic tone control and steering-wheel radio controls. Requires Luxury Pkg.		
12-disc CD changer, Limited	595	512
Cross lace alloy wheels	165	142
Includes 225/60R16 tires. Custom requires Luxury or Prestige Pkg. NA w/Gran Touring Pkg.		

BUICK PARK AVENUE

Buick Park Avenue Ultra

Front-wheel-drive near-luxury car

Base price range: $32,980-$37,490. Built in USA. **Also consider:** Chrysler LHS and 300M, Oldsmobile Aurora, Toyota Avalon

FOR • Acceleration • Passenger and cargo room • Steering/handling (Ultra) **AGAINST** • Fuel economy (supercharged V6) • Steering/handling (base suspension) • Rear visibility

Ultrasonic rear parking assist is a new option for Buick's 2001 flagship sedan, while leather upholstery is now standard on the base Park Avenues. Base models use a 205-horsepower V6, Ultras add a supercharger for 240 hp. Both have automatic transmission, antilock brakes, and self-leveling rear suspension. Optional is a Gran Touring suspension package that includes firmer suspension settings and more aggressive tire tread. Standard on Ultra and optional on the base Park Avenue is General Motors' StabiliTrak antiskid system, designed to sense an impending skid in a turn and apply the brakes to an individual wheel to keep the car on its intended course.

For '01, ultrasonic rear parking assist is optional on both models and

Prices are accurate at time of publication; subject to manufacturer's change.

BUICK

uses a series of lights visible in the inside mirror to warn of obstacles when the car is backing. Leather is now standard on both Park Avenues; it was optional on the base model. The base model also gains the Ultra's interior memory system, which allows a choice of two driver-programmed presets for climate controls, front seats, and outside mirrors. General Motor's OnStar assistance system is standard on Ultra and optional on the base Park Avenue.

PERFORMANCE Both Park Avenues are quiet, substantial-feeling cars with ample power over a broad speed range. Ultra's supercharged performance is impressive, but Buick recommends premium gas. In tests of 2000s, we averaged 15.3 mpg in mostly city driving with one Ultra, 19.5 in a more even mix of city and highway work with another. A base model averaged 19.8 mpg on regular fuel. Expect little change with '01 Park Avenues.

The standard chassis is calibrated for comfort, so steering is light at freeway speeds and the body floats a bit over undulations. The optional Gran Touring suspension provides better ride control while reducing body lean and front-end plowing in corners. It includes magnetic variable-effort steering (standard on Ultra) that responds quickly but feels a tad numb. We know StabiliTrak works well based on experience with Cadillacs, so we welcome its availability in the Park Avenue. Braking is strong and stable, but panic stops induce marked nosedive.

ACCOMMODATIONS Park Avenue has abundant head and leg room, but not quite enough shoulder width for three large adults front or back. Seats are comfortable, despite lacking good lateral support in turns. The outboard front safety belts anchor to the seat, so they're easy to reach and always fit comfortably. The dash layout is traditional but works well enough. Outward vision is good, and the roomy trunk has a low liftover.

OnStar and the tire-pressure monitor that's standard on Ultra and optional on the base model are worthwhile features. And rear parking assist proves helpful when backing in tight spaces. Our testers are divided on the usefulness of the available head up display, which projects speed and other readings onto the windshield. The grade of interior materials doesn't match that of most import-brand near-luxury competitors, but Park Avenues we've tested have had good overall fit and finish, although sub-freezing weather brought out some suspension creaking in one Ultra.

VALUE In a class dominated by imports, Park Avenue gives up some prestige in exchange for traditional American room, power, and amenities at a competitive price.

ENGINES

	ohv V6	Supercharged ohv V6
Size, liters/cu. in.	3.8/231	3.8/231
Horsepower @ rpm	205 @ 5200	240 @ 5200

Specifications begin on page 535.

BUICK

	ohv V6	Supercharged ohv V6
Torque (lb-ft) @ rpm	230 @ 4000	280 @ 3600
Availability	S[1]	S[2]
EPA city/highway mpg		
4-speed OD automatic	19/30	18/27

1. Base. 2. Ultra.

PRICES

Buick Park Avenue	Retail Price	Dealer Invoice
Base 4-door sedan	$32980	$29847
Ultra 4-door sedan	37490	33928
Destination charge	720	720

STANDARD EQUIPMENT:

Base: 3.8-liter V6 engine, 4-speed automatic transmission, dual front airbags, front side-impact airbags, antilock 4-wheel disc brakes, daytime running lights, heated mirrors w/passenger-side parallel park assist, air conditioning w/dual-zone automatic climate control, interior air filter, power steering, tilt leather-wrapped steering wheel, cruise control, leather upholstery, front split bench seat with driver- and passenger-side 10-way power, front storage armrest, cupholders, rear seat trunk pass-through, memory system (seats, mirrors, climate controls, radio), power mirrors w/driver-side automatic day/night, power windows, power door locks, remote keyless entry, overhead console, rear defogger, AM/FM/cassette, digital clock, tachometer, power remote decklid and fuel-door releases, map lights, illuminated visor mirrors, variable intermittent wipers, automatic headlights, auxiliary power outlet, floormats, automatic level-control suspension, theft-deterrent system with starter interrupt, cornering lights, 225/60R16 tires, alloy wheels.

Ultra adds: supercharged 3.8-liter V6 engine, traction control, antiskid system, OnStar System w/one year service (roadside assistance, emergency services; other services available), magnetic variable-assist power steering, leather-wrapped steering wheel w/radio and climate controls, Seating Pkg. (power lumbar adjustment, heated front seats, power front and manual rear articulating headrests), rear-seat storage armrest, automatic day/night rearview mirror, compass, rain-sensing windshield wipers, driver information center (tire-pressure monitor, oil-life/level monitor, low-washer-fluid, dual trip odometers, additional warning lights, and trip computer), AM/FM/cassette/CD player w/upgraded sound system, rear illuminated vanity mirrors, universal garage door opener.

OPTIONAL EQUIPMENT:
Major Packages

Gran Touring Pkg., Base	285	245

Prices are accurate at time of publication; subject to manufacturer's change.

BUICK

	Retail Price	Dealer Invoice
Ultra	$200	$172

Includes Gran Touring suspension, magnetic variable-assist power steering (Base), 225/60R16 touring tires, unique alloy wheels. Base requires 1SE Pkg., traction control.

1SE Prestige Pkg., Base	1692	1455

OnStar System w/one year service (roadside assistance, emergency services; other services available), AM/FM/cassette/CD player, steering wheel radio controls, 4-way power front lumbar adjustment, automatic day/night rearview mirror, compass, universal garage door opener, driver information center (tire-pressure monitor, oil-life/level monitor, dual trip odometers, additional warning lights, trip computer), heated power mirrors, rain-sensing wipers, 3-note horn.

Powertrains
Traction control, Base w/1SE Pkg.	175	151

Safety Features
StabiliTrak antiskid system, Base	495	426

Requires 1SE Pkg., traction control.

Comfort and Convenience
AM/FM/cassette/CD player, Base	200	172

Includes steering-wheel radio controls.

12-disc CD changer	595	512

Base requires 1SE Pkg., Concert Sound III speakers.

Concert Sound III speakers, Base w/1SE Pkg.	280	241
Power sunroof	1095	942

Base requires 1SE Pkg.

Heated front seats, Base	225	194
Convenience Console/Five Person Seating Pkg., Ultra	185	159

Bucket seats, console with writing surface and accommodations for phone and fax, cupholders, auxiliary power outlets.

Head-up display	275	237

Requires rear ultrasonic parking assist. Base requires 1SE Pkg.

Rear ultrasonic parking assist	295	254

Requires head-up instrument display.

Chrome alloy wheels	735	632

BUICK REGAL

Front-wheel-drive midsize car; similar to Buick Century, Chevrolet Impala, Oldsmobile Intrigue, and Pontiac Grand Prix

Base price range: $22,845-$26,095. Built in Canada. **Also consider:** Honda Accord, Nissan Maxima, Toyota Camry

Specifications begin on page 535.

BUICK

Buick Regal w/Olympic pkg.

FOR • Acceleration • Instruments/controls **AGAINST** • Fuel economy (supercharged V6)

Olympic-themed editions are new to Buick's upscale midsize sedan for 2001, while OnStar becomes standard instead of optional on the top Regal model. Regal shares its basic design with Buick's Century but is styled and equipped to appeal to younger buyers. It's also similar under the skin to the Chevrolet Impala, Oldsmobile Intrigue, and Pontiac Grand Prix.

Regal is offered in LS and uplevel GS models. The LS has a 200-horsepower V6, the GS adds a supercharger for 240 hp. Automatic transmission, antilock 4-wheel disc brakes, and traction control are standard. A firmer Gran Touring suspension with 16-inch wheels in place of 15s is standard on GS and optional on LS. A side airbag for the driver is standard on GS and included with optional leather upholstery on the LS; leather upholstery is standard on the GS. A split folding rear seatback is standard on both models.

The new Olympic editions come in LS and GS form and add special gold, silver, or graphite paint with a lighter lower body color, plus taupe leather interior, USA Olympic insignia, and the Gran Touring suspension. The Olympic cars' look is by clothing designer Joseph Abboud. Buick plans to introduce other Joseph Abboud inspired Regal models later in the 2001 model year. Now standard on the GS, General Motors' OnStar assistance system is available on the LS as part of its Prestige option package.

PERFORMANCE Regal's base V6 is smooth, quiet, and strong, and is backed by a well-mannered automatic transmission. The supercharged GS is fast, clocking 0-60 mph in 6.9 seconds, about a second quicker than the LS in our tests of 2000 models. Unfortunately, the GS suffers some steering-wheel tug—called torque steer—in hard takeoffs. It demands premium fuel, but is not much thirstier than the LS, averaging 16.9-20.1 mpg in our tests. We expect similar results from '01 Regals.

The LS's base suspension rides and handles nearly as well as the GS's Gran Touring setup. Both are controlled and comfortable, although

Prices are accurate at time of publication; subject to manufacturer's change.

BUICK

no Regal combines bump absorption and cornering balance as well as most European sport sedans. Wind and road noise are noticed but not intrusive at highway speeds.

ACCOMMODATIONS Like most midsize sedans, Regal carries four adults in comfort, five in a pinch. Front seats are supportive even in spirited driving, something encouraged by legible, well-placed gauges and controls. Minor lapses include a somewhat complex climate panel and a console-bin cover that can pinch fingers. The trunklid opens 90 degrees on hinges that don't intrude on the ample luggage space, but there's a wide bumper shelf to stretch over. Workmanship is generally solid and satisfying, but interior ambiance is compromised by too many hard plastic surfaces.

VALUE Regal is solid, competitively priced, and well-equipped, but falls just short of the cohesive feel that earns the Intrigue and Grand Prix our Recommended label.

ENGINES

	ohv V6	Supercharged ohv V6
Size, liters/cu. in.	3.8/231	3.8/231
Horsepower @ rpm	200 @ 5200	240 @ 5200
Torque (lb-ft) @ rpm	225 @ 4000	280 @ 3600
Availability	S[1]	S[2]
EPA city/highway mpg		
4-speed OD automatic	19/30	18/27

1. LS. 2. GS.

PRICES

Buick Regal	Retail Price	Dealer Invoice
LS 4-door sedan	$22845	$20903
GS 4-door sedan	26095	23876
Destination charge	600	600

STANDARD EQUIPMENT:

LS: 3.8-liter V6 engine, 4-speed automatic transmission, traction control, dual front airbags, antilock 4-wheel disc brakes, daytime running lights, emergency inside trunk release, variable-assist power steering, leather-wrapped tilt steering wheel, cruise control, air conditioning w/dual-zone manual climate control, interior air filter, cloth upholstery, front bucket seats, front console, cupholders, auxiliary power outlets, 6-way power driver seat, split folding rear seat, power mirrors w/heated driver-side, power windows, power door locks, remote keyless entry, tachometer, variable intermittent wipers, rear defogger, map lights, visor mirrors, AM/FM/cassette, digital clock, remote decklid release, automatic headlights, theft-deterrent system, fog lights, tire pressure monitor, 215/70R15 tires, wheel covers.

GS adds: supercharged 3.8-liter V6 engine, full traction control, driver-side

BUICK

side-impact airbag, OnStar System w/one year service (roadside assistance, emergency services; other services available), leather upholstery, dual-zone automatic climate control, AM/FM/cassette/CD player, illuminated visor mirrors, driver information center (supercharger boost gauge, oil-change monitor, additional warning lights, trip computer), floormats, Gran Touring Suspension, 225/60R16 tires, alloy wheels.

OPTIONAL EQUIPMENT:

	Retail Price	Dealer Invoice

Major Packages

Premium Pkg. 1SB, LS $412 $354
Includes AM/FM/cassette/CD player, illuminated visor mirrors, floormats, cargo net.

Luxury Pkg. 1SC, LS 1997 1717
Premium Pkg. 1SB plus dual-zone automatic climate control, automatic day/night rearview mirror and driver-side mirror, steering-wheel-mounted radio controls, alloy wheels.

Touring Pkg. 1SD, LS 2542 2186
Luxury Pkg. 1SC plus leather upholstery, driver-side side-impact airbag, Monsoon sound system.

Prestige Pkg. 1SE, LS 3286 2826
Touring Pkg. plus Gran Touring Pkg. (Gran Touring suspension, 225/60R16 tires, alloy wheels), OnStar System w/one year service (roadside assistance, emergency services; other services available), Driver Information Center (oil change light monitor, additional warning lights, trip computer), 6-way power passenger seat.

Olympic Pkg. 1SF, LS 3926 3376
Manufacturer's discount price 3426 2946
Touring Pkg. 1SD plus Gran Touring Pkg. (Gran touring suspension, 225/60R16 tires, alloy wheels), 6-way power passenger seat, power sunroof, Olympic logo floormats and badging.

Luxury Pkg. 1SH, GS 540 464
Steering-wheel-mounted radio controls, Monsoon sound system, automatic day/night rearview and outside mirrors.

Prestige Pkg. 1SJ, GS 870 748
Luxury Pkg. 1SF plus 6-way power passenger seat.

Olympic Pkg. 1SK, GS 1915 1647
Manufacturer's discount price 1415 1217
Prestige Pkg. 1SE plus power sunroof, Olympic logo floormats and badging.

Gran Touring Pkg., LS 600 516
Consists of Gran Touring suspension, 225/60R16 tires, alloy wheels. Requires option pkg.

Comfort and Convenience

Leather upholstery, LS 795 684
Includes driver-side side-impact airbag. Requires option pkg.

Prices are accurate at time of publication; subject to manufacturer's change.

BUICK • CADILLAC

	Retail Price	Dealer Invoice
Power sunroof	$695	$598
LS requires Luxury Pkg., Prestige Pkg., or Touring Pkg. GS requires Prestige Pkg.		
Heated front seats	225	194
LS requires leather upholstery.		
Alloy wheels, LS	350	301
16-inch chrome alloy wheels	650	559
LS requires Gran Touring Pkg.		

CADILLAC CATERA

Cadillac Catera Sport

Rear-wheel-drive near-luxury car

Base price: $31,305. Built in Germany. **Also consider:** Acura TL, BMW 3-Series, Infiniti I30, Lexus ES 300, Mercedes-Benz C-Class

FOR • Brake performance • Build quality **AGAINST** • Control layout

Alterations to the rear brakes are the only change to Cadillac's entry-level model for 2001. Built in Germany by General Motors' Opel subsidiary, Catera uses an Opel-designed V6 engine, a 4-speed automatic transmission, antilock 4-wheel disc brakes, traction control, and leather upholstery. Front side airbags are standard. An optional Sport package adds firmer suspension tuning and 17-inch wheels in lieu of 16s, plus a rear spoiler, high-intensity headlamps, heated seats, and a matte-chrome instead of black grille. GM's OnStar assistance system is standard. For '01, Cadillac replaces Catera's solid rear brake discs with vented ones aimed at improved braking performance.

EVALUATION Catera doesn't handle as well as most Euro-brand rivals, but its firm suspension delivers a reasonably comfortable ride and competent road manners. The powertrain provides adequate acceleration and decent fuel economy (20 mpg in our test of 2000s), but road noise

Specifications begin on page 535.

CADILLAC

and full-throttle engine drone are high for the near-luxury class. A brief preview drive of an '01 wasn't enough to determine whether the new vented rear brake discs significantly improve braking performance, but stopping power is strong, with good pedal modulation. Catera does boast a solid feel and decent room for four adults, but is only average for ergonomics, visibility, and entry/exit. It remains an also-ran in the near-luxury sales race.

ENGINES

	dohc V6
Size, liters/cu. in.	3.0/181
Horsepower @ rpm	200 @ 6000
Torque (lb-ft) @ rpm	192 @ 3400
Availability	S

EPA city/highway mpg
4-speed OD automatic	17/24

PRICES

Cadillac Catera	Retail Price	Dealer Invoice
Base 4-door sedan	$31305	$29112
Destination charge	640	640

STANDARD EQUIPMENT:

Base: 3.0-liter dohc V6 engine, 4-speed automatic transmission, traction control, dual front airbags, front side-impact airbags, antilock 4-wheel disc brakes, daytime running lights, air conditioning w/dual-zone automatic climate control, OnStar System w/one year service (roadside assistance, emergency services; other services available), variable-assist power steering, leather-wrapped tilt steering wheel, cruise control, leather upholstery, front bucket seats, 8-way power driver seat, passenger seat power height-adjustment, center console, cupholders, split folding rear seat w/trunk pass-through, heated power mirrors, power windows, power door locks, remote-keyless entry system, AM/FM/cassette, steering-wheel radio controls, digital clock, tachometer, variable intermittent wipers, auxiliary power outlets, outside temperature display, remote fuel-door and decklid release, rear defogger, automatic day/night rearview mirror, illuminated visor mirrors, map lights, automatic headlights, floormats, theft-deterrent system, cornering lights, fog lights, load-leveling suspension, full-size spare, 225/55HR16 tires, alloy wheels.

OPTIONAL EQUIPMENT:
Major Packages

Luxury Pkg.	995	846

Memory driver seat, memory outside and rearview mirrors, 8-way power passenger seat, universal garage door opener, theft-deterrent system w/alarm.

Prices are accurate at time of publication; subject to manufacturer's change.

CADILLAC

	Retail Price	Dealer Invoice
Sport Pkg.	$2510	$2134

Luxury Pkg. plus heated front seats, rear spoiler, high intensity discharge headlights, sport suspension, 235/45HR17 tires.

Comfort and Convenience

Heated front seats	425	361
Power sunroof	995	846
AM/FM/cassette/CD player	973	827

Includes weatherband, radio data system, Bose sound system.

Power rear sunshade	295	251

Appearance and Miscellaneous

Chrome alloy wheels	795	509

NA w/Sport Pkg.

CADILLAC DeVILLE

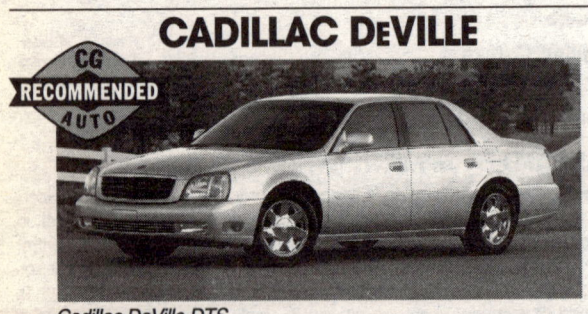

Cadillac DeVille DTS

Front-wheel-drive luxury car

Base price range: $40,495-$46,267. Built in USA. **Also consider:** Infiniti Q45, Lexus LS 430, Lincoln Town Car

FOR • Acceleration • Build quality • Entry/exit • Interior materials • Quietness • Passenger and cargo room **AGAINST** • Navigation system controls • Fuel economy • Rear visibility

Cadillac's largest car will soon offer an optional e-mail system, but begins the 2001 model year by adding a standard CD player on the base model and an optional tire pressure monitor. DeVille comes in base, DHS (DeVille High Luxury Sedan), and DTS (DeVille Touring Sedan) trim. All have a 4-speed automatic transmission and a V8 engine. The DTS has 300 horsepower, the others 275. Traction control and antilock 4-wheel disc brakes are standard. Standard on DTS and optional elsewhere is Cadillac's StabiliTrak antiskid system, designed to selectively apply the front brakes and vary steering effort to fight skids in

Specifications begin on page 535.

CADILLAC

turns. DTS also gets Cadillac's Continuously Variable Road Sensing Suspension. All DeVilles have front side airbags with a head/chest bag for the driver; lower-body rear side airbags are optional.

A navigation system with touch-screen display is optional on DHS/DTS. Due later in the model year is an Infotainment system combining the audio unit and text display of e-mail on a dashboard screen. The system responds to adjustments via the screen, a keypad, and voice commands. Cadillac's exclusive Night Vision is optional on DHS and DTS. It uses infrared technology to detect heat-generating objects beyond headlight range and projects a black-and-white image onto the windshield just above hood level. The new tire pressure monitor warns of low pressure in individual tires on an instrument panel display.

Base and DHS DeVilles a front bench seat with column shift, the DTS has buckets and console shift. The base model has digital instrumentation. DHS and DTS have analog gauges, plus standard leather upholstery and lumbar-massaging front seats. General Motor's OnStar assistance system is standard.

PERFORMANCE DeVille's ride is comfortable but controlled, and the poised DTS easily holds its own against large imported luxury sedans. All DeVilles benefit from available StabiliTrak and road-sensing suspension that reduces body motion in cornering and emergency maneuvers.

Acceleration is outstanding at about 7 seconds 0-60 mph. Our test DTS models averaged 14.6-16.7 mpg. Cadillac recommends 91-octane fuel, but says less-expensive regular is acceptable and doesn't hurt performance much. The transmission is smooth and responsive, wind and road noise are hushed, and the powertrain feels smooth and refined.

ACCOMMODATIONS Few sedans are more spacious or comfortable. Front seats provide fine support and stretch-out room in the outboard positions, although a middle rider on the front bench seat will feel squeezed. Rear seating impresses with limousinelike leg clearance, a firm, generous cushion, and width enough for three adults. Rear temperature control and the DHS's sunshades and adjustable lumbar are useful amenities, and all doors open exceptionally wide.

We prefer the analog gauges to the base model's dated digital array, but both are unobstructed and legible. Dashboard and steering wheel house an abundance of controls, but most are large and clearly labeled. Once programmed, the new navigation system is an aid, but fingerprints build up on its touch-screen display. Outward visibility is basically good, although thick rear roof pillars compromise over-the-shoulder vision. We have not yet tested the Infotainment system.

Night Vision works and is likely to be of most benefit to those who frequently drive in rural areas. A moving image that resembles a photographic negative is projected onto the lower left windshield. It's alien at first, but doesn't interfere with normal vision and can be adjusted for brightness or switched off.

Prices are accurate at time of publication; subject to manufacturer's change.

CADILLAC

Cabin materials and workmanship are competitive with imported luxury cars, and are noticeably better than other domestic brands—except for low-budget plastic trim in the dashboard's center and the crude movement of the vent adjusters. Interior storage space is good, and the 4-golf-bag trunk opens to bumper level.

VALUE Spacious and powerful, this Cadillac brims with space-age gizmos and is priced below most V8 luxury rivals. Affluent younger shoppers still tend to favor imports, but DeVille's many virtues make it worth considering.

ENGINES

	dohc V8	dohc V8
Size, liters/cu. in.	4.6/279	4.6/279
Horsepower @ rpm	275 @ 5600	300 @ 6000
Torque (lb-ft) @ rpm	300 @ 4000	295 @ 4400
Availability	S[1]	S[2]
EPA city/highway mpg		
4-speed OD automatic	16/27	16/27

1. DeVille, DHS. 2. DTS.

PRICES

Cadillac DeVille	Retail Price	Dealer Invoice
Base 4-door sedan	$40495	$37208
DHS 4-door sedan	46267	42489
DTS 4-door sedan	46267	42489
Destination charge	720	720

STANDARD EQUIPMENT:

Base: 4.6-liter dohc V8 275-horsepower engine, 4-speed automatic transmission, traction control, dual front airbags, front side-impact airbags, antilock 4-wheel disc brakes, daytime running lights, OnStar System w/one year service (roadside assistance, emergency services; other services available), air conditioning w/tri-zone automatic climate control, variable-assist power steering, tilt leather-wrapped steering wheel, cruise control, cloth upholstery, split front bench seat, 8-way power front seats, front storage armrest, cupholders, rear seat trunk pass-through, heated power mirrors w/driver-side automatic day/night, power windows, power door locks, remote keyless entry, AM/FM/cassette/CD player, digital clock, steering wheel radio and climate controls, trip computer, outside temperature indicator, illuminated front visor mirrors, variable intermittent wipers, power decklid release and power pull-down, remote fuel door release, rear defogger, automatic day/night rearview mirror, compass, map lights, automatic headlights, automatic parking brake release, floormats, theft-deterrent system, cornering lights, load-leveling suspension, 225/60SR16 tires, alloy wheels.

DHS adds: leather upholstery, heated front and rear seats, 12-way power

Specifications begin on page 535.

CADILLAC

front seats w/lumbar massage, front and rear power lumbar adjustment, memory system (driver seat, mirrors, steering wheel, climate control, radio), power tilt and telescoping wood and leather-wrapped steering wheel, wood shift knob, Bose sound system, analog instruments, tachometer, wood interior trim, rear illuminated visor mirrors, rain-sensing automatic wipers, power rear window sunshade, manual rear side sunshades, chrome alloy wheels.

DTS adds: 4.6-liter dohc V8 300-horsepower engine, StabiliTrak antiskid system, front bucket seats, center console, tilt leather-wrapped steering wheel, fog lights, Continuously Variable Road Sensing Suspension, 235/55HR17 tires, alloy wheels, Deletes: memory system, power tilt and telescoping wood and leather-wrapped steering wheel, wood shift knob, rear seat lumbar adjustment, rear illuminated visor mirrors, power rear window sunshade, manual rear side sunshades, chrome alloy wheels.

OPTIONAL EQUIPMENT:

	Retail Price	Dealer Invoice
Major Packages		
Comfort and Convenience Pkg., Base	$1095	$931
DTS	695	591
Heated front and rear seats, front seat lumbar adjustment (Base), memory system (driver seat, mirrors, steering wheel [DTS], climate controls, radio), power tilt and telescoping steering wheel (DTS), trunk mat.		
Safety and Security Pkg., Base, DHS	1045	888
DTS	550	468
StabiliTrak antiskid system (Base, DHS), ultrasonic rear parking assist, tire pressure monitor, universal garage door opener.		
Safety Features		
Rear side-impact airbags	295	251
Night Vision, DHS, DTS	2250	1913
Requires Safety and Security Pkg.		
Comfort and Convenience		
Navigation system, DHS, DTS	1995	1696
Navigation system with Global Positioning System, LCD screen, 6-disc CD changer.		
Power sunroof	1550	1318
DHS deletes rear illuminated visor mirrors.		
Leather upholstery, Base	785	667
Adaptive front seats,		
DHS, DTS	995	846
DTS requires Comfort and Convenience Pkg.		
6-disc CD changer	595	506
Wood Trim Pkg., DTS	595	506
Wood and leather-wrapped steering wheel, wood shift knob.		
Voice-activated cellular telephone	675	574
Chrome alloy wheels, DTS	795	509

Prices are accurate at time of publication; subject to manufacturer's change.

CADILLAC

CADILLAC ELDORADO

Cadillac Eldorado

Front-wheel-drive luxury car
Base price range: $40,036-$43,611. Built in USA. **Also consider:** Jaguar XK8, Mercedes-Benz CLK

FOR • Acceleration • Steering/handling • Interior materials
AGAINST • Fuel economy • Rear visibility • Climate controls (base model) • Rear-seat entry/exit

A rear-seat trunk-pass-through is standard on the base Eldorado, as the biggest 2001 change to Cadillac's slow-selling luxury coupe. Eldorado is offered in base Sport Coupe (ESC) and uplevel Touring Coupe (ETC) models. Both have automatic transmission and share Cadillac's 4.6-liter Northstar V8 with the Seville and DeVille sedans. Horsepower is 300 for ETC and 275 for ESC.

Antilock brakes and traction control are standard. But Eldorado is the only Cadillac without front side airbags. The ETC has Cadillac's Continuously Variable Road Sensing Suspension and StabiliTrak antiskid system, but they're older versions of the systems used by the Seville STS and DeVille DTS. Stabilitrak is optional for the ESC. General Motor's OnStar assistance system is standard. The seat pass-through had been exclusive to the ETC.

EVALUATION Eldorado is worth considering for those few who still like big, heavy coupes, especially since meager demand should mean sizable discounts. Both models accelerate swiftly, but the ETC is punchiest at highway speeds while the ESC is slightly stronger around town. In our tests we averaged around 18 mpg. Cadillac recommends 91-octane fuel, but says less-expensive regular is acceptable and doesn't hurt performance much. Noise levels are low. Road manners depend on model. The comfort-oriented ESC has an almost pillowy ride but leans a lot in corners. The ETC's firmer suspension offers better body control at the expense of some harshness over sharp bumps. StabiliTrak adds an extra measure of safety, especially on wet roads. Eldorado seats four in

Specifications begin on page 535.

CADILLAC

comfort and offers plenty of luggage room, but aft entry/exit demands the usual coupe contortions, and wide rear roof pillars impede visibility. Workmanship is good, but falls short of best-in-class brands like Lexus and Mercedes-Benz.

ENGINES

	dohc V8	dohc V8
Size, liters/cu. in.	4.6/279	4.6/279
Horsepower @ rpm	275 @ 5600	300 @ 6000
Torque (lb-ft) @ rpm	300 @ 4000	295 @ 4400
Availability	S[1]	S[2]
EPA city/highway mpg		
4-speed OD automatic	17/26	17/26

1. Sport Coupe. 2. Touring Coupe.

PRICES

Cadillac Eldorado	Retail Price	Dealer Invoice
ESC 2-door coupe	$40036	$36788
ETC 2-door coupe	43611	40059
Destination charge	720	720

STANDARD EQUIPMENT:

ESC: 4.6-liter dohc V8 275-horsepower engine, 4-speed automatic transmission, traction control, dual front airbags, antilock 4-wheel disc brakes, wiper-activated headlights, daytime running lamps, air conditioning w/dual-zone automatic climate control, OnStar System w/one year service (roadside assistance, emergency services; other services available), variable-assist power steering, leather-wrapped steering wheel with controls for radio and climate, tilt steering wheel, cruise control, leather upholstery, 8-way power front bucket seats, center console, cupholders, rear seat trunk pass-through, overhead console, heated power mirrors w/driver-side automatic day/night, power windows, power door locks, remote keyless entry, rear defogger, automatic day/night rearview mirror, compass, outside temperature indicator, AM/FM/cassette, power antenna, digital clock, tachometer, remote fuel-door release, remote decklid release w/power pull-down, trip computer, wood interior trim, variable intermittent wipers, automatic parking-brake release, automatic headlights, map lights, illuminated visor mirrors, floormats, automatic level control suspension, theft-deterrent system, fog lights, cornering lights, 225/60R16 tires, alloy wheels.

ETC adds: 4.6-liter dohc V8 300-horsepower engine, StabiliTrak antiskid system, Bose AM/FM/weatherband/cassette/CD player, 12-way power front seats, power lumbar adjustment, heated front seats, Memory Pkg. (memory seats, mirrors, climate control, and radio presets), passenger-side mirror tilt-down parking aid, rain-sensing windshield wipers, Continuously Variable Road Sensing Suspension, 235/60HR16 tires.

Prices are accurate at time of publication; subject to manufacturer's change.

CADILLAC

OPTIONAL EQUIPMENT:

	Retail Price	Dealer Invoice
Major Packages		
Comfort/Convenience Pkg., ESC	$950	$808
Memory Pkg. (memory seats, mirrors, climate control, and radio presets), power lumbar support, heated front seats.		
Safety Features		
StabiliTrak Antiskid system, ESC	495	421
Comfort and Convenience		
Power sunroof	1550	1318
Bose AM/FM/cassette/CD player, ESC	1219	1036
12-disc CD player	595	506
Leather-wrapped and wood steering wheel	395	336
Universal garage door opener	107	91
235/60ZR16 tires, ETC	250	213
Chrome alloy wheels	795	507

2002 CADILLAC ESCALADE

2002 Cadillac Escalade

Rear or four-wheel-drive full-size sport-utility vehicle; similar to GMC Yukon/Denali

Base price range: $49,290. Built in USA. **Also consider:** Lexus LX470, Lincoln Navigator, Mercedes-Benz ML430

FOR • Acceleration • Quietness • Passenger and cargo room • Trailer towing capability **AGAINST** • Steerin feel • Fuel economy • Entry/exit

Cadillac's SUV skips 2001 for redesigned '02 models built on the same platform as the GMC Yukon/Yukon XL and Chevy's Tahoe/Suburban. Sales begin in early 2001. Escalade remains an upmarket version of GMC's Denali, but offers no counterpart to the long-wheelbase XL Denali. The Cadillac gets distinct front-end styling and side cladding, a slightly different dash-

Specifications begin on page 535.

CADILLAC

board, more-upscale interior trim, and several unique features. For the first time, there's a 2-wheel-drive Escalade. With a mandatory 5.3-liter V8 and 4-speed automatic transmission, the 2WD model is expected to account for 30 percent of sales. The 4WD model gets a new 6.0-liter V8 and permanent 4WD. Respective horsepower jumps by 30 and 90 versus the previous 5.7 V8, and the 6.0 makes 20 more hp than in Denali. Towing capacity with 4WD improves to 8500 pounds from 6500; the 2WD rates 7700. Front side airbags, antilock 4-wheel disc brakes, traction control, and Cadillac's Road Sensing Suspension with auto-adjusting shock absorbers are standard. The 4WD adds an antiskid system. Also new for '02 are 17-inch wheels (replacing 16s), a 50/50 third-row bench seat, a 60/40 second-row bench that stows flat with the floor, a liftgate with separate opening window, Ultrasonic Rear Parking Assist that warns when backing up near obstacles, and a premium version of GM's OnStar service that "reads" information over the audio system.

EVALUATION Previews of 4WD prototypes show the new Escalade to be usefully faster than the old—Cadillac claims 8.6 seconds 0-60 mph, 9.5 for the 2WD—and very refined by truck standards. Indeed, it's quite pleasant to drive, with good noise isolation from all sources and a mostly absorbent ride. The 6.0 has ample midrange punch despite occasionally slow transmission downshifts. The steering is too light and slow, and the redesign brings extra weight that does nothing for handling, though the various electronic chassis controls keep things predictable. The 2WD earns slightly better EPA ratings than last year's 4WD Escalade, but the new 4WD borders on Ford Excursion thirsty. It's a little shorter on a trimmer wheelbase, but Escalade is nearly two inches wider now, which translates into ample second-row room for three adults. The third seat is best left to limber kids, but overall head room is fine and, unlike before, all seats are comfortably supportive. Entry/exit isn't super-easy, but acceptable for a big SUV. Drivers enjoy fine visibility and a well-arranged dashboard, though the steering-column shifter interferes with access to the audio controls. Maximum cargo volume increases more than 20 cubic feet, but there's precious little space behind the third seat, though that folds for extra room and goes in and out fairly easily. We'd make traction control available on the 2WD model, but permanent 4WD and more power are smart moves that combine with the new platform to make the new Escalade a serious contender among premium SUVs.

ENGINES

	dohc V8	dohc V8
Size, liters/cu. in.	4.6/279	4.6/279
Horsepower @ rpm	275 @ 5600	300 @ 6000

Prices are accurate at time of publication; subject to manufacturer's change.

CADILLAC

	dohc V8	dohc V8
Torque (lb-ft) @ rpm	300 @ 4000	295 @ 4400
Availability	S[1]	S[2]
EPA city/highway mpg		
4-speed OD automatic	14/17	
4-speed OD automatic		12/16

1. SLS. 2. STS.

Prices unavailable at time of publication.

CADILLAC SEVILLE

Cadillac Seville STS

Front-wheel-drive luxury car

Base price range: $41,935-$48,045. Built in USA. **Also consider:** BMW 5-Series, Lexus LS 430, Mercedes-Benz E-Class

FOR • Acceleration • Automatic transmission performance • Handling/roadholding • Interior storage space • Interior materials
AGAINST • Fuel economy • Rear visibility

Cadillac's sportiest large sedan for 2001 gets new option packages. Seville comes in 275-horsepower SLS and 300-hp STS models, both with Cadillac's 4.6-liter Northstar V8 and 4-speed automatic transmission. Front side airbags, antilock brakes and traction control are standard. So are Cadillac's Continuously Variable Road Sensing Suspension and StabiliTrak antiskid system. The latter is designed to selectively apply the front brakes and vary steering effort to fight skids in turns. Both Sevilles offer heated "adaptive" front seats, whose air bladders continuously adjust to occupant body contours, and lumbar-roller front seats that massage the lower back. General Motor's OnStar assistance system is standard. A satellite navigation system with touch-screen display is optional. New and standard for '01 are Cadillac's Torque Sensing power front windows, which automatically stop raising if an obstruction is in the way. A new text-based e-mail system is part of Cadillac's option-

Specifications begin on page 535.

CADILLAC

al Infotainment system which also incorporates an audio unit. Both are controlled using a dashboard-mounted color video display, a keypad, and voice commands. New for '01 are several Luxury and Premium option packages, which add to the SLS heated front and rear seats, a new dashboard mounted tire-pressure monitor, and an ultrasonic rear parking assist system. New packages for STS add performance tires, chrome alloy wheels, and a power sunroof. Some of these items are available seperately on both models.

EVALUATION Both Sevilles are quick but thirsty—only 14.8 mpg in our tests. Cadillac recommends 91-octane fuel, but says less-expensive regular doesn't hurt performance much. These heavy front-wheel-drive sedans aren't as nimble as most rear-drive rivals, and the magnetic steering system feels artificially heavy in turns. The SLS has a quiet, absorbent ride. The firmly damped STS thumps over bumps that don't disturb European rivals. Seville's plus points include comfortable room for four adults, a well-designed dashboard, and quality interior materials. The optional navigation system uses a dashboard mounted color video display. It can be useful once its programming is mastered, but the screen is difficult to read in direct sunlight and the system inconveniently incorporates some radio functions. Of Seville's two models, the SLS is the better value for its blend of performance and comfort.

ENGINES

	dohc V8	dohc V8
Size, liters/cu. in.	4.6/279	4.6/279
Horsepower @ rpm	275 @ 5600	300 @ 6000
Torque (lb-ft) @ rpm	300 @ 4000	295 @ 4400
Availability	S[1]	S[2]
EPA city/highway mpg		
4-speed OD automatic	NA	NA

1. SLS. 2. STS.

PRICES

Cadillac Seville	Retail Price	Dealer Invoice
SLS 4-door sedan	$41935	$38526
STS 4-door sedan	48045	44116
Destination charge	720	720

STANDARD EQUIPMENT:

SLS: 4.6-liter dohc V8 275-horsepower engine, 4-speed automatic transmission, traction control, dual front airbags w/automatic child recognition system, front side-impact airbags, antilock 4-wheel disc brakes, antiskid system, wiper-activated headlights, daytime running lights, OnStar

Prices are accurate at time of publication; subject to manufacturer's change.

CADILLAC

System w/one year service (roadside assistance, emergency services; other services available), air conditioning w/dual zone automatic climate control, outside temperature display, interior air filter, variable-assist power steering, leather-wrapped tilt steering wheel w/radio and climate controls, cruise control, leather upholstery, 10-way power front seats, front and rear articulating headrests w/power height adjustment for front headrests, center console, cupholders, overhead console, trunk pass-through, wood interior trim, heated power mirrors w/driver-side automatic day/night, power windows, power door locks, remote keyless entry, automatic day/night rearview mirror, compass, AM/FM/cassette/CD player, digital clock, tachometer, map lights, illuminated visor mirrors, automatic parking brake release, remote fuel door and decklid releases, variable intermittent wipers, automatic headlights, rear defogger, floormats, cornering lights, theft-deterrent system, variable suspension, automatic level control suspension, 235/60R16 tires, alloy wheels.

STS adds: 4.6-liter dohc V8 300-horsepower engine, Performance Shift Algorithm 4-speed automatic transmission, Memory Pkg. (two-driver memory seat, mirrors, steering wheel, climate control and radio presets), 14-way power front seats, power tilt and telescoping steering wheel, AM/FM/weatherband/cassette/CD player, w/Bose sound system, radio data system, parking-asist passenger-side mirror, rain-sensing automatic wipers, fog lights, STS suspension tuning, 235/60HR16 tires.

OPTIONAL EQUIPMENT:
Major Packages

	Retail Price	Dealer Invoice
1SB Luxury Pkg., SLS	$1100	$935

Heated front and rear seats, power tilt and telescoping steering wheel, Memory Pkg. (two-driver memory seat, mirrors, steering wheel, climate control and radio presets).

1SC Premium Luxury Pkg., SLS	3140	2669

Luxury Pkg. plus Bose sound system, ultrasonic rear parking assist, chrome alloy wheels.

1SD Luxury Pkg., STS	1985	1687

6-disc CD changer, wood trimmed steering wheel and shift knob, chrome alloy wheels.

1SE Premium Luxury Pkg., STS	2930	2491

Luxury Pkg. plus tire pressure monitor, ultrasonic rear parking assist, high intensity discharge headlights, 235/55HR17 tires.

1SF Premium Performance Pkg., STS	6400	5440

Premium Luxury Pkg. plus power sunroof, Infotainment Radio System (AM/FM/weatherband/cassette, radio data system, e-mail, text messaging), cellular telephone.

Safety Features

Ultrasonic rear parking assist, SLS	295	251

Specifications begin on page 535.

CADILLAC • CHEVROLET

Comfort and Convenience	Retail Price	Dealer Invoice
Infotainment Radio System, STS	$1995	$1696

Includes AM/FM/weatherband/cassette, radio data system, e-mail, text messaging. Requires cellular telephone.

Navigation system, SLS	2945	2503
STS	1995	1696

Navigation system w/Global Positioning System, LCD screen.

UM5 Bose sound system, SLS	950	808

Includes AM/FM/weatherband/cassette/CD w/radio data system, automatic volume control.

6-disc CD player	595	506

SLS requires option pkg.

Cellular telephone	675	574
Power sunroof	1550	1318

SLS requires opton group.

Wood Trim Pkg.	595	506

Wood trimmed steering wheel and shift knob.

Chrome alloy wheels	795	509
235/60ZR16 tires, STS	250	213

CHEVROLET ASTRO

Chevrolet Astro

Rear- or all-wheel-drive minivan; similar to GMC Safari

Base price range: $20,593-$25,056. Built in USA. **Also consider:** Chevrolet Venture, Dodge Caravan, Ford Windstar

FOR • Passenger and cargo room • Trailer towing capability
AGAINST • Fuel economy • Entry/exit • Ride

A tilt steering wheel, cruise control, CD player, remote keyless entry, and power windows, mirrors and locks are newly standard as Chevrolet's truck-based minivan enters its 18th model year. Astro is also sold as the near-identical GMC Safari. Astro comes in a single body length with a passenger-side sliding door and choice of LS and LT trim

Prices are accurate at time of publication; subject to manufacturer's change.

CHEVROLET

levels. A no-frills 2-seat Cargo Van returns for commercial users. Passenger models all come with 8-passenger seating courtesy of two front buckets and two 3-place rear benches. A 7-passenger setup with two second-row buckets is optional.

The sole powertrain is a 190-horsepower V6 and automatic transmission, the latter featuring a Tow/Haul mode for more efficient shifting when carrying heavy loads. Antilock brakes are standard, an all-wheel-drive system optional. The passenger model's added standard equipment encompasses items that had been optional and also includes a trip computer, outside temperature indicator, and rear privacy glass. And Chevrolet says the new high-output alternator is better suited to handling the electrical loads imposed by laptop computers and TVs.

PERFORMANCE General Motors is the only automaker to offer a distinct choice in minivans, and the Astro and Safari are better suited to heavy-duty work than front-drive offerings like Chevy's own Venture. For example, Astro's 5500-pound towing capacity exceeds Venture's by a full ton. But the penalty for this trucky brawn is a rougher ride. Steering and handling aren't as nimble either, though Astro and Safari aren't as ponderous as full-size vans. They do suffer more road and wind noise than sleeker car-based minivans, however.

The torquey V6 and smooth-shifting transmission provide good acceleration and passing response, but don't expect to average more than 15 mpg overall—less with the heavier all-wheel-drive models. At least the AWD requires no input from the driver, and is worth considering if you live in the snowbelt.

ACCOMMODATIONS Front entry/exit is hampered by a fairly tall step-up and narrow lower doorways. The front footwells are also uncomfortably narrow. Head room is abundant throughout, and there's good passenger space in the second and third rows, though getting to the third-row bench is difficult. Astro and Safari's seats aren't as easy to remove as the lighter modular seating in GM's front-drive minivans, but once out, there's plenty of cargo space. Unlike the swing-out rear doors, the optional Dutch doors allow an unobstructed rear view and include the convenience of a lift-up glass hatch and a defroster. An optional dual sound system allows front-seat passengers to listen to one audio source and rear-seaters another on headphones.

VALUE Consider Astro or Safari if you're looking for a minivan to haul cargo and handle light-duty towing. For primarily passenger use, go with one of the many front-drive alternatives, which typically offer better fuel economy, a more car-like driving feel, and more convenience features such as dual sliding side doors.

ENGINES

	ohv V6
Size, liters/cu. in.	4.3/262
Horsepower @ rpm	190 @ 4400

Specifications begin on page 535.

CHEVROLET

	ohv V6
Torque (lb-ft) @ rpm	250 @ 2800
Availability	S
EPA city/highway mpg	
4-speed OD automatic	16/20[1]

1. 15/19 w/AWD.

PRICES

Chevrolet Astro	Retail Price	Dealer Invoice
2WD 3-door Cargo van	$20593	$18637
AWD 3-door Cargo van	22993	20809
2WD LS 3-door van	23241	21033
AWD LS 3-door van	25056	22676
Destination charge	645	645

STANDARD EQUIPMENT:

Cargo: 4.3-liter V6 engine, 4-speed automatic transmission, dual front airbags, antilock brakes, daytime running lamps, front air conditioning, variable-assist power steering, vinyl upholstery, front bucket seats, cupholders, black rubber floor covering, variable intermittent wipers, AM/FM radio, digital clock, auxiliary power outlets, automatic headlights, theft-deterrent system, dual manual outside mirrors, 215/75R15 tires. **AWD** models add: permanent 4-wheel drive.

LS adds: tilt steering wheel, cruise control, cloth upholstery, 8-passenger seating with front bucket seats and two 3-passenger rear bench seats, carpeting, power mirrors, power windows, power door locks, remote keyless entry, AM/FM/CD player, overhead console, trip computer, compass, outside temperature indicator, illuminated visor mirrors, map lights, floormats, rear privacy glass, swing-out rear side windows, roof rack. **AWD** models add: permanent 4-wheel drive.

OPTIONAL EQUIPMENT:
Major Packages

LS Preferred Equipment Group 1SD, LS	1527	1313

Front and rear air conditioning, rear heater, 6-way power driver seat, AM/FM/cassette/CD player, rear defogger, rear Dutch doors.

LT Preferred Equipment Group 1SE, LS	3178	2733

LS Preferred Equipment Group plus leather-wrapped steering wheel, rear radio controls, headphone jacks, universal garage door opener, 215/75R15 white-letter tires, alloy wheels.

ZQ3 Convenience Pkg., Cargo	383	329

Tilt steering wheel, cruise control.

ZQ2 Convenience Group, Cargo	474	408

Power windows and door locks.

Prices are accurate at time of publication; subject to manufacturer's change.

CONSUMER GUIDE

CHEVROLET

	Retail Price	Dealer Invoice
Trailering Special Equipment	$309	$266
Platform trailer hitch, 8-lead wiring harness.		

Powertrains
Locking rear differential	252	217

Comfort and Convenience
Front and rear air conditioning, LS	523	450
Rear heater, LS	205	176
Dutch doors, LS	518	445
Includes rear defogger.		
7-passenger seating, LS	NC	NC
Front- and second-row bucket seats, third-row bench seat. Requires LT Group.		
Leather upholstery, LS	950	817
Requires LT Group.		
AM/FM/CD player, Cargo	407	350
Rear radio controls, LS	155	133
Includes headphone jacks. Requires LS Group 1SD.		

Appearance and Miscellaneous
Running boards, LS	400	344
Requires Preferred Equipment Group, alloy wheels.		
Alloy wheels, LS	25	22
Requires LS Group 1SD.		
Chrome styled steel wheels, LS	25	22

CHEVROLET BLAZER

Chevrolet Blazer LT 4WD 4-door wagon

Rear- or 4-wheel-drive midsize sport-utility vehicle; similar to GMC Jimmy and Oldsmobile Bravada

Base price range: $19,170-$32,125. Built in USA. **Also consider:** Dodge Durango, Ford Explorer, Toyota 4Runner

Specifications begin on page 535.

CHEVROLET

FOR • Acceleration • Cargo room **AGAINST** • Rear-seat comfort • Fuel economy • Rear-seat entry/exit (2-door)

Chevrolet's 2001 midsize SUV gains a sporty new variant and other Blazers get detail changes in preparation for an early 2002-model-year redesign. The new Blazer Xtreme is a 2-wheel-drive 2-door model with low-riding sport suspension; unique 5-spoke 16-inch aluminum wheels; body-colored grille, bumpers, and lower body cladding; and special trim. It joins the 2-door LS model and 4-doors in LS, LT, and top-line TrailBlazer trim. Optional on the 4-wheel-drive LS 2-door is the ZR2 package that includes an elevated off-road suspension. A 5-speed manual transmission is standard on 2-doors. Automatic transmission is optional on 2-doors and standard on 4-doors. All use a 190-horsepower V6 and offer rear-wheel drive or, except on Xtreme, 4WD. LT and TrailBlazer 4x4s get General Motors' Autotrac system, which can be used on dry pavement and automatically engages the front axle only when needed. Other 4x4s have GM's Insta-Trac, which is for use only on slippery surfaces. Both systems provide low-range 4WD gearing. GM's OnStar assistance system is standard on LT and TrailBlazer.

For 2001, Chevrolet says 4WD models have a tighter turning radius. There also are fewer suspension choices, with the middle-ground Touring setup standard except on ZR2 and Xtreme, which have their own settings. Blazer is built from the same design as the GMC Jimmy and the Oldsmobile Bravada. All are being redesigned for release as '02 models starting in early 2001. The new versions will be slightly larger and will offer a more powerful inline-6-cylinder engine, though Chevy and GMC will continue to offer some editions of the current models.

PERFORMANCE In all these SUVs, GM's 4.3-liter V6 furnishes lively takeoffs and good midrange passing power. Fuel economy is about par for midsize 6-cylinder SUVs, around 16.5 mpg overall in our tests. Recently tested TrailBlazers, however, averaged 12.6 mpg in mostly city driving and 17.7 in mostly highway use. We haven't tested the new Extreme version.

Autotrac puts Blazer and Jimmy in league with domestic and some import rivals in offering the convenience of 4WD that doesn't have to be disengaged on dry pavement. Note that Jimmy features GM's "tow/haul" transmission mode that automatically provides more efficient shift points when pulling a trailer. Blazer lacks this mode. Blazer and Jimmy have firm steering, adequate stopping ability, and good overall handling. Though some may miss the previous choice of suspensions, the Touring setup is a fine all-rounder and provides a smoother ride than most other truck-based midsize SUVs. Wind and road noise are moderate at highway speeds.

ACCOMMODATIONS GM's midsize SUVs aren't quite as roomy as a 2001 Explorer but have ample space for four adults. Some of our

Prices are accurate at time of publication; subject to manufacturer's change.

CHEVROLET

testers find the driver's seat too soft for best support, however, and others can't find comfortable seat/steering wheel positioning. Jimmy shares with TrailBlazer a floor-mounted automatic-transmission shift lever; all other automatic Blazers use a clumsier column shift, though the Xtreme offers a floor-shift option.

Front passengers in any version must contend with an intrusive footwell hump, necessary to clear part of the exhaust system. And as on the Ford, a short rear seatback compromises comfort. A low step-in eases front entry/exit, but rear-seat access is subpar even in 4-door models. Outward visibility is compromised by thick center and rear roof pillars and, at night, by deeply tinted rear windows.

The spare tire stows under the vehicle, so cargo room is good with the rear seatback up and generous with it folded. GM scores a point by offering two cargo-access choices, both with independent-opening upper glass. We don't like to stretch over a drop-down tailgate to get to the cargo hold, so we prefer the liftgate.

VALUE A capable engine is a Blazer/Jimmy asset, and ride quality is better than average for a midsize SUV. But Explorer, helped by its optional V8 and stouter overall feel, wins our Best Buy nod among direct competitors. Still, optioned thoughtfully, Blazer and Jimmy cost less than many rivals.

ENGINES

	ohv V6
Size, liters/cu. in.	4.3/262
Horsepower @ rpm	190 @ 4400
Torque (lb-ft) @ rpm	250 @ 2800
Availability	S
EPA city/highway mpg	
5-speed OD manual	17/23[1]
4-speed OD automatic	16/21[2]

1. 15/18 w/4WD. 2. 16/20 w/4WD.

PRICES

Chevrolet Blazer	Retail Price	Dealer Invoice
LS 2-door wagon, 2WD	$19170	$17349
LS 2-door wagon, 4WD	22170	20064
Xtreme 2-door wagon, 2WD	21235	—
LS 4-door wagon, 2WD	24770	22417
LS 4-door wagon, 4WD	26770	24227
LT 4-door wagon, 2WD	26925	24367
LT 4-door wagon, 4WD	29125	26358
TrailBlazer 4-door wagon, 2WD	30125	27263
TrailBlazer 4-door wagon, 4WD	32125	29073
Destination charge	600	600

Specifications begin on page 535.

CHEVROLET

Dealer invoice price for Xtreme not available at time of publication. TrailBlazer requires a Preferred Equipment Group.

STANDARD EQUIPMENT:

LS: 4.3-liter V6 engine, 5-speed manual transmission (2-door), 4-speed automatic transmission w/column shift (4-door), dual front airbags, antilock 4-wheel disc brakes, daytime running lights, variable-assist power steering, air conditioning, cloth upholstery, front bucket seats w/manual lumbar adjustment (2-door), front console (2-door), split front bench seat with storage armrest (4-door), cupholders, split folding rear seat, AM/FM/cassette, digital clock, tachometer, passenger-side visor mirror, auxiliary power outlets, automatic headlights, variable intermittent wipers, floormats, theft-deterrent system, roof rack, dual outside mirrors, tailgate, 6-lead trailer wiring harness, full-size spare tire, 235/70R15 tires, alloy wheels. **4WD** adds: Insta-Trac part-time 4-wheel drive, 2-speed transfer case, front tow hooks.

Extreme adds to LS 2-door: leather-wrapped steering wheel, color-keyed body cladding, fog lights, rear defogger, deep-tinted glass, heavy-duty trailer hitch, lowered sport suspension, 235/60R16 tires.

LT adds to LS 4-door: cruise control, tilt leather-wrapped steering wheel, OnStar System w/one year service (roadside assistance, emergency services; other services available), front bucket seats, 8-way power driver seat, heated power mirrors, power windows, power door locks, remote keyless entry, AM/FM/CD player, overhead console, compass, outside temperature indicator, automatic day/night rearview mirror, illuminated visor mirrors, cargo cover, rear defogger, rear wiper/washer, power liftgate release, liftgate/liftglass, deep-tinted rear glass. **4WD** adds: Autotrac full-time 4-wheel drive, 2-speed transfer case, front tow hooks.

TrailBlazer adds: leather upholstery, driver seat memory, 8-way power passenger seat, floor shifter, automatic climate control, automatic day/night driver-side mirror, universal garage door opener, fog lights. **4WD** adds: Autotrac full-time 4-wheel drive, 2-speed transfer case, front tow hooks, 235/75R15 on/off-road white-letter tires.

OPTIONAL EQUIPMENT:
Major Packages

	Retail Price	Dealer Invoice
1SB Preferred Equipment Group, LS 2-door	$1200	$1032
LS 4-door	1050	903

Tilt steering wheel, cruise control, heated power mirrors, power windows and door locks, AM/FM/cassette w/automatic tone control, rear defogger, rear wiper/washer, power tailgate window release, deep-tinted rear glass, bodyside moldings (4WD).

1SC Preferred Equipment Group, LS 2-door	2300	1978

1SB Preferred Equipment Group plus remote keyless entry, AM/FM/CD player, 6-way power driver seat, leather-wrapped steering wheel, overhead console, compass, outside temperature indicator, illuminated visor mirrors.

Prices are accurate at time of publication; subject to manufacturer's change.

CHEVROLET

	Retail Price	Dealer Invoice
1SC Preferred Equipment Group, LS 4-door	$1450	$1247

1SB Preferred Equipment Group plus overhead console, compass, outside temperature indicator, front bucket seats.

1SX Preferred Equipment Group, Xtreme	—	—

Tilt steering wheel, cruise control, heated power mirrors, power windows, power door locks, AM/FM/cassette w/automatic tone control, power tailgate window, rear defogger, rear wiper/washer.

1SY Preferred Equipment Group, Xtreme	—	—

1SX Preferred Equipment Group plus remote keyless entry, 6-way power driver seat, AM/FM/CD player, overhead console, compass, outside temperature indicator, illuminated visor mirrors.

1SE Preferred Equipment Group, LT	1000	860

Leather upholstery, automatic climate control, liftgate/liftglass.

1SF Preferred Equipment Group, LT	1900	1634

1SE Preferred Equipment Group plus driver seat memory, 8-way power passenger seat, automatic day/night driver-side mirror, trip computer, universal garage door opener, fog lights.

1SG Preferred Equipment Group, TrailBlazer	NC	NC
Manufacturer's discount price, (credit)	(500)	(430)
ordered w/Bose sound system (credit)	(750)	(645)
ordered w/Bose sound system and sunroof (credit)	(1000)	(860)

Standard equipment.

Power sunroof/Bose sound system discount, LS, LT (credit)	(500)	(430)

Requires power sunroof and Bose sound system. LS requires Preferred Equipment Group.

ZR2 Wide Stance Performance Pkg., 2-door 4WD	2000	1720

Heavy-duty wide stance chassis, heavy-duty suspension, raised ride height, Bilstein shock absorbers, Shield Pkg., heavy-duty differential gears and axles, fender flares.

Trailering Special Equipment	210	181

Includes platform hitch, heavy-duty flasher. 2WD models require automatic transmission. Std. Xtreme.

Powertrains

4-speed automatic transmission, LS 2-door	1000	860

Xtreme includes floor shifter when order w/1SX or 1SY Groups.

Locking rear differential	270	232
Autotrac full-time 4-wheel drive transfer case, LS 4WD	225	194

Comfort and Convenience

Heated front seats, LT, TrailBlazer	250	215

LT requires 1SF Preferred Equipment Group.

Specifications begin on page 535.

CHEVROLET

	Retail Price	Dealer Invoice
Power sunroof	$800	$688
LS 2-door requires Preferred Equipment Group.		
Deluxe overhead console, LS 2-door	130	112
Includes universal garage door opener, trip computer. Requires 1SC Preferred Equipment Group.		
AM/FM/CD player, LS 4-door	100	86
Xtreme	—	—
LS requires Preferred Equipment Group.		
AM/FM/cassette/CD player, LS w/1SB Group	200	172
LS 2-door w/1SC Group, LT	100	86
Requires automatic transmission.		
6-disc CD changer	395	340
Requires AM/FM/cassette, automatic transmission. LS 4-door requires 1SC Preferred Equipment Group.		
Bose sound system	495	426
NA with AM/FM/cassette/CD player. Requires automatic transmission. LS 4-door requires 1SC Preferred Equipment Group.		
Steering-wheel radio controls	125	108
LS requires automatic transmission, Preferred Equipment Group.		
Cargo management system, 4-door	125	107
Cargo cover, LS 4-door	69	59
Requires Preferred Equipment Group.		

Appearance and Miscellaneous

Fog lights, LS 2-door 2WD, LS 4-door, LT	115	99
LS requires Preferred Equipment Group.		
Rear liftgate/liftglass, LS 4-door	NC	NC
Requires a Preferred Equipment Group.		

Special Purpose, Wheels and Tires

Shield Pkg., 4WD	126	108
Includes transfer case and front differential skid plates, fuel tank and steering linkage shields.		
235/75R15 on/off-road white-letter tires, 4WD LS, 4WD LT	168	144

CHEVROLET CAMARO

Rear-wheel-drive sports coupe; similar to Pontiac Firebird

Base price range: $17,075-$28,750. Built in Canada. **Also consider:** Chevrolet Corvette, Ford Mustang, Mitsubishi Eclipse

FOR • Acceleration (Z28) • Handling **AGAINST** • Fuel economy (Z28) • Ride (Z28) • Rear-seat room • Wet weather traction (without traction control) • Rear visibility • Entry/exit

Prices are accurate at time of publication; subject to manufacturer's change.

CHEVROLET

Chevrolet Camaro Z28 2-door convertible

Camaro and its Pontiac Firebird cousin are slated to be retired after the 2002 model year, though Camaro may return beyond that in redesigned form. Meantime, Chevrolet's 2001 ponycar gets a bit more V8 power and a new base-model trim group.

Camaro continues as a convertible or hatchback coupe in base V6 and V8 Z28 form. All come with 4-wheel antilock disc brakes and offer optional traction control. Convertibles have a standard power top with glass rear window; a T-top is optional for coupes. Base models use a 5-speed manual transmission or optional automatic; the Z28 offers automatic or a 6-speed manual at no price difference. Also back is the Z28-based SS package with high-power V8, functional hood scoop, larger tires, different rear spoiler, and upgraded suspension. This year, V8s gain 5 horsepower, all Camaros get retuned shock absorbers that Chevrolet says aid ride and handling, and a new RS Package for the base model delivers body stripes and Z28-style exhaust. Firebird shares Camaro's mechanical components but has different styling.

PERFORMANCE V8 versions deliver torrid acceleration yet are relatively docile in traffic. Base Camaros and Firebirds have spirited acceleration and are cheaper to insure than V8 models. They use less fuel, too. In our tests, we averaged 18.6 mpg with a base 5-speed Camaro and 15.1 with an automatic Z28. A Camaro SS returned 14.7 mpg, a Ram-Air Formula Firebird 16.2, both with 6-speed manuals. GM recommends 91 octane premium fuel for the V8s, but says 87 octane regular is acceptable.

All these cars have sporty, responsive steering and handling, and even the high-power models aren't punishing over bumps, though their stiffly sprung tail can skip around on rough pavement, so the available traction control is a must on slippery surfaces. Brakes are strong, with good pedal modulation. We expect lots of mechanical ruckus in "muscle" cars, and V8 Camaros and Firebirds do have a tiresome exhaust rumble, plus noisy high-performance tires.

ACCOMMODATIONS Camaro/Firebird's zoomy styling results in a wide but low cockpit that feels cramped even in front. Long, heavy doors

Specifications begin on page 535.

CHEVROLET

aggravate entry/exit, and the "bathtub" seating combines with wide rear pillars to impede driver vision. As in most such cars, the back seat is fit only for kids. Instruments and controls are easy to locate and decipher, though Firebird's dashboard is unnecessarily over-styled. Cargo space is concentrated in a rectangular rear well big enough to swallow a set of golf clubs, and the rear seatback in coupes folds for extra versatility, but both body styles suffer high rear liftover. Only a Ram-Air Firebird among our recent test cars has suffered squeaks and rattles, though convertibles have more body flex over bumps than modern ragtops should.

VALUE Our Recommended rating is based on the fact that V8 Camaros and Firebirds are among the world's best high-performance values. Otherwise, this '60s-think Detroit design is out of step with today's tastes. Relatively speaking, Camaro gets our nod as the more sensible buy of the Chevy/Pontiac twosome, but Mustang outsells this pair combined, so if you take the GM plunge, demand a sizable discount.

ENGINES

	ohv V6	ohv V8	ohv V8
Size, liters/cu. in.	3.8/231	5.7/346	5.7/346
Horsepower @ rpm	200 @ 5200	310 @ 5200	325 @ 5200
Torque (lb-ft) @ rpm	225 @ 4000	340 @ 4000	350 @ 4000
Availability	S[1]	S[2]	S[3]
EPA city/highway mpg			
5-speed OD manual	19/30		
6-speed OD manual		19/28	18/27
4-speed OD automatic	19/29	17/24	17/25

1. Base. 2. Z28. 3. SS.

PRICES

Chevrolet Camaro	Retail Price	Dealer Invoice
Base 2-door hatchback	$17075	$15624
Base 2-door convertible	24370	22299
Z28 2-door hatchback	21645	19805
Z28 2-door convertible	28750	26306
Destination charge	575	575

STANDARD EQUIPMENT:

Base hatchback: 3.8-liter V6 engine, 5-speed manual transmission, dual front airbags, antilock 4-wheel disc brakes, daytime running lights, air conditioning, power steering, tilt steering wheel, cloth upholstery, front bucket seats, center console, cupholders, folding rear seat, intermittent wipers, AM/FM/cassette, digital clock, tachometer, auxiliary power outlet, map lights, visor mirrors, automatic headlights, front floormats, dual outside mirrors, theft-deterrent system, rear spoiler, 215/60R16 tires, wheel covers.

Base convertible adds: power mirrors, power windows, power door locks,

Prices are accurate at time of publication; subject to manufacturer's change.

CHEVROLET

remote keyless entry, rear defogger, Monsoon sound system, leather-wrapped steering wheel w/radio controls, cruise control, rear floormats, fog lights, power convertible top, 3-piece hard boot with storage bag.

Z28 adds to Base hatchback: 5.7-liter V8 310-horsepower engine, 4-speed automatic transmission, limited-slip differential, Monsoon sound system, performance ride and handling suspension, 235/55R16 tires, alloy wheels.

Z28 convertible adds: power mirrors, power windows, power door locks, remote keyless entry, rear defogger, leather-wrapped steering wheel w/radio controls, cruise control, 6-way power driver seat, rear floormats, fog lights, power convertible top, 3-piece hard boot with storage bag.

OPTIONAL EQUIPMENT:

	Retail Price	Dealer Invoice
Major Packages		
Preferred Equipment Group 1SB, Base hatchback	$1170	$1041

Cruise control, remote hatch release, power mirrors and windows, power door locks, remote keyless entry, theft-deterrent system w/alarm, fog lights.

Preferred Equipment Group 1SD, Z28 hatchback	1715	1526

Pkg. 1SB plus 6-way power driver seat, leather-wrapped steering wheel w/radio controls, rear floormats, bodyside moldings.

SS Performance/Appearance Pkg., Z28	3950	3516

Includes 325-horsepower engine, composite hood w/functional air scoop, forced-air induction system, low-restriction dual exhaust, power steering fluid cooler, special rear spoiler, Special High Performance Ride and Handling Pkg., 275/40ZR17 tires, special alloy wheels.

Sport Appearance Pkg., Base	1755	1562
Z28	1348	1200

Front and rear body moldings, 235/55R16 tires (Base), alloy wheels (Base).

Performance Handling Pkg., Base	275	245

Limited-slip differential, performance axle ratio (w/automatic transmission), dual exhaust, sport steering ratio. Requires Preferred Equipment Group 1SB, 235/55R16 tires, and alloy wheels.

RS Pkg., Base	—	—

Body stripes, badging, Z28 exhaust system, silver painted exhaust outlets. NA w/Sport Appearance Pkg.

Powertrains

4-speed automatic transmission, Base	815	725
6-speed manual transmission, Z28	NC	NC

Includes performance axle ratio.

Hurst shifter, Z28	325	289

Requires 6-speed manual transmission.

Traction control, Z28	450	401
Base	250	223

Requires Preferred Equipment Group. Base requires Performance Handling Pkg.

Specifications begin on page 535.

CHEVROLET

	Retail Price	Dealer Invoice
Performance axle ratio, Z28	$300	$267

Requires automatic transmission and 245/50ZR16 tires.

Comfort and Convenience

AM/FM/cassette w/Monsoon sound system, Base hatchback	350	312
AM/FM/CD player w/Monsoon sound system, Base hatchback	450	401
Base convertible, Z28	100	89
12-disc CD changer	595	530

Requires AM/FM/cassette with Monsoon sound system.

Leather-wrapped steering wheel, Base hatchback	170	151

Includes radio controls. Requires Preferred Group 1SB, optional radio.

6-way power driver seat, Base	270	240
Leather upholstery	500	445

Z28 hatchback requires preferred equipment group.

Rear defogger, hatchback	170	151
Removable roof panels, hatchback	995	886

Includes locks, storage provisions, and sun shade. NA Performance Pkg.

245/50ZR16 performance tires, Base convertible, Z28	225	200
245/50ZR16 all-season performance tires, Z28	225	200
Alloy wheels, Base	275	245

Requires 235/55R16 tires.

Chrome alloy wheels, Base	975	868
Base w/Sport Appearance Pkg. or Performance Handling, Z28	725	645

Base requires 235/55R16 tires.

CHEVROLET CAVALIER

Chevrolet Cavalier 2-door coupe

Front-wheel-drive subcompact car; similar to Pontiac Sunfire

Base price range: $13,160-$16,365. Built in USA and Mexico.

Prices are accurate at time of publication; subject to manufacturer's change.

CHEVROLET

Also consider: Dodge/Plymouth Neon, Ford Focus, Honda Civic
FOR • Fuel economy • Visibility **AGAINST** • Rear-seat room
• Interior materials • Rear-seat entry/exit (coupe)

General Motors' best-selling car gets upgraded audio systems for 2001 in what is otherwise a stand-pat year. Cavalier comes as a 2-door coupe in base and Z24 form, and as a 4-door sedan in base and LS trim. Cavalier shares its basic design with the Pontiac Sunfire. GM no longer builds convertible versions of these cars.

All Cavaliers have 4-cylinder engines. Base and LS come with 115 horsepower; a larger 150-hp unit is standard in Z24 and optional for LS. Manual transmission is standard on all but the LS sedan. A 3-speed automatic transmission is optional on base models. A 4-speed automatic and traction control are standard on LS and optional elsewhere. Antilock brakes are standard. Audio upgrades include a CD player instead of cassette as standard on LS and Z24, and a more-powerful 6-speaker AM/FM/CD/cassette system that's optional on all.

PERFORMANCE Cavalier and Sunfire's base 2.2-liter engine furnishes adequate acceleration, but has no power to spare with automatic transmission. The 2.4 is noticeably stronger and works better with automatic than do many twincam 4-cylinders. Shift action on the 5-speed manual isn't up to that of the best competitors. Both automatic transmissions are smooth, prompt operators. Base-trim automatic-transmission sedan versions of these cars averaged 20.8-23.8 mpg in our tests, and a 5-speed 2.4-liter coupe we tested averaged just 20.4. That's unimpressive for economy cars, though you can expect over 30 mpg on the highway. Engines are coarse and loud when pushed hard, but settle down at cruising. Highway wind and road noise are evident, but no more so than in most subcompacts.

Like counterpart Sunfire SEs, the base and LS Cavaliers corner with adequate grip and moderate body lean. Ride quality is above the subcompact-class average, though bumps and ruts trigger loud thumps. Z24s and Sunfire GTs ride more stiffly, but handling is above the class norm. Kudos to GM for giving these low-priced cars standard antilock brakes; they have good stopping power.

ACCOMMODATIONS Cavaliers and Sunfires are as roomy and accommodating as most any competitor, and the standard air conditioning and rear defroster are nice amenities. Low-to-the-floor front bucket seats create plenty of headroom and still allow shorter drivers to see over the dashboard. Rear room is adequate for two smaller adults or three children. Gauges and controls are unobstructed and clearly labeled. Interior storage includes a large glovebox and four cupholders. Cabins are characterized by lots of flimsy plastic trim. Both Cavalier and Sunfire have a trunk opening that's too small to easily accept large objects, but cargo space is good. All rear seatbacks fold, though there's

Specifications begin on page 535.

CHEVROLET

no lock to secure trunk from interior.

VALUE They fall far short of the refinement of Japanese subcompacts, but Cavalier and Sunfire include plenty of useful standard features and should be available with discounts. Cavalier edges out Sunfire as the better overall value.

ENGINES

	ohv I4	dohc I4
Size, liters/cu. in.	2.2/134	2.4/146
Horsepower @ rpm	115 @ 5000	150 @ 5600
Torque (lb-ft) @ rpm	135 @ 3600	155 @ 4400
Availability	S[1]	S[2]
EPA city/highway mpg		
5-speed OD manual	24/34	23/33
3-speed automatic	23/29	
4-speed OD automatic	23/31	22/30

1. Base and LS. 2. Z24; optional, LS.

PRICES

Chevrolet Cavalier	Retail Price	Dealer Invoice
Base 2-door coupe	$13160	$12305
Base 4-door sedan	13260	11398
LS 4-door sedan	14855	13889
Z24 2-door coupe	16365	15301
Destination charge	600	600

STANDARD EQUIPMENT:

Base: 2.2-liter 4-cylinder engine, 5-speed manual transmission, dual front airbags, antilock brakes, daytime running lights, air conditioning, power steering, cloth and vinyl reclining front bucket seats, folding rear seat, center console, cupholders, map lights, AM/FM radio, digital clock, intermittent wipers, rear defogger, left remote and right manual mirrors, theft-deterrent system, 195/70R14 tires, wheel covers.

LS adds: 4-speed automatic transmission, traction control, tilt steering wheel, cruise control, cloth upholstery, tachometer, AM/FM/CD player, visor mirrors, variable intermittent wipers, remote decklid release, floormats, 195/65R15 tires.

Z24 adds: 2.4-liter dohc 4-cylinder engine, 5-speed manual transmission, easy-entry front passenger seat, power mirrors, power windows, power door locks, remote keyless entry, sport suspension, rear spoiler, fog lights, 205/55R16 tires, alloy wheels, deletes 4-speed automatic transmission, traction control.

OPTIONAL EQUIPMENT:
Major Packages

1SB Preferred Equipment Group 1, Base coupe	430	387

Prices are accurate at time of publication; subject to manufacturer's change.

CHEVROLET

	Retail Price	Dealer Invoice
Base sedan	$413	$372

AM/FM/CD player, remote decklid release, variable intermittent wipers, easy-entry front passenger seat (coupe), visor mirrors, bodyside moldings, mud guards, cargo net, floormats, 195/65R15 tires (coupe).

1SC Preferred Equipment Group 2, Base coupe	1050	945

Group 1 plus cruise control, tilt steering wheel, rear audio woofer, special wheel covers.

1SD Preferred Equipment Group 3, Base coupe	1764	1588

Group 2 plus power mirrors and windows, power door locks, remote keyless entry, power decklid release, theft-deterrent system w/alarm.

Sport Pkg., Base coupe w/Group 1	235	212
Base coupe w/Group 2 or 3	135	122

Premium speakers, tachometer, rear spoiler.

1SB Preferred Equipment Group 1, LS	830	747

Power mirrors, power windows and door locks, remote keyless entry, power decklid release, theft-deterrent system w/alarm.

Powertrains

2.4-liter dohc 4-cylinder engine, LS	450	405
3-speed automatic transmission, Base	700	630

NA w/Preferred Equipment Groups.

4-speed automatic transmission, Base, Z24	780	702

Includes traction control.

Comfort and Convenience

Power sunroof, coupe	595	536

Includes map lights. Base requires Preferred Equipment Group.

Remote keyless entry, Base coupe	370	333
Base sedan, LS	410	369

Includes power door locks, power decklid release, theft-deterrent system w/alarm.

AM/FM/CD player, Base	165	149
AM/FM/cassette/CD player, Base w/Group 1, LS, Z24	230	207
Base coupe w/group 2 or 3	130	117
Premium speakers	100	90

Appearance and Miscellaneous

Rear spoiler, LS	150	135
Alloy wheels, Base coupe, LS	295	266

CHEVROLET CORVETTE

CG BEST BUY AUTO

Rear-wheel-drive sports and GT car
Base price range: $40,080-$47,855. Built in USA.
Also consider: Chevrolet Camaro, Dodge Viper

Specifications begin on page 535.

CHEVROLET

Chevrolet Corvette Z06

FOR • Acceleration • Steering/handling • Instruments/controls
AGAINST • Fuel economy • Ride (Z51, FE4 suspension) • Rear visibility

America's longest-lived sports car gains an extreme-performance variant for 2001, and all models get standard antiskid control. Corvette comes as a convertible with a manual folding top and glass rear window, as a hatchback with a removable center roof panel, and as a fixed-roof coupe. The coupe is renamed Z06 and given special performance tuning for '01.

All have a 5.7-liter V8. Hatchbacks and convertibles continue with the LS1 version, which for 2001 adds five horsepower, for 350. The LS1 teams with standard automatic transmission or optional 6-speed manual. Z06s have the new 385-hp LS6, named after an early-1970s high-performance Chevrolet V8. It comes only with 6-speed manual. Traction control is standard on all models.

Hatchbacks and convertibles have three suspension choices: base FE1, optional Z51 Performance Handling, or optional Selective Real Time Damping, in which the driver chooses from three preset levels of ride firmness. Z06s come only with a new FE4 suspension, designed to provide the best handling of all.

Corvette's antiskid Active Handling system is now standard instead of optional; it's designed to brake individual wheels and retard engine power to keep the car on course in fast turns. Antilock brakes are standard, too, but side-impact airbags are unavailable. Z06s get functional body side brake ducting, "Z06" seat embroidery, and exclusive-design alloy wheels with wider tires than other models. Among options available on hatchbacks and convertibles is a head-up instrument display that projects vehicle speed and other readouts onto the windshield. Corvettes do without a spare tire. Hatchbacks and convertibles use "run-flat" tires that can be driven on even when punctured. Run flats are unavailable on Z06s; a can of liquid tire sealer is provided instead.

PERFORMANCE All Corvettes have fierce acceleration. We haven't yet timed a 2001 model, but our test 2000s did 0-60 mph in about 5 sec-

Prices are accurate at time of publication; subject to manufacturer's change.

CHEVROLET

onds. Chevy says the Z06 does 0-60 in 4.0 seconds, which rings true based on our test drives. With lots of highway miles, our 6-speed test 2000s averaged about 20 mpg, though heavy city work dropped one to just 12.9 mpg. An automatic-transmission convertible averaged 16.4 mpg, a manual version 18.4. A Z06 returned 19 mpg.

All available suspensions have a rugged ride that invites tail hop in bumpy turns, but handling is racer-sharp. We favor the base FE1 tuning, which furnishes a firm but not punishing ride; the Z51 is harsh in every-day use, and the driver-adjustable Selective Real Time Damping option tends to feel too soft or too hard. The Z06's ultra-stiff FE4 suspension is clearly the best for all-out performance, but its advantages are only really appreciated on a race track. Corvettes have copious tire noise and lots of engine roar, and the Z06's exhaust system is louder than that of coupes and convertibles; some may find its rumble tiresome. We know from experience that the run-flat tires work as advertised, but have not yet tested the Z06's tire sealant. However, Chevy says Japanese export Corvettes have relied on it since '97.

ACCOMMODATIONS Corvette rides close to the road, but low door sills make entry/exit about as easy as in many taller coupes. There's generous room for two adults, and the dashboard is sensibly designed. The available head-up display helps keep tabs on speed, but some drivers may find it distracting; it can be turned off. The convertible's defrosted glass rear window is a plus, and the soft top folds neatly and quickly beneath a hard cover, but it must raised and lowered from outside the car. Top-down wind buffeting is not severe.

Thick roof pillars hurt visibility to all corners in any model, but the view forward is good. All body styles have sufficient cargo space for two golf bags, but liftover is high and there's no partition between luggage bay and passenger compartment. Cockpit storage is minuscule. Corvettes have solid structures, but a loose driver's seat, squeaking interior trim (some of which is chintzy for the car's price), and poor body-panel fit were among flaws in our model-year 2000 test cars.

VALUE No Corvette is inexpensive, but if you like your high-performance sports cars big, bold, and brawny, there's no better all-around performance value.

ENGINES

	ohv V8	ohv V8
Size, liters/cu. in.	5.7/346	5.7/346
Horsepower @ rpm	350 @ 5600	385 @ 6000
Torque (lb-ft) @ rpm	375 @ 4400	385 @ 4800
Availability	S[1]	S[2]
EPA city/highway mpg		
6-speed OD manual	19/28	19/28
4-speed OD automatic	18/26	

1. Base models; torque is 360 @ 4000 w/automatic. 2. Z06.

Specifications begin on page 535.

CHEVROLET

PRICES

Chevrolet Corvette	Retail Price	Dealer Invoice
Base 2-door hatchback	$40080	$35070
Base 2-door convertible	46605	40779
Z06 2-door coupe	47855	41873
Destination charge	645	645

STANDARD EQUIPMENT:

Base: 5.7-liter V8 350-horsepower engine, 4-speed automatic transmission, limited-slip differential, traction control, dual front airbags, antilock 4-wheel disc brakes, antiskid system, low tire-pressure warning system, daytime running lights, air conditioning, variable-assist power steering, tilt leather-wrapped steering wheel, cruise conrtrol, leather upholstery, bucket seats, 6-way power driver seat, center console, cupholders, heated power mirrors, power windows, power door locks, remote keyless entry, Bose AM/FM/cassette, digital clock, power antenna (convertible), tachometer, auxiliary power outlet, intermittent wipers, rear defogger, map lights, illuminated visor mirrors, remote decklid/hatch release, theft-deterrent system, body-colored removable roof panel (hatchback), manually folding convertible top (convertible), extended-mobility tires (245/45ZR17 front, 275/40ZR18 rear), alloy wheels.

Z06 adds: 5.7-liter V8 385-horsepower engine, 6-speed manual transmission, dual-zone automatic climate controls, Bose AM/FM/CD player, FE4 suspension, 265/40ZR17 front tires, 295/35ZR18 rear tires, deletes low tire-pressure warning system, fog lights, extended-mobility tires.

OPTIONAL EQUIPMENT:
Major Packages

Preferred Equipment Group 1, hatchback	1700	1462
convertible	1800	1548

Dual-zone automatic climate control, sport bucket seats, 6-way power passenger seat, Memory System (driver seat, mirrors, climate control, radio), cargo cover and net (hatchback), automatic headlights (convertible), automatic day/night rearview and driver-side mirrors (convertible), fog lights.

Preferred Equipment Group 2, hatchback	2700	2322
convertible	2600	2236

Preferred Equipment Group 1 plus power tilt/telescoping steering wheel w/memory, head-up instrument display, automatic day/night rearview and driver-side mirrors (hatchback), automatic headlights (hatchback).

Memory Pkg., Z06	150	129

Memory System (driver seat, mirrors, climate control, radio)

Selective Real Time Dampening Suspension,
Base	1695	1458

Adjustable ride control.

Prices are accurate at time of publication; subject to manufacturer's change.

CHEVROLET

	Retail Price	Dealer Invoice
Z51 Performance Handling Pkg., Base	$350	$301

Stiffer springs and stabilizer bars. Automatic transmission requires performance axle ratio. NA w/Selective Real Time Dampening Suspension.

Powertrains

6-speed manual transmission, Base	815	701
Includes performance axle ratio.		
Performance axle ratio, Base	300	258

Comfort and Convenience

AM/FM/CD player, Base	100	86
AM/FM/cassette, Z06, (credit)	(100)	(86)
12-disc CD changer, Base	600	516
Automatic day/night rearview and driver-side mirrors	120	103

Appearance and Miscellaneous

Transparent roof panel, hatchback	750	645
Dual roof panels, hatchback	1200	1032
Standard removable roof panel and transparent roof panel.		
Magnesium wheels, Base	2000	1720
Polished alloy wheels, Base	1200	1032

CHEVROLET IMPALA

Chevrolet Impala LS

Front-wheel-drive midsize car; similar to Buick Century and Regal, Oldsmobile Intrigue, and Pontiac Grand Prix

Base price range: $19,149-$23,225. Built in Canada. **Also consider:** Ford Taurus, Honda Accord, Toyota Camry

FOR • Passenger and cargo room • Handling/roadholding • Instruments/controls **AGAINST** • Rear-seat comfort • Road noise

Impala plays the role of Chevrolet's "traditional" midsize sedan, though the smaller but lower-priced Malibu sells in greater volume. Impala shares its basic understructure with the Buick Century and Regal, the

Specifications begin on page 535.

CHEVROLET

Oldsmobile Intrigue, and Pontiac's Grand Prix. A 3.4-liter V6 is standard on the base Impala. The upscale LS gets a 3.8 liter that's optional on the base. Both come with automatic transmission, 4-wheel-disc brakes, 16-inch wheels, air conditioning, and power windows and locks. Antilock brakes and a side airbag for the driver are standard on LS, optional on the base model; no front passenger side airbag is offered.

For 2001, General Motors' OnStar assistance system is optional on the base model and newly standard on the LS. Both models also gain emergency inside trunk releases. The LS includes a tire-inflation monitor, traction control, and a "firm ride" suspension, all of which are included in the base model's 3.8-liter option. The base Impala seats six via a front bench seat but can be ordered with the LS's buckets and floor shift console. Leather upholstery is available for both and includes a split-fold rear seatback.

PERFORMANCE It's not the V8 Super Sport of yore, but Impala acquits itself well in most areas. The base engine has adequate power, while the 3.8 delivers usefully stronger takeoffs and passing response. An alert, smooth-shifting transmission aids the cause, but neither engine sounds smooth or refined when pressed. The 3.8-liter LS we tested averaged 20.1 mpg with lots of highway miles. The smaller V6 works a little harder in this sizable sedan, and our test 3.4-liter Impala averaged 19.8 mpg in an even mix of driving.

A good ride/handling balance makes this family 4-door pleasing to drive. Even the Ride and Handling suspension that goes with the larger engine absorbs most bumps well while tempering much of the float and wallow that plague the base suspension over high-speed dips. It also enhances control and reduces body lean in turns, though any Impala furnishes good grip and balance, plus authoritative steering feel. ABS should be standard on the base model—as on Chevy's smaller Malibu—but stopping power is good, despite pedal feel that isn't firm enough to suit some of our testers. Wind noise is low, but tire roar intrudes some on coarse pavement.

ACCOMMODATIONS This spacious sedan has enough cabin length for 6-footers to ride in tandem without cramping anyone's legs. However, there's not quite enough rear-seat width for three large adults, and the rear seat cushion is far too soft, short, and lacking in contour for best comfort. Head room is good all around, even with the optional moonroof. Entry/exit is big-car easy. The flat-floor trunk should swallow a family's vacation gear, and its opening is low and wide.

Drivers enjoy a standard manual tilt wheel, conveniently high-set audio switchgear, and simple climate controls (with dual-zone temperature adjustment on LS). Quibbles include tall-tail styling that hurts rearward vision. Offsetting the puny in-dash glovebox are roomy front-door map pockets and additional storage in either a front console or a pull-

Prices are accurate at time of publication; subject to manufacturer's change.

CHEVROLET

down center armrest. Interior materials are nice, but not special. Our test Impalas had a tight assembly feel, but one car's heater fan emitted an annoying, high-pitched whistle.

VALUE Impala is a clear alternative to the Ford Taurus, featuring a comfort-oriented American style to Taurus's import-influenced approach. Impala leads in powertrain response, Taurus in safety features and rear-seat comfort. Both offer more room and equipment for the price than the Honda Accord and Toyota Camry, though those Japanese-brand rivals are more polished all-around cars.

ENGINES

	ohv V6	ohv V6
Size, liters/cu. in.	3.4/205	3.8/231
Horsepower @ rpm	180 @ 5200	200 @ 5200
Torque (lb-ft) @ rpm	205 @ 4000	225 @ 4000
Availability	S[1]	S[2]
EPA city/highway mpg		
4-speed OD automatic	20/32	20/29

1. Base. 2. LS; optional, Base.

PRICES

Chevrolet Impala	Retail Price	Dealer Invoice
Base 4-door sedan	$19149	$17521
LS 4-door sedan	23225	21251
Destination charge	610	610

STANDARD EQUIPMENT:

Base: 3.4-liter V6 engine, 4-speed automatic transmission, dual front airbags, 4-wheel disc brakes, daytime running lights, emergency inside trunk release, air conditioning, power steering, tilt steering wheel, cloth upholstery, front split bench seat, cupholders, overhead console, power mirrors, power windows, power door locks, AM/FM radio, digital clock, rear defogger, variable intermittent wipers, map lights, visor mirrors, power remote decklid release, automatic headlights, floormats, theft-deterrent system, 225/60R16 tires, wheel covers.

LS adds: 3.8-liter V6 engine, traction control, driver-side side-impact airbag, antilock brakes, OnStar System w/one year service (roadside assistance, emergency services; other services available), manual dual-zone climate controls, interior air filter, cruise control, leather-wrapped steering wheel, front bucket seats, 6-way power driver seat, center console, split folding rear seat, overhead console w/storage, heated power mirrors, remote keyless entry, AM/FM/cassette, tachometer, automatic day/night rearview mirror, illuminated visor mirrors, rear spoiler, fog lights, Ride and Handling Suspension, tire inflation monitor, 225/60R16 touring tires, alloy wheels.

Specifications begin on page 535.

CHEVROLET

OPTIONAL EQUIPMENT:
Major Packages

	Retail Price	Dealer Invoice
1SB Preferred Equipment Group 1, Base	$872	$776

Cruise control, remote keyless entry, AM/FM/cassette, overhead console w/storage, illuminated visor mirrors, cargo net.

1SC Preferred Equipment Group 2, Base 1903 1694

Preferred Equipment Group 1 plus OnStar System w/one year service (roadside assistance, emergency services; other services available), manual dual-zone climate controls, leather-wrapped steering-wheel w/radio controls, automatic day/night rearview mirror, alloy wheels.

1SB Preferred Equipment Group 1, LS 396 352

Steering-wheel radio controls, Driver Information/Convenience Center (trip computer, compass, outside temperature indicator, universal garage door opener, theft-deterrent system w/alarm).

Custom Cloth Trim, Base 765 681

Driver-side side-impact airbag, 6-way power driver seat, split folding rear seat. Requires Preferred Equipment Group.

Custom Cloth Seat Trim w/bucket seats, Base 815 725

Custom Cloth Seat Trim plus front bucket seats, center console, additional cupholder. Requires Preferred Equipment Group.

Leather Seat Trim, Base 1390 1237

Custom Cloth Seat Trim plus leather upholstery. Requires Preferred Equipment Group, steering-wheel radio controls. NA with front bucket seats.

Comfort Seating Pkg., LS 425 378

Heated front seats, 6-way power passenger seat. Requires Leather Seat Trim.

Powertrains

3.8-liter V6 engine, Base 986 878

Includes traction control, antilock brakes, tire inflation monitor, Ride and Handling Suspension. Requires Preferred Equipment Group, 225/60R16 touring tires, alloy wheels.

Safety Features

Antilock brakes, Base 600 534

Includes tire inflation monitor.

Comfort and Convenience

Power sunroof 700 623

Base requires Preferred Equipment Group.

Driver Information/Convenience Center, Base 275 245

Trip computer, compass, outside temperature indicator, universal garage door opener, theft-deterrent system w/alarm. Requires Preferred Equipment Group.

6-way power passenger seat 305 271

Requires Preferred Equipment Group. NA w/bucket seats.

Prices are accurate at time of publication; subject to manufacturer's change.

CHEVROLET

	Retail Price	Dealer Invoice
Leather Seat Trim, LS	$625	$556
AM/FM/CD player, Base	405	360
Base w/Preferred Equipment Group, LS	123	109
Includes premium speakers.		
AM/FM/cassette/CD player, Base	505	449
Base w/Preferred Equipment Group, LS	223	198
Includes premium speakers.		
Steering-wheel radio controls, Base	171	152
Includes leather-wrapped steering wheel. Requires Preferred Equipment Group 1.		
Alloy wheels, Base	300	267
225/60R16 touring tires, Base	45	40

CHEVROLET MALIBU

Chevrolet Malibu

Front-wheel-drive midsize car

Base price range: $17,020-$19,300. Built in USA. **Also consider:** Honda Accord, Oldsmobile Intrigue, Toyota Camry

FOR • Ride • Build quality **AGAINST** • Steering feel

A host of minor revisions update Chevrolet's import-flavored midsize sedan for 2001. Slotting below the larger Impala in price and market position, Malibu offers base and upscale LS models, both powered by a 3.1-liter V6 and automatic transmission. Unlike Impala, which can seat six, Malibu has standard front bucket seats for 5-passenger capacity. Both Malibu models come with floor-shift automatic transmission, antilock brakes, air conditioning, and tachometer. Leather upholstery is optional for the LS.

For 2001, power door locks and a rear defogger are standard on the base model as well as the LS. LS models gain seatback map pockets, and both Malibus now have retained accessory power and add Radio Data System functions to cassette and CD audio systems. The remote

Specifications begin on page 535.

CHEVROLET

keyless entry system that's optional on base and standard on LS now remembers programmed audio selections for each keyfob.

PERFORMANCE Malibu's V6 can't match the silky smoothness of rival Honda and Toyota engines, but it provides satisfying power. The transmission is smooth, but doesn't always downshift quickly enough for passing.

In normal driving, Malibu is maneuverable and secure. Aggressive cornering brings tire scrubbing and substantial body lean and makes the steering feel slow and vague. Rough pavement is easily absorbed, though the suspension and tires thump loudly over ruts and potholes. Wind and road noise are high enough to keep Malibu from qualifying as a serene long-distance cruiser. Stopping power is adequate and pedal modulation good.

ACCOMMODATIONS Malibu is spacious for its external size, with generous front head room and leg room that's more than adequate all around. Rear head room is sufficient for those under 6-feet tall. Front seats are firm and nicely contoured, but the rear bench is hard and flat. Instruments are unobstructed, stalks for wipers and headlamps convenient, audio and climate controls large and accessible. A tasteful blend of fabrics, plastics, and padded surfaces give Malibu the ambience of some costlier cars. Interior storage space is generous, and the large trunk has a flat floor, huge opening, and a near-bumper-level sill. Thin pillars and large outside mirrors provide good visibility, but the rear parcel shelf is high enough to impede vision directly astern.

VALUE It's no cut-rate Camry, but Malibu delivers a fine blend of utility, driving satisfaction, and features at an attractive price. It's a strong Recommend pick.

ENGINES

	ohv V6
Size, liters/cu. in.	3.1/191
Horsepower @ rpm	170 @ 5200
Torque (lb-ft) @ rpm	190 @ 4000
Availability	S

EPA city/highway mpg

4-speed OD automatic	20/30

PRICES

Chevrolet Malibu	Retail Price	Dealer Invoice
Base 4-door sedan	$17020	$15573
LS 4-door sedan	19300	17660
Destination charge	585	585

STANDARD EQUIPMENT:

Base: 3.1-liter V6 engine, 4-speed automatic transmission, dual front

Prices are accurate at time of publication; subject to manufacturer's change.

CHEVROLET

airbags, antilock brakes, daytime running lights, air conditioning, power steering, tilt steering wheel, cloth upholstery, front bucket seats, center console, cupholders, power door locks, AM/FM radio, digital clock, tachometer, variable intermittent wipers, rear defogger, visor mirrors, remote decklid release, auxiliary power outlet, automatic headlights, dual outside mirrors w/driver-side remote, theft-deterrent system, 215/60R15 tires, wheel covers.

LS adds: cruise control, 6-way power driver seat, split folding rear seat, power mirrors, power windows, remote keyless entry, AM/FM/cassette/CD player, passenger-side illuminated visor mirror, map lights, floormats, fog lights, alloy wheels.

OPTIONAL EQUIPMENT:

	Retail Price	Dealer Invoice
Major Packages		
1SB Preferred Equipment Group 1, Base	$995	$896
LS	1320	1188
Power windows, power mirrors, cruise control, AM/FM/cassette, map lights, floormats.		
Comfort and Convenience		
Cruise control, Base	240	216
Power sunroof, LS	650	585
Split folding rear seat, Base	195	176
Includes cargo net. Requires Preferred Equipment Group 1.		
Leather upholstery, LS	595	536
Includes leather-wrapped steering wheel.		
AM/FM/cassette, Base	220	198
AM/FM/CD player, Base	320	288
AM/FM/cassette/CD player, Base	200	180
Requires Preferred Equipment Group 1.		
Remote keyless entry, Base	150	135
Requires Preferred Equipment Group 1.		
Appearance and Miscellaneous		
Rear spoiler, LS	175	158
Alloy wheels, Base	310	279
Requires Preferred Equipment Group 1.		

CHEVROLET MONTE CARLO

Front-wheel-drive midsize car; similar to Pontiac Grand Prix

Base price range: $19,570-$22,400. Built in USA. **Also consider:** Dodge Stratus coupe, Honda Accord coupe, Toyota Solara

FOR • Acceleration (SS) • Steering/handling (SS) • Instruments/controls **AGAINST** • Engine noise • Road noise • Rear-seat entry/exit

Specifications begin on page 535.

CHEVROLET

Chevrolet Monte Carlo LS

Chevrolet's midsize coupe adds an available side air bag, optional appearance packages, and a standard inside trunk release for 2001. Monte Carlo shares its underskin design with the Chevy Impala. It has front bucket seats for 5-passenger capacity. The LS model uses a 180-horsepower 3.4-liter V6, the sporty SS a 200-hp 3.8-liter V6; both come with automatic transmission only. The SS has firmer suspension settings than the LS, plus standard alloy wheels. Antilock 4-wheel disc brakes are standard on both.

For 2001, the LS joins the SS with standard traction control, and a side airbag for the driver is newly standard on SS. GM's OnStar assistance system, optional on both models last year, is now standard on the SS, optional on LS. The inside trunk release is designed to free occupants trapped in the trunk. The new Sport Appearance Package for the LS includes 5-spoke aluminum wheels and a rear spoiler. The SS's similar High Sport Appearance Package carries lower body cladding, unique 5-spoke wheels and rear spoiler, and bright exhaust tips.

PERFORMANCE The LS version of this relatively large coupe has modest handling abilities, but feels reasonably balanced and secure in corners. The SS shines on twisty roads, showing minimal body lean and good grip. Both Montes have firm, accurate steering and a comfortable ride. They're also stable in freeway cruising.

A responsive automatic transmission works with the base V6 to provide adequate acceleration. The SS is no muscle car, but its bigger V6 provides brisk takeoffs and ready power for freeway merging or backroad passing. Alas, both engines in our test cars were loud and gruff in full-bore acceleration, and tire roar was prominent on coarse surfaces. We had no opportunity to measure fuel economy. Standard antilock disc brakes are a welcome feature; they feel strong and have good pedal modulation, but hard stops induce excessive nosedive.

ACCOMMODATIONS Most coupes these days are built off compact- or subcompact-sized platforms, so Monte Carlo's midsize dimensions give it a big advantage in interior space. Two adults can stretch out in front, and rear leg room is adequate for average-size adults. Head room

CHEVROLET

gets tight with the optional sunroof, but there's far more clearance than in such rivals as the Mercury Cougar or Dodge Stratus coupe. The cabin also feels roomier than that of Honda's 2-door Accord and the Toyota Solara. Cargo room is another advantage, Monte's trunk being tall, wide, and deep with a convenient bumper-height liftover.

The driver gets a comfortable bucket seat with plenty of lateral bolstering, but thick rear roof pillars impede over-the-shoulder vision. Gauge groupings and graphics are excellent, controls fall easily to hand, and driver and front passenger have individual temperature controls.

VALUE Monte Carlo is roomier than other sports coupes, and beats Accord and Solara on a features-per-dollar basis. It isn't as polished as the Japanese-brand rivals and won't hold its value as well, but this Chevy has its own American-car character.

ENGINES

	ohv V6	ohv V6
Size, liters/cu. in.	3.4/205	3.8/231
Horsepower @ rpm	180 @ 5200	200 @ 5200
Torque (lb-ft) @ rpm	205 @ 4000	225 @ 4000
Availability	S[1]	S[2]

EPA city/highway mpg
4-speed OD automatic	20/32	19/29

1. LS. 2. SS.

PRICES

Chevrolet Monte Carlo	Retail Price	Dealer Invoice
LS 2-door coupe	$19570	$17907
SS 2-door coupe	22400	20496
Destination charge	610	610

STANDARD EQUIPMENT:

LS: 3.4-liter V6 engine, 4-speed automatic transmission, traction control, dual front airbags, antilock 4-wheel disc brakes, daytime running lights, emergency inside trunk release, air conditioning, power steering, tilt steering wheel, cloth upholstery, front bucket seats, center console, cupholders, split folding rear seat, overhead console, AM/FM/cassette, digital clock, tachometer, tire inflation monitor, power mirrors, power windows, power door locks, auxiliary power outlet, rear defogger, variable intermittent wipers, power decklid release, map lights, automatic headlights, visor mirrors, floormats, theft-deterrent system, 225/60R16 tires, wheel covers.

SS adds: 3.8-liter engine, driver-side side-impact airbag, OnStar System w/one year service (roadside assistance, emergency services; other services available), dual-zone manual climate control, interior air filter, cruise control, leather-wrapped steering wheel w/radio controls, remote keyless entry, automatic day/night rearview mirror, illuminated visor mirrors, fog lights,

Specifications begin on page 535.

CHEVROLET

rear spoiler, sport suspension, 225/60SR16 tires, alloy wheels.

OPTIONAL EQUIPMENT:
Major Packages

	Retail Price	Dealer Invoice
1SB Preferred Equipment Group 1, LS	$735	$654

Dual-zone manual climate control, cruise control, remote keyless entry, cargo net, alloy wheels.

1SC Preferred Equipment Group 2, LS	1378	1226

Preferred Equipment Group 1 plus OnStar System w/one year service (roadside assistance, emergency services; other services available), automatic day/night rearview mirror, illuminated visor mirrors.

Sport Appearance Pkg., LS	495	441

Rear spoiler, 16-inch alloy wheels. Requires Preferred Equipment Group.

1SB Preferred Equipment 1, SS	615	547

Heated power mirrors, 6-way power driver seat, automatic day/night outside mirrors, Driver Information/Convenience Center (includes trip computer, compass, outside temperature indicator, universal garage door opener, theft-deterrent system w/alarm).

High Sport Appearance Pkg., SS	2000	1780

Ground effects body cladding, special rear spoiler, badging, unique alloy wheels.

Comfort and Convenience

Driver Information/Convenience Center	275	245

Trip computer, compass, outside temperature indicator, universal garage door opener, theft-deterrent system w/alarm. LS requires Preferred Equipment Group.

AM/FM/CD player	123	109

Includes 6-speaker sound system, Radio Display System.

AM/FM/cassette/CD player	223	198

Includes Radio Display System and 6-speaker sound system.

Steering wheel radio controls, LS	171	152

Includes leather-wrapped steering wheel. Requires Preferred Equipment Group.

Leather upholstery	625	556

Requires power driver seat.

Heated front seats	120	107

Requires leather upholstery, power driver and passenger seats.

6-way power driver seat	305	271
6-way power passenger seat	305	271

Requires leather upholstery and power driver seat.

Power sunroof	700	623

LS requires Preferred Equipment Group.

Alloy wheels, LS	300	267

Prices are accurate at time of publication; subject to manufacturer's change.

CHEVROLET

CHEVROLET PRIZM

Chevrolet Prizm

Front-wheel-drive subcompact car; similar to Toyota Corolla

Base price range: $13,995-$16,060. Built in USA. **Also consider:** Dodge/Plymouth Neon, Honda Civic, Mazda Protege

FOR • Fuel economy **AGAINST** • Rear-seat room • Automatic transmission performance

Lower anchors for rear child seats and an inside trunk release handle for freeing trapped occupants are 2001 additions to Chevrolet's version of the Toyota Corolla. Prizm offers base and uplevel LSi sedans powered by a Toyota-designed 1.8-liter 4-cylinder engine. Manual transmission is standard, 3- and 4-speed automatics are optional. Front side airbags and antilock brakes are optional.

Both Prizms come with air conditioning. Features standard on the LSi and optional on the base model include power windows/locks, cruise control, rear defogger, tilt steering wheel, and cassette player. Exclusive to LSi is a 60/40 split-fold rear seat. Despite their design similarity, Prizm is outsold by Corolla 4-1. Corolla gets a styling facelift for '01; this Chevy does not. Prizm's performance and accommodations mirror those of comparable Corolla models.

The Toyota Corolla report includes an evaluation of the Prizm.

ENGINES

	dohc I4
Size, liters/cu. in.	1.8/110
Horsepower @ rpm	125 @ 5800
Torque (lb-ft) @ rpm	125 @ 4000
Availability	S
EPA city/highway mpg	
5-speed OD manual	31/37
3-speed automatic	28/33
4-speed OD automatic	29/37

Specifications begin on page 535.

CHEVROLET

PRICES

Chevrolet Prizm	Retail Price	Dealer Invoice
Base 4-door sedan	$13995	$13323
LSi 4-door sedan	16060	14807
Destination charge	485	485

STANDARD EQUIPMENT:

Base: 1.8-liter dohc engine, 5-speed manual transmission, dual front airbags, daytime running lights, emergency inside trunk release, air conditioning, power steering, cloth reclining front bucket seats, center console, cupholders, AM/FM radio, digital clock, variable intermittent wipers, automatic headlights, visor mirrors, remote fuel door and decklid release, floormats, dual outside mirrors, wheel covers, 175/65R14 tires.

LSi adds: cruise control, tilt steering wheel, power mirrors, power windows, power door locks, remote keyless entry, AM/FM/cassette, tachometer, outside temperature indicator, rear defogger, map lights, split folding rear seat w/trunk pass-through, 185/65R14 tires.

OPTIONAL EQUIPMENT:

Major Packages

Preferred Equipment Group 2, Base	570	490
Cruise control, power door locks, AM/FM/cassette.		

Powertrains

3-speed automatic transmission	495	426
4-speed automatic transmission	800	688

Safety Features

Antilock brakes	645	555
Front side-impact airbags	295	254
Integrated child safety seat, LSi	125	108

Comfort and Convenience

Tilt steering wheel, Base	80	69
Rear defogger, Base	180	155
Power windows, Base	300	258
Power sunroof	675	581
Tachometer, Base	70	60
Includes outside temperature indicator.		
AM/FM/cassette, Base	165	141
AM/FM/CD player, Base	215	185
Base w/Preferred Group 2, LSi	50	43

Appearance and Miscellaneous

Alloy wheels	283	243

Prices are accurate at time of publication; subject to manufacturer's change.

CHEVROLET

CHEVROLET TAHOE AND SUBURBAN

Chevrolet Tahoe LS 4WD

Rear- or 4-wheel-drive full-size sport-utility vehicle; similar to Cadillac Escalade and GMC Yukon/Denali

Base price range: $24,941-$30,780. Built in Canada. **Also consider:** Ford Expedition, Toyota Land Cruiser and Sequoia

FOR • Passenger and cargo room • Towing ability **AGAINST** • Rear-seat entry/exit • Fuel economy

A sporty new off-road option package and more power for the heaviest-duty Suburbans are additions to Chevrolet's 2001 full-size SUVs. Tahoe and the longer Suburban are 4-door wagons with standard swing-open tail doors or a liftgate with separate-opening glass as a no-cost alternative.

GMC's Yukon and Denali and Cadillac's Escalade share this design. Tahoe comes in a half-ton 1500 payload series, Suburban in 1500 and ³/₄-ton 2500 models. All offer base, LS, and LT trim levels and standard V8 power. The base Tahoe uses a 4.8 liter with 275 horsepower. Suburban 1500s and Tahoe LS and LT use a 5.3 liter with 285 hp. Standard on Suburban 2500s is a revised 6.0 with a new camshaft and aluminum rather than cast iron cylinder heads that raise horsepower to 320 from 300. Newly optional for Suburban 2500s is an 8.1-liter V8 with 340 hp and 455 pound-feet of torque.

All models have an automatic transmission with GM's Tow/Haul mode designed to optimize shifts under heavy loads. Four-wheel drive versions get GM's Autotrac, which can be left engaged on dry surfaces. Traction control is optional for 2WD models. Rear load-leveling suspension is also optional, as is GM's Autoride, which continuously adjusts shock damping according to road conditions. Antilock brakes and front side airbags are standard. Third-row bench seats are optional on both Tahoe and Suburban and combined with the available front bench, create a 9-passenger capacity. A pair of second-row bucket seats are

Specifications begin on page 535.

CHEVROLET

optional on Suburban.

Tahoe and Suburban 4x4s are available with the sporty new Z71 package. It includes wheel flares, lower body moldings, color-keyed bumpers and grille, tubular side steps, exclusive shock absorbers, and 17-inch wheels in place of 16s. GM's OnStar assistance system is standard on LT and Z71 Tahoes and Suburbans and optional on LS versions.

PERFORMANCE Aided by the smooth transmission's astute shifting, acceleration is always adequate in these SUVs, even with a full complement of passengers and cargo. Poor fuel economy remains an issue. Our test Suburban averaged 11.5 mpg, our test Yukon 12.9; both had the 5.3 liter and 4WD. We haven't had an opportunity to test a Suburban 2500 with the new 8.1-liter V8. Maximum towing capacity is 8700 pounds on Tahoe/Yukon, 12,000 on Suburban/Yukon XL.

These big wagons don't corner like cars, but handling is better than their size implies. Balance in changes of direction is good and they're relatively easy to maneuver. Steering is reasonably precise but could use better road feel. The suspension absorbs bumps well and is sure-footed on rough pavement. There's strong stopping power with a firm, progressive pedal feel. Wind rush is not intrusive. Tire noise is low for full-size SUVs, but still audible at highway speeds. Engines are throaty but smooth under hard acceleration.

ACCOMMODATIONS Drivers get a commanding view of the road and unobstructed gauges and controls. Outward visibility and cargo room are impressive, thanks in part to the spare tire being mounted beneath the rear undercarriage.

Seats feel substantial and room in front is generous, even for the largest occupants. Second-row seating is similarly spacious. The difference between Tahoe/Yukon and the longer Suburban/Yukon XL is most obvious in the third-row seats. Suburban/Yukon XL have ample room for two grownups, while Tahoe/Yukon third-row seating is practical only for children or occasional adult use.

Step-in is lower than on Expedition and Excursion, but higher than a typical minivan. Running boards are an option we recommend, but modest lower door openings still hamper rear ingress and egress, especially on Tahoe/Yukon.

Suburban/Yukon XL have nearly 46 cubic feet of storage behind their third-row seat. Tahoe/Yukon have only enough room for a row of grocery bags, but their 50/50 split third-row seat is more versatile than Suburban/Yukon XL's one-piece bench. Third-row seats on both models fold easily. They also remove, aided by roller wheels and safety belts mounted to the seat frame. Hoisting Suburban/Yukon XL's heavy bench in or out is a 2-person operation. Tahoe/Yukon's third-row removes in two more-manageable 40-pound sections. In either, cargo room is expansive with rear seats folded or removed.

Prices are accurate at time of publication; subject to manufacturer's change.

CHEVROLET

VALUE Don't buy a big sport-utility wagon without testing GM's offerings. They're capable, comfortable, competitively priced, and their size fits nicely into gaps between Ford's Expedition and Excursion. Tahoe and Yukon are the best overall values in GM's line of big SUVs and rate as Best Buys in the full-size SUV class.

ENGINES

	ohv V8	ohv V8	ohv V8	ohv V8
Size, liters/cu. in.	4.8/292	5.3/325	6.0/364	8.1/496
Horsepower @ rpm	275 @ 5200	285 @ 5200	320 @ 5000	340 @ 4200
Torque (lb-ft) @ rpm	290 @ 4000	325 @ 4000	360 @ 4000	455 @ 3200
Availability	S[1]	S[2]	S[3]	O[3]
EPA city/highway mpg				
4-speed OD automatic	15/20[4]	14/18[5]	NA	NA

1. Base Tahoe. 2. Tahoe LS and LT, Suburban 1500. 3. Suburban 2500. 4. 14/18 w/4WD. 5. 14/16 w/4WD.

PRICES

Chevrolet Tahoe and Suburban	Retail Price	Dealer Invoice
Tahoe 4-door wagon, 2WD	$24941	$21823
Tahoe 4-door wagon, 4WD	27857	24375
Suburban 1500 4-door wagon, 2WD	25921	22681
Suburban 2500 4-door wagon, 2WD	27780	24308
Suburban 1500 4-door wagon, 4WD	28837	25232
Suburban 2500 4-door wagon, 4WD	30780	26933
Destination charge: Tahoe	730	730
Destination charge: Suburban	765	765

STANDARD EQUIPMENT:

Tahoe: 4.8-liter V8 engine, 4-speed automatic transmission, dual front airbags, front side-impact airbags, antilock 4-wheel disc brakes, daytime running lights, power steering, tilt steering wheel, vinyl upholstery, front split bench seat, second-row split folding bench seat, cupholders, power door locks, AM/FM radio, digital clock, tachometer, engine hour meter, passenger-side visor mirror, auxiliary power outlets, intermittent wipers, automatic headlights, vinyl floor covering, theft-deterrent system, rear cargo doors, 7-lead trailer harness, full-size spare tire, P245/75R16 tires. **4WD** models add: Autotrac full-time 4-wheel drive, 2-speed transfer case, variable-assist power steering, front tow hooks.

Suburban adds: 5.3-liter V8 engine (1500), 6.0-liter V8 engine (2500), second-row bench seat, P245/75R16E tires (1500), LT245/75R16E tires (2500). **4WD** models add: Autotrac full-time 4-wheel drive, 2-speed transfer case, variable-assist power steering (1500), front tow hooks.

Specifications begin on page 535.

CHEVROLET

OPTIONAL EQUIPMENT:
Major Packages

	Retail Price	Dealer Invoice
Appearance Pkg.	$717	$617

Chrome grille, bodyside moldings, roof rack, stainless steel wheels.

	Retail Price	Dealer Invoice
LS Equipment Group 1SB, Tahoe	6164	5301
Suburban	7423	6384

5.3-liter V8 engine (Tahoe), front and rear air conditioning, rear heater (Suburban), front and rear manual climate controls, cloth upholstery, front storage armrest, second-row split folding bench seat and third row bench seat (Suburban), leather-wrapped steering wheel, cruise control, heated power mirrors, power windows, remote keyless entry, AM/FM/CD player, overhead console, automatic day/night rearview mirror, compass, outside temperature indicator, illuminated visor mirrors, cargo cover and net, rear defogger, carpeting, vinyl floormats, theft-deterrent system w/alarm, deep-tinted glass, chrome grille, bodyside moldings, roof rack, alloy wheels.

	Retail Price	Dealer Invoice
LT Equipment Group 1SC, Tahoe	10638	9149
Tahoe ordered w/sunroof	10201	8773
Suburban 1500	11942	10270
Suburban 2500	11506	9895
Suburban 1500 ordered w/sunroof	11710	10071
Suburban 2500 ordered w/sunroof	11274	9696

LS Pkg. plus OnStar System w/one year service (roadside assistance, emergency services; other services available), leather upholstery, heated power front bucket seats w/power recliners and lumbar adjustment, driver seat memory, center console, automatic climate control, AM/FM/cassette/CD player, automatic day/night driver-side mirror, mirror puddle lights, universal garage door opener, carpeted floormats, fog lights, side steps, Premium Ride Suspension (Tahoe, Suburban 1500), 265/70R16 all-terrain tires (Tahoe, Suburban 1500).

	Retail Price	Dealer Invoice
Third Row Seat Pkg., Tahoe ordered w/LT Group	750	645
Tahoe ordered w/LT Group and sunroof	955	821
Tahoe ordered w/LS Group	921	792
Tahoe ordered w/LS Group and leather upholstery	1321	1136

Split folding third row seat, rear heater, rear liftgate w/wiper/washer, rear floormat, Premium Ride Suspension (LS Group).

	Retail Price	Dealer Invoice
Traction Pkg., 2WD	723	622
w/LS or LT Group	485	417

Traction control, limited-slip rear differential, cruise control, front tow hooks.

	Retail Price	Dealer Invoice
Climate Pkg.	1542	1326

Front air conditioning, rear defogger, cruise control, deep-tinted glass.

	Retail Price	Dealer Invoice
Convenience Pkg.	683	587
ordered w/sunroof	576	495

OnStar System w/one year service (roadside assistance, emergency services; other services available), universal garage door opener, driver-side automatic day/night rearview mirror, carpeted floormats. Requires LS Group.

Prices are accurate at time of publication; subject to manufacturer's change.

CONSUMER GUIDE

CHEVROLET

	Retail Price	Dealer Invoice
Snow Plow Prep Pkg., 2WD Suburban 2500	$190	$163
4WD Suburban 2500	253	218

Engine oil cooler, electrical connections, heavy-duty front springs (2WD), adjustable front springs (4WD). NA with LT Group.

Z71 Off-Road Pkg., 4WD	—	—

Price and contents price not available at time of publication.

Trailer Pkg., Tahoe, Suburban 1500	285	245
Suburban 2500	164	141

Trailer hitch platform, transmission oil cooler, trailer brake wiring harness, heavy-duty air cleaner (Tahoe, Suburban 1500).

Powertrains

8.1-liter V8 engine, Suburban 2500	600	516

Comfort and Convenience

Power sunroof	1095	942

LS includes universal garage door opener. LT deletes automatic climate control. Requires LS or LT Group.

Power front seats	480	413

Requires LS Group.

Front bucket seats	855	735

Includes dual 6-way power, center console. Requires LS Group.

Second row bucket seats, Suburban	390	335

Requires LT Group or LS Group, bucket seats, and leather upholstery.

Second-row split folding bench seat and third-row bench seat, Suburban	1230	1058
Leather upholstery, Tahoe	1755	1509
Suburban	2405	2068

Includes 6-way power front bucket seats, center console. Requires LS Group.

Rear liftgate	NC	NC

Includes rear wiper/washer. Requires LS or LT Group.

AM/FM/cassette	147	126
AM/FM/cassette/CD player	125	108

Requires LS Group, front bucket seats.

Rear radio controls, w/LT Group	150	129
w/LS Group	165	142

Includes headphone jacks. Requires front bucket seats.

Appearance and Miscellaneous

Side steps	395	340

Requires LS Group.

Wheel-flares	180	155

Std. 4WD Suburban 2500.

Fog lights	85	73

Requires LS Group.

Specifications begin on page 535.

CHEVROLET

Special Purpose, Wheels and Tires

	Retail Price	Dealer Invoice
Autoride Suspension, Tahoe, Suburban 1500	$700	$602
Suburban 2500	750	645
Includes variable rate shock absorbers, load-leveling rear suspension, P265/70R16 all-terrain tires (Tahoe, Suburban 1500). Requires LT Pkg.		
Premium Ride Suspension, Tahoe, Suburban 1500	366	315
Includes P265/70R16 all-terrain tires. Requires LS Group.		
Skid Plate Pkg., 4WD	95	82
Polished alloy wheels, Tahoe, Suburban 1500	110	95
Requires LT Group.		

CHEVROLET TRACKER

Chevrolet Tracker ZR2 4-door wagon

Rear- or 4-wheel-drive compact sport-utility vehicle; similar to Suzuki Vitara

Base price range: $15,235-$21,230. Built in Canada. **Also consider:** Honda CR-V, Subaru Forester, Toyota RAV4

FOR • Maneuverability • Cargo room **AGAINST** • Ride • Steering/handling • Rear-seat room • Rear visibility • Acceleration • Rear-seat entry/exit (2-door)

Available V6 power and higher levels of equipment highlight changes to Chevrolet's smallest SUV for 2001.

Tracker offers a 2-door convertible and a longer 4-door wagon. Both have body-on-frame construction designed by Suzuki, which markets its own versions as the Vitara. All models are available with rear-wheel drive or 4-wheel drive. The 4WD isn't for use on dry pavement, but does have 4-low gearing. Tracker's standard engine is a 127-horsepower 4-cylinder; gone is the 97-hp four that was standard in the convertible. Also newly standard on all is air conditioning and an AM/FM radio with cassette player. Newly optional on all convertibles are power windows, locks, and mirrors.

The V6 had been a Vitara exclusive. For '01, Tracker adds V6 wag-

Prices are accurate at time of publication; subject to manufacturer's change.

CHEVROLET

ons in two trim levels: luxury-oriented LT, and sporty new ZR2. Both come with Suzuki's 155-hp V6 and include standard power windows/locks/mirrors, cruise control, and aluminum wheels. LTs in 2- or 4-wheel drive get a chrome grille, CD player, and optional leather upholstery. ZR2 comes only in 4WD form with special ZR2 graphics along with charcoal-colored wheel flares and exterior trim. ZR2 also is offered as a 2-door convertible, but only with the 4-cylinder engine. Automatic transmission is standard with the V6 and optional with the 4-cylinder in place of a 5-speed manual.

PERFORMANCE The 4-cylinder engine has only passable power in the convertible and feels lethargic in the heavier wagon. It also sounds and feels gruff when worked hard. Though no ball of fire either, the new V6 adds a welcome dose of power. The automatic transmission is well behaved, but the standard manual suffers vague shift action with long throws. Our test average was 20.2 mpg with a 4-cylinder 5-speed 4WD soft-top—not grand for a bantam SUV. Wagons do slightly worse.

Tracker or Vitara, these vehicles are prone to fore-aft pitching even on fairly smooth roads, though they absorb most bumps without jarring. Handling is competent, but cornering grip only so-so. Overall driving feel is less composed than in a Honda CR-V or Ford Escape/Mazda Tribute, with the Subaru Forester tops for all-around maneuvering ease and ride comfort. Tracker's part-time 4WD isn't as convenient as the permanent systems offered by the aforementioned rivals, though the Chevy is likely to be more adept off-road.

ACCOMMODATIONS Escape and Tribute top the class for room and comfort. Trackers have decent room in front, but relatively low-set seats mean drivers don't get as commanding a view forward as in most SUVs, and the exterior-mount spare tire and tall rear headrests hamper vision directly aft. The rear bench seat in wagons is short on leg room unless the front seats are well forward; the convertible's back seat is cramped and park-bench hard. Step-in height is moderate, but narrow rear doors impede access in wagons while ragtops are hindered by their 2-door design. The wide running boards standard on the new LT are difficult to step over. Radio and climate controls are low enough to require a long look down to adjust, and the radio has annoyingly tiny buttons.

The Tracker wagon is nearly a foot shorter than the CR-V, and it shows in scant cargo room behind the rear seat, making the standard split/fold seatback more necessary than usual. Tailgates on both body styles open to the right, which hinders curbside loading.

VALUE Tracker has some off-road prowess going for it, but it's an also-ran among compact SUVs in the kind of driving most people do. The Ford, Mazda, Honda, and Subaru entries are much more pleasant and enjoyable, roomier, and have higher resale values.

Specifications begin on page 535.

CHEVROLET

ENGINES

	dohc I4	dohc V6
Size, liters/cu. in.	2.0/121	2.5/152
Horsepower @ rpm	127 @ 6000	155 @ 6500
Torque (lb-ft) @ rpm	134 @ 3000	160 @ 4000
Availability	S[1]	O[2]
EPA city/highway mpg		
5-speed OD manual	23/25[3]	
4-speed OD automatic	24/26[4]	18/20

1. Base, ZR2 conv. 2. ZR2 wagon, LT. 3. 22/25 w/4WD. 4. 23/25 w/4WD.

PRICES

Chevrolet Tracker

	Retail Price	Dealer Invoice
Base 2-door convertible, 2WD	$15235	$14351
Base 4-door wagon, 2WD	15855	14935
LT 4-door wagon, 2WD	20130	18962
Base 2-door convertible, 4WD	16335	15388
Base 4-door wagon, 4WD	16955	15972
ZR2 2-door convertible, 4WD	18185	17130
ZR2 4-door wagon, 4WD	20550	19358
LT 4-door wagon, 4WD	21230	19999
Destination charge	450	450

STANDARD EQUIPMENT:

Base: 2.0-liter dohc 4-cylinder engine, 5-speed manual transmission, dual front airbags, daytime running lights, air conditioning, power steering, cloth/vinyl upholstery, front bucket seats, center console, split folding rear seat (wagon), cupholders, folding rear seat (convertible), AM/FM/cassette, digital clock, tachometer, variable intermittent wipers, passenger-side visor mirror, map lights, auxiliary power outlet, rear defogger (wagon), rear wiper/washer (wagon), automatic headlights, cargo cover (wagon), floormats, dual outside mirrors, skid plate, front and rear tow hooks, rear-mounted full-size spare tire, 195/75R15 tires. **4WD** adds: part-time 4-wheel drive, 2-speed transfer case, 205/75R15 tires.

ZR2 convertible adds: part-time 4-wheel drive, 2-speed transfer case, tilt steering wheel, cruise control, power mirrors, power windows, power door locks, remote keyless entry, wheel flares, 215/75R15 white-letter tires, alloy wheels.

ZR2 wagon adds: 2.5-liter dohc V6 engine, 4-speed automatic transmission.

LT adds to Base: 2.5-liter dohc V6 engine, 4-speed automatic transmission, tilt steering wheel, cruise control, cloth upholstery, power mirrors, power windows, power door locks, remote keyless entry, AM/FM/CD player, roof rack, running boards, 215/70R15 tires, alloy wheels. **4WD** adds: part-time 4-wheel drive, 2-speed transfer case.

Prices are accurate at time of publication; subject to manufacturer's change.

CHEVROLET

OPTIONAL EQUIPMENT:

	Retail Price	Dealer Invoice
Major Packages		
Preferred Equipment Group 2, Base convertible	$1470	$1308
Base wagon	1415	1259

Power mirrors, power windows and door locks, remote keyless entry, cruise control, tilt steering wheel, cargo storage compartment (convertible), alloy wheels.

Powertrains
4-speed automatic transmission, Base, ZR2 convertible	1000	890

Safety Features
Antilock brakes	595	530

Comfort and Convenience
Leather upholstery, LT	595	530
AM/FM/CD player, Base, ZR2	100	89
Lockable storage compartment, Base convertible	125	111

Appearance and Miscellaneous
Roof rack, Base/ZR2 wagon	126	112

Special Purpose, Wheels and Tires
Alloy wheels, Base	365	325

CHEVROLET VENTURE

Chevrolet Venture

Front-wheel-drive minivan; similar to Oldsmobile Silhouette and Pontiac Montana

Base price range: $20,795-$30,315. Built in USA. **Also consider:** Dodge Caravan, Ford Windstar, Honda Odyssey

FOR • Ride • Passenger and cargo room **AGAINST** • Fuel economy • Rear-seat comfort

Specifications begin on page 535.

CHEVROLET

Chevrolet's front-wheel-drive minivan adds a stowable third-row seat, driver-side power door, 6-disc dashboard CD player, and rear parking aid for 2001. Regular-length and 14-inch-longer extended-length bodies are offered. Among extended models is a Warner Bros. Edition with a rear-seat video entertainment package; this year, its ceiling-mounted screen increases from 5.6 inches to 6.8 inches, and the headphones are cordless. Venture shares its design with the Oldsmobile Silhouette and Pontiac Montana.

All Ventures have dual sliding side doors. A power right-side door is available; due later in the model year is an optional power left-side door. (Montana already offers this option.) All models seat seven; some extendeds can optionally seat eight. The stowable third-row seat option due later in the model year comes with a rear floor-mounted covered storage tray. A second-row child seat is optional.

All Ventures have a 3.4-liter V6, automatic transmission, front side airbags, and antilock brakes. Optional on LS and standard on LT and Warner Bros. is the new Rear Parking Assist, which warns of objects behind the vehicle when backing up. The new 6-disc CD player is optional on LS, LT, and Warner Bros. On all models except the Value edition, GM's OnStar assistance system is standard and a universal garage-door opener is optional. Lower anchors for rear child seats are added, and cupholders move from the sides of the front seats to the dashboard. The Venture's cargo version has been dropped for 2001.

PERFORMANCE These Chevy, Olds, and Pontiac minivans have adequate acceleration, helped by a smooth, responsive transmission. Fuel economy is good for this class, averaging around 18 mpg in our tests, though a Montana got 15.7 in mostly city driving.

Venture, Silhouette, and Montana share a basic suspension that enables them to ride and handle much like cars. Most rivals do, too, but the GM models feel somewhat sportier than the minivan norm. Steering is accurate and communicative, cornering grippy and predictable, body lean modest. Most bumps are easily absorbed and the highway ride is stable. Montana's sport suspension, part of the optional Sport Performance and Handling Package, slightly improves agility but makes the ride jittery on urban streets. The load-leveling suspension available on all three brands is a useful feature.

Stopping is controlled and progressive, though a test Silhouette had a slightly mushy brake feel. Wind noise is prominent around the mirrors at highway speed, but road and engine sounds are well-muffled.

ACCOMMODATIONS These minivans make efficient use of interior space, providing good head and leg room at all positions. Each second-row bucket seat weighs just 39 pounds and is easy to remove or relocate. Even the 45-pound rear bench isn't overly cumbersome. To get

CHEVROLET

seats this light, however, GM uses less-substantial cushions than most rivals, and the seats are low enough that lanky adults sit with knees upright. The stowable third-row seat makes for a quick conversion, but does not disappear into the floor, as does the Honda Odyssey's and Mazda MPV's. Instead, it folds level with the convenience tray to form a flat surface that's about four inches higher than the actual floor.

Venture is the only model that offers a second-row 3-passenger bench seat, and Silhouette is alone in offering third-row captain's chairs. Entry/exit is step-in easy, though it's still a chore to get to the third-row seat.

The power rear passenger door is an appreciated Montana convenience, although Chrysler, Dodge, Ford, Honda, and Toyota already offer power sliding doors on both sides. Storage bins and cup/juice-box holders abound, and there's a handy storage net between the front seats. With all seats in place, cargo room is tight on regular-length models, good on extended versions. The tailgate is easier to manage than most. Visibility is excellent, helped by large outside mirrors. Drivers also enjoy clear, handy gauges and controls.

All three GM minivans offer essentially the same video package. Its ceiling-mounted screen is usefully larger this year and easy to see in all light conditions, and the infrared cordless headphones are a nice touch. However, the VCR is floor level at the base of the dashboard and is difficult to load or operate while driving, though it can be adjusted via remote control.

VALUE These minivans merit strong consideration. Venture is the best value of the three, but base prices on all are reasonable and include a fine array of standard features.

ENGINES

	ohv V6
Size, liters/cu. in.	3.4/207
Horsepower @ rpm	185 @ 5200
Torque (lb-ft) @ rpm	210 @ 4000
Availability	S

EPA city/highway mpg	
4-speed OD automatic	18/25

PRICES

Chevrolet Venture	Retail Price	Dealer Invoice
Value regular length 4-door van	$20795	$19402
Plus regular length 4-door van	24455	22132
Plus extended 4-door van	25455	23037
LS regular length 4-door van	25385	22973
LS extended 4-door van	26385	23878
LT extended 4-door van	28670	25946
Warner Bros Edition extended 4-door van	30315	27435

Specifications begin on page 535.

CHEVROLET

	Retail Price	Dealer Invoice
Destination charge	$640	$640

STANDARD EQUIPMENT:

Value: 3.4-liter V6 engine, 4-speed automatic transmission, dual front airbags, front side impact airbags, antilock brakes, daytime running lights, front air conditioning, power steering, tilt steering wheel, cloth upholstery, 7-passenger seating (front bucket seats, center 2-passenger and rear 3-passenger bench seats), center console, overhead consolette, cupholders, power door locks, dual sliding rear doors, AM/FM radio, digital clock, variable intermittent wipers, visor mirrors, auxiliary power outlet, automatic headlights, theft-deterrent system, dual outside mirrors, 215/70R15 tires, wheel covers.

Plus adds: OnStar System w/one year service (roadside assistance, emergency services; other services available), cruise control, heated power mirrors, power front windows, power door locks, remote keyless entry, center and third row split folding bench seats, overhead console, AM/FM/cassette, rear defogger, rear wiper/washer, floormats, deep-tinted rear glass.

LS adds: power rear quarter windows, AM/FM/CD player, illuminated visor mirrors, roof rack, alloy wheels.

LT adds: traction control, rear parking assist, front and rear air conditioning, 6-way power driver seat, two center row captain chairs, stowable third-row seat, power passenger-side sliding rear door, AM/FM/cassette/CD player, rear radio controls, rear headphone jacks, theft-deterrent system w/alarm, air inflation kit, touring suspension w/automatic load-leveling.

Warner Bros. Edition adds: cloth/leather upholstery, three center-row bucket seats, two third-row bucket seats, LCD screen, VCR player, remote control, deletes traction control, air inflation kit, touring suspension w/automatic load-leveling.

OPTIONAL EQUIPMENT:
Major Packages

Trailering Pkg., LS, Warner	720	619
LS/Warner w/self-sealing tires	570	490
LT	165	142

Includes heavy-duty engine and transmission oil cooling, touring suspension w/load-leveling, air inflation kit.

Safety Features

Rear parking assist, LS extended	150	129
Traction control, LS, Warner	195	168

Comfort and Convenience

Front and rear air conditioning, Plus extended, LS extended	475	409
Power passenger-side sliding door, Plus	770	662

Prices are accurate at time of publication; subject to manufacturer's change.

CHEVROLET • CHRYSLER

	Retail Price	Dealer Invoice
LS	$720	$620
Includes 6-way power driver seat, power rear quarter windows.		
2-center row captain chairs, LS regular	290	249
8-passenger seating, LS	525	452
Three second-row bucket seats, third-row 3-passenger stowable bench seat.		
Leather upholstery, LT	625	538
AM/FM/CD player, Plus	100	86
AM/FM/cassette/CD player, LS	100	86
AM/FM/cassette w/6-disc		
CD changer, LS	395	340
LT, Warner	295	254
Rear-seat audio controls, LS	155	133
Includes headphone jacks.		
Rear defogger, Value	305	262
Universal garage door opener,		
Plus regular, LS, LT, Warner	110	95

Appearance and Miscellaneous

Roof rack, Plus	225	194
Touring suspension, LS, Warner	555	477
LS/Warner w/self-sealing tires	405	348
Includes traction control, load-leveling suspension, air inflation kit, 215/70R15 touring tires.		
Self-sealing 215/70R15 tires, LS, Warner	300	258
LT	150	129
Alloy wheels, Plus	295	254

CHRYSLER CONCORDE

Chrysler Concorde LXi

Front-wheel-drive full-size car; similar to Chrysler LHS and 300M and Dodge Intrepid

Base price range: $22,510-$26,755. Built in Canada. **Also consider:** Buick LeSabre, Pontiac Bonneville, Toyota Avalon

Specifications begin on page 535.

CHRYSLER

FOR • Passenger and cargo room • Ride • Steering/handling
AGAINST • Rear visibility • Trunk liftover

Chrysler's full-size car gets several new safety features for 2001, including optional front side airbags and a 3-point safety belt for the rear-seat's middle position. Concorde shares its underskin design with the Dodge Intrepid and is the foundation for Chrysler's comfort-oriented LHS and sporty 300M near-luxury cars. It has standard seating for five and optional seating for six.

Base LX and uplevel LXi models are offered, both with V6 engines. The LX has 200 horsepower, the LXi 222. Automatic transmission is standard. Antilock brakes and traction control are optional on the LX, standard on LXi.

For 2001, the LX's 22D option package includes the LXi's standard alloy wheels. Also, the LXi's optional Infinity audio system gains steering-wheel mounted controls. The front side airbags are optional for both models. Concorde's performance and accommodations mirror those of like-equipped Intrepids.

The Dodge Intrepid report includes an evaluation of the Concorde.

ENGINES

	dohc V6	ohc V6
Size, liters/cu. in.	2.7/167	3.2/197
Horsepower @ rpm	200 @ 5800	222 @ 6400
Torque (lb-ft) @ rpm	190 @ 4850	222 @ 3950
Availability	S[1]	S[2]
EPA city/highway mpg		
4-speed OD automatic	19/28	18/26

1. LX. 2. LXi.

PRICES

Chrysler Concorde	Retail Price	Dealer Invoice
LX 4-door sedan	$22510	$20609
LXi 4-door sedan	26755	24387
Destination charge	610	610

STANDARD EQUIPMENT:

LX: 2.7-liter dohc V6 engine, 4-speed automatic transmission, dual front airbags, 4-wheel disc brakes, emergency inside trunk release, air conditioning, power steering, tilt steering wheel, cruise control, cloth upholstery, front bucket seats, 8-way power driver seat w/manual lumbar adjustment, center console, cupholders, trunk pass-through, power mirrors, power windows, power door locks, remote keyless entry, AM/FM/cassette, digital clock, tachometer, illuminated visor mirrors, rear defogger, auxiliary power outlet, variable intermittent wipers, power decklid release, map lights, floormats,

Prices are accurate at time of publication; subject to manufacturer's change.

CHRYSLER

225/60R16 tires, wheel covers.

LXi adds: 3.2-liter V6 engine, traction control, antilock brakes, variable-assist power steering, leather-wrapped steering wheel, leather upholstery, 8-way power passenger seat, AM/FM/cassette/CD player, automatic climate control, trip computer, automatic day/night rearview mirror, universal garage door opener, theft-deterrent system, full-size spare tire, alloy wheels.

OPTIONAL EQUIPMENT:
Major Packages

	Retail Price	Dealer Invoice
LX Pkg. 22D, LX	$1135	$1010
Premium sound system, automatic day/night mirror, universal garage door opener, trip computer, alloy wheels.		
LXi Pkg. 24F, LXi	NC	NC
Manufacturer's discount price, (credit)	(300)	(267)
LXi standard equipment.		
Leather Interior Group, LX	1075	957
Leather upholstery, 8-way power passenger seat, leather-wrapped steering wheel. Requires LX Pkg. 22D.		
Traction Control/Steering Group, LX	280	249
Traction control, variable-assist power steering. Requires LX Pkg. 22D, antilock brakes.		

Safety Features

Antilock brakes, LX	600	534
Front side-impact airbags	350	312

Comfort and Convenience

Power sunroof	895	797
Front split bench seat	100	89
8-way power passenger seat, LX	380	338
Requires LX Pkg. 22D.		
AM/FM/cassette/CD player, LX	575	512
LX w/LX Pkg.	225	200
Includes premium sound system.		
AM/FM/cassette w/in-dash 4-disc CD changer, LXi	575	512
Includes Infinity sound system, steering wheel radio controls.		
Smoker's group	20	18
Includes ashtrays and lighter.		
Alloy wheels, LX	390	347
Chrome alloy wheels, LXi	600	534

CHRYSLER LHS AND 300M

Front-wheel-drive near-luxury car; similar to Chrysler Concorde and Dodge Intrepid

Specifications begin on page 535.

CHRYSLER

Chrysler LHS

Base price range: $28,680-$29,640. Built in Canada. **Also consider:** Acura TL, Audi A6, Lexus GS 300

FOR • Acceleration • Passenger and cargo room • Ride/handling
AGAINST • Rear visibility • Trunk liftover

The LHS and 300M are, respectively, luxury and sports versions of Chrysler's Concorde. Optional front side airbags and a new luxury package with real wood trim keynote 2001 changes. LHS and 300M use the same front-wheel-drive chassis as the Concorde and similar Dodge Intrepid, but have distinct styling and the 300M has a special shortened body. LHS and 300M share a 253-horsepower V6 and automatic transmission; the 300M uses Chrysler's AutoStick automatic with separate gate for manual shifting. Antilock 4-wheel disc brakes and traction control are standard.

The 300M has sportier suspension and steering settings than the LHS, but the same tires. Both get new-design 17-inch alloy wheels, which are available with chrome finish on the 300M; the LHS's extra-cost bright wheels retain the previous style. A Performance Handling option gives the 300M more-aggressive tires, which for 2001 are on 17-inch wheels instead of 16s.

New standard features include steering wheel audio controls and a 3-point safety belt for the middle rear seat position. The new Luxury Group option package includes walnut interior trim and outside rear-view mirrors that automatically tilt down for better visibility when the car is shifted into reverse.

PERFORMANCE Acceleration is a match for any direct rival—and a clear step ahead of Concorde and Intrepid. LHS and 300M fall short of such competitors as the Lexus GS 300 and Acura TL in overall refinement, however. Their engine isn't quite as smooth, and road and wind noise, while not objectionable, aren't as well-isolated. Our extended-use-test '99 LHS had the same powertrain as the 2001, and averaged 21.6 mpg over 14,480 miles. A test 2000 300M averaged 18.6 mpg. Both figures are good for cars of this size, although the majority of our driving was on highways. The LHS has competent handling and a well-

Prices are accurate at time of publication; subject to manufacturer's change.

CHRYSLER

controlled ride. The 300M steers and turns with assertiveness and its base suspension absorbs bumps well. We haven't tested the optional Performance Handling Group with the 2001's new wheels and tires, but the previous setup made the ride jarring over bad pavement. Both models have strong brakes with fine pedal feel.

Our 300M test car suffered undue torque steer (pulling to one side in hard acceleration), and, along with our extended-use LHS, tended to drift to the left at freeway speeds. A dealer service department said it could find no alignment problems with the extended-use-test LHS, nor could it find evidence of any transmission malfunction when we complained that this test car would shift in and out of overdrive with a modest jolt in 40-mph cruising. The LHS was otherwise mechanically trouble-free.

ACCOMMODATIONS Concorde and Intrepid offer a front bench for 6-passenger capacity, but LHS and 300M are 5-passenger cars. Leather upholstery and heated front seats are standard, and the 300M has a 60/40 split folding rear seatback. No near-luxury rival equals their generous interior volume, though the 300M's slight rear leg-room deficiency compared to the LHS is apparent. On both models, rear-seat entry is hampered by the elongated door shape.

Controls are well-placed and have good tactile feel, but the gauges are poorly illuminated, making them hard to read at night. Interior materials and assembly are commendable, though not in a league with import rivals. Models with light-colored dashboard tops suffer annoying reflections in the windshield, and narrow rear windows make for poor aft visibility. The LHS's trunk is large and has a wide opening; the 300M's has less volume and a smaller opening.

VALUE LHS and 300M give up a measure of refinement to the top competition, and their cabin decor isn't as sophisticated. But no similarly priced rival matches this duo's blend of interior space and overall performance.

ENGINES

	ohc V6
Size, liters/cu. in.	3.5/215
Horsepower @ rpm	253 @ 6400
Torque (lb-ft) @ rpm	255 @ 3950
Availability	S
EPA city/highway mpg	
4-speed OD automatic	18/26

PRICES

Chrysler LHS and 300M	Retail Price	Dealer Invoice
LHS 4-door sedan	$28680	$26300
300M 4-door sedan	29640	27155
Destination charge	655	655

Specifications begin on page 535.

CHRYSLER

STANDARD EQUIPMENT:

LHS: 3.5-liter V6 engine, 4-speed automatic transmission, traction control, dual front airbags, antilock 4-wheel disc brakes, emergency inside trunk release, variable-assist power steering, tilt leather-wrapped steering wheel w/radio controls, cruise control, air conditioning w/automatic climate control, leather upholstery, heated 8-way power front bucket seats w/driver-side memory and manual lumbar adjustment, center console, cupholders, rear seat trunk pass-through, heated power mirrors w/memory, power windows, power door locks, remote keyless entry, Infinity AM/FM/cassette/CD player w/9-speakers and memory, analog clock, tachometer, trip computer, universal garage door opener, automatic day/night rearview mirror, rear defogger, power decklid release, variable intermittent wipers, illuminated visor mirrors, automatic headlights, map lights, floormats, theft-deterrent system, fog lights, 225/55R17 tires, alloy wheels.

300M adds: 4-speed automatic transmission w/manual-shift capability, firm-feel power steering, split folding rear seat, sport suspension, Deletes: variable-assist power steering, rear seat trunk pass-through.

OPTIONAL EQUIPMENT:

Major Packages

	Retail Price	Dealer Invoice
Luxury Pkg.	$520	$463

Wood interior trim, vehicle information center, outside-mirror tilt-down back-up aid, driver-side automatic day/night mirror.

Performance Handling Group, 300M	560	498

Includes unlimited top speed engine controller, performance antilock 4-wheel disc brakes, performance power steering and suspension, 225/55VR17 tires.

Safety Features

Front side-impact airbags	350	312

Comfort and Convenience

Power sunroof	895	797
AM/FM/cassette w/in-dash 4-disc CD changer	515	458

Includes 11-speaker Infinity sound system.

Smoker's Group	20	18

Ashtrays, lighter.

Chrome alloy wheels	750	668

CHRYSLER PT CRUISER

CG BEST BUY AUTO

Front-wheel-drive compact car

Base price: $15,935. Built in Mexico. **Also consider:** Honda CR-V, Subaru Outback, Volkswagen Passat

FOR • Handling/roadholding • Entry/exit • Passenger and cargo

Prices are accurate at time of publication; subject to manufacturer's change.

CHRYSLER

Chrysler PT Cruiser

room **AGAINST** • Acceleration w/automatic transmission

A sales hit even before it reached showrooms last spring as a 2001 model, this retro-styled 4-door wagon gets minor changes this fall, including available heated front seats and yellow pearl paint.

The PT (Personal Transportation) Cruiser is considered a truck under federal fuel-economy regulations, but is designed to blend carlike comfort and roadability with practical features borrowed from minivans and sport-utility vehicles. It seats five, and size-wise compares to Honda's CR-V compact SUV, with a similar wheelbase and only 2 cubic feet less cargo volume despite standing some 2 inches lower and nearly 9 inches shorter overall.

The PT Cruiser is built on an all-new unibody platform, and some of its mechanical components are similar to the subcompact Neon sedan's. The only engine is a 150-horsepower version of Chrysler's familiar 2.4-liter 4-cylinder, linked to 5-speed manual or optional 4-speed automatic transmissions. Standard features include a removable 65/35 split-fold rear seat, multi-position rear parcel shelf, air conditioning, tilt steering wheel, floor shift console, and rear wiper/washer on a one-piece liftgate. An optional Touring Group includes a firmer suspension and 16-inch wheels to replace the base 15s. Optional 4-wheel antilock disc brakes supplant rear drums and are bundled with traction control.

The Limited Edition package includes the Touring Group, plus leather upholstery, power moonroof, and a fold-flat front passenger seat. That seat is also included in the 2-F option package, and some of the other items are available separately. Front and rear power windows are standard. Both are now controlled by switches on the dashboard; previously the rears were operated only by switches at the base of the center console. Those switches remain for use by rear-seat passengers.

PERFORMANCE PT Cruiser is a pleasant, fairly refined car with predictable front-drive handling. Steering is responsive, with just the right amount of assistance. We haven't tested the base suspension, but the firmer Touring setup delivers surprisingly flat cornering, plus a comfortably controlled ride except on washboard surfaces, where it tends to jig-

Specifications begin on page 535.

CHRYSLER

gle a bit. Noise levels are generally low, but coarse pavement induces some road roar on the touring tires, wind noise starts to intrude at 65 mph, and the engine note rises above 4000 rpm. The engine is quite smooth but not very muscular, especially up long grades or in highway passing with more than two people aboard. It's fine in around-town cruising. The automatic transmission is pretty responsive, though it sometimes downshifts with a lurch. Cruiser's manual gearbox has a light but very positive shift action not unlike a Honda 5-speed. Braking feels strong with good pedal modulation. The automatic-transmission Cruiser we tested ranged from 18.5 to 23.0 mpg depending on conditions. Our test 5-speed averaged 21.7.

ACCOMMODATIONS This is where the Cruiser really shines. Chrysler claims 26 different seating/cargo configurations with the available fold-flat front passenger seat, but you'll have to fold or remove the rear bench for cargo of any size because there's only grocery-bag space with that seat in use. Both rear-seat sections have convenient carry handles and built-in rollers. They're still a bit cumbersome, but not unduly heavy: The larger portion weighs 60 pounds, the smaller 38. Tall and fairly wide rear doors provide plenty of space for slinging them in or out, to the added benefit of passenger access. The load floor is low and flat, and the rear wheel arches don't steal much space. Interior storage is plentiful.

Cruiser's cabin is plenty roomy for four adults and maybe a rear center-seater who doesn't mind a little crowding. The high body build gives all riders abundant head clearance even beneath the power moonroof. Seating is comfortably chair-height, and even 6-footers have good leg space behind a tall front occupant.

Chrysler carries Cruiser's sense of style into the instrument panel, which is tidy and generally well arranged. Audio units sit below simple dial-type climate controls and are easy to reach and operate.

Addition of dashboard switches for the rear power windows erases our biggest complaint about the control layout. Previously, the driver had to stretch awkwardly to the rear base of the center console to raise or lower the back power windows. Drivers have clear outward sightlines, although the rear head restraints are a minor obstruction.

Cruisers we tested felt solid on the road and looked great inside and out. Interior materials feel sturdier than Cruiser's price might suggest, though some of our testers wish for more "soft-feel" surfaces.

VALUE Chrysler says the Cruiser appeals to an unusually wide spectrum of buyers, and we agree. It's hard to beat this affordable vehicle's impressive combination of room, comfort, versatility, and driving pleasure. Mediocre acceleration is the only real flaw, and even that's about par versus other small wagons. Demand for the PT Cruiser currently outstrips supply, so expect to pay full retail well into the 2001 model year.

Prices are accurate at time of publication; subject to manufacturer's change.

CHRYSLER

ENGINES

	dohc I4
Size, liters/cu. in.	2.4/148
Horsepower @ rpm	150 @ 5500
Torque (lb-ft) @ rpm	162 @ 4000
Availability	S

EPA city/highway mpg

5-speed OD manual	20/26
4-speed OD automatic	20/25

PRICES

Chrysler PT Cruiser

	Retail Price	Dealer Invoice
Base 4-door wagon	$15935	$14767
Destination charge	565	565

STANDARD EQUIPMENT:

Base: 2.4-liter dohc 4-cylinder engine, 5-speed manual transmission, dual front airbags, air conditioning, power steering, tilt steering wheel, front bucket seats, center console, cupholders, split folding rear seat, power windows, AM/FM/cassette, tachometer, rear defogger, rear wiper/washer, visor mirrors, variable intermittent wipers, auxiliary power outlet, floormats, dual outside mirrors, 195/65R15 tires, wheel covers.

OPTIONAL EQUIPMENT:

Major Packages

Quick Order Pkg. 27F/28F	1365	1215
Manufacturer's discount price	775	690

Heated power mirrors, power door locks, remote keyless entry, illuminated visor mirrors, map lights, additional auxiliary power outlets, flood light, fold-flat front passenger seat, underseat storage, rear sear outboard headrests, assist handles, cargo net, deep tinted glass, theft-deterrent system w/alarm.

Limited Quick Order Pkg. 27G/28G	4605	4098
Manufacturer's discount price	3360	2990

Quick Order Pkg. 27F/28F plus front side-impact airbags, leather upholstery, driver-seat power height adjuster, cruise control, power sunroof, Luxury Touring Group (leather-wrapped steering and shift knob, floormats, bright exhaust tip, fog lights, touring suspension, 205/55R16 tires, chrome alloy wheels), overhead console, compass, outside temperature indicator, badging.

Luxury Touring Group	1215	1081
Manufacturer's discount price	1025	912

Leather-wrapped steering and shift knob, floormats, bright exhaust tip, badging, fog lights, touring suspension, 205/55R16 tires, chrome alloy wheels. Requires Quick Order Group 2-F.

Specifications begin on page 535.

CHRYSLER

	Retail Price	Dealer Invoice
Touring Group	$590	$525
Fog lights, touring suspension, 205/55R16 tires, painted alloy wheels.
Power Sunroof Group	925	823
Manufacturer's discount price	750	667
Power Sunroof Group, ordered w/Quick Order Pkg.27F/28F	725	645
Manufacturer's discount price	665	592
Power sunroof, Light Group, overhead console, compass, outside temperature indicator, assist handles.
| Light Group | 160 | 142 |
Illuminated visor mirrors, map lights, additional auxiliary power outlets.

Powertrains
4-speed automatic transmission	825	734

Safety Features
Front side-impact airbags	350	312
4-wheel Antilock Disc Brake Pkg.	790	703
Manufacturer's discount price	595	525
Antilock 4-wheel disc brakes, traction control.

Comfort and Convenience
Cruise control	225	200
AM/FM/cassette/CD player	225	200
Driver-seat power height adjuster	100	89
Requires Quick Order Group 27F/28F.
| Overhead console | 150 | 134 |
Includes compass, outside temperature indicator, map lights.

Appearance and Miscellaneous
Deep tinted glass	275	245

CHRYSLER SEBRING

Front-wheel-drive midsize car; similar to Dodge Stratus
Base price range: $17,945-$28,915. Built in USA. **Also consider:** Ford Taurus, Honda Accord, Toyota Camry/Solara

FOR • Steering/handling **AGAINST** • Acceleration (4-cylinder) • Rear-seat entry/exit (coupe) • Rear-seat comfort (coupe)

Chrysler's midsize line is redesigned for 2001, retaining its coupe and convertible models, but adding a sedan previously sold under the Cirrus nameplate. Wheelbases are unchanged, and exterior dimensions increase only slightly. The available V6 engines are new, the sedan offers side curtain airbags, and Chrysler claims numerous structural

Prices are accurate at time of publication; subject to manufacturer's change.

CHRYSLER

Chrysler Sebring LX sedan

changes to improve crashworthiness and reduce noise, vibration, and harshness.

The Sebring coupe again shares its platform and powertrains with the Mitsubishi Galant and Eclipse. It's built in Illinois alongside the similar Dodge Stratus coupe (which used to be called the Avenger). The Sebring LX coupe has a 147-horsepower 2.4-liter 4-cylinder engine. The LXi has a 3.0 V6 with 200 hp, 37 more than the V6 it replaces. Standard with the V6 is a 5-speed manual transmission. Optional with the V6 and standard with the 4-cylinder is a 4-speed automatic. In V6 models, the automatic has Chrysler's AutoStick manual-shift feature.

The Sebring sedan and convertible again share a Chrysler platform and powertrains. The sedan has a Dodge Stratus counterpart. Standard on Sebring LX sedans is a 150-hp 4-cylinder. Optional on the LX sedan and standard on the LXi is a 2.7-liter V6 with 200 hp, 32 more than the V6 it replaces.

The Sebring convertible comes in JX, JXi, and Limited models, all with the 2.7 V6. All sedans and convertibles have automatic transmission (sans AutoStick). Convertibles have a power top and heated glass rear window. The power side windows automatically raise and lower in tandem with the top. The sedan's optional curtain airbags drop down from above the side windows for head protection in a side impact. Lower-body side airbags are not offered.

Sedans, convertibles, and the LXi coupe come with 4-wheel disc brakes. Antilock brakes are standard on the Limited convertible, unavailable on the LX coupe, and optional on all other Sebrings.

Sedans and convertibles have lower anchors for rear child seats and an emergency release inside the trunk. Chrysler says new headlamps on coupes and sedans are 25-percent brighter than before, and that thicker window and door glass improves sound insulation.

Sebring sedans and coupes have performance and accommodations similar to those of comparably equipped Stratus sedans and coupes. Dodge does not offer a Staratus convertible.

The Dodge Stratus report includes an evaluation of the Sebring.

Specifications begin on page 535.

CHRYSLER

ENGINES

	ohc I4	dohc I4	dohc V6	ohc V6
Size, liters/cu. in.	2.4/143	2.4/148	2.7/167	3.0/181
Horsepower @ rpm	147 @ 5500	150 @ 5200	200 @ 5900	200 @ 5500
Torque (lb-ft) @ rpm	158 @ 4000	167 @ 4000	192 @ 4300	205 @ 4500
Availability	S[1]	S[2]	S[3]	S[4]
EPA city/highway mpg				
5-speed OD manual				20/27
4-speed OD automatic	21/27	21/29	20/28	19/27

1. LX coupe. 2. LX sedan. 3. LXi convertible/sedan; optional LX sedan. 4. LXi coupe; optional LX coupe.

PRICES

Chrysler Sebring	Retail Price	Dealer Invoice
LX 2-door coupe	$19910	$18250
LXi 2-door coupe	21475	19463
LX 4-door sedan	17945	16461
LXi 4-door sedan	20830	19029
JX 2-door convertible	24370	22309
JXi 2-door convertible	26830	24499
Limited 2-door convertible	28915	26354
Destination charge: coupes	585	585
Destination charge: sedans, convertibles	575	575

STANDARD EQUIPMENT:

LX coupe: 2.4-liter 4-cylinder engine, 4-speed automatic transmission, dual front airbags, air condtioning, power steering, tilt steering wheel, cruise control, cloth upholstery, front bucket seats w/height-adjustable driver seat, center console, cupholders, power mirrors, power windows, power door locks, remote keyless entry, AM/FM/cassette, tachometer, rear defogger, remote decklid release, variable-intermittent wipers, map lights, auxiliary power outlet, visor mirrors, floormats, theft-deterrent system, fog lights, 205/55HR16 tires, wheel covers.

LXi coupe adds: 3.0-liter V6 engine, 5-speed manual transmission, 4-wheel disc brakes, leather-wrapped steering wheel, Infinity AM/FM/cassette/CD player, automatic day/night rearview mirror, compass, 215/50R17 tires, alloy wheels.

LX sedan adds to LX coupe: 2.4-liter dohc 4-cylinder engine, 4-wheel disc brakes, emergency inside trunk release, split folding rear seat, automatic-off headlights, 205/65R15 tires, deletes remote keyless entry, map lights, theft-deterrent system.

LXi sedan adds: 2.7-liter dohc V6 engine, leather upholstery, 8-way power driver seat, leather-wrapped steering wheel, AM/FM/CD player, trip comput-

Prices are accurate at time of publication; subject to manufacturer's change.

CHRYSLER

er, automatic day/night rearview mirror, compass, rear spoiler, 205/60R16 tires, alloy wheels.

JX convertible adds to LX coupe: 2.7-liter dohc V6 engine, 4-wheel disc brakes, emergency inside trunk release, 6-way power drivers seat, heated power mirrors, illuminated visor mirrors, power convertible top, automatic-off headlights, 205/65R15 tires, deletes fog lights, theft-deterrent system.

JXi convertible adds: leather upholstery, leather-wrapped steering wheel, trip computer, universal garage door opener, AM/FM/CD player, automatic day/night rearview mirror, theft-deterrent system, fog lights, 205/60R16 tires, alloy wheels.

Limited convertible adds: antilock 4-wheel disc brakes, Infinity AM/FM/cassette w/in-dash 4-disc CD changer, two-tone paint, chrome alloy wheels.

OPTIONAL EQUIPMENT:

	Retail Price	Dealer Invoice
Major Packages		
Touring Group, LX coupe	$630	$561
6-way power driver seat, AM/FM/cassette/CD player, outside temperature indicator, compass.		
Leather Interior Group, LXi coupe	1045	930
Leather upholstery, 6-way power driver seat, universal garage door opener.		
Quick Order Group 24/28J, LX sedan	955	850
Manufacturer's discount price	830	739
AM/FM/CD player, remote keyless entry, 8-way power driver seat, illuminated visor mirrors, trip computer, low washer fluid warning light, map lights, rear passenger assist handles.		
Luxury Group, LXi sedan	1295	1153
4-speed automatic transmission w/manual-shift capability, remote keyless entry, theft-deterrent system w/alarm, upgraded sound system, universal garage door opener, cargo net, chrome alloy wheels.		
Security Group, LX/LXi sedan, JX	175	156
Theft-deterrent system w/alarm. LX requires Quick Order Group.		
Powertrains		
3.0-liter V6 engine, LX coupe	850	757
2.7-liter dohc V6 engine, LX sedan	800	712
4-speed automatic transmission, LXi coupe	825	734
Autostick manual-shift capabilty, LXi coupe	165	147
Requires 4-speed automatic transmission.		
Safety Features		
Front side-impact airbags, LX/LXi sedan	350	312
Antilock brakes, LXi coupe w/manual trans, sedans	565	503
LXi coupe w/automatic transmission	740	659
JX, JXi	—	—
LXi w/automatic transmission includes traction control.		

Specifications begin on page 535.

CHRYSLER

Comfort and Convenience

	Retail Price	Dealer Invoice
Power sunroof, LX/LXi coupe, LX/LXi sedan	$685	$610
LX sedan requires Quick Order Group.		
AM/FM/CD player, LX sedan	125	111
AM/FM/cassette w/in-dash 4-disc CD changer, LXi coupe, LX/LXi sedan, JX, JXi	250	223
LX sedan requires Quick Order Group.		
Premium sound system, LX/LXi sedan	350	312
Remote keyless entry, LX sedan	170	151
8-way power driver seat, LX sedan	380	338
Smokers Pkg., LX/LXi sedan, JX, JXi, Limited	20	18
Alloy wheels, LX coupe, JX	365	325
Alloy wheels w/205/60R16 tires, LX sedan	325	289
JX	—	—
Chrome alloy wheels, LXi coupe	750	668
LXi sedan	550	490
LXi coupe requires Leather Interior Group.		

CHRYSLER TOWN & COUNTRY AND VOYAGER

Chrysler Town & Country Limited

Front- or all-wheel-drive minivan; similar to Dodge Caravan

Base price range: $19,160-$37,175. Built in USA. **Also consider:** Chevrolet Venture, Ford Windstar, Honda Odyssey, Toyota Sienna

FOR • Available all-wheel drive • Entry/exit • Interior storage space • Passenger and cargo room **AGAINST** • Fuel economy • Acceleration (4-cylinder)

New styling, more-powerful engines, and some minivan firsts, includ-

Prices are accurate at time of publication; subject to manufacturer's change.

CHRYSLER

ing a power liftgate, highlight the redesigned 2001 Chrysler Town & Country and Voyager. With the demise of Plymouth, Voyager joined Town & Country in the Chrysler-brand stable late in 1999.

Wheelbases are unchanged from 2000, although Voyager is limited to the 113.3-inch chassis while Town & and Country uses only the longer 119.3-inch span. As in the past, the Dodge Caravan shares this design and most mechanical features; it's also redesigned for 2001 in both regular- and extended-length models.

Voyager offers base and LX trim, the Town & Country LX, LXi, and Limited models. All have front-wheel-drive, with the Town & Country available with all-wheel drive. A 4-cylinder engine is standard in the base Voyager and is unchanged from last year's power ratings. A 3.3-liter V6 is optional in the base Voyager and standard in the Voyager LX and Town & Country LX and LXi. This engine increases to 180 horsepower, from 158. A 3.8-liter V6 is standard in the Limited and with AWD and is optional in the LXi; it increases to 215 hp, from 180. Later in the 2001 model year, 2WD Limiteds will adopt as standard a 230-hp version of the 3.5-liter overhead-cam V6 from Chrysler's LHS and 300M sedans. The 4-cylinder engine teams with a 3-speed automatic transmission. Both V6s use a 4-speed automatic. Antilock brakes are optional on the base Voyager and standard on all other models.

The 2001 vans are about 2 inches wider than the 1996-2000 models, with regular-length versions also about 3 inches longer overall. All models seat seven and have two sliding side doors, with power operation for one or both side doors available. New wraparound taillamps, 50-percent larger headlights, and lower-body cladding on Town & Country LXi and Limited are among the styling changes. Alterations inside include new dashboards and a center console with an internal power outlet and the capability of being mounted between the front or second-row seats. A newly available rear parcel shelf can be fixed at floor or midlevel positions and includes pop-up storage dividers. Dashboard airbags gain dual-stage inflators. Front side airbags—a first-time feature on these vans—are standard on the Limited and optional on other Town & Country and Voyager models. An available in-dash 4-disc CD player is also new. A rear-seat entertainment system with 6.4-inch LCD screen, VCR, and wireless headphones is a dealer-installed option, as is a navigation system.

New for these vans are power sliding side doors, their unique feature being a manual override that allows them to be closed or opened by hand during the powered phase. A right-side power door is optional on the Voyager LX and Town & Country LX, while power operation for both sides is standard on LXi and Limited models. The new power liftgate is controlled by the keyfob or interior switches and has sensors designed to stop its movement if it encounters an obstruction. The power liftgate is standard on the Town & Country Limited and optional on the other

Specifications begin on page 535.

CHRYSLER

Town & Countrys.

Unlike the Honda Odyssey and Mazda MPV, the third-row bench seat does not fold away into the floor, but Chrysler does offer a new 50-50 split third-row bench; each portion weighs 55 pounds and removes individually and can also recline or fold flat.

PERFORMANCE Considering a Voyager? Go for the 3.3 V6, which furnishes the power required by a vehicle this size. Similarly, Town & Country requires the muscle of the 3.8 V6 to get off the line smartly and hold its own in highway passing and merging. We haven't tested a 3.5-liter Town & Country, but that engine does not have significantly more torque than the 3.8. Nor have we had an opportunity to measure fuel economy with any '01 DamilerChrylser minivan. Don't expect much deviation from the 17.7 mpg we averaged in tests of 2000 3.8-liter models and the 15.8 mpg we got with the overworked 3.3 in a Grand Caravan. SUV-intenders would do well to consider an AWD Town & Country as a sensible, comfortable alternative.

Town & County absorbs bumps better than any SUV and better than most minivans, Voyager included, though Voyager's ride isn't harsh. Bigger wheels and tires give Town & County an edge over Voyager in handling and roadholding, too, though both are carlike and friendly to drive. Town & Country brakes with more authority than Voyager thanks to its standard antilock 4-wheel discs, but Voyager's stopping power is adequate. Copious sound insulation makes Town & Country one of the quietest minivans, with fine suppression of wind, road, and engine noise. Voyager is average in this regard.

ACCOMMODATIONS Town & Country plays its luxury role to the hilt, with comfortably supportive and generously sized seating at all positions and available leather upholstery. Voyager's shorter wheelbase results in just-adequate leg room in the second- and third-row positions and in unexceptional cargo space with all seats in place. We like the easy-to-remove split third-row seats, but unlike stowable alternatives, you still must decide whether to take them out before you begin your trip.

The power side doors' manual-override function is a surprising convenience, while Town & Country's power liftgate (shared with the Grand Caravan) is a useful minivan innovation. Both systems stop and reverse direction quickly when encountering an obstruction, the liftgate's sensors proving particularly sensitive. The available movable center console, which is lighted and contains a power outlet, enhances versatility. So does the multi-position rear parcel shelf, though we're leery about the durability of its plastic pop-up dividers.

The revamped dashboard moves controls closer to the driver, but the front cupholders block access to the in-dash CD changer. With no provision for an integrated navigation system, the add-on screen mounts atop the dashboard. Town & Country has a unique "three-zone" climate system option that allows for independent control of driver, front-pas-

CHRYSLER

senger, and rear-seating settings.

VALUE DaimlerChrysler's lineup dominates the "shoulders" of the minivan market, accounting for 67 percent of sales under $20,000 and 50 percent of those over $30,000. That's testimony to the appeal of the entry-level Voyager and the luxury Town & Country, which, bolstered by the '01 redesign, are now stronger values than ever.

ENGINES

	dohc I4	ohv V6	ohv V6
Size, liters/cu. in.	2.4/153	3.3/202	3.8/231
Horsepower @ rpm	150 @ 5200	180 @ 5200	215 @ 5000
Torque (lb-ft) @ rpm	167 @ 4000	210 @ 4000	245 @ 4000
Availability	S[1]	S[2]	S[3]

EPA city/highway mpg
3-speed automatic	20/26		
4-speed OD automatic		18/24	17/23[4]

1. Base Voyager. 2. Voyager LX, Town & Country LX and LXi; optional base Voyager. 3. Town & Country Limited and AWD; optional Town & Country LXi. 4. 16/22 w/AWD.

PRICES

Chrysler Town & Country and Voyager

	Retail Price	Dealer Invoice
Voyager Base regular length 4-door van, FWD	$19160	$17784
Voyager LX regular length 4-door van, FWD	23525	21242
Town & Country LX extended 4-door van, FWD	24430	22253
Town & Country LX extended 4-door van, AWD	30850	27903
Town & Country LXi extended 4-door van, FWD	29175	26429
Town & Country LXi extended 4-door van, AWD	32715	29544
Town & Country Limited extended 4-door van, FWD	24850	31423
Town & Country Limited extended 4-door van, AWD	37175	33469
Destination charge	640	640

AWD denotes all-wheel drive. FWD denotes front-wheel drive.

STANDARD EQUIPMENT:

Voyager Base: 2.4-liter dohc 4-cylinder engine, 3-speed automatic transmission, dual front airbags, front air conditioning, power steering, cloth upholstery, front bucket seats, center console, cupholders, second row 2-passenger bench seat, third row 3-passenger bench seat, AM/FM/cassette, digital clock, variable intermittent wipers, visor mirrors, auxiliary power outlets, intermittent rear wiper/washer, dual outside mirrors, 215/70R15 tires, wheel covers.

Voyager LX adds: 3.3-liter V6 engine, 4-speed automatic transmission, antilock brakes, tilt steering wheel, cruise control, heated power mirrors, power windows, power door locks, rear defogger, floormats.

Town & Country LX FWD adds: antilock 4-wheel disc brakes, windshield wiper de-icer.

Specifications begin on page 535.

CHRYSLER

Town & Country LX AWD adds: 3.8-liter V6 engine, permanent all-wheel drive, 3-zone climate control, second row bucket seats, third row split-folding and tumble bench seat, remote keyless entry, AM/FM/cassette/CD player, automatic-off headlights, rear privacy glass, load-leveling height-control suspension.

Town & Country LXi adds to Town & Country LX FWD: 8-way power driver seat, second row bucket seats, third row split-folding and tumble bench seat, 3-zone automatic climate control (including rear controls), rear air conditioning and heater, interior air filter, remote keyless entry, power sliding driver- and passenger-side rear doors, AM/FM/cassette w/CD changer controls, Infinity speakers, illuminated visor mirrors, overhead console, trip computer, universal garage door opener, map lights, automatic-off headlights, rear privacy glass, fog lights, 215/65R16 tires. **AWD** adds: permanent all-wheel drive, 3.8-liter V6 engine, load-leveling height-control suspension, alloy wheels.

Town & Country Limited adds: 3.8-liter V6 engine, traction control, front side-impact airbags, leather upholstery, third row bench seat w/armrests, leather-wrapped steering wheel, memory system (driver seat, mirrors, radio), power rear liftgate, AM/FM/cassette/CD player, steering wheel radio controls, driver-side and rearview automatic day/night mirrors, automatic headlights, theft-deterrent system w/alarm, roof rack, load-leveling height-control suspension, full-size spare tire, chrome alloy wheels, deletes: third row split-folding and tumble bench seat. **AWD** adds: permanent all-wheel drive.

OPTIONAL EQUIPMENT:
Major Packages

	Retail Price	Dealer Invoice
Power Convenience Group, Base	$815	$693
Heated power mirrors, power windows and door locks.		
Deluxe Convenience Group, Base	375	319
Tilt steering wheel, cruise control.		
Climate Group II, Base	645	548
Base w/Power Convenience Group	680	578
Voyager LX	450	383
Heated power mirrors (Base), rear defogger (Base), windshield wiper de-icer, privacy glass.		
Climate Group III, Town & Country LX FWD	1085	922
3-zone manual climate control, interior air filter, privacy glass.		
Quick Order Pkg. 25H, Voyager LX	1080	918
Dual-zone air conditioning controls, windshield wiper de-icer, privacy glass, remote keyless entry, overhead console, trip computer, illuminated visor mirrors, glove box light, map lights, automatic-off headlights.		
Quick Order Pkg. 25K, Voyager LX	2955	2512
Manufacturer's discount price	2755	2342
Quick Order Pkg. 25H plus power sliding passenger-side rear door, 8-way power driver seat, third row split-folding bench seat, AM/FM/cassette/CD player.		

Prices are accurate at time of publication; subject to manufacturer's change.

CONSUMER GUIDE

CHRYSLER

	Retail Price	Dealer Invoice
Quick Order Pkg. 25H, Town & Country LX FWD	$1620	$1377

3-zone manual climate control, interior air filter, remote keyless entry, overhead console, trip computer, illuminated visor mirrors, automatic-off headlights, glove box light, map lights, privacy glass.

Quick Order Pkg. 25K,		
Town & Country LX FWD	3695	3141
Manufacturer's discount price	3495	2971

Quick Order Group 25H plus power sliding passenger-side rear door, 8-way power driver seat, second row bucket seats, third row split-folding bench seat, AM/FM/cassette/CD player.

Quick Order Pkg. 25/29U, LXi FWD	2125	1806
LXi AWD	1680	1428

Leather upholstery, power passenger seat, removable center console, leather-wrapped steering wheel, theft-deterrent system w/alarm, alloy wheels (FWD).

Trailer Tow Group, Town & Country LX/LXi FWD	610	519
LX/LXi AWD	320	272
Limited	175	149

Heavy-duty engine cooling, heavy-duty alternator and battery, trailer wiring harness, load-leveling height-control suspension (LX/LXi FWD), full-size spare tire (LX, LXi). LX FWD requires Quick Order Pkg.

Powertrains

3.3-liter V6 engine, Base	970	825
Requires 4-speed automatic transmission.		
3.8-liter V6 engine, LXi FWD	335	285
4-speed automatic transmission, Base	200	170
Requires 3.3-liter V6 engine.		
Traction control, LXi FWD	175	149

Safety Features

Antilock brakes, Base	565	480
Front side impact airbags	350	298
Std. Limited.		

Comfort and Convenience

AM/FM/CD player, Base	225	191
Voyager LX, Town & Country LX FWD	175	149
AM/FM/cassette/CD player,		
Voyager LX, Town & Country LX FWD, LXi	225	191
Includes Infinity speakers. Voyager LX requires Quick Order Pkg. 25H.		
In-dash 4-disc CD changer, LX	695	591
LXi	375	319
Limited	150	128
Includes Infinity speakers. LX requires Quick Order Pkg. 25K.		

Specifications begin on page 535.

CHRYSLER

	Retail Price	Dealer Invoice
Infinity speakers, LX	$495	$421
FWD models require Quick Order Pkg.		
Steering wheel radio controls, LXi	135	115
CYS 7-passenger seating,		
Voyager LX, Town and Country LX FWD	695	591
Quad bucket seats, third row bench seat. LX requires Quick Order Pkg. 25H.		
CYT 7-passenger seating,		
Voyager LX, Town & Country LX FWD	820	697
Quad bucket seats w/second row integrated child seat, third row bench seat. Requires Quick Order Pkg. 25H.		
CYL 7-passenger seating, LX, LXi	125	106
Quad bucket seats, second row integrated child seat, third row split-folding and tumble bench seat. LX FWD requires Quick Order Pkg. 25K. NA w/leather upholstery.		
CYK/CYR 7-passenger seating,		
Base, Voyager LX, Town & Country LX FWD	225	191
Front bucket seats, second row bench seat w/dual integrated child seats, third row bench seat.		
CYW 7-passenger seating, Limited	125	106
Quad bucket seats w/second row integrated child seat, third row bench w/armrests. Requires heated front seats.		
Leather upholstery, LXi	890	757
NA w/CYL 7-passenger seating.		
Heated front seats, LXi, Limited	250	213
LXi requires Quick Order Pkg., leather upholstery.		
Removable center console, Town & Country LX, LXi	195	166
Requires quad bucket seats. LX requires Quick Order Pkg.		
Power sliding passenger-side rear door,		
Town & Country LX FWD	385	327
Requires Quick Order Pkg.		
Power rear liftgate, Town & Country LX, LXi	295	251
LX FWD requires Quick Order Pkg., power sliding passenger-side rear door.		
Rear parcel shelf, Town & Country	—	—
Smoker's Group	20	17
Includes ashtray and lighter.		

Appearance and Miscellaneous

Theft-deterrent system w/alarm	175	149
Requires Quick Order Pkg. Std. Limited		
Roof rack	235	200
Std. Limited.		
Load-leveling height-control suspension	290	247
Base requires antilock brakes. Std. Limited and AWD.		

Prices are accurate at time of publication; subject to manufacturer's change.

CHRYSLER • DODGE

	Retail Price	Dealer Invoice
Touring Suspension Pkg., LXi FWD	$540	$459
Suspension upgraded for handling, alloy wheels.		
Alloy wheels, LXi FWD	445	378

DODGE CARAVAN

Dodge Grand Caravan ES

Front- or all-wheel-drive minivan; similar to Chrysler Town & Country and Voyager

Base price range: $19,160-$32,235. Built in USA and Canada.
Also consider: Chevrolet Venture, Ford Windstar, Honda Odyssey, Toyota Sienna

FOR • Available all-wheel drive • Entry/exit • Interior storage space • Passenger and cargo room **AGAINST** • Fuel economy • Acceleration (4-cylinder)

America's perennial best-selling minivan is redesigned for 2001. Fresh styling, more power, and innovations such as a power rear liftgate highlight the fourth-generation Caravan. Dodge again shares this minivan design with the Chrysler Town & Country and Voyager, which are similarly redesigned for 2001.

Caravan offers regular-length and extended-length Grand models. Wheelbases are unchanged from 1996-2000 versions, but the regular-length body is longer by 3 inches and both versions are about 2 inches wider. There are three models: regular-length SE, Sport models in both lengths, and Grand Caravan ES. All seat seven and have two sliding side doors; power operation for one or both side doors is new to Dodge.

Styling changes include wraparound taillamps and 50-percent larger headlights. The dashboard is revised and the new center console with internal power outlet can be placed between the front or second-row seats. Also new is an available rear parcel shelf with pop-up storage dividers that can be mounted at floor or midlevel positions. Front-side

Specifications begin on page 535.

DODGE

airbags are new options, while the dashboard airbags gain dual-stage inflators and the front seat belts get pretensioners.

Front-wheel drive is standard. All-wheel drive is available on Grand Caravans. Standard in the SE is a 4-cylinder engine unchanged in power from last year. Standard on all other front-drive models is a 3.3-liter V6 with 180 horsepower, an increase of 22 hp. Standard with AWD and optional on the front-drive ES is a 3.8-liter V6 with 215 hp, an increase of 35 hp. The 4-cylinder engine uses a 3-speed automatic transmission. The V6s use a 4-speed automatic. Both transmissions have a column-mounted gear lever, but the ES is available with Chrysler's AutoStick feature. This adds a toggle in the column shift lever, making it the only minivan with a separate control for manual gear changes. Antilock brakes are optional on the SE and standard on other models.

Power operation for one, or, on Grand models, both side doors is available. In a minivan exclusive shared with Voyager and Town & Country, the side doors can be closed or opened by hand even during the powered phase. The new power liftgate is another minivan first. It's controlled by the keyfob and interior switches and has sensors designed to stop its movement if it encounters an obstruction. It's optional on Grand Caravans and is also offered on Town & Country. Unlike the Honda Odyssey and Mazda MPV, Caravan's third-row seats do not fold into the floor, but Caravan offers a new 50-50 split third-row bench; each portion weighs 55 pounds, can be removed individually, and can recline or fold flat. A rear-seat video entertainment system and a naviagation system are dealer-installed options.

PERFORMANCE New convenience features account for the most-obvious improvements, leaving Caravan's performance upgraded incrementally in the '01 redesign. That's fine, because this was already among the most-capable minivans on the road.

Acceleration is good—with the right engine. In a vehicle this heavy, the 4-cylinder is acceptable only for light-duty, low-speed chores. The 3.3 V6 provides good power off the line and on the highway in a regular-length model, but feels overburdened in a Grand Caravan loaded for a family vacation. That makes the 3.8 the safest bet in the Grands, where it supplies substantial muscle in all conditions. It's the smoothest of these engines, as well, and while all work nicely with the 4-speed automatic, the AutoStick available with the 3.8 furnishes a sporty dimension absent in other minivans. And Caravan (along with Town & Country) is the only non-truck-based minivan with the all-weather security of available AWD.

Grands smooth out bumps better than the shorter-wheelbase models, but all Caravans ride comfortably. Still, you'll feel most pavement imperfections with the Touring suspension option, so try before you buy. Steering is nicely weighted, and straight-ahead stability is admirable. Caravans with the 15-inch wheels and tires are modest but predictable

Prices are accurate at time of publication; subject to manufacturer's change.

DODGE

handlers, while the 16- and 17-inch setups provide noticeably more grip and sharper response in turns. Stopping power is adequate, but pedal feel and confidence are improved with the 4-wheel disc brakes on ES and AWD Grands.

Heavy crosswinds and 75-mph cruising elevate wind rush, and certain road surfaces bring out marked tire noise, but neither is prominent enough to disturb conversation.

ACCOMMODATIONS The redesign enhances a package that was already roomier and more user-friendly than most minivans. All seats are comfortably padded and the driver and front passenger have ample room. Grands have generous knee and foot clearance in the second- and third-row seats, making them spacious where regular-length versions can be cramped. Same goes for cargo space behind the third-row seat, where regular Caravans fit just a single row of grocery bags. The new split third-row seats are invitingly simple to fold and remove, but still not quite as convenient as a fold-away design. The middle-row bucket seats tip forward with little effort to provide access to the rear while, cleverly, their side-mounted cupholders remain stationary.

The ability to easily stop or speed up the power side doors by hand is genuinely useful, as is the new power liftgate. Both systems respond quickly to obstructions, with the liftgate being especially sensitive. It reverses direction at the slightest touch. Movable center consoles with interior lighting and power outlets are a nice innovation. The new rear parcel shelf also is handy, though its pop-up dividers seem flimsy.

Caravan's gauges are unobstructed and its controls are easy to decipher and close to the driver. An exception is the available 4-disc in-dash CD changer, which is remote from the main audio controls and blocked when the front cupholders are in use. The available on-board navigation system uses a screen housing mounted atop the dashboard.

The available rear climate controls are centrally located and can be adjusted by either middle-seat passenger. And Caravan still offers integrated middle-row child safety seats.

VALUE Caravan's hold on the minivan sales title can only be strengthened by the '01 redesign, which adds desirable innovations such as the power liftgate to a vehicle that's hard to beat for refinement, utility, and carlike road manners. Don't buy a minivan without checking out Dodge's latest.

ENGINES

	dohc I4	ohv V6	ohv V6
Size, liters/cu. in.	2.4/153	3.3/202	3.8/231
Horsepower @ rpm	150 @ 5200	180 @ 5000	215 @ 5000
Torque (lb-ft) @ rpm	167 @ 4000	210 @ 4000	245 @ 4000
Availability	S[1]	S[2]	S[3]
EPA city/highway mpg			
3-speed automatic	20/26		
4-speed OD automatic		18/24	17/23[4]

1. SE. 2. Sport, ES; optional SE. 3. AWD; optional Grand Caravan ES. 4. 16/22 w/AWD

Specifications begin on page 535.

DODGE

PRICES

Dodge Caravan	Retail Price	Dealer Invoice
SE regular length 4-door van, FWD	$19160	$17784
Sport regular length 4-door van, FWD	23525	21242
Grand Sport 4-door van, FWD	24275	21957
Grand Sport 4-door van, AWD	29695	26727
Grand ES 4-door van, FWD	29110	26212
Grand ES 4-door van, AWD	32235	28962
Destination charge	640	640

AWD denotes all-wheel drive. FWD denotes front-wheel drive.

STANDARD EQUIPMENT:

SE: 2.4-liter dohc 4-cylinder engine, 3-speed automatic transmission, dual front airbags, front air conditioning, power steering, cloth upholstery, front bucket seats, center console, cupholders, second row 2-passenger bench seat, third row 3-passenger bench seat, AM/FM/cassette, digital clock, intermittent wipers, map lights, visor mirrors, auxiliary power outlets, intermittent rear wiper/washer, dual outside mirrors, 215/70R15 tires, wheel covers.

Sport FWD adds: 3.3-liter V6 engine, 4-speed automatic transmission, antilock brakes, tilt steering wheel, cruise control, heated power mirrors, power windows, power door locks, variable intermittent wipers, rear defogger, windshield wiper de-icer, floormats.

Sport AWD adds: 3.8-liter V6 engine, permanent all-wheel drive, antilock 4-wheel disc brakes, 3-zone climate control (including rear controls), interior air filter, rear air conditioning and heater, leather-wrapped steering wheel, remote keyless entry, tachometer, illuminated visor mirrors, overhead console, automatic-off headlights, fog lights, rear privacy glass, touring and load-leveling height-control suspension, 215/65R16 tires, alloy wheels.

ES adds to Sport FWD: antilock 4-wheel disc brakes, remote keyless entry, power sliding driver- and passenger-side rear doors, 3-zone automatic climate controls (including rear controls), rear air conditioning and heater, interior air filter, Infinity sound system, tachometer, trip computer, illuminated visor mirrors, leather-wrapped steering wheel, 8-way power driver seat, second row bucket seats, third row split-folding bench seat, universal garage door opener, automatic day/night rearview mirror, rear privacy glass, fog lights, 215/65R16 tires, alloy wheels. **AWD** adds: permanent all-wheel drive, 3.8-liter V6 engine, load-leveling height-control suspension.

OPTIONAL EQUIPMENT:
Major Packages

Power Convenience Group, SE	815	693

Heated power mirrors, power windows and door locks.

Prices are accurate at time of publication; subject to manufacturer's change.

DODGE

	Retail Price	Dealer Invoice
Deluxe Convenience Group, SE	$375	$319

Tilt steering wheel, cruise control.

Climate Group II, SE	645	548
SE w/Power Convenience Group	680	578

Heated power mirrors, rear defogger, windshield wiper de-icer, rear privacy glass.

Climate Group II, Sport FWD	450	383

Rear privacy glass.

Climate Group III, Grand Sport FWD	1085	922

Rear air conditioning, rear privacy glass.

Quick Order Pkg. 25H,

Sport FWD regular length	1080	918
Grand Sport FWD	1620	1377

Dual-zone climate controls, rear air conditioning (Grand), remote keyless entry, overhead console, illuminated visor mirrors, additional interior lights, automatic-off headlights, rear privacy glass.

Quick Order Pkg. 25K,

Sport FWD regular length	2955	2512
Manufacturer's discount price	2755	2342
Quick Order Pkg. 25K, Grand Sport FWD	3495	2971
Manufacturer's discount price	3295	2801

Quick Order Pkg. 25H plus power sliding passenger-side rear door, quad bucket seats, third row split-folding bench seat, 8-way power driver seat, AM/FM/cassette/CD player.

Touring Group, Sport FWD regular length	870	740
Grand Sport FWD	820	697
Grand Sport FWD w/Towing Group	770	655

Leather-wrapped steering wheel, 4-wheel disc brakes, fog lights, touring suspension, 215/65R16 tires, alloy wheels. Requires Quick Order Pkg.

Quick Order Pkg. 29S, ES FWD	1985	1687
ES AWD	1035	880

AutoStick automatic transmission w/manual-shift capability, traction control (FWD), steering wheel radio controls, removable center console, AM/FM/cassette/CD player, automatic day/night rearview mirror, touring suspension (FWD), full-size spare tire, 215/60R17 tires (FWD), chrome alloy wheels (FWD). ES FWD requires 3.8-liter V6 engine.

Towing Group, Grand Sport FWD	660	561
Grand Sport AWD, ES AWD	320	272
ES FWD	610	519
ES FWD w/Pkg. 29S	465	395

Heavy-duty engine cooling, heavy-duty alternator and battery, load-leveling height-control suspension (FWD), 4-wheel disc brakes, trailer wiring harness, full-size spare tire. Sport FWD requires Quick Order Pkg.

DODGE

Powertrains	Retail Price	Dealer Invoice
3.3-liter V6 engine, SE	$970	$825
Requires 4-speed automatic transmission.		
3.8-liter V6 engine, ES FWD	335	285
4-speed automatic transmission, SE	200	170
Requires 3.3-liter V6 engine.		
Traction control, ES FWD	175	149

Safety Features		
Antilock brakes, SE	565	480
Front side-impact airbags	350	298

Comfort and Convenience		
AM/FM/CD player, SE	225	195
Sport	175	149
AM/FM/cassette/CD player, Sport	225	191
Sport FWD requires Pkg. 25H.		
In-dash 4-disc CD changer, Sport FWD	695	591
ES	375	319
ES w/Pkg. 29S	150	128
Includes Infinity speakers. Sport requires Pkg. 25K.		
Infinity speakers, Sport	495	421
Requires AM/FM/cassette/CD player. Sport FWD requires Quick Order Pkg.		
Steering wheel radio controls, ES	75	64
CYK/CYR 7-passenger seating, SE, Sport	225	191
Front bucket seats, second row 2-passenger bench seat w/dual integrated child seats, third row 3-passenger bench seat. Sport FWD requires Quick Order Pkg.		
CYS 7-passenger seating, Sport	695	591
Quad bucket seats, third row 3-passenger folding bench seat. Sport FWD requires Pkg. 25H.		
CYT 7-passenger seating, Sport	820	697
Quad bucket seats w/integrated child seat, third row 3-passenger bench seat. Sport FWD requires Pkg. 25H.		
CYL 7-passenger seating, Sport FWD, ES	125	106
Quad bucket seats w/integrated child seat, third row 3-passenger split-folding bench seat. Sport requires Pkg. 25K. NA w/leather upholstery.		
Leather upholstery, ES	890	757
ES w/Pkg. 29S	1250	1063
Heated front seats, ES	250	213
Requires Quick Order Pkg., leather upholstery.		
Removable console, Grand	195	166
Sport FWD requires Quick Order Pkg. Sport AWD requires CYS or CYT seating.		
Rear defogger, SE	195	166

Prices are accurate at time of publication; subject to manufacturer's change.

CONSUMER GUIDE

DODGE

	Retail Price	Dealer Invoice
SE w/Power Convenience Group	$230	$196
Power sliding passenger-side rear door, Sport	385	327
Sport FWD requires Quick Order Pkg. 25H.		
Power liftgate, Grand	295	251
Sport FWD requires Quick Order Pkg., power sliding passenger-side rear door.		
Smoker's Group	20	17
Includes ashtrays, lighter.		

Appearance and Miscellaneous

Theft-deterrent system w/alarm, SE, Sport	175	149
Sport FWD requires Quick Order Pkg.		
Roof rack	235	200
Load-leveling height-control suspension, FWD	290	247
SE requires antilock brakes.		
Touring Suspension, ES FWD	95	81
Chrome alloy wheels, ES FWD	680	578
Includes 215/60R17 tires.		

DODGE DURANGO

Dodge Durango Sport SLT 4WD

Rear- or 4-wheel-drive midsize sport-utility vehicle

Base price range: $26,650-$28,770. Built in USA. **Also consider:** Chevrolet Blazer, Ford Explorer, Jeep Grand Cherokee

FOR • Passenger and cargo room • Acceleration (5.9-liter V8)
AGAINST • Rear-seat comfort • Fuel economy

Dodge's sport-utility vehicle loses one of its three available V8 engines for 2001, but gains a redesigned interior with a dashboard control for the 4-wheel-drive system. Durango is sized between the midsize and full-size SUV classes. It offers rear- or 4-wheel-drive Sport and SLT

DODGE

trim, and a 4WD R/T package. The base 4WD system is for slippery surfaces only. Included on the R/T and optional on other 4x4s is full-time 4WD that can remain engaged on all surfaces.

The 230-horsepower 5.2-liter overhead-valve V8 previously standard on 2WD Durangos is dropped for 2001. The newer 235-hp 4.7-liter overhead-cam V8 is standard on all but the R/T. The R/T requires a 245-hp 5.9-liter V8 that's optional on other Durangos. All engines use automatic transmission. Rear antilock brakes are standard, 4-wheel ABS is optional.

Front bucket seats and a 3-place rear bench are standard. A front bench is available, as is a 2-place third-row seat. Interior revisions include a new dashboard with an oil-level indicator, and a new center console. On 4x4s, the transfer case is now controlled by a dashboard switch rather than a floor lever. Heated front seats are a new component of the SLT Plus package, which again includes leather upholstery and 16-inch wheels with wheel-arch flares. Body-color exterior trim and fog lamps come with the SLT package. The R/T package builds on the SLT Plus package, adding special 17-inch alloy wheels, R/T emblems, unique shock absorber tuning, and leather and suede interior trim, among other features.

PERFORMANCE The 4.7 V8 is smoother than last year's 5.2, and just as strong, with a towing capacity of around 6000 pounds. Stronger yet is the 5.9; its 7400-pound towing rating matches that of some full-size SUVs. The transmission used with the 4.7 is newer than the one used with the 5.9. Both provide smooth, prompt upshifts, although 5.9-liter Durangos we tested suffered some sloppy, harsh downshifts. Fuel economy with either engine is poor. Our test 4x4 Durangos averaged only 11.8 mpg with the 4.7. A test 5.9-liter averaged just 11.2 mpg.

Durango doesn't feel ponderous despite the usual SUV body lean and nose plowing in fast turns. Its ride is absorbent and composed even on bumpy roads, and directional stability is good. But Durango's front-disc/rear-drum brakes don't stop this large vehicle with confidence. Braking is little improved with the 4-wheel ABS, which is standard on most rivals, but an option on Durango.

ACCOMMODATIONS Durango uses its size well, providing generous shoulder width and head room. Unfortunately, the available third-row seat is just as tight and hard to access as those in full-size SUVs. And seat padding is uncomfortably thin in both the second and third row. Demerits, too, for thick side pillars and rear headrests that impede driver vision.

On the plus side, large doors and modest step-in height make for easy entry/exit, there's enough space behind the third seat for a week's groceries, and the middle and rear benches fold flat in seconds to open up ample cargo room. Durango's redesigned interior has blockier styling than the previous version but functions just as well. Controls are simple

Prices are accurate at time of publication; subject to manufacturer's change.

CONSUMER GUIDE

DODGE

and handy, including the new dashboard-mounted 4WD switch which eliminates the bulky floor-mounted lever of previous Durangos. The quality of materials is good, although cruder than some rivals. Also, the door handles and some interior details have a flimsier, more plasticky feel than before.

VALUE Durango approaches full-size SUVs for roominess and power but sells at midsize-SUV prices. That merits our Recommended rating.

ENGINES

	ohc V8	ohv V8
Size, liters/cu. in.	4.7/287	5.9/360
Horsepower @ rpm	235 @ 4800	245 @ 4000
Torque (lb-ft) @ rpm	295 @ 3200	335 @ 3200
Availability	S	O[1]
EPA city/highway mpg		
4-speed OD automatic	15/20[2]	12/17[3]

1. Mandatory w/R/T. 2. 14/17 w/4WD. 3. 12/16 w/4WD.

PRICES

Dodge Durango	Retail Price	Dealer Invoice
Base 4-door wagon 2WD	$26650	$24057
Base 4-door wagon 4WD	28770	25958
Destination charge	585	585

STANDARD EQUIPMENT:

Base: 4.7-liter V8 engine, 4-speed automatic transmission, dual front airbags, rear antilock brakes, front air conditioning w/manual dual-zone controls, variable-assist power steering, tilt steering wheel, cruise control, cloth/vinyl upholstery, front split bench seat, split folding second row seat, cupholders, power mirrors, power windows, power door locks, remote keyless entry, AM/FM/cassette, digital clock, tachometer, visor mirrors, map lights, variable intermittent wipers, auxiliary power outlets, rear defogger, variable-intermittent rear wiper/washer, rear privacy glass, full-size spare, 235/75R15XL tires, alloy wheels. **4WD** model adds: part-time 4-wheel drive, 2-speed transfer case.

OPTIONAL EQUIPMENT:
Major Packages

SLT Quick Order Pkg. 26/28 G	1315	1118
Manufacturer's discount price	1000	850

Front bucket seats, cloth upholstery, 8-way power driver seat, center console, upgraded interior door panels, floormats, roof rack, fog lights, body-colored bumpers and bodyside moldings, 235/75R15XL white-letter tires.

SLT Plus Group, 2WD	3850	3323
Manufacturer's discount price, 2WD	3350	2848

Specifications begin on page 535.

DODGE

	Retail Price	Dealer Invoice
SLT Plus Group, 4WD	$3915	$3378
Manufacturer's discount price, 4WD	3415	2903

Leather upholstery, heated front seats, 8-way power passenger seat, heated power mirrors w/driver-side automatic day/night, AM/FM/cassette/CD player, Infinity sound system, steering wheel radio controls, woodgrain instrument panel, overhead console, trip computer, compass, outside temperature indicator, automatic day/night rearview mirror, illuminated visor mirrors, theft-deterrent system w/alarm, running boards, fender flares, 255/65R16 white-letter tires (2WD), 265/70R16 white-letter tires (4WD), cast alloy wheels. Requires SLT Quick Order Pkg.

R/T Sport Group, 4WD	1250	1063

Full-time 4WD transfer case, special axle ratio, limited-slip differential, sport-tuned exhaust, special bucket seats, suede door trim panels, running boards, fender flares, badging, performance shock absorbers, 275/60R17 tires, cast alloy wheels. Requires SLT Plus Group, 5.9-liter engine.

Overhead Convenience Group	415	353

Includes illuminated visor mirrors, automatic day/night rearview mirror, overhead console, compass, trip computer, outside-temperature indicator, reading lights. Requires SLT Quick Order Pkg.

Special Appearance Group	520	442
ordered w/SLT Quick Order Group	125	106

Bodyside moldings, pewter-accent running boards, cast alloy wheels. Requires Pkg. 26/28G. 2WD without SLT Plus Group requires Tire and Wheel Group. NA with R/T Sport Group.

Tire and Wheel Group, 2WD	470	400
4WD	495	421

Fender flares, 255/65R16 white-letter tires (2WD), 265/70R16 white-letter tires (4WD), cast alloy wheels.

Trailer Tow Group	590	502
ordered w/SLT Plus Group	465	395

Includes 7-wire harness, 4-pin wire adaptor, platform hitch, heavy-duty alternator and battery, heavy-duty engine and power steering fluid cooling, heated power mirrrors.

Powertrains

5.9-liter V8 engine	595	506

Requires SLT Quick Order Pkg.

Full-time 4WD, 4WD	395	336

Safety Features

Front and rear antilock brakes	495	421

Comfort and Convenience

Rear air conditioning	550	468

Requires third row seat.

Prices are accurate at time of publication; subject to manufacturer's change.

DODGE

	Retail Price	Dealer Invoice
Heated power mirrors	$210	$179
Includes driver-side automatic day/night. Requires SLT Quick Order Pkg.		
Front bucket seats	NC	NC
Third row split-folding seat	550	468
AM/FM/cassette/CD player	300	255
Infinity sound system	330	281

Appearance and Miscellaneous

Security Group	225	191
Theft-deterrent system w/alarm. Requires SLT quick Order Pkg.		
Running boards	395	336
Requires SLT Quick Order Pkg. 4WD requires Tire and Wheel Pkg.		

DODGE INTREPID

Dodge Intrepid ES

Front-wheel-drive full-size car; similar to Chrysler Concorde and LHS and 300M

Base price range: $20,910-$24,975. Built in Canada. **Also consider:** Buick LeSabre, Pontiac Bonneville, Toyota Avalon

FOR • Passenger and cargo room • Ride • Steering/handling
AGAINST • Trunk liftover • Rear visibility

Optional front side airbags headline changes to Dodge's full-size sedan for 2001. Intrepid shares its basic design with the Chrysler Concorde but has different styling.

The base Intrepid is renamed SE for 2001. Uplevel ES and performance-oriented R/T models continue. All have V6 engines. The standard 2.7 liter makes 200 horsepower. Optional on the ES is a 222-hp 3.2 liter. The R/T uses a 242-hp 3.5 liter. The only transmission is a 4-speed automatic, but the ES and R/T have Chrysler's Autostick, an automatic with a separate gate for manual shifting.

Antilock brakes are optional on SE and ES, standard on the R/T, which also includes firmer suspension tuning, unique trim, and 17-inch

Specifications begin on page 535.

DODGE

wheels. In addition to the newly optional front side airbags, Intrepid gets standard 3-point safety belts for the rear-middle seat position. Also, the split/fold rear seat that's standard on the ES is now optional on SE and R/T. Front bucket seats and a floor shift lever are standard on all models, but the SE offers an optional front bench seat and column shift for 6-passenger seating.

PERFORMANCE Poised and controlled, Intrepid and Concorde are among the best-handling full-size cars and share a ride that's firm and stable without being harsh over rough pavement. The R/T isn't European sports sedan athletic, but it feels more composed than other Intrepids and doesn't ride much harder.

While the R/T's 3.5 V6 is slightly stronger than the Intrepid/Concorde 3.2, both engines have good power at low speeds and in passing situations. The 2.7 provides adequate acceleration, but feels overworked in highway passing or merging. It does give this large car impressive fuel economy: 26.2 mpg in our most-recent test, which included lots of highway driving. Our test 3.2-liter models average about 21 mpg. We haven't had an opportunity to measure fuel economy in the R/T.

Intrepids we've evaluated tended to have slightly better stopping power and brake-pedal feel than test Concordes. But both cars benefit from Chrysler's efforts to reduce road noise and now are as quiet as most similarly priced competitors.

ACCOMMODATIONS The spacious Intrepid and Concorde have generous rear leg room and are among the few sedans wide enough to carry three adults in the back seat without uncomfortable squeezing. Both offer plenty of head room front and rear, though Concorde's taller roofline provides slightly more scalp clearance in back. Front seats are roomy, too, but some 6-footers don't have enough leg room to really stretch out. Only children are comfortable in the front bench seat's middle position, and they should sit in back, anyway. Doorways are big, but the rear door shape on both models hampers entry.

Dashboard layouts are similar and put the radio a bit too far from the driver. Other controls and gauges are close by and intelligently designed. Interior assembly is sound, although an abundance of hard plastic surfaces is at odds with the cabin's otherwise pleasing atmosphere. Intrepid has a larger rear window than Concorde, but a high rear parcel shelf on both cars hurts aft visibility.

Intrepid's available folding rear seatback is more versatile than Concorde's trunk pass-through, but both cars have a huge trunk whose flat floor extends so far forward that a sliding cargo bin would be a great idea. Both also have a high trunk liftover, and Intrepid's trunk opening is slightly narrower overall than Concorde's.

VALUE Intrepid targets the sportier buyer, while Concorde's message is one of stylish comfort. Both do their jobs well, being roomy, athletic, and

Prices are accurate at time of publication; subject to manufacturer's change.

DODGE

competitively priced. Their reputation for reliability lags behind that of such rivals as the Toyota Avalon and Buick LeSabre, but overall, Concorde and Intrepid are impressive values.

ENGINES

	dohc V6	ohc V6	ohc V6
Size, liters/cu. in.	2.7/167	3.2/197	3.5/215
Horsepower @ rpm	200 @ 5800	222 @ 6400	242 @ 6400
Torque (lb-ft) @ rpm	190 @ 4850	222 @ 3950	248 @ 3950
Availability	S[1]	O[2]	S[3]
EPA city/highway mpg			
4-speed OD automatic	19/28	18/26	18/26

1. SE, ES; 201 hp in ES. 2. ES. 3. R/T.

PRICES

Dodge Intrepid	Retail Price	Dealer Invoice
SE 4-door sedan	$20910	$19140
ES 4-door sedan	22605	20648
R/T 4-door sedan	24975	22758
Destination charge	610	610

STANDARD EQUIPMENT:

SE: 2.7-liter dohc V6 engine, 4-speed automatic transmission, dual front airbags, 4-wheel disc brakes, emergency inside trunk release, air conditioning, power steering, tilt steering wheel, cruise control, cloth upholstery, front bucket seats, center console, cupholders, power mirrors, power windows, power door locks, rear defogger, variable intermittent wipers, AM/FM/cassette, digital clock, tachometer, visor mirrors, map lights, power remote decklid release, automatic-off headlights, floormats, 225/60R16 tires, wheel covers.

ES adds: 4-speed automatic transmission w/manual-shift capability, driver seat lumbar adjustment, split folding rear seat w/trunk pass-through, leather-wrapped steering wheel, remote keyless entry, fog lights, alloy wheels.

R/T adds: 3.5-liter dohc V6 engine, traction control, antilock brakes, AM/FM/cassette/CD player, performance suspension, 225/55VR17 tires, Deletes: driver seat manual lumbar adjustment, split folding rear seat w/trunk pass-through, remote keyless entry.

OPTIONAL EQUIPMENT:
Major Packages

Quick Order Pkg. 23/24L, ES	NC	NC
Manufacturer's discount price, (credit)	(120)	(107)
Standard Equipment.		
Quick Order Pkg. 24M, ES	3140	2795

Specifications begin on page 535.

DODGE

	Retail Price	Dealer Invoice
Manufacturer's discount price	$2720	$2421

Leather upholstery, 8-way power front seats, automatic climate control, AM/FM/cassette w/4-disc CD changer and Infinity sound system, overhead console, automatic day/night rearview mirror, trip computer, illuminated visor mirrors, universal garage door opener, theft-deterrent system w/alarm, full-size spare tire. Requires 3.2-liter V6 engine.

Quick Order Pkg. 25S, R/T	1795	1598

Leather upholstery, 8-way power front seats, split folding rear seat, rear center armrest w/cupholder.

Driver's Convenience Group, R/T	605	538

8-way power driver seat, split folding rear seat, remote keyless entry.

Powertrains

3.2-liter V6 engine, ES	500	445

Safety Features

Antilock brakes, SE, ES	600	534
ES w/Quick Order Pkg. 24M	775	690

ES with Quick Order Pkg. 24M includes traction control.

Front side-impact airbags	350	312

Comfort and Convenience

Power sunroof	895	797
Remote keyless entry, SE, R/T	225	200
AM/FM/cassette/CD player, SE, ES	575	512

Includes premium sound system.

AM/FM/cassette w/in-dash 4-disc CD changer, R/T	575	512

Includes Infinity sound system, steering wheel radio controls.

Front split bench seat, SE	100	89
8-way power driver seat, SE	380	338
Split folding rear seat, SE	210	187
Smoker's Group	20	18

Includes ashtrays and lighter.

Alloy wheels, SE	390	347

DODGE/PLYMOUTH NEON

CG RECOMMENDED AUTO

Front-wheel-drive subcompact car
Base price: $12,715. Built in USA. **Also consider:** Ford Focus, Honda Civic, Toyota Corolla

FOR • Fuel economy • Steering/handling **AGAINST** • Noise • Automatic transmission performance

Available front side airbags, leather upholstery, and two new perfor-

Prices are accurate at time of publication; subject to manufacturer's change.

DODGE

Plymouth Neon

mance-oriented models are additions to Neon for 2001. This subcompact is sold by Dodge and Plymouth dealers, though the Plymouth-badged version will be dropped after the 2001 model year.

A 4-door sedan is the sole body style. Base models are called SE by Dodge and simply Neon by Plymouth. The better-equipped trim level is tagged ES by Dodge and LX by Plymouth. For 2001, Dodge adds performance-oriented R/T and ACR (American Club Racer) option packages, the latter intended for organized competition. Neon's only engine is a 2.0-liter 4-cylinder. The version in the R/T and ACR makes 150 horsepower. The version in the other models makes 132. Manual transmission is standard, a 3-speed automatic is optional on all but the R/T and ACR.

Antilock 4-wheel disc brakes are packaged with traction control and are standard on R/T and ACR, optional on other models. The new front side airbags are included with the new optional leather upholstery; Dodge offers them on ES and R/T versions, Plymouth on the LX.

PERFORMANCE R/T and ACR Neons furnish good acceleration, but other models feel sluggish, especially with the 3-speed automatic transmission; most rivals offer a 4-speed automatic for better acceleration from a stop. Our test 2000 Neons averaged 24 mpg with automatic transmission in mostly highway driving, and 25.3 with manual in a more-even mix of city and freeway work. We haven't had an opportunity to measure fuel economy on the R/T and ACR. Neon absorbs most bumps well and has enjoyably sporty handling. Wind and road noise are noticeable but are not as intrusive as the engine, which groans loudly under hard throttle.

ACCOMMODATIONS Neon's seats are fairly comfortable, and leg room is sufficient for most adults, front and rear. Head clearance is generous in front, but tight in the back seat for those over 5-foot-8 or so. Gauges are generously sized and look dressy, but lose contrast in dim light with the headlamps on. A high parcel shelf restricts the driver's view directly aft.

Seat fabrics feel rich, and while there's a surplus of hard plastic on

Specifications begin on page 535.

DODGE

Neon's dashboard and doors, it doesn't look or feel cheap. Doorways are fairly large, but the rear-door shape hinders entry and exit. Trunk volume is good for this class, but liftover is high and the lid hinges dip into the load area.

VALUE Tepid acceleration on the volume models notwithstanding, Neon is well-equipped and capable enough to earn our Recommended label. Sales are slow, so don't buy without taking advantage of factory incentives and/or dealer discounts on Neon's already attractive prices.

ENGINES

	ohc I4	ohc I4
Size, liters/cu. in.	2.0/122	2.0/122
Horsepower @ rpm	132 @ 5600	150 @ 6500
Torque (lb-ft) @ rpm	130 @ 4600	135 @ 4400
Availability	S	S[1]
EPA city/highway mpg		
5-speed OD manual	28/35	28/35
3-speed automatic	25/31	

1. R/T, ACR.

PRICES

Dodge/Plymouth Neon	Retail Price	Dealer Invoice
Dodge SE/Plymouth Base 4-door sedan	$12715	$11729
Destination charge	560	560

STANDARD EQUIPMENT:

SE/Base: 2.0-liter 4-cylinder 132-horsepower engine, 5-speed manual transmission, dual front airbags, emergency inside trunk release, power steering, tilt steering wheel, cloth upholstery, front bucket seats, center console, cupholders, split folding rear seat, AM/FM/cassette w/CD changer controls, variable intermittent wipers, rear defogger, visor mirrors, auxiliary power outlet, floormats, dual outside mirrors, 185/65R14 tires, wheel covers.

OPTIONAL EQUIPMENT:

Major Packages

Value/Fun Group	725	645
Manufacturer's discount price	595	529
Power sunroof, Light Group. Requires ES/LX Pkg. or R/T Pkg.		
ES/LX Pkg. 21G/22G	2485	2212
Manufacturer's discount price	1820	1620

Air conditioning, leather-wrapped steering wheel and shift knob, upgraded upholstery, heated power mirrors, power front windows, Sentry Group (power door locks, remote keyless entry, power trunk release, tachometer, theft-deterrent system), fog lights, ES badging (Dodge), LX badging (Plymouth), 185/60R15 tires. NA w/150-horsepower engine.

Prices are accurate at time of publication; subject to manufacturer's change.

DODGE

	Retail Price	Dealer Invoice
R/T Pkg. 25H, Dodge	$4430	$3973
Manufacturer's discount price	3570	3178

Air conditioning, traction control, antilock 4-wheel disc brakes, tachometer, power mirrors, power windows and door locks, remote keyless entry, power decklid release, special bucket seats, leather-wrapped steering wheel and shifter, illuminated visor mirrors, map lights, additional courtesy lights, fog lights, rear spoiler, unique front fascia, body cladding, performance steering, sport suspension, high speed engine controller, 195/50VR16 tires, alloy wheels. Requires 150-horsepower engine.

ACR Pkg. 25E, Dodge	2125	1891
Manufacturer's discount price	1880	1673

Traction control, antilock 4-wheel disc brakes, tachometer, leather-wrapped steering wheel and shifter, unique front fascia, high speed engine controller, performance steering, competition suspension, 185/60HR15 tires, alloy wheels. Deletes AM/FM/cassette w/CD changer controls, floormats. Requires 150-horsepower engine.

Driver's Convenience Group, Dodge w/ACR Pkg.	2160	1922
Manufacturer's discount price	1745	1553

Air Conditioning, Light Group, Sentry Key Security Group, AM/FM/cassette w/CD changer controls, floormats.

Sun/Sound Group	1195	1064
Manufacturer's discount price	795	708

Power sunroof, in-dash 4-disc CD changer, Light Group, 185/60R15 tires. Requires air conditioning. NA w/ES/LX Pkg., R/T Pkg. or ACR Pkg.

Antilock Brake Group	840	748
ordered w/ES/LX Pkg., Security Group, or Sport Appearance Group	740	659
Manufacturer's discount price	595	530

Antilock 4-wheel disc brakes, traction control, tachometer.

Power Convenience Group	380	338

Power front windows, heated power mirrors. Requires Sentry Key Security Group, air conditioning.

Sentry Key Security Group	730	650
Manufacturer's discount price	315	281

Power door locks, remote keyless entry, power decklid release, tachometer, theft-deterrent system. Requires air conditioning. Competition Group requires Driver Convenience Group.

Sport Appearance Group	1765	1571
Manufacturer's discount price	1085	966
Sport Appearance Group, ordered w/Sun/Sound Group	1710	1064
Manufacturer's discount price	1030	917
Sport Appearance Group, ordered w/ES/LX Pkg.	1610	1433

Specifications begin on page 535.

DODGE

	Retail Price	Dealer Invoice
Manufacturer's discount price..	$985	$877

Antilock Brake Group, tachometer, rear spoiler, performance steering, sport suspension, 195/50VR16 tires, alloy wheels. NA Plymouth.

Light Group	130	116

Illuminated visor mirrors, additional courtesy, map lights. Requires air conditioning.

Powertrains

2.0-liter 4-cylinder 150-horsepower engine........................	250	223
Requires R/T Pkg. or ACR Pkg.		
3-speed automatic transmission..	600	534
NA w/150-horsepower engine.		

Safety Features

Front side-impact airbags...	350	312

Comfort and Convenience

Air conditioning..	1000	890
Cruise control..	225	200
NA w/Competition Pkg.		
Leather upholstery..	1010	899
Manufacturer's discount price...	850	757
Includes front side-impact airbags. Requires ES/LX Pkg. or R/T Pkg.		
In-dash 4-disc CD changer..	375	334
NA w/ACR Pkg.		
Alloy wheels...	410	365
ordered w/ES/LX Pkg. or Sun/Sound Group.................	355	316
Includes 185/60R15 tires. Requires air conditioning.		

DODGE STRATUS

Dodge Stratus ES

Front-wheel-drive midsize car; similar to Chrysler Sebring
Base price range: $17,800-$20,705. Built in USA. **Also con-**

Prices are accurate at time of publication; subject to manufacturer's change.

DODGE

sider: Chevrolet Malibu, Honda Accord, Toyota Camry/Solara

FOR • Steering/handling **AGAINST** • Acceleration (4-cylinder)
• Rear-seat entry/exit (coupe) • Rear-seat comfort (coupe)

Dodge's midsize sedans and coupes are redesigned for 2001, with fresh styling, new V6 engines, and optional side curtain airbags for sedans. The Stratus coupe, formerly known as the Dodge Avenger, shares its design with the similarly redesigned Chrysler Sebring coupe; both use powertrains and platforms derived from the Mitsubishi Eclipse and Galant. The Stratus sedan again shares its Chrysler-bred design with the Chrysler Sebring sedan and convertible. No Stratus convertible is planned.

Styling is familiar, despite all-new sheetmetal. Exterior and interior dimensions change little, though coupes are lighter by about 100 pounds and sedans heavier by the same amount. Sedans come in SE and ES models. SE sedans retain a 2.4-liter 4-cylinder engine. Optional on those models and standard on the ES is the 2.7-liter V6 from the Dodge Intrepid. Both engines come only with a 4-speed automatic transmission. ES models use Dodge's Autostick with a separate gate for manual shifting.

Stratus coupes offer SE and R/T models. Standard on SE coupes is a 2.4-liter 4-cylinder. Optional on SE coupes and standard on R/Ts is a 3.0-liter V6 new to the Stratus line. Both coupes use a 5-speed manual or optional 4-speed automatic; R/T automatics get Autostick. The sedans' powertrains are built by Chrysler. The coupes' powertrains are from Mitsubishi and are shared with Eclipse and Galant.

The optional curtain airbags on sedans deploy from above the side windows and are designed to inflate in side collisions and protect the upper body. No lower-body side airbags are offered. Antilock brakes are optional on all models except the SE coupe. Standard on sedans are lower anchors for rear child seats and an emergency release inside the trunk. Wheel diameter on sedans increases by one inch over last year. Chrysler says new headlamps on these coupes and sedans are 25-percent brighter than before and that thicker front door glass improves sound insulation.

PERFORMANCE The new V6 engines in Sebring and Stratus are a clear step forward in both power and refinement, with the Chrysler-made 2.7 feeling smoother than the Mitsubishi 3.0. Though not as quite as fast as domestic and import rivals with larger V6s, any V6 Sebring or Stratus has acceleration that's easily adequate for most needs.

Four-cylinder owners are still relegated to life in the slow and noisy lane, even though both 2.4s are an improvement over last year. Regardless of engine, automatic transmission performance improves, with smoother upshifts and prompt downshifts. The optional Autostick is a welcome addition to coupe models and the Stratus ES. We haven't yet

Specifications begin on page 535.

DODGE

measured fuel economy, but expect it to reflect the 21.0 mpg we averaged in a test of a '99 V6 Dodge Stratus.

Uplevel models handle noticeably better than base models, with little penalty in ride quality. All feel competent on twisty roads—with better grip and less body lean than Camry—and comfortably absorb most bumps. The new coupes are slightly more nimble than the sedans, but don't filter out bad pavement as well. The Sebring convertible feels solid enough, despite some cowl shake and flex on undulating pavement. Steering feedback is good, though we'd like less around-town assist on the 4-cylinder versions. All models we tested had the optional ABS and stopping power was a high point, feeling sure and stable with good pedal modulation.

Overall refinement still isn't up to that of Japanese-brand rivals, but noise levels and drivetrain vibration are greatly reduced from the previous generation. Sedans no longer have an annoying tire thunk over expansion joints, and coupes lose their transmission whine. Suppression of wind noise is admirable.

ACCOMMODATIONS Stratus and Sebring sedans have uncommonly roomy interiors for their exterior size, despite a slight loss of rear head clearance compared to last year. Sebring convertible front seating is spacious, while in the coupes, taller front-seat occupants might want a touch more head room.

With a little squeezing, three adults can fit in the sedans' back seat, and they'll enjoy generous leg and foot room. The convertible has rear seating for two, and it's surprisingly comfortable. The coupes have three rear seat belts, but even two adults will feel crowded, and the seat cushion is uncomfortably low. Availability of side curtain air bags in sedans is a plus and unusual in this class, but we'd also like to see some side airbag protection for the coupes.

Sedan and convertible gauges are clear and readable. The coupes' mirror the gimmicky design of the Mitsubishi Eclipse. Coupe drivers sit low to the floor, while the sedan and convertible have airy-feeling cockpits, though lane changes in all models would be easier with larger outside mirrors. The quality of interior materials are a step up from before and are competitive with most rivals—though the coupes still suffer lots of hard plastic surfaces.

It's easy to get in or out of the sedans, but a low roof line hampers entry/exit to the coupes' front seat, and interference from the front seat belts worsens the already cumbersome ingress and egress to the back. Convertibles mount their front shoulder belts to the seats, so they don't hamper rear access.

Cargo space is average for the class (which means good for a convertible), though the coupes' trunklid hinges dip into the luggage bay. Interior storage is adequate in the 2-door models. Sedans have a small center console and lack rear-door map pockets.

Prices are accurate at time of publication; subject to manufacturer's change.

DODGE

VALUE Despite improvements in driveline smoothness and overall refinement, the new Stratus and Sebring sedans and coupes lack the polished feel of import-brand rivals. While all three body styles offer competitive value, the real prize here is the Sebring convertible, which is roomier than like-priced ragtops and quite the pleasant cruiser.

ENGINES

	ohc I4	dohc I4	dohc V6	ohc V6
Size, liters/cu. in.	2.4/143	2.4/148	2.7/167	3.0/181
Horsepower @ rpm	147 @ 5500	150 @ 5200	200 @ 5900	200 @ 5000
Torque (lb-ft) @ rpm	158 @ 4000	167 @ 4000	192 @ 4300	205 @ 4500
Availability	S[1]	S[2]	S[3]	S[4]

EPA city/highway mpg

5-speed OD manual	23/30			20/27
4-speed OD automatic	21/27	21/29	20/28	19/27

1. SE coupe. 2. SE sedan. 3. ES; optional SE sedan. 4. R/T; optional SE coupe.

PRICES

Dodge Stratus	Retail Price	Dealer Invoice
SE 2-door coupe	$17810	$16296
R/T 2-door coupe	20705	18872
SE 4-door sedan	17800	16302
ES 4-door sedan	20435	18647
Destination charge: coupes	585	585
Destination charge: sedans	575	575

STANDARD EQUIPMENT:

SE coupe: 2.4-liter 4-cylinder engine, 5-speed manual transmission, dual front airbags, air conditioning, power steering, tilt steering wheel, cruise control, cloth upholstery, front bucket seats, height-adjustable driver seat, center console, cupholders, split folding rear seat, power mirrors, power windows, power door locks, AM/FM/cassette, digital clock, tachometer, variable intermittent wipers, rear defogger, auxiliary power outlet, visor mirrors, remote decklid release, floormats, theft-deterrent system, 205/55HR16 tires, wheel covers.

R/T adds: 3.0-liter V6 engine, 4-wheel disc brakes, leather-wrapped steering wheel, remote keyless entry, Infinity AM/FM/cassette/CD player, automatic day/night rearview mirror, compass, illuminated visor mirrors, fog lights, sport suspension, 215/50HR17 tires, alloy wheels.

SE sedan adds to SE coupe: 2.4-liter dohc 4-cylinder engine, 4-speed automatic transmission, 4-wheel disc brakes, emergency inside trunk release, 205/65TR15 tires.

ES adds: 2.7-liter dohc V6 engine, 4-speed automatic transmission w/man-

Specifications begin on page 535.

DODGE

ual-shift capability, leather-wrapped steering wheel, 8-way power driver seat, remote keyless entry, AM/FM/CD player, trip computer, universal garage door opener, compass, illuminated visor mirrors, map lights, outside temperature indicator, fog lights, 205/60TR16 tires, alloy wheels.

OPTIONAL EQUIPMENT:

	Retail Price	Dealer Invoice
Major Packages		
Touring Group, SE coupe	$690	$614
Remote keyless entry, AM/FM/cassette/CD player, theft-deterrent system w/alarm.		
Leather Interior Group, R/T	1045	930
Leather upholstery, 6-way power driver seat, universal garage door opener.		
Quick Order Pkg. 24/28C, SE sedan	955	850
Manufacturer's discount price	830	739
Remote keyless entry, illuminated entry, map lights, 8-way power driver seat, AM/FM/CD player, illuminated visor mirrors, trip computer, premium headliner module, low washer fluid warning light, rear assist handles.		
Security Group, SE sedan, ES	175	156
Central locking system, theft-deterrent system.		
Powertrains		
3.0-liter V6 engine, SE coupe	850	757
2.7-liter dohc V6 engine, SE sedan	800	712
4-speed automatic transmission, SE coupe	855	734
R/T	990	881
R/T includes manual-shift capability.		
Safety Features		
Front side-impact airbags, SE sedan, ES	350	312
Antilock brakes, R/T 5-speed, SE sedan, ES	565	503
R/T automatic	740	659
R/T automatic includes traction control.		
Comfort and Convenience		
Leather upholstery, ES	580	516
8-way power driver seat, SE sedan	380	338
Power sunroof	685	610
SE sedan requires Quick Order Pkg. 24/28C.		
Remote keyless entry, SE sedan	170	151
AM/FM/CD player, SE sedan	125	111
AM/FM/cassette w/in-dash 4-disc CD changer,		
SE sedan, ES	250	223
R/T	NC	NC
SE requires Quick Order Pkg. 24/28C.		
Premium sound system, SE sedan, ES	350	312
SE requires Quick Order Pkg. 24/28C.		

Prices are accurate at time of publication; subject to manufacturer's change.

DODGE • FORD

	Retail Price	Dealer Invoice
Smoker's Group, SE sedan, ES	$20	$18
Ash tray, lighter.		
Alloy wheels, SE coupe	365	325
SE sedan	350	312
Chrome alloy wheels, ES	550	490

FORD CROWN VICTORIA

Ford Crown Victoria

Rear-wheel-drive full-size car; similar to Mercury Grand Marquis

Base price range: $21,965-$24,080. Built in Canada. **Also consider:** Buick LeSabre, Dodge Intrepid, Toyota Avalon

FOR • Passenger and cargo room **AGAINST** • Fuel economy

Added power and adjustable pedals head the short list of changes to Ford's full-size sedan. Crown Victoria, Mercury's similar Grand Marquis, and the related Lincoln Town Car are the only full-size cars still built in the traditional body-on-frame, rear-wheel-drive layout. Other 2001 changes include front airbags that adjust deployment based on crash severity, and headlights that turn on automatically with the wipers.

Crown Victoria comes in base and LX models with standard automatic transmission. Its 4.6-liter V8 gains 20 horsepower this year, yielding 220 in base form and 235 with optional dual exhausts, which are part of a Handling and Performance Package that also includes firmer suspension, low-profile tires, and a higher numerical rear-axle ratio. However, torque on both engines drops by 10 pound-feet. Antilock brakes are optional on the base model and standard on LX. The switch to deactivate the optional traction control system moves from inside the glovebox to the dashboard. Headlamps are now controlled via the windshield wiper stalk and turn on automatically with the wipers. This eliminates the dashboard headlamp switch. The new adjustable brake and accelerator pedals provide a three-inch range of travel via a switch on

Specifications begin on page 535.

FORD

the instrument panel.

PERFORMANCE Ford's overhead-cam V8 runs quietly and provides Crown Vic and Grand Marquis with smooth, strong acceleration and good passing power. The transmission is unobtrusive except for pronounced downshifts in passing situations. We averaged 14.7 mpg in a test of a 2000 model with the Handling and Performance Package; expect the base engine, with its more fuel-efficient axle ratio, to average 16-17 mpg.

Though not sloppy handlers, these big sedans don't change direction with as much poise as trimmer front-drive rivals from Dodge, Chrysler, or General Motors. The base suspension keeps float and wallow over pavement undulations to reasonable levels. While the Handling Package brings no great improvement in road manners, neither does it hurt ride quality. Steering effort is too light for our tastes. The optional traction control system doesn't match the grip of front-wheel drive, but without it, these rear-drive sedans can become virtually immobilized on slick roads.

ACCOMMODATIONS Crown Vic and Grand Marquis have that good-old big-car feel, with easy access to all seats and adult-size room front and rear. The center driveshaft tunnel intrudes on foot space, however, and the bench seats do a poor job holding occupants in place during fast turns. The new power adjustable foot pedals, optional on the LX, are particularly useful for shorter drivers and allow them to sit a safe distance from the steering wheel airbag.

We prefer the standard analog gauges, but the optional digital instruments are easy to read day or night. Controls are generously sized, though the driver must stretch to reach those for the climate system. A mix of plastic and vinyl panels and seats of cloth or leather create a conservative, serviceable interior decor. The trunk holds plenty of luggage, but the space is concentrated in a deep center well, so some bulky items are a tough fit.

VALUE We favor the more-modern approach of front-wheel-drive rivals such as the Buick LeSabre and Dodge Intrepid, but rear-drive, V8 traditionalists won't be disappointed with the reasonably priced Crown Victoria and Grand Marquis.

ENGINES

	ohc V8	ohc V8
Size, liters/cu. in.	4.6/281	4.6/281
Horsepower @ rpm	220 @ 4750	235 @ 4750
Torque (lb-ft) @ rpm	265 @ 4000	275 @ 4000
Availability	S	O
EPA city/highway mpg		
4-speed OD automatic	18/25	18/25

Prices are accurate at time of publication; subject to manufacturer's change.

FORD

PRICES

Ford Crown Victoria	Retail Price	Dealer Invoice
Base	$21965	$20793
LX 4-door sedan	24080	22738
Destination charge	680	680

STANDARD EQUIPMENT:

Base: 4.6-liter V8 220-horsepower engine, 4-speed automatic transmission, dual front airbags, 4-wheel disc brakes, emergency inside trunk release, air conditioning, variable-assist power steering, tilt steering wheel, cruise control, cloth upholstery, front split bench seat, cupholders, AM/FM/cassette, digital clock, power mirrors, power windows, power door locks, power decklid release, rear defogger, intermittent wipers, passenger-side visor mirror, wiper-activated automatic headlights, theft-deterrent system, 225/60SR16 tires, wheel covers.

LX adds: upgraded interior trim, 6-way power driver seat with power recliner and power lumbar support, illuminated visor mirrors, map lights, remote keyless entry.

OPTIONAL EQUIPMENT:

Major Packages

Comfort Group, LX	900	801

Antilock brakes, automatic climate control, 6-way power passenger seat with power lumbar support, leather-wrapped steering wheel, automatic day/night rearview mirror with compass, alloy wheels.

Comfort Plus Group, LX	1900	1691

Comfort Group plus leather upholstery, trip computer, digital instrumentation, Premium Audio System.

Handling and Performance Pkg., Base	935	832
LX	740	658
LX w/Comfort Group or Comfort Plus Group	615	547

Includes 235-horsepower engine, dual exhaust, performance springs, shocks and stabilizer bars, rear air suspension, 3.27 axle ratio, 225/60TR16 touring tires, alloy wheels.

Safety Features

Antilock brakes w/traction control	775	690
Antilock brakes	600	534

Comfort and Convenience

Power adjustable pedals, LX	120	107
Remote keyless entry, Base	240	213
Leather upholstery, LX	795	708

Requires Comfort Group.

FORD

	Retail Price	Dealer Invoice
6-way power driver seat, Base	$360	$321
AM/FM/CD player	140	124
6-disc CD changer, LX	350	312
Premium Audio System, LX	360	321
Upgraded amplifier and six speakers. Requires Comfort Group.		
Universal garage door opener, LX	115	102

Appearance and Miscellaneous

225/60SR16 whitewall tires	80	71
NA with Handling and Performance Pkg.		

FORD ESCAPE

Ford Escape

Front- or 4-wheel-drive compact sport-utility vehicle; similar to Mazda Tribute

Base price range: $17,645-$20,820. Built in USA. **Also consider:** Honda CR-V, Subaru Forester, Toyota RAV4

FOR • Cargo room • Maneuverability • Visibility **AGAINST** • Control layout (automatic transmission)

Answering the Honda CR-V and Toyota RAV4, Ford's compact SUV went on sale this summer as another 4-door unibody wagon with front-wheel drive or permanent 4WD. However, Escape offers V6 as well as 4-cylinder power; its Honda and Toyota rivals have only 4-cylinder engines. Escape is 4.6 inches shorter than the CR-V but virtually equal in other dimensions. Escape was developed jointly with Ford partner Mazda, which gets its own version called the Tribute. Their new carlike platform is a Mazda design, but their shared engines are Ford's. Escape has more rugged styling than Tribute and will account for 75 percent of the 135,000 annual output at the Ford plant in Missouri that builds them both.

Escape comes in XLS and uplevel XLT models. The 4-cylinder engine is from the subcompact Focus line and teams only with a floor-

FORD

shifted manual transmission. The optional V6 is from the midsize Taurus and mates only with a column-shifted 4-speed automatic. Escape's 4WD automatically sends up to 50 percent power aft when front-wheel slip is detected, but a 50/50 split can be locked in with a dashboard switch. There's no low-range gearing. Antilock brakes are standard on XLT and optional on XLS. Front side airbags are optional on both. Standard equipment includes a rear liftgate with glass hatch and wiper, air conditioning, front bucket seats with console, and a CD player. A 60/40 split-fold rear seatback is standard on XLT. Fifteen-inch wheels are standard on both models; 16s are optional on V6 XLTs.

PERFORMANCE Escape and Tribute are today's most capable all-around compact SUVs, and among the most refined, too. Their available V6 power and locked-in 50/50 4WD give them a power and traction advantage over the similarly sized but 4-cylinder CR-V and RAV4. Those qualities, plus ground clearance and roominess, put them ahead of the Subaru Forester, though the new Hyundai Santa Fe is a good match for space and V6 power.

The majority of Escapes and Tributes are expected to have the V6 and most will also have 4WD. The 4WD V6 models we tested summoned more power throughout the speed range than any of their 4-cylinder rivals, and felt quicker than other compact V6 SUVs, Santa Fe included. Zero-60 mph times were 8.9 seconds. Around-town acceleration, highway merging, and two-lane passing are stress-free, though some of our testers wished for more muscle to climb long grades. We haven't had an opportunity to measure fuel economy with a 4-cylinder model, but 4WD V6 Tributes and Escapes averaged 18-19.2 mpg in our tests, good figures for an SUV of this size and just slightly less than we average with automatic-transmission CR-Vs. The Escape/Tribute automatic transmission shifts smoothly and promptly, but feels somewhat indecisive on lengthy uphill grades. The 4WD system provides sufficient traction to climb steep gravely hillsides, but absence of low-range gearing or even all-terrain tires rules out serious off-roading.

These new SUVs certainly don't approach sport-sedan handling—fast, tight turns can trigger front-end plowing. But their steering is exceptionally direct, and stability at 75 mph is good even in gusty crosswinds. Balance and grip are quite good in most changes of direction, with less body lean than other SUVs of similar build. The suspension, while different in tuning, feels markedly taut in both . Escape and Tribute. Both resist wallow and float over dips and swells, though some sharp bumps register abruptly. Braking is controlled and satisfactorily strong, though some of our testers say nosedive in simulated panic stops is too pronounced. Noise levels are not objectionable, but wind roar is prominent at speed, and the tires whine on coarse pavement. Tribute seems to muffle engine noise better than Escape, too.

ACCOMMODATIONS An airy, comfortable cabin belies Escape/

FORD

Tribute's compact exterior dimensions. Taller riders will wish for more head room in sunroof-equipped models, but clearance is otherwise generous. The rear seat has generous leg room—more than in some midsize SUVs—and outstanding foot room beneath the front seats. The rear bench itself furnishes well-contoured support, even in the middle position, which benefits from a nearly flat floor and enough width to nicely accommodate an adult on short trips. Doorways are wide, but step-in is higher than on most compact SUVs.

The driver gets an elevated view of the road ahead, and unimpeded vision to the sides and rear. Positioning to the steering wheel and pedals is comfortable on a firm seat. Gauges and controls are legible and well-placed, but the long automatic-transmission shift lever can be awkward to operate and it interferes with the driver's reach to the radio. The Ford climate system used on both vehicles doesn't allow independent control of air recirculation or air conditioning, and some test drivers say the dashboard vents direct too much cold air directly to their hands.

Tribute's interior furnishings are slightly upscale to those of Escape, but both cabins feel solidly assembled with durable materials. No other compact SUV has more usable cargo room than these new arrivals. The rear seatbacks easily fold flat once the headrests are removed. And the standard separate-opening rear glass is an added convenience.

VALUE Substantial feeling, roomy, comfortable, and even fun to drive, Escape and Tribute earn a slot on the compact SUV all-star team right off the bat. Priced in the mid-$20,000 range fully equipped, they're also imminently sensible alternatives to any number of midsize SUVs, especially truck-based wagons that are less efficient in their use of space and fuel.

ENGINES

	dohc I4	dohc V6
Size, liters/cu. in.	2.0/121	3.0/182
Horsepower @ rpm	130 @ 5400	200 @ 6000
Torque (lb-ft) @ rpm	135 @ 4500	200 @ 4750
Availability	S	O
EPA city/highway mpg		
5-speed OD manual	22/26	
5-speed OD automatic		18/24

PRICES

Ford Escape	Retail Price	Dealer Invoice
XLS 4-door wagon, 2WD	$17645	$16566
XLS 4-door wagon, 4WD	19270	18046
XLT 4-door wagon, 2WD	19195	17978
XLT 4-door wagon, 4WD	20820	19456
Destination charge	540	540

Prices are accurate at time of publication; subject to manufacturer's change.

FORD

STANDARD EQUIPMENT:

XLS 2.0-liter dohc 4-cylinder engine, 5-speed manual transmission, dual front airbags, air conditioning, power steering, tilt steering wheel, cloth upholstery, front bucket seats, console, cupholders, folding rear seat, power mirrors, power windows, power door locks, remote keyless entry, AM/FM/CD player, digital clock, tachometer, overhead console, intermittent wipers, auxiliary power outlet, rear wiper/washer, automatic-off headlights, theft-deterrent system, roof rack, 225/70R15 tires. **4WD** adds: full-time 4-wheel drive.

XLT adds: antilock brakes, cruise control, height-adjustable driver seat w/adjustable lumbar support, split folding rear seat, AM/FM/cassette/CD player, map lights, visor mirrors, cargo cover, floormats, theft-deterrent system w/perimeter alarm, fog lights, 225/70R15 white-letter tires. **4WD** adds: full-time 4-wheel drive.

OPTIONAL EQUIPMENT:

Major Packages

	Retail Price	Dealer Invoice
Convenience Group, XLS	$325	$293

Cruise control, cargo cover, floormats, perimeter alarm system.

Leather Comfort Group, XLT	870	783

Leather upholstery, 6-way power driver seat, front under-seat storage compartment, leather-wrapped steering wheel, deluxe overhead console w/storage.

Trailer Towing Pkg.	350	316

Trailer hitch, 7-wire harness, wiring kit, oil cooler. Requires 3.0-liter V6 engine.

Powertrains

3.0-liter dohc V6 engine, XLT	1480	1332
XLS	1400	1260

Requires 4-speed automatic transmission. XLT includes upgraded center console w/armrest.

4-speed automatic transmission	NC	NC

Requires 3.0-liter V6 engine.

Safety Features

Front side-impact airbags	345	310
Antilock brakes, XLS	575	517

Comfort and Convenience

Power sunroof, XLT	585	527
AM/FM/cassette/CD player, XLS	130	117
Mach sound system, XLT	505	454
Mach sound system w/6-disc CD changer, XLT	585	527

Appearance and Miscellaneous

Side step bars	275	248
Rear privacy glass, XLT	275	248

Specifications begin on page 535.

FORD

Special Purpose, Wheels and Tires	Retail Price	Dealer Invoice
Alloy wheels, XLS	$375	$337
Includes 225/70R15 white-letter tires.		
235/70R16 white-letter tires, XLT	175	157
Includes wheel lip moldings. Requires 3.0-liter V6 engine.		

FORD EXCURSION

Ford Excursion

Rear- or 4-wheel-drive full-size sport-utility vehicle

Base price range: $34,245-$40,985. Built in USA. **Also consider:** Chevrolet Tahoe and Suburban, GMC Yukon/Denali

FOR • Passenger and cargo room • Trailer towing capability • Seat comfort **AGAINST** • Fuel economy • Maneuverability • Rear visibility

For 2001, the world's largest, heaviest SUV gets additional power for its diesel engine. Compared to its nearest competitor, the Chevrolet Suburban, Excursion is 1900 pounds heavier and more than 6 inches larger in almost all exterior dimensions. Excursion seats up to nine, has four side doors, and center-opening rear half-doors below a one-piece top-hinged tailgate window. It comes in XLT and Limited models and with 2- or 4-wheel drive. Automatic transmission and antilock 4-wheel disc brakes are standard. Due later in the 2001 model year are available power adjustable pedals.

A V8 is the base engine. A V10 is standard with 4WD and optional with 2WD. Available with either drivetrain is a turbocharged diesel V8 that for '01 gains 15 horsepower. The 4WD system shifts between 2WD and 4-high and 4-low via a dashboard switch, but is not for use on dry pavement. General Motors rivals and Ford's Expedition offer 4WD that need not be disengaged on dry pavement.

Excursion has dashboard airbags, but no side airbags. Front bucket seats are standard on Limited and available for XLT in lieu of a 3-place

Prices are accurate at time of publication; subject to manufacturer's change.

FORD

bench. Both have a fold-down second-row bench and a removable third-row bench. Leather upholstery is standard on Limited, optional on XLT. Same for a reverse sensing system that sounds an alert of objects in Excursion's path when backing up. For '01, the Limited gets standard fog lamps and outside mirrors with built-in turn signals.

In response to safety and environmental critics, Ford says all Excursion engines meet low-emission-vehicle standards and that the SUV makes extensive use of recycled materials. Excursion also has Ford's BlockerBeam, a steel cross member below the front bumper designed to prevent cars from sliding under in a crash. In back is a standard trailer hitch intended for the same purpose.

PERFORMANCE Sixty percent of Excursions are ordered with 4WD, with the V10 XLT the top-selling version. Our tests of 2000 models were done with just a driver and no more than four passengers. Under these conditions, either the V10 or the diesel engine gets this 7000-pound SUV to cruising speed fairly quickly. We expect slightly better performance with the '01 diesel's additional power. Highway passing response is adequate, too, aided by the transmission's smooth, prompt downshifts. A 2WD V10 Limited averaged 10.8 mpg in our tests, one of the lowest figures we've recorded. We haven't tested a V8 model.

Excursion is a stable straight-line cruiser and isn't disturbed by most broken pavement, although bigger bumps and ridges register fairly sharply. On twisting roads or in traffic, this enormous wagon feels ponderous, responding lazily to steering inputs. The steering itself is as light as that of most cars, but curb-to-curb turning diameter is almost 50 feet, so it can be a chore to maneuver on side streets and in parking lots. The brakes are easily modulated and feel strong, but drivers need to acclimate to longer stopping distances. Suppression of wind rush and road roar is quite good. The diesel idles noisily, but cruises without fuss, and the gas engines intrude only under full throttle.

ACCOMMODATIONS Excursion carries eight adults without painful squeezing. Second-row passengers get the roomiest accommodations, highlighted by exceptional leg space. The third-row seat is more confining, but not inhospitable to grownups. The driver's seat is comfortable, but the wide transmission tunnel intrudes somewhat into the front passenger's footwell.

Maximum cargo volume is an unmatched 146.4 cubic feet. Even with all seats in place, Excursion has a class-leading 48 cubic feet of luggage space. The one-piece third-row bench folds nearly flat, or it can be removed, though it's heavy and cumbersome despite small roller wheels. The second-row bench splits 70/30 and also folds. There are plenty of bins and cubbies, and up to 10 cupholders and 5 power outlets. The rear "Dutch" doors are a clever solution to cargo-bay access, though neither works with the liftglass closed.

Gauges are easy to see. Some of our testers had to stretch to reach

Specifications begin on page 535.

FORD

the audio and climate controls, and the steering wheel partially hides the 4WD switch. The driver gets a big-rig perspective of the road, and notches cut into the forward portion of the front-door sills enhance the view out the side mirrors. But extra care is still needed to be certain nothing's hiding along Excursion's long, tall flanks and tail. The reverse sensing system is a smart option, especially since the deep-tinted windows reduce rear visibility at night. Four-wheel-drive Excursions ride three inches higher than 2WD models, but ingress and egress are no harder than for other big SUVs, and easier than some. Standard running boards provide useful footholds, the rear doors are exceptionally long, and there's adequate clearance to the third-row seat.

VALUE Excursion's size and weight are serious drawbacks if you use it as a "suburban utility vehicle." But if you tow up to 10,000 pounds, need 4WD, and can abide abysmal fuel economy, base prices in the $33,400-$41,000 range actually make it a good SUV value.

ENGINES

	ohc V8	ohc V10	Turbodiesel ohc V8
Size, liters/cu. in.	5.4/330	6.8/415	7.3/444
Horsepower @ rpm	255 @ 4500	310 @ 4250	250 @ 2600
Torque (lb-ft) @ rpm	350 @ 2500	425 @ 3250	505 @ 1600
Availability	S[1]	S[2]	O
EPA city/highway mpg			
4-speed OD automatic	NA	NA	NA

1. 2WD. 2. 4WD; optional 2WD.

PRICES

Ford Excursion	Retail Price	Dealer Invoice
XLT 4-door wagon, 2WD	$34245	$30380
XLT 4-door wagon, 4WD	37560	33232
Limited 4-door wagon, 2WD	37885	33512
Limited 4-door wagon, 4WD	40985	36178
Destination charge	750	750

STANDARD EQUIPMENT:

XLT: 5.4-liter V8 engine, 4-speed automatic transmission, dual front airbags, antilock 4-wheel disc brakes, front and rear air conditioning, power steering, tilt leather-wrapped steering wheel, cruise control, cloth upholstery, front split bench seat, second-row reclining split-folding bench seat, third-row folding bench seat, cupholders, overhead console, heated power mirrors, power front windows, power door locks, remote keyless entry, AM/FM/cassette/CD player, digital clock, tachometer, automatic day/night rearview mirror, map lights, illuminated visor mirrors, intermittent wipers, rear defogger, auxiliary power outlets, intermittent rear wiper/washer, floormats, theft-deterrent system, rear liftgate w/lower Dutch doors, roof rack, privacy glass, running boards, front tow hooks, 7-lead trailer harness, Class IV trailer hitch, full-size

Prices are accurate at time of publication; subject to manufacturer's change.

FORD

spare tire, LT265/75R16D white-letter tires, chrome steel wheels. **4WD** adds: part-time 4-wheel drive, 2-speed transfer case w/electronic control, 6.8-liter V10 engine.

Limited adds: reverse sensing system, leather upholstery, front captain chairs, 6-way power driver seat, center console, trip computer, rear radio controls, outside-mirror mounted turn signal lights, power rear quarter windows, variable intermittent wipers, illuminated running boards, fog lights, alloy wheels. **4WD** adds: part-time 4-wheel drive, 2-speed transfer case w/electronic control, 6.8-liter V10 engine.

OPTIONAL EQUIPMENT:	Retail Price	Dealer Invoice
Major Packages		
Comfort and Convenience Group, XLT	$1160	$986
Captain's chairs, 6-way power driver seat, trip computer, power rear quarter windows, illuminated running boards, bodyside stripes.		
Powertrains		
6.8-liter V10 engine, 2WD	595	506
7.3-liter turbodiesel V8 engine, 2WD	4660	3961
4WD	4065	3455
5.4-liter V8 engine, 4WD	NC	NC
Limited-slip differential	250	213
Requires 6.8- or 7.3-liter engine.		
Safety Features		
Reverse sensing system, XLT	245	208
Comfort and Convenience		
Telescoping heated power trailer tow mirrors	95	81
Leather upholstery, XLT	1360	1156
Requires Comfort and Convenience Group.		
Heated front seats, Limited	290	247
In-dash 6-disc CD changer	255	217
Special Purpose, Wheels and Tires		
Skid plates, 4WD	75	64
Polished alloy wheels, XLT	310	263
Requires optional tires.		
LT265/75R16D all-terrain white-letter tires	130	111
XLT requires alloy wheels.		

FORD EXPEDITION
Rear- or 4-wheel-drive full-size sport-utility vehicle; similar to Lincoln Navigator

CG AUTO BEST BUY

Base price range: $29,845-$40,400. Built in USA. **Also consider:** Chevrolet Tahoe and Suburban, GMC Yukon/Denali

Specifications begin on page 535.

FORD

Ford Expedition

FOR • Acceleration (5.4-liter) • Passenger and cargo room • Visibility • Towing ability • Build quality **AGAINST** • Fuel economy • Entry/exit (4WD models)

An available entertainment package and upgraded equipment lists are the 2001 changes of note to the market's best-selling full-size SUV. Expedition offers XLT and Eddie Bauer models. Front bucket seats are standard on Eddie Bauer and optional on XLT in place of a front bench. Three-passenger second- and third-row bench seats are standard on both. Optional on Eddie Bauers is a pair of second-row buckets (without a center console). Power adjustable gas and brake pedals are standard on both models.

Newly standard features include privacy glass, and, on Eddie Bauers, a Homelink universal transmitter. Eddie Bauer 4x4s also gain a standard tow package. Newly optional on Eddie Bauers is a rear-seat entertainment system with VCR and 6.8-inch screen. XLT's Comfort and Convenience option package adds heated mirrors and 16-inch alloy wheels, while the Premium Sport package now includes alloy rather than chrome wheels.

XLTs and 2-wheel-drive Eddie Bauers come with a 4.6-liter V8. Optional on those models and standard on 4WD Eddie Bauers is a 5.4-liter V8. Both team only with automatic transmission. Expedition's 4WD system can be left engaged on dry pavement and has low-range gearing. Antilock 4-wheel disc brakes are standard, front side airbags and Reverse Sensing System are optional.

Lincoln's Navigator shares Expedition's basic design, but has a more-powerful V8, more luxury features, and offers a navigatio system.

PERFORMANCE Expedition and Navigator aren't agile, but they drive easily enough for their size. Body lean is modest as long as cornering speeds are. Rear-drive models and XLT Expeditions with the 16-inch wheels have a stable, relatively soft ride. The 4x4s and versions with 17-inch wheels—Eddie Bauer Expeditions and all Navigators—ride stiffly and are not impressively composed over bumps.

The 5.4 V8 provides robust acceleration and is our recommendation if you order 4WD or tow trailers weighing more than 3000 pounds. Note

Prices are accurate at time of publication; subject to manufacturer's change.

CONSUMER GUIDE 171

FORD

that Navigator gets standard a twincam 5.4 with 300 horsepower, 40 more than Expedition's version. Expedition's 4.6 is adequate for most tasks, but doesn't have enough low-speed muscle for swift passing in this 2.5-ton wagon. We averaged just 12.6 mpg in tests of a 5.4-liter Expedition and 12.5 in a Navigator. Wind and road noise are well-muffled, as is engine thrash except in hard acceleration.

ACCOMMODATIONS Front-seat space is bountiful, and Expedition and Navigator are wide enough for comfortable 3-across adult seating in the second row, where the nearly flat floor means no one straddles a hump. Both Navigator and Expedition both offer second-row buckets, though Lincoln fits a useful center console while Ford opts for a narrow channel to the third-row seat. That third-row seat is Crampsville for adults, and there's only a foot-wide trench of luggage space behind. However, cargo room gets ever-more cavernous as you fold the second-row seats or remove the third-row bench. Unfortunately, removing that big, heavy bench is a 2-person task. The tailgate glass opens separately, but the weighty liftgate is a chore to raise and lower—and side-opening cargo rear doors, as on General Motors rivals, aren't offered. Interior step-in is higher than on the big GM SUVs, too.

Navigator has fancier standard trim but the same user-friendly dashboard design as Expedition. An exception is Navigator's navigation system, which is more difficult to program than most and, in our test model, suffered a frustrating delay in providing voice directions.

A button adjacent to the steering column quickly powers the pedal cluster forward as much as three inches, enough to fine-tune the driving position: It's a welcome feature for shorter drivers. We also recommend the Reverse Sensing System, which sounds a warning of unseen objects behind when backing up. Storage bins abound and include an enormous center-console box. Most of our test examples have had impressively solid build quality, but our last test Navigator suffered ill-fitting interior trim.

VALUE Expedition and Navigator have strong rivals in the Suburban and Yukon XL, while the slightly smaller Chevy Tahoe and GMC Yukon may also draw away some sales. All that competition should be to your benefit when negotiating a deal.

ENGINES

	ohc V8	ohc V8
Size, liters/cu. in.	4.6/281	5.4/330
Horsepower @ rpm	215 @ 4400	260 @ 4500
Torque (lb-ft) @ rpm	290 @ 3250	350 @ 2500
Availability	S[1]	S[2] |ри
EPA city/highway mpg		
4-speed OD automatic	15/20[3]	13/18[4]

1. XLT and Eddie Bauer 2WD. 2. Eddie Bauer 4WD, optional others. 3. 14/18 w/4WD. 4. 12/16 w/4WD.

Specifications begin on page 535.

FORD

PRICES

Ford Expedition

	Retail Price	Dealer Invoice
XLT 4-door wagon, 2WD	$29845	$26511
XLT 4-door wagon, 4WD	32715	28980
Eddie Bauer 4-door wagon, 2WD	36255	32025
Eddie Bauer 4-door wagon, 4WD	40400	36589
Destination charge	715	715

STANDARD EQUIPMENT:

XLT: 4.6-liter V8 engine, 4-speed automatic transmission, dual front airbags, antilock 4-wheel disc brakes, front air conditioning, variable-assist power steering, tilt steering wheel, cruise control, cloth upholstery, front split bench seat, 6-way power driver seat w/manual lumbar support, second-row split-folding-reclining bench seat, third row folding bench seat, cupholders, power-adjustable pedals, power mirrors, power front windows, power door locks, remote keyless entry, AM/FM/cassette, digital clock, tachometer, map lights, passenger-side visor mirror, variable intermittent wipers, rear defogger, rear wiper/washer, auxiliary power outlet, floormats, theft-deterrent system, rear privacy glass, rear liftgate with flip-up glass, roof rack, 4-lead trailer harness, full-size spare tire, 255/70R16 tires, styled steel wheels. **4WD** adds: Control Trac full-time 4-wheel drive, 2-speed transfer case, front tow hooks, 30-gallon fuel tank.

Eddie Bauer adds: automatic climate control, rear air conditioning and heater w/rear controls, leather upholstery, front captain chairs, driver seat and power adjustable pedal memory, leather-wrapped steering wheel, front storage console, rear radio controls and headphone jacks, overhead storage console (trip computer, compass, storage), heated power mirrors w/memory, automatic day/night rearview mirror, universal garage door opener, Mach sound system system, 6-disc CD changer, illuminated visor mirrors, power rear-quarter windows, automatic headlights, illuminated running boards, outside-mirror mounted turn signal lights, fog lights, 275/60R17 white-letter tires, chrome styled steel wheels. **4WD** adds: Control Trac full-time 4-wheel drive, 2-speed transfer case, 5.4-liter V8 engine, 30-gallon fuel tank, front tow hooks, 7-lead trailer harness, frame-mounted hitch, 265/70R17 all-terrain white-letter tires.

OPTIONAL EQUIPMENT:
Major Packages

Comfort/Convenience Pkg., XLT	1935	1645

Captain's chairs, floor console, rear air conditioning and heater w/rear controls, automatic day/night rearview mirror, illuminated visor mirrors, rear radio controls, heated power mirrors, illuminated running boards, 255/70R16 all-terrain tires.

Premium Sport Appearance Group, XLT 2WD	860	731

Prices are accurate at time of publication; subject to manufacturer's change.

FORD

	Retail Price	Dealer Invoice
XLT 4WD	$960	$816

Captain's chairs, color-keyed bumpers and grille, side step bars, wheel lip moldings, fog lights, skid plates (4WD), 275/60R17 white-letter tires (2WD), 265/70R17 all-terrain white-letter tires (4WD). Requires Comfort/Convenience Group.

No Boundaries Group, 2WD XLT	860	705
4WD XLT	960	816

Captain's chairs, illuminated running boards, fog lights, chrome mirrors and grille surround, color-keyed bodyside and wheel lip moldings, 275/60R17 white-letter tires (2WD), 265/70R17 white-letter tires (4WD), alloy wheels. Requires Comfort/Convenience Pkg.

Class III Trailer Tow Group, 2WD	880	748
4WD XLT	390	332

7-lead trailer wiring harness, frame-mounted hitch, auxiliary transmission-oil cooler, 30-gallon fuel tank (2WD), rear load-leveling suspension (2WD). Std. 4WD Eddie Bauer.

Powertrains

5.4-liter V8 engine, XLT, Eddie Bauer 2WD	695	591
Limited-slip differential	255	217

Safety Features

Front side-impact airbags	395	335

Requires Reverse Sensing System. XLT requires Comfort/Convenience Pkg.

Reverse Sensing System	200	170

Requires front side-impact airbags.

Comfort and Convenience

Rear Entertainment System, Eddie Bauer	1345	1143

Videocassette player, LCD screen.

Power sunroof	800	680

XLT requires Premium Sport Appearance Group.

Heated front seats, Eddie Bauer	295	251
Leather captain chairs, XLT	1360	1156
Second row captain chairs, Eddie Bauer	795	676
6-disc CD changer, XLT	495	421

Requires Comfort/Convenience Group.

Special Purpose, Wheels and Tires

Load-leveling suspension, 4WD	815	692
Skid plates, 4WD	105	89

Specifications begin on page 535.

FORD

FORD EXPLORER

Ford Explorer 4-door wagon

Rear- or 4-wheel-drive midsize sport-utility vehicle; similar to Mercury Mountaineer

Base price range: $20,840-$34,565. Built in USA. **Also consider:** Chevrolet Blazer, Jeep Grand Cherokee, Toyota 4Runner

FOR • Cargo room • Build quality **AGAINST** • Ride • Fuel economy

America's best-selling SUV starts a short 2001 model year with its lowest priced wagons getting standard instead of optional automatic transmission and a more powerful V6 engine. Four-door Explorers are available in XLS, XLT, Eddie Bauer, and Limited versions. Also available are the 2-door Explorer Sport and the Explorer Sport Trac. The latter has a 4-door SUV cabin, but in lieu of an enclosed cargo area it uses a 4-foot-long pickup-truck bed that has a drop-down tailgate. Sport and Sport Trac come in a single trim level. All Explorers are available with rear- or 4-wheel drive. Antilock brakes are standard and front side airbags are optional on all but Sport Trac.

The 160-hp overhead-valve V6 previously standard on XLS and XLT is dropped for '01, so the standard engine linewide is a 210-hp (203 hp on Sport) overhead-cam V6. Optional on XLT, Eddie Bauer, and Limited is a 215-hp V8. Manual transmission is standard on Sport and Sport Trac. Automatic is optional on those models, standard on all other Explorers including the XLS and XLT, which previously had standard 5-speed manual. Standard on V6 4x4s is Ford's Control Trac system with 4WD that need not be disengaged on dry pavement. V8 4x4s have permanently engaged 4WD.

Optional on 4-door models (except Sport Trac) is an audible Reverse Sensing System that warns of obstacles when backing up. Rear load-leveling is an option for 4WD XLT, Eddie Bauer, and Limited models. Mercury markets a slightly retrimmed version of the 4-door Explorer

Prices are accurate at time of publication; subject to manufacturer's change.

FORD

wagon as the Mountaineer. Due in January 2001 as '02 models are redesigned 4-door versions of both; they will be slightly larger than the current design and offer three rows of seats.

PERFORMANCE Sport Trac's wheelbase is more than a foot longer than the 4-door Explorer's and its frame is stiffer—by 40 percent, says Ford. And it has a specially tuned suspension. That adds up to what's arguably the best-driving version of this popular SUV. Sport Trac takes bumps with less harshness than 4-door Explorers and Mountaineers, and lacks the bouncy ride motions that afflict the 2-door Sport. Sport Trac also has more accurate steering and takes corners with slightly less body lean than other models, though all Explorers and Moutaineers handle with reasonable balance and confidence.

Teamed with the alert 5-speed automatic, the V6 provides good off-the-line power and fine around-town response, feeling overtaxed only in highway overtaking maneuvers or on mountain upgrades. The V8 is best in those situations and for heavy towing, but is gruffer than the V6. Expect to average 15-16 mpg with the V6. The last AWD V8 we tested averaged an abysmal 12.4 mpg.

Like rival systems from General Motors, Jeep, and Dodge, Control Trac automatically sends power to the wheels with the best traction so there's no need for the driver to constantly evaluate road conditions and decide whether to be in 2WD or 4WD. The V8's AWD affords similar freedom. Braking on any of these Ford/Mercury models feels strong and is easily modulated. Sport Trac is nearly car quiet, but while other Explorers and Mountaineers don't muffle mechanical sounds and wind and road noise as well as some SUVs, they're not so noisy as to disrupt conversation.

ACCOMMODATIONS All 4-door Explorers and Mountaineers—Sport Trac included—have ample space for four adults, and three can fit in back with some squeezing. That gives Sport Trac a back seat that's roomier and more comfortable than any similarly sized crew-cab pickup truck's, including the Dodge Dakota and Nissan Frontier. The 2-door Sport's rear seat is cramped and difficult to get into and out of. What all these vehicles have in common is a rather hard rear seat with subpar shoulder support.

Step-in height is slightly taller than the SUV norm, so it's a little more work to get in or out of an Explorer or Mountaineer. All have a comfortable driving position, though it's a mild stretch to the climate controls. Power window switches are illuminated for easy nighttime use, and the view of surrounding traffic is unimpeded. Available side airbags and the reverse-warning system are laudable features and rare in this class, and Sport Trac's standard power rear window is clever and practical.

In-cabin storage is good, although removing Sport Trac's console pouch leaves a behind useless cavity; we'd opt for the conventional center console. Enclosed models have ample cargo room, separate-open-

Specifications begin on page 535.

FORD

ing liftglass, and, like Sport Trac, undercarriage spare-tire storage. On all, the split rear seatback folds in a single motion without removing the headrests. Sport Trac's cargo box is shorter than a traditional pickup's, though its sidewalls are usefully tall and the molded-in bedliner a smart touch. We recommended the flip-over cargo cage (available through the dealer), and also the optional plastic wall that divides the box into two compartments. In all, Sport Trac seems an astute compromise between SUV comfort and truck utility.

VALUE An array of engine and 4WD choices, sound ergonomics, and competitive prices keep the '01 Explorer and Mountaineer among our Recommended picks. But competition is tough, and redesigned versions are coming, so angle for a good deal. A slew of SUV/pickup crossovers are on the horizon, but Sport Trac is currently without direct competition, so while its base prices are reasonable, don't expect much of a discount.

ENGINES

	ohc V6	ohv V8
Size, liters/cu. in.	4.0/245	5.0/302
Horsepower @ rpm	210 @ 5250	215 @ 4200
Torque (lb-ft) @ rpm	240 @ 3250	288 @ 3300
Availability	S[1]	S[2]

EPA city/highway mpg

4-speed OD automatic		14/19
5-speed OD automatic	15/19	

1. 203 hp w/Sport. 2. Standard w/AWD; optional XLT, Eddie Bauer, and Limited 2WD.

PRICES

Ford Explorer

	Retail Price	Dealer Invoice
Sport 2-door wagon, 2WD	$20840	$19147
Sport 2-door wagon, 4WD	23860	21836
Sport Trac 4-door crew cab, 2WD	21665	19882
Sport Trac 4-door crew cab, 4WD	24435	22347
XLS 4-door wagon, 2WD	25115	23072
XLS 4-door wagon, 4WD	26995	24746
XLT 4-door wagon, 2WD	27915	25564
XLT 4-door wagon, 4WD	29880	27314
XLT 4-door wagon, AWD	30090	27500
Eddie Bauer 4-door wagon, 2WD	31930	29138
Eddie Bauer 4-door wagon, 4WD	33895	30887
Eddie Bauer 4-door wagon, AWD	34310	31256
Limited 4-door wagon, 2WD	32185	29365
Limited 4-door wagon, 4WD	34150	31114
Limited 4-door wagon, AWD	34565	31483
Destination charge	600	600

Prices are accurate at time of publication; subject to manufacturer's change.

FORD

XLT, Eddie Bauer, and Limited require a Series Code Pkg.

STANDARD EQUIPMENT:

XLS: 4.0-liter V6 engine, 5-speed automatic transmission, antilock 4-wheel disc brakes, dual front airbags, air conditioning, power steering, cloth upholstery, front captain chairs, center console, cupholders, split folding rear seat, power mirrors w/puddle lights, power windows, power door locks, power liftgate release, variable intermittent wipers, auxiliary power outlet, AM/FM/cassette, digital clock, tachometer, map light, rear defogger, intermittent rear wiper/washer, passenger-side visor mirror, theft-deterrent system, roof rack, full-size spare tire, 235/75R15 all-terrain white-letter tires, alloy wheels. **4WD** models add: Control Trac full-time 4-wheel drive, 2-speed transfer-case.

Sport/Sport Trac adds: 5-speed manual transmission, rear drum brakes (Sport Trac), AM/FM/CD player, power rear window (Sport Trac), rear privacy glass, rear cargo box (Sport Trac), 4-wire trailering harness, 235/75R15 white-letter tires, styled steel wheels (Sport Trac), Deletes: power liftgate release. **4WD** adds: Control Trac full-time 4-wheel drive, 2-speed transfer-case, transfer case skid plate (Sport Trac), front tow hooks (Sport Trac), 235/75R15 all-terrain white-letter tires.

XLT adds to XLS: leather-wrapped steering wheel, front bucket seats w/manual lumbar support, 6-way power driver seat, high series floor console (armrest, cupholders, rear radio/air conditioning controls), overhead console (compass, outside temperature display, front and rear reading lights), AM/FM/CD player, illuminated visor mirrors, floormats, fog lights. **4WD** adds: Control Trac full-time 4-wheel drive, 2-speed transfer case. **AWD** adds: permanent 4-wheel drive, 5.0-liter V8 engine, 4-speed automatic transmission.

Eddie Bauer adds: tilt leather-wrapped steering wheel, cruise control, automatic climate control, steering wheel radio/climate controls, remote keyless entry, automatic day/night rearview mirror, universal garage door opener, Travelnote digital memo recorder, automatic headlights, cargo cover, rear privacy glass, running boards, 255/70R16 all-terrain white-letter tires. **4WD** adds: Control Trac full-time 4-wheel drive, 2-speed transfer-case. **AWD** adds: permanent 4-wheel drive, 5.0-liter V8 engine, 4-speed automatic transmission.

Limited adds: heated power mirrors w/puddle lights. **4WD** adds: Control Trac full-time 4-wheel drive, 2-speed transfer-case. **AWD** adds: permanent 4-wheel drive, 5.0-liter V8 engine, 4-speed automatic transmission.

OPTIONAL EQUIPMENT:
Major Packages

	Retail Price	Dealer Invoice
Comfort Group, Sport, Sport Trac	$935	$795

Front low-back bucket seats, 6-way power driver seat, overhead console, outside temperature indicator, compass. Requires Convenience Group, 5-speed automatic transmission.

Specifications begin on page 535.

FORD

	Retail Price	Dealer Invoice
Comfort Group w/leather upholstery, Sport, Sport Trac	$1495	$1271

Leather upholstery, front low-back bucket seats, 6-way power driver seat, overhead console, outside temperature indicator, compass, high series floor console, rear climate controls, rear radio controls. Requires Convenience Group, 5-speed automatic transmission.

Premium Sport Group, 2WD Sport	550	468
4WD Sport, Sport Trac	700	595

Side step bars, fog lights, front tow hooks, 235/75R15 all-terrain white-letter tires (2WD Sport), 255/70R16 tires (4WD Sport, Sport Trac), bright cast alloy wheels (4WD Sport, Sport Trac). Sport requires Convenience Group.

Convenience Group, Sport, Sport Trac	830	706

Cruise control, tilt leather-wrapped steering wheel, remote keyless entry w/keypad, automatic door locks (w/automatic transmission), puddle lights.

Convenience Group, XLS	750	638

Tilt steering wheel, cruise control, remote keyless entry, cargo cover, rear privacy glass.

Sport Group, XLS	1500	1275
Manufacturer's discount price	1000	850

Special cloth captain chairs, AM/FM/CD player, storage bag, side step bars, fog lights, wheel lip moldings, chrome steel wheels.

Series Code Pkg., XLT	750	638
Manufacturer's discount price	NC	NC

Tilt steering wheel, cruise control, remote keyless entry, cargo cover, rear privacy glass.

Sport Group, XLT	1095	931
Manufacturer's discount price	795	676

Color-keyed grille, platinum-colored bumpers and wheel lip moldings, side step bars, limited slip differential (w/5.0-liter engine), special axle ratio, Eddie Bauer-style wheels, 255/70R16 tires.

Series Code Pkg., Eddie Bauer	1615	1373
Manufacturer's discount price	NC	NC

AM/FM/cassette/CD player w/Mach Audio System, leather upholstery, 6-way power passenger seat.

Series Code Pkg., Limited	1870	1590
Manufacturer's discount price	NC	NC

AM/FM/cassette/CD player, Mach Audio System, leather upholstery, heated front seats, power passenger seat, driver seat memory.

Trailer Towing Prep Group, XLS, XLT, Eddie Bauer, Limited	355	302

Wiring harness, trailer hitch, heavy-duty flasher, limited-slip differential, special axle ratio.

Prices are accurate at time of publication; subject to manufacturer's change.

FORD

Powertrains	Retail Price	Dealer Invoice
5.0-liter V8 engine, XLT 2WD	$775	$659
Eddie Bauer 2WD, Limited 2WD	420	358
Requires 4-speed automatic transmission.		
4-speed automatic transmission, XLT, Eddie Bauer, Limited	NC	NC
NA 4WD. Requires 5.0-liter V8 engine.		
5-speed automatic transmission, Sport, Sport Trac	1095	931
Limited-slip differential, Sport, Sport Trac	355	302

Safety Features

Front side-impact airbags,		
XLS, XLT, Eddie Bauer, Limited	395	336
Sport	390	332
Sport requires Comfort Group. XLS requires cloth sport bucket seats.		
Reverse Sensing System, XLT, Eddie Bauer, Limited	255	217

Comfort and Convenience

Cloth sport bucket seats, XLS	280	238
Leather sport bucket seats, XLT	950	808
Includes power front seats.		
Heated seats, Eddie Bauer	255	217
Automatic day/night mirror, XLT	185	158
Includes automatic headlights.		
Power sunroof, Sport, Sport Trac, XLT, Eddie Bauer, Limited	800	680
Includes front overhead console with rear reading lamps. Sport and Sport Trac require Comfort Group or Convenience Group, 5-speed automatic transmission.		
AM/FM/CD player, XLS	100	85
AM/FM/cassette/CD player, XLS, XLT	130	111
XLT	665	565
Pioneer AM/FM/cassette, Sport, Sport Trac	510	433
Includes in-dash 6-disc CD changer. Requires Convenience Group, 5-speed automatic transmission.		
6-disc CD changer, XLT	395	336
Universal garage door opener, XLT	215	185
Includes Travelnote digital memo recorder.		

Appearance and Miscellaneous

Running boards, XLT	395	336
Locking tonneau cover, Sport Trac	590	502
Rear privacy glass, XLS	295	251

Special Purpose, Wheels and Tires

Rear load leveling suspension,		
XLT, Eddie Bauer, Limited	350	298
NA 2WD, AWD. XLT requires leather sport bucket seats.		

Specifications begin on page 535.

FORD

2002 FORD EXPLORER

2002 Ford Explorer 4-door wagon

Rear- or 4-wheel-drive midsize sport-utility vehicle; similar to Mercury Mountaineer

Base price range: $24,020-$34,055. Built in USA. **Also consider:** Chevrolet Trailblazer, Jeep Grand Cherokee, Toyota 4Runner

Ford's Explorer helped launch the SUV revolution in 1991, and its second redesign since then brings a restyled wagon with available 7-passenger seating. The similarly redesigned '02 Mercury Mountaineer again shares Explorer's basic design, but looks more distinct than ever from its Ford cousin.

Explorer remains a midsize 4-door and is the same overall length as the 1995-2001 version it replaces. Wheelbase is longer by about two inches, however, and track is wider by 2.5. That allows addition of optional third-row seating, a feature absent in Explorer's Jeep and General Motors midsize competitors.

Sold alongside the '02 Explorer are the 2-door Explorer Sport model and the Explorer Sport Trac SUV/pickup truck crossover, which are based on the previous-generation Explorer design.

Explorer retains a body-on-frame design but trades a solid rear axle for independent rear suspension, which Ford says improves ride and handling. Ground clearance increases slightly while front-bumper height is lowered more than two inches to be compatible with passenger cars.

XLS, XLT, Eddie Bauer and Limited trim levels return with a standard 200-horsepower overhead-cam V6. Their optional V8 is the 240-hp overhead-cam 4.6 liter from the larger Expedition. It replaces a 215-hp overhead-valve 5.0 V8. Manual transmission is standard on XLS. Optional on XLS and standard on the others is a 5-speed automatic, which was previously reserved for V6 Explorers.

Prices are accurate at time of publication; subject to manufacturer's change.

FORD

All come with 2-wheel drive or Ford's Control Trac 4WD, which can remain engaged on dry pavement and features low-range gearing. V8 versions can tow up to 7400 pounds. Due later in the model year is Ford's AdvanceTrac system, which is designed to prevent skids by automatically applying braking selectively to each wheel. In response to the Firestone tire controversy, Ford says 2002 Explorer buyers can have their choice of Michelin, Goodyear, or non-recalled-model Firestone tires, depending on equipment level.

Front side airbags are again optional and are supplemented by newly optional curtain side airbags for side-collision protection. Due later in the model year is a system designed to deploy the curtain airbags to prevent injury in a rollover accident. A tilt/telescoping steering wheel is optional, as are adjustable brake and accelerator pedals.

Rear seats fold flat with the cargo floor. Seven-passenger models get a 40/20/40 split second-row with tip-forward outboard sections intended to help third-row ingress and egress. Rear-parking assist is a new option. The one-piece liftgate's separate-opening glass section dips lower than before—Ford says to the height of a shopping cart—in an effort to ease loading. Full prices were not announced in time for this report, but base prices range from $24,020 to $34,055. We have not tested a 2002 Explorer and so cannot provide an evaluation or ratings.

ENGINES

	ohc V6	ohc V8
Size, liters/cu. in.	4.0/245	4.6/281
Horsepower @ rpm	210 @ 5250	240 @ 4750
Torque (lb-ft) @ rpm	250 @ 4000	280 @ 4000
Availability	S	O
EPA city/highway mpg		
5-speed OD automatic	16/22	15/20

2001 prices unavailable at time of publication.

FORD FOCUS

Front-wheel-drive subcompact car
Base price range: $12,125-$16,235.
Built in USA and Mexico. **Also consider:**
Honda Civic, Mazda Protege, Toyota Corolla

FOR • Control layout • Handling/roadholding • Fuel economy • Cargo room (wagon) **AGAINST** • Acceleration • Engine noise • Rear-seat entry/exit (hatchback)

Optional antiskid control and a sporty new Street Edition package highlight Ford's "new edge" subcompact for 2001. Focus comes in three body styles: a 2-door hatchback in sporty ZX3 trim; a 4-door sedan in LX, SE, and top ZTS form; and a 4-door SE wagon.

Specifications begin on page 535.

FORD

Ford Focus ZTS

A 110-horsepower 4-cylinder engine is standard in LX sedans and in SE models. A 130-hp twincam version is optional in the SE sedan and is newly optional in the SE wagon. The 130-hp engine is standard in ZTS and ZX3. Both engines team with manual transmission or 4-speed automatic on all models; the wagon had come only with automatic. Antilock brakes are standard on ZTS, optional on the others. Head/chest front side airbags are optional, and all models come with upper and lower rear child-seat anchors.

Ford's AdvanceTrac antiskid system, which is designed to counter skids in turns, is optional on ZTS and ZX3 and comes with rear disc brakes in place of drums. The new Street Edition option is for SE sedans and wagons equipped with the twincam engine and includes sport bucket seats, in-dash CD changer, and 16-inch alloy wheels. Also for 2001, ZX3 gets an optional Premium Group that includes 16-inch alloys and other features.

PERFORMANCE Focus has terrific road manners but fairly ordinary engines. It tackles twisty roads with linear, communicative steering, controlled body lean, and good grip from the 15-inch tires standard on most models. Bumps register with a thump, as in many European cars, but their impact seldom disturbs the cabin. Highway ride is wallow-free. Simulated panic stops with ABS is stable and fairly swift, with only moderate nosedive, but some early Focuses we tested suffered unprogressive pedal action. We haven't yet had the opportunity to test a Focus with the AdvanceTrac antiskid system.

The SE sedan is the most popular Focus, and we'd recommend those buyers spring for the $470 Sport Group with the twincam engine option, which provides slightly better acceleration than the tepid base engine. Still, even with the slick-shifting manual transmission, neither engine is more than adequate for fast freeway merging or climbing long grades. Our test 5-speed ZTS did 0-60 mph in a so-so 9.5 seconds, hampered by short gearing that requires two shifts instead of one to reach that speed. Focus's automatic provides fuss-free gear changes and isn't a huge drag on overall performance, though it does dull takeoffs. Our extended-use-test ZTS 5-speed is averaging 26.2 mpg over its

Prices are accurate at time of publication; subject to manufacturer's change.

FORD

first 9834 miles. We averaged 23.2 mpg with a test automatic ZTS. (Unfortunately, buyers ordering a manual-transmission wagon get no price break, paying the same as if they ordered the automatic transmission.)

Focus suffers noticeable wind rush around the front side windows and some testers find its high-speed engine note unpleasant. Noise is acceptable otherwise, and engines are tolerably smooth.

ACCOMMODATIONS Focus is quite roomy for a subcompact. All occupants sit comfortably high, yet have bountiful head clearance. Rear leg room is among the best in class, but still none too generous; this is still a subcompact car. The standard height-adjustable driver's seat enhances already good outward visibility, but the adjustment is by a tedious crank handle sited ahead of the seat bottom. More convenient is the available tilt/telescopic steering wheel, a rare feature in this class.

The dashboard echoes the exterior's edgy look and works well. Controls are conspicuous and smooth-working, and the air conditioner isn't tied to one or two distribution modes, though the air vents are not ideally placed. And lack of a tachometer redline is curious in cars with high-winding 4-cylinder engines.

Stirrup-type exterior door handles and large front-door frames assist entry/exit, but rear doors should open wider. All Focuses, the wagon in particular, have generous cargo holds and rear seats that flip/fold flat. Liftovers are low, and the sedan's trunklid uses strut-type hinges that don't intrude into the luggage area—a feature many costlier cars lack.

Our several test cars have had a solid on-road feel. However, our extended-use ZTS was built without the model's standard tilt/telescopic steering wheel, which had to be retrofitted by a dealer service department. It also was the subject of emissions systems and cruise control recalls, and a creaking suspension led to the warranty replacement of an upper strut bearing. Other Focus test cars have had poor-fitting interior panels.

VALUE Focus is not as refined as the class-topping Honda Civic, but offers generous subcompact passenger and cargo room. Ford's newest is fun to drive, too, despite the timid engines, and prices are very competitive. Put it on your small-car shopping list.

ENGINES

	ohc I4	dohc I4
Size, liters/cu. in.	2.0/121	2.0/121
Horsepower @ rpm	110 @ 5000	130 @ 5300
Torque (lb-ft) @ rpm	125 @ 3750	135 @ 4500
Availability	S[1]	S[2]
EPA city/highway mpg		
5-speed OD manual	28/38	25/34
4-speed OD automatic	27/35	24/32

1. LX, SE sedan. 2. SE wagon, ZX3, ZTS; optional SE sedan.

Specifications begin on page 535.

FORD

PRICES

Ford Focus

	Retail Price	Dealer Invoice
LX 4-door sedan	$12385	$11770
SE 4-door sedan	14040	13292
SE 4-door wagon	16235	15311
ZTS 4-door sedan	15260	14414
ZX3 2-door hatchback	12125	11530
Destination charge	490	490

STANDARD EQUIPMENT:

LX: 2.0-liter 4-cylinder engine, 5-speed manual transmission, dual front airbags, emergency inside trunk release, power steering, cloth upholstery, front bucket seats, height-adjustable driver seat, center console, cupholders, split folding rear seat, AM/FM/cassette, digital clock, auxiliary power outlet, visor mirrors, rear defogger, intermittent wipers, remote decklid release, floormats, theft-deterrent system, dual outside mirrors, 185/65R14 tires, wheel covers.

ZX3 adds: 2.0-liter dohc 4-cylinder engine, AM/FM/CD player, leather-wrapped steering wheel, tachometer, rear wiper/washer, fog lights, 195/60R15 tires, alloy wheels.

SE sedan adds to LX: air conditioning, power mirrors, power windows, power door locks, remote keyless entry, AM/FM/CD player, variable intermittent wipers, 195/60R15 tires, alloy wheels.

SE wagon adds: 2.0-liter dohc 4-cylinder engine, 4-speed automatic transmission, cargo cover, rear wiper/washer, roof rack.

ZTS adds to SE sedan: 2.0-liter dohc 4-cylinder engine, antilock brakes, tilt/telescoping leather-wrapped steering wheel, cruise control, driver-seat lumbar adjustment, tachometer, front armrest, map lights, fog lights, 205/50R16 tires.

OPTIONAL EQUIPMENT:
Major Packages

Comfort Group, SE	345	307

Cruise control, tilt/telescoping steering wheel, map lights.

Sport Group, SE	470	418

2.0-liter dohc 4-cylinder engine, tachometer, rear spoiler, fog lights. SE wagon requires Street Edition.

Street Edition, SE	775	690

Sport bucket seats, AM/FM radio w/in-dash 6-disc CD changer, 205/50R16 tires, 6-spoke alloy wheels. Requires Sport Group.

Power Group, ZX3	740	658

Power mirrors and windows, power door locks, remote keyless entry.

Premium Group, ZX3	1095	975

Air conditioning, tilt/telescoping steering wheel, cruise control, front center armrest, map lights, 205/50R16 tires, 6-spoke alloy wheels.

Prices are accurate at time of publication; subject to manufacturer's change.

CONSUMER GUIDE

FORD

Powertrains	Retail Price	Dealer Invoice
4-speed automatic transmission	$815	$725
Std. SE wagon.		

Safety Features
Antilock brakes, LX, SE, ZX3	400	356
Advance Trac, ZX3, ZTS	1225	1091
Includes antiskid system, traction control. ZX3 requires antilock brakes, Premium Group.		
Front side-impact airbags	350	312

Comfort and Convenience
Air conditioning, LX, ZX3	795	708
Leather upholstery, ZTS	695	619
Power sunroof, ZX3	495	441
Requires Premium Group.		

FORD MUSTANG

Ford Mustang GT 2-door coupe

Rear-wheel-drive sports coupe
Base price range: $16,805-$26,695. Built in USA. **Also consider:** Chevrolet Camaro, Pontiac Firebird

FOR • Acceleration (GT, Cobra) • Steering/handling **AGAINST** • Rear visibility (convertible) • Fuel economy (GT, Cobra) • Rear-seat room • Wet weather traction (without traction control) • Rear-seat entry/exit

Return of the high-performance Cobra and minor line-wide changes mark the 2001 edition of the original "ponycar." Mustang offers base, GT, and Cobra versions; all come as coupes or as convertibles with a power top and glass rear window. The Cobra is back after being pulled from the lineup mid last year amid performance complaints.

Base Mustangs have a 190-hp V6, GTs a 260-hp single-overhead-cam V8, Cobras a 320-hp twincam V8. A 5-speed manual transmission

Specifications begin on page 535.

FORD

is standard, automatic is optional, except on the Cobra. All models have 4-wheel disc brakes; antilock control is standard on GT and Cobra, optional on the base Mustang. Traction control is standard on Cobra, optional elsewhere. Cobras feature an independent rear suspension in place of the other models' less-sophisticated solid-axle design.

Changes for 2001 include a new floor console; repositioned front cupholder; larger rear cupholder; and the addition of a power point, tissue holder, and parking-brake boot. A rear defroster is now standard, the optional Mach 460 sound system is available with a 6-disc in-dashboard CD player, and GTs get standard 17-inch alloy wheels in place of 16s. Also, GT and Cobra get new hood and side scoops.

PERFORMANCE Mustang proves there's still life in one of Detroit's oldest designs. V6 versions are the most popular in terms of sales, and even they accelerate strongly. The GT's V8 has tire-smoking muscle and effortless passing power; our test 5-speed convertible did 0-60 mph in 6.5 seconds. Still, you'll need the Cobra to keep up with V8-powered Chevrolet Camaros or Pontiac Firebirds. Our 5-speed GT test cars averaged 15.5 mpg.

Mustang has a ride-comfort edge over its GM rivals, though bad pavement comes through distinctly in the stiff-riding V8 models. Mustang has plenty of lateral grip and good steering feel, but all these ponycars tend to get skittish in bumpy corners. Traction control enhances wet-weather safety; we recommend it. Stopping power is strong, pedal modulation good with the standard 4-wheel discs—although ABS is optional on base models and standard on Camaro and Firebird. Wind rustle is low, but hard acceleration brings out lots of engine noise and, with the V8, substantial exhaust roar. The convertible has enough top insulation to keep it from being uncomfortably noisy with its roof raised.

ACCOMMODATIONS With its relatively upright design, Mustang is easier to get into and out of than most competitors, although its long doors and tight rear-seat entry/exit are common coupe drawbacks. Mustang's reasonably supportive front seats offer good room for two and are positioned higher than those in its GM rivals, though rear visibility is still constricted, especially with the convertible's top up. The rear bench best suits children. Build quality is nothing special, and hard plastic dominates the interior decor. Trunk space is meager, and convertibles lack the coupe's handy split folding rear seatback.

VALUE Mustang handily outsells its GM competition because it has broader appeal. This is still an impractical car, but easily fulfills its core mission: Deliver sporty performance and looks for a reasonable price.

ENGINES

	ohv V6	ohc V8	dohc V8
Size, liters/cu. in.	3.8/232	4.6/281	4.6/281
Horsepower @ rpm	190 @ 5250	260 @ 5250	320 @ 6000

Prices are accurate at time of publication; subject to manufacturer's change.

FORD

	ohv V6	ohc V8	dohc V8
Torque (lb-ft) @ rpm	220 @ 2750	302 @ 4600	317 @ 4750
Availability	S[1]	S[2]	S[3]
EPA city/highway mpg			
5-speed OD manual	20/29	17/24	NA
4-speed OD automatic	20/27	17/23	

1. Base. 2. GT. 3. Cobra.

PRICES

Ford Mustang	Retail Price	Dealer Invoice
Base 2-door coupe	$16805	$15644
Base 2-door convertible	22220	20518
GT 2-door coupe	22440	20716
GT 2-door convertible	26695	24546
Cobra 2-door coupe	—	—
Cobra 2-door convertible	—	—
Destination charge	600	600

Cobra prices not available at time of publication.

STANDARD EQUIPMENT:

Base coupe: 3.8-liter V6 engine, 5-speed manual transmission, dual front airbags, 4-wheel disc brakes, emergency inside trunk release, power steering, tilt steering wheel, air conditioning, cloth upholstery, bucket seats, split folding rear seat, center console, cupholders, power mirrors, power windows, power door locks, remote keyless entry, AM/FM/cassette/CD player, digital clock, tachometer, visor mirrors, rear defogger, intermittent wipers, auxiliary power outlet, power remote decklid release, theft-deterrent system, 205/65R15 tires, alloy wheels.

Base convertible adds: power convertible top, cruise control, 6-way power driver seat, illuminated visor mirrors, floormats, Deletes: split folding rear seat.

GT coupe adds to base coupe: 4.6-liter V8 engine, limited-slip differential, antilock 4-wheel disc brakes, leather-wrapped steering wheel, cruise control, 6-way power driver seat, illuminated visor mirrors (convertible), power convertible top (convertible), floormats, fog lights, rear spoiler, GT Suspension Pkg., 245/45ZR17 tires, Deletes: split folding rear seat (convertible).

Cobra adds: 4.6-liter dohc V8 engine, traction control, leather/cloth upholstery, remote keyless entry, Mach AM/FM radio w/in-dash 6-disc CD changer, illuminated visor mirrors, Cobra Suspension Pkg., Deletes: rear spoiler.

OPTIONAL EQUIPMENT:
Major Packages

110A Deluxe Series Order Code, Base coupe	565	509

Cruise control, 6-way power driver seat, floormats, rear spoiler.

Specifications begin on page 535.

FORD

	Retail Price	Dealer Invoice
120A Premium Series Order Code, Base coupe	$1795	$1616

Deluxe Series Order Code plus traction control, anti-lock brakes, AM/FM radio w/in-dash 6-disc CD changer, Mach sound system, leather-wrapped steering wheel, accent stripe, 225/55R16 tires.

160A Premium Series Order Code, Base convertible	2565	2309

4-speed automatic transmission, traction control, anti-lock brakes, leather upholstery, leather-wrapped steering wheel, Mach AM/FM radio w/in-dash 6-disc CD changer, accent stripes, rear spoiler.

140A Premium Series Order Code, GT	1150	1035

Leather upholstery, Mach AM/FM radio w/in-dash 6-disc CD changer, premium alloy wheels.

Sport Appearance Group, Base coupe	250	223

Accent stripes, 225/55R16 tires. Requires 110A Deluxe Series Order Code.

Powertrains
4-speed automatic transmission, Base, GT	815	725

Safety Features
Antilock brakes, Base	730	650

Includes traction control. Base coupe requires 110A Deluxe Series Order Code.

Comfort and Convenience
Leather upholstery, Base, GT	500	445

Base coupe requires 120A Premium Series Order Code.

Mach AM/FM radio w/in-dash 6-disc CD changer, Base, GT	550	490

Base coupe requires 110A Deluxe Series Order Code.

Appearance and Miscellaneous
Rear spoiler, Cobra	—	—
Polished alloy wheels, Cobra	—	—

FORD TAURUS

CG RECOMMENDED AUTO

Front-wheel-drive midsize car; similar to Mercury Sable

Base price range: $18,260-$21,535. Built in USA.
Also consider: Chevrolet Impala, Honda Accord, Pontiac Grand Prix, Toyota Camry

FOR • Handling/roadholding • Rear-seat comfort • Cargo room
AGAINST • Low-speed acceleration

After a major design update last year, Ford's best-selling car slides into 2001 with only minor changes: Taurus gains lower anchors for rear child seats and the fuel tank grows from 16 gallons to 18.

Prices are accurate at time of publication; subject to manufacturer's change.

FORD

Ford Taurus 4-door sedan

Sedans come in LX, SE, SES, and SEL trim, the wagon in SE form. Taurus seats six with the available front bench seat, five with front buckets. A 2-passenger rear-facing third-row seat is a wagon option.

The base overhead-valve V6 has 155 horsepower. Standard on SEL and optional for SES and the SE wagon is a 200-hp twincam V6. A 4-speed automatic is the only transmission. Traction control and head/chest front side airbags are optional. Antilock brakes are standard on SES and SEL, optional on other Tauruses. Adjustable gas and brake pedals that power fore and aft about three inches are available on all but the LX model.

Taurus again shares its underskin design and mechanical components with the similar Mercury Sable.

PERFORMANCE Taurus and Sable perform well for mainstream midsize cars, a shortage of ready acceleration being their principal shortfall. Floor the throttle from a standstill and pickup is good; our test 200-hp Sable LS did 0-60 mph in 8.2 seconds. But both engines are slow to respond in the 25-50 mph range and feel weaker at those speeds than the larger V6s in such General Motors rivals as the Chevrolet Impala and Pontiac Grand Prix. Our test twincam Tauruses and Sables returned 18.4 mpg on average, about par for the class. We haven't measured the base engine's fuel economy. Both V6s use regular gas.

Taurus and Sable are balanced and stable even in rapid direction changes. The steering has fine on-center sense, but turning effort isn't always linear. Resistance to wallow and float is impressive, but rough-road ride is mediocre: Potholes, expansion joints, and pavement patches register sharply.

Brakes feel strong in everyday use and are easily modulated, though a test Sable sedan didn't stop impressively short in simulated panic stops. Also, we'd like to see 4-wheel disc brakes available for sedans, not just wagons. Engine and wind noise are low enough that tire thrum seems fairly prominent, though it doesn't require a raised voice to overcome.

ACCOMMODATIONS Taurus and Sable are synonymous with "fam-

Specifications begin on page 535.

FORD

ily car," and they shine in this role. Particularly notable is back-seat comfort, where head clearance is generous, and leg and foot space is plentiful. The rear seat is substantial and comfortably contoured. The Taurus wagon's fold-away rear-facing third seat is designed for children under 80 pounds.

Front outboard seating positions are uncrowded and adequately bolstered. The center portion of the front-bench suits only toddlers—who should ride in back anyway—but it flip-folds into a handy console/armrest that doesn't block the lower instrument panel. The movable pedals adjust easily via a control on the outboard seat bottom. They permit shorter drivers to sit further from the steering-wheel airbag, and team with standard tilt steering for an easily tailored driving position. The available driver-seat lumbar adjustment also helps comfort, but its control knob is awkwardly located on the seat front.

Gauges include a tachometer and are unobstructed, but their analog markings may be too small for some drivers to easily read at a glance. And it would be nice if bucket-seat models repeated the transmission-position readout within the gauge cluster. Controls are easy to see and use, though the climate systern can't run the air conditioning in all vent modes.

Both body styles have generous luggage space. The sedan's trunk is among the largest in class and includes useful grocery-bag hooks. But the lid's hinges and adjustment brackets intrude into the cargo area, and the opening isn't that large. Sedans are available with split-fold rear seatbacks, but they don't lock to protect trunk contents.

VALUE Taurus and Sable deliver good road manners, terrific utility, and an array of safety features at competitive prices. Acceleration and ride comfort aren't tops, but these sedans and wagons merit a place on any midsize-car shopping list.

ENGINES

	ohv V6	dohc V6
Size, liters/cu. in.	3.0/182	3.0/181
Horsepower @ rpm	155 @ 4900	200 @ 5650
Torque (lb-ft) @ rpm	185 @ 3950	200 @ 4400
Availability	S	O[1]
EPA city/highway mpg		
4-speed OD automatic	19/28	20/28

1. SE wagon, SES; standard SEL.

PRICES

Ford Taurus	Retail Price	Dealer Invoice
LX 4-door sedan	$18260	$17092
SE 4-door sedan	19035	17606
SE 4-door wagon	20190	18646
SES 4-door sedan	20050	18521

Prices are accurate at time of publication; subject to manufacturer's change.

FORD

	Retail Price	Dealer Invoice
SEL 4-door sedan	$21535	$19856
Destination charge	625	625

STANDARD EQUIPMENT:

LX: 3.0-liter V6 engine, 4-speed automatic transmission, dual front airbags, emergency inside trunk release, air conditioning, variable-assist power steering, tilt steering wheel, cloth upholstery, 5-passenger seating, front bucket seats, column shift, center console, cupholders, power mirrors, power windows, power door locks, AM/FM radio, digital clock, tachometer, variable intermittent wipers, auxiliary power outlets, visor mirrors, rear defogger, remote decklid release, theft-deterrent system, 215/60R16 tires, wheel covers.

SE sedan adds: remote keyless entry, cruise control, AM/FM/cassette, alloy wheels.

SE wagon adds: 4-wheel disc brakes, 6-passenger seating, front split bench seat w/flip-fold seating console, split folding rear seat, power antenna, rear/wiper washer, roof rack.

SES adds to SE sedan: antilock brakes, 6-passenger seating, front split bench seat w/flip-fold seating console, 6-way power driver seat, split folding rear seat, AM/FM/CD player, illuminated visor mirrors.

SEL adds: 3.0-liter dohc V6 engine, leather-wrapped steering wheel, automatic climate control, AM/FM/cassette w/in-dash 6-disc CD changer, remote keyless entry w/keypad, heated power mirrors, automatic headlights.

OPTIONAL EQUIPMENT:
Major Packages

LX Plus Pkg., LX	585	521

Cruise control, remote keyless entry, AM/FM/cassette, alloy wheels. Available only in California, Hawaii, and Orlando region.

SES Group, SE wagon	1040	925

Antilock brakes, AM/FM/CD player, 6-way power driver seat, illuminated visor mirrors. Requires Wagon Group.

Wagon Group, SE wagon	300	267

Rear facing third seat, cargo cover.

SES Wagon Plus Group, SE Wagon	435	387

3.0-liter dohc V6 engine, power-adjustable pedals. Available only in California, Hawaii, and Orlando region.

SES Plus Group, SES	435	387

3.0-liter V6 engine, power-adjustable pedals, 5-passenger seating, console, floor shift. Available only in California, Hawaii, and Orlando region.

SEL Group, SEL	50	45

Power-adjustable pedals, 5-passenger seating, console, floor shift, Mach Audio system. Available only in California, Hawaii, and Orlando region.

Specifications begin on page 535.

FORD

Powertrains	Retail Price	Dealer Invoice
3.0-liter dohc V6 engine, SE wagon, SES	$695	$619
Traction control, SE, SES, SEL	175	156
Requires antilock brakes. SE wagon requires SES Group.		

Safety Features		
Front side-impact airbags	390	347
LX requires power door locks.		
Antilock brakes, LX, SE	600	534

Comfort and Convenience		
6-passenger seating, LX, SE sedan	NC	NC
Front split bench seat w/flip-fold seating console.		
5-passenger seating, SES, SEL	105	93
Includes floor shift.		
Leather upholstery, SE wagon, SES, SEL	895	797
Includes 5-passenger seating. Wagon requires SES Group.		
6-way power driver seat, SE	395	352
Includes lumbar adjustment.		
6-way power passenger seat, SEL	350	312
Requires leather upholstery and front side-impact airbags.		
Split folding rear seat, SE sedan	140	124
Power-adjustable pedals3669	120	107
NA LX. SE requires power driver seat.		
AM/FM/CD player, SE	140	124
Premium Audio Group, SE wagon, SES	530	472
AM/FM/cassette w/in-dash 6-disc CD changer, Mach Premium Sound. Wagon requires SES Group and Wagon Group.		
Mach Premium Sound, SEL	320	285
Power sunroof, SES, SEL	890	792
Heated power mirrors, SE wagon, SES	35	31

Appearance and Miscellaneous		
Rear spoiler, SES, SEL	230	205
Requires 5-passenger seating.		

FORD WINDSTAR

Front-wheel-drive minivan

CG RECOMMENDED AUTO

Base price range: $19,910-$33,455.
Built in Canada. **Also consider:** Chevrolet Venture, Dodge Caravan, Honda Odyssey, Toyota Sienna

FOR • Passenger and cargo room   **AGAINST** • Fuel economy

New safety features, including a minivan-first antiskid system, highlight changes to the 2001 Windstar. Ford's minivan also shelves last year's

Prices are accurate at time of publication; subject to manufacturer's change.

FORD

Ford Windstar SE Sport

base 3.0-liter V6, making a 3.8-liter V6 the standard engine for all models.

Windstar comes in a single body length and this year has a slightly restyled nose and tail. LX, SE, SE Sport, SEL, and Limited models are offered. Dual sliding doors are standard except on the base LX. Power operation for both side doors is available. Antilock brakes and automatic transmission are standard. Most models come with traction control, and head/chest front side airbags are standard on Limiteds, optional on other Windstars. All seat seven; a center console is now included with the available second-row bucket seats. Power adjustable gas and brake pedals, a reverse sensing system that sounds a warning of obstacles while backing up, and a rear seat video entertainment system (now with removable VCR) are available.

New safety features include sensors that deploy the dashboard airbags based on crash severity and the positioning of the driver and front passenger. Also, a strobe light in the driver's outside mirror now warns approaching traffic that the left-side sliding door is opened. Due later in the model year, the available antiskid system applies a rear brake and reduces engine power to enhance control in turns. A low-tire-pressure warning system is newly standard on passenger models, Limiteds gain a wood-and-leather steering wheel, and SE and SE Sport models join SEL and Limited with standard 16-inch wheels and tires. The SE Sport is a new model and includes a black grille.

PERFORMANCE Good riddance to the underpowered 3.0 V6. Windstar is a good performer with the 3.8, which furnishes sufficient power even with a full load of passengers, but is gruff under hard throttle. In mostly city driving, our test 2000 3.8 example averaged 14.8 mpg—below average for a minivan.

Windstar's wheelbase is among the longest of any minivan and helps provide a stable ride, though some bumps and ruts register harshly. Handling is confident, but Windstar's steering feels artificial and doesn't respond as quickly as that of the Honda Odyssey or General Motors minivans. Worse, our SEL test model exhibited annoying torque steer—

Specifications begin on page 535.

FORD

a tug on the steering wheel in fast take-offs. Brake-pedal feel is good, but overall stopping power is mid-pack.

ACCOMMODATIONS Windstar has a friendly dashboard design, roomy seating, and even the manual side doors are easy to open and close thanks to easy-grip interior handles. Likewise, the rear hatch raises and lowers with a light touch, although separate-opening rear glass isn't available. The new strobe warning is a thoughtful item, as is the second-row console.

The power adjustable pedals help a range of drivers position themselves a safe distance from the steering wheel airbag. But some of our testers find the driver's seat itself uncomfortable. The second- and third-row seats are substantial and supportive, but they're heavy—the benches weigh more than 100 pounds apiece, the buckets 65 pounds each—so removal and installation demand muscle and technique. Second- and third-row seatbacks fold fore and aft for great cargo and passenger versatility. Second-row outboard shoulder belts are height-adjustable. No integrated child seat is offered.

Audio controls are too busy, but we like the climate system's ability to run air conditioning in all vent modes. Switches for the available power-operated rear quarter windows are on the driver's door panel, inaccessible to the front passenger. And instead of a rear-seat video screen mounted at ceiling height, as in rivals, Windstar's is near floor-level and is not visible to those in the third-row seat. The Reverse Sensing System is worth considering because the base of Windstar's rear window is not visible to the driver, complicating backing up.

VALUE Minivans from Dodge, Chrysler, and Honda are our Best Buys, but the roomy Windstar boasts some noteworthy safety and convenience features.

ENGINES

	ohv V6
Size, liters/cu. in.	3.8/232
Horsepower @ rpm	200 @ 4900
Torque (lb-ft) @ rpm	240 @ 3600
Availability	S

EPA city/highway mpg

4-speed OD automatic	17/23

PRICES

Ford Windstar	Retail Price	Dealer Invoice
Cargo 3-door van	$19910	$18370
LX 3-door van	21875	20556
LX 4-door van	24690	22624
SE Sport 4-door van	27125	24792
SE 4-door van	28285	25824
SEL 4-door van	30805	28066

Prices are accurate at time of publication; subject to manufacturer's change.

FORD

	Retail Price	Dealer Invoice
Limited 4-door van	$33455	$30425
Destination charge	655	655

STANDARD EQUIPMENT:

Cargo: 3.8-liter V6 engine, 4-speed automatic transmission, dual front airbags, antilock brakes, air conditioning, power steering, 2-passenger seating (cloth front buckets), front passenger area carpeting and cloth headliner, cupholders, power mirrors, power windows, power door locks, AM/FM radio, digital clock, tachometer, intermittent wipers, rear defogger, rear wiper/washer, auxiliary power outlets, visor mirrors, theft-deterrent system, full-size spare tire, 215/70R15 tires, wheel covers.

LX 3-door adds: low tire-pressure warning light, 7-passenger seating (front bucket seats, 2-place second row bench seat and 3-place third row bench seat), rear passenger area carpeting and cloth headliner, Light Group (front map/dome lights, glovebox light, second row reading and B-pillar lights, Sleeping Baby Mode lights), floormats, deletes full-size spare.

LX 4-door adds: tilt steering wheel, cruise control, driver-side sliding rear door, remote keyless entry, second and third row adjustable seat-tracks and rollers, AM/FM/cassette.

SE Sport adds: automatic climate control, rear air conditioning w/rear climate controls, leather-wrapped steering wheel, second row bucket seats w/console, overhead console (conversation mirror, coin holder, garage door opener/sunglasses holders, dome/reading lights), key pad entry, roof rack, rear privacy glass, 225/60R16 tires, alloy wheels.

SE adds: quad bucket seats, 6-way power driver seat w/power lumbar adjustment, power adjustable pedals, heated power mirrors w/open sliding door warning strobe-light, premium AM/FM/cassette/CD player w/rear audio controls, illuminated visor mirrors, cornering lights, 215/65R16 tires, Deletes: second row console.

SEL adds: power sliding rear doors, leather upholstery, 6-way power passenger seat w/power lumbar adjustment, automatic day/night rearview mirror, universal garage door opener, compass, automatic headlights.

Limited adds: traction control, front side-impact airbags, reverse sensing system, wood/leather-wrapped steering wheel, driver seat and mirror memory, in-dash 6-disc CD changer, Travelnote digital memo recorder, perimeter alarm, heavy-duty battery and cooling, trailer wiring harness, full-size spare tire, self-sealing tires.

OPTIONAL EQUIPMENT:
Major Packages

Van Value Group, Cargo 910 773
  Tilt steering wheel, cruise control, remote keyless entry, AM/FM/cassette,

Specifications begin on page 535.

FORD

privacy glass.

	Retail Price	Dealer Invoice
Value Group, LX 3-door	$545	$463

Tilt steering wheel, cruise control, AM/FM/cassette.

Comfort Group, LX 4-door	1060	901

Rear air conditioning, automatic climate control, rear climate controls, roof rack, privacy glass.

Power Group, LX 4-door	445	378

Power adjustable pedals, 6-way power driver seat. Requires Comfort Group.

Convenience Group, SE Sport	605	514

Adjustable pedals, 6-way power driver seat, center console, heated power mirrors w/turn signal lights, storage nets.

Electronics Group, SE	360	306

Automatic day/night rearview mirror, compass, additional warning messages, automatic headlights.

Family Security Group I, LX 4-door	455	387

Traction control, perimeter alarm, self-sealing tires.

Family Security Group II, SE Sport, SE, SEL	600	510

Traction control, reverse sensing system theft-deterrent system w/perimeter alarm, 215/65R16 self-sealing tires.

Class II Trailer Towing Pkg., LX 4-door, SE Sport, SE	470	400
SEL	445	378

Heavy-duty battery, trailer tow wiring, full-size spare tire.

Safety Features

Front side-impact air bags	390	332

NA Cargo. Std. Limited.

Comfort and Convenience

Rear Seat Entertainment System,		
SE Sport, SE, SEL, Limited	995	846

Videocassette player, LCD screen, two headphones, headphone jacks, remote control. NA w/floor console.

Power driver- and passenger-side sliding rear doors,		
SE Sport, SE	900	765

SE Sport requires leather upholstery.

Floor console,		
LX 4-door, SE Sport, SE, SEL	155	132
AM/FM/cassette/CD player, LX 4-door	250	213
SE Sport	300	255

SE Sport includes rear radio controls. SE Sport requires Convenience Group.

In-dash 6-disc CD changer, SE Sport	300	255
SE, SEL	NC	NC

Prices are accurate at time of publication; subject to manufacturer's change.

FORD

Quad bucket seats, LX 4-door	745	633
Requires Power Group.		

	Retail Price	Dealer Invoice
Second row low back bucket seats, SE Sport (credit)	($145)	($123)
Deletes second row console. Requires Convenience Group.		
Second row bucket seats w/console, SE, SEL	145	123
Leather upholstery, SE Sport, SE	865	735
Includes power front seats. SE Sport includes low back bucket seats. SE Sport requires Convenience Group.		

Appearance and Miscellaneous

Liftgate spoiler, SE Sport	195	166
Alloy wheels, LX 4-door	415	352

FORD ZX2

Ford ZX2

Front-wheel-drive sports coupe

Base price: $12,050. Built in Mexico. **Also consider:** Ford Focus ZX3, Honda Prelude, Volkswagen New Beetle

FOR • Fuel economy **AGAINST** • Rear-seat room • Noise • Rear-seat entry/exit

This little coupe is based on Ford's 1997-2000 Escort, and for 2001, it drops the sporty S/R option package. ZX2 uses a 4-cylinder engine teamed with manual transmission or optional 4-speed automatic. Antilock brakes are optional. Standard features include 15-inch alloy wheels and tires, cassette player, power mirrors, and rear defroster. The departed S/R package included performance exhaust, sport suspension, larger tires, 4-wheel disc brakes, and yellow paint, none of which remain available. ZX2's only other change of note for 2001 is the addition of an emergency trunk release.

EVALUATION ZX2's ride is firm but not punishing, and its road man-

Specifications begin on page 535.

FORD

ners are enjoyably competent, although it's not as nimble as the Focus ZX3 hatchback, which shares its engine. Acceleration is good, especially with manual transmission, but the engine is buzzy and there's considerable road noise, making for tiresome driving. Our test automatic ZX2 averaged a laudable 29.0 mpg, a 5-speed got 24.5 in harder driving. ZX2 is smaller inside than the Focus ZX3. Front-seat space is adequate, although some testers complain of insufficient fore-aft seat travel. Rear-seat room is better than in many sports coupes, but it's still tight for adults, and rear entry/exit is tricky. Controls are handy and logical, but the standard fixed steering wheel doesn't suit all drivers (tilt is optional), and over-the-shoulder visibility is poor. Cargo room is good for a subcompact coupe, but the trunk opening is small and the lid hinges cut into load space. The ZX2 looks sportier than it performs. Honda's new Civic coupe or the ZX3 rate far higher overall.

ENGINES

	dohc I4
Size, liters/cu. in.	2.0/121
Horsepower @ rpm	130 @ 5750
Torque (lb-ft) @ rpm	127 @ 4250
Availability	S

EPA city/highway mpg
5-speed OD manual	25/33
4-speed OD automatic	25/33

PRICES

Ford ZX2	Retail Price	Dealer Invoice
Base 2-door coupe	$12050	$11432
Destination charge	465	465

STANDARD EQUIPMENT:

Base: 2.0-liter dohc 4-cylinder engine, 5-speed manual transmission, dual front airbags, emergency inside trunk release, power steering, cloth upholstery, bucket seats, center console, cupholders, split folding rear seat, power mirrors, AM/FM/cassette, digital clock, tachometer, rear defogger, variable intermittent wipers, auxiliary power outlet, visor mirrors, rear spoiler, 185/60R15 tires, alloy wheels.

OPTIONAL EQUIPMENT:

Major Packages

Power Group	395	352
Power windows and door locks, remote keyless entry. Requires air conditioning.		
Comfort Group	395	352
Cruise control, tilt leather-wrapped steering wheel, map lights.		

Prices are accurate at time of publication; subject to manufacturer's change.

FORD • GMC

Powertrains
4-speed automatic transmission... 815 725

	Retail Price	Dealer Invoice

Safety Features
Antilock brakes.. $400 $356

Comfort and Convenience
Air conditioning... 795 708
Leather upholstery.. 395 352
Premium AM/FM/cassette w/6-disc CD changer 295 263
Power sunroof.. 595 530

Appearance and Miscellaneous
Chrome alloy wheels... 595 530
Includes 185/65R14 tires.

2002 GMC ENVOY

2002 GMC Envoy

Rear- or 4-wheel-drive midsize sport-utility vehicle; similar to Chevrolet Trailblazer and Oldsmobile Bravada

Base price range: NA. Built in USA. **Also consider:** Acura MDX, Dodge Durango, Ford Explorer, Mercury Mountaineer

GMC drops its familiar Jimmy and Envoy for 2002 in favor of a significantly larger new midsize SUV with more room and power. To be sold only under the Envoy name, it rolls out this spring, ahead of Chevrolet's related 2002 TrailBlazer but behind Oldsmobile's similarly revamped '02 Bravada. All are 4-door 5-passenger wagons with a new body-on-frame General Motors platform. They vary in styling, pricing, and standard and optional features and the only shared exterior body panels are the roof, front doors, and tailgate. GMC's entry is positioned in the market between the other two, but is slightly more upscale than previous Envoys.

Like its '02 linemates, the new Envoy measures some 10 inches longer overall, 6 inches longer in wheelbase, 5 inches wider, and nearly

Specifications begin on page 535.

GMC

5 inches higher than its predecessor.

Replacing the previous model's 4.3-liter overhead-valve V6 engine is a new 4.2-liter inline 6-cylinder with dual overhead camshafts and 80 more horsepower. Most rivals offer V8s, but GM says its new six is as powerful and more economical. The only transmission is a 4-speed automatic. Rear-wheel drive is offered along with GM's all-surface Autotrac 4WD. Maximum tow capacities are 6100 pounds with 4WD and 6300 on 4x2s. GMC claims car-like ride comfort from a new rear suspension with coil instead of leaf springs, though it retains a solid axle. The redesigned 2002 Ford Explorer and Mercury Mountaineer have independent rear suspension, as well as three rows of seats for 7-passenger capacity, a feature Envoy won't match for at least a year.

Antilock 4-wheel disc brakes remain standard, but the '02 Envoy one-ups TrailBlazer with standard 17-inch wheels instead of 16s. It also comes with rear audio controls, heated power front seats, and GM's OnStar assistance system. OnStar is optional for TrailBlazer.

Both the Chevy and GMC have standard front side airbags, plus dual-stage dashboard airbags that deploy with one of two force levels as signaled by sensors monitoring crash severity and occupant position. Other specifics weren't available for this report, but Envoy should offer more comfort, convenience and trim features than TrailBlazer, but not so many standard items to upstage the costlier Olds Bravada. Due later, but not before model year 2003, is a longer-wheelbase Envoy with standard seating for seven via the addition of a third-row bench, plus rear doors longer than the fronts and a standard 5.3-liter V8 borrowed from GM's full-size pickups and SUVs.

We have not yet driven the 2002 Envoy and thus cannot provide ratings or a road-test evaluation.

ENGINES

	dohc I6
Size, liters/cu. in.	4.2/256
Horsepower @ rpm	270 @ 6000
Torque (lb-ft) @ rpm	275 @ 3600
Availability	S
EPA city/highway mpg	
4-speed OD automatic	16/21

Prices unavailable at time of publication.

GMC SAFARI

Rear- or all-wheel-drive minivan; similar to Chevrolet Astro

Base price range: $20,593-$25,056. Built in USA. **Also consider:** Chevrolet Venture, Dodge Caravan, Ford Windstar

FOR • Passenger and cargo room • Trailer towing capability
AGAINST • Fuel economy • Entry/exit • Ride

Prices are accurate at time of publication; subject to manufacturer's change.

GMC

GMC Safari SLT

Safari and its Chevrolet Astro twin are America's only rear-wheel-drive truck-based minivans, and they receive only minor changes for 2001. Both come as passenger and cargo versions in a single body length with passenger-side sliding door and are available with rear-wheel drive or all-surface 4-wheel drive. Passenger models offer the choice of two side-hinged panel doors at the back or swing-out half-height "Dutch" doors. Antilock brakes and daytime running lights are standard.

This year, Safari loses its base passenger model, leaving SLE and SLT trim levels. It also gets a stronger alternator that GMC says helps supply more power for laptop computers and TVs. Eight-passenger seating is standard, while a seven-passenger option replaces the second-row bench seat with twin buckets. The only powertrain is a 4.3-liter V6 and automatic transmission; the transmission has a Tow/Haul mode that optimizes shift points for heavy hauling and towing. Safari's optional 4WD system drives the rear wheels until they start to slip, then automatically engages the front axle to restore traction. Safari's performance and accommodations mirror those of similarly equipped Astros.

The Chevrolet Astro report includes an evaluation of the Safari.

ENGINES

	ohv V6
Size, liters/cu. in.	4.3/262
Horsepower @ rpm	190 @ 4400
Torque (lb-ft) @ rpm	250 @ 2800
Availability	S
EPA city/highway mpg	
4-speed OD automatic	16/20[1]

1. 15/19 with AWD.

PRICES

GMC Safari	Retail Price	Dealer Invoice
2WD Cargo 3-door van	$20593	$18637
AWD Cargo 3-door van	22993	20809
2WD SLE 3-door van	23241	21033
AWD SLE 3-door van	25056	22676
Destination charge	655	655

Specifications begin on page 535.

GMC

AWD denotes all-wheel drive.

STANDARD EQUIPMENT:

Cargo: 4.3-liter V6 engine, 4-speed automatic transmission, antilock brakes, dual front airbags, daytime running lights, variable-assist power steering, front air conditioning, vinyl upholstery, front bucket seats, cupholders, AM/FM radio, digital clock, rubber floor covering, intermittent wipers, carpeting, auxiliary power outlets, theft-deterrent system, rear panel doors, dual outside mirrors, 215/75R15 tires. **AWD** adds: Autotrac permanent 4-wheel drive.

SLE adds: cloth upholstery, 8-passenger seating (front bucket seats, two 3-passenger rear bench seats), tilt steering wheel, cruise control, power mirrors, power windows, power door locks, remote keyless entry, AM/FM/CD player, overhead console, trip computer, compass, outside temperature indicator, map lights, illuminated visor mirrors, automatic headlights, carpeting, floormats, roof rack, 6-wire trailering harness. **AWD** adds: Autotrac permanent 4-wheel drive.

OPTIONAL EQUIPMENT:

	Retail Price	Dealer Invoice
Major Packages		
SLE Marketing Option Pkg. 1SD, SLE	$1527	$1313
Front and rear air conditioning, rear heater, 6-way power driver seat, AM/FM/cassette/CD player, rear Dutch doors, rear defogger.		
SLT Marketing Option Pkg. 1SE, SLE	3178	2733
SLE Marketing Option Pkg. 1SD plus leather-wrapped steering wheel, universal garage door opener, rear radio controls, 215/75R15 white-letter tires, alloy wheels.		
ZQ2 Convenience Pkg., Cargo	474	408
Power door locks, power windows.		
ZQ3 Convenience Pkg., Cargo	383	329
Tilt steering wheel, cruise control.		
Heavy Duty Trailering Equipment	309	266
Platform hitch, 8-lead wiring harness.		
Powertrains		
Limited-slip differential	252	217
Comfort and Convenience		
Rear air conditioning, SLE	523	450
Rear heater, SLE	205	176
Rear Dutch doors, Cargo	518	445
SLE	459	395
Includes rear defogger.		
7-passenger seating, SLE	NC	NC
Front bucket seats w/lumbar support, middle bucket seats, 3-passenger rear seat. Requires SLT Pkg. 1SE.		
Leather upholstery, SLE	950	817
Requires SLT Pkg. 1SE.		

Prices are accurate at time of publication; subject to manufacturer's change.

CONSUMER GUIDE

GMC

	Retail Price	Dealer Invoice
AM/FM/CD player, Cargo	$407	$350
Requires Convenience Pkg. ZQ2.		
Rear headphone jacks/radio controls, SLE	125	108
Requires SLE Pkg. 1SD.		

Appearance and Miscellaneous

Running boards, SLE	400	344
Requires option pkg., alloy wheels.		
Alloy wheels, SLE	25	21
Requires SLE Pkg. 1SD.		
Chrome steel wheels, Cargo	248	213

GMC YUKON/DENALI

GMC Yukon

Rear- or 4-wheel-drive full-size sport-utility vehicle; similar to Chevrolet Tahoe and Suburban and Cadillac Escalade

Base price range: $32,200-$47,450. Built in USA. **Also consider:** Ford Excursion, Ford Expedition, Toyota Land Cruiser

FOR • Acceleration (Denali) • Passenger and cargo room • Trailer towing capability **AGAINST** • Steering feel • Fuel economy

Redesigned luxury models and more available power highlight 2001 news for GMC's full-size SUVs. Yukon and the longer Yukon XL are basically retrimmed versions of Chevrolet's Tahoe and Suburban, respectively. This year, the upscale Yukon Denali moves to the same platform and offers a first-ever XL version.

Yukon XLs come in half-ton 1500 and three-quarter-ton 2500 models; the regular Yukon and both Denalis are half-tons only. A third-row bench seat is standard on XL and Denalis, optional for regular Yukons. Second-row reclining bucket seats are available for the XLs, while heated front seats are standard on Denali, optional elsewhere. Both Yukons offer a no-cost choice of side-opening rear cargo doors or an aluminum liftgate with independent-opening glass hatch; the latter is standard for

Specifications begin on page 535.

GMC

Denalis. Front side airbags, antilock 4-wheel disc brakes, and V8 power feature across the board.

Regular Yukons come with a 4.8-liter V8 or optional 5.3. XL 1500s get the 5.3. Standard for XL 2500s and both Denalis is a 6.0-liter V8 with 20 more horsepower than last year. An 8.1-liter V8 is newly optional for XL 2500s. The only transmission is a 4-speed automatic with GM's Tow/Haul mode that adjusts shift points to accommodate heavy loads or trailers.

Yukons offer rear-wheel drive or GM's Autotrac 4-wheel drive, which can be used on dry pavement and includes locked-in 4WD High and Low ranges. Denalis come with a new permanent 4WD system requiring no driver intervention. A limited-slip rear axle and traction control are available for 2WD Yukons and are standard on XL 4x2s. Optional for Yukons is an SLT package that includes GM's OnStar assistance system, which is standard for Denalis. The upmarket models also get slightly different exterior styling, 17-inch wheels instead of 16s, GM's Autoride system with auto-adjusting shock absorbers, leather interior trim, and premium Bose audio with 6-disc in-dash CD changer. Besides the second-row buckets, a sunroof is the only Denali option. Many standard Denali items are optional for other Yukons, whose performance and accommodations mirror those of like-equipped Tahoes and Suburbans.

PERFORMANCE Mainstream Yukon and XLs drive much like their Chevy counterparts, so our Tahoe/Suburban evaluation applies to them too. Denalis are a bit different, being closer to Cadillac's similarly redesigned 2002 Escalade for acceleration and refinement. That's no surprise, as the luxury GMCs share many design features with the latest Cadillac SUV.

As a result, the Denalis have similarly strong acceleration from most any speed, even though they have 25 fewer horsepower than the '02 Escalade. Denali's pleasantly absorbent ride is free of the unwanted rough-surface wheel patter that mars so many big SUVs. Handling is assured, helped by the new permanent 4WD, but these remain heavy, high-built rigs with marked body lean in tight, fast corners and numb, over-light steering action. We've so far had no chance to measure fuel economy, but it's bound be as grim as with other sumo-class SUVs. The upside is great towing ability: up to 8500 pounds on the regular Denali, 8400 for the XL.

Like GM's other big SUVs, ABS disc brakes give Denalis good stopping power, though pedal action was touchy on the two preview models we drove. Noise levels are low for the class. Wind rush is noticed in gusty conditions, but there's not much tire noise even on coarse pavement, and though the V8 growls above 4000 rpm, it's never intrusive.

Incidentally, the XL Denali doesn't feel much different behind the wheel versus the shorter model. The only time you're really aware of its extra length is in crowded urban conditions and tight parking spots.

Prices are accurate at time of publication; subject to manufacturer's change.

GMC

ACCOMMODATIONS Like mainstream Yukons, the Denalis deliver fine driver visibility from a high-riding command post featuring clear gauges and mostly intuitive, well-placed controls. Entry/exit is big-SUV typical, but standard running boards help, especially for those with shorter legs.

Denalis naturally boast the same relatively cavernous interiors as their less costly cousins. They're visibly dressier, if not quite luxury-car posh, but have the same generous front- and middle-row space for even the largest occupants. Similarly, the third-row seat in the longer XL Denali is far more habitable for adults than in the shorter Denali, though two persons is the limit in either. The bigger rig claims nearly 46 cubic feet of storage behind that seat, where the regular Denali barely takes a row of grocery bags. However, its 50/50 split back bench offers more versatility than the XL's one-piece affair, and the middle- and third-row seats fold easily on both models. Only the third seats are removable in either Denali; a 2-person task in the XL but fairly easy with the standard model's twin 40-pound sections. Both Denalis offer expansive cargo space with rear seats folded or removed.

VALUE The Best Buy tag on this report refers to the basic Yukon, which offers fine value in base form and most of the sensible luxury options anyone could want. The '01 Denalis mix the basic virtues of those mainstream Yukons with more standard power, extra amenities, and the convenience of permanent 4WD that only Cadillac matches among large domestic SUVs. Alas, Denalis are pricey—$45,950 base for the standard model, $47,450 for the XL—and they're as fuelish as anything in the class. Still, this recipe of style, luxury, and overall competence makes them good alternatives to a Lincoln Navigator or Toyota Land Cruiser.

ENGINES

	ohv V8	ohv V8	ohv V8	ohv V8
Size, liters/cu. in.	4.8/294	5.3/325	6.0/364	8.1/496
Horsepower @ rpm	275 @ 5200	285 @ 5200	320 @ 5000	340 @ 4200
Torque (lb-ft) @ rpm	290 @ 4000	325 @ 4000	360 @ 4000	455 @ 3200
Availability	S[1]	S[2]	S[3]	O[4]
EPA city/highway mpg				
4-speed OD automatic	14/17	14/16	12/16	NA

1. Yukon 2. Yukon XL 1500; optional Yukon. 3. Denali, Yukon XL 2500. 4. Yukon XL 2500.

PRICES

GMC Yukon/Denali

	Retail Price	Dealer Invoice
Yukon 2WD 4-door wagon	$32200	$28175
Yukon 4WD 4-door wagon	35078	30693
Denali AWD 4-door wagon	45950	40206
Yukon XL 1500 2WD 4-door wagon	35552	31108

Specifications begin on page 535.

GMC

	Retail Price	Dealer Invoice
Yukon XL 1500 4WD 4-door wagon	$37983	$33235
Denali XL AWD 4-door wagon	47450	41519
Yukon XL 2500 2WD 4-door wagon	36924	32309
Yukon XL 2500 4WD 4-door wagon	39439	34509
Destination charge: Yukon, Denali	730	730
Destination charge: Yukon XL, Denali XL	765	765

STANDARD EQUIPMENT:

Yukon: 4.8-liter V8 engine, 4-speed automatic transmission, dual front airbags, front side-impact airbags, antilock 4-wheel disc brakes, daytime running lights, front and rear air conditioning w/rear climate controls, interior air filter, rear heater, power steering, tilt leather-wrapped steering wheel, cruise control, cloth upholstery, split front bench seat, 6-way power front seats, cupholders, second row split folding seat, heated power mirrors, power windows, power door locks, remote keyless entry, AM/FM/CD player, digital clock, tachometer, engine hour meter, overhead console, illuminated visor mirrors, intermittent wipers, map lights, auxiliary power outlets, rear defogger, rear wiper/washer, automatic day/night rearview mirror, compass, outside temperature indicator, automatic headlights, carpeting, floormats, theft-deterrent system, fog lights, roof rack, rear liftgate/liftglass, deep-tinted rear glass, 7-lead trailer wiring harness, front tow hooks, full-size spare tire, P265/70R16 all-terrain tires, alloy wheels. **4WD adds:** Autotrac full-time 4-wheel drive, 2-speed transfer case, variable-assist power steering.

Denali/Denali XL add: 6.0-liter V8 engine, permanent 4-wheel drive, traction control (XL), limited-slip differential, OnStar System w/one year service (roadside assistance, emergency services; other services available), front and rear automatic climate controls, leather upholstery, heated 10-way power front bucket seats w/driver seat memory, third row split folding seat, Bose AM/FM/cassette/CD player w/6-disc CD changer, steering wheel radio controls, rear radio controls, rear headphone jacks, driver-side automatic day/night mirror, trip computer, universal garage door opener, cargo cover, running boards, Autoride suspension, trailer hitch platform, brake wiring harness, P265/70R17 tires.

Yukon XL: adds to Yukon: 5.3-liter V8 engine (1500), 6.0-liter V8 engine (2500), traction control, limited-slip rear differential, third row bench seat, trailer hitch platform, brake wiring harness, LT245/75R16E tires (2500). **4WD adds:** Autotrac full-time 4-wheel drive, 2-speed transfer case, variable-assist power steering (1500). Deletes: traction control, limited slip differential.

OPTIONAL EQUIPMENT:
Major Packages

SLT Marketing Option Pkg. 1SC, Yukon	1400	1204

Prices are accurate at time of publication; subject to manufacturer's change.

GMC

	Retail Price	Dealer Invoice
Yukon XL	$2050	$1763

Leather upholstery, front bucket seats, center console, AM/FM/cassette/CD player.

SLT Marketing Option Pkg. 1SD, Yukon	2818	2423
Yukon XL	2968	2552

SLT Pkg. 1SC plus OnStar System w/one year service (roadside assistance, emergency services; other services available), front and rear automatic climate control, heated 10-way power front seats, driver seat memory, rear seat radio controls and headphone jacks, universal garage door opener, driver-side automatic day/night rearview mirror.

Z71 Off-Road Suspension Pkg., 4WD Yukon	170	146

Gas shock absorbers, skid plates. NA with third row seat.

Heavy-Duty Trailering Equipment, 2WD Yukon	616	530
4WD Yukon	169	145

Traction control (2WD), limited-slip rear differential (2WD), trailer hitch platform, brake wiring harness. 2WD requires special axle ratio w/4.8-liter engine.

Powertrains

5.3-liter V8 engine, Yukon	700	602
8.1-liter V8 engine, Yukon XL 2500	600	516

Deletes std. Trailering Pkg.

Traction control, 2WD Yukon	195	168

Requires limited-slip rear differential.

Limited-slip rear differential, Yukon, 4WD Yukon XL	252	217
Special axle ratio, Yukon, Yukon XL	50	43

Comfort and Convenience

Power sunroof, Yukon, Yukon XL	1170	1006
Yukon/Yukon XL ordered w/SLT Pkg. 1SD	938	807
Denali, Denali XL	900	774

Yukon/Yukon XL include universal garage door opener. Deletes rear air conditioning controls.

Front and rear automatic climate controls, Yukon, Yukon XL	125	108

NA with power sunroof.

Front bucket seats, Yukon, Yukon XL	375	323

Includes floor console.

Second-row bucket seats, Yukon XL, Denali XL	290	250

Yukon XL requires front bucket seats or SLT Pkg.

Third-row split folding rear seat, Yukon	350	301
Yukon w/SLT Pkg.	750	645

Includes floormat. Deletes cargo cover.

AM/FM/cassette/CD player, Yukon, Yukon XL	125	108

Requires bucket seats.

Specifications begin on page 535.

GMC • HONDA

	Retail Price	Dealer Invoice
Rear seat radio controls, Yukon, Yukon XL	$165	$142

Includes headphone jacks. Requires front bucket seats.

Appearance and Miscellaneous

	Retail Price	Dealer Invoice
Rear panel doors, Yukon, Yukon XL	NC	NC
NA with Yukon third-row seat. Deletes rear wiper/washer.		
Running boards, Yukon, Yukon XL	395	340
Skid Plates, 4WD	95	82
Autoride Suspension, Yukon, Yukon XL 1500	700	602
Yukon XL 2500	750	645
Polished alloy wheels, Yukon, Yukon XL	110	95
Requires SLT Pkg.		
LT245/75R16C on/off-road white-letter tires, 4WD Yukon	258	222
Requires Z71 Off-Road Suspension Pkg.		
P265/70R16 all-terrain white-letter tires, Yukon, Yukon XL 1500	125	108
NA w/Z71 Off-Road Suspension Pkg.		

HONDA ACCORD

Honda Accord LX 4-door sedan

Front-wheel-drive midsize car

Base price range: $15,400-$25,100. Built in USA. **Also consider:** Dodge Stratus, Ford Taurus, Oldsmobile Intrigue, Toyota Camry/Solara

FOR • Acceleration (V6 models) • Quietness • Instruments/controls • Steering/handling • Build quality • Exterior finish • Interior materials
AGAINST • Automatic transmission performance • Rear-seat entry/exit (2-door)

Traction control for V6 models and "smart" front airbags are 2001 changes of note to one of America's perennial favorites. Honda's top-selling car line also gets minor appearance and equipment changes.

Prices are accurate at time of publication; subject to manufacturer's change.

HONDA

Accord returns with 4-cylinder and V6 coupes and sedans in LX and upscale EX trim, plus a price-leader 4-cylinder DX sedan. The 2.3-liter 4-cylinder delivers 135 horsepower in the DX and 150 in LX and EX models. Accord's 3.0-liter V6 has 200 hp. All models are certified as Low Emissions Vehicles (LEVs) nationwide, and a special California-only sedan meets that state's Super Ultra LEV standard.

Four-cylinder models offer manual or extra-cost automatic transmission; V6s come only with automatic. Antilock brakes are standard on V6s and 4-cylinder EXs, optional for the automatic 4-cylinder LX sedan. Leather upholstery is included on EX V6s and available for 4-cylinder EXs.

Front side airbags are standard on V6 models and leather-equipped 4-cylinder EXs. Both the passenger-side front and side airbags are now designed to automatically deactivate if seat-mounted sensors detect that a passenger is too small or out of position. In other changes, traction control is newly standard for V6 models but unavailable elsewhere, and Honda claims "engineering refinements" to reduce road and wind noise. All models get a subtle restyling front and rear, and all but the DX sedan add lighted power-window switches. EX V6s add standard automatic climate control, in-dash CD changer, and 4-way power passenger seat; 4-cylinder EXs also get the in-dash changer, while LXs are upgraded to 6-speaker audio with a single-disc in-dash player.

PERFORMANCE Both Accord engines are silky, revvy, quiet, and punchy. We timed a 5-speed 4-cylinder EX at 8.5 seconds to 60 mph, a V6 EX sedan at 7.6. However, Accord's automatic transmission sometimes shifts with a jolt and can be painfully slow to downshift for passing. Typical of Hondas, economy is good. Our extended-use 4-cylinder manual coupe returned 23.8 mpg over more than 8100 city/highway miles. We've also averaged 24.7 mpg with an automatic 4-cylinder sedan and between 20.7-24 mpg with V6 sedans.

Ride is firm but comfortable and controlled. Accords are capable handlers, too, with precise steering and fine balance, though ultimate cornering grip is modest on 4-cylinder models because of narrow tires. Braking is short, quick, and stable, but one V6 test sedan showed unusually heavy nosedive in simulated panic stops. Wind rush is modest, but overall noise suppression is only average; the '01s may be better in that respect, though we haven't yet tested them. Accords impress as solid and carefully constructed. Our extended-use car was trouble-free, though a recent test sedan's power front-passenger window worked only intermittently.

ACCOMMODATIONS Accord sedans are about as spacious as 4-door Toyota Camrys, but neither Honda body style seats five large adults without squeezing. Seat comfort itself is first-rate, especially up front. Though several competitors also offer front side airbags, Accord is one of the few mid-priced cars offering "smart" technology designed to reduce airbag-induced injuries.

As usual, Accord's dashboard is very user-friendly, though the ill-

HONDA

defined detent between the automatic transmission's top two gears could have some drivers cruising in third instead of fourth. Outward vision is good except over-the-shoulder, where a high parcel shelf inhibits sightlines. Entry/exit is easy on sedans, crouch-and-crawl to the rear in coupes. Interior storage space is decent, and both body styles have wide, flat-floor trunks. Liftover is a bit high in coupes, which also have slightly less cargo volume.

VALUE As a perennial Best Buy, Accord is a must-see midsize: roomy, very well built from top-grade materials, and with road manners a cut above the family-car norm. Demand is strong, so don't expect much discounting, but reliability and resale value are terrific.

ENGINES

	ohc I4	ohc I4	ohc V6
Size, liters/cu. in.	2.3/137	2.3/137	3.0/183
Horsepower @ rpm	135 @ 5400	150 @ 5700	200 @ 5500
Torque (lb-ft) @ rpm	145 @ 4700	152 @ 4900	195 @ 4700
Availability	S[1]	S[2]	S[3]
EPA city/highway mpg			
5-speed OD manual	23/30	25/31	
4-speed OD automatic	22/29	23/30	20/28

1. DX models. 2. LX, SE, EX models. 3. V6 models.

PRICES

Honda Accord	Retail Price	Dealer Invoice
DX 4-door sedan, 5-speed	$15400	$13715
DX 4-door sedan, automatic	16200	14426
DX 4-door sedan w/side airbags, 5-speed	15650	13937
DX 4-door sedan w/side airbags, automatic	16450	14684
VP 4-door sedan, automatic	17200	15315
VP 4-door sedan w/side airbags, automatic	17450	15537
LX 2-door coupe, 5-speed	18790	16727
LX 2-door coupe, automatic	19590	17438
LX 2-door coupe w/side airbags, 5-speed	19040	16950
LX 2-door coupe w/side airbags, automatic	19840	17661
LX 4-door sedan, 5-speed	18790	16727
LX 4-door sedan, automatic	19590	17438
LX 4-door sedan w/side airbags, 5-speed	19040	16950
LX 4-door sedan w/side airbags, automatic	19840	17661
LX 4-door sedan w/ABS, automatic	20590	18327
LX 4-door sedan w/ABS and side airbags, automatic	20840	18549
LX V6 2-door coupe, automatic	22400	19935
LX V6 4-door sedan, automatic	22400	19935
EX 2-door coupe, 5-speed	21400	19047
EX 2-door coupe, automatic	22200	19758
EX 2-door coupe w/leather, 5-speed	22550	20069

Prices are accurate at time of publication; subject to manufacturer's change.

HONDA

EX 2-door coupe w/leather, automatic	23350	20780
EX 4-door sedan, 5-speed	21400	19047
EX 4-door sedan, automatic	22200	19758
EX 4-door sedan w/leather, 5-speed	22550	20069
EX 4-door sedan w/leather, automatic	23350	20780
EX V6 2-door coupe, automatic	25100	22335
EX V6 4-door sedan, automatic	25100	22335
Destination charge	440	440

STANDARD EQUIPMENT:

DX: 2.3-liter 4-cylinder 135-horsepower engine, 5-speed manual or 4-speed automatic transmission, dual front airbags, emergency inside trunk release, variable-assist power steering, tilt steering wheel, cloth upholstery, front bucket seats, center console, cupholders, folding rear seat, AM/FM/cassette, digital clock, tachometer, intermittent wipers, rear defogger, remote fuel-door and decklid releases, visor mirrors, dual outside mirrors, theft-deterrent system, 195/70R14 tires, wheel covers.

VP adds: air conditioning, interior air filter, AM/FM/cassette/CD player, floormats.

LX adds to DX: 2.3-liter 4-cylinder VTEC 150-horsepower engine, cruise control, air conditioning, power mirrors, power windows, power door locks, AM/FM/CD player, illuminated visor mirrors, driver seat manual height adjustment, map lights, rear seat w/trunk pass-through (sedan), split folding rear seat (coupe), variable intermittent wipers, 195/65HR15 tires.

LX V6 adds: 3.0-liter V6 engine, 4-speed automatic transmission, traction control, front side-impact airbags, antilock 4-wheel disc brakes, 8-way power driver seat, floormats, 205/65VR15 tires.

EX adds to LX: front side-impact airbags, antilock 4-wheel disc brakes, power sunroof, remote keyless entry, driver seat power height adjustment, driver seat adjustable lumbar support, AM/FM/cassette w/in-dash 6-disc CD changer, automatic-off headlights, power decklid release, floormats, alloy wheels.

EX w/leather adds: leather upholstery, leather-wrapped steering wheel w/radio controls, 8-way power driver seat.

EX V6 adds: 3.0-liter V6-cylinder engine, 4-speed automatic transmission, traction control, automatic climate control, 4-way power passenger seat, universal garage door opener, 205/65VR15 tires.

Options are available as dealer-installed accessories.

HONDA CIVIC
Front-wheel-drive subcompact car

CG BEST BUY AUTO

Base price range: $12,760-$17,960. Built in USA, Canada and Japan. **Also consider:** Ford Focus, Mazda Protege, Toyota Corolla, Volkswagen Jetta/Golf

Specifications begin on page 535.

HONDA

Honda Civic EX 4-door sedan

FOR • Fuel economy • Visibility • Build quality • Ride **AGAINST** • Steering feel • Rear-seat entry/exit (coupes)

This perennial Best Buy begins its seventh design generation this fall with all-new 2001 models offering front side airbags as a first-time option, plus larger interiors and trunks. Sedan and coupe body styles return, but the Civic hatchback is gone. The lineup consists of DX, LX, and top-rung EX coupes and sedans. The LX coupe is new. There's also a high-mileage HX coupe and a low-emissions GX sedan that runs on compressed natural gas (CNG). Last year's sporty Si coupe is gone, but should return for Œ02.

Civic's previous 1.6-liter 4-cylinder engines give way to 1.7-liter derivatives with 9 more horsepower for DX, LX, and GX models and 2 more for the HX. EXs are unchanged in power but gain a little torque. All models have longer oil-change and tune-up intervals.

Manual transmission is standard. The extra-cost automatic is a conventional 4-speed unit except for the HX coupe, which again offers Honda's continuously variable transmission (CVT) with a belt-and-pulley system providing an infinite number of "gears."

Wheelbases are unchanged, but overall length is marginally shorter and all models are taller and have slightly larger cabins and trunks. The standard dual-stage airbags are designed to deploy with force appropriate to occupant size and weight. Front side airbags are a linewide option and include a sensor that deactivates the passenger bag if the occupant is not positioned for proper protection. Antilock brakes are standard on EX models but unavailable elsewhere. Pricing increases less than $100 over comparable 2000 models.

PERFORMANCE Civic has long been tops for small-car refinement and driving fun, and the '01s shape up as the best yet. Our experience has so far been limited to preview runs in four prototypes. All seemed to have much less tire noise on coarse pavement than previous Civics, plus similarly smooth engines, little wind noise, and a generally solid feel (Honda claims greater structural rigidity). However, uniformly spongy throttle action took the subjective edge off acceleration. The two sedans we tried, an automatic LX and manual EX, felt sluggish off the line, were

Prices are accurate at time of publication; subject to manufacturer's change.

CONSUMER GUIDE

HONDA

slow to rev (though the engines were likely not fully broken in), and suffered an un-Hondalike resonance above 4000 rpm. The manual EX and CVT HX coupes were quieter, but still not eager to rev.

On the plus side, Civic's manual transmission remains a model of slick, light precision and the conventional automatic is smooth and responsive. The CVT feels improved, providing adequate pickup without as much needless engine revving and consequent noise, though its operating characteristics take getting used to.

Regardless of model, handling remains nimble and assured, with only modest lean and good grip in hard cornering. The steering is a bit numb and overassisted for our taste: Better-quality tires would improve feel and feedback. Suspension tuning is on the soft side, so there's mild float over large humps and dips, but also enough suppleness to smother sharp bumps. Braking was good in our previews, but we're dismayed that only the top-line EXs offer ABS. We had no opportunity to measure fuel economy, but the '01s should be at least as thrifty as previous Civics, which generally averaged between 26 and 30 mpg in our tests of DX, LX, and EX models.

ACCOMMODATIONS With its added interior volume, Civic moves from the EPA's subcompact to its compact size category. A flat rear-seat floor area in both '01 body styles is a highlight of the new design. Though shoulder room is still lacking for three grownups in back, sedans have comfortable leg and head room for two 6-footers even with the front seats fully aft. Coupes offer less rear head room and much less rear leg room than sedans, though pre-teens shouldn't feel cramped. As usual, entry/exit is simple in sedans, aided by their newly elevated roofline, but a squeeze to the rear in coupes.

Civic drivers sit on slightly higher and wider seats in the '01s, which should aid long-distance comfort. Visibility is clear to all quarters, though the driver can't see the cars' rear corners when parking. The new dashboard puts most gauges and controls up high and handy. Honda's exemplary ergonomics keep everything simple, but one of our testers found the center dash vents tricky to adjust.

Trunks are of the low-lip, flat-floor sort and roomy for this exterior package. But old-fashioned sickle-shaped hinges steal space and could crunch your cargo, while the aperture won't swallow big boxes. Workmanship seemed fine on our test prototypes. However, interior decor is rather uninspired even on top-line EXs, the doors and trunklid close with a slight clang, and minor body drumming occurs on really rough surfaces.

VALUE The '01s represent an improved Civic in most ways and, with prices increasing only slightly, more car for the money. Gains in refinement, comfort, and space are obvious, though performance is not all it should be. Still, Honda's subcompact, bolstered by solid resale values and a fine reliability record, is a hands-down Best Buy.

Specifications begin on page 535.

HONDA

ENGINES

	ohc I4	ohc I4	ohc I4
Size, liters/cu. in.	1.7/102	1.7/102	1.7/102
Horsepower @ rpm	115 @ 6100	117 @ 6100	127 @ 6300
Torque (lb-ft) @ rpm	110 @ 4500	110 @ 4500	114 @ 4800
Availability	S[1]	S[2]	S[3]
EPA city/highway mpg			
5-speed OD manual	32/39	36/44	32/37
4-speed OD automatic	30/38		31/38

1. DX, LX. 2. HX. 3. EX.

PRICES

Honda Civic	Retail Price	Dealer Invoice
DX 2-door coupe, 5-speed	$12760	$11542
DX 2-door coupe, automatic	13560	12264
DX 2-door coupe w/side airbags, 5-speed	13010	11768
DX 2-door coupe w/side airbags, automatic	13810	12489
DX 4-door sedan, 5-speed	12960	11723
DX 4-door sedan, automatic	13760	12444
DX 4-door sedan w/side airbags, 5-speed	13210	11948
DX 4-door sedan w/side airbags, automatic	14010	12670
HX 2-door coupe, 5-speed	13560	12264
HX 2-door coupe, CVT	14560	13166
HX 2-door coupe w/side airbags, 5-speed	13810	12489
HX 2-door coupe w/side airbags, CVT	14810	13392
LX 2-door coupe, 5-speed	14810	13392
LX 2-door coupe, automatic	15610	14113
LX 2-door coupe w/side airbags, 5-speed	15060	13617
LX 2-door coupe w/side airbags, automatics	15860	14339
LX 4-door sedan, 5-speed	15010	13572
LX 4-door sedan, automatic	15810	14294
LX 4-door sedan w/side airbags, 5-speed	15260	13798
LX 4-door sedan w/side impact airbags, automatic	16060	14520
EX 2-door coupe, 5-speed	16410	14835
EX 2-door coupe, automatic	17210	15557
EX 2-door coupe w/side airbags, 5-speed	16660	15061
EX 2-door coupe w/side airbags, automatic	17460	15782
EX 4-door sedan, 5-speed	16910	15286
EX 4-door sedan, automatic	17710	16008
EX 4-door sedan w/side impact airbags, 5-speed	17160	15512
EX 4-door sedan w/side impact airbags, automatic	17960	16234
Destination charge	440	440

STANDARD EQUIPMENT:

DX: 1.7-liter 4-cylinder 115-horsepower engine, 5-speed manual or 4-speed

Prices are accurate at time of publication; subject to manufacturer's change.

HONDA

automatic transmission, dual front airbags, emergency inside trunk release, power steering, tilt steering wheel, cloth upholstery, front bucket seats, cupholders, split folding rear seat, AM/FM radio, digital clock, rear defogger, remote fuel-door and decklid releases, intermittent wipers, visor mirrors, auxiliary power outlet, theft-deterrent system, dual remote outside mirrors, 185/70R14 tires, wheel covers.

HX adds: 1.7-liter 4-cylinder VTEC 117-horsepower engine, 5-speed manual or Continuously Variable Transmission (CVT), cruise control, power mirrors, power door locks, AM/FM/cassette, tachometer, alloy wheels.

LX adds to DX: air conditioning, interior air filter, cruise control, power mirrors, power windows, power door locks, AM/FM/cassette, tachometer, map lights.

EX adds: 1.7-liter 4-cylinder VTEC 127-horsepower engine, antilock brakes, height-adjustable driver seat, center console, power sunroof, AM/FM/CD player, remote keyless entry, 185/65R15 tires.

Options are available as dealer-installed accessories.

HONDA CR-V

Honda CR-V SE

Front- or 4-wheel-drive compact sport-utility vehicle

Base price range: $18,750-$22,800. Built in Japan. **Also consider:** Ford Escape, Hyundai Santa Fe, Mazda Tribute, Subaru Forester

FOR • Maneuverability • Cargo room • Build quality • Exterior finish
AGAINST • Rear-seat entry/exit • Acceleration

Though facing more competition than ever, Honda's compact SUV enters 2001 with rear child-seat tethers the only notable change. CR-V comes as a base front-wheel-drive LX model and with 4WD in LX, EX, and top-line SE trim. The SE, added during 2000, comes with leather upholstery among several exclusive features.

The 4WD LX and EX offer manual or automatic transmission, other models automatic only. All use a 146-horsepower 4-cylinder engine.

Specifications begin on page 535.

HONDA

Honda's Real-Time 4WD normally drives the front wheels, directing power aft only in response to front wheelspin; it's not intended for hard off-road use, lacking locked-in 4WD and separate low-range gearing. Antilock brakes are standard on EX and SE, unavailable on LXs. CR-V is reportedly being redesigned for model-year 2002.

PERFORMANCE Though no powerhouse, CR-V's smallish engine is adequate for the vehicle's weight. We clocked a manual-shift 4WD at 9.3 seconds 0-60 mph, though that was with just a driver aboard, but that was also a few ticks better than we got with a 2WD Nissan Xterra V6/automatic. Unfortunately, CR-V's automatic saps enough low-rpm torque to hamper both standing-start acceleration and mid-range passing, especially in the heavier 4x4s. Note, too, that most rival compact SUVs offer the option of extra V6 muscle. Fuel economy is respectable all things considered, our manual 4WD averaging 22.5 mpg.

Being based on Honda's Civic subcompact, the CR-V is more pleasant to drive than than the truck-based Xterra, but not Hyundai's new car-based Santa Fe. Steering is a bit inert on-center, though precise enough. Modest body lean in tight turns allows the CR-V to be tossed around much like any small wagon, and its handy size is appreciated in urban traffic and tight parking spots. Ride is good except for annoying hop on rippled surfaces and thump on freeway expansion joints. Wind noise and tire thrum are reasonable, but engine boom around 4000 rpm—equal to about 70 mph—is wearing on long trips.

ACCOMMODATIONS The CR-V is spacious for its size, with ample head and leg room but not enough interior width for three adults in back. Step-in height is reasonable given the 8-inch ground clearance, but rear doorways are narrow for large folk. A standard tilt steering wheel and manual seat-height adjuster help tailor a sound basic driving position, but the wiper stalk gets in the way of the automatic's column shifter.

All models have a 50/50 split rear seat that double-folds to form a flat load floor; with the seat up, however, there's space behind for only about 10 grocery bags. The reclining rear seatback on EX and SE is a nice touch, and all models have a plastic cargo-floor panel that transforms into a picnic table with fold-down legs. Workmanship is solid and rattle-free, with fine detail finish and sturdy—though not fancy—interior decor.

VALUE CR-V is America's best-selling compact SUV, but newer-design competitors like Santa Fe and the Ford Excape/Mazda Tribute have an edge in performance, refinement, and driving ease, if not off-road ability. But the CR-V is a Honda, which is enough for many buyers, and still an appealing small SUV that's very easy to like.

ENGINES

	dohc I4
Size, liters/cu. in.	2.0/122
Horsepower @ rpm	146 @ 6200
Torque (lb-ft) @ rpm	133 @ 4500

Prices are accurate at time of publication; subject to manufacturer's change.

HONDA

	dohc I4
Availability	S
EPA city/highway mpg	
5-speed manual	22/25
4-speed OD automatic	22/25

PRICES

Honda CR-V	Retail Price	Dealer Invoice
LX 2WD 4-door wagon, automatic	$18750	$17138
LX 4WD 4-door wagon, 5-speed	19150	17502
LX 4WD 4-door wagon, automatic	19950	18232
EX 4WD 4-door wagon, 5-speed	20750	18962
EX 4WD 4-door wagon, automatic	21550	19692
SE 4WD 4-door wagon, automatic	22800	20833
Destination charge	440	440

STANDARD EQUIPMENT:

LX: 2.0-liter dohc 4-cylinder engine, 5-speed manual or 4-speed automatic transmission, dual front airbags, air conditioning, interior air filter, variable-assist power steering, tilt steering column, cruise control, cloth upholstery, front bucket seats w/driver-seat height adjustment, cupholders, split folding rear bench seat, power mirrors, power windows, power door locks, AM/FM/cassette, digital clock, tachometer, intermittent wipers, visor mirrors, map lights, remote fuel filler/hatch release, lift-out folding picnic table, auxiliary power outlets, rear defogger, intermittent rear wiper/washer, outside-mounted full-size spare tire, 205/70R15 tires. **4WD** models add: full-time all-wheel drive.

EX adds: full-time all-wheel drive, antilock brakes, AM/FM/CD player, remote keyless entry, reclining rear seat, floormats, alloy wheels.

SE adds: 4-speed automatic transmission, leather upholstery, leather-wrapped steering wheel, AM/FM/cassette/CD player, rear privacy glass.

Options are available as dealer-installed accessories.

HONDA INSIGHT

Front-wheel-drive subcompact car

Base price range: NA. Built in Japan. **Also consider:** Ford Focus ZX3, Toyota Celica, Toyota Prius

FOR • Fuel economy • Steering/handling **AGAINST** • Acceleration • Rear visibility • Road noise • Ride

Unchanged for its second year, this 2-seat hatchback coupe has a hybrid gas/electric powertrain, lightweight aluminum-intensive construc-

HONDA

Honda Insight

tion, and the EPA's top mileage ratings. Insight uses a small electric motor to assist a 3-cylinder gasoline engine in hard acceleration. When coasting or braking, the motor recharges a nickel-metal-hydride battery pack, so no external recharging is needed. A fuel-saving "idle-stop" feature shuts off the engine at stops. The only transmission is 5-speed manual, air conditioning the sole option. An optional continuously variable automatic transmission is due later in the model year. Toyota's somewhat larger Prius sedan has a different hybrid system that can use any combination of gas engine or electric motor depending on driving conditions.

EVALUATION Like a low-power Honda Civic, Insight is fun to drive but tiresome after a while. We clocked 0-60 mph at a yawning 11.3 seconds—marginal for passing and safe freeway merging—but averaged a remarkable 57.3 mpg overall and as high as 71 mpg in mostly city driving. Trouble is, that fuel thrift comes partly through low weight and minimal soundproofing, resulting in mediocre crosswind stability and relatively high noise levels. Ride suffers too: choppy and thumpy except on glassy pavement, aggravated by a short wheelbase that also makes the cockpit cozy, though far from cramped. Cockpit storage is meager, though, and luggage must be lifted onto a high deck that limits cargo to grocery-bag height. Plus points include decently comfortable seats, clear and convenient minor controls, acceptable all-round visibility, and attractive but not lavish interior trim. Insight is far more practical than any pure electric vehicle, but is compromised in too many ways by its maximum-mpg design. And at over $20,000 with air conditioning, it's not a great value when the same money buys a loaded top-line Civic.

ENGINES

	ohc I3/ electric
Size, liters/cu. in.	1.0/61
Horsepower @ rpm	73 @ 5700
Torque (lb-ft) @ rpm	91 @ 2000
Availability	S
EPA city/highway mpg	
5-speed OD manual	61/70

2001 prices unavailable at time of publication.

Prices are accurate at time of publication; subject to manufacturer's change.

HONDA

PRICES

2000 Honda Insight	Retail Price	Dealer Invoice
Base 2-door hatchback	$18880	$17439
Base w/air conditioning 2-door hatchback	20080	18546
Destination charge	440	440

STANDARD EQUIPMENT:

Base: 1.0-liter 3-cylinder gasoline engine/electric motor, 5-speed manual transmission, dual front airbags, antilock brakes, interior air filter, variable-assist power steering, front bucket seats, cupholders, power mirrors, power windows, power door locks, remote keyless entry, AM/FM/cassette, digital clock, trip computer, intermittent wipers, rear defogger, rear wiper/washer, map lights, driver-side visor mirror, auxiliary power outlet, remote fuel door release, 165/65R14 tires, alloy wheels.

Base w/air conditioning adds: air conditioning w/automatic climate control.

Options are available as dealer-installed accessories.

HONDA ODYSSEY

Honda Odyssey EX

Front-wheel-drive minivan

Base price range: $23,900-$28,400. Built in Canada. **Also consider:** Chrysler Town & Country, Dodge Grand Caravan, Ford Windstar, Toyota Sienna

FOR • Entry/exit • Passenger and cargo room   **AGAINST** • Navigation system controls • Rear visibility

Additional standard features highlight this strong-selling minivan for 2001. One of the largest, most powerful offerings in the class, Odyssey continues in LX and uplevel EX models with a 210-horsepower V6, automatic transmission, antilock brakes, and dual sliding rear side doors. The EX adds dual power sliding doors. Both models seat seven with front buckets, a pair of removable second-row buckets that can slide

Specifications begin on page 535.

HONDA

together to make a bench seat, and a third-row bench that folds away into the floor.

This year, both models add as standard an intermittent rear wiper, floormats, new front stereo speakers, and child-seat anchors/tethers in the second and third rows. LX also adds a manual driver-seat height adjuster and the traction control that was already standard on EX. The EX itself gets a security system integrated with its standard remote keyless locking.

No other minivan offers a factory-installed navigation system. Odyssey's is optional on the EX model and features an in-dash color touch-screen for displaying a map or driving directions; the latter can also be delivered as audio prompts. The system employs satellite positioning and DVD mapping, and is similar to that available in models from Honda's upscale Acura division.

PERFORMANCE Odyssey is tops for overall minivan dynamic competence. Handling is alert and confident, aided by good steering feel, and acceleration is spirited for the class. Our test EX clocked 0-60 mph in just over 9 seconds, though low and midrange passing response suffers by the transmission's slight reluctance to downshift. Fuel economy is as expected. We averaged 18.6 mpg with lots of highway miles, 16.8 mpg in hard city/freeway driving. Honda recommends premium fuel, but says the V6 will tolerate regular with a slight loss of power.

That engine is always smooth and quiet; only the Toyota Sienna beats Odyssey for minivan powertrain refinement. Wind noise is low, but tire rumble and even body drumming occur on coarse or broken pavement. Emergency stops are swift and stable, although one test model's rear brakes squealed in low-speed stops.

The one flaw is rather taut damping that allows some big bumps to jolt and produces marked wheel patter on expansion joints and pavement breaks. But that's with just a driver aboard. Add some weight and Odyssey absorbs most rough stuff with fine comfort and control.

ACCOMMODATIONS Odyssey's spacious cabin is easy to access thanks to a low step-in and large doorways. The EX's power-sliding side doors are convenient, if slower-acting than those in Ford and General Motors rivals.

Drivers have a commanding view ahead, but a headrest at every seating position leaves few clear rear sightlines. The driver's seat has too much backrest bolstering for some of our testers, too little for others, and seems too firm or too soft to suit all body types. Control placement is generally good, but the column-mount shifter tends to slide past Drive into third gear when moving from Park; it also blocks the driver's reach to some audio controls. And the power outlet is mounted at nearly floor level. The EX's available navigation system takes time to learn, but is a worthwhile feature in a family vehicle.

Second-row passengers have plenty of room, and we like the

HONDA

bench/bucket format. The third-row bench is a squeeze for three unless they're kids, and leg room there is tight unless the middle seats are moved well forward. The hideaway third seat is a very smart idea, but stowing it exposes two metal sidewall anchors that could damage cargo. The design also mandates a "space-saver" spare tire that stores in a covered well behind the front seats, which means a flat full-size tire must be carried in the passenger or cargo area.

All passengers get a reading light and air vent, and power rear vent windows are standard. Less likable were the interior rattles that afflicted one test Odyssey, including a persistent clicking from that versatile second-row seat.

VALUE It's not perfect, and it lacks some features against 2001 Chrysler and Dodge rivals. But Honda's minivan is a solid Best Buy: roomy, refined, reasonably priced, and a fine performer. No wonder it's been a virtual sell-out.

ENGINES

	ohc V6
Size, liters/cu. in.	3.5/212
Horsepower @ rpm	210 @ 5200
Torque (lb-ft) @ rpm	229 @ 4300
Availability	S

EPA city/highway mpg
4-speed OD automatic 18/25

PRICES

Honda Odyssey	Retail Price	Dealer Invoice
LX 4-door van	$23900	$21268
EX 4-door van	26400	23490
EX 4-door van w/navigation system	28400	25267
Destination charge	440	440

STANDARD EQUIPMENT:

auxiliary power outlet.

LX: 3.5-liter V6 engine, 4-speed automatic transmission, traction control, dual front airbags, antilock brakes, front and rear air conditioning, interior air filter, power steering, tilt steering wheel, cruise control, cloth upholstery, 7-passenger seating, front bucket seats, height-adjustable driver seat, center storage console, cupholders, two second-row bucket seats, third row 3-passenger folding bench seat, power mirrors, power windows, power door locks, AM/FM/cassette, digital clock, tachometer, variable intermittent wipers, rear defogger, rear intermittent wiper/washer, illuminated visor mirrors, map lights, remote fuel door release, floormats, theft-deterrent system, rear privacy glass, 215/65R16 tires, wheel covers, remote keyless entry.

Specifications begin on page 535.

HONDA

EX adds: 8-way power driver seat, dual power-sliding rear doors, automatic climate control, AM/FM/CD player, steering wheel radio controls, universal garage door opener, automatic-off headlights, alloy wheels.

Options are available as dealer-installed accessories.

HONDA PASSPORT

Honda Passport LX

Rear- or 4-wheel-drive midsize sport-utility vehicle; similar to Isuzu Rodeo

Base price range: NA. Built in USA. **Also consider:** Dodge Durango, Ford Explorer, Toyota 4Runner

FOR • Cargo room • Acceleration **AGAINST** • Road and wind noise • Fuel economy • Ride • Rear-seat entry/exit

Honda's larger SUV gets several added standard features for an otherwise carryover 2001. This clone of the Isuzu Rodeo offers LX, ritzier EX, and top-shelf EX-L models with rear- or 4-wheel drive. It has a left-hinged tailgate with separate-opening top-hinged glass. EX-L includes leather upholstery, 2-tone paint, color-matched fender flares, in-dash CD changer and, for '01, a 4-way power driver's seat.

All Passports use an Isuzu-designed V6. LXs come with manual transmission and offer an optional automatic that's standard on other models. Towing capacity is 4500 pounds. Passport's 4WD system isn't for dry pavement, but shifts between 2WD and 4-High via a dashboard button. It also has separate low-range gearing and, for '01, limited-slip rear differential. All Passports have antilock brakes, with rear discs now replacing drums on 4WDs. Rounding out '01 changes, all models get floormats, rear child-seat tethers, 8-speaker audio, and UV-reflecting front-door and tailgate glass as standard equipment.

Passport is built alongside Rodeo at the Subaru-Isuzu plant in Indiana, though the Isuzu version outsells it almost 3 to 1. Rodeo offers an electronically controlled shock-absorber system, but Passport's performance and accommodations otherwise mirror those of comparably

Prices are accurate at time of publication; subject to manufacturer's change.

CONSUMER GUIDE

HONDA

equipped Rodeos.

The Isuzu Rodeo report includes an evaluation of the Passport.

ENGINES

	dohc V6
Size, liters/cu. in.	3.2/193
Horsepower @ rpm	205 @ 5400
Torque (lb-ft) @ rpm	214 @ 3000
Availability	S

EPA city/highway mpg
5-speed OD manual	16/20
4-speed OD automatic	16/21[1]

1. 16/20 w4WD.

2001 prices unavailable at time of publication.

PRICES

2000 Honda Passport	Retail Price	Dealer Invoice
LX 2WD 4-door wagon, 5-speed	$22800	$20358
LX 2WD 4-door wagon, automatic	23950	21383
LX 4WD 4-door wagon, 5-speed	25950	23167
LX 4WD 4-door wagon, automatic	27100	24193
EX 2WD 4-door wagon, automatic	26600	23747
EX 4WD 4-door wagon, automatic	29050	25933
EX-L 2WD 4-door wagon, automatic	27700	24728
EX-L 4WD 4-door wagon, automatic	30150	26914
Destination charge	440	440

STANDARD EQUIPMENT:

LX: 3.2-liter dohc V6 engine, 5-speed manual or 4-speed automatic transmission, dual front airbags, antilock brakes, air conditioning, variable-assist power steering, tilt steering wheel, cruise control, cloth upholstery, front bucket seats, center console, cupholders, split folding rear seat, power mirrors, power windows, power door locks, AM/FM/cassette, digital clock, tachometer, map lights, visor mirrors, variable intermittent wipers, power tailgate release, cargo cover, rear defogger, intermittent rear wiper/washer, roof rack, skid plates, outside-mounted full-size spare tire, 225/75R16 tires. **4WD** models add: part-time 4-wheel drive, 2-speed transfer case, limited-slip differential, 4-wheel disc brakes, 245/70R16 tires, alloy wheels.

EX adds: 4-speed automatic transmission, power sunroof, leather-wrapped steering wheel, heated power mirrors, remote keyless entry, illuminated visor mirrors, theft-deterrent system, fog lights, rear privacy glass, under-floor full-size spare tire, 245/70R16 tires, alloy wheels. **4WD** models add: part-time 4-wheel drive, 2-speed transfer case, limited-slip differential, 4-wheel disc brakes.

EX-L adds: leather upholstery, in-dash 6-disc CD changer, two-tone paint,

Specifications begin on page 535.

HONDA

fender flares, bodyside moldings. **4WD** models add: part-time 4-wheel drive, 2-speed transfer case, limited-slip differential, 4-wheel disc brakes.

Options are available as dealer-installed accessories.

HONDA PRELUDE

Honda Prelude SH

Front-wheel-drive sports coupe
Base price range: NA. Built in Japan.   **Also consider:** Mitsubishi Eclipse, Toyota Celica, Volkswagen New Beetle

FOR • Acceleration • Steering/handling • Build quality • Exterior finish **AGAINST** • Road noise • Rear-seat room • Rear-seat entry/exit

Standard floormats, rear child-seat tethers, and emergency in-trunk opener are the main 2001 changes for this slow-selling sporty coupe. Prelude continues in base and SH models powered by a 2.2-liter 4-cylinder with dual overhead camshafts and Honda's VTEC variable-valve-timing system. Only the base model offers optional automatic transmission, which can be shifted manually. Both Preludes include antilock brakes. The SH features Honda's Active Torque Transfer System (ATTS) that counters the tendency of front-drive cars to plow, or understeer, in hard cornering.

EVALUATION Prelude's engine has more low-end torque than most like-size twincam fours, but still needs to rev high for best performance. We timed 0-60 mph at about 8 seconds with automatic, just over 7 with manual. Those test cars averaged around 23 mpg on the required premium fuel. We prefer the slick-shifting manual, but the automatic works well enough, though high-rpm downshifts can induce a jerky lunge. Handling is go-kart sharp. ATTS keeps the SH from running wide in hard turns, but is no substitute for proper traction control, which isn't available. Ride is reasonably supple for a sports coupe, though most bumps come through. Drivers sit low in a well-bolstered seat and enjoy good visibility and a convenient dashboard spoiled only by cheap-feeling slider-type climate controls. Rear-seat space is very limited, as is trunk room. The

Prices are accurate at time of publication; subject to manufacturer's change.

HONDA • HYUNDAI

pricey Prelude is in a sales free-fall, but we're still impressed enough by its polished road manners and sophisticated engineering to keep it on our sports-coupe Best Buy list.

ENGINES

	dohc I4
Size, liters/cu. in.	2.2/132
Horsepower @ rpm	200 @ 7000
Torque (lb-ft) @ rpm	156 @ 5250
Availability	S[1]
EPA city/highway mpg	
5-speed OD manual	22/27
4-speed OD automatic	21/26

1. 195 hp @ 6600 rpm with automatic transmission.

2001 prices unavailable at time of publication.

PRICES

2000 Honda Prelude	Retail Price	Dealer Invoice
Base 2-door coupe, 5-speed	$23500	$20982
Base 2-door coupe, automatic	24500	21874
SH 2-door coupe, 5-speed	26000	23212
Destination charge	440	440

STANDARD EQUIPMENT:

Base: 2.2-liter 4-cylinder dohc engine, 5-speed manual or 4-speed automatic transmission w/manual-shift capability, dual front airbags, antilock 4-wheel disc brakes, air conditioning, interior air filter, variable-assist power steering, leather-wrapped tilt steering wheel, cruise control, cloth upholstery, front bucket seats w/driver-seat height adjustment, folding rear seat, center console, cupholders, power mirrors, power windows, power door locks, remote keyless entry, power sunroof, AM/FM/CD player, digital clock, tachometer, visor mirrors, map lights, rear defogger, remote fuel-door and decklid release, variable intermittent wipers, auxiliary power outlet, theft-deterrent system, 205/50VR16 tires, alloy wheels.

SH adds: 5-speed manual transmission, Active Torque Transfer System, leather-wrapped shifter, rear spoiler.

Options are available as dealer-installed accessories.

HYUNDAI ACCENT
Front-wheel-drive subcompact car

Base price range: $8,999-$10,499. Built in South Korea. **Also consider:** Ford Focus, Honda Civic, Toyota Echo

FOR • Fuel economy • Visibility **AGAINST** • Noise • Acceleration • Ride • Rear-seat entry/exit (2-door)

Specifications begin on page 535.

HYUNDAI

Hyundai Accent 4-door sedan

Hyundai's lowest priced car gets a larger engine as its main change for 2001. Accent comes as the base L and uplevel GS 2-door hatchback and as a top-line GL 4-door sedan. The L stays with a single-cam 92-horsepower 1.5-liter 4-cylinder engine, but GS and GL adopt a twincam 105-hp 1.6-liter version. The L comes only with manual transmission; automatic is optional for other models. Accent is among the few mainstream passenger cars not offering antilock brakes, but the L now joins other models in having standard power brakes. This South Korean automaker offers one of the industry's longest warranty programs: 5-years/60,000-miles bumper-to-bumper, 10-years/100,000-miles powertrain.

PERFORMANCE We haven't yet tested the 1.6-liter models, but their larger engine is welcome because previous Accents had barely acceptable acceleration even with manual transmission; our test 2000 sedan did 0-60 mph in 11.2 seconds. If nothing else, the 1.6 will have an easier time with the optional automatic transmission, which does a nice job of resisting erratic shifting on hills. Even so, passing with either gearbox will still likely require noisy full-throttle operation. Economy remains a plus. Our 2000 manual GS hatchback averaged 29.6 mpg, the like-equipped sedan a commendable 30.4.

Small bumps are absorbed acceptably well, but like most subcompacts, Accent can be a rough-rider; large potholes are jolting, and the going is jiggly on washboard surfaces. Cornering grip is modest thanks to low-achiever tires, but Accent handles with predictable assurance. It also manages reasonably short simulated panic stops without ABS, this despite some rear-wheel lockup, marked but not alarming nosedive, and a little too much free play in the brake pedal. No car in this class is really quiet, but Hyundai keeps Accent's noise and vibration to class-competitive levels.

ACCOMMODATIONS Not much room to stretch here. Front seats are comfortable and supportive for everyday commuting, though longer trips still prove tiring. The back seat is too narrow for three adults, too flat for good support, and too cramped to give anyone over 6-feet tall much leg and head room. Rear entry/exit is tight too, even in the 4-door.

Prices are accurate at time of publication; subject to manufacturer's change.

HYUNDAI

Clearly marked controls are within easy reach. A higher rear deck than in many subcompacts pinches the view through the back window, but visibility is otherwise good. Trunk space is good for the exterior size, but limited by absolute standards. Our recent test models have been solid, generally well detailed, and had decent paint.

VALUE Accent is worth considering if you're shopping bargain-basement commuter cars, being affordable without seeming cheap and backed by that generous warranty. Remember, though, that Hyundai still lags most every other non-Korean brand in resale values.

ENGINES

	dohc I4	ohc I4
Size, liters/cu. in.	1.6/98	1.5/91
Horsepower @ rpm	105 @ 5800	92 @ 5500
Torque (lb-ft) @ rpm	106 @ 3000	97 @ 3000
Availability	S[1]	S[2]
EPA city/highway mpg		
5-speed OD manual	27/37	28/36
4-speed OD automatic	25/35	NA

1. GS, GL. 2. L.

PRICES

Hyundai Accent	Retail Price	Dealer Invoice
L 2-door hatchback, 5-speed	$8999	$8610
GS 2-door hatchback, 5-speed	9399	8797
GS 2-door hatchback, automatic	9999	9359
GL 4-door sedan, 5-speed	9899	9265
GL 4-door sedan, automatic	10499	9827
Destination charge	435	435

STANDARD EQUIPMENT:

L: 1.5-liter 4-cylinder engine, 5-speed manual transmission, dual front airbags, power steering, cloth upholstery, front bucket seats, center console, cupholders, folding rear seat, AM/FM/cassette, rear defogger, remote fuel-door release, variable intermittent wipers, auxiliary power outlet, dual remote outside mirrors, 175/70R13 tires, wheel covers.

GS and GL add: 1.6-liter dohc 4-cylinder engine, 5-speed manual or 4-speed automatic transmission, height-adjustable driver seat w/lumbar support, split folding rear seat, tachometer, digital clock, passenger-side visor mirror, cargo cover (GS), remote decklid release (GL), rear wiper/washer (GS).

OPTIONAL EQUIPMENT:
Major Packages

Option Pkg. 2	750	686
Air conditioning		

Specifications begin on page 535.

HYUNDAI

	Retail Price	Dealer Invoice
Option Pkg. 3, GS, GL	$1150	$1053

Air conditioning, power mirrors, power windows and door locks, AM/FM/CD player.

Powertrains
California and Northeast emissions	75	70

Required on cars purchased in Calif., N.H., N.Y., Mass.

Appearance and Miscellaneous
Rear spoiler	395	264

Post production options also available.

HYUNDAI ELANTRA

Hyundai Elantra 4-door sedan

Front-wheel-drive subcompact car

Base price range: $12,499-$13,299. Built in South Korea. **Also consider:** Dodge/Plymouth Neon, Ford Focus, Honda Civic, Mazda Protege, Nissan Sentra

FOR • Fuel economy • Maneuverability • Refinement • Ride/handling **AGAINST** • Acceleration (auto. trans.)

Hyundai's larger subcompact is redesigned for 2001 around carryover powertrains and a slightly larger package with new styling and standard front side airbags. Elantra loses its wagon and base sedan models this year, leaving a GLS sedan measuring 2.3 inches longer in wheelbase, 3.1 inches longer overall, and 1.2 inches taller than before. Curb weight is little changed. So are interior dimensions, though head and leg room are slightly reduced in back and slightly increased in front by Hyundai's measurements.

A 2.0-liter 4-cylinder remains the only engine, teamed with manual or optional automatic transmissions. Wheel diameter grows an inch to 15, shock absorbers are upgraded from hydraulic to gas-filled, and antilock

Prices are accurate at time of publication; subject to manufacturer's change.

HYUNDAI

4-wheel disc brakes are now a stand-alone option; the regular non-ABS system has rear drum brakes. Like all Hyundais, Elantra comes with one of the industry's longest warranties: 5-years/60,000-miles bumper-to-bumper, 10-years/100,000-miles powertrain.

Also standard are air conditioning, power windows/locks/mirrors, cassette stereo, tachometer, tilt steering wheel, manual 6-way driver's seat, front-seat lumbar support adjustment, intermittent wipers, and split-fold rear seat. Cruise control, 100-watt CD stereo, and sunroof are optional.

Coming next spring, as an early '02 entry, is a 4-door European-flavored GT hatchback with firmer suspension, standard rear disc brakes and alloy wheels, and somewhat different appearance. Hyundai will also restore Elantra's wagon body style for 2002.

PERFORMANCE We've not yet fully tested an '01 Elantra, but a preview drive in an automatic GLS sedan shows Hyundai has made great strides with this car. Acceleration is still nothing special by seat-of-the-pants, but the Elantra now has class-competitive refinement. Tire rumble and impact harshness are impressively low, wind noise modest. There's also far less engine ruckus than in previous models, an apparent result of exhaust system changes and new engine mounts. The automatic transmission seems better too: prompt and generally smooth-shifting. Equally laudable, fuel economy has improved by 2 mpg with either transmission in the EPA city test and by 2 mpg highway with automatic. Our previous test Elantras averaged 22-plus mpg despite hard driving.

Chassis tuning still favors ride comfort in the sedan, which is pretty good for a subcompact: firm yet supple enough to absorb most rough stuff with ease, let down only by minor freeway jiggle. We haven't yet tried the forthcoming GT hatchback, but it should ride almost as well as the GLS and have slightly sportier handling, though the sedan hustles along with assured front-drive stability and good body control. Braking was fine during our test session.

ACCOMMODATIONS Elantra's interior package now allows 6-footers to ride in tandem without the rear occupant's knees digging into the front seat. There's still not enough cabin width for three grownups in back, but head room is no problem, underseat foot space is adequate, and you can even indulge in a little leg stretching. Entry/exit is good too, even to the rear, despite fairly narrow threshholds.

Gauges, controls and driving position are typical Asian small car but nicely done, though the steering wheel may not tilt high enough for some and it takes much effort to turn the handwheel that adjusts rear cushion angle on the driver's seat. Overall visibility is fine in the sedan, slightly better in the sloped-tail hatchback. Both models have good small-items storage inside, plus roomy, flat-floor cargo holds, and the sedan trunk is roomy.

Elantra is one of the few subcompacts with standard front side

Specifications begin on page 535.

HYUNDAI

airbags, and it's also quite well finished inside and out. Switches move with a pleasing, almost Honda-like precision that belies the price, and major plastic moldings look like something from a more expensive car. Reliability hasn't been a problem with Hyundais we've tested, and our extended-use Elantra '99 wagon was virtually trouble-free over 25,000 miles.

VALUE Though still no Honda Civic or Toyota Corolla, Elantra is now very close to those segment leaders and, we think, a potential alternative to them for the first time. In addition to that long warranty, it enjoys a substantial price advantage comparably equipped, yet is no less pleasant or capable in most ways. A drawback is the low resale values associated with Korean vehicles, which partly cancels its initial cost advantage. But with products like this new Elantra and the Santa Fe SUV, Hyundai stands a chance of correcting that deficit too.

ENGINES

	dohc I4
Size, liters/cu. in.	2.0/121
Horsepower @ rpm	140 @ 6000
Torque (lb-ft) @ rpm	133 @ 4800
Availability	S

EPA city/highway mpg

5-speed OD manual	25/33
4-speed OD automatic	24/33

PRICES

Hyundai Elantra	Retail Price	Dealer Invoice
GLS 4-door sedan, 5-speed	$12499	$11504
GLS 4-door sedan, automatic	13299	12236
Destination charge	435	435

GT prices and equipment not available at time of publication.

STANDARD EQUIPMENT:

GLS: 2.0-liter dohc 4-cylinder engine, 5-speed manual or 4-speed automatic transmission, dual front airbags, front side-impact airbags, air conditioning, variable-assist power steering, tilt steering wheel, cloth upholstery, front bucket seats, manual 6-way adjustable driver seat w/lumbar adjustment, center console, cupholders, split folding rear seat, power mirrors, power windows, power door locks, AM/FM/cassette, digital clock, tachometer, visor mirrors, variable intermittent wipers, rear defogger, remote fuel-door and decklid release, map lights, 195/60HR15 tires, wheel covers.

OPTIONAL EQUIPMENT:
Major Packages

Option Pkg. 2	400	344

Cruise control, remote keyless entry, theft-deterrent system w/alarm.

Prices are accurate at time of publication; subject to manufacturer's change.

HYUNDAI

	Retail Price	Dealer Invoice
Option Pkg. 3	$750	$633
Option Pkg. 2 plus AM/FM/CD player.		
Option Pkg. 4	1400	1174
Option Pkg. 3 plus power sunroof.		
Option Pkg. 5	1150	1046
Option Pkg. 2 plus traction control, antilock 4-wheel disc brakes.		

Powertrains

California and Northeast emissions	100	94
Required on cars purchased in Calif., N.H., N.Y., Mass.		

Post production options also available.

HYUNDAI SANTA FE

Hyundai Santa Fe

Front- or 4-wheel-drive compact sport-utility vehicle

Base price range: $16,499-$21,999. Built in South Korea. **Also consider:** Ford Escape, Honda CR-V, Mazda Tribute, Subaru Forester

FOR • Instruments/controls • Entry/exit • Cargo room • Ride/handling **AGAINST** • Acceleration • Interior materials

The first SUV from South Korea's leading automaker is a 4-door 5-seat wagon loosely based on its compact Sonata sedan. Santa Fe is priced to compete with car-based compact SUVs like Honda's CR-V and the new Ford Escape/Mazda Tribute, but it's wider and heavier and has the largest cargo capacity in the class.

Santa Fe offers front-wheel drive or permanently engaged 4-wheel drive. The base GL model uses Sonata's 4-cylinder engine and manual transmission or an optional automatic with Hyundai's Shiftronic manual shift gate. Automatic is the only choice for the GL V6, the GLS, and the top-line LX, which use a version of Sonata's V6. Not intended for severe off-roading, Santa Fe's 4WD lacks low-range gearing. It normally splits power 60/40 front/rear, but can redirect it to the wheels with the greatest

Specifications begin on page 535.

HYUNDAI

traction. Optional on GLS and LX is traction control that works with both front drive and 4WD.

All Santa Fes have 16-inch alloy wheels, separate-opening tailgate window, air conditioning, power windows, CD stereo, 60/40 split-fold rear seat, and a sensor that deactivates the right-front airbag if a small child or no occupant is detected. Front side airbags are unavailable. Antilock brakes are optional and add rear discs instead of drums on 4-cylinder models; V6 models come with rear discs. Leather upholstery is exclusive to the LX.

PERFORMANCE Our Santa Fe exposure thus far has been in a 4WD V6, but it's clear this new SUV scores in most respects, especially for the price. Standing-start acceleration is no prize at 10.3 seconds in our 0-60 mph test, but midrange passing power is adequate, though this V6 doesn't seem to have much in reserve when faced with a sizable passenger or cargo load. We haven't tested a 4-cylinder model, but would guess it to have marginal overall performance. On the plus side, the automatic transmission is smooth and responsive, and the Shiftronic feature is helpful in some situations. We averaged a commendable 22.3 mpg despite gas-eating performance tests; that figure compares very favorably with the 18-20 mpg we got in similar driving with 4x4 V6 Ford Escapes.

Santa Fe's apparent sluggishness reflects hefty construction that helps impart a solid on-road feel, yet the ride/handling mix is decidedly more car than truck. Cornering is stable and not tippy-feeling, helped by responsive steering with fine feel and feedback. Ride is comfortably absorbent even on patchy pavement, though expansion joins and sharp ridges can jolt. Our ABS-equipped prototype made short work of our simulated emergency stops, but its sluggish, mushy initial pedal action didn't inspire confidence.

Refinement is generally good. The V6 groans at full throttle but is decently quiet otherwise, and wind rush and tire roar are both well controlled. The 4WD Santa Fe has a competitive 8.1 inches of ground clearance, and coped easily with a short off-road course we drove that included badly rutted trails and a couple of very steep grades.

ACCOMMODATIONS Santa Fe looks compact outside but is midsize spacious inside. In maximum cargo volume, for example, it beats Nissan's Xterra and even the Jeep Grand Cherokee. Santa Fe is also one of the wider compact SUVs, but three adults won't be uncrowded in back. However, rear leg room is pretty good even with the front seats pushed fully aft, all-around head room is ample, and lowish step-in height contributes to easy entry/exit despite fairly narrow rear door bottoms. The cargo deck isn't back-strain high, though length behind the rear seat is unexceptional. A full-size spare is standard; as on many other SUVs it mounts below the body in a wind-down cradle, making tire changes a potentially dirty task.

Prices are accurate at time of publication; subject to manufacturer's change.

CONSUMER GUIDE

HYUNDAI

Drivers enjoy good visibility from a typical SUV elevation. Most switches have unusual shapes but are logically arrayed. However, limited rearward seat travel may leave some larger drivers feeling crowded at the wheel, the inboard levers for front-seat lumbar adjustment are hemmed in by the center console and tough to grasp, and the outboard handwheels for driver-cushion tilt/height adjustment require tedious turning.

Most buyers will be happy with Santa Fe's generally solid feel. Still, dashboard plastic and the standard cloth upholstery are a tad utilitarian.

VALUE Santa Fe needs more V6 muscle and maybe better interior detailing, but it's still impressive with its pleasant carlike nature, high features-per-dollar factor, and generous 5-year/60,000-mile basic warranty with 10/100,000 powertrain coverage. Hyundai thinks Santa Fe will lift its image in America and thus improve the brand's resale values. It just might.

ENGINES

	dohc I4	dohc V6
Size, liters/cu. in.	2.4/143	2.7/165
Horsepower @ rpm	150 @ 5500	185 @ 6000
Torque (lb-ft) @ rpm	156 @ 3000	187 @ 4000
Availability	S[1]	S[2]

EPA city/highway mpg

5-speed OD manual	21/28	
4-speed OD automatic	20/27	19/26[3]

1. Base. 2. GLS, LX. 3. 19/23 w/4WD.

PRICES

Hyundai Santa Fe	Retail Price	Dealer Invoice
2WD GL 4-door wagon, 5-speed	$16499	$15443
2WD GL 4-door wagon, automatic	17299	16192
2WD GL V6 4-door wagon, automatic	18299	17128
4WD GL V6 4-door wagon, automatic	19799	18532
2WD GLS 4-door wagon, automatic	19299	18064
4WD GLS 4-door wagon, automatic	20799	19468
2WD LX 4-door wagon, automatic	20499	19187
4WD LX 4-door wagon, automatic	21999	20591
Destination charge	435	435

STANDARD EQUIPMENT:

GL: 2.4-liter dohc 4-cylinder engine, 5-speed manual or 4-speed automatic transmission w/manual-shift capability, dual front airbags, air conditioning, power steering, tilt steering wheel, cloth upholstery, front bucket seats, 8-way manually adjustable driver seat, center console, cupholders, split folding rear seat, power windows, AM/FM/CD player, digital clock, tachometer, variable intermittent wipers, visor mirrors, map lights, auxiliary power outlet, rear

HYUNDAI

defogger, remote fuel door release, roof rails, dual outside mirrors, full-size spare wheel, 225/70R16 tires, alloy wheels.

GL V6 adds: 2.7-liter dohc V6 engine, 4-speed automatic transmission w/manual-shift capability, 4-wheel disc brakes. **4WD** adds: full-time 4-wheel drive.

GLS adds: heated power mirrors, leather-wrapped steering wheel, cruise control, power door locks, remote keyless entry, AM/FM/cassette/CD player, rear wiper/washer, cargo cover, fog lights. **4WD** adds: full-time 4-wheel drive.

LX adds: limited-slip rear differential, leather upholstery. **4WD** adds: full-time 4-wheel drive.

OPTIONAL EQUIPMENT:
Major Packages

	Retail Price	Dealer Invoice
Option Pkg. 2, GL, GL V6	$995	$931
Cruise control, heated power mirrors, power door locks, remote keyless entry, rear wiper/washer, cargo cover and net, theft-deterrent system w/alarm, first aid kit, bodyside cladding.		
Option Pkg. 3, 4WD GL V6	1245	1165
Option Pkg. 2 plus limited-slip rear differential.		
Option Pkg. 4, GL	1545	1446
Option Pkg. 2 plus antilock 4-wheel disc brakes.		
Option Pkg. 5, GL V6	1490	1394
Option Pkg. 2 plus antilock brakes.		
Option Pkg. 10, GLS	250	234
Limited-slip rear differential.		
Option Pkg. 11, GLS	595	557
Traction control, antilock brakes.		
Option Pkg. 12, LX	295	261
Heated front seats, automatic day/night rearview mirror.		
Option Pkg. 13, LX	890	818
Option Pkg. 12 plus traction control, antilock brakes.		

HYUNDAI SONATA

Front-wheel-drive compact car

Base price range: $14,999-$18,824. Built in South Korea. **Also consider:** Chevrolet Malibu, Dodge Stratus, Mazda 626, Nissan Altima

FOR • Ride **AGAINST** • Automatic transmission performance • Rear-seat comfort

A new top-line model is the 2001 newsmaker for Sonata. This compact is no longer Hyundai's largest sedan, ceding that honor to the new midsize XG300. Sonata returns with a 4-cylinder base model and an uplevel V6 GLS. New this year is the GLS Leather, basically a GLS with

Prices are accurate at time of publication; subject to manufacturer's change.

HYUNDAI

Hyundai Sonata

equipped with a former option package; it upgrades the GLS with leather upholstery, power driver's seat, and premium CD/cassette stereo.

All Sonatas offer manual or optional automatic transmission. Optional on the GLS Leather and unavailable on other models are antilock 4-wheel disc brakes, which team with traction control. All models have standard front side airbags and a sensor system that deactivates both passenger airbags if a child or empty seat is detected. Hyundai's basic warranty is among the industry's longest: 5-years/60,000-miles bumper-to-bumper, 10/100,000 powertrain.

PERFORMANCE Sonata's suspension easily irons out most bumps, and rivals larger, costlier cars for overall comfort. The downside is that the soft damping doesn't control body motions too well. Dips and crests can induce moderate bounding, while lane changes at highway speeds are decidedly sloppy. (Higher-effort steering would help the latter. There's also more nosedive in emergency stops than there should be.)

The V6 provides decent punch—our automatic test car ran 0-60 mph in 9 seconds—but passing power is modest, and performance isn't helped by the transmission's reluctance to kick down; it also "hunts" too much between gears in hilly terrain. We haven't yet tested a 4-cylinder Sonata, but suspect it will need about 10 seconds 0-60 and be even more lackluster on the highway. At least V6 fuel economy is better than average: 22-23 mpg in our tests.

Sonata's 4-wheel disc brakes are easy to modulate for reasonably quick stops, though pedal action on one test GLS became mushy after a few hard stops. There's tire thrum on coarse pavement and some wind noise from the door mirrors, but this is otherwise a fairly quiet car.

ACCOMMODATIONS Sonata's driving position is comfortably high and adaptable enough, enhanced by supportive front seats and good visibility except to the rear corners. Front head and leg room are fine for a compact sedan. The aft cabin has adequate head clearance for 6-footers and good leg room, but a short, low seat cushion forces a knees-up posture. As usual with 4-doors this size, entry/exit is a bit tight aft, easy fore.

Specifications begin on page 535.

HYUNDAI

Most switches are easy to see and use, especially the large climate dials and buttons, but some of us find the audio controls too small for safe operation while driving. Front-door map pockets, a decently sized glovebox, and a useful center console provide ample interior storage. The roomy trunk has a low sill, and the standard folding rear seatbacks are useful, though the trunk pass-through isn't very big. Our recent test Sonatas have had a pleasingly solid feel, though interior materials were a cut below those of Japanese rivals.

VALUE Sonata's main deficits are tepid acceleration, unsporty handling, and the low resale values associated with South Korean brands. On the other hand, this well-equipped compact is priced like a premium subcompact and carries a reassuring warranty. Sonata isn't inspiring, but it offers more than fair value.

ENGINES

	dohc I4	dohc V6
Size, liters/cu. in.	2.4/146	2.5/152
Horsepower @ rpm	149 @ 5500	170 @ 6000
Torque (lb-ft) @ rpm	156 @ 3000	166 @ 4000
Availability	S[1]	S[2]
EPA city/highway mpg		
5-speed OD manual	22/30	20/28
4-speed OD automatic	21/28	20/27

1. Base. 2. GLS.

PRICES

Hyundai Sonata	Retail Price	Dealer Invoice
Base 4-door sedan, 5-speed	$14999	$13805
Base 4-door sedan, automatic	15499	14304
GLS 4-door sedan, 5-speed	16999	15116
GLS 4-door sedan, automatic	17499	15615
GLS Leather 4-door sedan, 5-speed	18324	16294
GLS Leather 4-door sedan, automatic	18824	16793
Destination charge	435	435

STANDARD EQUIPMENT:

Base: 2.4-liter dohc 4-cylinder engine, 5-speed manual or 4-speed automatic transmission, dual front airbags, front side-impact airbags, air conditioning, variable-assist power steering, tilt steering wheel, cruise control, cloth upholstery, front bucket seats w/driver seat lumbar adjustment, center console, cupholders, split folding rear seat, power mirrors, power windows, power door locks, AM/FM/cassette, digital clock, tachometer, driver-side visor mirror, illuminated passenger-side visor mirror, remote fuel-door and decklid releases, rear defogger, auxiliary power outlet, variable intermittent wipers, 205/60R15 tires, alloy wheels.

GLS adds: 2.5-liter dohc V6 engine, 4-wheel disc brakes, heated power mir-

Prices are accurate at time of publication; subject to manufacturer's change.

HYUNDAI

rors, AM/FM/CD player, power antenna, map lights.

GLS Leather adds: leather upholstery, power driver seat, AM/FM/cassette/CD player.

OPTIONAL EQUIPMENT:

	Retail Price	Dealer Invoice
Major Packages		
Option Pkg. 2, Base	$800	$679
Power sunroof, AM/FM/CD player.		
Option Pkg. 10, GLS	975	834
Power sunroof, AM/FM/cassette/CD player.		
Option Pkg. 12, LS Leather	550	458
Power sunroof.		
Option Pkg. 13, GLS Leather	1250	1113
Option Pkg. 12 plus antilock brakes, traction control.		
Powertrains		
California and Northeast emissions	100	100
Required on cars purchased in Calif., N.H., N.Y., Mass.		
Comfort and Convenience		
Remote keyless entry	180	120
Appearance and Miscellaneous		
Rear spoiler	440	295

Post production options also available.

HYUNDAI TIBURON

Hyundai Tiburon

Front-wheel-drive sports coupe

Base price range: $14,499-$15,299. Built in South Korea. **Also consider:** Ford Focus ZX3, Honda Civic coupe,

FOR • Steering/handling • Ride **AGAINST** • Passing power (automatic transmission) • Rear-seat room • Entry/exit

Hyundai's sporty coupe returns in a single hatchback model with

Specifications begin on page 535.

HYUNDAI

4-passenger capacity, 4-cylinder engine, manual and optional automatic transmissions, and 4-wheel disc brakes available with extra-cost antilock control. For 2001, Tiburon's base price is unchanged but includes a rear spoiler that had been a $345 option. Also new are metal-look interior trim and revised front bucket seats with manual 6-way driver's adjustment. New engine mounts and a stiffer dashboard are claimed to reduce noise, vibration, and harshness. Air conditioning, power windows/mirrors, and cruise control remain standard. Options again include sunroof, CD stereo, and leather seat inserts. Hyundai offers one of the industry's longest warranties: 5-years/60,000-miles bumper-to-bumper, 10-years/100,000-miles powertrain.

EVALUATION Handling is Tiburon's strong point, and its ride is taut without being brittle except on bombed-out pavement. Acceleration is fairly brisk with manual shift but weak with automatic. Typical of small coupes, this one has a low, snug driving position and a rear seat better suited to parcels than people. The visually interesting dashboard works well, but has some oddly shaped switches whose operation isn't intuitive. Distinctive styling and good road manners aside, Tiburon is not a standout sporty coupe choice unless a rock-bottom price is your top priority.

ENGINES

	dohc I4
Size, liters/cu. in.	2.0/122
Horsepower @ rpm	140 @ 6000
Torque (lb-ft) @ rpm	133 @ 4800
Availability	S

EPA city/highway mpg
5-speed OD manual	23/32
4-speed OD automatic	22/30

PRICES

Hyundai Tiburon	Retail Price	Dealer Invoice
Base 2-door hatchback, 5-speed	$14499	$13194
Base 2-door hatchback, automatic	15299	13926
Destination charge	435	435

STANDARD EQUIPMENT:

Base: 2.0-liter dohc 4-cylinder engine, 5-speed manual or 4-speed automatic transmission, dual front airbags, 4-wheel disc brakes, air conditioning, power steering, tilt steering wheel, cruise control, cloth upholstery, front bucket seats, center console, cupholders, split folding rear seat w/trunk pass-through, power mirrors, power windows, power door locks, AM/FM/cassette, digital clock, tachometer, rear defogger, remote hatch and fuel-door releases, passenger-side visor mirror, variable intermittent wipers, map lights, rear spoiler, 195/55HR15 tires, alloy wheels.

Prices are accurate at time of publication; subject to manufacturer's change.

HYUNDAI

OPTIONAL EQUIPMENT:
Major Packages

	Retail Price	Dealer Invoice
Option Pkg. 2	$1124	$935
Power sunroof, AM/FM/cassette/CD player.		
Option Pkg. 3	599	561
Leather upholstery, leather-wrapped steering wheel.		
Option Pkg. 4	1074	956
Leather upholstery, leather-wrapped steering wheel, AM/FM/cassette/CD player.		
Option Pkg. 5	1723	1496
Power sunroof, AM/FM/cassette/CD player, leather upholstery, leather-wrapped steering wheel.		
Option Pkg. 6	2222	1963
Option Pkg. 5 plus antilock brakes.		

Comfort and Convenience

Driver door remote keyless entry................................ — —
   Includes theft-deterrent system.

Post production options also available.

HYUNDAI XG300

Hyundai XG 300

Front-wheel-drive midsize car

Base price range: $23,499-$24,999. Built in South Korea. **Also consider:** Ford Taurus, Honda Accord, Toyota Camry

FOR • Ride/handling • Front-seat room/comfort **AGAINST** • Rear-seat entry/exit

South Korea's biggest automaker moves upscale for 2001 with a new U.S. flagship sedan. The XG300 is essentially a stretched version of Hyundai's Sonata, but is positioned above that compact sedan in size, price, and features. It uses a 192-horsepower 3.0-liter version of

Specifications begin on page 535.

HYUNDAI

Sonata's 2.5 V6. The only transmission is a 5-speed automatic with manual shift gate. Dimensionally, XG300 is similar to midsize favorites Honda Accord and Toyota Camry, and at $23,499, it costs about the same as those rivals' V6 sedans.

Standard equipment includes front side airbags, antilock 4-wheel disc brakes, automatic climate control, leather upholstery, CD audio, cruise control, and 15-inch alloy wheels. An extra $1500 buys an XG300 L with sunroof, heated front seats, CD/cassette stereo, woodgrain steering wheel, and auto-dimming inside mirror. An XGL version due in early calendar 2001 will add 16-inch alloy wheels to the other models' 15s.

The XG300 has been on sale for several years in South Korea and, more recently, in European markets. Like the Santa Fe compact SUV, its introduction here is part of Hyundai's effort to attract new customers while improving its stature, particularly in resale values, which remain lower than average for all Korean-brand vehicles.

PERFORMANCE This bigger new Hyundai offers a nice blend of ride comfort and predictable front-drive handling. Extreme bumps and ruts register sharply, but the XG soaks up most broken pavement with good body control and assured straightline stability. It's no BMW in the corners, but there's only moderate body lean in hard turns, and steering is responsive and properly weighted, though a trifle numb on-center. Our preview test didn't afford an opportunity to give the brakes a real workout, but they seem more than adequate for the available performance.

Indeed, "available performance" is a key term here. For a modern V6 midsize, the XG300's perceived acceleration isn't that strong, either off the line or when needed to merge or pass in the 40-55-mph range. The automatic transmission is generally smooth and alert, and its manual shift feature helps you get the most from the engine. But the car never feels very peppy, thanks to a relative lack of low-end torque for the vehicle's weight. Economy is also nothing special, at least by EPA estimates.

Refinement earns mixed marks. Tire noise is fairly high on coarse pavement, and noticeable wind rush in gusty conditions suggests the need for better sealing around the frameless door glass. The V6 is muted at cruise, but when pushed, it's a little louder than similar Honda and Toyota engines.

ACCOMMODATIONS Like its exterior, the XG300 is deliberately conservative inside, which isn't all bad. Front occupants have good room in all dimensions on supportive, well-shaped seats. In back, though, grownups have limited leg space with a front seat pushed very far aft, and there's not quite enough width for uncrowded three-abreast travel, though a small child might not complain about riding in the middle. Rear head room is only adequate for 6-footers, too. Entry/exit is okay but unexceptional.

Gauges and controls are easily deciphered and placed where drivers expect in a modern Asian midsize, though the dashboard looks a bit

Prices are accurate at time of publication; subject to manufacturer's change.

HYUNDAI

busy. Visibility is fine save invisible rear corners, as in most cars. A fairly large glovebox, bi-level center console bin, and door map pockets provide good small-items storage inside. The trunk is a roomy, flat-floor affair, but suffers the common malady of sickle-shaped trunklid hinges that steal space and could damage cargo.

Workmanship seems appropriate for the price, while interior materials, which include the standard leather upholstery, are a cut above the mid-$20,000 class.

VALUE The XG300 takes Hyundai into uncharted price and image territory in the U.S. Even Hyundai admits it doesn't know whether Americans are ready for a $24,000 Korean midsize, one reason only 15,000 XGs will be available for '01. That seems reasonable given the car's pleasant, if dated nature and lackluster acceleration. On the other hand, this bigger Hyundai sedan delivers plenty of features for the money, plus one of the best warranties around. Though no threat to Lexus, the XG300 is no dud either, just cautiously dull.

ENGINES

	dohc V6
Size, liters/cu. in.	3.0/181
Horsepower @ rpm	192 @ 6000
Torque (lb-ft) @ rpm	178 @ 4000
Availability	S

EPA city/highway mpg
5-speed OD automatic 19/27

PRICES

Hyundai XG300	Retail Price	Dealer Invoice
Base 4-door sedan	$23499	$21018
L 4-door sedan	24999	22359
Destination charge	435	435

STANDARD EQUIPMENT:

Base: 3.0-liter dohc V6 engine, 5-speed automatic transmission w/manual-shift capability, traction control, dual front airbags, front side-impact airbags, antilock 4-wheel disc brakes, air conditioning w/automatic climate control, variable-assist power steering, tilt leather-wrapped steering wheel, cruise control, leather upholstery, power front bucket seats, center console, cupholders, heated power mirrors, power windows, power door locks, remote keyless entry, AM/FM/CD player, digital clock, tachometer, trip computer, rear defogger, illuminated visor mirrors, map lights, auxiliary power outlets, variable intermittent wipers, remote fuel door/decklid release, 205/65VR15 tires, alloy wheels.

L adds: power sunroof, heated front seats, driver seat memory, woodgrain/leahter-wrapped steering wheel, AM/FM/cassette/CD player, automatic day/night rearview mirror.

Specifications begin on page 535.

HYUNDAI • INFINITI

OPTIONAL EQUIPMENT:
Major Packages

	Retail Price	Dealer Invoice
Option Pkg. 1, (credit)	($500)	($447)
Manual air conditioning. Deletes automatic climate control.		
Option Pkg. 2, Base	250	177
Manual air conditioning, power sunroof.		
Option Pkg. 4, L	NC	NC
Manual air conditioning, 8-disc CD changer.		
Option Pkg. 6, Base	750	624
Power sunroof.		
Option Pkg. 7, L	500	477
8-disc CD changer.		

INFINITI G20

Infiniti G20

Front-wheel-drive near-luxury car

Base price range: $21,395-$24,895. Built in Japan. **Also consider:** Acura TL, Audi A4, Volvo 40 series

FOR • Steering/handling • Instruments/controls • Visibility • Exterior finish **AGAINST** • Automatic transmission performance • Engine noise

Leather upholstery and a power sunroof are newly standard for 2001 on the G20 Touring version. G20 is the entry-level sedan from Nissan's upscale Infiniti division; '01 is likely the final model year for this slow-selling sedan. Luxury and sportier Touring (G20t) models are offered. Both have a 2.0-liter 4-cylinder engine, manual or optional automatic transmission, front side airbags, and antilock 4-wheel disc brakes. Touring adds a rear spoiler, foglights, limited-slip differential, and slightly lower-profile tires. The Leather and Sunroof package is optional on the Luxury model and standard this year on the Touring. Available for both is the Infiniti Communicator navigation and assistance system, which does not feature a dashboard display..

Prices are accurate at time of publication; subject to manufacturer's change.

INFINITI

EVALUATION G20 is peppy enough once up to speed. But weak low-speed torque means lackluster off-the-line acceleration for a 0-60-mph time of around 10 seconds with automatic transmission in our tests. At least fuel economy is better than the near-luxury norm; 22.8-26.9 mpg in our tests. Handling is agile and front-drive assured, ride surprisingly absorbent for a compact-sized car. Braking is swift and sure. Alas, the engine is vocal when worked hard and never sounds pleasant, while tire roar is noticed on coarse pavement. Seats are comfortable but things feels crowded with four adults aboard; most rivals offer more room. Gauges and controls are where you'd expect. Standard split folding rear seatbacks augment a useful trunk. Exterior fit and finish are excellent, but the cabin has a faint economy-car look and feel even with leather upholstery. Infiniti gives great customer service, but, this well-equipped 4-cylinder compact is not a great value versus a similarly equipped and priced midsize Honda Accord or Toyota Camry. However, Infiniti dealers should be willing to discount heavily on what is now a lame-duck model.

ENGINES

	dohc I4
Size, liters/cu. in.	2.0/122
Horsepower @ rpm	145 @ 6000
Torque (lb-ft) @ rpm	136 @ 4800
Availability	S

EPA city/highway mpg
4-speed OD automatic	23/30
5-speed OD automatic	24/31

PRICES

Infiniti G20	Retail Price	Dealer Invoice
Luxury 4-door sedan, 5-speed	$21395	$19522
Luxury 4-door sedan, automatic	22195	20252
Touring 4-door sedan, 5-speed	24095	21738
Touring 4-door sedan, automatic	24895	22460
Destination charge	525	525

STANDARD EQUIPMENT:

Luxury: 2.0-liter dohc 4-cylinder engine, 5-speed manual or 4-speed automatic transmission, dual front airbags, front side-impact airbags, antilock 4-wheel disc brakes, air conditioning, variable-assist power steering, tilt steering wheel, cruise control, cloth upholstery, front bucket seats, center console, cupholders, split folding rear seat, Bose AM/FM/cassette/CD player, power antenna, digital clock, tachometer, power mirrors, power windows, power door locks, remote keyless entry, rear defogger, remote fuel door

Specifications begin on page 535.

INFINITI

release, power decklid release, illuminated-visor mirrors, variable intermittent wipers, automatic-off headlights, floormats, theft-deterrent system, 195/65R15 tires, alloy wheels.

Touring adds: limited-slip differential, automatic climate control, interior air filter, leather upholstery, 4-way power driver seat, leather-wrapped steering wheel, power sunroof, universal garage door opener, fog lights, rear spoiler, 195/60R15 tires.

OPTIONAL EQUIPMENT:

	Retail Price	Dealer Invoice
Major Packages		
Leather and Sunroof Pkg., Luxury	$1500	$1132
Leather upholstery, 4-way power driver seat, leather-wrapped steering wheel, automatic climate control, power sunroof, universal garage door opener.		
Seat Pkg.	420	362
Heated front seats, heated mirrors. Luxury requires Leather and Sunroof Pkg.		
Comfort and Convenience		
Infiniti Communicator	1599	1378
Includes Global Positioning System, cellular telephone, roadside assistance, emergency services, four years service fees. Luxury requires Leather and Sunroof Pkg.		
6-disc CD changer	460	337

INFINITI I30

Infiniti I30

Front-wheel-drive near-luxury car

Base price range: $29,465–$31,540. Built in Japan. **Also consider:** Acura TL, BMW 3-Series, Lexus ES 300

FOR • Acceleration • Build quality • Instruments/controls • Quietness • Seat comfort • Handling/roadholding **AGAINST** • Rear visibility

After being redesigned for 2000 along with sibling Nissan Maxima,

Prices are accurate at time of publication; subject to manufacturer's change.

INFINITI

Infiniti's best-selling sedan adds a few new standard items for '01. I30 shares Maxima's underskin design, interior layout, and basic powertrain. But offers several features Maxima doesn't, plus more conservative styling, 5 more standard horsepower, and automatic transmission with no manual option.

This year, both the base I30 and sportier Touring (I30t) add steering-wheel audio controls, self-dimming inside mirror with compass, and an in-the-trunk emergency release as standard. Both models come with front head/chest side airbags, active front head restraints designed to minimize whiplash injury, antilock 4-wheel disc brakes, power sunroof, power rear-window sunshade (unavailable on Maxima), leather upholstery, automatic climate control, and remote keyless entry. The I30t has a firmer suspension with 17-inch wheels in place of 16s. Options include traction control packaged with heated front seats, and a cellphone/satellite navigation and assistance system.

PERFORMANCE While Maxima tilts toward exhuberant driving, I30 takes a softer, gentler approach befitting its near-luxury role. More sound insulation makes it quieter than Maxima, and isolation from road, wind, and engine noise is better than in an Acura TL, though not the class-leading Lexus ES 300. Ride is firm but absorbent, again putting I30 midway between the Acura and Lexus. Handling does too, with the Infiniti exhibiting fine grip and balance in hard cornering despite noticeable body lean. The I30t's tighter suspension and larger tires provide crisper handling than the base model enjoys, and with little penalty in ride.

Acceleration and throttle response are rewarding around town and on the freeway, and an easy match for the rival TL and ES. Without the optional traction control, though, the I30 can pull to one side in brisk getaways, which is rather annoying. Fuel economy is par for the class. We averaged 20.9 mpg on the recommended premium. Braking power and feel are very good, and the I30s we've tested felt solid and rattle-free over large, sharp bumps.

ACCOMMODATIONS I30 was styled in Japan, Maxima in the U.S., but they're obvious relatives despite sharing only window glass and roof. Interior differences are equally subtle. The Infiniti has modestly different seat padding that's comfortable and supportive. The dashboard is the Maxima's efficient design with slightly rearranged climate and audio controls whose size and markings are excellent. But the I30 also gets a foot-pedal parking brake that we find less convenient than Maxima's pull-up central lever.

Detailing aside, this is a roomy cabin, with plenty of adult-size leg space all-round. Rear head clearance is tight for those over 5-foot-10, but the seat cushion is nicely contoured. Conveniences include a height-adjustable center front armrest and a right-front cupholder positioned so a dashboard vent can cool (or heat) a beverage. The

Specifications begin on page 535.

INFINITI

rear sunshade is another thoughtful touch. Still, the interior isn't particularly imaginative, and the plastic wood trim looks low-budget. Standard split-fold rear seatbacks augment a large trunk, though the sickle-shaped trunklid hinges steal space. Our test cars were not equipped with the cell-phone/satellite communications system.

VALUE We're disappointed that heated seats and traction control aren't standard, but the I30 counts performance, comfort, solidity, and reasonable prices among its many assets. Add in Infiniti's sterling reputation for customer satisfaction and you have a sound near-luxury buy.

ENGINES

	dohc V6
Size, liters/cu. in.	3.0/181
Horsepower @ rpm	227 @ 6400
Torque (lb-ft) @ rpm	217 @ 4000
Availability	S

EPA city/highway mpg	
4-speed OD automatic	20/28

PRICES

Infiniti I30	Retail Price	Dealer Invoice
I30 4-door sedan	$29465	$26935
I30t 4-door sedan	31540	28079
Destination charge	525	525

STANDARD EQUIPMENT:

I30: 3.0-liter dohc V6 engine, 4-speed automatic transmission, dual front airbags, front side-impact airbags, front seat active head restraints, antilock 4-wheel disc brakes, emergency inside trunk release, air conditioning w/automatic climate control, interior air filter, variable-assist power steering, tilt leather-wrapped steering wheel, cruise control, leather upholstery, front bucket seats, 8-way power driver seat w/manual lumbar adjustment and memory, 4-way power passenger seat, center console, cupholders, split folding rear seat, power mirrors, power windows, power door locks, remote keyless entry, power sunroof, Bose AM/FM/cassette/CD player, steering wheel radio controls, analog clock, tachometer, rear defogger, automatic day/night rearview mirror, outside temperature indicator, compass, variable intermittent wipers, illuminated visor mirrors, universal garage door opener, auxiliary power outlet, power rear sunshade, automatic headlights, remote fuel door and decklid release, theft-deterrent system, fog lights, cornering lights, 215/55R16 tires, alloy wheels.

I30t adds: limited-slip differential, Xenon headlights, sport suspension, 225/50R17 tires.

Prices are accurate at time of publication; subject to manufacturer's change.

INFINITI

OPTIONAL EQUIPMENT:
Major Packages

	Retail Price	Dealer Invoice
Navigation System and Audio Pkg.	$2400	$2166
Navigation system, 6-disc CD changer.		
Heated Seats Pkg.	420	374
Heated front seats, heated mirrors, heavy-duty battery.		
Touring Sport Pkg., I30t	1000	887
Rear spoiler, side sill spoilers.		
Sunroof and Sunshade Pkg. delete, (credit)	(1000)	(868)
Deletes power sunroof, power rear sunshade.		

Powertrains

Traction control	300	268
Requires Heated Seats Pkg. NA w/Sunroof and Sunshade delete.		

Comfort and Convenience

Infiniti Communicator	1599	1378
Includes Global Positioning System, cellular telephone, roadside assistance, emergency services, four years service. NA w/Sunroof and Sunshade delete.		
6-disc CD changer	460	336

Appearance and Miscellaneous

Xenon headlights, I30	500	416
NA w/Sunroof and Sunshade delete.		
Side sills, I30t	500	445

INFINITI QX4

Infiniti QX4

Rear- or 4-wheel-drive midsize sport-utility vehicle; similar to Nissan Pathfinder

Base price range: $34,150-$35,550. Built in Japan. **Also consider:** Lexus RX 300, Mercedes-Benz M-Class, Toyota 4Runner

FOR • Cargo room • Build quality • Acceleration **AGAINST** • Rear-

Specifications begin on page 535.

INFINITI

seat comfort • Entry/exit

Still an upscale Pathfinder from Nissan's luxury division, the QX4 was updated for a spring 2000 debut as an early '01 model (as was Pathfinder). Heading the changes are a new twincam 3.5-liter V6 with 240 horsepower versus the previous 170-hp single-cam 3.3, plus revised exterior styling, a new dashboard, and, for the first time, a 2-wheel-drive version. Dimensions don't change, but the '01 sports subtly rounded lines, a new grille and bumpers, and brighter high-intensity-discharge headlamps instead of halogens. Interior changes include standard front side airbags and a new instrument panel with electro-fluorescent gauges and analog clock. A leather/simulated-wood steering wheel, heated rear seats, and navigation system are among several new options.

Automatic transmission and antilock brakes remain standard. QX4's All-Mode 4WD can be used on dry pavement and has separate low-range gearing. The new 2WD version is intended as a sales-boosting lower-cost alternative. QX4 performance and accommodations mirror those of the Pathfinder.

The Nissan Pathfinder report includes an evaluation of the QX4.

ENGINES

	dohc V6
Size, liters/cu. in.	3.5/214
Horsepower @ rpm	240 @ 6000
Torque (lb-ft) @ rpm	265 @ 3200
Availability	S

EPA city/highway mpg
4-speed OD automatic 15/19

PRICES

Infiniti QX4	Retail Price	Dealer Invoice
Base 2WD 4-door wagon	$34150	$30987
Base 4WD 4-door wagon	35550	32253
Destination charge	525	525

STANDARD EQUIPMENT:

Base: 3.5-liter dohc V6 engine, 4-speed automatic transmission, dual front airbags, front side-impact airbags, antilock brakes, air conditioning w/automatic climate control, interior air filter, variable-assist power steering, tilt leather-wrapped steering wheel, cruise control, leather upholstery, power front bucket seats, center console, cupholders, reclining split-folding rear seat, wood interior trim, heated power mirrors, power windows, power door locks, remote keyless entry, tachometer, Bose AM/FM/cassette/CD player, power antenna, analog clock, overhead console, outside temperature indicator, map lights, variable intermittent wipers, automatic-off headlights, auxiliary power outlets, universal garage door opener, illuminated visor mirrors, remote fuel door and hatch release, cargo cover, rear defogger, variable

Prices are accurate at time of publication; subject to manufacturer's change.

INFINITI • ISUZU

intermittent rear wiper/washer, floormats, theft-deterrent system, Xenon headlights, fog lights, step rails, roof rack, rear privacy glass, skid plates, full-size spare tire, 245/70SR16 tires, alloy wheels. **4WD** model adds: full-time 4-wheel drive.

OPTIONAL EQUIPMENT:

	Retail Price	Dealer Invoice
Major Packages		
Premium Pkg.	$600	$450
Memory driver seat, leather/wood-grain steering wheel, 245/65SR17 tires.		
Sport Pkg., 4WD	900	813
Heated front and rear seats, limited-slip rear differential. Requires Premium Pkg.		
Towing Pkg.	400	307
Comfort and Convenience		
Navigation system	2000	1805
Requires Premium Pkg., sunroof.		
Infiniti Communicator	1599	1378
Includes 4-year service fee. Requires Premium Pkg., sunroof. 2WD requires heated seats. 4WD requires Sport Pkg.		
Power sunroof	950	858
Requires Premium Pkg.		
Heated front and rear seats, 2WD	600	541
Requires Premium Pkg.		

Post production options also available.

ISUZU RODEO

Isuzu Rodeo

Rear- or 4-wheel-drive midsize sport-utility vehicle
Base price range: NA. Built in USA. **Also consider:** Dodge Durango, Ford Explorer, Toyota 4Runner

---

FOR • Cargo room • Acceleration (V6) **AGAINST** • Wind noise • Fuel economy • Ride • Rear-seat entry/exit

Specifications begin on page 535.

ISUZU

Addition of an Anniversary Edition and a revised Ironman Package are main changes to Isuzu's midsize SUV for 2001. Rodeo offers S, LS, and LSE trim levels, rear- or 4-wheel-drive, and standard antilock brakes.

A V6 with manual or automatic transmission is standard on all but the base 2WD Rodeo S model, which uses a 4-cylinder and manual transmission. The LSE comes only with automatic transmission. Rodeo's 4WD is not for use on dry pavement but has 4-wheel-low gearing. Maximum towing capacity is 4500 pounds. Rodeos have a side-hinged tailgate with separate flip-up rear window. The 4WD models have an outside-mount spare tire that is a no-charge alternative to internal storage on 2WD versions.

Celebrating the 85th anniversary of Isuzu Motors Limited, the Anniversary Edition is based on LS trim and adds 18-inch chrome wheels, chrome tube side steps, a power sunroof, roof spoiler, beige leather upholstery, and the choice of 2-tone exterior paint. Also optional for the LS, the Ironman Package (named for an Isuzu-sponsored triathlon competition) features special graphics and 2-tone paint, and this year adds 18-inch alloy wheels painted gray, tube side steps, a subwoofer, roof spoiler, and other features.

LSE, Anniversary, and Ironman Rodeos come with Isuzu's Intelligent Suspension Control. This computer-controlled system automatically varies shock-absorber firmness in an effort to optimize ride comfort.

Honda sells a retrimmed Rodeo as the Passport. Both are built by Isuzu in Indiana, but Passport doesn't offer the adjustable shock absorbers.

PERFORMANCE Without the auto-adjusting shocks, both Rodeo and Passport ride poorly, feeling choppy on rough pavement and harsh over big bumps and potholes. Rodeos with Intelligent Suspension Control hardly feel more compliant, and still showed plenty of jiggle on rippled surfaces. Handling, by contrast, is fairly agile for a midsize SUV, though there's still plenty of body lean and early tire squeal in hard cornering, another area where the Isuzu's adjustable suspension doesn't make much difference.

V6 models provide decently strong takeoffs—we timed our LSE at 9.3 seconds to 60 mph—and have good passing power. The automatic transmission is generally smooth and alert, though it does dither a bit in full-throttle kickdown shifts from mid-range speeds. Fuel economy is par for a 6-cylinder midsize SUV. A test 4WD LS averaged 15.8 mpg, while our near-new LSE managed only 14.5. The Isuzu-engineered 4WD is pushbutton-easy to operate, but most rivals offer systems that don't need to be disengaged on dry pavement.

Prices are accurate at time of publication; subject to manufacturer's change.

ISUZU

ACCOMMODATIONS Rodeo and Passport have OK passenger room apart from limited rear toe space. The driver's seat isn't height-adjustable and doesn't have enough rear travel for those with longer legs, but the seat itself offers comfortably firm support. The dashboard looks a bit dated but works well enough, though the factory audio system suffers a few cryptic controls. Interiors look durable but fairly plain, even the LSE with its standard leather upholstery and gratuitous mock-wood dash and door trim.

Step-in height is a little lower than the midsize-SUV norm, but narrow rear-door openings hinder back-seat entry/exit. Forward visibility is fine, but the outside spare tire interferes with rear vision. The side-opening tailgate demands cumbersome two-handed operation: To open it, you must first raise the window; to close it, you must reach into the hinge area and release a lever to free the door.

VALUE V6 Rodeos and Passports emphasize the sport in sport-utility, but there's no outstanding feature that sets either above the competition. Dated 4WD, poor ride quality, and prices that are no bargain detract from their value.

ENGINES

	dohc I4	dohc V6
Size, liters/cu. in.	2.2/134	3.2/193
Horsepower @ rpm	129 @ 5200	205 @ 5400
Torque (lb-ft) @ rpm	144 @ 4000	214 @ 3000
Availability	S[1]	S[2]
EPA city/highway mpg		
5-speed OD manual	21/24	16/20
4-speed OD automatic		18/21[3]

1. 2WD S. 2. S V6, LS, LSE. 3. 18/20 w/4WD.

2001 prices unavailable at time of publication.

PRICES

2000 Isuzu Rodeo	Retail Price	Dealer Invoice
S 4-cylinder 2WD 4-door wagon, 5-speed	$18080	$17176
S V6 2WD 4-door wagon, 5-speed	20985	19036
S V6 2WD 4-door wagon, automatic	21985	20226
S V6 4WD 4-door wagon, 5-speed	23440	21565
S V6 4WD 4-door wagon, automatic	24440	22485
LS 2WD 4-door wagon, 5-speed	23435	21325
LS 2WD 4-door wagon, automatic	24435	22235
LS 4WD 4-door wagon, 5-speed	26120	23769
LS 4WD 4-door wagon, automatic	27120	24678
LSE 2WD 4-door wagon, automatic	28790	26055
LSE 4WD 4-door wagon, automatic	31265	28295

Specifications begin on page 535.

ISUZU

	Retail Price	Dealer Invoice
Destination charge	$495	$495

STANDARD EQUIPMENT:

S: 2.2-liter dohc 4-cylinder engine, 5-speed manual transmission, dual front airbags, antilock brakes, variable-assist power steering, cloth upholstery, front bucket seats, center console, cupholders, split folding rear seat, 4-speaker AM/FM/cassette, digital clock, tachometer, intermittent wipers, visor mirrors, rear defogger, auxiliary power outlet, map lights, dual outside mirrors, skid plates, full-size spare tire, 225/75R16 tires.

S V6 adds: 3.2-liter dohc V6 engine, 5-speed manual or 4-speed automatic transmission, tilt steering wheel, cruise control, 245/70R16 tires. **4WD** adds: part-time 4-wheel drive, 2-speed transfer case, 4-wheel disc brakes, transfer-case skid plate, outside-mounted spare tire.

LS adds: air conditioning, power mirrors, power windows, power door locks, remote keyless entry, 6-speaker sound system, variable intermittent wipers, intermittent rear wiper/washer, cargo cover, floormats, theft-deterrent system, roof rack. **4WD** adds: part-time 4-wheel drive, 2-speed transfer case, limited-slip differential, 4-wheel disc brakes, transfer-case skid plate, outside-mounted spare tire.

LSE adds: 4-speed automatic transmission, leather upholstery, leather-wrapped steering wheel, AM/FM/cassette w/6-disc CD changer, power sunroof, fog lights, cross rails for roof rack, rear privacy glass, adjustable shock absorbers, alloy wheels. **4WD** adds: part-time 4-wheel drive, 2-speed transfer case, limited-slip differential, 4-wheel disc brakes, transfer-case skid plate, outside-mounted spare tire.

OPTIONAL EQUIPMENT:

Major Packages

Preferred Equipment Pkg. 1, S, S V6	1145	—
Manufacturer's discount price	1010	899

Air conditioning, roof rack. Requires rear wiper/washer.

Ironman Pkg., LS	1052	936

Adjustable shock absorbers, unique floormats, cross rails for roof rack, grey bumpers and fender flares, grey bodyside moldings, Ironman Triathalon badging and graphics, unique spare tire cover.

Gold Pkg., LSE	400	316

Gold badging, special alloy wheels w/gold accents, gold lettered spare tire cover. Requires outside-mounted spare tire.

Power sunroof, LS 2WD automatic, LS 4WD	700	623
6-disc CD changer, LS	353	314

Appearance and Miscellaneous

Brush guard	298	236

Prices are accurate at time of publication; subject to manufacturer's change.

ISUZU

	Retail Price	Dealer Invoice
Running boards	$360	$283
Side steps	355	281

Special Purpose, Wheels and Tires
Outside-mounted spare tire, 2WD	NC	NC
Trailer hitch	253	200
Alloy wheels, LS	400	356

Post production options also available.

ISUZU RODEO SPORT

Isuzu Rodeo Sport wagon

Rear- or 4-wheel-drive compact sport-utility vehicle; similar to Isuzu Rodeo

Base price range: $15,715-$20,360. Built in USA. **Also consider:** Ford Escape, Honda CR-V, Mazda Tribute

FOR • Cargo room • Acceleration (V6) **AGAINST** • Acceleration (4-cyl) • Ride • Noise • Entry/exit

Isuzu changes the name of its 2-door SUV for 2001, from Amigo to Rodeo Sport. The new badge is intended to position this convertible and hardtop as sportier, off-road-oriented versions of the larger, more popular 4-door Isuzu Rodeo. The Sport is essentially a shortened version of the Rodeo. They share engines, but the Sport offers two body styles: a hardtop and a semi-convertible with a folding soft top over the back seat. The convertible has a pop-up sunroof over the front seat and the hardtop has a pop-up sunroof over the rear seat. Both come with a 4-cylinder engine in rear-wheel drive, or with a V6 and a choice of rear- or 4-wheel drive. Both engines come with manual or automatic transmission for 2001; the 4-cylinder had been manual only. The 4WD system isn't for use on dry pavement, but has a pushbutton transfer case and low-range gearing. Antilock brakes are standard. Available on Rodeo Sports ordered with the Preferred Equipment option is the Iron-

Specifications begin on page 535.

ISUZU

man appearance package, named for Isuzu's sponsorship of the Ironman triathlon competition. It includes Isuzu's Intelligent Suspension Control, which uses a dashboard switch to choose "sport" or "comfort" shock-absorber damping. For '01, the Preferred Equipment package adds a rear cargo tray, V6 models gain a 2-speed variable intermittent windshield wipers, and the available alloy wheels mimic those on the Rodeo.

EVALUATION Rodeo Sport is far from perfect, but it is more substantial than some other small SUVs, and more refined than a Jeep Wrangler. Our test V6 5-speed 4x4 convertible ran 0-60 mph in 8.5 seconds—impressive for a compact SUV. It averaged 17.3 mpg. An automatic V6 averaged 16.9. With the standard suspension, small bumps are easily absorbed, but Rodeo Sport bounces and bounds over wavy pavement, potholes, and frost heaves. Ironman models with the Intelligent Suspension Control have improved ride control with little additional harshness. Passenger room in front is adequate, but it's a high step-up into the interior and the rear seat is tough to get to and not very spacious. Working the vinyl soft-top is as much a chore as on any rival.

ENGINES

	dohc I4	dohc V6
Size, liters/cu. in.	2.2/134	3.2/193
Horsepower @ rpm	130 @ 5200	205 @ 5400
Torque (lb-ft) @ rpm	144 @ 4000	214 @ 3000
Availability	S	O
EPA city/highway mpg		
5-speed OD manual	21/24[1]	18/21
4-speed OD automatic		17/21

1. 20/23 w/4WD.

PRICES

Isuzu Rodeo Sport

	Retail Price	Dealer Invoice
2WD S 4-cylinder 2-door convertible, 5-speed	$15715	$15241
2WD S 4-cylinder 2-door convertible, automatic	16835	16302
2WD S 4-cylinder 2-door wagon, 5-speed	15440	14974
2WD S 4-cylinder 2-door wagon, automatic	16560	16035
2WD S V6 2-door convertible, automatic	18410	17160
2WD S V6 2-door wagon, automatic	18135	16904
4WD S V6 2-door convertible, 5-speed	19750	18405
4WD S V6 2-door convertible, automatic	20750	19337
4WD S V6 2-door wagon, automatic	20360	18974
Destination charge	520	520

STANDARD EQUIPMENT:

2WD S 4-cylinder convertible: 2.2-liter dohc 4-cylinder engine, 5-speed manual or 4-speed automatic transmission, dual front airbags, antilock brakes, variable-assist power steering, cloth uphol-

Prices are accurate at time of publication; subject to manufacturer's change.

ISUZU

stery, front bucket seats, center console, cupholders, folding rear seat, AM/FM/cassette, digital clock, tachometer, manual front sunroof, auxiliary power outlets, driver-side visor mirror, intermittent wipers, map lights, rear folding top, dual outside mirrors, skid plates, outside-mounted full-size spare tire, 7-wire trailer harness, front and rear tow hooks, 245/70R16 tires.

S 4-cylinder wagon adds: manual rear sunroof, rear defogger, rear intermittent wiper. *Deletes:* rear folding top.

S V6 adds to S 4-cylinder convertible and S 4-cylinder wagon: 3.2-liter dohc V6 engine, tilt steering wheel, cruise control, variable intermittent wipers.
4WD models add: part-time 4-wheel drive, 2-speed transfer case, limited-slip differential, 4-wheel disc brakes.

OPTIONAL EQUIPMENT:

	Retail Price	Dealer Invoice
Major Packages		
Preferred Equipment Pkg. 2, V6	$2795	$2140
Manufacturer's discount price	2195	1713

Air conditioning, heated power mirrors, power windows and door locks, remote keyless entry, upgraded sound system, in-dash 6-disc CD changer, center armrest, courtesy lights, cargo tray, cargo net, floormats, dual note horns, theft-deterrent system.

Ironman Pkg., V6	1520	1301
Manufacturer's discount price	1215	1039

Adjustable shock absorbers, unique floormats, Ironman Triathlon graphics, titan gray exterior trim, fender flares, side steps, hood protector, bodyside moldings. Requires Preferred Equipment Pkg. 2. NA 2WD convewrtible.

Comfort and Convenience
Air conditioning, *4-cylinder, 2WD V6 wagon*	950	845

Appearance and Miscellaneous
Fog lights	70	56
NA 2WD wagon 5-speed.		
Fender flares	225	200
NA 2WD wagon 5-speed.		

Special Purpose, Wheels and Tires
Alloy wheels	400	356
NA 2WD wagon 5-speed.		

ISUZU TROOPER
Rear- or 4-wheel-drive full-size sport-utility vehicle

Base price range: $27,170-$34,813. Built in Japan. **Also consider:** Chevrolet Tahoe/GMC Yukon, Ford Expedition, Toyota Land Cruiser

Specifications begin on page 535.

ISUZU

Isuzu Trooper

FOR • Passenger and cargo room **AGAINST** • Fuel economy • Ride

Addition of an Anniversary Edition package highlights Isuzu's SUV flagship for 2001. Trooper is a 4-door wagon with swing-out rear doors split 70/30. S, LS, and Limited models are offered, all with rear- or 4-wheel drive. The only engine is a 3.5-liter V6 linked to manual or automatic transmission. The 4WD system used with manual-transmission is not for use on dry pavement. Used with automatic is Isuzu's Torque On Demand 4WD, which does not require that 4WD be disengaged on dry pavement. Antilock 4 wheel disc brakes are standard. Maximum towing capacity is 5000 pounds. Marking Isuzu Motors Limited's 85th anniversary, the Anniversary Package is available on LS Troopers and includes exclusive pearl white paint, white-accented 12-spoke alloy wheels, chrome side steps, leather upholstery, and a Nakamichi audio system.

EVALUATION Trooper displays fine throttle response throughout the speed range and Torque On Demand allows 2WD cruising or set-and-forget 4WD convenience. But our automatic-transmission test model averaged a poor 13.5 mpg. Handling is competent, although Trooper's tall build makes it feel more top-heavy than most SUVs in tight turns and it hurts directional stability in crosswinds. It also contributes to considerable wind noise at highway speeds. Ride is stable, but big bumps can register with a jolt. There's loads of passenger space and back-seat width for three adults. Step-in height is not unreasonable, and the tall build combines with large windows for fine outward visibility. Some testers object to the steering wheel's bus-like angle, and others complain of insufficient fore-aft driver-seat travel. Some minor controls are haphazardly placed, and the audio system is too recessed and has undersized buttons. Overall, this is a roomy SUV with a smooth powertrain, but it's priced against even larger V8 rivals that seat more than five.

ENGINES

	dohc V6
Size, liters/cu. in.	3.5/213
Horsepower @ rpm	215 @ 5400

Prices are accurate at time of publication; subject to manufacturer's change.

ISUZU

	dohc V6
Torque (lb-ft) @ rpm	230 @ 3000
Availability	S

EPA city/highway mpg
5-speed OD manual	16/19
4-speed OD automatic	15/19

PRICES

Isuzu Trooper	Retail Price	Dealer Invoice
S 4-door 2WD wagon, automatic	$27170	$24724
S 4-door 4WD wagon, 5-speed	27620	24859
S 4-door 4WD wagon, automatic	29170	26253
LS 4-door 2WD wagon, automatic	28765	25889
LS 4-door 4WD wagon, automatic	30765	27689
Limited 4-door 2WD wagon, automatic	32813	29204
Limited 4-door 4WD wagon, automatic	34813	30984
Destination charge	520	520

STANDARD EQUIPMENT:

S: 3.5-liter dohc V6 engine, 4-speed automatic transmission, dual front airbags, antilock 4-wheel disc brakes, air conditioning w/automatic climate control, variable-assist power steering, tilt steering wheel, cruise control, cloth upholstery, front bucket seats, center console, cupholders, split folding and reclining rear seat, AM/FM/cassette, digital clock, tachometer, heated power mirrors, power windows, power door locks, remote keyless entry, rear defogger, intermittent rear wiper/washer, remote fuel door release, intermittent wipers, illuminated visor mirrors, cargo cover, floormats, cornering lights, theft-deterrent system, skid plates, front and rear tow hooks, outside-mounted full-size spare tire, 245/70R16 tires, alloy wheels. **4WD** adds: part-time 4-wheel drive system (5-speed), full-time 4-wheel drive (automatic), 2-speed transfer case, limited slip differential.

LS adds: limited-slip differential, leather-wrapped steering wheel, heated front seats, 8-way power driver seat, 4-way power passenger seat, in-dash 6-disc CD changer, variable intermittent wipers, map lights, fog lights, rear privacy glass. **4WD** adds: full-time 4-wheel drive, 2-speed transfer case.

Limited adds: leather upholstery, power sunroof, compass, outside temperature indicator, barometer, altimeter. **4WD** adds: full-time 4-wheel drive, 2-speed transfer case.

OPTIONAL EQUIPMENT:
Major Packages

Anniversary Edition Pkg., LS	—	—

Leather upholstery, Nakamichi sound system, wood interior trim, special alloy wheels w/white accents.

Specifications begin on page 535.

ISUZU • JAGUAR

Comfort and Convenience	Retail Price	Dealer Invoice
Power sunroof, LS	$1100	$979
Cargo tray	60	47

Appearance and Miscellaneous

Gold Pkg., Limited	400	316
Gold badging and accented wheels.		

JAGUAR S-TYPE

Jaguar S-Type

Rear-wheel-drive luxury car; similar to Lincoln LS

Base price range: NA. Built in England. **Also consider:** BMW 5-Series, Lexus GS 300/430, Mercedes-Benz E-Class

FOR • Acceleration (V8) • Handling/roadholding • Quietness • Ride **AGAINST** • Automatic transmission performance (V6) • Cargo room

Ford-owned Jaguar builds the S-Type in Britain on the Lincoln LS platform with mostly Jaguar-specific components. Both the V6 3.0 and V8 4.0 models have 5-speed automatic transmission, traction control, antilock 4-wheel disc brakes, and front head/chest side airbags. Rear child-seat anchors join the list for '01, along with Jaguar's Reverse Park Control, a former option that warns of nearby objects when backing up. The 4.0 also gets a new premium audio system with standard 6-disc CD changer, another prior option, which now mounts in the trunk instead of the glovebox. The changer remains optional for the 3.0. An available Weather Package includes Jaguar's antiskid Dynamic Stability Control. A Sport Package offers computer-controlled shock absorbers, 17-inch wheels, and high-speed tires. A Deluxe Communications Package bundles navigation system, emergency assistance, and voice-activated phone, audio, and

Prices are accurate at time of publication; subject to manufacturer's change.
CONSUMER GUIDE

JAGUAR

climate controls. All '01 models are newly classed as Low Emissions Vehicles.

EVALUATION Like any Jaguar, the retro-styled S-type is quick and quiet, competent on twisty roads, and pretty serene on rough ones. Jaguar says the V6 version does 0-60 mph in 8 seconds, the V8 in 6.6, both good numbers that ring true in our tests. In our tests, we averaged 17.5 mpg with the V8 and 19.5 mpg with the V6. Both engines require premium gas. The firmer Sport Package suspension sharpens handling without much harm to ride. One major irritation is an automatic transmission prone to slow, erratic shifting. Inside, there's decent room and high comfort for four adults, but also restricted rear visibility, and, with the optional navigator, a fairly busy dashboard. Our test cars felt substantial but were let down by some interior plastic not in keeping with this car's price or status. The S-Type offers traditional Jaguar charm and—so far as we can tell—Ford reliability, but the V8 can cost as much as a BMW 5-Series with just a few options added, none of which make it BMW sporty.

ENGINES

	dohc V6	dohc V8
Size, liters/cu. in.	3.0/181	4.0/244
Horsepower @ rpm	240 @ 6800	281 @ 6100
Torque (lb-ft) @ rpm	221 @ 4500	287 @ 4300
Availability	S[1]	S[2]
EPA city/highway mpg		
5-speed OD automatic	18/26	17/23

1. 3.0. 2. 4.0.

2001 prices unavailable at time of publication.

PRICES

2000 Jaguar S-Type	Retail Price	Dealer Invoice
3.0 4-door sedan	$42500	$37128
4.0 4-door sedan	48000	41932
Destination charge	595	595

STANDARD EQUIPMENT:

3.0: 3.0-liter dohc V6 engine, 5-speed automatic transmission, traction control, dual front airbags, front side-impact airbags, antilock 4-wheel disc brakes, air conditioning w/dual-zone automatic climate control, interior air filter, variable-assist power steering, tilt/telescoping steering wheel, wood/leather-wrapped steering wheel, cruise control, leather upholstery, 8-way power front bucket seats, split folding rear seat, wood interior trim, power mirrors, power windows, power door locks, remote keyless entry, AM/FM/cassette w/CD changer controls, steering wheel

Specifications begin on page 535.

JAGUAR

radio controls, digital clock, tachometer, trip computer, rear defogger, heated wiper park, automatic headlights, floormats, theft-deterrent system, front and rear fog lights, full-sized spare tire, 225/55HR16 tires, alloy wheels.

4.0 adds: 4.0-liter dohc V8 engine, power sunroof, memory driver seat and mirrors, front seat power lumbar supports, power tilt/telescoping steering wheel w/memory, automatic day/night rearview mirror, compass, universal garage door opener.

OPTIONAL EQUIPMENT:

	Retail Price	Dealer Invoice
Major Packages		
Power/Memory Pkg., 3.0	$1900	$1596
Power sunroof, memory driver seat and mirrors, front seat lumbar supports, power tilt/telescoping steering wheel w/memory, automatic day/night rearview mirror, compass, universal garage door opener.		
Deluxe Communications Pkg.	4300	3644
Integrated navigation system, emergency services, voice activated controls (telephone, climate control, audio), portable cellular telephone.		
Sport Pkg.	1100	924
Computer-controlled shock absorbers, 235/50ZR17 tires, special alloy wheels.		
Weather Pkg.	1200	1008
Antiskid system, heated front seats, rain-sensing wipers, heated windshield, headlight washers, engine block heater.		
Safety Features		
Reverse park control	400	336
Comfort and Convenience		
Integrated navigation system	2000	1680
6-disc CD changer w/premium sound system	1500	1260

JAGUAR XJ SEDAN

Rear-wheel-drive luxury car

Base price range: NA. Built in England. **Also consider:** BMW 7-Series, Cadillac Seville, Infiniti Q45, Lexus LS 430, Mercedes-Benz S-Class/CL-Class

FOR • Ride • Acceleration • Quietness • Build quality • Exterior finish • Interior materials **AGAINST** • Fuel economy • Cargo space

Addition of a standard reverse-parking warning system highlights Jaguar's 2001 flagship sedans. This line features XJ8, XJ8L, luxury-oriented Vanden Plas and Vanden Plas Supercharged, and sporty XJR models. All are V8-powered, with the L and both Vanden Plas versions on a longer wheelbase. XJR and Vanden Plas Supercharged have 370

Prices are accurate at time of publication; subject to manufacturer's change.

JAGUAR

Jaguar XJ8

horsepower, other models 290. All have a 5-speed automatic transmission, antilock 4-wheel disc brakes, traction control, front side airbags and, for 2001, Jaguar's Reverse Park Control, which uses radar-like sensors to warn of obstacles when backing up. The Vanden Plas Supercharged uses 17-inch wheels, the XJR 18s, other models 16s. The Vanden Plas Supercharged also includes Jaguar's Computer Active Technology Suspension, basically computer-controlled shock absorbers. A satellite navigation system is newly standard on Vanden Plas Supercharged and remains optional for other XJs. In other changes, a CD changer is standard for XJ8/XJ8L as well as other models, the XJR adds a heated rear seat, and heated front/rear seats are now standard for the regular Vanden Plas as well as the Supercharged.

EVALUATION Even without supercharging, a silky V8 moves XJ's 2-ton heft with authority. Ride is as comfortable and compliant as any rival's, and noise levels are very low. The XJR shows the least cornering lean, but all models handle with surprising agility. Straight-line stability in crosswinds could be better, though. Interiors are cozy and elegant, but the dashboard layout is dated and messy, head room minimal for 6-footers, and the rear seat too low for comfort. Aft leg space is tight except in the L and Vanden Plas, which also afford easier entry/exit with their longer rear doors, though some crouching is still required. Cargo space is subpar for the class. For the individualist, however, these may be attractive alternatives to more staid luxury sedans like the Lexus LS and Mercedes-Benz E-Class—especially now that Jaguar ranks near them in customer satisfaction.

ENGINES	dohc V8	Supercharged dohc V8
Size, liters/cu. in.	4.0/244	4.0/244
Horsepower @ rpm	290 @ 6100	370 @ 6150
Torque (lb-ft) @ rpm	290 @ 4250	387 @ 3600
Availability	S[1]	S[2]
EPA city/highway mpg		
5-speed OD automatic	17/24	16/22

1. XJ8, XJ8L, Vanden Plas. 2. XJR, Vanden Plas Supercharged.

2001 prices unavailable at time of publication.

Specifications begin on page 535.

JAGUAR

PRICES

2000 Jaguar XJ Sedan	Retail Price	Dealer Invoice
XJ8 4-door sedan	$55650	$48616
XJ8L 4-door sedan	60700	53028
Vanden Plas 4-door sedan	64750	56566
XJR 4-door sedan	68550	59886
Vanden Plas Supercharged 4-door sedan	80650	70456
Destination charge	595	595

XJR and Vanden Plas Supercharged retail price includes $1300 Gas Guzzler tax.

STANDARD EQUIPMENT:

XJ8: 4.0-liter dohc V8 engine, 5-speed automatic transmission, traction control, driver- and passenger-side side airbags, front side-impact airbags, antilock 4-wheel disc brakes, variable-assist power steering, power tilt/telescopic steering wheel, cruise control, air conditioning w/automatic climate control, leather upholstery, wood interior trim, 12-way power front bucket seats with power lumbar adjusters, front storage console, overhead console, cupholders, driver memory system (driver seat, steering wheel, outside mirrors), automatic headlights, power sunroof, heated power mirrors, power windows, power door locks, remote keyless entry, trip computer, outside-temperature indicator, automatic day/night rearview mirror, AM/FM/cassette, steering wheel radio controls, analog clock, rear defogger, remote fuel-door and decklid releases, illuminated visor mirrors, universal garage-door opener, map lights, rain-sensing variable intermittent wipers, floormats, theft-deterrent system, chrome hood ornament, front and rear fog lights, full-size spare tire, 225/60ZR16 tires, alloy wheels.

XJ8L adds: 4.9-inch longer wheelbase.

Vanden Plas adds: wood and leather-wrapped steering wheel, wood shift knob, wood picnic trays on front seatbacks, upgraded leather upholstery and wood interior trim, lamb's wool floormats.

XJR adds to XJ8: supercharged 4.0-liter dohc V8 engine, Alpine sound system w/6-disc CD changer, heated front seats, wood and leather-wrapped steering wheel, sport suspension, 255/40ZR18 tires.

Vanden Plas Supercharged adds to Vanden Plas: supercharged 4.0-liter dohc V8 engine, heated front and rear seats, Alpine sound system w/6-disc CD changer, computer-controlled shock absorbers, 235/50ZR17 tires.

OPTIONAL EQUIPMENT:
Comfort and Convenience

Navigation system	1500	1260

XJ8, XJ8L requires Alpine sound system or CD changer.

Prices are accurate at time of publication; subject to manufacturer's change.

JAGUAR

	Retail Price	Dealer Invoice
Heated front and rear seats, XJ8, XJ8L, Vanden Plas	$500	$420
6-disc CD changer, XJ8, XJ8L, Vanden Plas	800	672
Alpine sound system w/CD changer, XJ8, XJ8L, Vanden Plas	1800	1512

JAGUAR XK8

Jaguar XK8 coupe

Rear-wheel-drive luxury car
Base price range: $66,200-$81,800. Built in England. **Also consider:** BMW Z8, Cadillac Eldorado, Mercedes-Benz SL-Class

FOR • Acceleration • Ride • Quietness • Build quality • Exterior finish • Interior materials **AGAINST** • Passenger and cargo room • Entry/exit • Rear visibility

Special editions and some new features alter the lineup of this luxury/performance 4-seater for 2001. Coupe and convertible body styles return, the latter with a power soft top and glass rear window with defroster. Each now comes in three flavors, all with 4.0-liter V8s. XK8s have 290 horsepower, while XKRs have a 370-hp supercharged engine, functional louvered hood, rear spoiler, 18-inch wheels (versus XK8's 17s), and Jaguar's Computer Active Technology Suspension (computer-controlled shock absorbers). New for 2001 are the Silverstone coupe and convertible, basically XKRs with 20-inch wheels, larger brakes, and unique cosmetic touches; the coupe includes a performance handling package. All models have a 5-speed automatic transmission, antilock 4-wheel disc brakes, traction control, and front side airbags that now deploy from the seatbacks instead of the doors. New ultrasonic front-occupant sensors are designed to provide more accurate triggering of both side and dashboard airbags. All models also get minor revisions to styling and seats, plus Jaguar's Reverse Park Control that warns of obstacles when backing up. XK8s now include heated front seats and

Specifications begin on page 535.

JAGUAR

premium audio with CD changer like XKRs. XKRs also make an in-dash navigation system standard; it remains optional for XK8s.

EVALUATION Though too large and heavy for genuine sports-car moves, these Jags can entertain on twisty roads. XKRs don't match the XK8's impressively absorbent ride, but they aren't harsh. Jaguar's V8 is a gem: strong, nearly silent at idle, and never louder than a muted, expensive-sounding snarl. Our test XK8 coupe scaled 0-60 mph in under 7 seconds and averaged 15 mpg. The XKRs we tested felt true to Jaguar's 0-60 claim of under 6 seconds and averaged 16.2 mpg. But beware the XK if you're tall or claustrophobic. Room is tight even in front, the back seat is toddler size, and entry/exit is difficult. At least the front seats are quite comfortable, and the dashboard is attractive and well arranged. Solid workmanship is another plus, convertible included. XKs are elegant, refined grand tourers and quite desirable, but they cost, though resale values may compensate some.

ENGINES

	dohc V8	Supercharged dohc V8
Size, liters/cu. in.	4.0/244	4.0/244
Horsepower @ rpm	290 @ 6100	370 @ 6150
Torque (lb-ft) @ rpm	290 @ 4250	387 @ 3600
Availability	S[1]	S[2]

EPA city/highway mpg

5-speed OD automatic	17/25[3]	16/23

1. XK8. 2. XKR. 3. 17/24 w/convertible.

2001 prices unavailable at time of publication.

PRICES

2000 Jaguar XK8	Retail Price	Dealer Invoice
XK8 2-door coupe	$66200	$57832
XK8 2-door convertible	71200	62200
XKR 2-door coupe	76800	67092
XKR 2-door convertible	81800	71460
Destination charge	595	595

STANDARD EQUIPMENT:

XK8: 4.0-liter dohc V8 engine, 5-speed automatic transmission, traction control, dual front airbags, antilock 4-wheel disc brakes, air conditioning w/automatic climate control, variable-assist power steering, power tilt/telescopic steering wheel, wood/leather-wrapped steering wheel, cruise control, power top (convertible), leather upholstery, 12-way power front bucket seats w/power lumbar support, memory system (driver seat, steering wheel, outside mirrors), cupholders, wood interior trim and shifter, tachometer, trip computer, outside-temperature indicator, automatic headlights, AM/FM/cassette, steering wheel radio controls, analog clock, heated power mirrors, power

Prices are accurate at time of publication; subject to manufacturer's change.

JAGUAR • JEEP

windows, power door locks, remote keyless entry, universal garage-door opener, illuminated visor mirrors, automatic day/night rearview mirror, rear defogger, remote fuel-door and decklid release, rain-sensing variable intermittent windshield wipers, map lights, floormats, theft-deterrent system, front and rear fog lights, full-size spare tire, 245/50ZR17 tires, alloy wheels.

XKR adds: supercharged 4.0-liter dohc V8 engine, heated front seats, Alpine sound system, 6-disc CD changer, headlight washers, computer-controlled shock absorbers, 245/45ZR18 front tires, 255/45ZR18 rear tires, deletes full-size spare tire.

OPTIONAL EQUIPMENT:

	Retail Price	Dealer Invoice
Major Packages		
All-Weather Pkg., XK8	$500	$420
Heated front seats, headlight washers.		
Comfort and Convenience		
Navigation system	2400	2016
XK8 requires Alpine sound system or CD changer.		
6-disc CD changer, XK8	800	672
Alpine sound system w/CD changer, XK8	1800	1512
Appearance and Miscellaneous		
18-inch alloy wheels, XK8	500	420
Includes 245/45ZR18 front tires, 255/45ZR18 rear tires, space-saver spare tire.		

JEEP CHEROKEE

Jeep Cherokee Classic

Rear- or 4-wheel-drive midsize sport-utility vehicle
Base price range: $19,370-$23,385. Built in USA. **Also consider:** Ford Explorer, Nissan Xterra, Toyota 4Runner

FOR • Acceleration • Cargo room **AGAINST** • Fuel economy • Ride • Rear-seat entry/exit (2-door)

Specifications begin on page 535.

JEEP

The older and less-expensive of Jeep's two midsize SUVs loses its 4-cylinder engine and trims its lineup for 2001. A redesigned Cherokee successor with new, rounded styling is due this summer as a 2002 model.

The current design dates from 1984 and closes its run with 2- and 4-door Sport models and 4-door Limited versions. Both come with a 190-horsepower inline 6-cylinder and manual or automatic transmission. Both offer rear-wheel drive and two 4WD systems: part-time Command-Trac and full-time Selec-Trac. Selec-Trac does not require that 4WD be disengaged on dry pavement. Antilock brakes are optional and both models gain rear child seat anchors for '01. Gone along with the 4-cylinder engine are base SE and uplevel Classic models.

PERFORMANCE Cherokee's 6-cylinder is strong throughout the speed range with fuel economy typical of a midsize SUV: about 15 mpg with automatic, 17 with manual in our tests.

Good balance and tidy dimensions make Cherokee quite maneuverable in most situations. It's not exactly smooth-riding, but the base suspension absorbs most bumps without jarring. The optional off-road oriented Up Country Suspension Group makes for a rough ride; spend instead for optional antilock brakes. Cherokee suffers powertrain and road resonances absent in most rivals. Wind noise at speed also is high.

ACCOMMODATIONS Cherokee shows its age in a low-roof passenger compartment with no surplus of front shoulder room, a shortage of rear knee clearance, and fairly lofty step-in. Rear entry/exit is tight, thanks to narrow lower doorways. The dashboard is convenient, and outward vision is good, though larger door mirrors would help lane-changing. Mounting the spare tire inside eats up cargo room, but there's still decent space with the rear seat in use, and a long load floor with it folded. An outside spare is available through Jeep dealers. Recent test Cherokees had occasional interior rattles and wide panel gaps around the hood and tailgate.

VALUE Cherokee is capable on-road and off, and not too expensive, provided you go easy on options. Still, being way behind the times in room, ride, and refinement, this is the "blue light special" of midsize SUVs.

ENGINES

	ohv I6
Size, liters/cu. in.	4.0/242
Horsepower @ rpm	190 @ 4600
Torque (lb-ft) @ rpm	225 @ 3000
Availability	S

EPA city/highway mpg

5-speed OD manual	18/23[1]
4-speed OD automatic	16/21[2]

1. 17/22 w/4WD. 2. 15/20 w/4WD.

Prices are accurate at time of publication; subject to manufacturer's change.

JEEP
PRICES

Jeep Cherokee	Retail Price	Dealer Invoice
Sport 2-door wagon 2WD	$19370	$17536
Sport 2-door wagon 4WD	20880	18884
Sport 4-door wagon 2WD	20405	18466
Sport 4-door wagon 4WD	21915	19815
Limited 4-door wagon 2WD	21870	19756
Limited 4-door wagon 4WD	23385	21109
Destination charge	585	585

STANDARD EQUIPMENT:

Sport: 4.0-liter 6-cylinder engine, 5-speed manual transmission, dual front airbags, power steering, cloth upholstery, front bucket seats, center console, cupholders, folding rear seat, AM/FM/cassette, digital clock, tachometer, variable intermittent wipers, auxiliary power outlets, rear defogger, remote outside mirrors, 225/75R15 all-terrain white-letter tires. **4WD** models add: Command-Trac part-time 4-wheel drive, 2-speed transfer case, alloy wheels.

Limited adds: 4-speed automatic transmission, leather-wrapped steering wheel, power mirrors, rear wiper/washer, floormats, roof rack, 225/70R16 tires. **4WD** adds: Command-Trac part-time 4-wheel drive, 2-speed transfer case.

OPTIONAL EQUIPMENT:
Major Packages

Sport Value Group, Sport 2-door	2170	1845
Sport 4-door	2345	1993
Manufacturer's discount price	NC	NC

Air conditioning, automatic-off headlights, illuminated visor mirrors, map lights, underhood light, power mirrors, power windows and door locks, remote keyless entry, intermittent rear wiper/washer, leather-wrapped tilt steering wheel, floormats, roof rack.

Limited Value Group, Limited	1825	1551
Manufacturer's discount price	NC	NC

Air conditioning, automatic-off headlights, illuminated visor mirrors, map lights, underhood light, power windows and door locks, remote keyless entry, tilt steering wheel.

Leather Interior Group, Limited	1440	1224
Manufacturer's discount price	1190	1011

Leather upholstery, heated power front seats, woodgrain interior trim.

Up Country Suspension Group, Sport 4WD w/alloy wheels	845	718
Sport 4WD	780	663
Limited 4WD	725	616

Limited-slip rear differential, maximum engine cooling, off-road suspension, tow hooks, skid plates, rear stabilizer bar delete, 225/75R15 white-letter all-terrain tires, full-size spare tire.

Specifications begin on page 535.

JEEP

	Retail Price	Dealer Invoice
Trailer Tow Group	$365	$310
4WD w/Up Country Suspension Group	245	208

Equalizer hitch, 7-wire receptacle, 4-wire trailer adapter, maximum engine cooling. Requires full-size spare tire. Sport requires automatic transmission.

Powertrains

4-speed automatic transmission, Sport	945	803
Selec-Trac full-time 4WD, 4WD	540	459
Sport 4WD w/alloy wheels	605	514
4WD w/Up Country Suspension	395	336

Includes full-size spare tire. Requires automatic transmission.

Limited-slip rear differential	285	242

Requires full-size spare tire.

Safety Features

Antilock brakes	600	510

Comfort and Convenience

6-way power driver seat, Limited	300	255
Overhead console, Limited	235	200

Outside temperature indicator, trip computer, sunglasses/garage door opener holder.

Cruise control	250	213
Heated power mirrors	45	38
AM/FM/cassette/CD player	410	349
Infinity sound system,		
Limited	350	298

Requires AM/FM/cassette/CD player.

Cargo cover	75	64
Smokers Group	20	17

Ash tray, lighter.

Appearance and Miscellaneous

Theft-deterrent system	75	64
Deep-tinted glass,		
Sport 2-door	375	319
Sport 4-door, Limited	270	230
Fog lights, Sport,		
Classic, Limited	110	94

Special Purpose, Wheels and Tires

Alloy wheels, Sport	245	208
Full-size spare tire, Sport	145	123
Sport w/alloy wheels,		
Limited	210	179

Prices are accurate at time of publication; subject to manufacturer's change.

JEEP

JEEP GRAND CHEROKEE

Jeep Grand Cherokee Limited

Rear- or 4-wheel-drive midsize sport-utility vehicle

Base price range: $27,300-$35,095. Built in USA. **Also consider:** Ford Explorer, Lexus RX 300, Mercedes-Benz M-Class

FOR • Acceleration • Cargo room **AGAINST** • Fuel economy

Interior revisions, a 5-speed automatic transmission, and larger wheels keynote changes to Jeep's flagship SUV for 2001. Grand Cherokee comes in Laredo and Limited models, both with a 6-cylinder engine or optional V8. The six comes with a 4-speed automatic, the V8 with a new 5-speed automatic.

Both models are offered with rear-drive or one of three 4WD systems, all of which are usable on dry pavement. Selec-Trac provides 2WD or full-time 4WD. Permanently engaged Quadra-Trac II apportions power between front and rear axles. Quadra-Drive is also permanently engaged 4WD, but can send 100 percent of the engine's power to any one wheel to maintain traction.

The V8's new 5-speed automatic adds a second overdrive top gear intended to increase highway fuel economy. This transmission replaces a 4-speed, but retains an extra gear ratio between second and third gears designed to improve passing response and provide smoother downshifts.

Also for '01, Limited models trade standard 16-inch wheels for 17s, which are newly optional on Laredos. Aluminum-finish interior trim is added, and the available universal garage door opener is backlit for easier nighttime viewing. A rear storage net, rear child-seat anchors, and a connector for electric trailer brakes are newly standard.

PERFORMANCE Handling and off-road ability are Grand Cherokee's strengths. Control in directional changes is good despite a fair amount of body lean. Steering feels natural in turns, but requires frequent corrections at highway speeds. As for ride quality, Grand Cherokee easily absorbs most bumps and potholes but it allows queasy side-to-side and

JEEP

fore-and-aft pitching motions over uneven pavement.

Acceleration is adequate with the 6-cylinder, robust with the V8. Our extended-use-test 6-cylinder 4WD 2000 Laredo is averaging 15.9 mpg over its first 9717 miles; that's on the high side of average for a midsize 6-cylinder SUV. In lots of highway driving, a test 2000 V8 Limited averaged 16.1 mpg, but in mostly city work, another V8 Grand Cherokee returned just 12.7 mpg. We have not measured fuel economy with the new 5-speed automatic, but EPA estimates are unchanged from last year. No SUV offers this range of 4WD systems, and all provide Grand Cherokee with excellent traction on-road and off.

Our extended-use Grand Cherokee has not required any unscheduled service. However, its Quadra-Drive system, like those of other Grand Cherokees we've tested, suffers lots of gear whine and occasional front-wheel binding in tight, low-speed turns. And in one V8 test model, Quadra-Drive generated a pronounced shudder when coming to a stop. Braking is strong and smooth, pedal modulation good. Engines are well-muffled, but wind rush and tire roar can intrude at highway speeds.

ACCOMMODATIONS Four adults fit easily, but Grand Cherokee isn't wide enough to seat three grownups comfortably in the rear. Moreover, the rear seatback is too upright for best comfort and there's little toe space under the front seats. All seats are too soft for optimal support. The dashboard has a generally convenient layout, and Limited models add handy steering-wheel audio controls. Roof pillars are too thick for best outward vision, though large outside mirrors help. Bins and pockets provide plenty of small-items storage. Cargo room, though adequate, is at the low end for this class, and the rear seatbacks are more difficult to fold than in most SUVs. Back-seat entry and exit is hampered by narrow rear door bottoms. Grand Cherokee's overall structure feels solid, and interior materials range from pleasingly solid to budget-grade plasticky.

VALUE Performance and overall design are good, and prices are competitive. But questions about the long-term mechanical reliability of this line of Jeeps keeps Grand Cherokee from the Recommended category. Our extended-use test of a Laredo will help address those concerns.

ENGINES

	ohv I6	ohc V8
Size, liters/cu. in.	4.0/242	4.7/284
Horsepower @ rpm	195 @ 4600	235 @ 4800
Torque (lb-ft) @ rpm	230 @ 3000	295 @ 3200
Availability	S	O
EPA city/highway mpg		
4-speed OD automatic	16/21	
5-speed OD automatic		15/20[1]

1. 15/19 w/4WD.

Prices are accurate at time of publication; subject to manufacturer's change.

JEEP
PRICES

Jeep Grand Cherokee

	Retail Price	Dealer Invoice
Laredo 4-door wagon 2WD	$27300	$24729
Laredo 4-door wagon 4WD	29270	26498
Limited 4-door wagon 2WD	32665	29450
Limited 4-door wagon 4WD	35095	31624
Destination charge	585	585

STANDARD EQUIPMENT:

Laredo: 4.0-liter 6-cylinder engine, 4-speed automatic transmission, dual front airbags, antilock 4-wheel disc brakes, air conditioning, power steering, tilt steering wheel, cruise control, cloth upholstery, front bucket seats, split folding rear seat, center console, cupholders, overhead console (compass, trip computer, outside temperature indicator, map lights), power mirrors, power windows, power door locks, AM/FM/cassette, digital clock, tachometer, variable intermittent wipers, auxiliary power outlet, visor mirrors, rear defogger, intermittent rear wiper/washer, theft-deterrent system, rear privacy glass, roof rack, 225/75R16 tires, alloy wheels. **4WD** adds: Selec-Trac full-time 4-wheel drive, 2-speed transfer case.

Limited adds: dual-zone automatic climate control, leather upholstery, leather-wrapped steering wheel w/radio controls, 10-way power front seats w/driver-side memory, heated power mirrors w/driver-side memory and automatic day/night, remote keyless entry, AM/FM/cassette/CD player w/Infinity sound system, automatic day/night rearview mirror, universal garage door opener, illuminated visor mirrors, automatic headlights, cargo cover, floormats, fog lights, 235/65R17 tires. **4WD** adds: Quadra-Trac II permanent 4-wheel drive, 2-speed transfer case.

OPTIONAL EQUIPMENT:
Major Packages

Quick Order Pkg. 26F/28F, Laredo	2330	1981
Manufacturer's discount price	1830	1556

Remote keyless entry, 6-way power front seats, automatic day/night rearview mirror, automatic headlights, leather-wrapped steering wheel, AM/FM/cassette CD player, universal garage door opener, illuminated visor mirrors, cargo cover and net, floormats, theft-deterrent system w/alarm, 225/75R16 white-letter tires.

Quick Order Pkg. 26S/28S	4335	3685
Manufacturer's discount price	3540	3009

Quick Order Pkg. 26F/28F plus leather upholstery, heated power mirrors, fog lights, bodyside stripes, 235/65R17 tires, special alloy wheels.

Quick Order Pkg. 26G/28G, Limited	NC	NC
Manufacturer's discount price, (credit)	(500)	(425)

Standard equipment.

Specifications begin on page 535.

JEEP

	Retail Price	Dealer Invoice
Quick Order Pkg. 26K/28K, Limited 2WD	$1510	$1284
Manufacturer's discount price	1010	859
Quick Order Pkg. 26K/28K, Limited 4WD	2060	1751
Manufacturer's discount price	1560	1326

Heated front seats, power sunroof, 10-disc CD changer, Quadra-Drive permanent 4-wheel drive (4WD), full-size spare tire.

Convenience Group, Laredo	640	544
Manufacturer's discount price	140	119

Remote keyless entry, cargo cover and net, floormats, 225/75R16 white-letter tires.

Cold Weather Group, Laredo	300	255

Heated power mirrors, heated 10-way power front seats. Laredo requires Quick Order Group and leather upholstery.

Luxury Group, Laredo	750	638

6-way power front seats, automatic day/night rearview mirror, automatic headlights. Requires Infinity sound system or 10-disc CD changer.

Cold Weather Group, Limited	250	213

Heated power mirrors, heated 10-way power front seats. Laredo requires Quick Order Group and leather upholstery.

Up-Country Suspension Group,		
Laredo 4WD w/26F/28F Pkg.	575	489
Laredo 4WD w/26S/28S Pkg.	390	332
Limited 4WD	410	349
Limited w/26K/28K Pkg.	250	213

Heavy-duty suspension, Skid Plate Group, full-size spare tire, 245/70R16 all-terrain white-letter tires, 235/65R17 all-terrain white-letter tires (Limited, Laredo w/26S/28S Pkg.).

Class III Trailer Tow Prep Group	105	89

Trailer wiring harness, mechanical cooling fan. Requires 4.0-liter engine.

Trailer Tow Group	360	306

Frame mounted receiver hitch, 7-wire connector, 7-way round to 4-way flat plug adapter, power steering cooler. Requires 4.0-liter engine.

Trailer Tow Group IV, 4WD	255	217

Trailer Tow Group ordered with 4.7-liter engine. Laredo requires option pkg.

Powertrains

4.7-liter V8 engine, Laredo 4WD	1165	990
Laredo 2WD, Limited	1070	910

Requires 5-speed automatic transmission. Laredo requires Quick Order Pkg. 4WD includes Quadra-Trac II permanent 4WD.

Manufacturer's discount price, Limited	370	315

Requires 5-speed automatic transmission. Laredo requires Quick Order Pkg. 4WD includes Quadra-Trac II permanent 4WD.

Prices are accurate at time of publication; subject to manufacturer's change.

JEEP

Major Packages	Retail Price	Dealer Invoice
5-speed automatic transmission	$75	$64
Requires 4.7-liter V8 engine.		
Quadra-Trac II permanent 4WD, Laredo 4WD	445	378
Quadra-Drive permanent 4WD, Laredo w/4.0-liter engine	995	846
Laredo w/4.7-liter engine, Limited	550	468
Quadra-Trac II plus Vari-Lok progressive axles.		
Limited-slip differential, 2WD	285	242
NA with 4.7-liter engine in combination w/Up-Country Suspension Group.		

Comfort and Convenience

Power sunroof	800	680
Leather upholstery, Laredo	795	676
Includes 10-way power front seats. Requires Quick Order Pkg. 26F/28F.		
AM/FM/cassette/CD player, Laredo	335	285
10-disc CD changer, Laredo w/Pkg. 26F/28F	710	604
Laredo w/Pkg. 26S/28S, Limited	300	255
Includes Infinity sound system.		
Infinity sound system, Laredo	410	349
Requires Quick Order Pkg. 26F/28F.		

Special Purpose, Wheels and Tires

Skid Plate/Tow Hook Group, 4WD	200	170
245/75R16 all-terrain white-letter tires, Laredo	185	157
Requires Convenience Group or Pkg. 26F/28F.		

JEEP WRANGLER

Jeep Wrangler Sport

4-wheel-drive compact sport-utility vehicle

Base price range: $14,890-$22,435. **Built in USA.** **Also consider:** Honda CR-V, Subaru Forester, Toyota RAV4

FOR • Cargo room • Maneuverability **AGAINST** • Fuel economy

JEEP

• Acceleration (4-cylinder w/automatic) • Noise • Ride • Entry/exit

Jeep's tradition-bound compact SUV gets revised interior features and a thicker soft top with available deep-tint windows for 2001.

Wranglers come with a soft top and plastic side windows; a hardtop with glass windows is optional. The base SE model has a 4-cylinder engine, uplevel Sport and Sahara models use Jeep's 4.0-liter inline 6-cylinder. Manual transmission is standard; a 3-speed automatic is optional. All Wranglers have 4-wheel drive for use only on slippery surfaces. Antilock brakes are optional on 6-cylinder models.

Intermittent windshield wipers are standard for 2001, and Sahara adds standard air conditioning. Also new is a revised center console with rear cupholders, an available subwoofer for the audio system, and a plastic instead of metal Add-a-Trunk rear storage compartment that can now slide forward or be removed. Tinted soft-top windows are available. And Jeep says a new tilt steering-wheel mechanism offers greater range and finer adjustments. The reengineered soft top is more durable and insulates better against noise, Jeep says.

PERFORMANCE Wrangler is fun to drive, but not if you like comfort or quiet. A short wheelbase and off-road-ready suspension trigger abrupt vertical ride motions even on apparently smooth roads. Likewise, cornering is skittish on bumpy surfaces and the steering isn't very precise. Wrangler is quite maneuverable, however, and the optional antilock brakes stop it with fine control; too bad they're not offered on the 4-cylinder SE. Even with this year's revised soft top, wind noise is intrusive in the convertible, even with the top up. Hardtops are quieter, but not much.

The 4-cylinder feels underpowered with automatic transmission. It accelerates well enough in town with manual shift, but must be worked to its limits on short freeway on-ramps and in two-lane passing. The 6-cylinder delivers fine power with either transmission but doesn't make the 3000-pound Wrangler a hot rod; we timed a Sahara with automatic at 9.8 seconds 0-60 mph. A test 5-speed Sahara averaged 15.2 mpg, an automatic averaged 17.6 in mostly highway driving. Both figures are slightly better than we've averaged with the 4-cylinder.

ACCOMMODATIONS Head room is terrific with either top and front seats are chair-height comfortable, but elbow room is tight and there are no door armrests. Two adults fit in back without touching shoulders, but knee room is tight and the seat isn't very comfortable. Gauges and controls are logically grouped, outward vision is good. Only a few grocery bags fit behind the back seat, which folds or removes to create steamer-trunk-sized load space. Raising or lowering the soft top is a time-consuming struggle with zippers, fasteners, and struts. Workmanship is solid, materials more durable than fancy.

VALUE Wrangler isn't comfortable, but few vehicles have more personality or better off-road ability. Six-cylinder models can quickly top

JEEP

$22,000, but all versions have strong resale value.

ENGINES

	ohv I4	ohv I6
Size, liters/cu. in.	2.5/150	4.0/242
Horsepower @ rpm	120 @ 5400	190 @ 4600
Torque (lb-ft) @ rpm	140 @ 3500	235 @ 3200
Availability	S[1]	S[2]
EPA city/highway mpg		
5-speed OD manual	18/20	16/19
3-speed automatic	16/18	15/18

1. SE. 2. Sport, Sahara.

PRICES

Jeep Wrangler	Retail Price	Dealer Invoice
SE 2-door convertible	$14890	$14268
Sport 2-door convertible	19155	17276
Sahara 2-door convertible	22435	20163
Destination charge	585	585

STANDARD EQUIPMENT:

SE: 2.5-liter 4-cylinder engine, 5-speed manual transmission, Command-Trac part-time 4-wheel drive, 2-speed transfer case, dual front airbags, roll bar, power steering, vinyl upholstery, front bucket seats, tachometer, front carpeting, mini floor console, cupholder, variable intermittent wipers, dual outside mirrors, skid plates, 205/75R15 all-terrain tires, styled steel wheels.

Sport adds: 4.0-liter 6-cylinder engine, folding rear bench seat, AM/FM/cassette with rear sound bar and speakers, digital clock, rear carpeting, 215/75R15 all-terrain tires.

Sahara adds: air conditioning, tilt leather-wrapped steering wheel, cloth upholstery, full storage console, AM/FM/CD player, front floormats, fog lights, deep-tinted rear glass, bodyside steps, front and rear tow hooks, outside-mounted full-size spare tire, 225/70R16 all-terrain tires, alloy wheels.

OPTIONAL EQUIPMENT:
Major Packages

Pkg. 22N/23N, SE	1310	1114

AM/FM/cassette, rear sound bar w/speakers, folding rear seat, rear carpeting.

Pkg. 24D/25D, Sport	620	527

Tilt leather-wrapped steering wheel, cloth upholstery, full storage console w/cupholders, coutesy and underhood lights, full-size spare tire.

ADC Convenience Group, SE, Sport	165	140

Full storage console w/cupholders, courtesy, underhood lights.

Fog Lights and Tow Hook Group, SE, Sport	180	153

Specifications begin on page 535.

JEEP

Powertrains	Retail Price	Dealer Invoice
3-speed automatic transmission	$625	$531
Limited-slip rear differential	285	242
Requires full-size spare tire. Sport requires Tire and Wheel Group.		
Dana 44 rear axle, Sport, Sahara	595	506
Requires full-size spare. NA with antilock brakes. Sport Requires Tire and Wheel Group.		

Safety Features

Antilock brakes, Sport, Sahara	600	510

Comfort and Convenience

Hard top, SE, Sport	920	782
Sahara	1160	986
Includes full metal doors with roll-up windows, rear wiper/washer, deep-tinted glass (SE, Sport), rear defogger, cargo light.		
Soft and hard tops, SE, Sport	1560	1326
Sahara	1800	1560
Includes hard doors.		
Full metal doors w/roll-up windows	125	106
Air conditioning, SE, Sport	895	761
Cloth reclining front bucket seats with rear seat, SE	745	633
SE w/Pkg. 22N/23N, Sport	150	128
SE includes rear carpeting.		
AAC Convenience Group 1, SE, Sport	190	162
Tilt leather-wrapped steering wheel.		
Cruise control, SE, Sport	300	255
SE/Sport w/Convenience Group 1, Sahara	250	213
Includes leather-wrapped steering wheel.		
AM/FM/cassette, SE	715	608
Includes rear sound bar with speakers.		
AM/FM/CD player, SE w/22N/23N, Sport	125	106
Includes rear sound bar with speakers.		
Additional speakers w/subwoofer, SE, Sport	200	170
Requires ADC Convenience Group. SE requires Pkg. 22N/23N. Std. Sahara.		

Appearance and Miscellaneous

Theft-deterrent system	75	64
Add-A-Trunk lockable storage	125	106
SE requires rear seat.		
Deep-tinted rear glass, SE/Sport w/hard top	240	204
SE/Sport w/soft and hard tops	365	310
Tinted soft top windows, SE, Sport	125	106
Bodyside steps, SE, Sport	75	64

Prices are accurate at time of publication; subject to manufacturer's change.

CONSUMER GUIDE

JEEP • KIA

Special Purpose, Wheels and Tires

	Retail Price	Dealer Invoice
Full Face Tire and Wheel Group, SE	$700	$595
Sport	425	361
Sport w/Pkg. 24D/25D	310	264

Full-size spare tire, 225/75R15 all-terrain tires, full-face steel wheels.

Grizzly Tire and Wheel Group, SE	965	820
Sport	690	587
Sport w/Pkg. 24D/25D	575	489

Full-size spare tire, 225/75R15 all-terrain tires, alloy wheels.

30-Inch Tire and Wheel Group, Sport w/5-speed	785	667
Sport w/Pkg. 24D and automatic	670	570
Sport w/Pkg. 25D and 5-speed	850	723
Sahara w/automatic	360	306
Sahara w/5-speed	540	459

Five alloy wheels, full-size spare (Sport), heavy-duty shock absorbers and rear axle, Dana 44 rear axle (w/5-speed), 30x9.5R15 all-terrain white-letter tires.

KIA RIO

Kia Rio

Front-wheel-drive subcompact car

Base price range: $8595-$9470. Built in South Korea. **Also consider:** Daewoo Lanos, Hyundai Accent, Nissan Sentra, Toyota Echo

FOR • Fuel economy • Maneuverability **AGAINST** • Engine noise • Passenger room • Rear seat entry/exit • Acceleration

Kia's new entry-level car is a 4-door sedan sized and priced below its Sephia and Spectra subcompacts. At $8595 to start, Rio is one of the least expensive cars on the U.S. market. The only engine is a 1.5-liter twincam 4-cylinder with manual or optional 4-speed automatic transmissions. Rear-window defroster, center console, and full cloth interior are standard. Options include antilock brakes, air conditioning, rear

KIA

spoiler, alloy wheels, and an "Upgrade Package" that includes power steering with tilt wheel. Kia's new Long Haul Warranty duplicates the Hyundai Advantage program; Kia is owned by Hyundai, South Korea's largest automaker. Coverage includes 5 years/60,000 miles basic, 10/100,000 powertrain, and 5/100,000 against rust, plus 5 years/unlimited miles roadside assistance.

EVALUATION Rio is a nice enough little sedan, but not a compelling choice even as basic transportation. Our automatic-transmission test car coped well with normal street traffic given a heavy throttle foot. It struggled to reach cruising speed, however, and we doubt it would break 11 seconds 0-60 mph. We weren't able to measure fuel economy for this report, but it likely won't be stellar for the subcompact class. Rio drives without surprises, but soft damping and slim standard tires produce only modest grip and lots of front-end plowing in tight, fast corners. Braking is competent, but there's the usual small-car ride choppiness on washboard surfaces, plus mild bounce on large moguls and dips. The engine drones in hard acceleration and at higher cruising speeds; the low-achiever tires are noisy on most surfaces. Rio's trim size is a boon for parking, but makes the interior cozy for adults, especially in back. Rear entry/exit is tight, too. Some larger drivers will feel crowded at the wheel, but gauges and controls are simple and convenient. Cargo space is good for the exterior size, but the trunk opening is small and a fold-down seatback is unavailable. Assembly quality is better than might be expected for the price, though budget-grade dashboard plastic marks the interior. Our test car stickered at $11,432 with options, a long way from the advertised $8595 base and enough to buy a larger, fancier used car in good condition.

ENGINES

	dohc I4
Size, liters/cu. in.	1.5/91
Horsepower @ rpm	96 @ 5800
Torque (lb-ft) @ rpm	98 @ 4500
Availability	S

EPA city/highway mpg	
5-speed manual	27/32
4-speed OD automatic	25/31

PRICES

Kia Rio	Retail Price	Dealer Invoice
Base 4-door sedan, 5-speed	$8595	$7900
Base 4-door sedan, automatic	9470	8700
Destination charge	450	450

STANDARD EQUIPMENT:

Base: 1.5-liter dohc 4-cylinder engine, 5-speed manual or 4-speed auto-

Prices are accurate at time of publication; subject to manufacturer's change.

KIA

matic transmission, dual front airbags, manual steering, cloth upholstery, front bucket seats w/height-adjustable driver seat, center console, cupholders, rear defogger, intermittent wipers, front floormats, dual outside mirrors, 175/70R13 tires.

OPTIONAL EQUIPMENT:

	Retail Price	Dealer Invoice
Major Packages		
Upgrade Pkg.	$380	$315
Variable-assist power steering, tilt steering wheel, visor mirrors, bodyside moldings, wheel covers.		
Safety Features		
Antilock 4-wheel disc brakes	400	350
Comfort and Convenience		
Air conditioning	750	650
AM/FM/cassette	320	250
AM/FM/CD player	395	325
Appearance and Miscellaneous		
Rear spoiler	85	65
Alloy wheels	275	225
Includes 175/65TR14 tires.		

KIA SEPHIA/SPECTRA

Kia Sephia

Front-wheel-drive subcompact car

Base price range: $14,395-$20,640. Built in South Korea. **Also consider:** Ford Focus, Honda Civic, Toyota Echo

FOR • Fuel economy **AGAINST** • Acceleration (automatic) • Noise • Rear seat room • Cargo room

Longer warranties and larger front brakes head a short list of 2001 changes to the larger of two subcompact lines from this South Korean maker. Sephia is a 4-door sedan sold in base and better-equipped LS

Specifications begin on page 535.

KIA

versions. Spectra is a 4-door hatchback derivative in GS and uplevel GSX models. Each has slightly different styling, standard features, and pricing. All use the same 1.8-liter 4-cylinder engine and manual or optional automatic transmissions. Side airbags aren't available, but antilock brakes are optional for Spectra and Sephia LS.

This year, both get larger front disc brakes. Dual vanity mirrors, gas cap tether, and coin tray are being added as running changes. But the big news is Kia's Long Haul Warranty, instituted last summer and a duplicate of the Hyundai Advantage program. Kia is owned by Hyundai, South Korea's largest vehicle maker. Basic coverage goes from 3 years/36,000 miles to 5/50,000, powertrain coverage from 5/60,000 to 10/100,000, and roadside assistance from 3/36,000 to 5/unlimited miles. Corrosion is warranted for 5/100,000.

PERFORMANCE The longer warranties may enhance sales appeal and owner peace of mind, but they do nothing for performance. Acceleration, for example, is just average, our test Sephia LS manual clocking 9.2 seconds 0-60 mph; the automatic adds about two seconds. Highway passing power is just OK too, and the engine loses steam on long upgrades. Sephia/Spectra's manual transmission has longish throws but a light progressive clutch. The automatic is smooth and prompt, but relatively weak engine torque means it's constantly shifting between fourth and third gears to maintain speed.

Fuel economy is also unremarkable at 22.7 mpg in our tests, though that included some very hard driving. Braking is adequate without the optional ABS, much better with the 4-wheel disc brakes that come with the ABS. This year's bigger front brakes may improve stopping performance, but won't change the marked nosedive that occurs in emergency stops.

These Kias are pleasantly "tossable" on twisty roads, with quick, responsive steering and safe, if uninspired, front-drive moves. Ride is okay, but excessive tire thump detracts from comfort on rippled freeways. Wind and road noise are surprisingly modest for the budget league, and the engine gets raucous only above 4000 rpm, though that's a shame because peak power is only available above that point.

ACCOMMODATIONS Front leg room is Sephia/Spectra highlight. Even 6-foot drivers may not need all the seat travel available, and the standard tilt steering wheel and height-adjustable driver's seat on upper-trim versions allow most everyone to find the right stance. Head room is also good in front, but the bucket seats aren't that comfortable on longer trips despite firm bolstering. Rear-seat room is limited in all dimensions, though two smaller adults shouldn't complain on shorter trips. Smallish doors impede aft entry/exit, though.

Dashboards are simple and orderly, and Kia's recent switch to larger, more user-friendly audio controls is welcome. All-around visibility is fine.

Cargo room is small-car normal in Sephia, slightly better in the hatch-

Prices are accurate at time of publication; subject to manufacturer's change.

KIA

back Spectra. Both have fold-down back seats for extending the load floor, but the Sephia's can't be locked.

Workmanship seems to have improved greatly in the past couple of years. Interiors feature nice soft-touch plastics and quality-look fabrics, and our recent test cars have been tight and rattle-free. Even the tinny door chime has been relaced with a more-expensive sounding bell.

VALUE Sephia and Spectra are low-priced but not cut-rate. They're not class leaders in any respect, but they now boast some of the industry's longest warranties, which should be a sales-booster that could eventually help improve Kia's lowly resale values.

ENGINES

	dohc I4
Size, liters/cu. in.	1.8/109
Horsepower @ rpm	125 @ 6000
Torque (lb-ft) @ rpm	108 @ 4500
Availability	S
EPA city/highway mpg	
5-speed OD manual	25/30
4-speed OD automatic	22/31

PRICES

Kia Sephia/Spectra	Retail Price	Dealer Invoice
Sephia Base 4-door sedan, 5-speed	$10595	$9596
Sephia Base 4-door sedan, automatic	11570	10456
Sephia LS 4-door sedan, 5-speed	12195	10959
Sephia LS 4-door sedan, automatic	13170	11819
Spectra GS 4-door hatchback, 5-speed	10795	9796
Spectra GS 4-door hatchback, automatic	11770	10656
Spectra GSX 4-door hatchback, 5-speed	12995	11795
Spectra GSX 4-door hatchback, automatic	13970	12655
Destination charge	450	450

STANDARD EQUIPMENT:

Sephia Base/Spectra GS: 1.8-liter dohc 4-cylinder engine, 5-speed manual or 4-speed automatic transmission, dual front airbags, variable-assist power steering, cloth upholstery, front bucket seats, driver seat front cushion tilt, center console, cupholders, split folding rear seat, AM/FM/cassette, tachometer (Spectra GS), . rear defogger, passenger-side visor mirror (Spectra GS), remote fuel-door/decklid release, intermittent wipers, dual remote outside mirrors, 185/65R14 tires, wheel covers.

Sephia LS adds to Sephia Base: air conditioning, tilt steering wheel, power windows, power door locks, tachometer, passenger-side visor mirror.

Spectra GSX adds to Spectra GS: air conditioning, tilt leather-wrapped steering wheel, power windows, power door locks, rear spoiler, bodyside

Specifications begin on page 535.

KIA

cladding, alloy wheels.

OPTIONAL EQUIPMENT:	Retail Price	Dealer Invoice
Major Packages		
Cruise Pkg., LS, GSX	$400	$350
Cruise control, power mirrors, variable intermittent wipers, upgraded sound system.		
Safety Features		
Antilock brakes, LS, GSX	800	745
Includes 4-wheel disc brakes.		
Comfort and Convenience		
Air conditioning, Base, GS	900	745
AM/FM/CD player, LS, GSX	295	245
CD changer, LS, GSX	335	270
Requires AM/FM/CD player.		
Appearance and Miscellaneous		
Alloy wheels, LS	340	274

KIA SPORTAGE

Kia Sportage Limited 4-door wagon

Rear- or 4-wheel-drive compact sport-utility vehicle
Base price range: $14,395-$20,640. Built in South Korea. **Also consider:** Ford Escape, Honda CR-V, Hyundai Santa Fe

FOR • Cargo room • Maneuverability • Visibility **AGAINST**
• Acceleration (4-door) • Ride • Noise • Interior materials • Rear-seat entry/exit (2-door)

Longer warranties and a luxury wagon trim option make 2001 news for this South Korean-built compact SUV. Sportage offers a 4-door wagon in base and EX trim and a shorter 2-door semi-convertible with a manual-fold cloth top over the rear seat. All offer optional antilock brakes and the industry's only standard driver's knee airbag. The only engine is a

Prices are accurate at time of publication; subject to manufacturer's change.

KIA

2.0-liter 4-cylinder. Wagons offer rear-wheel drive or 4WD and manual or optional automatic transmissions. The convertible comes as an automatic 2WD or manual 4x4. Sportage's 4WD isn't for use on dry pavement but has low-range gearing.

This year, EX wagons get a $545 Limited trim/equipment package that includes premium 6-speaker AM/FM/CD/cassette stereo, remote keyless entry, unique alloy wheels, color-keyed bumpers and side cladding, chrome roof rack, hard-shell spare tire cover, and platinum-color gauge. Another $800 delivers 2-tone leather seats with embroidered Limited logos.

Like other 2001 Kias, Sportages are backed by the company's new Long Haul Warranty that duplicates the Hyundai Advantage program. Kia is owned by Hyundai, South Korea's largest automaker. Basic coverage goes from 3 years/36,000 miles to 5/50,000, powertrain coverage from 5/60,000 to 10/100,000, and roadside assistance from 3/36,000 to 5/unlimited miles. Corrosion is warranted for 5/100,000.

PERFORMANCE Sportage competes with the popular Honda CR-V and Toyota RAV4, as well as the Suzuki Vitara/Chevrolet Tracker. The Kia is more like the latter than the car-based Honda and Toyota, whose 4WD doesn't kick in unless the front wheels lose traction. Sportage's 4WD must be manually engaged and then only for slippery conditions. At least it has shift-on-the fly operation and, like the Vitara/Tracker setup, separate low-range gearing for off-road.

Unfortunately, Sportage is a sluggish performer, especially with automatic transmission. Convertibles are a bit sprightlier than wagons, but not much, and the engine in any model is quite gruff when worked even moderately hard. We averaged 19 mpg with a manual 4WD wagon, which is just slightly less than we've recorded with various CR-Vs.

Handling in any Sportage is a nice surprise, thanks to a relatively wide stance that means good stability and relatively modest body lean in tight turns. Ride is more trucky than carlike, however, and noise levels are fairly high from all sources even in gentle cruising, especially in the convertible.

ACCOMMODATIONS The Sportage wagon is larger than it looks and has OK room for four adults. Head clearance is good, even for 6-footers. Entry/exit is reasonable thanks to largish doors and a relatively low step-in, but the convertible makes rear access much tighter and trickier, and it offers scant rear leg space with the front seats pushed back. Still, the convertible Sportage is no worse in these areas than the soft-top Vitara/Tracker. The Kia's top is time-consuming to raise or lower, despite few snaps and numerous Velcro fastenings, though it fits well.

Wagon or convertible, Sportage drivers enjoy a carlike dash and seating position. Visibility is generally good, but the wagon's outside spare tire is in the way directly aft and the convertible's wide center roof posts interfere at some intersections. Both models offer good cargo space for their

Specifications begin on page 535.

KIA

exterior size, but only with rear seats folded. All Sportages feel solid enough on the road, and materials and workmanship seem to have improved lately to near-Japanese levels, but Kia still ranks low in consumer surveys of reliability and satisfaction.

VALUE The Sportage wagon is a questionable value even as a budget-priced SUV, while the convertible is more weekend plaything than practical daily driver. CR-V and RAV4 offer better long-term value, especially at trade-in time, plus superior refinement and workmanship, though they cost somewhat more. And parent Hyundai now has the car-based Santa Fe, a larger, more comfortable wagon available with both V6 power and full-time 4WD for little more than a well-optioned Sportage—and with the same commendably long warranties. Also consider the new Ford Escape.

ENGINES

	dohc I4
Size, liters/cu. in.	2.0/122
Horsepower @ rpm	130 @ 5500
Torque (lb-ft) @ rpm	127 @ 4000
Availability	S

EPA city/highway mpg
5-speed OD manual	19/22[1]
4-speed OD automatic	18/21

1. Wagons; 20/22 mpg on convertibles.

PRICES

Kia Sportage	Retail Price	Dealer Invoice
2WD Base 2-door convertible, automatic	$14395	$13124
2WD Base 4-door wagon, 5-speed	15295	13941
2WD Base 4-door wagon, automatic	16295	14851
4WD Base 2-door convertible, 5-speed	14895	13458
4WD Base 4-door wagon, 5-speed	16795	15170
4WD Base 4-door wagon, automatic	17795	16080
2WD EX 4-door wagon, 5-speed	17895	16180
2WD EX 4-door wagon, automatic	18895	17090
4WD EX 4-door wagon, 5-speed	19095	17100
4WD EX 4-door wagon, automatic	20095	18010
2WD Limited 4-door wagon, 5-speed	18440	16635
2WD Limited 4-door wagon, automatic	19440	17545
4WD Limited 4-door wagon, 5-speed	19640	17555
4WD Limited 4-door wagon, automatic	20640	19465
Destination charge	450	450

STANDARD EQUIPMENT:

Base: 2.0-liter dohc 4-cylinder engine, 5-speed manual or 4-speed automatic transmission, dual front airbags, driver-side knee airbag, variable-

Prices are accurate at time of publication; subject to manufacturer's change.

KIA • LAND ROVER

assist power steering, tilt steering wheel, cloth upholstery, front bucket seats w/driver-side lumbar adjuster, center console, cupholders, folding rear seat (convertible), split folding rear seat (wagon), power mirrors, power windows, power door locks, tachometer, digital clock, rear defogger (wagon), remote fuel-door release, intermittent wipers, auxiliary power outlet, rear folding soft top (convertible), rear-mounted full-size spare tire, 205/75R15 tires. **4WD** models add: part-time 4-wheel drive, 2-speed transfer case, alloy wheels.

EX adds: air conditioning, leather-wrapped steering wheel, cruise control, AM/FM/CD player, visor mirrors, variable intermittent wipers, rear wiper/washer, rear privacy glass, roof rack, alloy wheels. **4WD** models add: part-time 4-wheel drive, 2-speed transfer case.

Limited adds: remote keyless entry, AM/FM/cassette/CD player, floormats. **4WD** models add: part-time 4-wheel drive, 2-speed transfer case.

OPTIONAL EQUIPMENT:	Retail Price	Dealer Invoice
Safety Features		
Antilock brakes	$490	$410
Comfort and Convenience		
Air conditioning, Base	900	745
AM/FM/cassette, Base	320	250
AM/FM/CD player, Base	475	375
CD changer, Base, EX	335	270
Leather upholstery, EX	900	760
Limited	800	680
Appearance and Miscellaneous		
Roof rack, Base wagon	195	150
Special Purpose, Wheels and Tires		
Alloy wheels, 2WD Base	340	274

LAND ROVER DISCOVERY
4-wheel-drive midsize sport-utility vehicle

Base price: $33,350-$36,350. Built in England. **Also consider:** Ford Explorer, Lexus RX 300, Mercedes-Benz M-Class

FOR • Ride • Exterior finish • Cargo room **AGAINST** • Instruments/controls • Fuel economy • Noise • Entry/exit

A return to three trim levels marks the lower-priced Land Rover for 2001. Discovery continues as a 4-door sport-utility wagon with permanent 4-wheel drive and standard seating for five, but last year's single model is replaced by SD, LE, and top-line SE versions in ascending order of price, trim, and equipment. An optional Rear Seat Package expands capacity to seven via two forward-facing third-row seats and

LAND ROVER

Land Rover Discovery

changes badging to SD7, LE7, and SE7. All models retain a 4.0-liter V8, 4-speed automatic transmission, antilock 4-wheel disc brakes, and 16-inch wheels. The 4WD has separate low-range gearing and electronic traction control that brakes individual wheels to limit spin in severe conditions. Also standard is Land Rover's Hill Descent Control that automatically applies the brakes to limit speed when descending steep grades in Low range. An optional for SE/SE7 Performance Package delivers 18-inch wheels and Land Rover's Active Cornering Enhancement (ACE), which replaces anti-roll bars with hydraulic rams intended to reduce body lean in hard turns. A rear Self-Leveling Suspension is standard for "7" models and available for LE and SE. Leather interior trim is standard for SE/SE7, as is a new 10-speaker, 220-watt premium audio system. Ford recently purchased Britain's Land Rover from German automaker BMW.

EVALUATION Without ACE, this tall, relatively narrow SUV suffers copious body lean in tight turns. With ACE, it corners with fine control and balance. Too bad the technology is available only on the pricey top-line models. Ride is choppy on closely spaced bumps, but most imperfections are soaked up without jarring. Braking is sure, acceleration okay for the class; our last test model did 0-60 mph in 10.2 seconds. Wind, engine, and axle noise are intrusive, though, and we averaged just 12.5 mpg on required premium fuel. The optional third-row seat feels cramped, but overall people and package space are good. A tall step-in and narrow doorways make entry/exit tough even for an SUV, especially to the rear. Workmanship remains patchy; one recent test model had numerous squeaks and rattles. Optional 7-seat capacity is a plus, but the BMW X5, Mercedes M-Class, and Lexus RX 300 offer better performance, handling, refinement, and quality without the Discovery's English eccentricities.

ENGINES

	ohv V8
Size, liters/cu. in.	4.0/241
Horsepower @ rpm	188 @ 4750
Torque (lb-ft) @ rpm	250 @ 2600

Prices are accurate at time of publication; subject to manufacturer's change.

LAND ROVER

	ohv V8
Availability	S
EPA city/highway mpg	
4-speed OD automatic	13/17

PRICES

Land Rover Discovery	Retail Price	Dealer Invoice
SD 4-door wagon	$33350	$29685
LE 4-door wagon	34350	30570
SE 4-door wagon	36350	32350
Destination charge	625	625

STANDARD EQUIPMENT:

SD: 4.0-liter V8 engine, 4-speed automatic transmission, permanent 4-wheel drive, 2-speed transfer case, traction control, Hill Descent Control, dual front airbags, antilock 4-wheel disc brakes, air conditioning w/dual-zone control, outside temperature indicator, power steering, leather-wrapped tilt steering wheel, cruise control, vinyl upholstery, 8-way power front bucket seats, center console, cupholders, split folding rear seat, heated power mirrors, power windows, power door locks, remote keyless entry, AM/FM/cassette, digital clock, steering wheel radio controls, tachometer, rear defogger, rear wiper/washer, illuminated visor mirrors, automatic day/night rearview mirror, compass, map lights, auxiliary power outlets, variable intermittent wipers, remote fuel-door release, rear fog lights, theft-deterrent system, rear-mounted full-size spare tire, 255/65HR16 tires, alloy wheels.

LE adds: cloth/leather upholstery, wood interior trim, front fog lights, headlight washers.

SE adds: leather upholstery, front seat power lumbar adjustment, dual power sunroofs, Phillips/Lear sound system, in-dash 6-disc CD changer, universal garage door opener, cargo cover, Class III towing hitch receiver.

OPTIONAL EQUIPMENT:
Major Packages

Rear Seat Pkg.	1750	1558

Forward-facing third-row seats, hydraulic rear step, remote radio controls (SE), self-leveling rear suspension.

Performance Pkg., SE	2900	2581

Active Cornering Enhancement, 255/55HR18 tires, special alloy wheels.

Cold Climate Pkg.	500	445

Heated windshield, heated front seats.

Specifications begin on page 535.

LAND ROVER

Comfort and Convenience	Retail Price	Dealer Invoice
Dual power sunroofs, SD, LE	$1500	$1335
Rear air conditioning, LE, SE	750	668
Special Purpose, Wheels and Tires		
Self-leveling rear suspension, LE, SE	750	668

LAND ROVER RANGE ROVER

Land Rover Range Rover 4.6 HSE

4-wheel-drive full-size sport-utility vehicle

Base price range: $62,000-$68,000. Built in England. **Also consider:** BMW X5, Lexus LX 470, Mercedes-Benz M-Class

FOR • Ride • Passenger and cargo room • Build quality **AGAINST** • Fuel economy • Entry/exit

Britain's flagship sport-utility continues in two models, but last year's 4.0 SE adopts the larger V8 of the uplevel 4.6 HSE to become a 4.6 SE. Both have permanent 4-wheel drive with low-range gearing, automatic transmission, antilock 4-wheel disc brakes, traction control, front side airbags, and a driver-adjustable self-leveling suspension. The HSE has standard 18-inch wheels instead of 16s, additional wood and leather interior trim, a satellite-linked navigation system, and a new 6-speaker 460-watt premium audio system with steering-wheel controls and CD changer. All are available for the SE. Also for 2001, the nav system adds several features designed for off-road use, and the HSE gets a no-cost "Luxurious Carpets" trim option with carpeting and seat piping that complement specific paint colors. Range Rover is built alongside the less expensive Discovery by Land Rover, which Ford recently purchased from Germany's BMW. A redesigned Range Rover is slated for 2002.

EVALUATION These vehicles are marvelous off-road and comfortable on-road. The SE always deserved the HSE's larger V8, but even that gives only adequate acceleration, plus dismal "economy": just 13.1 mpg in mostly highway driving, a dismal 11.8 overall in our tests. Handling is predictable but not much fun, and lots of steering correction is needed to stay on course at highway speeds. The cabin is roomy and the seats

Prices are accurate at time of publication; subject to manufacturer's change.

LAND ROVER

cushy, though the lack of third-row seating is a competitive deficit. Control layout and operation are unorthodox; the navigation system is particularly tricky. Recent test models have exhibited prominent gear whine. Overall, Range Rover offers little of tangible value that you can't get in rival SUVs for thousands less.

ENGINES

	ohv V8
Size, liters/cu. in.	4.6/278
Horsepower @ rpm	222 @ 4750
Torque (lb-ft) @ rpm	300 @ 2600
Availability	S

EPA city/highway mpg
4-speed OD automatic 12/15

PRICES

Land Rover Range Rover	Retail Price	Dealer Invoice
4.6 SE 4-door wagon	$62000	$54870
4.6 HSE 4-door wagon	68000	60180
Destination charge	625	625

STANDARD EQUIPMENT:

4.6 SE: 4.6-liter V8 engine, 4-speed automatic transmission, full-time 4-wheel drive, 2-speed transfer case, locking center differential, front and rear traction control, dual front airbags, front side-airbags, antilock 4-wheel disc brakes, variable-assist power steering, tilt/telescopic leather-wrapped steering wheel, cruise control, air conditioning w/dual-zone automatic climate control, interior air filter, leather upholstery, heated 10-way power front bucket seats w/memory, center console, cupholders, split folding rear seat, wood interior trim, heated power mirrors w/memory and automatic day/night, outside mirror tilt-down back-up aid, power windows, power door locks, remote keyless entry, Harman/Kardon AM/FM/weatherband/cassette w/in-dash 6-disc CD changer, steering-wheel radio controls, tachometer, power sunroof, trip computer, automatic day/night rearview mirror, universal garage-door opener, remote fuel-door release, rear defogger, variable intermittent wipers, variable-intermittent rear wiper/washer, illuminated visor mirrors, map lights, cargo cover, theft-deterrent system, headlight wiper/washers, front and rear fog lights, trailer hitch and wiring harness, height-adjustable and automatic load-leveling suspension, full-size spare tire, 265/65HR16 tires, alloy wheels.

4.6 HSE adds: navigation system, upgraded Harman/Kardon sound system, upgraded leather and wood interior trim, 255/55HR18 tires.

OPTIONAL EQUIPMENT:
Comfort and Convenience

Wood/leather-wrapped steering wheel, HSE.................. 400   354

Specifications begin on page 535.

LAND ROVER • LEXUS

	Retail Price	Dealer Invoice
Color-keyed carpets/seat piping, HSE	$750	$550

Major Packages

Navigation/Audio Pkg., SE	3000	2650

Includes upgraded Harman/Kardon sound system.

LEXUS ES 300

Lexus ES 300

Front-wheel-drive near-luxury car

Base price: $31,505. Built in Japan. **Also consider:** Acura TL, Infiniti I30, Mercedes-Benz C-Class

FOR • Acceleration • Ride • Quietness • Build quality • Exterior finish • Interior materials **AGAINST** • Rear visibility • Steering feel

An emergency in-trunk opener and revised option packages mark the 2001 edition of the front-wheel drive sedan from Toyota's luxury brand. The ES 300 is a visually distinct cousin to the V6 Toyota Camry sedan, but has slightly more power and more standard features, including front side airbags and traction control. Lexus now offers a second near-luxury model in the slightly smaller rear-drive IS 300, but that one targets the enthusiast market against the Audi A4 and BMW 3-Series. The ES aims at luxury-minded buyers.

ES offers options unavailable on Camry, including Lexus's Vehicle Skid Control (VSC) stability system, a Brake Assist feature that provides full stopping power in response to strong, quick brake-pedal movement, and a "semi-active" Adaptive Variable Suspension that adjusts shock-absorber damping within driver-selected soft, normal, and sport modes. For 2001, ES replaces its previous major option groups with six new ones, each with leather-trim interior in combination with various other popular extras. The newly standard in-trunk release has a glow-in-the-dark handle and is intended to prevent someone from being accidentally trapped in the trunk.

PERFORMANCE Quietness and comfort remain the ES 300's signature assets. Wind and road noise are muted, and the V6 is nearly silent at idle, silken under power. Acceleration is brisk at under 7.5 seconds

Prices are accurate at time of publication; subject to manufacturer's change.

LEXUS

0-60 mph in our tests. Less likable is an automatic transmission that's reluctant to kick down from overdrive fourth at midrange speeds, which frustrates passing. Fuel economy is acceptable but not outstanding; we averaged 20.5 mpg overall on the required premium gas. Braking is swift and vice-free save marked nosedive in simulated panic stops.

In ride and handling, the ES 300 is more "little limo" than sports sedan. Steering is quick but short on road feel, and though the car corners capably, it does so with marked body lean and relatively modest grip. Ride is soft and isolating, but some sharp bumps do register. The optional Adaptive Variable Suspension—basically computer-controlled shock absorbers—has little functional advantage over the normal chassis, but the optional VSC antiskid system is worth the money.

ACCOMMODATIONS The ES interior is an inviting place for four adults. Six-footers can sit comfortably in tandem, although those in back must ride knees-up and have little toe room beneath the front seats. The trunk is modestly sized bit usefully shaped and benefits from a low liftover. Drivers get ample seat and steering-wheel adjustments, clear gauges, and handy switchgear. Outward visibility is fine except for hard-to-see rear corners, a penalty of the high-tail styling. Workmanship and materials are generally first-rate, although the last ES 300 we tested had some misaligned dashboard panels—very un-Lexus.

VALUE The ES now feels dated against newer-design rivals like the Acura TL, BMW 3-Series, and Mercedes C-Class, and an Infiniti I30 costs somewhat less with comparable equipment. But if you value comfort and elegance over sporty road manners in your near-luxury car, the ES is still hard to beat, and its resale values are golden.

ENGINES

	dohc V6
Size, liters/cu. in.	3.0/181
Horsepower @ rpm	210 @ 5800
Torque (lb-ft) @ rpm	220 @ 4400
Availability	S

EPA city/highway mpg
4-speed OD automatic	20/28

PRICES

Lexus ES 300	Retail Price	Dealer Invoice
Base 4-door sedan	$31505	$27365
Destination charge	545	545

STANDARD EQUIPMENT:

Base: 3.0-liter dohc V6 engine, 4-speed automatic transmission, traction control, dual front airbags, front side-airbags, antilock 4-wheel disc brakes, daytime running lights, emergency inside trunk

Specifications begin on page 535.

LEXUS

release, air conditioning w/automatic climate control, variable-assist power steering, tilt steering wheel, cruise control, cloth upholstery, front bucket seats, 10-way power driver seat w/power lumbar support, 8-way power passenger seat, center console, cupholders, rear seat trunk pass-through, wood interior trim, heated power mirrors w/driver-side automatic day/night, power windows, power door locks, remote keyless entry, AM/FM cassette, digital clock, tachometer, automatic day/night rearview mirror, overhead console, outside-temperature indicator, rear defogger, variable intermittent wipers, illuminated visor mirrors, remote fuel-door and decklid releases, auxiliary power outlet, automatic headlights, floormats, theft-deterrent system, fog lights, full-size spare tire, 205/65VR15 tires, alloy wheels.

OPTIONAL EQUIPMENT:

	Retail Price	Dealer Invoice

Major Packages

	Retail Price	Dealer Invoice
Leather Trim Pkg.	$1885	$1508

Leather upholstery, leather-wrapped steering wheel, memory driver seat and outside mirrors, interior air filter, universal garage door opener.

VP Value Pkg.	1965	1769

Leather Trim Pkg. plus power sunroof, in-dash 6-disc CD c hanger.

VK Value Pkg. w/Nakamichi Audio	2515	2264

Value Pkg. plus Nakamichi premium sound system.

Safety Features

Antiskid system	550	440

Comfort and Convenience

Power sunroof	1000	800
Heated front seats	440	352

Requires Leather Trim Pkg.

Nakamichi premium audio system	1630	1277

Includes in-dash 6-disc CD changer.

In-dash 6-disc CD changer	1080	864
Wood steering wheel	300	240

Requires Leather Trim Pkg.

Appearance and Miscellaneous

High intensity headlights	515	412
Adaptive Variable Suspension	620	496

Requires Leather Trim Pkg.

Chrome alloy wheels	1740	870

Includes 205/60VR16 tires.

Prices are accurate at time of publication; subject to manufacturer's change.

LEXUS

	Retail Price	Dealer Invoice
205/60VR16 tires	$40	$32

LEXUS GS 300/430

Lexus GS 300

Rear-wheel-drive luxury car
Base price range: $38,555-$47,355. Built in Japan. **Also consider:** BMW 5-Series, Jaguar S-Type, Mercedes-Benz E-Class

FOR • Acceleration • Steering/handling • Quietness • Build quality • Exterior finish • Interior materials **AGAINST** • Fuel economy • Navigation system controls

Lexus's midrange sedans are now the 6-cylinder GS 300 and the new GS 430, which replaces last year's GS 400 model and uses the same new 4.3-liter V8 as Lexus's larger LS 430 sedan. For 2001, both GS models sport subtle styling changes, including new high-intensity headlamps as standard for the 430 and optional for the 300. A 5-speed automatic remains the only transmission, but the GS 300 now comes with the V8's "E-Shift" steering-wheel control buttons. Window-curtain side airbags are newly standard for both versions, joining lower-body side airbags. Lexus's Vehicle Skid Control (VSC) stability system, traction control, and antilock brakes are standard. A navigation system is optional. Both models add standard steering-wheel audio controls for '01, plus electronic compass, and additional wood interior trim. The top audio option is now a premium 8-speaker Mark Levinson system, similar to that available on the LS 430.

V8 or six, the GS delivers swift, silky performance and powerful braking. We haven't yet timed a new 430, but our last 400 ran 0-60 mph in only 6 seconds; the 300 takes around 7.6. Our GS 400s average 17.9-19.0 mpg; the 430 should be little if any

Specifications begin on page 535.

LEXUS

thirstier. A test 300 averaged 17.2 mpg with lots of city driving. Premium fuel is recommended for both engines. The smooth automatic transmission is responsive, but not everyone gets the hang of the E-shift control buttons. Both models are very quiet, though minor tire roar is noticed with optional 17-inch rubber. Either GS corners with grippy precision and only moderate body lean, but overall ride, handling, and brake-pedal feel don't quite match those of German rivals. Ride is supple on the 300, a bit thumpy on the V8 model over tar strips and expansion joints. Interiors offer fine comfort for four adults, though rear head room is tight for 6-footers and not all drivers will find a suitable position despite multiple power adjustments. Vision astern is limited. The optional in-dash navigator absorbs some audio and climate controls, which can complicate driving. Trunk space isn't exceptional. Cabin materials are gorgeous and overall workmanship top-notch, but recent test cars have had some minor interior rattles and one had ripply looking paint beneath its glossy clearcoat. Either GS is a good alternative to German sports sedans, with the 300 a better overall value than the rapid 430.

ENGINES

	dohc I6	dohc V8
Size, liters/cu. in.	3.0/183	4.3/262
Horsepower @ rpm	220 @ 5800	300 @ 5600
Torque (lb-ft) @ rpm	220 @ 3800	325 @ 3400
Availability	S[1]	S[2]
EPA city/highway mpg		
5-speed OD automatic	18/24	18/23

1. GS 300. 2. GS 430.

PRICES

Lexus GS 300/430	Retail Price	Dealer Invoice
GS 300 4-door sedan	$38555	$33489
GS 430 4-door sedan	47355	40655
Destination charge	545	545

STANDARD EQUIPMENT:

GS 300: 3.0-liter dohc 6-cylinder engine, 5-speed automatic transmission w/manual shift-capability, traction control, dual front airbags, front side-airbags, front side curtain airbags, antilock 4-wheel disc brakes, anti-skid system, daytime running lights, air conditioning w/automatic dual-zone climate control, interior air filter, variable-assist power steering, power tilt/telescopic leather-wrapped steering wheel, cruise control, cloth upholstery, 10-way power front bucket seats with power lumbar support, center console, cupholders, wood

LEXUS

interior trim, heated power mirrors w/automatic day/night, power windows, power door locks, remote keyless entry, AM/FM/cassette, digital clock, automatic day/night rearview mirror, compass, variable intermittent wipers, rear defogger, outside-temperature indicator, illuminated visor mirrors, universal garage door opener, remote fuel-door and trunk releases, map lights, automatic headlights, floormats, theft-deterrent system, fog lights, 215/60VR16 tires, alloy wheels.

GS 430 adds: 4.0-liter dohc V8 engine, leather upholstery, memory system (driver seat, steering wheel, outside mirrors), high-intensity headlights, 225/55VR16 tires. *Deletes:* manual shift-capability.

OPTIONAL EQUIPMENT:

	Retail Price	Dealer Invoice
Major Packages		
LA Leather Trim Pkg., GS 300	$1660	$1328
Leather upholstery, memory system (driver seat, steering wheel, outside mirrors).		
PM Premium Pkg., GS 300	3760	3008
Leather Trim Pkg., power sunroof, in-dash 6-disc CD changer, heated front seats, high-intensity headlights.		
PM Premium Pkg., GS 430	2540	2032
Heated front seats, power sunroof, in-dash 6-disc CD changer.		
ND Navigation System Pkg., GS 300	6715	5472
GS 430	4540	3732
Premium Pkg. plus navigation system.		
NL Navigation/Mark Levinson Radio System Pkg., GS 300	7965	6410
GS 430	5790	4670
Navigation System Pkg. plus Premium Mark Levinson Radio System Pkg.		
LI Premium Mark Levinson Radio System Pkg., GS 300	5965	4710
GS 430	3790	2970
Premium Pkg. plus Mark Levinson sound sytem.		
Comfort and Convenience		
Heated front seats, GS 300	440	352
Requires Premium Pkg.		
In-dash 6-disc CD changer	1080	864
Power sunroof	1020	816

Specifications begin on page 535.

LEXUS

	Retail Price	Dealer Invoice
Wood/leather-wrapped steering wheel, GS 430	$300	$240

Appearance and Miscellaneous

Rear spoiler, GS 430	440	352
235/45ZR17 tires, GS 430	215	172
Chrome alloy wheels	1700	850

LEXUS IS 300

Lexus IS 300

Rear-wheel-drive near-luxury car

Base price: $30,500. Built in Japan. **Also consider:** Acura TL, Audi A4, BMW 3-Series, Mercedes-Benz C-Class

FOR • Acceleration • Brake performance • Handling **AGAINST** • Automatic transmission controls • Rear-seat room • Road noise

Toyota's luxury division takes on the Audi A4, BMW 3-Series and other premium sporty compacts with this new rear-drive sedan. The IS 300 uses the same 3.0-liter inline 6-cylinder engine as Lexus's larger GS 300 sedan, though with a bit less power and torque. Initially, the only transmission is a 5-speed automatic with Lexus's E-Shift steering-wheel buttons for manual gear changes. A 5-speed manual transmission is slated for early 2001, likely as a no-charge option. Against the target 3-Series, the IS 300 is similar in overall length and height, but stands about an inch narrower on a 2-inch shorter wheelbase.

Standard equipment includes antilock 4-wheel disc brakes, 17-inch wheels with performance tires, traction control, front side airbags, heated mirrors, high-intensity headlamps, automatic climate control, and an in-dash 6-disc CD changer. Options are limited to leather and suede upholstery, heated front seats, sunroof, limited-slip differential, and, at no extra cost, 16-inch wheels with all-season tires.

PERFORMANCE Like a good welterweight boxer, the IS 300 is light on

LEXUS

its feet and packs a solid punch. Lexus claims 7.1 seconds for the 0-60-mph dash, which seems right to us after our initial test drives. We averaged 17.2 mpg on the required premium gas.

The responsive automatic transmission helps performance with greased-lightning shifts in both manual and automatic modes. One test car, however, sometimes upshifted when it wasn't supposed to. And some of our test drivers find it difficult to become acclimated to E-Shift, which uses two buttons on the steering-wheel face for downshifts, two on the backside for changing up. The floor shift gate has slots for third gear and fifth, but not fourth, which discourages working the lever manually

The IS handles with agility and tracks accurately regardless of wheel/tire choice. Cornering too fast risks an easy tail-slide, but it's readily corrected with the quick, informative steering. Overall, credit this behavior more to the car's nimble size and good tires rather than a suspension in a league with the best of Europe. That's brought home in a ride that's firm and occasionally thumpy, though the car copes well with broken pavement at higher speeds. Simulated panic stops showed little dive and good stability, though braking isn't as confident as BMW's. Tire noise is the main disturbance of the peace, and then not much. Lexus says the IS engine is tuned for a throatier sound versus the GS 300 six, but it's still subdued at lower rpm and always creamy smooth and pleasant to the ear.

ACCOMMODATIONS The IS 300 is compact-car small inside, so two passengers is the practical limit in the rear seat, and 6-footers won't want to ride back there for any length of time. Narrow doorways make getting in or out of the rear seat a squeeze. Front occupants fare better, but rearward seat travel is only adequate for long-legged drivers. The front buckets are relatively thin shells with subpar lumbar bolstering and cushions too short for proper thigh support.

Drivers have things pretty easy otherwise, with clear sightlines except to the rear (because high-tail styling) and simple, well-spotted controls. The jazzy "chronograph-style" gauge cluster works well enough, but we'd prefer more straightforward gauges.

In-cabin storage is subcompact-size, but OK. So is cargo room, though the usefully cubic trunk has U-shape hinges that eat into the space and could crunch your Louis Vuitton. Workmanship on the cars we tested was up to Lexus's usual standard, but the IS 300 doesn't feel quite as substantial as a BMW 3-Series or A4, even though it weighs about the same. And the odd ribbed dashtop trim looks low-class.

VALUE As a smaller, more agile Lexus, the IS 300 gives the brand a new weapon to begin shifting its image away from soft-riding luxury cars with little enthusiast appeal. But it really doesn't exceed expectations on any front. The 3-Series is tough competition, and the IS is clearly an upstart imitator without "built for the autobahn" cachet. Still, this is a nifty

Specifications begin on page 535.

LEXUS

little sedan, and Lexus should have no problem with the modest 25,000 units per year it hopes to sell. Give the IS 300 a whirl, but check out the 3-Series, A4, and Acura's satisfying, high-value TL.

ENGINES

	dohc I6
Size, liters/cu. in.	3.0/183
Horsepower @ rpm	215 @ 5800
Torque (lb-ft) @ rpm	218 @ 3800
Availability	S

EPA city/highway mpg

5-speed OD automatic	18/23

PRICES

Lexus IS 300	Retail Price	Dealer Invoice
Base 4-door sedan	$30500	$26492
Destination charge	495	495

STANDARD EQUIPMENT:

Base: 3.0-liter dohc 6-cylinder engine, 5-speed automatic transmission w/manual-shift capability, traction control, dual front airbags, front side-impact airbags, antilock 4-wheel disc brakes, daytime running lights, emergency inside trunk release, air conditioning w/automatic climate control, interior air filter, variable-assist power steering, tilt leather-wrapped steering wheel, cruise control, cloth upholstery, front bucket seats, center console, cupholders, trunk pass-through, heated power mirrors, power windows, power door locks, remote keyless entry, AM/FM/cassette/in-dash 6-disc CD changer, digital clock, tachometer, rear defogger, map lights, visor mirrors, remote decklid release, theft-deterrent system, Xenon headlights, fog lights, 215/45ZR17 tires, alloy wheels.

OPTIONAL EQUIPMENT:

Major Packages

Leather Pkg.	1705	1364

Leather/suede upholstery, 8-way power front seats, universal garage door opener.

Luxury Leather Pkg.	1805	1444

Leather Pkg. plus special seat trim, wood interior trim.

Powertrains

Limited-slip differential	390	312

Comfort and Convenience

Power sunroof	1000	800
Heated front seats	440	352

Requires option pkg.

Prices are accurate at time of publication; subject to manufacturer's change.

LEXUS

Appearance and Miscellaneous

	Retail Price	Dealer Invoice
Polished alloy wheels	$400	$320
205/55VR16 tires	NC	NC

LEXUS LS 430

Lexus LS 430

Rear-wheel-drive luxury car

Base price: $54,005. Built in Japan. **Also consider:** Audi A8, BMW 7-Series, Mercedes-Benz S-Class

FOR • Acceleration • Ride • Quietness • Build quality **AGAINST** • Automatic transmission performance • Instruments/controls

Lexus turned the luxury-car market on its ear in 1989 with its original LS 400. Offering hushed accommodations, V8 muscle, and Camry-like dependability starting at $35,000, the first premium sedan from Toyota's upscale division undercut European rivals by thousands of dollars. The 2001 Lexus LS 430 aims for a similar breakthrough.

Named for its new 4.3-liter V8, this second-generation LS has more interior room than the original thanks to a 3-inch longer wheelbase and a taller roofline. Horsepower remains 290, but the new LS has more torque in a quest for improved throttle response. One of the few returning components is the 5-speed automatic transmission.

The '01 comes in three basic states of trim: base, base with Euro-Tuned suspension, and Ultra-Luxury. All have side curtain airbags, front lower-body side airbags, High Intensity Discharge headlamps, leather upholstery, and antiskid control. Also available is Lexus Link, an assistance service provided in conjunction with the similar General Motors OnStar system.

The Euro-Tuned version gets tauter suspension tuning in combination with 17-inch wheels and tires in place of 16s. The $12,290 Ultra-Luxury package includes an dual-mode air suspension, navigation system, Mark Levinson audio, laminated side glass, power door closers, heated and cooled front seats, and upgraded leather and wood trim with

Specifications begin on page 535.

LEXUS

suede headliner. The package adds to the rear passenger compartment separate audio and climate controls; seat adjusters with memory, heat, and massage; refrigerated armrest; power sunshade, and manual side window shades. Some of these features are available separately. The LS 430 also offers front and rear parking assist and a laser cruise control system designed to maintain a set distance from the vehicle ahead.

PERFORMANCE The 430 carries on the LS tradition of silent but swift acceleration. Lexus claims a 0-60 mph in 6.3 seconds. That's actually a tick slower than the 6.1 of our test 2000 model, but fast nonetheless, and still whisper quiet, even under full throttle. Sadly, acceleration is handicapped in passing situations by a slow-to-downshift transmission. We didn't have an opportunity to measure fuel economy, but EPA estimates are unchanged and we expect the '01 to average about 17 mpg.

Ride quality is another LS hallmark and the 430 is supple on even the harshest surfaces. The Ultra's air suspension is even smoother.

Steering feel and overall roadholding, shortcomings in the past, are improved—especially with the sport setup. Still, the LS can't match the athletic feel of the BMW 7-Series and Audi A8. The brakes on the LS 430s we tested were disappointing. Stopping power feels modest, and pedal action is mushy rather than firm. The antiskid system works well, helping maintain control in slippery turns. We were unable to evaluate the new laser cruise control system, but are interested to test a device that changes vehicle speed without driver input.

ACCOMMODATIONS There's ample room for four large adults and entry/exit is a snap. Well positioned, supportively contoured, and power adjustable 14 ways, the driver's seat is among the most inviting in the industry. Add the optional air heating/cooling and you ride for hours without discomfort. The standard rear seats are comfortable, and the Ultra-Luxury's adjustable/massaging rear seats and other amenities make for a remarkably soothing experience.

Gauges are legible, interior storage space is plentiful, outward visibility is excellent, and the fore/aft park assist takes the worry out of maneuvering in tight places. On the downside, all this technology results in a daunting jumble of buttons, switches, and dials—especially on models with the navigation system, where even activating the voice-command function requires pressing a button.

Interior materials and assembly are average for the premium class—except on the Ultra-Luxury, which raises the luxury-car bar for quality, fit, and finish. Trunk space is among best-in-class, though the Ultra-Luxury's separate rear air conditioning system cuts its volume to 17.5 cubic feet.

VALUE The LS 430 is priced close to the $54,005 list of the 2000 LS 400, though the Ultra-Luxury adds $12,290. Despite some techo-overload, Lexus's latest flagship again sets the standard for comfort, coddling, and isolation among premium luxury sedans.

Prices are accurate at time of publication; subject to manufacturer's change.

LEXUS

ENGINES

	dohc V8
Size, liters/cu. in.	4.3/262
Horsepower @ rpm	290 @ 5600
Torque (lb-ft) @ rpm	320 @ 3400
Availability	S

EPA city/highway mpg

5-speed OD automatic 18/25

PRICES

Lexus LS 430	Retail Price	Dealer Invoice
Base 4-door sedan	$54005	$46363
Destination charge	545	545

STANDARD EQUIPMENT:

Base: 4.3-liter dohc V8 engine, 5-speed automatic transmission, traction control, dual front airbags, front side-impact airbags, front and rear side-head-protection system, antilock 4-wheel disc brakes, antiskid system, emergency inside trunk release, daytime running lights, variable-assist power steering, power tilt/telescoping steering wheel, leather-wrapped/wood steering wheel, cruise control, air conditioning w/dual zone automatic climate control, leather upholstery, 14-way power driver seat, 10-way power passenger seat, front power headrests and lumbar adjustment, memory system (driver seat and headrest, steering wheel, mirrors), center console, cupholders, wood interior trim, heated power mirrors w/tilt-down back-up aid, automatic day/night rearview and outside mirrors, power windows, power door locks, remote keyless entry, AM/FM/cassette w/in-dash 6-disc CD changer, steering wheel radio controls, digital clock, tachometer, outside temperature indicator, trip computer, compass, rear defogger, illuminated visor mirrors, universal garage door opener, map lights, rain-sensing variable intermittent wipers, remote fuel-door and decklid release, auxiliary power outlet, automatic headlights, floormats, theft-deterrent sytem, high-intensity discharge headlights, fog lights, tool kit, full-size spare tire, 225/60HR16 tires, alloy wheels.

OPTIONAL EQUIPMENT:
Major Packages

Ultra Luxury Pkg. 12290   9870
Navigation system w/Lexus Link, rear air conditioning w/rear climate control and interior air filter, climate controlled front seats, heated rear seats, rear seat power adjusters and massage, rear seat cooler box in armrest, power sunroof, suede headliner, Mark Levinson sound system, rear radio controls, dynamic laser cruise control (maintains distance from vehicle in front of car), power rear sunshade, manual rear side-window sunshades, power door closer, laminated side glass, front and rear parking sensing system, self-adjusting air suspension.

Specifications begin on page 535.

LEXUS

	Retail Price	Dealer Invoice
Navigation System Pkg.	$4000	$3300
Navigation system, power sunroof, heated front and rear seats.		
Mark Levinson Radio System Pkg.	3240	2530
Mark Levinson sound system, power sunroof, heated front and rear seats.		
Navigation System/Radio System	5240	4230
Navigation System Pkg. plus Mark Levinson sound system.		

Comfort and Convenience

Lexus Link	1215	1015
Emergency and roadside assistance, travel advice and information. Includes one year service fee.		
Power sunroof	1120	896
Heated front and rear seats	880	704
Nappa Leather Interior Pkg.	1460	1168
Upgraded leather upholstery. Requires Ultra Luxury Pkg.		
Nappa Leather/Semi Anilin Leather Interior Pkg.	2105	1684
Upgraded leather upholstery. Requires Ultra Luxury Pkg.		

Appearance and Miscellaneous

Euro-Tuned Suspension	NC	NC
Requires 225/55R17 tires.		
225/55R17 tires	100	80
Chrome alloy wheels	1800	900
Includes 225/55R17 tires.		

LEXUS LX 470

Lexus LX 470

4-wheel-drive full-size sport-utility vehicle; similar to Toyota Land Cruiser

Base price: $61,405. Built in Japan. **Also consider:** BMW X5, Lincoln Navigator

FOR • Acceleration • Passenger and cargo room • Ride • Build quality • Exterior finish • Interior materials **AGAINST** • Fuel economy

Prices are accurate at time of publication; subject to manufacturer's change.

LEXUS

• Rear entry/exit

A few added features and an exclusive navigation/entertainment option mark the 2001 upscale version of the Toyota Land Cruiser. LX 470 stands apart with Lexus styling cues, a higher price, and more standard equipment, but both these big SUVs come with V8 power, traction control and antiskid systems, antilock brakes with full-power Brake Assist, and permanent 4-wheel drive with low-range gearing and locking center differential. Exclusive to the LX is a standard Adaptive Variable Suspension with computer-controlled shock absorbers and Automatic Height Control with three driver-selectable elevations. Other standards include sunroof, lighted running boards, leather/wood interior trim, rear air conditioning, and CD changer.

New for '01 is a 9-speaker Mark Levinson sound system, replacing last year's premium Nakamichi option, and the LX's first optional navigation system. The latter displays map data from a DVD drive that will also play DVD movies on the in-dash screen—an industry first—though only with the transmission in Park. The DVD drive integrates with the normal CD changer and will play movie audio tracks with the vehicle in motion. Newly standard is a leather/wood steering wheel (optional before), second-row child-seat anchorages, new dual rear cupholders, and revised keys and locks designed to better resist tampering.

LX 470 performance and accommodations are similar to those of the Land Cruiser.

The Toyota Land Cruiser report includes an evaluation of the LX 470.

ENGINES

	dohc V8
Size, liters/cu. in.	4.7/285
Horsepower @ rpm	230 @ 4800
Torque (lb-ft) @ rpm	320 @ 3400
Availability	S

EPA city/highway mpg

4-speed OD automatic	13/16

PRICES

Lexus LX 470	Retail Price	Dealer Invoice
Base 4-door wagon	$61405	$52716
Destination charge	545	545

STANDARD EQUIPMENT:

Base: 4.7-liter dohc V8 engine, 4-speed automatic transmission, full-time 4-wheel drive, locking center differential and limited-slip rear differential, traction control, dual front airbags, antiskid system, antilock 4-wheel disc brakes, daytime running lights, front and rear air conditioning w/front and rear automatic climate controls, interior air filter, variable-assist power steering, power

Specifications begin on page 535.

LEXUS

tilt and telescoping steering wheel w/memory, wood/leather-wrapped steering wheel, cruise control, leather upholstery, heated power front bucket seats with driver-side lumbar support and memory, center console, cupholders, reclining and split folding middle seat, split folding third-row seat, wood interior trim, heated power mirrors w/driver-side automatic day/night and memory, passenger-side mirror w/tilt-down back-up aid, power windows, power door locks, remote keyless entry, AM/FM/cassette w/in-dash 6-disc CD changer, overhead console, power antenna, digital clock, tachometer, power sunroof, universal garage door opener, rear defogger, intermittent rear wiper/washer, outside temperature display, auxiliary power outlets, automatic day/night rearview mirror, compass, illuminated visor mirrors, map lights, variable intermittent wipers, automatic headlights, remote fuel-door release, floormats, running boards, rear privacy glass, fog lights, theft-deterrent system, adaptive-variable and height-adjustable suspension, full-size spare tire, 275/70HR16 tires, alloy wheels.

OPTIONAL EQUIPMENT:

	Retail Price	Dealer Invoice
Major Packages		
Navigation/Radio System	$4280	$3510
Navigation system, Mark Levinson sound system, DVD/CD changer in console.		
Comfort and Convenience		
Mark Levinson Radio System	1280	960
Appearance and Miscellaneous		
Roof rack	603	375
Chrome alloy wheels	1300	350

Post production options also available.

LEXUS RX 300

CG BEST BUY AUTO

Lexus RX 300

Front- or 4-wheel-drive midsize sport-utility vehicle; similar to Toyota Highlander

Base price range: $33,005-$34,605. Built in Japan. **Also consider:** Acura MDX, BMW X5, Mercedes-Benz M-Class

Prices are accurate at time of publication; subject to manufacturer's change.

LEXUS

FOR • Ride • Passenger and cargo room • Build quality • Exterior finish • Interior materials **AGAINST** • Audio and climate controls

A standard antiskid system and several detail updates take the best-selling Lexus into its third model year. A pioneer "crossover" vehicle blending truck and car attributes, the RX 300 continues as a 5-passenger, 4-door sport-utility wagon available with front-wheel drive or permanent all-wheel drive. The AWD lacks separate low-range gearing, but the RX isn't designed for severe off-road use. The sole powertrain again comprises a 4-speed automatic transmission and a 3.0-liter V6 with variable valve timing. Towing capacity is 3500 pounds. For 2001, standard front side airbags and antilock 4-wheel disc brakes are joined by Lexus's Vehicle Skid Control (VSC) that modulates brakes and engine power to maintain stability in slippery conditions. Also newly standard in Lexus's Brake Assist feature that applies full brake force in response to rapid brake-pedal movement in emergency stops.

Other standard equipment changes for '01 include a fuel tank enlarged by 2.6 gallons, an alloy spare wheel (replacing a steel rim), 3-point rear center seatbelt, rear child-seat anchors, an extra rear cupholder (in the center armrest), and modified grille. New options include all-black leather interior trim, wood steering wheel and shift knob, and heated front seats with two warmth levels instead of one. An available navigation system returns.

RX 300 is loosely based on the Lexus ES 300/Toyota Camry sedan platform. Toyota's new 2001 Highlander is essentially an RX with different styling, 4- and 6-cylinder power, fewer standard features, and a lower base price.

PERFORMANCE The RX behaves better than most SUVs—more like a luxury car or minivan. Though too big and heavy to have really agile handling, it corners with fine stability and little body lean for an SUV, helped by responsive steering. We haven't yet sampled an '01 model with VSC, but we know it works based on experience with it in other Lexus models, and we applaud its being made standard for the RX. Ride is perhaps even more impressive, the RX smothering bumps large and small with ease—better than many cars, in fact.

The front-drive RX is snappy off the line—we clocked one at 8.2 seconds 0-60 mph—and has good power throughout the speed range. The slightly heavier 4WD version does almost as well. The V6 is a paragon of refinement, but the transmissions in two 4WD test models exhibited some uneven shifting until warmed up, after which they were flawless. Between those two vehicles we averaged 16.3 mpg, just slightly better than the norm for midsize 4x4 SUVs. A front-driver returned 19.2 mpg. Routine braking is good, though some of our testers find pedal action a trifle spongy. Tire noise is noticed on coarse pavement, but the RX is pleasingly quiet overall—except with the optional sunroof open at high-

Specifications begin on page 535.

LEXUS

way speeds, when the pop-up air deflector creates mighty wind roar.

ACCOMMODATIONS Sophisticated shapes, comfortable seats, and rich materials characterize the RX 300 cabin. Entry/exit is a simple matter, and there's ample room and comfort for adults, even at the middle-rear position. Drivers sit commandingly high, but some may find the roof pillars too thick for best outward vision, even in front, and the tilt steering wheel doesn't go up high enough to suit our 6-foot testers. The unusual video-type display for climate and audio settings seems gimmicky, but works well enough. Other instruments and controls are large, clear, and close by.

Handy touches include four auto-up/down power windows, a pair of useful drawers in the center console, and large map pockets in each door. Out back are two small underfloor bins flanking a covered spare-tire well. Rear-seat conversion is convenient, but the load deck isn't that long with the seat up, and liftover is relatively high even on the 2WD version.

VALUE More "suburban utility vehicle" than traditional SUV, the RX 300 is posh, refined, roomy, and pleasant to drive. The main drawback to this Best Buy is nearly nonexistent dealer discounting in the face of justifiably strong demand.

ENGINES

	dohc V6
Size, liters/cu. in.	3.0/183
Horsepower @ rpm	220 @ 5800
Torque (lb-ft) @ rpm	222 @ 4400
Availability	S

EPA city/highway mpg
4-speed OD automatic	19/24[1]

1. 19/22 w/4WD.

PRICES

Lexus RX 300	Retail Price	Dealer Invoice
Base 2WD 4-door wagon	$33005	$28668
Base 4WD 4-door wagon	34605	30058
Destination charge	495	495

STANDARD EQUIPMENT:

Base: 3.0-liter dohc V6 engine, 4-speed automatic transmission, dual front airbags, front side-impact airbags, antilock 4-wheel disc brakes, daytime running lights, air conditioning w/automatic climate control, variable-assist power steering, tilt leather-wrapped steering wheel, cruise control, cloth upholstery, front bucket seats, 10-way power driver seat w/power lumbar support, 4-way power passenger seat, center console, cupholders, split folding rear seat, overhead console, wood interior trim, AM/FM/cassette, power antenna, digital clock, tachometer, heated

Prices are accurate at time of publication; subject to manufacturer's change.

LEXUS • LINCOLN

power mirrors, power windows, power door locks, remote keyless entry, variable intermittent wipers, trip computer, outside temperature indicator, illuminated visor mirrors, rear defogger, intermittent rear wiper/washer, remote fuel door release, automatic headlights, map lights, auxiliary power outlets, cargo cover, floormats, theft-deterrent system, rear privacy glass, fog lights, trailer wiring harness, tow hitch receiver, 225/70SR16 tires, alloy wheels. **4WD** model adds: permanent 4-wheel drive.

OPTIONAL EQUIPMENT:

	Retail Price	Dealer Invoice
Major Packages		
Limited Pkg.	$1820	$1456
Includes Leather Trim Pkg., driver seat memory, universal garage door opener, interior air filter.		
Premium Pkg.	1920	1536
Limited Pkg. plus automatic day/night rear view and outside mirrors.		
Convenience Pkg.	516	323
Roof rack, rear wind deflector.		
Powertrains		
Traction control, 2WD	300	240
Locking rear differential, 4WD	390	312
Comfort and Convenience		
Power moonroof	1000	800
Leather Trim Pkg.	1280	1024
Heated front seats	440	352
Requires Limited or Premium Pkg.		
6-disc CD changer	1080	864
Premium audio system	1630	1277
Includes 6-disc CD changer, upgraded speakers, and amplifiers.		
Special Purpose, Wheels and Tires		
Towing hitch	306	193

Post production options also available.

LINCOLN CONTINENTAL

Front-wheel-drive luxury car

Base price: $39,380. Built in USA. **Also consider:** Acura RL, LS 400, Mercedes-Benz E-Class

FOR • Acceleration • Passenger and cargo room **AGAINST** • Rear-seat comfort

Free regularly scheduled maintenance for the first 3-years/36,000 miles tops the changes to the 2001 Continental. The lone front-wheel drive Lincoln has a V8 engine, 4-speed automatic transmission, traction

Specifications begin on page 535.

LINCOLN

Lincoln Continental

control, antilock 4-wheel disc brakes, and front side airbags. Front bucket seats are standard; a front bench for 6-passenger seating is a no-cost option. Optional is Lincoln's Driver Select System, which includes driver-adjusted "plush," "normal," and "firm" suspension settings. Regular shock absorbers with automatic rear leveling are standard, as are three driver-selected levels of power-steering assist. A universal garage door opener is standard. Options include a tire-pressure alert system and run-flat tires Discontinued is RESCU, Lincoln's satellite/cell phone-based emergency assistance and concierge service. Introduction of a Telematics system with more features, including e-mail, is delayed, possibly until the 2002 model year.

PERFORMANCE We appreciate Continental's strong power, but are unimpressed with the variable suspension and steering systems. Though this V8 isn't as brawny—or smooth—as Cadillac's similarly sized Northstar engine, Continental provides fine acceleration from all speeds and effortless cruising ability. It's also relatively thrifty, our extended-use test car averaging 18.5 mpg during the 10,300 miles we drove it. Lincoln requires 91-octane fuel.

We prefer the soft but non-gimmicky base suspension. Despite its various settings, the Driver Select System can't deliver the blend of comfort and control befitting cars of this class, and the adjustable steering never feels natural. The engine note is pleasing, but tire rumble is evident on concrete surfaces, and some test drivers say wind noise is high for a luxury car. Stopping power is strong and pedal modulation good.

ACCOMMODATIONS Continental has adequate room for four adults, though rear leg room is not generous and toe space under the front seats is tight. Bench seat or buckets, the interior isn't wide enough for 3-across seating without rubbing shoulders. And the seat cushions—front and rear—are too soft for comfortable long-distance support.

The dashboard design is unimaginative, but nothing is obstructed or hard to use, and the bright, electronically defined gauge markings can be read easily in direct sunlight. Convenient steering-wheel climate and radio controls are included with the Driver Select System. Headrests

Prices are accurate at time of publication; subject to manufacturer's change.

LINCOLN

and hefty roof pillars impede vision to the rear corners. The cabin has real wood trim and overall build quality seems a pllus; the only problem with our extended-use car was a minor dashboard rattle.

VALUE It's quiet and powerful, but Continental is a near-luxury also-ran in terms of comfort, room, and image. This slow-seller is worth considering only if you can get a hefty discount.

ENGINES

	dohc V8
Size, liters/cu. in.	4.6/281
Horsepower @ rpm	275 @ 5750
Torque (lb-ft) @ rpm	275 @ 4750
Availability	S

EPA city/highway mpg

4-speed OD automatic	17/25

PRICES

Lincoln Continental	Retail Price	Dealer Invoice
Base 4-door sedan	$39380	$36412
Destination charge	745	745

STANDARD EQUIPMENT:

Base: 4.6-liter dohc V8 engine, 4-speed automatic transmission, traction control, dual front airbags, front side-impact airbags, antilock 4-wheel disc brakes, emergency inside trunk release, programmable variable-assist power steering, tilt leather-wrapped steering wheel, cruise control, air conditioning w/automatic climate control, interior air-filter, leather upholstery, front bucket seats w/power lumbar adjusters, 6-way power front seats, memory system for driver seat and outside mirrors, center console, cupholders, overhead console, wood interior trim, heated power mirrors w/tilt-down back-up aid, power windows, power door locks, remote keyless entry, key pad entry, rear defogger, automatic day/night rearview mirror, compass, variable intermittent wipers, wiper-activated headlights, AM/FM/cassette, analog clock, tachometer, remote fuel-door and decklid releases, map lights, auxiliary power outlet, illuminated visor mirrors, universal garage door opener, automatic headlights, automatic parking brake release, floormats, automatic load leveling suspension, theft-deterrent system, cornering lights, 225/60R16 tires, alloy wheels.

OPTIONAL EQUIPMENT:
Major Packages

Driver Select System	605	526

Semi-active suspension, selectable ride control, Memory Profile System (includes power steering assist and ride control), steering wheel with radio and climate controls, automatic day/night driver-side mirror. Requires Alpine sound system.

Specifications begin on page 535.

LINCOLN

	Retail Price	Dealer Invoice
Luxury Appearance Pkg.	$1105	$961

Wood-trimmed steering wheel, unique seat trim and floormats, special grille, chrome alloy wheels. Requires Driver Select System. NA w/Personal Security Pkg.

Personal Security Pkg.	640	557

Tire pressure monitor, run-flat tires. NA w/Luxury Appearance Pkg. Requires polished alloy wheels.

Comfort and Convenience

Power sunroof	1525	1327
Front split bench seat	NC	NC
Heated front seats	400	348
Voice-activated cellular telephone	800	696
Requires Alpine Audio System.		
Alpine Audio System	575	501
Digital signal processing, subwoofer amplifier, additional speakers.		
6-disc CD changer	605	526
Requires Alpine Audio System.		
Chrome alloy wheels	855	744
Polished alloy wheels	360	313
ordered in Calif. or Hawaii	NC	NC

LINCOLN LS

Lincoln LS

Rear-wheel-drive near-luxury car; similar to Jaguar S-Type
Base price range: $31,665-$35,695. Built in USA. **Also consider:** Acura TL, Lexus ES 300, Mercedes-Benz C-Class

FOR • Acceleration (V8) • Ride/handling • Seat comfort **AGAINST** • Automatic transmission performance • Climate controls

No charge for regularly scheduled maintenance for the first 3 year/36,000 miles, plus standard traction control, are among the

Prices are accurate at time of publication; subject to manufacturer's change.

LINCOLN

changes to Lincoln's rear-wheel-drive luxury/sport sedan. The LS shares a platform with Jaguar's S-Type, but is built in Michigan and differs from the British car in styling and equipment. The two share the same basic engines: a Ford-based V6 and a Jaguar-designed V8. Both LS engines team with a 5-speed automatic transmission (also used by the S-Type), but the V6 LS can be ordered with a 5-speed manual. Front side airbags, antilock 4-wheel disc brakes, wood and leather interior trim, and power tilt/telescopic steering are standard. Traction control is standard on all models for 2001; it had been included only with automatic-transmission. The optional antiskid system also is now available with both transmissions. A firmer-suspension Sport Package replaces 16-inch wheels with 17s and high-performance tires. All manual-transmission LSs have the Sport Package; automatic models with that option get a separate shift gate for manual gear changes. Options include a sunroof. A newly-optional 6-disc in-dash CD player rounds out the '01 changes. Introduction of a Telematics system with more features, including e-mail, is delayed, possibly until the 2002 model year. Discontinued is Lincoln's RESCU cell phone/satellite assistance system.

PERFORMANCE The LS is the dynamic equal of some costlier import sedans. Low-speed steering feel could be firmer, but the LS turns in crisply, corners with grippy precision and modest lean, and shows impressive highway stability even in gusty crosswinds. The optional Sport Package enhances body control without undue harm to the firm but generally supple ride. Engines make muted, classy sounds when pushed. Tire noise intrudes on coarse surfaces and mostly drowns out wind rush on any surface. Braking is swift and sure despite indecisive pedal action. Traction control is an important safety feature on any rear-drive car, and we're happy to see it available on manual-transmission LS's for '01.

V8 acceleration is strong, our test car running 0-60 mph in 7.3 seconds (Lincoln lists 7.7). The automatic V6 needs 9.3 seconds, Lincoln says, which isn't outstanding, though there's more than adequate muscle except on steep inclines or when real passing punch is required. V8 or V6, the LS's automatic transmission is a slow to kickdown for passing, though it's more responsive than in S-Type Jaguars we've tested, and it's not as smooth as expected of near-luxury cars. The manual has a notchy, unpleasant shift action is matched by a slightly heavy, indistinct clutch movement. Fuel economy is OK, but wins no prizes. We averaged 16.3 mpg with one V8 LS, 16 with another, and 19.6 with a manual V6. Both engines require 91-octane gas.

ACCOMMODATIONS The LS feels less cramped than the S-Type, but four adults is still the practical limit. Head clearance is okay, and there's good rear leg space even behind tall front occupants. Some of our testers couldn't dial in an acceptable driving position in one manual-shift car, and no one liked the climate system controls, but a fast 1000-

Specifications begin on page 535.

LINCOLN

mile highway trip showed the front seats to be comfortable for at least 3 hours at a stretch. Large door mirrors offset visibility lost to thick rear roof pillars. Interior storage is confined to small door map pockets and a puny console bin; the optional CD changer is being moved from the glovebox, where it takes up virtually all space, to beneath the right front seat. SelectShift and manual models have but a single front cupholder. Trunk volume looks good on paper, but only small suitcases can stand upright, there's not much fore/aft length, and bulky u-shaped trunk hinges are potential luggage crunchers.

Our various test cars have been generally solid and well finished. However, coarse pavement can induce minor body drumming, and two LSs tested in California had loose driver's-door mirrors and front windows that made minor but disturbing creak-cracking noises when operated and in rough-road driving. Against other near-luxury cars, the LS interior is unimaginative in design and disappointing in the execution of certain details.

VALUE Ordinary interior furnishings are its most obvious flaw, but the LS includes lots of features for the money, has capable road manners, and is among the few near-luxury cars available with a V8 engine. It merits consideration.

ENGINES

	dohc V6	dohc V8
Size, liters/cu. in.	3.0/181	3.9/235
Horsepower @ rpm	210 @ 6500	252 @ 6100
Torque (lb-ft) @ rpm	205 @ 4750	267 @ 4300
Availability	S[1]	S[2]
EPA city/highway mpg		
5-speed manual	18/25	
5-speed OD automatic	18/25	17/23

1. LS V6. 2. LS V8.

PRICES

Lincoln LS	Retail Price	Dealer Invoice
LS V6 4-door sedan, automatic	$31665	$29383
LS V6 4-door sedan, manual	33445	30986
LS V8 4-door sedan, automatic	35695	33011
Destination charge	610	610

STANDARD EQUIPMENT:

LS V6 automatic: 3.0-liter dohc V6 engine, 5-speed automatic transmission, traction control, dual front airbags, front side-impact airbags, antilock 4-wheel disc brakes, emergency inside trunk release, air conditioning w/dual-zone automatic climate control, interior air filter, variable-assist power steering, power tilt/telescoping wood/leather-wrapped steering wheel, cruise control, leather upholstery, 8-way power driver seat, 6-way power passenger seat,

Prices are accurate at time of publication; subject to manufacturer's change.

LINCOLN

center console, cupholders, split folding rear seat, heated power mirrors, power windows, power door locks, remote keyless entry, AM/FM/cassette, steering-wheel radio controls, tachometer, map lights, illuminated visor mirrors, rear defogger, variable intermittent wipers, automatic headlights, remote fuel door/decklid release, floormats, theft-deterrent system, fog lights, 215/60HR16 tires, brushed alloy wheels.

LS manual adds: 5-speed manual transmission, Sport Pkg. (leather-wrapped steering wheel, Alpine AM/FM radio w/in-dash 6-disc CD changer, color-keyed bumpers, engine oil cooler, upgraded steering and brakes, sport suspension, full-size spare tire, 235/50VR17 Super Silver Alloy Wheels).

LS V8 adds to LS V6 automatic: 3.9-liter dohc V8 engine, memory driver seat, memory steering wheel and mirrors, front power lumbar supports, automatic day/night rearview mirror, universal garage door opener, rain-sensing wipers, trip computer, compass, 215/60VR16 tires.

OPTIONAL EQUIPMENT:

	Retail Price	Dealer Invoice
Major Packages		
Sport Pkg., automatics	$1990	$1732

Leather-wrapped steering wheel, automatic transmission w/manual-shift capability, Alpine AM/FM radio w/in-dash 6-disc CD changer, color-keyed bumpers, engine oil cooler, upgraded steering and brakes, sport suspension, 235/50VR17 Super Silver Alloy Wheels.

Convenience Pkg., LS V6	960	835

Memory driver seat, memory steering wheel and mirrors, front power lumbar supports, automatic day/night rearview mirror, universal garage door opener, rain-sensing wipers.

Safety Features		
Antiskid system	735	640
Comfort and Convenience		
Power sunroof	1005	874
Heated front seats	400	348
Portable cellular telephone	705	613
Alpine Audiophile Radio System, LS V6 auto., LS V8	575	501
Alpine AM/FM radio w/in-dash 6-disc CD changer, automatics	605	526
Polished alloy wheels, automatics	405	348
Chrome alloy wheels, LS V6 manual	845	735

LINCOLN NAVIGATOR

Rear- or 4-wheel-drive full-size sport-utility vehicle; similar to Ford Expedition

Base price range: $43,645-$47,395. Built in USA. **Also consider:** Cadillac Escalade, GMC Yukon Denali and XL Denali, Lexus LX 470

Specifications begin on page 535.

LINCOLN

Lincoln Navigator

FOR • Passenger and cargo room • Instruments/controls • Build quality • Interior materials **AGAINST** • Fuel economy • Entry/exit • Maneuverability

As on all 2001 Lincolns, regularly scheduled maintenance on the Navigator is provided free of charge for the first 3 years/36,000 miles. Navigator is the luxury version of the Ford Expedition and like its cousin, also gains a rear-seat video entertainment system option this year.

Navigator comes with a 300-horsepower edition of the 260-hp 5.4-liter V8 available in Expedition. Automatic transmission, self-leveling shock absorbers, front side airbags, and antilock 4-wheel disc brakes are standard. Available is rear-wheel drive or Ford's Control Trac 4-wheel drive, which can be left engaged on dry pavement. Standard seating consists of front- and second-row buckets, each with a center console, and a 3-passenger third-row bench. A 3-passenger second-row bench is available at no charge. The standard power-adjustable pedal cluster is linked to the driver-seat memory system. Navigators have leather upholstery and wood interior trim and this year gain standard auxliary rear climate controls.

The new entertainment system includes a VCR and a 6.5-inch video screen. Also optional is a satellite navigation system with dashboard screen (Planned introduction of a Telematics system with e-mail capability is delayed, possibly until the 2002 model year.) Other options include "climate-controlled" front seats that encorporate small internal fan and heat pump, and an audible warning system sounds as the vehicle approaches an obstacle while reversing.

Expedition doesn't offer the 300-hp engine, but Navigator's performance and accommodations are otherwise comparable to those of its Ford sibling.

The Ford Expedition report includes an evaluation of the Navigator.

ENGINES

	dohc V8
Size, liters/cu. in.	5.4/330
Horsepower @ rpm	300 @ 5000

Prices are accurate at time of publication; subject to manufacturer's change.

LINCOLN

	dohc V8
Torque (lb-ft) @ rpm	355 @ 2750
Availability	S

EPA city/highway mpg

4-speed OD automatic 13/18

PRICES

Lincoln Navigator	Retail Price	Dealer Invoice
4-door wagon, 2WD	$43645	$38650
4-door wagon, 4WD	47395	41875
Destination charge	715	715

STANDARD EQUIPMENT:

2WD: 5.4-liter dohc V8 engine, 4-speed automatic transmission, limited-slip differential, antilock 4-wheel disc brakes, dual front airbags, front side-impact airbags, air conditioning w/front and rear automatic climate controls, variable-assist power steering, wood/leather-wrapped steering wheel w/radio and climate controls, tilt steering column, cruise control, power-adjustable pedals w/memory, leather upholstery, 7-passenger seating w/quad bucket seats, 6-way power front seats w/power lumbar adjustment, driver seat memory, third-row folding bench seat, wood interior trim, front floor console (rear audio controls and headphone jack, rear air conditioning/heater outlet), second row floor console, overhead console, trip computer, compass, cupholders, heated power mirrors w/memory and turn signal lights, power windows, power door locks, remote keyless entry, key pad entry, automatic day/night rearview mirror, AM/FM/cassette, digital clock, tachometer, illuminated visor mirrors, auxiliary power outlets, universal garage door opener, automatic headlights, variable intermittent wipers, automatic parking brake release, rear defogger, intermittent rear wiper/washer, map lights, floormats, theft-deterrent system, rear privacy glass, fog lights, roof rack, illuminated running boards, rear self-leveling suspension, Trailer Towing Group (7-wire harness, hitch, heavy-duty flasher, engine-oil cooler, auxiliary transmission-oil cooler), full-size spare tire, 275/60R17 white-letter tires, alloy wheels.

4WD adds: Control Trac full-time 4-wheel drive, front and rear self-leveling suspension, front tow hooks, 255/75R17 all-terrain white-letter tires.

OPTIONAL EQUIPMENT:

Safety Features

Reverse Sensing System	255	219

Comfort and Convenience

Voice activated cellular telephone	660	567
Requires 6-disc CD changer.		
Navigation system	1995	1716
Requires 6-disc CD changer.		

Specifications begin on page 535.

LINCOLN

	Retail Price	Dealer Invoice
Rear Entertainment System	$1280	—
Fold-down LCD screen, videocassette player, two wireless headphones. NA with navigation system, power sunroof, climate control seats, cellular telephone.		
Power folding mirrors	145	125
Power sunroof	1495	1286
Replaces overhead console with mini overhead console. NA with navigation system.		
Climate control front seats	595	521
8-passenger seating	NC	NC
Second row 3-passenger split bench seat.		
Alpine AM/FM/cassette	580	499
6-disc CD changer	595	512
Chrome alloy wheels	595	512

LINCOLN TOWN CAR

Lincoln Town Car Cartier L

Rear-wheel-drive luxury car

Base price range: $39,145-$48,510. Built in USA. **Also consider:** Acura RL, Cadillac DeVille, Lexus LS 430

FOR • Passenger and cargo room • Quietness **AGAINST** • Fuel economy • Rear visibility

More horsepower, power adjustable pedals, and no charge for regularly scheduled maintenance for the first 3 years/36,000 miles are Town Car's 2001 headliners. This last American-brand, rear-drive full-size luxury sedan comes in regular- and extended-length "L" form. L versions have a 6-inch longer wheelbase and an additional 6 inches of rear leg room, plus wider rear-door openings, heated rear seats and rear audio and climate controls. The L version is available in base Executive and top-line Cartier trim and is intended to help Town Car maintain its leadership in the "livery" market, where it accounts for 85 percent of non-

Prices are accurate at time of publication; subject to manufacturer's change.

LINCOLN

stretch limousine sales.

All Town Cars have a 4.6-liter V8 that makes 225 horsepower in Executive and Signature models, 240 with standard dual exhausts in Cartier versions. Those are gains of 25 horsepower for each version. A Touring Sedan package for Signatures includes the 240-hp engine, plus firmer suspension. All models have a 4-speed automatic transmission, antilock 4-wheel disc brakes, traction control, leather upholstery, and 40/20/40 front bench seat.

Gas and brake pedals that power fore and aft about three inches are newly standard and the headlamp switch moves from the dashboard to the windshield-wiper stalk as part of a new feature that turns on the headlights with the wipers. All Lincolns get the free scheduled maintenance for 2001. Introduction of a Telematics communications system with e-mail capability is delayed, possibly until the 2002 model year.

PERFORMANCE This big 4-door suffers more cornering lean and less grip than imported luxury sedans allow—enough that you'll want to slow down in fast turns. The steering is reasonably accurate, if too light for our tastes. Ride is absorbent and hushed, spoiled by mild float over humps and minor tire pattering on some freeway surfaces. Refinement is a plus, with little road noise and just a muted engine note. Wind rush rises above 60 mph, but doesn't intrude.

The "L" version adds 200 pounds to the regular Town Car but doesn't feel significantly slower. Indeed, despite this year's horsepower boost, no Town Car can match Cadillac DeVille for acceleration, but all models are sufficiently quick at under 10 seconds 0-60 mph in our tests. The transmission smoothly changes gears, but it sometimes takes a deep helping of throttle to coax a downshift. Fuel economy is about par for the class at around 17 mpg in our tests of both regular and L models.

Standard traction control enhances grip, but Town Car isn't as mobile in deep snow as front-drive rivals, and the system can interrupt engine power, making it tricky to accelerate across a slippery intersection. Braking is short and stable for such a softly sprung heavyweight, but pedal action isn't progressive and nosedive is pronounced.

ACCOMMODATIONS Lincoln says Town Car relies on fleet buyers for about 40 percent of its sales. With 47.1 inches of rear leg room—tops among factory-built automobiles—the L package should quell any complaints livery drivers have about back-seat space. Standard models have good rather than great rear leg room, but any Town Car has generous head clearance. Still, three adults across is a squeeze, and the ill-formed rear cushion isn't the sofa-comfortable seat it should be. Power adjustable pedals allow shorter drivers to sit a safer distance from the steering-wheel airbag. Gauges are analog and legible, controls user-friendly. Visibility is compromised by thick side and rear pillars and a high rear deck. Entry/exit is easy.

Specifications begin on page 535.

LINCOLN

Trunk volume looks fine on paper, but is concentrated in a deep center well that makes loading and unloading heavy objects a strain. Workmanship on our test Cartier was faultless, though interior materials are less substantial than those in Cadillacs and imported luxury cars.

VALUE Cadillac's DeVille is a better car, but Town Car delivers traditional American luxury-car values of spaciousness and isolation, and its base prices are the lowest in this class.

ENGINES

	ohc V8	ohc V8
Size, liters/cu. in.	4.6/281	4.6/281
Horsepower @ rpm	225 @ 4750	240 @ 4750
Torque (lb-ft) @ rpm	275 @ 4000	285 @ 4000
Availability	S[1]	S[2]
EPA city/highway mpg		
4-speed OD automatic	17/24	17/24

1. Executive, Signature. 2. Cartier; optional Signature.

PRICES

Lincoln Town Car	Retail Price	Dealer Invoice
Executive 4-door sedan	$39145	$36211
Executive L 4-door sedan	43255	39909
Signature 4-door sedan	41315	38163
Cartier 4-door sedan	43700	40310
Cartier L 4-door sedan	48510	44639
Destination charge	745	745

STANDARD EQUIPMENT:

Executive: 4.6-liter V8 225-horsepower engine, 4-speed automatic transmission, traction control, dual front airbags, front side-impact airbags, antilock 4-wheel disc brakes, emergency inside trunk release, variable-assist power steering, tilt leather-wrapped steering wheel, cruise control, air conditioning w/automatic climate control, leather upholstery, dual 8-way power front seat split bench seat w/power recliners and lumbar support, power-adjustable pedals, cupholders, heated power mirrors, power windows, power door locks, remote keyless entry, key pad entry, auxiliary power outlet, rear defogger, AM/FM/cassette, digital clock, remote fuel-door release, power decklid pulldown, headlight-activated variable-intermittent wipers, illuminated visor mirrors, map lights, automatic headlights, automatic parking brake release, floormats, theft-deterrent system, cornering lights, 225/60SR16 tires, alloy wheels.

Executive L adds: 6-inch longer wheelbase, rear radio and climate controls, rear illuminated visor mirrors, 225/70R16 tires.

Signature adds to Executive: memory system (driver seat, mirrors, pedals), wood steering wheel w/radio and climate controls, automatic day/night

Prices are accurate at time of publication; subject to manufacturer's change.

LINCOLN • MAZDA

rearview and driver-side mirrors, compass, universal garage-door opener, Premium sound system.

Cartier adds: 4.6-liter V8 240-horsepower engine, upgraded leather upholstery, heated front seats, Alpine sound system, analog clock, gold pkg., dual exhaust, chrome alloy wheels.

Cartier L adds: 6-inch longer wheelbase, rear radio and climate controls, heated rear seats, rear illuminated visor mirrors, 225/70R16 tires.

OPTIONAL EQUIPMENT:

	Retail Price	Dealer Invoice
Major Packages		
Mirrors and Compass Group, Executive, Executive L	$245	$213
Automatic day/night driver-side and rearview mirrors, compass.		
Touring Pkg., Signature	710	618
Upgraded suspension, 4.6-liter V8 240-horsepower engine, dual exhaust, performance axle ratio and torque converter, perforated leather upholstery, special grille and body cladding, 235/60TR16 tires, unique alloy wheels.		
Premium Pkg., Signature, Cartier	2130	1854
Manufacturer's discount price	1595	1388
CD changer, power sunroof.		
Comfort and Convenience		
Heated front seats, Signature	400	348
CD changer, Signature, Cartier, Cartier L	605	526
Voice-activated cellular telephone, Signature, Cartier, Cartier L	800	696

MAZDA 626

Mazda 626 LX

Front-wheel-drive compact car

Base price range: $18,735-$22,935. Built in USA. **Also consider:** Mitsubishi Galant, Nissan Altima, Volkswagen Passat

FOR • Acceleration (V6) • Steering/handling • Build quality

Specifications begin on page 535.

MAZDA

AGAINST • Automatic transmission performance • Road noise

Mazda's best-selling car is essentially unchanged for 2001. The 626 is offered in LX and uplevel ES trim, both with 4-cylinder or optional V6 power. The 4-cylinder ES comes with automatic transmission; other models offer manual or optional automatic. V6 models have 4-wheel disc brakes. Antilock brakes are optional across the board, packaged with front side airbags, and, on V6 models, traction control.

PERFORMANCE Four-cylinder 626s have adequate acceleration with manual transmission, but feel sluggish with automatic. V6s are lively either way, but are most enjoyable with manual. Regardless of engine, Mazda's automatic sometimes downshifts with a jolt. We got a pleasing 22.5 mpg from our test manual-shift V6; expect slightly less with automatic. We haven't had an opportunity to measure 4-cylinder economy.

Any 626 is quiet, though tire roar intrudes over coarse pavement. Ride is absorbent and well controlled, though high-speed dips induce some float. Handling isn't sport-sedan crisp, but body lean in turns is mild. Braking is good, with little nosedive and steady tracking in hard stops.

ACCOMMODATIONS Though technically a compact, the 626 rivals some midsize sedans with room for 6-footers to ride in tandem without the rear passenger's knees digging into the front seats. There's also good underseat foot room and adequate rear head clearance even for 6-footers. Still, tall drivers might want a little more rearward seat travel to get further from the steering wheel. The cabin is a bit narrow for uncrowded 3-abreast travel in back, but fairly large doorways make for easy enough entry/exit all around.

As for outward visibility, driver seating, and dash layout, the 626 is competitive but no more. Interior materials are better than the compact-class norm, however, and this Mazda feels solid on the road and exhibits fine detail finish.

VALUE Although not the the sportiest compact sedan, 626 is competent enough to earn our Recommended mark. LXs offer better dollar value than EXs, but both 626 models tend to be overlooked by consumers. That, combined with stiff competition, means you shouldn't have to pay full retail for either.

ENGINES

	dohc I4	dohc V6
Size, liters/cu. in.	2.0/122	2.5/152
Horsepower @ rpm	130 @ 5500	170 @ 6000
Torque (lb-ft) @ rpm	130 @ 3000	163 @ 5000
Availability	S[1]	S[2]
EPA city/highway mpg		
5-speed OD manual	26/33	21/27
4-speed OD automatic	22/28	20/26

1. LX 4-cylinder, ES 4-cylinder. 2. LX V6, ES V6.

Prices are accurate at time of publication; subject to manufacturer's change.

MAZDA

PRICES

Mazda 626	Retail Price	Dealer Invoice
LX 4-cylinder 4-door sedan	$18735	$17088
LX V6 4-door sedan	19935	18181
ES 4-cylinder 4-door sedan	20935	19091
ES V6 4-door sedan	22935	20911
Destination charge	480	480

STANDARD EQUIPMENT:

LX: 2.0-liter dohc 4-cylinder engine, 5-speed manual transmission, dual front airbags, air conditioning, variable-assist power steering, tilt steering wheel, cruise control, cloth upholstery, front bucket seats w/driver seat height adjustment, center console, cupholders, split folding rear seat, power mirrors, power windows, power door locks, remote keyless entry, AM/FM/CD player, digital clock, tachometer, variable intermittent wipers, rear defogger, auxiliary power outlets, map lights, illuminated visor mirrors, automatic-off headlights, remote fuel-door and decklid releases, 205/60R15 tires, wheel covers.

LX V6 adds: 2.5-liter dohc V6 engine, 4-wheel disc brakes.

ES adds to LX: 4-speed automatic transmission, leather upholstery, leather-wrapped steering wheel and shifter, floormats, alloy wheels.

ES V6 adds: 2.5-liter dohc V6 engine, 5-speed manual transmission, 4-wheel disc brakes, 6-way power driver seat, Bose AM/FM/cassette/CD player, heated mirrors, power sunroof, theft-deterrent system, 205/55R16 tires.

OPTIONAL EQUIPMENT:

Major Packages

Luxury Pkg., LX 4-cylinder	1800	1440
ES 4-cylinder	1300	1040

Power sunroof, 6-way power driver seat, heated mirrors, theft-deterrent system w/alarm, floormats (LX), alloy wheels (LX).

Premium Pkg., LX V6	1850	1480

Power sunroof, 6-way power driver seat, heated mirrors, floormats, theft-deterrent system w/alarm, 205/55R16 tires, alloy wheels.

Powertrains

4-speed automatic transmission, LX, ES V6	800	696

Safety Features

Antilock brakes w/traction control, LX V6 automatic, ES V6 automatic	700	560
Antilock brakes w/front side-impact airbags, LX 4-cylinder, ES 4-cylinder	800	640

Antilock brakes w/front side-impact airbags, traction control,

Specifications begin on page 535.

MAZDA

	Retail Price	Dealer Invoice
LX V6, ES V6	950	760
Front side-impact airbags, LX V6 automatic	$250	$200

Comfort and Convenience

AM/FM/cassette/CD player, LX, ES 4-cylinder	200	170
Audio Pkg., LX V6	600	480
AM/FM/cassette/CD player w/Bose sound system. Requires Premium Pkg.		
6-disc CD changer, ES V6	225	180

Appearance and Miscellaneous

Rear spoiler	395	295
Fog lights	250	200
Alloy wheels, LX 4-cylinder	450	383
16-inch alloy wheels, LX V6	595	505
Includes 205/55R16 tires.		

MAZDA MIATA

Mazda Miata

Rear-wheel-drive sports and GT car

Base price range: $21,180-$23,930. Built in Japan. **Also consider:** BMW Z3 Series, Honda S2000, Toyota MR2 Spyder

FOR • Acceleration • Steering/handling • Fuel economy **AGAINST** • Cargo room • Noise • Entry/exit

Mazda's 2-seat sports car gets more power for 2001, plus a revised interior and restyled front fascia. Miata comes in base and uplevel LS versions, both with a 4-cylinder engine that for '01 gains 15 horsepower, to 155. Five-speed manual transmission is standard, 6-speed manual is optional on the LS. Automatic is optional on both models. Antilock brakes are unavailable on the base model, optional on LS. Both get brake revisions aimed at improved stopping and chassis modifications to increase rigidity.

Prices are accurate at time of publication; subject to manufacturer's change.

MAZDA

Base Miatas gain standard 15-inch wheels instead of 14s. Standard on LS are 16-inch wheels, a Miata first. A manual-folding soft top with a heated glass rear window is standard. A removable hardtop is optional. Interior changes include redesigned seats, a new center console, and chrome gauge bezels.

EVALUATION Miata represents front-engine sports-car tradition, while its new Toyota MR2 rival is a mid-engine design. Both are terrific fun to drive, with Miata offering slightly more cargo room and, in base form, somewhat better value. The '01's additional power makes this lightweight roadster feel more gutsy, especially at low speeds and in passing. We'd expect it to shave a few tenths from the last model's 0-60-mph time of around 8 seconds. We didn't experience a huge difference in performance between the 5- and 6-speed manuals, though automatic-transmission versions aren't nearly as responsive as either. Expect fuel economy to mirror the 25.8 mpg we averaged in a 5-speed test car with the previous 140-hp engine. Road, wind, and engine noise are prominent. The '01 brake improvements go unnoticed in everyday driving, but stopping power is strong and easily modulated. Rigidity does feel enhanced, despite continued cowl scuttle over rippled pavement. Handling is a delight, steering a model of accuracy, but the factory tires furnish poor traction in snow. Four Goodyear Ultra Grip Ice winter tires installed on our Chicago-based test car provided unerring bite in snow and adequate cornering grip on dry surfaces. Miata's not quite as spacious as the MR2 but has decent room for two medium-size adults. Entry/exit is bend and twist, and small windows hamper visibility. The trunk holds a couple of soft overnight bags. Workmanship is good, with quality materials and tight assembly.

ENGINES

	dohc I4
Size, liters/cu. in.	1.8/112
Horsepower @ rpm	155 @ 7000
Torque (lb-ft) @ rpm	125 @ 5500
Availability	S

EPA city/highway mpg

5-speed OD manual	23/28
6-speed OD manual	23/28
4-speed OD automatic	22/28

PRICES

Mazda Miata	Retail Price	Dealer Invoice
Base 2-door convertible	$21180	$19331
LS 2-door convertible	23930	21836
Destination charge	480	480

Specifications begin on page 535.

MAZDA

STANDARD EQUIPMENT:

Base: 1.8-liter dohc 4-cylinder engine, 5-speed manual transmission, dual front airbags, 4-wheel disc brakes, air conditioning, variable-assist power steering, leather-wrapped steering wheel, cloth upholstery, bucket seats, center console, cupholders, power mirrors, power windows, AM/FM/CD player, power antenna, digital clock, tachometer, intermittent wipers, rear defogger, remote fuel-door and decklid releases, passenger-side visor mirror, floormats, theft-deterrent system, windblock panel, fog lights, 195/50VR15 tires, alloy wheels.

LS adds: limited-slip differential, cruise control, leather upholstery, power door locks, remote keyless entry, Bose sound system, 205/45WR16 tires.

OPTIONAL EQUIPMENT:

	Retail Price	Dealer Invoice
Major Packages		
Convenience Pkg., Base	$795	$668
Cruise control, power door locks, remote keyless entry, upgraded sound system.		
Suspension Pkg., Base	1095	861
LS	395	332
Sport suspension w/Bilstein shock absorbers, limited slip differential (Base), 205/45WR16 tires (Base).		
Powertrains		
6-speed manual transmission, LS	650	565
4-speed automatic transmission, Base, LS	900	872
LS requires antilock brakes.		
Limited-slip differential, Base	395	332
Safety Features		
Antilock brakes, LS	550	468
Comfort and Convenience		
AM/FM/cassette/CD player	150	120
Appearance and Miscellaneous		
Detachable hardtop	1500	1215
Rear spoiler	295	236

MAZDA MILLENIA
Front-wheel-drive near-luxury car

Base price range: $28,025-$31,025. Built in Japan. **Also consider:** Acura TL, Infiniti I30, Lexus ES 300

FOR • Acceleration (S model) • Steering/handling • Build quality • Exterior finish • Interior materials   **AGAINST** • Transmission performance • Rear visibility

Prices are accurate at time of publication; subject to manufacturer's change.
CONSUMER GUIDE

MAZDA

Mazda Millenia

Standard front side airbags and revised styling are the prime 2001 additions to the top-line Mazda. Millenia is a 4-door near-luxury sedan offered as the base model—renamed "P" for '01—with a 170-horsepower V6 and in uplevel S form with a 210-hp supercharged V6. The only transmission is a 4-speed automatic. Traction control is standard on the S, optional on the P. Antilock brakes are standard on both. Millenia for '01 gets altered front and rear styling, which adds 1.8 inches to overall length. Also, the P model gains standard instead of optional leather upholstery and power sunroof. Linewide interior additions include a power-lumber driver's seat, leather-wrapped shift knob, new center console with 10-CD storage, new cupholders (two front, two rear), and 2-tone trim. Mazda also says added sound insulation reduces noise levels and structural reinforcements serve to improve handling.

EVALUATION Its updated looks are quite contemporary but can't erase the fact that Millenia dates from 1995. That puts it among the oldest near-luxury cars, eclipsed overall by the newer, more-refined Lexus ES 300, Infiniti I30, and Acura TL. Acceleration is adequate in the P: 0-60 mph in a respectable 9.4 seconds in our tests. Our test S model did 0-60 in just 7.8 seconds, despite some throttle lag. The S averaged 18.9 mpg in mostly highway driving; we didn't have an opportunity to measure fuel economy with the P model. Millenia pays for its stable road manners with a firm ride on uneven pavement, though it does a good job of isolating wind and road noise. Front side airbags were overdue in a tastefully designed cabin that has good room in front. In back, space is tight for larger adults, and three across is a squeeze.

ENGINES	dohc V6	Supercharged dohc V6
Size, liters/cu. in.	2.5/152	2.3/138
Horsepower @ rpm	170 @ 5800	210 @ 5300
Torque (lb-ft) @ rpm	160 @ 4800	210 @ 3500
Availability	S[1]	S[2]
EPA city/highway mpg		
4-speed OD automatic	20/27	20/28

1. Base. 2. S.

Specifications begin on page 535.

MAZDA

PRICES

Mazda Millenia

	Retail Price	Dealer Invoice
P 4-door sedan	$28025	$25604
S 4-door sedan	31025	28340
Destination charge	480	480

STANDARD EQUIPMENT:

P: 2.5-liter dohc V6 engine, 4-speed automatic transmission, dual front airbags, front side-impact airbags, antilock 4-wheel disc brakes, air conditioning w/automatic climate control, variable-assist power steering, leather-wrapped power tilt steering wheel w/memory, cruise control, leather upholstery, 8-way power front bucket seats, driver seat power lumbar adjustment, center console, cupholders, rear seat trunk pass-through, power mirrors, power windows, power door locks, remote keyless entry, power sunroof, AM/FM/cassette/ CD player, steering wheel radio controls, digital clock, tachometer, outside-temperature indicator, illuminated visor mirrors, variable intermittent wipers, rear defogger, auxiliary power outlets, automatic-off headlights, remote fuel-door and decklid releases, floormats, theft-deterrent system, fog lights, 215/55VR16 tires, alloy wheels.

S adds: 2.3-liter dohc supercharged V6 engine, traction control, Bose sound system, upgraded suspension, 215/50VR17 tires.

OPTIONAL EQUIPMENT:
Major Packages

4-Seasons Pkg., P	600	504
S	300	252

Traction control (P), heated front seats, heated mirrors, heavy-duty wipers, heavy-duty battery, extra-capacity windshield-washer tank.

Comfort and Convenience

Bose audio system, P	800	672
In-dash 6-disc CD changer	500	420

Appearance and Miscellaneous

Two-tone paint	380	319
Chrome alloy wheels, S	500	420

MAZDA MPV

Front-wheel-drive minivan

Base price range: $20,675-$26,280. Built in Japan. **Also consider:** Dodge Caravan, Honda Odyssey, Toyota Sienna

FOR • Handling/roadholding • Passenger and cargo room • Instruments/controls **AGAINST** • Acceleration • Automatic transmission performance

Prices are accurate at time of publication; subject to manufacturer's change.

MAZDA

Mazda MPV LX

Mazda's minivan for 2001 stands pat following last year's redesign. MPV is offered in base DX, mid-level LX, and top-shelf ES models. All use a 2.5-liter dual-overhead cam V6 based on a design from Ford, Mazda's parent company. A 4-speed automatic is the only transmission. Antilock brakes are standard on LX and ES, unavailable on DX. Front side airbags are standard on ES, optional for LX. All MPVs seat seven and have second-row bucket seats that slide together to create a 2-passenger bench. The 3-place third-row bench folds into the floor. Optional for LX and ES is a sporty appearance package with fog lights and aero body addenda. Leather upholstery is exclusive to and standard for the ES.

EVALUATION Being smaller than most rivals gives the new MPV unusually agile minivan handling, abetted by fine visibility and a suspension that provides a generally supple, comfortable ride. But the engine is small too, so MPV struggles more than most minivans up hills, in passing sprints, and from standstill (we clocked a yawning 11.2 seconds 0-60 mph). Tardy transmission response doesn't help. Being underpowered compromises mileage too; one test MPV returned 19 mpg, another only 15.9. The Ford V6 sounds coarse even at moderate throttle, though overall noise levels are modest. Despite its compact exterior, MPV has decent second- and third-row leg space for 6-footers, plus more cargo room behind than many larger minivans claim. Step-in height is a tad higher than the minivan norm, and the sliding doors aren't so large, but the second- and third-row seats are quick and easy to fold or stow, and the driver's station is well laid out, though the column shift lever can be a minor obstruction. In all, the new MPV shines for its roomy, versatile seating package and almost sporty road manners, but it's not outstanding dollar value and it needs more power—which is coming for 2002 with a more muscular 3.0-liter V6. Until then, it will be on our minivan B-list.

ENGINES

	dohc V6
Size, liters/cu. in.	2.5/152
Horsepower @ rpm	170 @ 6250
Torque (lb-ft) @ rpm	165 @ 4250

Specifications begin on page 535.

MAZDA

	dohc V6
Availability	S
EPA city/highway mpg	
4-speed OD automatic	18/23

PRICES

Mazda MPV	Retail Price	Dealer Invoice
DX 4-door van	$20675	$19003
LX 4-door van	22800	20835
ES 4-door van	26280	24009
Destination charge	480	480

STANDARD EQUIPMENT:

DX: 2.5-liter dohc V6 engine, 4-speed automatic transmission, dual front airbags, front air conditioning, variable-assist power steering, tilt steering wheel, cloth upholstery, front bucket seats, center console, cupholders, two center row bucket seats, stowable third row 3-passenger bench seat, overhead console, visor mirrors, variable intermittent wipers, AM/FM/CD player, digital clock, tachometer, rear intermittent wiper/washer, auxiliary power outlet, 205/65R15 tires, wheel covers.

LX adds: antilock brakes, heated power mirrors, power windows, power door locks, remote keyless entry, cruise control, height-adjustable driver seat, AM/FM/cassette/CD player, illuminated visor mirrors, rear privacy glass.

ES adds: front side-airbags, front and rear air conditioning, leather upholstery, leather-wrapped steering wheel, premium sound system, floormats, theft-deterrent system, 215/60R16 tires, alloy wheels.

OPTIONAL EQUIPMENT:
Major Packages

1DX Power Pkg., DX	1325	1140

Cruise control, heated power mirrors, power windows, power door locks, floormats, bodyside moldings, alloy wheels.

1LX Security Pkg., LX	980	843

Front side-impact airbags, floormats, theft-deterrent system, alloy wheels.

2LX Touring Pkg., LX	1855	1595

Security Pkg. plus premium sound system w/9 speakers, wood-tone interior trim.

1GT GFX Pkg., LX, ES	595	512

Front spoiler, fog lights, side sill extensions, rear underspoiler. LX requires Touring Pkg.

2GT GFX Pkg., LX	895	770

1GT GFX Pkg. plus 215/60HR16 tires, alloy wheels. Requires Security Pkg.

Prices are accurate at time of publication; subject to manufacturer's change.

MAZDA

	Retail Price	Dealer Invoice
4-Seasons Pkg., LX, ES	$400	$344

Rear heater, heavy-duty rear defogger, larger washer tank, transmission oil cooler, heavy-duty battery and radiator, additional cooling fan. LX requires Security Pkg. or Touring Pkg.

Comfort and Convenience

Rear entertainment system	1595	1372

Videocassette player, LCD screen, jacks for DVD player and game system.

Television tuner	50	—

Requires rear entertainment system.

Rear air conditioning, DX, LX	595	512

DX requires Power Pkg.

Power sunroof, LX, ES	700	602

LX requires Touring Pkg.

In-dash 6-disc CD changer, LX, ES	450	387

LX requires Touring Pkg.

Appearance and Miscellaneous

Roof Rack	200	172
Fog lights	250	215

MAZDA PROTEGE

CG RECOMMENDED AUTO

Mazda Protege ES

Front-wheel-drive subcompact car

Base price range: NA. Built in Japan. **Also consider:** Ford Focus, Honda Civic, Volkswagen Jetta

FOR • Fuel economy • Ride • Quietness **AGAINST** • Noise • Acceleration (with automatic transmission)

The 2001 version of Mazda's smallest sedan bowed in January with a new front-end appearance and sportier emphasis for the top-line model.

Dimensions and pricing change little from 2000, and base DX, uplevel LX, and top-line ES models return. All have a 4-cylinder engine. DX and LX retain a 105-horsepower 1.6 liter. Standard on the ES and avail-

Specifications begin on page 535.

MAZDA

able on the LX is a 130-hp 2.0 liter borrowed from Mazda's larger 626 model. It replaces a 122-hp 1.8. Manual transmission is standard, automatic is optional. Antilock brakes are optional on LX and ES and are unavailable on the DX; same goes for front side airbags. The ES model also has standard rear disc brakes to the others' rear drums, 16-inch alloy wheels to the others' 15-inch wheels, and a monochromatic black interior treatment.

PERFORMANCE Protege takes a sportier approach to road manners than many subcompacts, mirroring the Ford Focus and Volkswagen Jetta rather than the tamer, softer Honda Civic. But the tradeoff is a slightly stiffer ride and a markedly higher level of engine, road, and wind noise than most rivals, especially Civic. DX and LX Proteges take most bumps with firm control and provide accurate steering and agile handling. The ES shares their suspension and adds larger tires that sharpen handling, but allow road imperfections to be felt even more.

Acceleration in the 1.6-liter models is adequate with the manual transmission, but disappointing with the automatic, especially in highway passing situations. We have not yet tested an LX or ES with the 2.0, but the previous 1.8 could scoot through traffic well enough, and the 2.0 should also help remedy that engine's shortage of highway passing power. A 2000-model test 5-speed ES averaged 26.6 mpg with lots of highway driving.

ACCOMMODATIONS Protege is among the more spacious subcompact sedans, with relatively abundant front head room and rear leg room. The dashboard is well laid out, though the climate system's rotary knobs are just out of the driver's easy reach and a bit too small to easily use. Visibility is good to all corners. Interior storage space is good, with open and covered bins, two cupholders, front-door map pockets, and a large glovebox. Trunk space is about average for the class, though all models come with a 60/40 split folding rear seatback for carrying longer items. The Protege is attractively finished, and even the base DX is fitted with a nice blend of fabrics and textured plastic surfaces. Assembly and paintwork on the cars we tested were nearly the equal of Honda, Toyota, and VW subcompacts.

VALUE Mazda hopes the new front-end appearance and sportier 2.0-liter engine help raise Protege's profile. Indeed, this is a car that tends to get overlooked by subcompact buyers. That's a shame, because in terms of room and driving pleasure it equals, even exceeds, many rivals, Civic included. It's easy to recommend, with the DX in particular a cut above most base-model subcompacts.

ENGINES

	dohc I4	dohc I4
Size, liters/cu. in.	1.6/97	2.0/122
Horsepower @ rpm	105 @ 5500	130 @ 5500
Torque (lb-ft) @ rpm	107 @ 4000	130 @ 3000

Prices are accurate at time of publication; subject to manufacturer's change.

MAZDA

	dohc I4	dohc I4
Availability	S[1]	S[2]
EPA city/highway mpg		
5-speed OD manual	29/34	NA
4-speed OD automatic	26/33	NA

1. DX, LX. 2. LX 2.0, ES.

2001 prices unavailable at time of publication.

PRICES

2000 Mazda Protege	Retail Price	Dealer Invoice
DX 4-door sedan	$12115	$11584
LX 4-door sedan	13415	12547
ES 4-door sedan	15215	14070
Destination charge	480	480

STANDARD EQUIPMENT:

DX: 1.6-liter dohc 4-cylinder engine, 5-speed manual transmission, dual front airbags, variable-assist power steering, tilt steering wheel, cloth reclining front bucket seats, center console, split folding rear seat, cupholders, rear defogger, remote fuel-door release, intermittent wipers, visor mirrors, auxiliary power outlet, remote outside mirrors, 185/65R14 tires, wheel covers.

LX adds: cruise control, AM/FM/CD, digital clock, sport front bucket seats w/height adjustment, remote decklid release, tachometer, power mirrors, power windows, power door locks, map lights.

ES adds: 1.8-liter dohc 4-cylinder engine, air conditioning, remote keyless entry, theft-deterrent system, 195/55R15 tires, alloy wheels.

OPTIONAL EQUIPMENT:

Major Packages

Convenience Pkg., DX	1575	1292
Air conditioning, AM/FM/CD player, digital clock, floormats.		
Comfort Pkg., LX	1145	939
Air conditioning, floormats.		
Premium Pkg., LX	1600	1312
ES	1580	1296
Front side-impact airbags, power sunroof, remote keyless entry, antilock brakes. Requires Comfort Pkg.		

Powertrains

4-speed automatic transmission	800	720

Comfort and Convenience

Power sunroof, LX, ES	700	560
LX requires remote keyless entry.		

MAZDA

	Retail Price	Dealer Invoice
AM/FM/cassette/CD player	$250	$213
DX requires Convenience Pkg.		
Remote keyless entry, LX	100	80
Includes theft-deterrent system.		

Appearance and Miscellaneous

Rear spoiler	330	246
Fog lights	195	156

MAZDA TRIBUTE

Mazda Tribute

Front- or 4-wheel-drive compact sport-utility vehicle; similar to Ford Escape

Base price range: $17,005-$23,025. Built in USA. **Also consider:** Honda CR-V, Subaru Forester, Toyota RAV4

FOR • Cargo room • Maneuverability • Steering/handling
AGAINST • Control layout (automatic transmission)

Mazda's first SUV since the old Ford Explorer-based Navajo is a slightly upscale version of the Ford Escape. Both Tribute and Escape have more available power than the Honda CR-V, Toyota RAV4, and similar compacts. They're built at a Ford plant in Missouri on a new purpose-designed Mazda platform and with Ford-sourced powertrains. Styling and suspension settings are unique to each.

Like CR-V and RAV4, Tribute has car-type unibody construction, 4-wheel independent suspension, and choice of front- or 4-wheel drive. The base DX model uses manual transmission and the same 4-cylinder engine that powers Ford's subcompact Focus. A V6 borrowed from the midsize Taurus is optional on Tribute DX and standard on LS and ES models. The V6 teams only with 4-speed automatic. As on Escape, Tribute's 4WD automatically directs up to 50 percent of the power aft if front-wheel slip occurs. A dashboard switch allows locking in a fixed 50/50 split, but, as on CR-V and RAV4, there's no 4WD low range.

Prices are accurate at time of publication; subject to manufacturer's change.

MAZDA

Tributes have a rear liftgate with opening hatch window. LX and ES models have 60/40 split-fold rear seatbacks; the ES has standard leather upholstery. Antilock brakes and front side airbags are optional on LX and ES and unavailable on the DX. Sixteen-inch wheels and tires are an option for Escape's top-trim model only but are standard on all Tributes. Tribute's performance and accommodations reflect those of similarly equipped Escapes.

The Ford Escape report includes an evaluation of the Tribute.

ENGINES

	dohc I4	dohc V6
Size, liters/cu. in.	2.0/121	3.0/182
Horsepower @ rpm	130 @ 6000	200 @ 6000
Torque (lb-ft) @ rpm	135 @ 4500	200 @ 4750
Availability	S[1]	S[2]
EPA city/highway mpg		
5-speed OD manual	22/26	
4-speed OD automatic		18/24

1. DX. 2. DX V6, LX, ES.

PRICES

Mazda Tribute	Retail Price	Dealer Invoice
DX 4-cylinder 4-door wagon, 2WD	$17005	$15721
DX 4-cylinder 4-door wagon, 4WD	18705	17289
DX V6 4-door wagon, 2WD	19140	17693
DX V6 4-door wagon, 4WD	20540	18984
LX 4-door wagon, 2WD	20820	19241
LX 4-door wagon, 4WD	22020	20348
ES 4-door wagon, 2WD	21825	20170
ES 4-door wagon, 4WD	23025	21276
Destination charge	515	515

STANDARD EQUIPMENT:

DX 4-cylinder: 2.0-liter dohc 4-cylinder engine, 5-speed manual transmission, dual front airbags, air conditioning, variable-assist power steering, tilt steering wheel, cloth upholstery, front bucket seats, center console, cupholders, folding rear seat, power mirrors, power windows, power door locks, AM/FM/CD player, digital clock, tachometer, variable intermittent wipers, visor mirrors, rear defogger, rear wiper/washer, map lights, auxiliary power outlets, automatic headlights, remote fuel door/hatch release, floormats, rear privacy glass, roof rack, 215/70R16 tires. **4WD** adds: full-time 4-wheel drive.

DX V6 adds: 3.0-liter V6 engine, 4-speed automatic transmission. **4WD** adds: full-time 4-wheel drive.

LX adds: cruise control, remote keyless entry, split folding rear seat, cargo cover, fog lights, 235/70R16 tires, alloy wheels. **4WD** adds: full-time 4-wheel

MAZDA • MERCEDES-BENZ

drive.

ES adds: leather upholstery, 6-way power driver seat, leather-wrapped steering wheel, overhead console. **4WD** adds: full-time 4-wheel drive.

OPTIONAL EQUIPMENT:	Retail Price	Dealer Invoice
Major Packages		
Popular Equipment Pkg., DX 4-cylinder	$700	$609
DX V6	845	735
Remote keyless entry, rear privacy glass, wheel lip moldings (DX V6), 235/70R16 tires (DX V6), alloy wheels.		
Luxury Pkg., LX, ES	1090	948
Power sunroof, overhead console, Premium Audio Pkg.		
Trailer Tow Pkg., DX V6, LX, ES	350	305
Engine oil cooler, tow bar, hitch, trailer wiring harness.		
Safety Features		
Front side-impact airbags and antilock brakes, LX, ES	495	431
Comfort and Convenience		
Premium Audio Pkg., LX, ES	505	439
AM/FM/cassette, in-dash 6-disc CD changer, premium speakers.		
Cassette player	200	160
Appearance and Miscellaneous		
Alarm system	115	69
DX requires Popular Equipment Pkg.		

MERCEDES-BENZ C-CLASS

Mercedes-Benz C240

Rear-wheel-drive near-luxury car
Base price range: $29,950-$36,950. Built in Germany. **Also consider:** Acura TL, Audi A4, BMW 3-Series

FOR • Acceleration (C320) • Build quality • Steering/handling • Quietness • Seat comfort **AGAINST** • Automatic transmission per-

Prices are accurate at time of publication; subject to manufacturer's change.

MERCEDES-BENZ

formance (C240)

Mercedes redesigns its entry-level sedans for 2001, giving the new C-Class standard V6 power, new safety features, and styling modeled on the flagship S-Class.

Again a compact-sized near-luxury 4-door, this second-generation C-Class is about an inch longer in wheelbase and overall than the 1994-2000 models. Interior dimensions grow slightly, trunk volume diminishes nearly one cubic foot.

The C240 has a 168-horsepower 2.6-liter V6. It supplants the C230, which used a 185-hp supercharged 4-cylinder. The 215-hp C320 borrows its 3.2-liter V6 from Mercedes' midsize E320. It replaces the C280, which used a 194-hp 2.8 V6. Both engines meet Low Emissions Vehicle standards in all 50 states. They require premium gas.

Standard on the C240 is a 6-speed manual transmission, with a 5-speed automatic optional. The previous C-Class did not offer a manual transmission, unlike the rival BMW 3-Series and Audi A4. The C320 uses only the automatic, which features Mercedes' Touch Shift that allows manual gear changes by moving the shift lever slightly left or right. Traction control, an antiskid system, and antilock 4-wheel disc brakes are standard. Standard wheel and tire size increases to 16 inches from 15, and both C-Class models are available with an optional Sport package that includes firmer suspension calibrations, slightly wider tires, aluminum interior details, and aero body trim.

Every C-Class comes with head protection curtain side airbags for front and rear passengers, dual-stage front air bags, and front and rear side airbags. Also included are Mercedes' Tele Aid assistance system and BabySmart child seat recognition system; the latter disables the front passenger airbags in the presence of a special child seat.

Among other standard features are a tilt/telescoping steering wheel (power on the C320) and wood interior trim. Full leather upholstery is optional on both models in place of the standard leather/vinyl. Other options include Xenon gas discharge headlights, a glovebox CD changer, and satellite navigation system. The redesigned interior features a new steering wheel with built in controls that Mercedes says can govern more than 50 different functions, including the trip computer, audio system, and interior and exterior lighting.

PERFORMANCE The rock-solid bearing and confident manner that made Mercedes famous comes through undiluted in the new C-Class. If not as nimble as the more overtly sporting A4 and 3-Series, this sedan is nonetheless responsive and composed no matter the situation or road condition. Steering is firm and linear, the car is unwavering on long straights and balanced and steady in turns, with sufficient body lean to communicate the build-up of cornering forces, but not feel sloppy. Isolation from road imperfections isn't absolute. Bumps register, but never disturb comfort or upset control. Braking is sure, pedal pressure

Specifications begin on page 535.

MERCEDES-BENZ

informatively progressive. The Sport setup furnishes more grip and slightly sharper steering, but it increases road noise from background to foreground on coarse surfaces. Wind rush is impressively muted.

Both these V6s are buttery smooth, but the larger engine delivers distinctly better throttle response at all speeds and works seamlessly with the automatic transmission. Mercedes says the C320 does 0-60 mph in just 6.9 seconds, and based on our initial test drives, it does indeed feel like one of the faster cars in the near-luxury class.

The C240 does 0-60 in 8.7 seconds with automatic transmission and in 8.2 with manual, says Mercedes. Both are unexceptional figures for this class, though acceleration is sufficient for everyday driving. Unlike the C320, however, the C240 requires the automatic transmission to downshift with annoying frequency when moving through fast traffic or in hilly terrain. Touch Shift is inviting to use and helps get the most from each engine. The smooth-shifting manual transmission lends the C240 a sportier, more responsive feel, but fewer than 10 percent of buyers are expected to order it. Our test C320 averaged 22.7 mpg. We've had no opportunity to measure fuel economy with a C240.

ACCOMMODATIONS True to its compact-size dimensions, the C-Class has fine room for two adults in front and adequate space for a pair of adults in back. Only those over 6-feet tall will lack for rear-seat head room. Knee clearance gets tight if the front seats are more than halfway back, however, and there's little room for feet under the front seats.

Front or rear, seats are firmly bolstered and supportive. The driver is well-positioned thanks to the tilt/telescope wheel and multiple seat adjustments, though the C240's standard mix of manual and power controls are not as inviting to use. Power window and lock switches are conveniently placed on the door panels. Mercedes relies on two rocker switches on the steering wheel spokes to control or fine-tune a multitude of functions, such as the trip odometer. The switches are illuminated, but their operation isn't always self evident and the system requires the driver to scroll between "windows" in the main instrument cluster to access some information. Those windows appear in a screen that occupies much of the instrument cluster, the only actual instruments being a large, arcing speedometer face, a fuel gauge, and, squeezed in at the far left, a small tachometer.

Cabin assembly and materials match the car's high overall level, though the relatively lightweight govebox latch, some plastic control surrounds, and visible mold seams in the door pulls are letdowns. Interior storage is good and the usefully shaped trunk holds more than its 12-cubic-foot volume would suggest.

VALUE The C-Class finally has its own identity, no longer a "baby Benz" as much as a new near-luxury sedan desirable in its own right. As a bonus, it competes head-on with the best in class for driving enjoyment, features, and value.

Prices are accurate at time of publication; subject to manufacturer's change.

MERCEDES-BENZ

ENGINES

	ohc V6	ohc V6
Size, liters/cu. in.	2.6/159	3.2/195
Horsepower @ rpm	168 @ 5500	215 @ 5700
Torque (lb-ft) @ rpm	177 @ 4500	221 @ 3000
Availability	S[1]	S[2]
EPA city/highway mpg		
6-speed OD manual	18/27	
5-speed OD automatic	20/26	19/26

1. C240. 2. C320.

PRICES

Mercedes-Benz C-Class	Retail Price	Dealer Invoice
C240 4-door sedan	$29950	$27854
C320 4-door sedan	36950	34364
Destination charge	645	645

Complete option prices not available at time of publication.

STANDARD EQUIPMENT:

C240: 2.6-liter V6 engine, 6-speed manual transmission, traction control, dual front airbags w/automatic child seat recognition system, front and rear side-impact airbags, front and rear side-head-protection system, antilock 4-wheel disc brakes, antiskid system, TeleAid emergency assistance system, power tilt/telescoping steering wheel w/radio and additional controls, variable-assist power steering, tilt/telescoping steering wheel, cruise control, air conditioning w/dual-zone automatic climate control, interior air filter, vinyl upholstery, front bucket seats, driver seat power height adjustment and recliner, wood interior trim, power mirrors, power windows, power door locks, remote keyless entry, AM/FM/cassette, digital clock, tachometer, trip computer, automatic headlights, rear defogger, front and rear fog lights, 205/55HR16 tires, alloy wheels.

C320 adds: 3.2-liter V6 engine, 5-speed automatic transmission w/manual-shift capability, leather upholstery, power driver seat, memory system (driver seat, mirrors, steering wheel, climate control), Bose sound system.

OPTIONAL EQUIPMENT:
Major Packages

Sport Pkg.	2950	2744

Sport leather seats, aluminum interior trim, unique gauge faces, body cladding, firmer suspension, 225/50R16 tires, unique alloy wheels.

Powertrains

5-speed automatic transmission w/manual-shift capability, C240	1300	1209

Specifications begin on page 535.

MERCEDES-BENZ

Comfort and Convenience	Retail Price	Dealer Invoice
Navigation system	$2035	$1893
Leather upholstery, C240	—	—
Power front seats, C240	1200	1116
Includes memory for driver seat, mirrors, steering wheel.		
Heated seats and headlight washers	800	744
Split folding rear seat	425	395
Bose sound system, C240	595	553
Cellular telephone and 6-disc CD changer	1795	1038

Appearance and Miscellaneous

Xenon headlights	850	791

MERCEDES-BENZ CLK

Mercedes-Benz CLK55 AMG 2-door coupe

Rear-wheel-drive luxury car

Base price range: $41,950-$67,400. Built in Germany. **Also consider:** BMW 3-Series, Saab 9-3, Volvo 70 Series

FOR • Steering/handling • Acceleration **AGAINST** • Rear-seat and cargo room • Rear-seat entry/exit

A new high-performance coupe and added electronic features highlight Mercedes' sporty compact 2-doors for 2001. Joining the V6 CLK320 coupe and convertible and their V8 CLK430 counterparts is the CLK55 AMG coupe packing a 342-horsepower 5.5-liter V8, plus styling tweaks, interior treatment, brakes, suspension tuning, and special 17-inch wheels designed by Mercedes' AMG performance division. Mercedes claims the CLK55 as its fastest production car ever at 5.2 seconds 0-60 mph. All CLKs have 5-speed automatic transmission with Mercedes' Touch Shift manual gearchange feature, antilock brakes, traction control with Mercedes' antiskid ESP system, front side airbags, and Mercedes' TeleAid emergency assistance system. This year, TeleAid adds door unlocking, vehicle diagnostics and alarm-system monitoring to the services available by cell link from Mercedes' staffed

Prices are accurate at time of publication; subject to manufacturer's change.

MERCEDES-BENZ

24-hour assistance center. Newly optional is Mercedes' integrated COMAND system that controls audio and available satellite navigation and phone functions from a dashboard screen. Offered separately is an Internet-based "InfoServices" option that uses the COMAND screen to display news, sports, weather and other owner-selected information.

EVALUATION The new CLK55 is the quickest factory Mercedes ever, at around 5 seconds 0-60 mph, and even the V6s are quick, a test 320 coupe doing 0-60 mph in about 7 seconds and averaging 21.6 mpg. Structural stiffening makes convertibles reasonably solid over bumps, but adds enough weight to blunt performance. The lighter 430 coupe rockets to 60 in a claimed 6.1 seconds; our test convertible averaged 20.2 mpg. All CLKs have that substantial Mercedes driving feel, near viceless handling, and a firmly absorbent ride, but the available performance tires find little grip in snow despite the standard traction control. Noise levels are low save rough-pavement tire thump and rumble. Front-seat room is snug for larger folk, rear room tight for most anyone. Interior decor is tasteful, but the steering wheel only telescopes and some controls are poorly marked and placed. The convertible has just 5.8 cubic feet of trunk space with the top lowered and quivers more on rough roads than we expected. Even so, any CLK is a highly capable and comfortable tourer with typical Mercedes virtues—and prices.

ENGINES

	ohc V6	ohc V8	ohc V8
Size, liters/cu. in.	3.2/195	4.3/260	5.4/322
Horsepower @ rpm	215 @ 5700	275 @ 5750	342 @ 5500
Torque (lb-ft) @ rpm	229 @ 3000	295 @ 3000	376 @ 3000
Availability	S[1]	S[2]	S[3]
EPA city/highway mpg			
5-speed OD automatic	21/29	18/25	17/24

1. CLK 320. 2. CLK 430. 3. CLK 55.

PRICES

Mercedes-Benz CLK	Retail Price	Dealer Invoice
CLK320 2-door coupe	$41950	$39014
CLK320 2-door convertible	48900	45477
CLK430 2-door coupe	49650	46175
CLK430 2-door convertible	56500	52545
CLK55 2-door coupe	67400	62682
Destination charge	645	645

STANDARD EQUIPMENT:

CLK320: 3.2-liter V6 engine, 5-speed automatic transmission w/manual-shift capability, traction control, dual front airbags w/automatic child seat recognition system, front side-impact airbags, antilock 4-wheel disc brakes, antiskid

Specifications begin on page 535.

MERCEDES-BENZ

system, automatic roll bar (convertible), TeleAid emergency assistance system, air conditioning w/dual-zone automatic climate control, interior air filter, power steering, telescoping leather-wrapped steering wheel w/radio controls, cruise control, leather upholstery, 10-way power front seats w/driver seat memory, center console, cupholders, split folding rear seat, wood interior trim, heated power mirrors w/memory, driver-side mirror w/automatic day/night, passenger-side mirror w/tilt-down back-up aid, power windows, power door locks, remote keyless entry, power convertible top (convertible), wind deflector (convertible), Bose AM/FM/cassette/weatherband w/CD changer controls, digital clock, tachometer, outside temperature indicator, intermittent wipers, illuminated visor mirrors, rear defogger, automatic day/night rearview mirror, universal garage door opener, floormats, theft-deterrent system, front and rear fog lights, full-size spare tire, 205/55R16 tires, alloy wheels.

CLK430 adds: 4.3-liter V8 engine, lower-body cladding, 225/45ZR17 front tires, 245/40ZR17 rear tires.

CLK55 adds: 5.4-liter V8 engine, power sunroof, heated multi-contour front seats, rain-sensing wipers, power rear sunshade, Xenon headlights w/washers, sport suspension.

OPTIONAL EQUIPMENT:
Major Packages

	Retail Price	Dealer Invoice
Option Pkg. K2	$1795	$1038
Integrated portable cellular telephone, 6-disc CD changer.		
Option Pkg. K2A	2190	1355
Voice-activated cellular telephone, 6-disc CD changer.		
Option Pkg. K3, 320/430 coupe	1340	1246
Power sunroof, rain-sensing wipers, power rear window sunshade.		
Option Pkg. K4, 320/430 coupe	1545	1437
convertible	1650	1535
Heated front seats, rain-sensing wipers (convertible), Xenon headlights w/washers.		
Designo Espresso Edition	6050	5627
Light brown seat trim, light brown/charcoal steering wheel and floormats, natural maple wood console trim. Requires heated front seats or Option Pkg K4.		
Designo Slate Blue Edition	6850	6371
Charcoal maple console trim, dark blue/charcoal seat trim, steering wheel, and floormats. Requires heated front seats or Option Pkg. K4.		

Comfort and Convenience

COMAND System	2035	1893
Navigation system, CD player. Deletes cassette player.		
Multi-contour front seats, 320, 430	725	674
Heated front seats, 320, 430	620	577

Prices are accurate at time of publication; subject to manufacturer's change.

MERCEDES-BENZ

MERCEDES-BENZ E-CLASS

Mercedes-Benz E320 4-door wagon

Rear- or all-wheel-drive luxury car

Base price range: $47,850-$70,300. Built in Germany. **Also consider:** Audi A6/allroad quattro, BMW 5-Series, Jaguar S-Type, Lexus GS 300/430

FOR • Cargo room (wagon) • Acceleration • Steering/handling • Ride • Available all-wheel drive • Build quality • Exterior finish
AGAINST • Fuel economy (E430, E55) • Navigation system controls

Mercedes' 2001 focus is on the new C-Class, so the best-selling E-Class group sees only minor changes. Models again comprise the V6 E320 sedan and wagon, V8 E430 sedan, and the limited-production high-performance E55 AMG sedan with a 5.4-liter V8. The only transmission is a 5-speed automatic with Mercedes' Touch Shift manual gearchange feature. The E430 and both E320s can be ordered with Mercedes' 4Matic all-wheel drive in lieu of rear drive. Wagons seat seven via a rear-facing third-row seat.

Like all 2001 Mercedes, every E-Class comes with Mercedes' antiskid Electronic Stability Program, TeleAid emergency assistance system, side-window curtain airbags, and lower-body side airbags front and rear. Newly optional for E320 and E430 sedans is a Sport Package with firmer suspension, special upsized wheels and tires, and "aero" lowerbody styling. Returning linewide extras include voice-activated cell phone, in-dash satellite navigation system, and rear parking assist. This year, the standard TeleAid assistance system adds vehicle diagnosis, door unlocking, and alarm-system monitoring as new services. A revised lock/ignition system now automatically adjusts the driver's seat and door mirrors to preset positions that can be programmed to each master key.

PERFORMANCE Any E-Class is more athletic than the typical luxury 4-door, if not so nimble as a 5-Series BMW. Steering is firm and precise, body lean modest in hard cornering. The suspension provides a model blend of ride comfort and dynamic control and easily smothers most

Specifications begin on page 535.

MERCEDES-BENZ

bumps. Quietness is another asset. 4Matic furnishes great traction but adds about 200 pounds for a slight sacrifice in acceleration and fuel economy.

Acceleration is satisfying in any model. Our subjective experience on test drives suggests Mercedes is truthful in claiming 0-60 mph of 7.1 seconds for the E320 sedan and 7.8 for the E320 wagon. AWD adds about a half-second. The V8 E430 does 0-60 in a claimed 6.4 seconds and feels usefully faster than the V6 sedan, with outstanding highway passing power. The E55 has stirring acceleration—5.4 seconds 0-60, says Mercedes—and the sportiest handling, though it's not as nimble as the rival BMW M5. A test E55 returned 19.2 mpg, helped by lots of highway miles.

ACCOMMODATIONS There's ample room for four adults, but the transmission tunnel precludes long-distance comfort for a rear center-seater. Both body styles have good cargo capacity, flat load floors, and low liftovers. The wagon's third seat folds easily for cargo, but is deliberately sized for kids. Gauges and controls are generally well done, but some buttons have cryptic markings and the console-mount power window controls may not be to everyone's liking. All models offer good visibility from a comfortable, easily tailored driver's post, plus craftsmanship that's solid on the road and nearly impeccable to the eye.

VALUE Quality, resale value, performance, and safety features make E-Class models unqualified luxury car Best Buys. The wagon and available AWD are added attractions for superior traction and/or increased cargo capacity. E320s are the best values, with the E430 a stellar rival for the BMW 540i.

ENGINES

	ohc V6	ohc V8	ohc V8
Size, liters/cu. in.	3.2/195	4.3/260	5.4/322
Horsepower @ rpm	221 @ 5500	275 @ 5750	349 @ 5500
Torque (lb-ft) @ rpm	232 @ 3000	295 @ 3000	391 @ 3000
Availability	S[1]	S[2]	S[3]

EPA city/highway mpg
| 5-speed OD automatic | 21/30[4] | 18/24[5] | 16/23 |

1. E320. 2. E430. 3. E55 AMG. 4. 20/27 w/wagon, 20/26 w/4matic wagon, 20/28 w/4Matic sedan. 5. 17/23 w/4matic.

PRICES

Mercedes-Benz E-Class	Retail Price	Dealer Invoice
E320 4-door sedan	$47850	$44501
E320 4-door wagon	48650	45245
E320 AWD 4-door sedan	50700	47151
E320 AWD 4-door wagon	51500	47895
E430 4-door sedan	53200	49476
E430 AWD 4-door sedan	56050	52127

Prices are accurate at time of publication; subject to manufacturer's change.

MERCEDES-BENZ

	Retail Price	Dealer Invoice
E55 4-door sedan	$70300	$65379
Destination charge	645	645

AWD denotes all-wheel drive. E55 gas guzzler tax not available at time of publication.

STANDARD EQUIPMENT:

E320 sedan: 3.2-liter V6 engine, 5-speed automatic transmission w/manual-shift capability, traction control, dual front airbags w/automatic child seat recognition system, front and rear side-impact airbags, front and rear side head-protection, antilock 4-wheel disc brakes, antiskid system, TeleAid emergency assistance system, air conditioning w/dual-zone automatic climate control, interior air filter, variable-assist power steering, power tilt/telescopic steering wheel w/memory feature, leather-wrapped steering wheel, cruise control, leather upholstery, 10-way power front bucket seats w/memory feature, center console, cupholders, wood interior trim, trip computer, heated power mirrors w/memory feature and driver-side automatic day/night, passenger-side mirror tilt-down parking aid, power windows, power door locks, remote keyless entry, automatic day/night rearview mirror, outside-temperature indicator, AM/FM/cassette w/CD changer controls, digital clock, tachometer, rear defogger, illuminated visor mirrors, auxiliary power outlet, remote fuel door and decklid releases, universal garage-door opener, variable intermittent wipers, map lights, floormats, theft-deterrent system, front and rear fog lights, full-size spare tire, 215/55HR16 tires, alloy wheels. **AWD** adds: permanent all-wheel drive.

E320 wagon adds: cloth and leather upholstery, folding third seat, cargo cover, intermittent rear wiper and heated washer, automatic rear load leveling suspension, roof rails. **AWD** adds: permanent all-wheel drive.

E430 adds to E320 sedan: 4.3-liter V8 engine, Bose sound system, 235/45WR17 tires. **AWD** adds: permanent all-wheel drive.

E55 adds: 5.4-liter V8 engine, power sunroof, heated multi-contour front seats, rain-sensing automatic wipers, power rear window sunshade, aerodynamics package, Xenon headlights w/washers, sport suspension, 245/40ZR18 front tires, 275/35ZR18 rear tires.

OPTIONAL EQUIPMENT:
Major Packages

E1 Option Pkg., E320, E430	1100	1023
Heated front seats, Xenon headlamps, heated headlight washers.		
E2 Option Pkg., E320	1610	1497
Bose sound system, power sunroof, rain-sensing wipers.		
E3 Option Pkg., E320, E430	4090	3804
Front air dam, side sill skirts, rear apron, projector beam fog lights, 235/45WR17 tires, special alloy wheels. NA AWD.		

Specifications begin on page 535.

MERCEDES-BENZ

	Retail Price	Dealer Invoice
K2 Option Pkg.	$1795	$1038
Integrated portable cellular telephone, 6-disc CD changer.		
K2A Option Pkg.	2190	1355
Voice-activated integrated portable cellular telephone, 6-disc CD changer.		
Designo Espresso Edition, E320 sedan, E430	6050	5627
E320 wagon	6650	6185
E55	5300	4929
Elm wood console trim, elm wood/charcoal leather steering wheel, Nappa leather upholstery (E320, E430), charcoal/light brown floormats. Requires heated front seats. Not available AWD.		
Designo Silver Edition, E320 sedan, E430	6050	5627
E320 wagon	6650	6185
E55	5300	4929
Maple wood console trim, maple wood/charcoal leather steering wheel, Nappa leather upholstery (E320, E430), charcoal/dark green floormats. Requires heated front seats. Not available AWD.		
COMAND System	2035	1893
Navigation system, AM/FM/CD player, steering wheel radio controls.		

Comfort and Convenience

Power sunroof, E320, E430	1160	1079
Full leather upholstery, E320 wagon	1375	1279
Multi-contour power front seats, E320, E430	725	674
Active ventilated front seats	1150	1070
Includes heated seats. Wagons require full leather upholstery.		
Heated front seats, E320, E430	620	577
Power rear window sunshade, E320 sedan, E430	420	391

MERCEDES-BENZ M-CLASS

2001 Mercedes-Benz M-Class

4-wheel-drive midsize sport-utility vehicle
Base price range: $35,800-$65,900. Built in USA. **Also con-**

Prices are accurate at time of publication; subject to manufacturer's change.

MERCEDES-BENZ

sider: BMW X5, Ford Explorer, Jeep Grand Cherokee, Lexus RX 300

FOR • Acceleration (ML430, ML55) • Steering/handling • Build quality • Cargo room **AGAINST** • Fuel economy • Ride (ML430, ML55)

Hill descent control leads the short list of 2001 additions to Mercedes' SUV. The M-Class offers V6 ML320, V8 ML430, and high-performance ML55 models; the last features a larger V8, bigger brakes, exclusive 18-inch wheels with low-profile tires, and sport front bucket seats. All have a 5-speed automatic transmission with Mercedes' Touch Shift manual shift gate, plus permanent 4-wheel drive with separate low-range gearing controlled by a dashboard button.

This year, the 4WD adds "downhill traction control" that automatically limits vehicle speed when descending steep grades. Four lower-body side airbags are standard, as are dashboard airbags that now deploy with full or partial force depending on impact severity. A 2-passenger third-row seat is optional except for the ML55, and all models come with an in-dash video display for controlling audio and, where equipped, cell phone and satellite navigation. Mimicking GM's OnStar system, the standard TeleAid communications and emergency assistance system is expanded for '01 to provide vehicle diagnostics, door unlocking, and alarm system monitoring.

PERFORMANCE Although the Lexus RX 300 and BMW X5 are more car-like, few true SUVs are more pleasant to drive than the M-Class. The smooth automatic transmission helped a test ML320 do 0-60 mph in a decent 9.1 seconds, though acceleration slows with heavier loads. Typical of 6-cylinder SUVs, we've averaged 13.9-15 mpg with several ML320s. V8 models are noticeably faster; Mercedes pegs the ML430 at 8 seconds 0-60. Off-the-line punch isn't great, but the 430 gathers speed quickly and has good highway passing power. The ML55 mirrors those traits, but delivers even more thrust underway; our test model clocked a class-leading 6.4 seconds to 60. Over 15,500 miles, our extended-use 1999 ML430 averaged 15.7 mpg, which is better than we get with most V8 SUVs. It requires premium fuel, as does the ML55, which returned just 12.9 mpg in our test. Both V8s emit a throaty roar under hard throttle; the V6 just sounds coarse.

MLs are poised and stable for SUVs, with less cornering lean than most. Steering is precise and linear, though self-centering is weak. Ride is comfortably absorbent in the ML320; firmer suspensions and low-profile tires make other models jiggly but not punishing over bumps.

The 4WD system brakes any combination of wheels to maintain traction, but isn't as effective as traditional setups in heavy snow and on demanding off-road trails. It's also hard on the brakes. Wind and road noise are low for an SUV but higher than in a family sedan—or the rival Lexus and BMW. Braking is strong and stable, especially in the ML55. Our extended-use ML430 was mechanically trouble-free, but had poor AM radio reception in urban areas.

ACCOMMODATIONS The M-Class has a manageably low step-in,

Specifications begin on page 535.

MERCEDES-BENZ

exceptionally wide doors, and room enough for five adults, though rear leg space gets tight with the front seats fully aft. This is also among the few mid-size SUVs with third-row seating, but that's still only intended for children or occasional adult use. Markings on some controls are not obvious, but ergonomics are otherwise good. So is visibility, except directly aft due to the rear headrests. Load volume is ample, but it takes some practice to master the multiple folding options for the second-row seat. Interior decor is now more in line with what's expected of a Mercedes in both fit-and-finish and the look and feel of materials. Sturdy overall construction is evident, despite occasional body shudder on rough surfaces and something less than Mercedes' usual granite-solid driving feel.

VALUE Among true SUVs, the M-Class is one of the best for refinement, handling, and overall competence. Prices are steep, but high resale values boost the appeal of this Recommended pick.

ENGINES

	ohc V6	ohc V8	ohc V8
Size, liters/cu. in.	3.2/195	4.3/260	5.4/332
Horsepower @ rpm	215 @ 5500	268 @ 5500	342 @ 5500
Torque (lb-ft) @ rpm	233 @ 3000	288 @ 3000	376 @ 3000
Availability	S[1]	S[2]	S[3]
EPA city/highway mpg			
5-speed OD automatic	16/20	15/19	14/18

1. ML320. 2. ML430. 3. ML55.

PRICES

Mercedes-Benz M-Class	Retail Price	Dealer Invoice
ML320 4-door wagon	$35800	$33294
ML430 4-door wagon	44200	41106
ML55 4-door wagon	65900	61287
Destination charge	645	645

STANDARD EQUIPMENT:

ML320: 3.2-liter V6 engine, 5-speed automatic transmission w/manual-shift capability, full-time 4-wheel drive, 2-speed transfer case, traction control, dual front airbags w/automatic child seat recognition system, front and rear side-airbags, anti-skid system, antilock 4-wheel disc brakes, TeleAid emergency assistance system, navigation system, passenger-side under-seat storage drawer, air conditioning, interior air filter, power steering, tilt leather-wrapped steering wheel, cruise control, cloth upholstery, manual 6-way front bucket seats, center console, split folding rear seat, cupholders, wood interior trim, heated power mirrors, power front windows, power door locks, intermittent wipers, remote keyless entry, rear defogger, intermittent rear wiper/washer, AM/FM/cassette w/CD changer controls, digital clock, tachometer, universal garage door opener, auxiliary power outlets, illuminated visor mirrors, map lights, cargo cover, floormats, theft-deterrent system, roof rack, rear fog

Prices are accurate at time of publication; subject to manufacturer's change.

MERCEDES-BENZ

lights, front and rear tow hooks, 255/65R16 tires, alloy wheels.

ML430 adds: 4.3-liter V8 engine, leather upholstery, heated 8-way power front seats, automatic day/night driver-side and rearview mirrors, trip computer, rear privacy glass, 275/55R17 tires.

ML55 adds: 5.5-liter V8 engine, power sunroof, dual front seat memory, Bose sound system, power rear quarter windows, Xenon headlights, front fog lights, 285/50WR18 tires.

OPTIONAL EQUIPMENT:

	Retail Price	Dealer Invoice
Major Packages		
M1 Luxury Pkg., ML320	$1600	$1488
Leather upholstery, heated 8-way power front seats, rear privacy glass. Requires sunroof or Skyview roof.		
M2 Convenience Pkg., ML320	1150	1070
Trip computer, automatic day/night driver-side and rearview mirrors, power folding outside mirrors, rain-sensing wipers, dual front seat memory, locking under-passenger-seat compartment. Requires M1 Luxury Pkg.		
M3 Convenience Pkg., ML430	695	646
Dual front seat memory, rain-sensing wipers, power folding mirrors. Requires sunroof or Skyview roof.		
M6 Sport Pkg., ML320, ML430	3300	3069
Sport bumpers, bodyside cladding, fender flares, fog lights, chrome exhaust tips, 275/55R17 tires, special alloy wheels. Requires sunroof or Skyview roof.		
M7 Seat Pkg., ML320 w/M1 Pkg., ML430	1350	1256
ML320	1150	1070
Two third row seats, power rear quarter windows. Deletes cargo cover.		
Designo Cognac Edition	4000	3720
Bourbon exterior color, cognac/charcoal interior color, special wood interior trim and floormats. ML320 requires heated front seats, M1 Luxury Pkg.		
Designo Mystic Green Edition, ML320, ML430	4000	3720
Mystic green exterior color, Java/Borneo interior color, special wood interior trim and floormats. ML320 requires heated front seats, M1 Luxury Pkg.		
Comfort and Convenience		
Power sunroof, ML320, ML430	1095	1018
Skyview roof, ML320, ML430	2450	2279
8-square foot power sunroof.		
Bose sound system, ML320, ML430	1075	1000
Includes 6-disc CD changer.		
Heated front seats, ML320	620	577
Appearance and Miscellaneous		
Xenon headlights, ML320, ML430	850	791
Requires M6 Sport Pkg.		

Specifications begin on page 535.

MERCEDES-BENZ

MERCEDES-BENZ S-CLASS/ CL-CLASS

Mercedes-Benz S-Class

Rear-wheel-drive luxury car

Base price range: $70,800-$117,200. Built in Germany. **Also consider:** Audi A8, BMW 7-Series, Lexus LS 430

FOR • Acceleration • Build quality • Entry/exit (S-Class) • Passenger room (S-Class) • Refinement • Ride **AGAINST** • Rear-seat room (CL-Class) • Rear-seat entry/exit (CL-Class) • Fuel economy • Navigation system controls

V12 and high-performance V8 models, plus added electronic features, make 2001 news for Mercedes' flagship line. Joining the V8 S430 and S500 sedans and the CL500 coupe are the limited-edition V12 S600 sedan and CL600 coupe. Their V12 deactivates 6 cylinders to save fuel when full power isn't needed and they have exclusive interior trim and wheels. The new S55 and CL55 share a more-powerful V8, 18-inch wheels, and aero body addenda. An available Sport Package delivers this look and firmer suspension to the S430, S500, and CL500. Optional on S430 and S500 and standard for CLs, S55, and S600 is Mercedes' Active Body Control designed to counteract body roll in hard cornering. All models have a 5-speed automatic transmission with separate manual shift gate, antilock 4-wheel disc brakes with Mercedes' Brake Assist and antiskid systems. Also standard is Mercedes' Teleaid assistance system and dashboard video control for audio, navigation, and phone. All models have rear side torso airbags and side curtain airbags. Newly available is Mercedes' Distronic "smart" cruise control designed to use radar sensors to automatically adjust speed and maintain a distance from vehicles ahead. Also new is an Internet-based "InfoServices" option for displaying news, sports, weather, and other user-selected information on the dashboard screen. Finally, TeleAid expands to include door unlocking, vehicle diagnostics, and alarm

Prices are accurate at time of publication; subject to manufacturer's change.

MERCEDES-BENZ

monitoring.

EVALUATION Coupe or sedan, Mercedes' flagships are silken, hushed performers with strong acceleration, confident handling, superb brakes, and a mostly unruffled ride. We haven't yet tested the new V12s or sport models. Size and heft preclude truly agile handling, but all models are poised on twisty backroads, and the anti-lean suspension is impressively effective. All models demand premium gas but aren't frighteningly "fuelish." We've recorded 16-17 mpg in town and up to 26 on the highway with the S430 and the two 500s. All have spacious front seating and competitive cargo space. Sedans are roomy in back—especially for legs—but aren't quite wide enough for three grownups. High tech abounds, so there's a daunting array of buttons, switches and displays, many of which take time to figure out and can distract the driver. These Mercedes remain among the world's best luxury cars, are fairly priced for high-end machinery, and enjoy resale values that are like money in the bank.

ENGINES

	ohc V8	ohc V8	ohc V8	ohc V12
Size, liters/cu. in.	4.3/260	5.0/303	5.4/322	5.8/353
Horsepower @ rpm	275 @ 5750	302 @ 5000	354 @ 5500	362 @ 5500
Torque (lb-ft) @ rpm	295 @ 3000	339 @ 2700	391 @ 3000	391 @ 4000
Availability	S[1]	S[2]	S[3]	S[4]
EPA city/highway mpg				
5-speed OD automatic	17/24	16/23	17/24	15/23

1. S430. 2. S500, CL500. 3. S55 AMG, CL55 AMG. 4. S600, CL600.

PRICES

Mercedes-Benz S-Class/CL-Class

	Retail Price	Dealer Invoice
S430 4-door sedan	$70800	$65844
S500 4-door sedan	78950	73424
S55 4-door sedan	98000	91140
S600 4-door sedan	114000	106020
CL500 2-door coupe	87500	81375
CL55 2-door coupe	99500	92535
CL600 2-door coupe	117200	108996
Destination charge	645	645

S500 and CL500 add Gas Guzzler Tax $1000. S600 and CL600 add Gas Guzzler Tax $1300. S55 and CL55 Gass Guzzler Tax not available at time of publication.

STANDARD EQUIPMENT:

S430: 4.3-liter V8 engine, 5-speed automatic transmission w/manual-shift

Specifications begin on page 535.

MERCEDES-BENZ

capability, dual front airbags w/automatic child seat recognition system, front and rear side-impact airbags, traction control, front and rear side head-protection system, COMAND navigation system, TeleAid emergency assistance system, antiskid system, antilock 4-wheel disc brakes, daytime running lights, air conditioning w/dual-zone automatic climate control, interior air filter, variable-assist power steering, power tilt/telescoping leather-wrapped steering wheel w/memory, cruise control, leather upholstery, 14-way power front bucket seats w/adjustable lumbar support and memory, center console, cupholders, wood interior trim, heated power mirrors w/memory and driver-side automatic day/night and passenger-side tilt-down parking aid, power windows, power door locks, remote keyless entry, AM/FM/cassette/CD player w/Bose sound system, steering wheel radio controls, tachometer, power sunroof, automatic day/night rearview mirror, universal garage door opener, front and rear illuminated visor mirrors, rain-sensing intermittent wipers, map lights, automatic headlights, floormats, theft-deterrent system, front and rear fog lights, outside-mirror mounted turn signal lights, self-leveling air suspension, 225/60R16 tires, alloy wheels.

S500 adds: 5.0-liter V8 engine, upgraded leather upholstery, heated front seats, Xenon headlights, headlight washers.

CL500 adds: 6-disc CD changer, wood/leather-wrapped steering wheel, power rear sunshade, active suspension, 225/55HR17 tires. *Deletes*: rear visor mirrors, self-leveling air suspension.

S55/CL55 add to S500: 5.4-liter engine, wood/leather-wrapped steering wheel (CL55), 6-disc CD changer, power rear sunshade, multicontour and active ventilated front seats, active suspension, 245/45YR18 front tires, 275/40YR18 rear tires. *Deletes*: self-leveling air suspension.

S600/CL600 adds: 6.0-liter V12 engine, rear dual-zone automatic climate controls (S600), wood/leather wrapped steering, power adjustable heated rear seats w/lumbar adjustment (S600), cellular telephone, additional leather interior trim, alcantara headliner, parktronic parking aid, 225/55ZR17 tires, polished alloy wheels.

OPTIONAL EQUIPMENT:
Major Packages

	Retail Price	Dealer Invoice
Designo Espresso Edition, S430	$9500	$8835
S500, S55	8700	8091
S600	7500	6975

Special light brown leather seat trim w/two-tone door panels, elm wood interior trim, unique floormats, Designo Expresso paint. Requires climate comfort rear seats or heated rear seats.

Designo Silver Edition, S430	10450	9719
S500	9750	9068
S600	8550	7952

Shell-colored leather interior trim, maple wood interior trim, unique floormats, Designo Silver paint. Requires Active ventilated seats or heated rear seats, power rear seats or Four Place Seating Pkg.

Prices are accurate at time of publication; subject to manufacturer's change.

MERCEDES-BENZ

	Retail Price	Dealer Invoice
Designo Espresso Edition, CL500, CL55	$9800	$9114
CL600	8300	7719

Special mocha leather interior trim, natural maple wood trim on console and doors, unique floormats. CL500 requires CL3 Comfort Pkg.

Designo Silver Edition, CL500, CL55	9800	9114
S600	8300	7719

Platinum leather interior trim, natural maple wood door and console trim, unique floormats. CL500 requires CL3 Comfort Pkg.

S5/CL2 Sport Pkg., S430, S500, CL 500, S600	4900	4557

Front spoiler, side skirts, rear apron, 245/45YR18 front tires, 275/YR18 rear tires, AMG Monoblock Wheels.

K2A Option Pkg., S430, S500	2190	1355

Voice-activated integrated cellular telephone, 6-disc CD changer.

Comfort and Convenience

Keyless go	995	925

Remote keyless entry and ignition starting system.

S3 Comfort Pkg., S430	1960	1823

Multi-contour front seats w/pulsating air chambers, and active lumbar support, heated and active ventilated front seats.

S3/CL3 Comfort Pkg., S500, CL500	1460	1358

Multi-contour front seats w/pulsating air chambers, and active lumbar support, heated and active ventilated front seats.

Active ventilated seats, S430, S500, S55	1530	1423
S600	910	846

Includes heated rear seats. Requires power rear seat adjusters or Four Place Seating Pkg.

Power rear adjusters, S430, S500, S55	1785	1660
Four Place Seating Pkg., S500	5655	5259
S600	3870	3599

Includes rear bucket seats, power reclining seatbacks, wood console.

Heated front seats, S430	620	577
Heated rear seats, S430, S500, S55	620	577
Rear dual-zone climate control, S430, S500, S55	1840	1711
Distronic cruise control	2800	2604
Parktronic	995	925
Power rear window sunshade, S430, S500, S55	495	460
Rear side sunshades	300	279
Power trunk closer	450	419

Appearance and Miscellaneous

Xenon headlights w/washers, S430	1130	1051
Tire pressure monitoring system, S430, S500, S600, CL500, CL600	600	558
Active suspension, S430, S500	2900	2697

Specifications begin on page 535.

MERCURY

MERCURY COUGAR

Mercury Cougar

Front-wheel-drive sports coupe
Base price range: $16,700-$22,050. Built in USA. **Also consider:** Honda Prelude, Volkswagen New Beetle

FOR • Exterior finish **AGAINST** • Rear visibility • Rear-seat room

Revised appearance inside and out and introduction of a high-performance model make 2001 news for Mercury's sporty coupe. The base 125 horsepower 4-cylinder version of this 4-seat hatchback comes only with manual transmission. The plusher 170-hp V6 version gets manual or automatic. Due after the start of the model year, the 196-hp V6 Cougar S comes only with manual, and adds a sport suspension with 17-inch wheels and tires, and special trim. Optional on all Cougars are front side airbags and antilock brakes. A Sport Group for the 170-hp V6 model includes rear disc brakes (versus drums) and 16-inch wheels in place of 15s. Front fascia, grille, and headlamps are new for '01, V6 Sport Group and S models get aluminum pedals, all Cougars have a new steering wheel and altered instrument faces, and a 6-disc in-dash CD changer is a new option.

PERFORMANCE We haven't yet tested an S model, but Cougar's base powerteam is reasonably peppy. The 170-hp V6 adds some low-end muscle, but its passing power is unimpressive, as is its 0-60-mph acceleration (9.9 seconds for our automatic test car). Neither engine matches comparable Japanese units for refinement or high-revving fun. The automatic transmission is acceptably smooth but hunts annoyingly between gears in hilly terrain. And manual shift action is notchy. We aver-

Prices are accurate at time of publication; subject to manufacturer's change.

MERCURY

aged 19.9 mpg with a 5-speed V6, 20.7 with an automatic version. Mercury recommends 91-octane for the V6s.

Cougar handles well, but it lacks the twisty-road agility of most import brand rivals, and its steering feels artificially heavy and non-linear. The V6 Sport Group delivers flatter, grippier cornering at the expense of a thumpy, nervous ride on bad pavement. The softer base suspension is more comfortable, but doesn't absorb bumps well, either. Brake-pedal feel is inconsistent—mushy on one test car, touchy on another—though stopping power is adequate. High levels of road rumble and exhaust noise bespeak sportiness to some, but just sound unpleasant to us.

ACCOMMODATIONS Most sport-coupe interiors feel claustrophobic and Cougar's is no exception. The front cabin provides adequate head and leg room and the bucket seats afford good lateral support, though none of our test drivers gives them high marks for comfort. The cramped rear seat is a preteen environment, with a poorly shaped cushion making it particularly inhospitable. Tip-slide front seats aid rear access without making it easy. The over styled dashboard takes time to sort out, the radio is inconveniently low, and there's no tachometer redline—an odd omission with manual shift. The cabin is further flawed by lots of hard, cheap looking plastic. The hatchback design and split-folding seatbacks provide generous cargo space, but liftover is high. Paint quality and exterior fit and-finish have been very good on Cougars we've tested.

VALUE It has an edgy attitude, but this Mercury is only average in most ways. The most-direct rival is the Mitsubishi Eclipse, which costs slightly more but handles better. Also consider the roomier but more conservative Dodge Stratus coupe, with the pricey but exciting-to-drive Honda Prelude still the class of this class.

ENGINES

	dohc I4	dohc V6	dohc V6
Size, liters/cu. in.	2.0/121	2.5/155	2.5/155
Horsepower @ rpm	125 @ 5500	170 @ 6250	196 @ 6750
Torque (lb-ft) @ rpm	130 @ 4000	165 @ 4250	168 @ 5500
Availability	S	O[1]	S[2]

EPA city/highway mpg

5-speed OD manual	24/34	19/28	NA
4-speed OD automatic		20/29	

1. V6 model. 2. S model.

PRICES

Mercury Cougar	Retail Price	Dealer Invoice
4-cylinder 2-door hatchback	$16700	$15505

Specifications begin on page 535.

MERCURY

	Retail Price	Dealer Invoice
V6 2-door hatchback	$17200	$15955
S 2-door hatchback	22050	20321
Destination charge	475	475

STANDARD EQUIPMENT:

4-cylinder: 2.0-liter dohc 4-cylinder engine, 5-speed manual transmission, dual front airbags, emergency inside trunk release, air conditioning, interior air filter, variable-assist power steering, tilt steering wheel, cloth upholstery, front bucket seats, power height-adjustable driver seat, split folding rear seat, heated power mirrors, power windows, power door locks, AM/FM/CD player, digital clock, tachometer, trip computer, outside temperature indicator, auxiliary power outlet, driver-side visor mirror, rear defogger, cupholder, variable intermittent wipers, power decklid release, front floormats, theft-deterrent system, 205/60R15 tires, alloy wheels.

V6 adds: 2.5-liter dohc V6 170-horsepower engine, upgraded suspension.

S adds: 2.5-liter dohc V6 high-output engine, traction control, antilock 4-wheel disc brakes, leather upholstery, 6-way power driver seat, leather-wrapped steering wheel, cruise control, remote keyless entry, AM/FM/ cassette/CD player, illuminated visor mirrors, map lights, rear wiper/ washer, rear spoiler, fog lights, sport suspension, 215/50ZR17 tires.

OPTIONAL EQUIPMENT:
Major Packages

Convenience Group,

4-cylinder	615	547
V6	660	588

Cruise control, remote keyless entry, AM/FM/cassette/CD player (V6), rear wiper/washer.

Sport Group, V6	865	770

Leather-wrapped steering wheel and shift knob, upgraded sport seats w/adjustable headrests, alloy pedals, center armrest, passenger-side visor mirror, driver-side illuminated visor mirror, map lights, glove box light, additional warning lights, fog lights, rear spoiler, 4-wheel disc brakes, 215/50ZR16 tires.

Powertrains

4-speed automatic transmission, V6	815	725
Traction control, V6	235	209

Requires antilock brakes.

Prices are accurate at time of publication; subject to manufacturer's change.

MERCURY

Safety Features	Retail Price	Dealer Invoice
Antilock brakes, 4-cylinder, V6	$500	$445
Front side-impact airbags	390	347

Comfort and Convenience

Power sunroof	615	547
6-way power driver seat, V6	235	209
Requires Sport Group.		
Leather upholstery, V6	895	797
Requires Sport Group and power driver seat.		
AM/FM/cassette/CD player, 4-cylinder, V6	80	71
In-dash 6-disc CD changer, V6	210	187
V6 w/Convenience Group	130	116
Smoker's Pkg.	15	13
Includes ashtray, lighter.		

Appearance and Miscellaneous

Rear spoiler, 4-cylinder	235	209
Machined alloy wheels, V6	250	223
Requires Sport Group.		

MERCURY GRAND MARQUIS

Mercury Grand Marquis

Rear-wheel-drive full-size car; similar to Ford Crown Victoria

Base price range: $22,805-$25,525. Built in Canada. **Also consider:** Buick LeSabre, Chrysler Concorde, Dodge Intrepid

FOR • Passenger and cargo room **AGAINST** • Fuel economy

More power and adjustable pedals are the top 2001 changes to Mercury's largest car. Grand Marquis shares its design with the Ford Crown Victoria and Lincoln Town Car—the only traditional full-size rear-drive sedans available from a North American manufacturer.

Specifications begin on page 535.

MERCURY

Grand Marquis comes in GS and uplevel LS versions with a 220-horsepower V8 and automatic transmission. An optional Handling Package includes dual exhausts for 235 hp, plus a numerically higher rear-axle ratio for faster getaways, performance tires, firmer damping, and rear load leveling air springs. Both engines gain 20 hp this year. Four-wheel disc brakes are standard. Antilock brakes and traction control are optional. Maximum trailer weight is 2000 pounds.

Dashboard airbags now adjust deployment based on crash severity. The adjustable pedals power fore and aft about three inches and are controlled by a dashboard switch. Also for Œ01, the traction control switch moves from inside the glovebox to the instrument panel. Headlamps are now controlled via the windshield wiper stalk and turn on automatically with the wipers. This eliminates the dashboard headlamp switch. Grand Marquis' performance and accommodations mirror those of the Crown Victoria.

The Ford Crown Victoria report includes an evaluation of the Grand Marquis.

ENGINES

	ohc V8	ohc V8
Size, liters/cu. in.	4.6/281	4.6/281
Horsepower @ rpm	220 @ 4750	235 @ 4750
Torque (lb-ft) @ rpm	265 @ 4000	275 @ 4000
Availability	S	O
EPA city/highway mpg		
4-speed OD automatic	17/24	17/24

PRICES

Mercury Grand Marquis	Retail Price	Dealer Invoice
GS 4-door sedan	$22805	$21595
GS w/Group 60C 4-door sedan	23285	22038
LS 4-door sedan	24705	23343
LS w/Group 60L 4-door sedan	25525	24098
Destination charge	680	680

STANDARD EQUIPMENT:

GS: 4.6-liter V8 220-horsepower engine, 4-speed automatic transmission, dual front airbags, 4-wheel disc brakes, emergency inside trunk release, air conditioning, variable-assist power steering, tilt steering wheel, cruise control, cloth upholstery, front split bench seat, 8-way power driver seat w/power recliner, cupholders, power mirrors, power windows, power door locks, AM/FM/cassette, digital clock, variable intermittent wipers, rear defogger, passenger-side visor mirror, wiper-activated automatic headlights, remote fuel

MERCURY

door/decklid release, floormats, cornering lights, 225/60SR16 whitewall tires, wheel covers.

LS adds to GS: upgraded upholstery, power driver-seat lumbar adjuster and recliner, remote keyless entry, key pad entry, map lights, illuminated visor mirrors, bodyside stripes.

OPTIONAL EQUIPMENT:
Major Packages

	Retail Price	Dealer Invoice
Handling Pkg., GS, LS	$855	$761
LS w/Premium Pkg.	535	476

Upgraded suspension, load-leveling rear air-suspension, performance axle ratio, 235-horsepower engine, dual exhaust, 225/60R16 handling tires, alloy wheels.

Regional Group 60C, GS	NC	NC

Remote keyless entry, illuminated visor mirrors, front and rear reading lights, body stripes. Available only in California, Arizona, Nevada, Hawaii.

Premium Pkg., LS	1120	997

Automatic climate control, power adjustable pedals, power passenger seat w/power lumbar and recliner, leather-wrapped steering wheel, automatic day/night rearview mirror, compass, alloy wheels.

Ultimate Pkg., LS	2520	2243

Premium Pkg. plus antilock brakes, traction control, digital instrumentation, Premium AM/FM/cassette.

Regional Group 60L, LS	NC	NC

Premium Pkg. plus leather upholstery, Premium AM/FM/cassette, universal garage door opener, digital instrumentation, trip computer. Available only in California, Arizona, Nevada, Hawaii.

Safety Features

Antilock brakes	600	534
Antilock brakes w/traction control	775	690

Comfort and Convenience

Power adjustable pedals	120	107
Automatic climate control, LS	175	156

Includes outside-temperature indicator.

Electronic instrumentation, LS	425	379

Digital instrumentation, trip computer. Requires automatic climate control.

Luxury Light Group, GS	190	169

Includes front and rear reading lights, visors, illuminated visor mirrors.

Remote keyless entry, GS	240	213

Includes key pad entry.

Leather upholstery, LS	795	708

Requires Premium Pkg. or Ultimate Pkg.

Premium AM/FM/cassette, LS	360	321

Requires automatic climate control.

Specifications begin on page 535.

MERCURY

	Retail Price	Dealer Invoice
AM/FM/CD player, GS	$140	$124
6-disc CD changer, LS	350	312
Requires Premium AM/FM/cassette.		
Rear air suspension, LS	270	240
Tuned for softer ride.		
Alloy wheels, LS	320	285

MERCURY MOUNTAINEER

Mercury Mountaineer

Rear- or 4-wheel-drive midsize sport-utility vehicle; similar to Ford Explorer

Base price range: $27,655-$30,120. Built in USA. **Also consider:** Dodge Durango, Lexus RX 300, Toyota 4Runner

FOR • Acceleration • Cargo room • Visibility • Build quality
AGAINST • Ride • Fuel economy

Rear childseat tether anchors are the sole additions for 2001 as Mercury's upscale version of the 4-door Ford Explorer begins a short model year. Redesigned versions of Mountaineer and Explorer are due in January '01 as 2002 models; they're larger than the 1995-2001 editions and will have new styling and offer seating for up to eight passengers on three rows.

For '01 Mountaineer offers rear- and 4-wheel drive with a choice of an overhead-cam V6 with a 5-speed automatic transmission or a V8 with 4 speed automatic. V6 models with 4WD get Ford's Control Trac system, which need not be disengaged on dry pavement. V8 versions have permanently engaged 4WD. Options include front side airbags, rear load leveling suspension, and Ford Motor Company's Reverse Sensing System, which signals an audible warning when the vehicle backs up close to an object.

Luxury options groups are called Monterey and, for V8 mod-

Prices are accurate at time of publication; subject to manufacturer's change.

MERCURY

els only, Premiere. Both include woodgrain interior trim and color-keyed bodyside moldings, running boards, and bumpers, among other amenities. The Premiere adds a color-keyed grille, special spruce green paint, and exclusive 16-inch tires on 5-spoke alloy wheels in place of standard 15 inch wheels. Included with the optional universal garage door opener is an integrated digital memo recorder. Mountaineer's performance and accommodations mirror those of comparably equipped Explorers.

The Ford Explorer report includes an evaluation of the Mountaineer.

ENGINES

	ohc V6	ohv V8
Size, liters/cu. in.	4.0/245	5.0/302
Horsepower @ rpm	210 @ 5250	215 @ 4200
Torque (lb-ft) @ rpm	240 @ 3250	288 @ 3300
Availability	S	O

EPA city/highway mpg

4-speed OD automatic		14/19
5-speed automatic	15/20[1]	

1. 15/19 w/4WD.

PRICES

Mercury Mountaineer	Retail Price	Dealer Invoice
4-door wagon, 2WD	$27655	$24369
4-door wagon, 4WD	29655	27149
4-door wagon, AWD	30120	27563
Destination charge	575	575

STANDARD EQUIPMENT:

2WD: 4.0-liter V6 engine, 5-speed automatic transmission, dual front airbags, antilock 4-wheel disc brakes, air conditioning, power steering, tilt leather-wrapped steering wheel, cruise control, cloth upholstery, front captain chairs, split folding rear seat, center console, cupholders, power mirrors, power windows, power door locks, intermittent rear wiper/washer, rear defogger, AM/FM/cassette, digital clock, tachometer, illuminated visor mirrors, variable intermittent wipers, auxiliary power outlets, cargo cover, map lights, floormats, theft-deterrent system, running boards, roof rack, rear privacy glass, fog lights, full-size spare tire, 235/70R15 all-terrain tires, alloy wheels.

4WD adds: Control Trac full-time 4-wheel drive, 2-speed transfer case.

AWD adds: 5.0-liter V8 engine, 4-speed automatic transmission, permanent 4-wheel drive, limited-slip differential, Trailer Tow Pkg. (heavy-duty flasher, trailering harness), 235/75R15 all-terrain white-letter tires.

Specifications begin on page 535.

MERCURY

OPTIONAL EQUIPMENT:

	Retail Price	Dealer Invoice

Major Packages

Convenience Group $1195 $1016
Cloth sport bucket seats, 6-way power driver seat, AM/FM/cassette/CD player, rear radio and climate controls, rear headphone jacks, remote keyless entry, key pad entry, autolock/relock system, overhead console w/compass and outside temperature indicator, illuminated visor mirrors, automatic day/night rearview mirror, high series floor console, rear vent w/fan, additional cupholders, automatic headlights, puddle lights.

Luxury Group 1495 1271
Leather upholstery, 6-way power front sport bucket seats, automatic climate control, message center (trip computer, oil-life monitor, additional warning lights), Mach AM/FM/cassette/CD player, steering wheel radio/climate controls. Requires Convenience Group.

Monterey Feature Group... 495 421
Woodgrain interior trim, unique floormats, light tan lower body, badging. Requires Convenience Group and Luxury Group.

Premiere Feature Group, 2WD, AWD..................... 595 506
Woodgrain interior trim, unique floormats, Spruce Green or Wedgewood Blue metallic paint, color-keyed grille, bodyside moldings, bumpers and running boards, 255/70R16 white letter tires, special alloy wheels. Requires Convenience Group, Luxury Group. 2WD requires 5.0-liter engine.

Powertrains

5.0-liter V8 engine, 2WD 465 395
Includes 4-speed automatic transmission, limited-slip differential, 3.73 axle ratio, Trailer Tow Pkg., 235/75R15 all-terrain white-letter tires. NA 4WD.

Limited-slip differential, 2WD, 4WD........................ 355 302
Includes Trailer Tow Pkg. (heavy-duty flasher, trailering harness) and 3.73 axle ratio.

Safety Features

Front side-impact airbags.. 395 336
Requires Convenience Group.

Reverse Sensing System... 255 217
Requires Convenience Group.

Comfort and Convenience

Automatic climate control 590 502
Includes steering wheel climate/radio controls, message center (trip computer, oil-life monitor, additional warning lights). Requires Convenience Group and Mach AM/FM/cassette/CD player.

Leather sport bucket seats...................................... 950 808
Includes 6-way power front seats. Requires Convenience Group.

Universal garage door opener 215 182
Includes Travelnote digital memo recorder.

Prices are accurate at time of publication; subject to manufacturer's change.

MERCURY

	Retail Price	Dealer Invoice
Power sunroof	$800	$680
Requires Convenience Group.		
6-disc CD changer	395	336
Requires Convenience Group.		
Mach AM/FM/cassette/CD player	440	374
Requires Convenience Group.		

Special Purpose, Wheels and Tires

Rear load-leveling suspension, 4WD, AWD	395	336
Requires Convenience Group, leather sport bucket seats.		
Chrome alloy wheels	495	421
235/75R15 all-terrain white-letter tires, 2WD, 4WD	230	196

2002 MERCURY MOUNTAINEER

2002 Mercury Mountaineer

Rear- or 4-wheel-drive midsize sport-utility vehicle; similar to Ford Explorer

Base price range: $28,630-$30,610. Built in USA. **Also consider:** Acura MDX, Dodge Durango, Lexus RX 300

Mountaineer was introduced as a 1997 model, cloning the 4-door Ford Explorer but making due with only minor trim differences in its bid to attract a tonier audience. Mountaineer is redesigned along with Explorer for 2002, and now has substantially different styling than its Ford cousin, a look Mercury hopes will enhance its appeal to upscale SUV buyers, especially women.

Mountaineer shares the new Explorer's body-on-frame design and both are the same overall length as the outgoing 2001 versions on a wheelbase longer by about two inches and a track wider by 2.5. Body shells are identical, but Mountaineer employs what Mercury terms "architectural styling cues," most prominent in its different-looking nose and grille. Interior and exterior trim with a satin aluminum finish is another Mountaineer design theme.

Specifications begin on page 535.

MERCURY

Adoption of independent rear suspension in place of a solid rear axle lowers the rear load floor by seven inches and allows installation of third-row seating—standard on Mountaineer, optional on Explorer—that increases passenger capacity from five to seven. Where Explorer offers four levels of trim, Mountaineer comes as a single model with options such as leather upholstery and sunroof. And Mercury says different tire design and shock-absorber valving give Mountaineer its own character.

As in Explorer, rear-wheel-drive and 4-wheel drive are offered, but Mountaineer's 4WD system is permanently engaged. It requires no action from the driver to activate, though it is without low-range gearing. Antilock 4-wheel disc brakes are standard; an optional antiskid system is due later in the year. The base engine is again a 4.0-liter overhead-cam V6. Replacing a 215-horsepower overhead-valve 5.0 as the optional V8 is a 240-hp overhead-cam 4.6 liter. A 5-speed automatic transmission is standard with both engines; V8 Mountaineers previously used a 4-speed automatic. V8 versions can tow up to 7300 pounds.

Front side airbags are again optional and are joined by newly optional curtain side airbags for side-collision protection; a related system available later in the year uses sensors to detect an impending rollover and deploys the curtain airbags. A tilt/telescoping steering wheel is standard, adjustable brake and accelerator pedals optional. We have not yet tested a 2002 Explorer or Mountaineer and so cannot provide an evaluation or ratings.

ENGINES

	ohc V6	ohc V8
Size, liters/cu. in.	4.0/245	4.6/281
Horsepower @ rpm	210 @ 5250	250 @ 4750
Torque (lb-ft) @ rpm	250 @ 4000	280 @ 4000
Availability	S	O

EPA city/highway mpg
4-speed OD automatic		16/22
5-speed automatic	15/20[1]	

1. 15/19 w/4WD.

Prices unavailable at time of publication.

MERCURY SABLE

Front-wheel-drive midsize car; similar to Ford Taurus

Base price range: $19,185-$22,685. Built in USA. **Also consider:** Honda Accord, Toyota Camry

FOR • Handling/roadholding • Rear-seat comfort • Cargo room
AGAINST • Low-speed acceleration

A two-gallon increase in fuel-tank volume, to 18 gallons, lower rear

Prices are accurate at time of publication; subject to manufacturer's change.

MERCURY

Mercury Sable 4-door sedan

child-seat anchors, and an optional single-disc CD player are additions for 2001 to Mercury's midsize car. Sable and its near-twin, the Ford Taurus, received a major design update for 2000, including fresh front and rear styling.

Sable sedans and wagons come in GS and uplevel LS and LS Premium trim. Standard is a 153-horsepower overhead-valve 3.0-liter V6; a 200-hp twincam V6 is standard on LS Premium, optional on LS. A 4-speed automatic is the only transmission. Sixteen-inch wheels and tires are standard, antilock brakes and traction control are optional. Five-passenger seating with front buckets or 6-passenger seating with a front bench are available. Unlike the Taurus wagon, Sable's doesn't offer a 2-place third-row seat. Power-adjusting foot pedals are standard on LSs, optional on GS.

Front head/chest side airbags are optional, and all Sables get Ford's Advanced Restraints System. This is designed to minimize airbag injuries to front-seat occupants by gauging the severity of a crash, recognizing variables such as seat position, then deciding whether to deploy the front airbags and at what power. The system does not control the side airbags, but does modulate the seatbelt pretensioners for both front seats. Sedans have an emergency trunklid release designed to free anyone trapped in the trunk. Sable's performance and accommodations mirror those of similarly equipped Tauruses.

The Ford Taurus report includes an evaluation of the Sable.

ENGINES

	ohv V6	dohc V6
Size, liters/cu. in.	3.0/182	3.0/181
Horsepower @ rpm	155 @ 4900	200 @ 5650
Torque (lb-ft) @ rpm	185 @ 3950	200 @ 4400
Availability	S	S[1]

EPA city/highway mpg

4-speed OD automatic	19/28	20/28

1. LS Premium; optional LS.

Specifications begin on page 535.

MERCURY

PRICES

Mercury Sable	Retail Price	Dealer Invoice
GS 4-door sedan	$19185	$17777
GS 4-door wagon	20985	19397
LS 4-door sedan	20285	18767
LS Premium 4-door sedan	21585	19937
LS Premium 4-door wagon	22685	20927
Destination charge	625	625

STANDARD EQUIPMENT:

GS: 3.0-liter V6 engine, 4-speed automatic transmission, dual front airbags, 4-wheel disc brakes (wagon), emergency inside trunk release (sedan), air conditioning, interior air filter, variable-assist power steering, tilt steering wheel, cruise control, cloth upholstery, 6-passenger seating, split front bench seat, column shift, split folding rear seat (wagon), third row seat (wagon), cupholders, power mirrors, power windows, power door locks, remote keyless entry, AM/FM/cassette, digital clock, power antenna (wagon), tachometer, variable intermittent wipers, rear defogger, visor mirrors, auxiliary power outlets, map lights, remote decklid release (sedan), cargo cover (wagon), rear wiper/washer (wagon), floormats, theft-deterrent system, roof rack (wagon), 215/60R16 tires, wheel covers (sedan), alloy wheels (wagon).

LS adds: cloth/leather upholstery, 5-passenger seating w/front bucket seats, center console, floor shift, 6-way power driver seat w/manual lumbar adjustment, split folding rear seat, power-adjustable pedals, leather-wrapped steering wheel, alloy wheels.

LS Premium adds: 3.0-liter dohc V6 engine, automatic climate control, keypad entry, heated power mirrors, illuminated visor mirrors, automatic headlights, theft-deterrent system w/alarm, fog lights.

OPTIONAL EQUIPMENT:

Major Packages
Secure Group	995	886

Traction control, front side-impact airbags, antilock brakes.

Powertrains
3.0-liter dohc V6 engine, LS	695	619
Traction control, LS, LS Premium	175	156

Requires antilock brakes.

Safety Features
Front side-impact airbags	390	347
Antilock brakes	600	534

Prices are accurate at time of publication; subject to manufacturer's change.

MERCURY

Comfort and Convenience

	Retail Price	Dealer Invoice
5-passenger seating, GS sedan	$105	$93
Includes center console, floor shift.		
6-passenger seating, LS Premium	NC	NC
Requires leather upholstery.		
Leather upholstery, LS Premium	NC	NC
Power driver seat, GS	395	352
Includes manual lumbar support		
Power passenger seat, LS Premium	350	312
Requires front side-impact airbags, leather upholstery.		
Power-adjustable pedals, GS	120	107
Power sunroof, LS, LS Premium	890	792
Manufacturer's discount price, LS Premium	NC	NC
Manufacturer's discount price available only in California, Hawaii, New York City, Boston, Philadelphia, Pittsburgh, and Washington, DC.		
Audio Group, LS, LS Premium	670	597
6-disc CD changer, Mach sound system.		
AM/FM/CD player, GS, LS	140	120

Appearance and Miscellaneous

Alloy wheels, GS sedan	395	352
Chrome alloy wheels, LS, LS Premium	295	263

MERCURY VILLAGER

Mercury Villager

Front-wheel-drive minivan; similar to Nissan Quest

Base price range: $22,510-$27,210. Built in USA. **Also consider:** Dodge Caravan, Honda Odyssey, Toyota Sienna

FOR • Passenger and cargo room • Control layout **AGAINST** • Interior materials • Fuel economy

A restyled grille and front fascia and a revised liftgate appearance are

Specifications begin on page 535.

MERCURY

the main changes to Villager for 2001. Mercury's minivan shares its design with the Nissan Quest and both manufacturers have announced that production of these vehicles will cease during model-year 2002.

Villager comes in base, Sport, and luxury Estate models. All have dual sliding rear doors, a 3.3-liter V6 engine, and automatic transmission. All seat seven. Second-row seating consists of a 2-person bench on base models and a pair of bucket seats on Sport and Estate. All Villagers have a 3-passenger third-row bench that slides fore and aft on floor tracks. Standard on Sport and Estate and unavailable on the base model is an adjustable-height rear parcel shelf behind the third-row seat.

Side airbags and power sliding doors aren't available. An optional rear seat entertainment system includes a VCR with remote control, 6.4-inch flip-down screen, and headphones. Quest offers this system at no extra charge. Remote keyless entry is standard on all Villagers, and leather upholstery is standard on Estate. For '01, Sport and Estate alloy wheels are restyled.

PERFORMANCE Villager and Quest are reasonably snappy away from a stop. But power in the 35-55-mph range is unimpressive, and highway passing response borders on inadequate with a full load and the air conditioning on. As in Nissan trucks that use this engine, there's marked engine roar under heavy throttle. Wind and tire noise aren't car-quiet, but are no louder than in other minivans. Our test Quest averaged 16.9 mpg, slightly better than the class average.

The relatively compact Villager and Quest have above-average minivan maneuverability, abetted by firm steering with ample feel. Base models have 15-inch tires, but the 16s on the Villager Estate and Sport and the Quest SE provide notably crisper cornering response. All use the same suspension and it soaks up sharp bumps decently well, but overall ride quality doesn't match that of longer-wheelbase minivans like the Dodge Grand Caravan and Toyota Sienna.

ACCOMMODATIONS These minivans are relatively cozy, with scant clearance between any of the seats. The front seatbacks are narrow, although supportive cushions make for good overall comfort. Step-in is low, but third-row entry/exit is tighter than in most minivans due to a lowish roof and narrow passageways.

Cargo room is slim with the third seat in its normal position, though the handy available adjustable-height rear parcel shelf greatly enhances versatility in stowing smaller items. The third-row bench doesn't remove, but can slide up to the front seats to free up a large cargo hold; too bad its release handle is so difficult to reach. The second-row seats are easy to take in and out, and maximum cargo space is good for the exterior size.

Interior storage includes a removable net between the front seats, double front-door pockets, and numerous bins and beverage holders, including a dual front cupholder that doesn't block any controls when in use.

Prices are accurate at time of publication; subject to manufacturer's change.

MERCURY

Villager and Quest target an upscale audience but undercut that goal with an abundance of hard-surfaced interior plastic, industrial-looking switchgear, unfinished edges around door handles and map pockets, and some sharp-edge seat mounts. The Villager we tested also suffered a rattling rear seat.

VALUE Like Mazda's MPV, Villager and Quest are smaller outside and inside than most rivals, but are more maneuverable. The absence of available side airbags and power sliding doors in the Mercury and Nissan are telling omissions for modern minivans, however. And acceleration and refinement need to be more competitive, too. None of these deficiencies is likely to be remedied before production of these vans ends.

ENGINES

	ohc V6
Size, liters/cu. in.	3.3/200
Horsepower @ rpm	170 @ 4800
Torque (lb-ft) @ rpm	200 @ 2800
Availability	S

EPA city/highway mpg
4-speed OD automatic 17/24

PRICES

Mercury Villager	Retail Price	Dealer Invoice
Base 4-door van	$22510	$20654
Sport 4-door van	25735	23525
Estate 4-door van	27210	24837
Destination charge	655	655

STANDARD EQUIPMENT:

Base: 3.3-liter V6 engine, 4-speed automatic transmission, dual front airbags, front air conditioning, power steering, tilt steering wheel, cruise control, cloth upholstery, 7-passenger seating (front bucket seats, 2-passenger second row bench seat, 3-passenger third row folding bench seat), center console, cupholders, dual sliding rear doors, power mirrors, power front windows, power door locks, remote keyless entry, AM/FM/cassette, digital clock, tachometer, variable intermittent wipers, illuminated visor mirrors, rear defogger, intermittent rear wiper/washer, auxiliary power outlets, floormats, theft-deterrent system, roof rack, cornering lights, 215/70R15 tires, wheel covers.

Sport adds: front and rear air conditioning, interior air filter, 6-way power driver seat, second row bucket seats, leather-wrapped steering wheel w/radio controls, rear radio controls, rear headphone jacks, power rear quarter windows, overhead console w/conversation mirror, universal garage door opener, Travelnote digital memo recorder, adjustable rear parcel shelf, map lights, privacy glass, fog lights, flip-open liftgate, two-tone paint, handling suspen-

Specifications begin on page 535.

MERCURY

sion, 225/60R16 tires, alloy wheels.

Estate adds: leather upholstery, memory driver seat and mirrors, 4-way power passenger seat, Premium sound system, heated power mirrors, automatic headlights.

OPTIONAL EQUIPMENT:

	Retail Price	Dealer Invoice
Major Packages		
Convenience Group, Base	$995	$846

Power rear windows, 6-way power driver seat, overhead console, map lights, rear reading lights, additional courtesy lights, flip-open liftgate, privacy glass. Requires rear air conditioning.

Rear Seat Entertainment System, Sport, Estate	1295	1101

Videocassette player, headphones, remote control, video game outlet, rear passenger controls, headphones. Requires Supersound AM/FM/cassette/CD player or Entertainment Premium AM/FM/casstte. NA w/power sunroof.

Trailer Tow Prep Group	250	213

Trailer tow module and jumper harness, heavy-duty battery, full-size spare tire.

Safety Features

Antilock brakes	590	502

Comfort and Convenience

Rear air conditioning, Base	495	421

Includes interior air filter, rear radio controls.

Automatic climate control, Estate	245	208
Power sunroof, Sport, Estate	775	659
Electronic instrument cluster, Estate	295	251

Digital speedometer, digital odometer and dual trip odometers, outside temperature indicator, trip computer. Requires automatic air conditioning.

586 Premium AM/FM/cassette, Base, Sport	310	263

Includes rear radio controls and headphone jacks. NA w/Rear Seat Entertainment System.

58M Entertainment Premium AM/FM/cassette, Sport, Estate	310	263

Includes upgraded sound system. Requires Rear Seat Entertainment System.

58K Supersound AM/FM/cassette/CD player, Sport, Estate	865	735

Includes 6-disc CD changer, upgraded sound system and more powerful headphone system.

6-disc CD changer	370	314
Leather upholstery, Sport	795	676
Alloy wheels, Base	395	336

Prices are accurate at time of publication; subject to manufacturer's change.

MITSUBISHI

MITSUBISHI DIAMANTE

Mitsubishi Diamante LS

Front-wheel-drive near-luxury car
Base price range: $25,387-$28,407. Built in Australia. **Also consider:** Acura TL, Infiniti I30, Lexus ES 300

FOR • Acceleration • Quietness • Ride **AGAINST** • Rear head room

Unchanged save the addition of rear child-seat anchors, Diamante returns for 2001 as Mitsubishi's U.S. flagship. ES and luxury LS sedans are offered, the latter with standard leather upholstery, power sunroof, and 16-inch alloy wheels to ES's 15-inch steel wheels. Standard on LS are foglamps, which had been part of an All-Weather option package. That package is still available for the LS and includes heated mirrors and front seats, plus traction control. Antilock 4-wheel disc brakes are standard, but side airbags are unavailable. The sole powertrain is a 3.5-liter V6 engine and 4-speed automatic transmission.

EVALUATION Diamante survives in a very competitive class mostly on feature-per-dollar value. Its torquey V6 provides satisfying performance. Our test took 8.1 seconds 0-60 mph and averaged 19.7 mpg with a healthy dose of highway driving. We recommend the optional traction control because the front tires can spin wildly on damp pavement; too bad this safety feature only comes in an option package for the uplevel LS. Wind and road noise are low, but the engine isn't as smooth as the near-luxury norm. Most bumps are easily absorbed, but there's some float over fast humpbacks, and marked body lean in tight turns. Four adults won't lack leg or foot space, but with the sunroof, head clearance is marginal for 6-footers. Interior storage space is subpar, the pop-out cupholders are flimsy, and the busy dashboard is saddled with too-small radio buttons. Outward visibility is good, however, and the trunk usefully roomy and easy to load, though the lid hinges steal space. Detail assembly is thorough and materials generally look good, but door closings are a bit tinny.

Specifications begin on page 535.

MITSUBISHI

ENGINES

	ohc V6
Size, liters/cu. in.	3.5/213
Horsepower @ rpm	205 @ 5000
Torque (lb-ft) @ rpm	231 @ 4000
Availability	S

EPA city/highway mpg
4-speed OD automatic 18/24

PRICES

Mitsubishi Diamante	Retail Price	Dealer Invoice
ES 4-door sedan	$25387	$23100
LS 4-door sedan	28407	25845
Destination charge	520	520

STANDARD EQUIPMENT:

ES: 3.5-liter V6 engine, 4-speed automatic transmission, dual front airbags, antilock 4-wheel disc brakes, air conditioning w/automatic climate control, variable-assist power steering, tilt steering wheel, cruise control, cloth upholstery, manual 10-way adjustable front bucket seats, center console, cupholders, power mirrors, power windows, power door locks, remote keyless entry, variable intermittent wipers, AM/FM/CD player, power antenna, digital clock, tachometer, illuminated visor mirrors, rear defogger, map lights, auxiliary power outlets, remote fuel-door and decklid releases, automatic-off headlights, floormats, theft-deterrent system, full-size spare tire, 205/65HR15 tires, wheel covers.

LS adds: leather upholstery, 8-way power driver seat w/memory and power lumbar support, 4-way power passenger seat, leather-wrapped steering wheel w/radio controls, Infinity sound system, power sunroof, universal garage door opener, fog lights, 215/60VR16 tires, alloy wheels.

OPTIONAL EQUIPMENT:

Major Packages
All Weather Pkg., LS...................... 720 584
  Traction control, heated front seats and mirrors.

MITSUBISHI ECLIPSE

Front-wheel-drive sports coupe

Base price range: $17,987-$26,407. Built in USA. **Also consider:** Acura Integra, Honda Prelude, Toyota Celica, Volkswagen New Beetle

---

FOR • Acceleration (V6) • Handling/roadholding **AGAINST** • Road noise • Rear-seat room • Rear visibility • Rear-seat entry/exit

Prices are accurate at time of publication; subject to manufacturer's change.

MITSUBISHI

Mitsubishi Eclipse Spyder

Eclipse comes as a hatchback coupe and Spyder convertible, with the coupe getting a few minor feature changes for 2001. Both body styles come in GS and GT trim, and there's a price-leader RS coupe. GTs have a standard V6, other Eclipses a 4-cylinder engine. Manual transmission is standard for all, with automatic optional; the GT automatic has a separate gate for manual shifting. Spyders include a power soft top with glass rear window. Linewide standards include alloy wheels, air conditioning, CD stereo, power windows and locks, and engine immobilizer. The RS has 15-inch wheels and tires, GS models 16s, and GTs add 17-inch wheels, lower-body skirts, and rear disc brakes instead of drums. Front side airbags are available only for GTs in a Premium Package option along with antilock brakes and, with automatic transmission, traction control. Antilock brakes are standard on the GT Spyder. Leather upholstery is available for GTs and the GS Spyder.

For 2001, coupes add rear child-seat anchors, and the GS and GT gain a standard rear spoiler. Also new is a GS coupe Sun and Sound package comprising sunroof and premium audio; a similar Sun, Sound and Leather package with leather upholstery is available for the GT coupe.

PERFORMANCE Eclipses are relatively mature-feeling sporty compacts, not quite as refined as the costlier Honda Prelude, but less coltish than the Toyota Celica. Regardless of tire size, ride is pliant and comfortable for this type of car. Handling is alert and responsive, with little cornering lean and grippy front-drive predictability, though low-speed maneuverability is hampered by a large turning circle. There's some wheel patter on washboard roads, but it's not bothersome. Braking is good, too, but ABS should be available on all models, not just GTs.

Eclipse's 4-cylinder is generally smooth and quiet and packs a respectable punch with the smooth-shifting manual transmission. The automatic is responsive enough, and Mitsubishi's Sportronic manual shift feature helps get the most from the V6. GTs aren't rockets, but are satisfyingly quick. Our extended-use automatic GT coupe does 0-60 mph in 8.6 seconds and is averaging 21.8 mpg over its first 6023 miles. An automatic GT convertible averaged 20.6 mpg in our tests.

Specifications begin on page 535.

MITSUBISHI

Spyders perform much like equivalent coupes, though they weigh a bit more. Cowl shake is noticed over bumps in ragtop models, but structural stiffness is acceptable and the top seals tightly and insulates well. Eclipse's V6 is little quieter than its 4-cylinder, and there's noticeable tire noise on some surfaces. Wind rush, by contrast, is nicely tamed in coupes despite the retention of frameless door glass. Our extended-test Eclipse has required no unscheduled maintenance.

ACCOMMODATIONS This is a cozy 2+2 with a Yoda-size rear seat and limbo-dancer entry/exit. At least the front buckets hug the torso and are comfortable on long rides. The driving position is low-slung, and visibility remains difficult directly aft—especially top-up in Spyders with their teensy back windows. Some taller drivers may wish the standard tilt steering wheel adjusted higher, but all models have seat-height adjustment. Gauges and most switchgear are clear and handy. Clock/audio readouts are eye-level in a central pod, but can be tough to see in daytime. Ditto the air conditioning and recirculation indicator lights.

Luggage space is generous in coupes with the rear seat folded, limited in Spyders (though not by the folded top). Load lips are lofty in both body styles, and the coupe hatch lid is rather heavy. Workmanship is generally solid, but many interior materials feel too lightweight and doors close with a clang.

VALUE A relatively conservative nature serves the latest Eclipse well, broadening its market while keeping most drivers entertained. Spyders have little direct competition in their price league. Coupe or convertible, a GT would be our pick, but you won't feel penalized in one of the less expensive 4-cylinder models.

ENGINES

	ohc I4	ohc V6
Size, liters/cu. in.	2.4/143	3.0/181
Horsepower @ rpm	147 @ 5500	200 @ 5500
Torque (lb-ft) @ rpm	158 @ 4000	205 @ 4000
Availability	S[1]	S
EPA city/highway mpg		
5-speed OD manual	23/31	20/28
4-speed OD automatic	20/28	20/27

1. RS, GS; 140 horsepower and 155 lb-ft with automatic transmission.

PRICES

Mitsubishi Eclipse

	Retail Price	Dealer Invoice
RS 2-door hatchback, 5-speed	$17987	$16460
RS 2-door hatchback, automatic	18787	17192
GS 2-door hatchback, 5-speed	18797	17196
GS 2-door hatchback, automatic	19797	18111
GS Spyder 2-door convertible, 5-speed	23407	21409
GS Spyder 2-door convertible, automatic	24407	22319

Prices are accurate at time of publication; subject to manufacturer's change.

MITSUBISHI

	Retail Price	Dealer Invoice
GT 2-door hatchback, 5-speed	$20947	$19168
GT 2-door hatchback, automatic	21947	20083
GT Spyder 2-door convertible, 5-speed	25407	23245
GT Spyder 2-door convertible, automatic	26407	24155
Destination charge	520	520

STANDARD EQUIPMENT:

RS: 2.4-liter 4-cylinder engine, 5-speed manual or 4-speed automatic transmission, dual front airbags, variable-assist power steering, tilt steering wheel, air conditioning, interior air filter, cloth upholstery, front bucket seat w/driver height adjustment, center console, cupholders, folding rear seat, power windows, power door locks, AM/FM/CD player, digital clock, tachometer, variable-intermittent wipers, map lights, auxiliary power outlets, remote hatch release, visor mirrors, rear defogger, cargo cover, automatic-off headlights, floormats, theft-deterrent system, dual outside mirrors, 195/65HR15 tires, alloy wheels.

GS hatchback adds: 5-speed manual or 4-speed automatic transmission w/manual-shift capability, cruise control, leather-wrapped steering wheel, power mirrors, split folding rear seat, rear spoiler, 205/55HR16 tires.

GS convertible adds: Infinity sound system, remote keyless entry, non-folding rear seat, power convertible top, fog lights.

GT adds to GS hatchback or GS convertible: 3.0-liter V6 engine, 4-wheel disc brakes, power antenna (convertible), sport suspension, fog lights, 215/50VR17 tires.

OPTIONAL EQUIPMENT:

Major Packages

P3 Premium Pkg., GT hatchback	2760	2402

Antilock brakes, front side-airbags, Infinity AM/FM/cassette w/in-dash 4-disc CD changer, leather front bucket seats, 8-way power driver seat, remote keyless entry, power sunroof, compass, outside temperature indicator, rear wiper/washer, theft-deterrent system w/alarm.

P4 Premium Pkg., GT hatchback automatic	3050	2652

P3 Premium Pkg. plus traction control.

P5/P6 Premium Pkg., GT convertible 5-speed	2370	2057
GT convertible automatic	2650	2308

Antilock brakes, traction control (automatic), front side-airbags, leather front bucket seats, 6-way power driver seat, Infinity AM/FM/cassette w/in-dash 4-disc CD changer.

P1/P2 Sun and Sound Pkg., GS/GT hatchback	1080	936

Infinity sound system, power sunroof.

Specifications begin on page 535.

MITSUBISHI

	Retail Price	Dealer Invoice
P5 Sun, Sound and Leather Pkg., GT hatchback	$1690	$1458
Sun and Sound Pkg. plus leather front bucket seats.		

Comfort and Convenience

Leather front bucket seats, GS convertible, GT	600	525

MITSUBISHI GALANT

Mitsubishi Galant GTZ

Front-wheel-drive compact car

Base price range: $17,557-$24,007. Built in USA. **Also consider:** Mazda 626, Nissan Altima, Volkswagen Passat

FOR • Ride • Steering/handling **AGAINST** • Rear-seat entry/exit

The addition of rear child-seat anchors and one new option package are the only changes to Mitsubishi's compact sedan. Galant returns in 4-cylinder DE and ES models and in V6 ES, LS, and sporty GTZ versions. All come with 4-speed automatic transmission, and all but the DE include an anti-theft system and driver-seat lumbar adjustment. Front side airbags are standard for LS and GTZ, optional for ES models. Antilock brakes are standard in V6 models and available for the 4-cylinder ES. GTZ stands apart with a body-color grille, rear-deck spoiler, and white-faced gauges.

Traction control remains standard for LS and GTZ, and is available on the ES models, packaged with heated door mirrors and alloy wheels. Besides the new rear child-seat anchors, all Galants are now certified as 50-state Low Emissions Vehicles, with 4-cylinder models rating Ultra LEV status if sold in states requiring California emissions standards.

PERFORMANCE Galant is a surprisingly entertaining compact sedan, especially with V6 power. Both engines are smooth performers. The 4-cylinder is decently strong, becomes vocal only at higher rpm, and furnished 0-60 mph in 10.3 seconds in our tests. The smoother, quieter V6 took a test GTZ 0-60 mph in 8.3 seconds. The V6 also works well with the automatic transmission to provide throttle response as good as any in this class. Galant's V6 is fairly thrifty too, averaging 21-22.2 mpg in our tests, though it requires premium fuel.

Prices are accurate at time of publication; subject to manufacturer's change.
CONSUMER GUIDE

MITSUBISHI

With slightly more highway driving, our 4-cylinder automatic ES averaged 24 mpg on regular.

Aside from some minor tail hop over sharp lateral ridges, Galant's ride is comfortably compliant and controlled. Handling is predictable and balanced, and straight-line tracking is good. The GTZ telegraphs small bumps more clearly than other models, but has slightly less body lean in tight corners and more precise steering. Regardless of model, simulated panic stops are short, true, and level, even without antilock control. Wind rush is muted, but tire roar intrudes on coarse pavement.

ACCOMMODATIONS Galant has only average compact-class room for four adults, five in a pinch. Rear entry/exit could be better, but front seats are long-haul supportive. As usual with compacts, adult rear-seaters have just enough head room for comfort, but not enough leg space to avoid riding knees-up.

Gauges and controls are well placed, while visibility is hindered only to the rear by the high-tail styling. The flat-floor low-liftover trunk is spacious enough, and all models except the base DE come with a folding rear seatback—though only the right side folds. Galant's driving feel is satisfyingly solid, but the trunk lid feels flimsy, and minor dash rattles plagued two examples we tested. Exterior finish appears fine. Interior materials are pedestrian but pleasant, falling just shy of "upscale" even on the toney LS and GTZ.

VALUE An agreeable, competent family 4-door, Galant offers much of the driving satisfaction—if not the top-notch workmanship—of a Honda Accord or Toyota Camry at lower cost.

ENGINES

	ohc I4	ohc V6
Size, liters/cu. in.	2.4/143	3.0/181
Horsepower @ rpm	140 @ 5500	195 @ 5500
Torque (lb-ft) @ rpm	155 @ 4000	205 @ 4000
Availability	S[1]	S[2]
EPA city/highway mpg		
4-speed OD automatic	21/28	20/27

1. DE, ES. 2. ES V6, LS, GTZ.

PRICES

Mitsubishi Galant	Retail Price	Dealer Invoice
DE 4-door sedan, automatic	$17557	$16151
ES 4-door sedan, automatic	18407	16749
ES V6 4-door sedan, automatic	20307	18481
LS 4-door sedan, automatic	23907	21750
GTZ 4-door, automatic	24007	21842
Destination charge	520	520

STANDARD EQUIPMENT:

DE: 2.4-liter 4-cylinder engine, 4-speed automatic transmission, dual

Specifications begin on page 535.

MITSUBISHI

front airbags, air conditioning, interior air filter, power steering, tilt steering wheel, cloth upholstery, front bucket seats, manual 8-way adjustable driver seat, center console, cupholders, power windows, power door locks, AM/FM/CD player, digital clock, tachometer, rear defogger, variable intermittent wipers, driver-side visor mirror, map lights, remote fuel door and decklid releases, auxiliary power outlets, automatic-off headlights, floormats, theft-deterrent system, dual remote outside mirrors, 195/60HR15 tires, wheel covers.

ES adds: cruise control, leather-wrapped steering wheel, remote keyless entry, split folding rear seat, power mirrors, illuminated visor mirrors, fog lights.

ES V6 adds: 3.0-liter V6 engine, antilock 4-wheel disc brakes, 205/55HR16 tires.

LS adds: traction control, front side-airbags, leather upholstery, 8-way power driver seat w/lumbar adjustment, heated power mirrors, power sunroof, Infinity sound system, theft-deterrent system w/alarm, alloy wheels.

GTZ adds: sport suspension, rear spoiler.

OPTIONAL EQUIPMENT:

Major Packages

	Retail Price	Dealer Invoice
Premium Pkg., ES 4-cylinder	$2600	$2261
ES V6	2400	2082

Front side-airbags, antilock brakes (ES 4-cylinder), power sunroof, Infinity sound system, leather-wrapped steering wheel, driver seat adjustable lumbar, rear heat ducts, heated mirrors, alloy wheels.

All Weather Pkg., ES V6	310	270

Traction control, heated mirrors.

Comfort and Convenience

Power sunroof, ES	850	697

MITSUBISHI MONTERO

Mitsubishi Montero XLS

4-wheel-drive full-size sport-utility vehicle

Prices are accurate at time of publication; subject to manufacturer's change.

MITSUBISHI

Base price range: $31,297-$35,297. Built in Japan. **Also consider:** Chevrolet Tahoe/GMC Yukon, Ford Expedition, Toyota Land Cruiser

FOR • Passenger and cargo room **AGAINST** • Fuel economy • Acceleration • Ride • Steering/handling

Mitsubishi's senior sport-utility vehicle is redesigned for 2001. Compared to the 1992-2000 generation, it's longer, lower, and wider, with a new independent rear suspension and unibody construction instead of body-on-frame. A 3.5-liter V6 returns with slightly more torque. The base XLS has a 4-speed automatic transmission and part-time 4-wheel drive; the costlier Limited gets a 5-speed automatic with a separate gate for manual shifting, plus Mitsubishi's ActiveTrac 4WD that can be used on dry pavement. Antilock brakes and front side airbags are standard, as is seating for seven with a 2-passenger third-row bench that folds into the rear cargo floor. Both models have 16-inch alloy wheels.

EVALUATION Despite a more car-like design than prior models, the '01 Montero is no less trucky to drive. It's pleasingly stable in straight-line cruising, but slow steering contributes to a ponderous feel around town, body lean is copious in fast cornering, and the hard ride is the least forgiving among full-size SUVs. Brakes feel strong, but hard stops dip the nose severely. Acceleration is lethargic in anything less than near-full-throttle application. A Limited averaged 17.1 mpg in our tests, not bad for a big SUV; Mitsubishi recommends premium fuel. The large tires hum loudly on most surfaces, and wind noise is intrusive above 60 mph. First- and second-row seating is roomy and comfortable. The third-row bench suits pre-teens. Doors open wide, but step-in is quite high and access to the third seat is for the young and limber. We like the stowable third seat, but not the side-hinged cargo door or that the climate system's status is displayed only as it's being adjusted. Montero's styling sets it apart, and it is spacious, but a harsh ride and mediocre acceleration and handling make alternatives such as the Chevrolet Tahoe more attractive values.

ENGINES

	ohc V6
Size, liters/cu. in.	3.5/213
Horsepower @ rpm	200 @ 5000
Torque (lb-ft) @ rpm	235 @ 3500
Availability	S

EPA city/highway mpg

4-speed OD automatic	14/17
5-speed OD automatic	13/18

PRICES

Mitsubishi Montero	Retail Price	Dealer Invoice
XLS 4-door wagon	$31297	$28495

Specifications begin on page 535.

MITSUBISHI

	Retail Price	Dealer Invoice
Limited 4-door wagon	$35297	$32135
Destination charge	520	520

STANDARD EQUIPMENT:

XLS: 3.5-liter V6 engine, 4-speed automatic transmission, part-time 4-wheel drive, 2-speed transfer case, dual front airbags, front side-impact airbags, antilock 4-wheel disc brakes, air conditioning, variable-assist power steering, tilt steering wheel, cruise control, cloth upholstery, front bucket seats, height adjustable driver seat, center console, cupholders, split folding second row seat, folding third row seat, power mirrors, power windows, power door locks, remote keyless entry, AM/FM/CD player, digital clock, variable intermittent wipers, rear defogger, intermittent rear wiper/washer, auxiliary power outlets, visor mirrors, map lights, cargo cover, automatic-off headlights, remote fuel door release, floormats, theft-deterrent system, roof rack, rear privacy glass, tow hooks, skid plates, full-size spare tire, 265/70R16 tires, alloy wheels.

Limited adds: 5-speed automatic transmission w/manual-shift capability, permanent 4-wheel drive, limited-slip differential, power sunroof, leather upholstery, heated front seats, 10-way power driver seat, wood/leather-wrapped steering wheel, heated power mirrors, Infinity sound system, power antenna, compass, outside temperature display, trip computer, fog lights.

OPTIONAL EQUIPMENT:
Major Packages

P1 Preferred Equipment Group, XLS	1150	1001
Limited-slip differential, power sunroof.		
P2 Preferred Equipment Group, Limited	900	783
Automatic climate controls, rear air conditioning w/rear controls.		

MITSUBISHI MONTERO SPORT

Mitsubishi Montero Sport Limited

Rear- or 4-wheel-drive midsize sport-utility vehicle

Prices are accurate at time of publication; subject to manufacturer's change.

MITSUBISHI

Base price range: $22,747-$32,777. Built in Japan. **Also consider:** Ford Explorer, Nissan Xterra, Toyota 4Runner

FOR • Cargo room • Instruments/controls • Build quality **AGAINST** • Ride/handling • Fuel economy • Rear-seat entry/exit • Engine noise

A new sport-trimmed model and additional safety features highlight Mitsubishi's volume-selling sport-utility wagons for 2001. Montero Sport comes in ES, LS, XLS models, new 3.5XS trim, and top-line Limited form. All are available with rear-wheel drive or with 4-wheel drive; the ES was previously not sold with 4WD. The 4WD system has low range gearing but is not for use on dry pavement.

ES, LS, and XLS have a 3.0-liter V6. Limiteds and the new 3.5XS use a 3.5-liter V6 borrowed from the full-size Montero. The 3.5XS is distinguished by matte-black fender flares, side steps, and roof rails, plus projector-beam headlamps and special wheels. All models come with automatic transmission. Antilock 4-wheel disc brakes are standard on Limiteds and all 4WD models.

In other changes, all Montero Sports get rear child-seat anchors, driver's seatbelt pretensioner, front seatbelt load-force limiters, and structural strengthening designed to reduce the forces reaching occupants in an offset crash. LS models add standard keyless entry, and the power windows on XLS and Limited can now be operated briefly after ignition shutoff. Finally, like some other '01 Mitsubishis, Montero Sports now qualify as Low Emissions Vehicles in all 50 states.

PERFORMANCE Montero Sport's rear suspension switched from leaf springs to a more sophisticated coil-spring arrangement last year. Our test drives show it makes for much smoother going, reducing tail jiggle on washboard surfaces and improving body control over large humps and dips. Springs and shock absorbers remain truck-tight, however, so don't expect a carlike ride. Same goes for handling, which is OK for a high-built SUV but doesn't inspire confidence on fast twisty roads, thanks to fairly vague steering and a somewhat tippy cornering feel. Crosswind stability at highway speeds isn't great on most SUVs, and it isn't here. There's also marked wind rush above about 60 mph. Road noise, by contrast, is fairly low.

Acceleration is nothing special. The 3.0-liter models feel lazy from standstill but cruise comfortably and have decent passing punch. The 3.5-liter engine delivers fine acceleration at all speeds, though it's scarcely quieter than the smaller V6, suffering marked fan noise when worked hard. Fuel economy is typical for midsize SUVs: 14-17 mpg for 3.0-liter test models, 16.8 with a 2WD Limited.

ACCOMMODATIONS The high floor and low roof that give Montero Sport a somewhat distinctive look pay no dividends in room or comfort. Ingress and egress are relatively tough, thanks to a fairly lofty step-in and, in back, narrow lower door openings. Tubular side steps are stan-

Specifications begin on page 535.

MITSUBISHI

dard on LS, XLS, Limited and then new 3.5XS, but are more decorative than useful. Aft head clearance is only adequate for 6-footers, and the rear bench is short in the backrest and too narrow for uncrowded three-adult travel. However, rear legroom is generous even behind a tall front-seater. The cargo deck is rather high, but the available space is useful and rear-seat folding straightforward.

Drivers enjoy a carlike dash, but the front seats are low to the floor, forcing a legs-out position. Visibility suffers some from thickish rear roof pillars. All models have a tilt steering wheel, but it doesn't raise high enough to give some taller drivers an unobstructed view of the gauges. Montero Sport has a reassuring trucklike solidity, backed up by fine detail finish and attractive interior materials.

VALUE It's a bit noisy, stiff-riding, and, in 3.0-liter form, slightly underpowered, but Montero Sport is priced right and should carry deeper discounts than more popular rivals like Dodge Durango and Toyota 4Runner. The new 3.5XS adds spice to the 2001 menu, but costs almost as much as a Limited.

ENGINES

	ohc V6	ohc V6
Size, liters/cu. in.	3.0/181	3.5/213
Horsepower @ rpm	165 @ 5250	197 @ 5000
Torque (lb-ft) @ rpm	186 @ 4000	223 @ 3500
Availability	S[1]	S[2]
EPA city/highway mpg		
4-speed OD automatic	19/22[3]	17/20[4]

1. ES, LS, XLS. 2. Limited. 3. 18/21 w/4WD. 4. 16/20 w/4WD.

PRICES

Mitsubishi Montero Sport	Retail Price	Dealer Invoice
ES 2WD 4-door wagon	$22747	$20699
ES 4WD 4-door wagon	24947	22700
LS 2WD 4-door wagon	25627	23317
LS 4WD 4-door wagon	27657	25167
3.5XS 2WD 4-door wagon	26637	24236
3.5XS 2WD 4-door wagon	28667	26077
XLS 2WD 4-door wagon	27397	24926
XLS 4WD 4-door wagon	29307	26668
Limited 2WD 4-door wagon	31317	28500
Limited 4WD 4-door wagon	32777	29821
Destination charge	520	520

STANDARD EQUIPMENT:

ES: 3.0-liter V6 engine, 4-speed automatic transmission, dual front airbags, air conditioning, power steering, tilt steering wheel, cloth upholstery, front

Prices are accurate at time of publication; subject to manufacturer's change.

MITSUBISHI • NISSAN

bucket seats w/driver-side lumbar adjustment, center console, cupholders, folding rear seat, overhead console, power mirrors, power windows, power door locks, AM/FM/CD player, digital clock, tachometer, auxiliary power outlets, intermittent wipers, rear defogger, rear wiper/washer, map lights, visor mirrors, floormats, theft-deterrent system, front and rear tow hooks, skid plates, full-size spare, 235/75R15 tires. **4WD** adds: part-time 4-wheel drive, 2-speed transfer case, antilock 4-wheel disc brakes.

LS adds: cruise control, remote keyless entry, split folding rear seat, variable-intermittent wipers, side steps, roof rails, rear privacy glass, 255/70R16 tires, alloy wheels. **4WD** adds: part-time 4-wheel drive, 2-speed transfer case, antilock 4-wheel disc brakes.

3.5XS adds: 3.5-liter V6 engine, fog lights. **4WD** adds: part-time 4-wheel drive, 2-speed transfer case, antilock 4-wheel disc brakes.

XLS adds to LS: leather-wrapped steering wheel, automatic day/night rearview mirror, compass, outside temperature indicator, cargo cover. **4WD** adds: part-time 4-wheel drive, 2-speed transfer case, antilock 4-wheel disc brakes.

Limited adds: 3.5-liter V6 engine, limited-slip differential, antilock 4-wheel disc brakes, leather upholstery, heated front seats, heated power mirrors, Infinity sound system, power antenna, power sunroof, illuminated visor mirrors, fog lights. **4WD** adds: part-time 4-wheel drive, 2-speed transfer case.

OPTIONAL EQUIPMENT:
Major Packages

	Retail Price	Dealer Invoice
P1 Preferred Equipment Pkg., XLS	$1660	$1440
Limited-slip rear differential, power sunroof, Infinity sound system, power antenna.		
P2 Preferred Equipment Pkg., XLS	2660	2310
P1 Preferred Pkg. plus leather upholstery.		

NISSAN ALTIMA

Nissan Altima GLE

Front-wheel-drive compact car
Base price range: $15,140-$20,390. Built in USA. **Also con-**

NISSAN

sider: Mazda 626, Mitsubishi Galant, Volkswagen Passat

FOR • Steering/handling • Instruments/controls **AGAINST** • Rear-seat comfort • Automatic transmission performance

Only minor trim and equipment changes mark Nissan's best-selling car line for the third year of its current design. Altima continues in base XE, volume GXE, sporty SE, and luxury GLE sedans, all with a 2.4-liter 4-cylinder engine. Automatic transmission is standard for GLE and optional elsewhere in place of 5-speed manual. Antilock brakes are optional except for the base model, and front side airbags are standard on GLE and optional for GXE and SE.

Last year's Altimas got revised steering, suspension, and styling. Changes this year are minor. Included are an in-the-trunk emergency release for all models and an in-dash CD changer as standard for SE and optional for GLE. A new GXE Limited Edition package includes an 8-way power driver's seat, remote entry/alarm and all items in the GXE's Value Option Package. The Limited Edition option replaces last year's GXE Appearance and Convenience Package. Leather upholstery remains standard for GLE, available for SE.

PERFORMANCE Altima's recent engineering work made the engine smoother and free of its previous high-rpm boom. It also improved handling. Body lean is reduced to moderate, so there's a little extra cornering grip, especially with the 16-inch tires included on SE and GLE. Despite this, ride hasn't suffered. Even the sport-tuned SE soaks up rough stuff without thumpiness or drumming while providing reasonable absorbency. Steering, however, remains a bit numb on-center and requires more correcting than we like in straight-line highway cruising. Wind noise is tolerably low, but Altima still isn't quite as refined as a Honda Civic.

We've not yet been able to clock the latest Altimas, but 0-60 mph should take about 9 seconds with automatic based on our '99-model test results—adequate but no more. The automatic transmission itself performed admirably in one test SE, but in other Altimas we've driven it was hesitant to downshift at midrange speeds and sometimes slurred upshifts. A 5-speed GXE we tested averaged 20.4 mpg, also no great shakes for this class. Simulated panic stops are undramatic but not exceptionally short.

ACCOMMODATIONS Altima has good front-seat room even for 6-footers, who also have sufficient rear knee clearance but little toe space beneath the seat. The reach bench seat is short, and too soft and ill-shaped to offer much support. Narrow lower rear door openings make for entry/exit slightly confined, but that's true of most like-sized rivals.

The dashboard is convenient apart from low-mounted audio controls, and complements a well judged driving position enhanced by support-

NISSAN

ive, nicely bolstered bucket seats. All but base Altimas have a standard front/rear cushion tilt, which also helps driver comfort, though the dual handwheel adjusters are awkwardly placed and not that easy to operate. Visibility suffers a bit from high-tail styling and wide roof posts. Trunk space is good, though a broad sill can make for back-straining reaches and the sickle-shaped lid hinges intrude into the load area. Altimas we tested had a solid on-road feel and good all-around fit-and-finish.

VALUE Altima is a competent, competitively priced family compact offering enough model and equipment variations to satisfy most any budget. It's not top of the class in any one respect, but it earns our Best Buy label as a good all-rounder with no serious drawbacks.

ENGINES

	dohc I4
Size, liters/cu. in.	2.4/146
Horsepower @ rpm	155 @ 5600
Torque (lb-ft) @ rpm	156 @ 4400
Availability	S

EPA city/highway mpg

5-speed OD manual	23/31
4-speed OD automatic	21/28

PRICES

Nissan Altima	Retail Price	Dealer Invoice
XE 4-door sedan, 5-speed	$15140	$14547
XE 4-door sedan, automatic	15940	15315
GXE 4-door sedan, 5-speed	16340	15016
GXE 4-door sedan, automatic	17140	15751
SE 4-door sedan, 5-speed	18640	16935
SE 4-door sedan, automatic	19440	17662
GLE 4-door sedan, automatic	20390	18525
Destination charge	520	520

STANDARD EQUIPMENT:

XE: 2.4-liter 4-cylinder engine, 5-speed manual or 4-speed automatic transmission, dual front airbags, emergency inside trunk release, power steering, tilt steering wheel, cloth upholstery, front bucket seats, center console, cupholders, power mirrors, power windows, tachometer, intermittent wipers, rear defogger, passenger-side visor mirror, remote fuel door and decklid release, theft-deterrent system, 195/65R15 tires, wheel covers.

GXE adds: split folding rear seat, 205/60R15 tires.

SE adds: 4-wheel disc brakes, air conditioning, leather-wrapped steering wheel, cruise control, power door locks, remote keyless entry, AM/FM radio w/in-dash 6-disc CD changer, digital clock, power antenna, variable intermit-

Specifications begin on page 535.

NISSAN

tent wipers, illuminated visor mirrors, overhead console, map lights, universal garage door opener, auxiliary power outlet (automatic), sport-tuned suspension, fog lights, rear spoiler, 205/55R16 tires, alloy wheels.

GLE adds to SE: 4-speed automatic transmission, front side-impact airbags, leather upholstery, 8-way power driver seat, AM/FM/cassette/CD player, luxury suspension, 205/55TR16 tires, Deletes: 4-wheel disc brakes, rear spoiler.

OPTIONAL EQUIPMENT:

	Retail Price	Dealer Invoice

Major Packages

	Retail Price	Dealer Invoice
XE Option Pkg., XE	$1999	$1734

AM/FM/CD player with digital clock, air conditioning, cruise control.

Value Option Pkg., GXE	999	918

Air conditioning, AM/FM/CD player, power door locks, illuminated entry, illuminated visor mirrors, rear cupholders (automatic), variable intermittent wipers, auxiliary power outlet (automatic), battery saver system, glove box and map lights.

Limited Edition Pkg., GXE	1375	1263

Value Option Pkg. plus 8-way power driver seat, remote keyless entry, floormats.

Safety Features

	Retail Price	Dealer Invoice
Antilock brakes, GXE, SE, GLE	499	454

GXE, SE require front side-impact airbags. SE, GLE require power sunroof. GXE requires Limited Edition Pkg.

Front side-impact airbags, GXE, SE	249	227

GXE requires Limited Edition Pkg. SE requires Power sunroof.

Comfort and Convenience

	Retail Price	Dealer Invoice
Leather upholstery, SE	1299	1126

Includes 8-way power driver seat. Requires power sunroof.

8-way power driver seat, SE	399	346

Requires power sunroof, mud guards.

Power sunroof, GXE, SE, GLE	849	737

GXE requires Limited Edition Pkg.

Remote keyless entry, GXE	199	172

Requires Value Option Pkg.

AM/FM/cassette/CD player, GXE	399	346

Requires Limited Edition Pkg.

In-dash 6-disc CD changer, GLE	399	346

Appearance and Miscellaneous

	Retail Price	Dealer Invoice
Rear spoiler, GXE, GLE	339	293
Mud guards, GXE, SE, GLE	79	69

SE, GLE require power sunroof.

Post production options also available.

Prices are accurate at time of publication; subject to manufacturer's change.

NISSAN

NISSAN MAXIMA

Nissan Maxima SE

Front-wheel-drive midsize car; similar to Infiniti I30

Base price range: $21,249-$27,649. Built in Japan. **Also consider:** Honda Accord, Pontiac Grand Prix, Toyota Camry

FOR • Acceleration • Steering/handling • Ride **AGAINST** • Manual shift action

A special SE 20th Anniversary model is the big addition to Nissan's 2001 flagship sedans. Maxima comes in GXE, sporty SE, and luxury GLE versions with a 222-horsepower 3.0-liter V6. The new 20th Anniversary Edition gets the 227-hp version of this engine also used in the related I30 from Nissan's upscale Infiniti Division. The GLE comes with automatic transmission that is optional for other models in place of 5-speed manual. All Maximas have antilock 4-wheel disc brakes. Traction control is available except on GXE. Front side airbags are included in a new Meridian Edition option package; heated seats come with them, but GXE and SE require ordering a separate Comfort & Convenience package.

Sixteen-inch alloy wheels are standard on SE and GLE and optional in place of 15s for GXE. Leather upholstery is standard on GLE, optional for SE. SEs have a standard rear spoiler and firmer suspension.

The 20th Anniversary is basically the regular SE equipped with the Leather Trim and Comfort & Convenience options—the latter including 17-inch wheels. It adds the higher-power engine, limited-slip differential, bronze-finish headlamp lenses, lower-body "aero" kit, and aluminum trim on the shift knob, pedals, and door sills. Finally, steering-wheel audio controls are a new SE/GLE standard and a GXE option.

PERFORMANCE This is a swift, polished performer. Maxima corners with grippy assurance and only mild body lean. The SE is a tad crisper in turns thanks to its sport suspension, but all models are agile and have quick, informative steering. However, the SE suffers some ride choppiness over bumps that other models comfortably absorb. Credit Nissan

Specifications begin on page 535.

NISSAN

for giving all models standard antilock 4-wheel disc brakes, which scrub off speed quickly and consistently with excellent control.

Our test GXE with automatic transmission did 0-60 mph in a satisfying 7.9 seconds. Manual-transmission models feel even faster, and all Maximas enjoy a responsive powertrain. This V6 feels downright muscular, with fine punch off the line and enticingly strong passing power. Our test models averaged 20-22.5 mpg, good for this level of performance, though Nissan recommends premium fuel.

Most Maximas are sold with automatic transmission, and Nissan's latest version of this transmission is free of the annoying lurch in full-throttle downshifts we criticized before. The manual, however, still suffers imprecise clutch takeup and slightly stiff shift action. Another dynamic quibble is annoying steering-wheel tug in hard takeoffs unless the front wheels are perfectly straight. This torque-steer effect isn't entirely cancelled even with the available traction control—which should be at least optional for the base GXE.

ACCOMMODATIONS Like most cars its size, Maxima is a roomy 4-seater for grownups. Taller adults have enough head clearance beneath the optional moonroof to avoid crunched coiffs, and a fairly upright rear seatback pays comfort dividends on long trips. Rear leg space is ample for most folks, but 6-footers will be knees-up behind a similarly tall front occupant.

Gauges and switchgear are simple and generally attractive, though lookalike knobs for audio volume and temperature can be confusing, and some of our test drivers find it too long a stretch to the main radio and climate controls. On the other hand, there's more rearward seat travel than even the lankiest drivers should need. Visibility is fine except directly astern. A 60/40 folding rear seatback improves on the narrow pass-through of old, and a wide, low opening allows no-sweat trunk access. Our test models were generally solid and well-finished, though we noted minor body shudder over rough disturbances, plus a couple of annoying rattles inside.

VALUE Maxima is a natural rival for top-line V6 Toyota Camrys and Honda Accords, and it answers those tough opponents with an appealing blend of performance, handling, ride comfort, and near-luxury-league refinement and amenities. Add in competitive prices and you have a strong Recommended choice that deserves serious consideration.

ENGINES

	dohc V6
Size, liters/cu. in.	3.0/183
Horsepower @ rpm	222 @ 6400
Torque (lb-ft) @ rpm	217 @ 4000
Availability	S[1]

Prices are accurate at time of publication; subject to manufacturer's change.

NISSAN

EPA city/highway mpg
5-speed OD manual 22/27
4-speed OD automatic 19/26

1. 227 hp on 20th Anniversary Edition.

PRICES

Nissan Maxima	Retail Price	Dealer Invoice
GXE 4-door sedan, 5-speed	$21249	$19430
GXE 4-door sedan, automatic	22949	20745
SE 4-door sedan, 5-speed	23849	21433
SE 4-door sedan, automatic	24349	21882
SE 20th Anniversary Edition 4-door sedan, 5-speed	27149	24342
SE 20th Anniversary Edition 4-door sedan, automatic	27649	24791
GLE 4-door sedan, automatic	26449	23769
Destination charge	520	520

STANDARD EQUIPMENT:

GXE: 3.0-liter dohc V6 222-horsepower engine, 5-speed manual or 4-speed automatic transmission, dual front airbags, antilock 4-wheel disc brakes, emergency inside trunk release, air conditioning, variable-assist power steering, tilt steering wheel, cruise control, cloth upholstery, front bucket seats, front console, cupholders, split folding rear seat, power mirrors, power windows, power door locks, remote keyless entry, AM/FM/cassette, digital clock, tachometer, auxiliary power outlets, illuminated visor mirrors, variable intermittent wipers, rear defogger, automatic headlights, remote decklid and fuel door releases, map lights, theft-deterrent system, 205/65R15 tires, wheel covers.

SE adds: AM/FM/cassette/CD player, leather-wrapped steering wheel w/radio controls, fog lights, rear spoiler, sport-tuned suspension, 215/55R16 tires, alloy wheels.

SE 20th Anniversary Edition: adds: 3.0-liter dohc V6 227-horsepower engine, limited-slip differential, 8-way power driver seat, power sunroof, automatic day/night rearview mirror, universal garage door opener, floormats, aerodynamic body cladding, badging, 225/50VR17 tires.

GLE adds to GXE: 4-speed automatic transmission, automatic climate control, outside temperature display, leather upholstery, 8-way power driver seat, 4-way power passenger seat, leather-wrapped steering wheel w/radio controls, Bose AM/FM/cassette/CD player, universal garage door opener, power decklid release, fog lights, 215/55R16 tires, alloy wheels.

OPTIONAL EQUIPMENT:

Major Packages

Meridian Edition, GXE automatic, SE, SE 20th Anniv., GLE   539   467
Front side-impact airbags, heated front seats and mirrors, low windshield washer fluid warning light. GXE, SE require Comfort and Convenience Pkg.

NISSAN

	Retail Price	Dealer Invoice
GXE Comfort and Convenience Pkg., GXE automatic.....	$1069	$950

AM/FM/cassette/CD player upgraded sound system, steering wheel radio controls, 8-way power driver seat, automatic day/night rearview mirror, universal garage door opener, height-adjustable armrest, cargo net, 215/55R16 tires, alloy wheels.

SE Comfort and Convenience Pkg., SE............................	1799	1598

Power sunroof, 8-way power driver seat, universal garage door opener, automatic day/night rearview mirror, cargo net, 225/50VR17 tires.

Leather Trim Pkg., SE, SE 20th Anniv.	1349	1171

Leather upholstery, 4-way power passenger seat, automatic climate control, outside temperature display.

Powertrains
Traction control, SE/SE 20th Anniv. automatic, GLE	299	259

Comfort and Convenience
Bose sound system, SE, SE 20th Anniv.	899	798

SE requires Comfort and Convenience Pkg.

6-disc CD changer...	459	338

GXE requires Comfort and Convenience Pkg. NA GXE 5-speed.

Power sunroof, GXE automatic, GLE	899	779

GXE requires Comfort and Convenience Pkg.

Appearance and Miscellaneous
Rear spoiler, GXE, GLE	479	360

Post production options also available.

NISSAN PATHFINDER

Nissan Pathfinder SE

Rear- or 4-wheel-drive midsize sport-utility vehicle; similar to Infiniti QX4

Base price range: $27,349-$31,799. Built in Japan. **Also consider:** Ford Explorer, Lexus RX 300, Toyota 4Runner

Prices are accurate at time of publication; subject to manufacturer's change.

NISSAN

FOR • Acceleration • Cargo room • Build quality **AGAINST** • Rear-seat room • Rear-seat entry/exit

Nissan's premium sport-utility wagon adopts several options once reserved for its upscale Infiniti sister, the QX4. Pathfinder began 2001 last spring in base XE, sporty SE, and top-line LE versions with added standard features and a new twincam 3.5-liter V6 replacing a single-cam 3.3. Horsepower is 240 with automatic transmission and 250 with manual versus the previous 170; respective torque is 265/240 pound-feet versus 200. Towing capacity is unchanged at 5000 pounds. Only the SE is available with manual shift. All models offer rear drive or part-time 4WD; the latter has low-range gearing and is for slick surfaces only. Newly optional for LE is the QX4's on-demand "All-Mode" 4WD, which is useable on dry pavement via settings for 2WD, Auto 4WD, and locked-in 4WD High and Low. Antilock brakes are standard across the board. Front side airbags are available in the Leather option package for SE and LE.

The 2001 Pathfinders also get a restyled dashboard and console, standard cruise control and power windows/locks/mirrors for all models, and newly available steering-wheel audio controls and memory power seats. Now, SEs and LEs with in-dash CD changer offer the QX4's optional satellite-linked navigation system with dashboard touch-screen and audible route instructions. Also newly optional for LEs and automatic-equipped SEs with available Bose audio is a rear-seat entertainment system with video player, flip-down LCD screen, separate audio controls, and game port.

Base prices change little for 2001, with only XEs seeing an increase. The QX4 also gets the bigger V6 and a revised dashboard this year, but has side airbags and the All-Mode 4WD as standard.

PERFORMANCE Once performance also-rans among midsize SUVs, Pathfinder and QX4 are now more than competitive, with good power throughout the speed range. Nissan claims 0-60 mph at 8.8 seconds, 2.1 seconds quicker than the 2000s. Tapping full power, though, requires a determined throttle foot, and the automatic transmission in our SE 4x4 was slow to downshift for passing. In our tests, the '01 QX4 and Pathfinder averaged 15.6-16.5 mpg, about par for this class, but the new V6 needs premium gas; the old one used regular.

Offering the QX4's more sophisticated 4WD is welcome on Pathfinder LEs, but the regular 4WD is dated against those offered by most every one of Pathfinder's rivals, lacking dry-pavement capability and pushbutton transfer-case control. Despite a larger turning radius than most rivals, handling is a Pathfinder/QX4 plus. Their taut suspension aids control and keeps body lean in turns moderate. The steering feels properly weighted in turns but suffers vague on-center feel at highway speeds. Both the Nissan and Infiniti ride firmly, though the QX4 is

Specifications begin on page 535.

NISSAN

acceptably comfortable over bumps and ridges that feel jarring in the Pathfinder. Wind and road noise are well muffled in any model. The V6 signals its newfound muscle with a throaty roar in hard acceleration, but cruises quietly. Braking feels strong enough, with minimal nosedive in hard stops.

ACCOMMODATIONS Head room is good all around, but rear leg space is barely adequate for adults with the front seats pushed more than halfway back. The rear seat itself is low to the floor and deficient in back support. Step-in height is relatively high, and narrow rear-door openings further complicate entry/exit.

Pathfinder and QX4 share a basic redesigned dashboard that's functionally sound. The new navigation system is nicely integrated and works well once you master its programming. Thick rear roof pillars impede the driver's over-the shoulder vision. Cargo volume is good, and the new separate-opening tailgate window is handy, but folding the rear seat is more complicated than usual. All these SUVs feel solidly built, and the QX4 is distinguished by top-notch interior materials and standard front side airbags. On Pathfinder, front side airbags are available only in tandem with optional leather upholstery, which isn't offered on either the XE or on the SE with manual transmission.

VALUE Acceleration is improved, and QX4 benefits from Infiniti's high customer satisfaction ratings, but antiquated 4WD weighs against the Pathfinder unless you splurge for a top-line LE with the extra-cost QX4 system, in which case you might as well get the Infiniti. Regardless of model or equipment, these SUVs still don't have everything it takes to be compelling values.

ENGINES

	dohc V6
Size, liters/cu. in.	3.5/214
Horsepower @ rpm	240 @ 6000
Torque (lb-ft) @ rpm	265 @ 3200
Availability	S[1]
EPA city/highway mpg	
5-speed OD manual	17/19[2]
4-speed OD automatic	16/19[3]

1. 250 hp, 240 ft-lb w/manual transmission. 2. 16/19 w/4WD. 3. 15/19 w/4WD.

PRICES

Nissan Pathfinder	Retail Price	Dealer Invoice
XE 2WD 4-door wagon, automatic	$27649	$25138
XE 4WD 4-door wagon, automatic	29649	26956
SE 2WD 4-door wagon, 5-speed	27349	24865
SE 2WD 4-door wagon, automatic	28349	25774
SE 4WD 4-door wagon, 5-speed	29349	26683
SE 4WD 4-door wagon, automatic	30349	27592

Prices are accurate at time of publication; subject to manufacturer's change.

NISSAN

	Retail Price	Dealer Invoice
LE 2WD 4-door wagon, automatic	$29299	$26637
LE 4WD 4-door wagon, automatic	31799	28910
Destination charge	520	520

STANDARD EQUIPMENT:

XE: 3.5-liter dohc V6 engine, 4-speed automatic transmission, dual front airbags, antilock brakes, air conditioning, power steering, tilt leather-wrapped steering wheel, cruise control, cloth upholstery, front bucket seats, center console, cupholders, split folding rear seat, heated power mirrors, power windows, power door locks, remote keyless entry, AM/FM/cassette/CD player, digital clock, tachometer, variable intermittent wipers, passenger-side visor mirror, rear defogger, rear intermittent wiper/washer, auxiliary power outlets, map lights, automatic headlights, cargo cover, roof rack, theft-deterrent system, rear privacy glass, roof rails, tow hooks, skid plate, full-size spare tire, 245/70R16 tires, alloy wheels. **4WD** models add: part-time 4-wheel drive, 2-speed transfer case.

SE adds: 5-speed manual or 4-speed automatic transmission, limited-slip differential (5-speed), height-adjustable front bucket seats w/adjustable lumbar support, Bose AM/FM/cassette/CD player w/in-dash 6-disc CD changer, steering-wheel radio controls, fog lights, roof rack, tubular step rails, 255/65R16 tires. **4WD** models add: part-time 4-wheel drive, 2-speed transfer case.

LE adds: 4-speed automatic transmission, automatic climate control, power sunroof, universal garage door opener, outside temperature indicator, compass, illuminated visor mirrors, running boards. **4WD** models add: full-time 4-wheel drive, 2-speed transfer case.

OPTIONAL EQUIPMENT:

Major Packages

Sunroof Pkg., SE	1099	953

Power sunroof, universal garage door opener, illuminated visor mirrors, compass, outside temperature indicator.

Leather Pkg., SE 2WD automatic, LE 2WD	1799	1560
SE 4WD automatic, LE 4WD	1999	1734

Leather upholstery, 8-way power driver seat w/memory, 4-way power passenger seat, heated front seats (4WD), front side-impact airbags. SE requires Sunroof Pkg.

Powertrains

Limited-slip differential, SE 4WD automatic, LE 4WD	249	216

Comfort and Convenience

Navigation system, SE automatic, LE	1999	1734
Mobile entertainment system, SE, LE	1299	1126

Specifications begin on page 535.

NISSAN

Special Purpose, Wheels and Tires	Retail Price	Dealer Invoice
Tow hitch	$389	$305

Post production options also available.

NISSAN QUEST

Nissan Quest GXE

Front-wheel-drive minivan; similar to Mercury Villager
Base price range: NA. Built in USA. **Also consider:** Dodge Caravan, Ford Windstar, Honda Odyssey, Toyota Sienna

FOR • Passenger and cargo room • Control layout **AGAINST**
• Interior materials

A styling update and revised equipment mark the final changes for Quest and the related Mercury Villager. Nissan and Ford agreed last summer to end their minivan joint venture, so both versions cease production in late 2001 after a short run of '02s. Nissan says it will have a new minivan for 2004.

Meanwhile, Quest again offers a single body size in GXE, SE, and top GLE trim with Nissan V6 power, automatic transmission, and dual rear sliding side doors. Antilock brakes are standard, but side airbags and power sliding doors remain unavailable. All models have a 3-person third-row bench seat that slides on floor tracks. SE and GLE have two second-row buckets, the GXE a removable 2-place second-row bench optionally available with child safety seats.

Like Villagers, 2001 Quests get a cosmetic touchup outside, plus a revised dashboard. The GLE gains an in-dash CD changer, rear cargo shelf, 16-inch wheels, and rear antiroll bar as standard, thus matching other models, while the SE gets a retuned sports suspension. Heated seats are now standard for SE and GLE, as is a new 130-watt "Super Sound" system. Models without the available sunroof now offer an optional rear-seat entertainment system with flip-down ceiling-mount screen, concealed VCR, and separate audio controls. A similar floor-console system, new last year, remains optional for sunroof-equipped

Prices are accurate at time of publication; subject to manufacturer's change.

NISSAN

SE and GLE models.

Quest and Villager are assembled by Ford in Ohio using a high percentage of Nissan parts. Quest's performance and accommodations mirror those of similarly equipped Villagers.

The Mercury Villager report includes an evaluation of the Quest.

ENGINES

	ohc V6
Size, liters/cu. in.	3.3/201
Horsepower @ rpm	170 @ 4800
Torque (lb-ft) @ rpm	200 @ 2800
Availability	S

EPA city/highway mpg

4-speed OD automatic	17/23

2001 prices unavailable at time of publication.

PRICES

2000 Nissan Quest	Retail Price	Dealer Invoice
GXE 4-door van	$22259	$20236
SE w/cloth 4-door van	24399	21927
SE w/leather 4-door van	26699	23994
GLE 4-door van	26399	23725
Destination charge	520	520

STANDARD EQUIPMENT:

GXE: 3.3-liter V6 engine, 4-speed automatic transmission, dual front airbags, antilock brakes, front air conditioning, variable-assist power steering, tilt steering wheel, cruise control, cloth upholstery, 7-passenger seating, front bucket seats, second-row 2-passenger bench seat, third-row sliding 3-passenger bench seat, front storage console, under passenger-seat storage, cupholders, two sliding rear doors, heated power mirrors, power front windows, power door locks, remote keyless entry, AM/FM/cassette, digital clock, tachometer, variable intermittent wipers, illuminated visor mirrors, rear defogger, intermittent rear wiper/washer, remote fuel door/hatch releases, floormats, theft-deterrent system, rear privacy glass, cornering lights, roof rack, 215/70R15 tires, wheel covers.

SE w/cloth adds: rear air conditioning, interior air filter, rear climate controls, AM/FM/cassette/CD player, leather-wrapped steering wheel w/radio controls, rear audio controls, conversation mirror, reading lights, second row captain chairs, auxiliary power outlet, automatic headlights, sport suspension, 225/60R16 tires, alloy wheels.

SE w/leather adds: leather upholstery, 6-way power driver seat w/manual lumbar support, 4-way power passenger seat, memory system for driver seat and mirrors, reclining second row captain chairs, power rear quarter windows, universal garage door opener, adjustable rear parcel shelf, flip-up rear hatch glass.

Specifications begin on page 535.

NISSAN

GLE adds: automatic climate control w/front and rear controls, 215/70R15 tires, deletes adjustable rear parcel shelf, flip-up rear glass hatch, sport suspension.

OPTIONAL EQUIPMENT:

	Retail Price	Dealer Invoice
Major Packages		
Comfort Plus Pkg., GXE	$899	$779
Leather-wrapped steering wheel w/radio controls, rear air conditioning controls, reading lights, conversation mirror, auxiliary power outlet, adjustable rear parcel shelf, heavy-duty battery, alloy wheels.		
Convenience Pkg., SE w/cloth	799	693
6-way power driver seat w/lumbar adjustment, power rear quarter windows, universal garage door opener, automatic headlights, adjustable rear parcel shelf, flip-up rear hatch glass.		
Popular Pkg., GLE	500	433
Adjustable rear parcel shelf, 6-disc CD changer, flip-up rear hatch glass, full-size spare tire, trailer wiring harness.		
Audio Upgrade Pkg., GXE	349	303
SE	359	311
AM/FM/cassette/CD player. Requires Comfort Plus Pkg.		
Towing Pkg., GXE, SE	169	—
Full-size spare tire, trailering harness.		
Safety Features		
Two integrated child seats, GXE	229	199
NA with Audio Upgrade Pkg.		
Comfort and Convenience		
Video Entertainment System	1099	—
Manufacturer's discount price	NC	NC
Videocassette player, LCD screen, jacks for headphones and games.		
Power sunroof, SE, GLE	899	779
SE requires Convenience Pkg.		
Appearance and Miscellaneous		
Fog lights, GXE	379	283
SE, GLE	389	287
Running boards w/bumper step pad	529	373
Tow hitch	419	305
GXE and SE requires Towing Pkg. GLE requires Popular Pkg.		

Post production options also available.

NISSAN SENTRA
Front-wheel-drive subcompact car

CG RECOMMENDED AUTO

Base price range: $11,649-$15,699. Built in Mexico.
Also consider: Ford Focus, Honda Civic, Toyota Echo

Prices are accurate at time of publication; subject to manufacturer's change.

NISSAN

Nissan Sentra GXE

FOR • Fuel economy **AGAINST** • Rear-seat entry/exit

An in-the-trunk emergency release is the one change of note for Nissan's 2001 subcompact sedans. XE and uplevel GXE Sentras use a 1.8-liter 4-cylinder engine, the sportier SE a 2.0-liter version. Both engines team with manual or optional automatic transmission. There's also a special California-only Sentra CA model that meets that state's Super Ultra Low Emission Vehicle requirements.

Antilock brakes and front side airbags are optional as a package for GXE and SE. The SE has standard 4-wheel disc brakes and is the only Sentra available with a sunroof. XE and GXE come with 14-inch tires on steel wheels; SEs get 15-inch alloy rims and offer 16-inchers in a Performance Package that also includes a firmer-yet suspension, upgraded audio system and interior trim, and security system. An in-dash CD changer is optional for SE and GXE only. XE loses its driver-seat height adjuster, but all Sentras gain an in-trunk emergency release designed to free anyone trapped inside.

PERFORMANCE Sentras don't exactly feel underpowered, but our test GXE with manual shift needed a none-too-lively 9.9 seconds to go 0-60 mph, and automatic transmission will add at least a second to that. With its larger engine, the SE is quicker, but not much unless you get manual transmission, which helps this small sedan feel quite spunky. Sentra's automatic transmission is responsive and smooth enough. But some 5-speed models we tested suffered imprecise shift action and overly sharp clutch engagement that made smooth driving tricky. With manual transmission, our test GXE averaged 24.9 mpg and an SE 28.5. Expect slightly less with automatic.

Sentra's base suspension delivers safe, predictable front-drive handling, but only modest cornering grip on the standard all-season tires. There's some bounding at higher speeds, and marked wheel patter on washboard freeways. The ride isn't really bad, but is decidedly less absorbent than rivals such as the Honda Civic, Volkswagen Jetta, and Toyota Echo. A firmer suspension gives the Sentra SE sportier handling with a slight additional loss of ride comfort. No model is really quiet, with

Specifications begin on page 535.

NISSAN

tire roar in particular higher than the class norm. Our test GXE lacked optional ABS but completed our simulated 60-mph panic stops with reasonably short distances, little nosedive, and easy pedal modulation, though the right-rear wheel was prone to sudden lockup. We think ABS is a worthwhile option that should be available on all models.

ACCOMMODATIONS Interior space isn't generous enough to make Sentra the "compact sedan" Nissan advertises. That's most noticeable in the rear, where 6-footers can sit upright but have little leg or foot space if a front seat is pushed all the way aft. Worse, the front seats don't go that far back, so tall drivers might also feel cramped. Still, most should be able to get comfortable via the standard tilt wheel and—except on the XE—a height-adjustable seat. Entry/exit is hindered by small rear door openings, particularly at foot level.

The dashboard and interior decor are typical of entry-level Japanese cars: a bit drab but nicely put together with sturdy-feeling materials. Gauges and controls are simple, handy, and familiar. The radio is top-dead center, but smallish buttons and markings make it harder to use than it should be. Interior storage is above average, but trunk room isn't, aggravated by a moderate-size aperture, space-robbing trunklid hinges, and scant height beneath the rear parcel shelf.

VALUE It's not a refined as a Honda Civic or as roomy as a Ford Focus, but Sentra is solid enough and priced right to merit a spot on your subcompact-car shopping list.

ENGINES

	dohc I4	dohc I4
Size, liters/cu. in.	1.8/110	2.0/122
Horsepower @ rpm	126 @ 6000	145 @ 6400
Torque (lb-ft) @ rpm	129 @ 2400	136 @ 4800
Availability	S[1]	S[2]
EPA city/highway mpg		
5-speed OD manual	27/35	24/31
4-speed OD automatic	26/33	24/30

1. XE and GXE. 2. SE.

PRICES

Nissan Sentra	Retail Price	Dealer Invoice
XE 4-door sedan, 5-speed	$11649	$10956
XE 4-door sedan, automatic	12399	11661
GXE 4-door sedan, 5-speed	13499	12343
GXE 4-door sedan, automatic	14299	13075
CA 4-door sedan, automatic	14799	14106
SE 4-door sedan, 5-speed	14899	13624
SE 4-door sedan, automatic	15699	14355
Destination charge	520	520

Prices are accurate at time of publication; subject to manufacturer's change.

NISSAN

CA only available in California.

STANDARD EQUIPMENT:

XE: 1.8-liter dohc 4-cylinder engine, 5-speed manual or 4-speed automatic transmission, dual front airbags, emergency inside trunk release, power steering, tilt steering wheel, cloth upholstery, front bucket seats, center console, cupholders, rear defogger, remote decklid and fuel-door releases, dual outside mirrors, 185/65R14 tires, wheel covers.

GXE adds: air conditioning, cruise control, height-adjustable driver seat, AM/FM/CD player, digital clock, tachometer, power mirrors, power windows, power door locks, variable intermittent wipers, visor mirrors.

CA adds: 4-speed automatic transmission, remote keyless entry, 195/60HR15 tires, alloy wheels.

SE adds to GXE: 2.0-liter dohc 4-cylinder engine, 4-wheel disc brakes, leather-wrapped steering wheel, remote keyless entry, split folding rear seat, fog lights, sport suspension, 195/60HR15 tires, alloy wheels.

OPTIONAL EQUIPMENT:

Major Packages

	Retail Price	Dealer Invoice
XE Option Pkg., XE	$1199	$1040

Air conditioning, AM/FM/cassette, digital clock.

GXE Convenience Pkg., GXE	150	131

Remote keyless entry, power decklid release, split folding rear seat, cargo net, rear auxiliary power outlet, valet key.

GXE Luxury Pkg., GXE	649	563

Illuminated visor mirrors, upgraded sound system, overhead storage console, map lights, theft-deterrent system, 195/60HR15 tires, alloy wheels. Requires GXE Convenience Pkg.

SE Performance Pkg., SE w/automatic	699	606
SE w/5-speed	899	779

Limited-slip differential (5-speed), upgraded sound system, illuminated visor mirrors, upgraded upholstery, overhead storage console, map lights, rear spoiler, theft-deterrent system, Stage II Sport Suspension, 195/55R16 tires.

Safety Features

Front side-impact airbags and antilock brakes, GXE, SE.	699	606

Comfort and Convenience

P04 upgraded sound system, SE	190	170
In-dash 6-disc CD changer, GXE, SE	399	346

GXE requires GXE Luxury Pkg. SE requires upgraded sound system or SE Performance Pkg.

Power sunroof, SE	599	519

Requires upgraded sound system.

Specifications begin on page 535.

NISSAN

Appearance and Miscellaneous

	Retail Price	Dealer Invoice
Theft-deterrent system, GXE, SE	$299	$259
GXE requires Convenience Pkg.		
Rear spoiler, XE, GXE, SE	339	259

NISSAN XTERRA

Nissan Xterra SE

Rear- or 4-wheel-drive midsize sport-utility vehicle
Base price range: $17,999-$26,099. Built in USA. **Also consider:** Dodge Durango, Ford Explorer, Toyota 4Runner

FOR • Cargo room **AGAINST** • Ride/handling • Acceleration (4-cyl.) • Rear-seat entry/exit • Wind noise

A sales success in debut 2000, Nissan's junior midsize SUV gets minor revisions to the instrument cluster among a handful of changes for 2001. Priced against compact SUVs like the Honda CR-V, Xterra is a midsize based on Nissan's Frontier pickup. It's designed to appeal to young buyers who favor function and rugged appearance over comfort and amenities.

The base XE model has a 4-cylinder engine, manual transmission, and 2-wheel drive. XE V6 and top-line SE models come with the Frontier's 3.3-liter V6 and offer manual or automatic transmission, 2WD or 4WD. Xterra's 4WD is not for use on dry pavement. All models come with antilock brakes, air conditioning, and engine/transmission skid plates. SEs add a manual sunroof and, for '01, standard 16-inch wheels and tires in place of 15s and a new sound system with in-dash 5-disc CD changer and steering-wheel audio controls.

PERFORMANCE Xterra aims to be back-pack functional and hip-hop cool, yet it's performance is rather stodgy. Acceleration is plodding with the 4-cylinder, only adequate with the V6. We clocked an automatic 2WD SE at 9.6 seconds 0-60 mph versus 9.3 for a test manual-shift 4WD CR-V. At least the automatic transmission works well, as do the brakes.

Prices are accurate at time of publication; subject to manufacturer's change.

NISSAN

Even with 2WD, Xterra's suspension is stiff enough to cause noticeable jiggle on bumpy pavement, though rough stuff won't pummel your kidneys. Cornering grip is decent for a high, narrowish SUV, but the steering is vague on-center, and Xterra is easily outmaneuvered by true compact SUVs. Fuel economy is assuredly midsize SUV: 14.6-17.2 mpg in the 2WD V6 models we've tested. That test 5-speed CR-V averaged 22.5 mpg.

While it doesn't match CR-V or Toyota's RAV4 with the convenience of all-surface 4WD, Xterra is designed to better them in off-road capability and includes a 4WD-low range that the Honda and Toyota do not. Indeed, Xterra made short work of difficult mountain trails in our tests. But it's no quieter than a compact SUV. The V6 drones under hard throttle, and a nagging wind whistle from the prominent available roof rack adds to intrusive highway noise levels.

ACCOMMODATIONS Xterra's nothing-you-don't-need approach is evident in utilitarian cabin furnishings. To keep prices down, for example, Nissan omits a folding mechanism for the rear seat cushions. They simply lift out so the rear seatbacks can flop forward. Likewise, most interior trim panels are visibly thin, as is the door glass, though seat fabrics seem durable.

Drivers will like the generally well arranged dashboard, but lanky ones might wish for more rearward seat travel, and the "umbrella handle" parking brake is an old-fashioned chore. Lowish front seats mean good front head room for tall occupants, but also a slightly legs-out posture that's tough on long-distance comfort. Head room is terrific in back, where the kicked-up roofline allows the bench seat to stand higher than the front buckets, giving riders a better view ahead. Alas, three grownups won't fit in back without crowding, and rear leg room is minimal without the front seats pushed up some. The rear bench is both hard and short on leg support, too. Step-in is high, and narrow rear door bottoms hamper entry/exit. Cargo space is better than in a CR-V or RAV4 with the rear seat up, and ample with it fully stowed.

VALUE It's less pleasant than a CR-V or Ford Escape in everyday driving, but Xterra offers truck toughness and off-road ability those car-based rivals lack, plus, unlike the Honda, a V6 engine. Better still, the midsize V6 Xterra is priced lower than some 4WD versions of less-roomy 4-cylinder compact SUVs.

ENGINES

	ohc I4	ohc V6
Size, liters/cu. in.	2.4/146	3.3/200
Horsepower @ rpm	143 @ 5200	170 @ 4800
Torque (lb-ft) @ rpm	154 @ 4000	200 @ 2800
Availability	S[1]	S[2]
EPA city/highway mpg		
5-speed OD manual	19/24	16/18

Specifications begin on page 535.

NISSAN

	ohc I4	ohc V6
4-speed OD automatic		15/19

1. XE. 2. XE V6, SE.

PRICES

Nissan Xterra

	Retail Price	Dealer Invoice
2WD XE 4-door wagon, 5-speed	$17999	$16740
2WD XE V6 4-door wagon, 5-speed	19049	17717
2WD XE V6 4-door wagon, automatic	20049	18647
4WD XE V6 4-door wagon, 5-speed	21049	19577
4WD XE V6 4-door wagon, automatic	22049	20507
2WD SE 4-door wagon, 5-speed	23099	21242
2WD SE 4-door wagon, automatic	24099	22161
4WD SE 4-wagon, 5-speed	25099	23081
4WD SE 4-wagon, automatic	26099	24001
Destination charge	520	520

STANDARD EQUIPMENT:

XE: 2.4-liter dohc 4-cylinder engine, 5-speed manual transmission, dual front airbags, antilock brakes, air conditioning, power steering, cloth upholstery, front bucket seats, center console, cupholders, split folding rear seat, AM/FM/CD player, digital clock, tachometer, rear defogger, roof rack, dual outside mirrors, rear privacy glass, skid plates, full-size spare tire, 235/70R15 tires.

XE V6 adds: 3.3-liter V6 engine, 5-speed manual or 4-speed automatic transmission. **4WD** models add: part-time 4-wheel drive, 2-speed transfer case.

SE adds: limited-slip differential, power mirrors, power windows, power door locks, remote keyless entry, manual sunroof, tilt leather-wrapped steering wheel w/radio controls, cruise control, AM/FM radio w/in-dash 6-disc CD changer, auxiliary power outlets, passenger-side visor mirror, variable intermittent wipers, map lights, cargo cover, rear wiper, theft-deterrent system, tubular step rails, first aid kit, fog lights, front tow hooks, 255/70R16 tires, alloy wheels. **4WD** models add: part-time 4-wheel drive, 2-speed transfer case.

OPTIONAL EQUIPMENT:

Major Packages

Utility Pkg., XE	599	519
XE V6	699	606

Tilt steering wheel, variable intermittent wipers, cargo cover, rear wiper, ceiling tie clips, first aid kit, auxiliary power outlets, tubular step rails, fender lip moldings (XE V6), 265/70R15 tires (XE V6).

Power Pkg., XE V6	1299	1126

Power mirrors, power windows, power door locks, remote keyless entry, cruise control, map lights, cloth door inserts, theft-deterrent system. Requires Utility Pkg.

Prices are accurate at time of publication; subject to manufacturer's change.

NISSAN • OLDSMOBILE

	Retail Price	Dealer Invoice
Sport Pkg., XE V6	$849	$737

AM/FM/cassette/CD player, fog lights, limited-slip differential, front tow hooks, alloy wheels. Requires Power Pkg.

Comfort and Convenience
In-dash 6-disc CD changer, XE, XE V6	439	355
Automatic day/night rearview mirror	219	161

Appearance and Miscellaneous
Grille/taillight guards	609	310

Special Purpose, Wheels and Tires
Tow hitch, XE	399	289
XE V6, SE	349	238

Post production options also available.

OLDSMOBILE ALERO

Oldsmobile Alero 4-door sedan

Front-wheel-drive compact car; similar to Pontiac Grand Am

Base price range: $17,210-$22,190. Built in USA. **Also consider:** Chrysler Sebring, Mazda 626, Volkswagen Passat

FOR • Acceleration (V6) • Control layout • Passenger and cargo room • Quietness **AGAINST** • Engine noise (4-cylinder) • Rear visibility (2-door) • Rear-seat entry/exit (2-door)

Wider availability of the V6 engine and more standard equipment are the 2001 changes to Oldsmobile's compact coupe and sedan. Base Alero GX, GL1, GL2, and top line GLS models continue; last year's GL3 is dropped. GX, GL1, and GL2 have a 4-cylinder engine. The GLS has a V6 that for '01 is optional on GL1 and GL2. Automatic transmission is standard, a 5-speed manual is a credit option on 4-cylinder GXs and GL2s. All Aleros have antilock 4-wheel disc brakes and traction control.

Specifications begin on page 535.

OLDSMOBILE

For '01, GXs gain standard power windows, and cruise control and a CD player are standard instead of optional. The GL1 gains map lights and standard instead of optional keyless remote entry. The GL's Sport option package is dropped, but its sport suspension, wider tires, alloy wheels, and rear spoiler are newly standard on the GL2. Also, a new Sun and Sound option package for GLs adds a power sunroof and upgraded audio system with cassette and CD player. Alero shares its basic design with the Pontiac Grand Am.

PERFORMANCE Acceleration with the V6 engine is perhaps Alero's best feature. The V6 feels gutsy from a stop and responds quickly in passing situations. At around 8 seconds 0-60 mph, a V6 Alero is among the faster compacts. The downside? Torque steer—sideways pulling under hard acceleration—and a lack of refinement compared to rival Japanese V6s. Alero's 4-cylinder isn't nearly as fast as its V6, but it's okay in most everyday tasks. Test V6 Aleros averaged 21.6-23.7 mpg; we have not had an opportunity to measure the 4-cylinder's fuel economy. With either engine, the automatic transmission provides smooth, prompt downshifts. The manual transmission adds a dash of sportiness to 4-cylinder Aleros, but it doesn't shift as smoothly as that in such rivals as Honda and Toyota.

Alero's ride and handling won't be confused with those of an import-brand sport sedan. There's good grip in steady-state cornering. But the steering feels artificially heavy and is somewhat nervous on center, and Alero can feel unsure in quick transitions. Neither suspension rides harshly over bumps, but neither impresses with its compliance or ability to enhance control. Braking is drama-free and pedal action reassuringly firm, but stopping power feels no more than adequate. Both engines sound and feel coarse under hard throttle, and the 4-cylinder we tested vibrated at idle. Wind noise is modest, although the tires drum and thrum on any but the smoothest of pavement.

ACCOMMODATIONS Gauges are clear and compact. Major controls are nicely grouped around the driver, and the easy-to-use climate system features independent air conditioning and recirculation modes. There's no indicator that the available fog lamps are on, however, and no control feels particularly rich or satisfying to use. Padded dashboard and door panels are a nice touch, but at odds with Alero's upscale aspirations are the dashboard vents, which suffer a crude, notchy movement and can't be aimed above the horizontal. Visibility is good in sedans but hampered in coupes by thick roof pillars.

Front head and leg room are good, and rear-seat space rivals that of a few midsize cars. However, seat comfort is compromised by insubstantial foam padding that offers little long-distance support. Rear-seat entry/exit is the usual squeeze in the coupes. Trunks are wide and deep but don't extend that far forward and have smallish openings. All models come with split-fold rear seatbacks to expand the cargo area. Aleros

Prices are accurate at time of publication; subject to manufacturer's change.

OLDSMOBILE

we tested felt solid and rattle-free.

VALUE Strong V6 acceleration and a long list of standard features at competitive prices are Alero's virtues. It feels more mature than cousin Grand Am, but still can't match import-brand rivals in refinement and in interior design and materials.

ENGINES

	dohc I4	ohv V6
Size, liters/cu. in.	2.4/146	3.4/207
Horsepower @ rpm	150 @ 5600	170 @ 4800
Torque (lb-ft) @ rpm	155 @ 4400	200 @ 4000
Availability	S[1]	S[2]
EPA city/highway mpg		
5-speed OD manual	21/29	
4-speed OD automatic	20/30	21/32

1. GX, GL1, GL2. 2. GLS, optional GL1, GL2.

PRICES

Oldsmobile Alero	Retail Price	Dealer Invoice
GX 2-door coupe	$17210	$16091
GX 4-door sedan	17210	16091
GL1 2-door coupe	18620	17037
GL1 4-door sedan	18620	17037
GL2 2-door coupe	19525	17865
GL2 4-door sedan	19525	17865
GLS 2-door coupe	22190	20082
GLS 4-door sedan	21965	19878
Destination charge	575	575

STANDARD EQUIPMENT:

GX: 2.4-liter dohc 4-cylinder engine, 4-speed automatic transmission, traction control, dual front airbags, antilock 4-wheel disc brakes, daytime running lights, air conditioning, power steering, tilt steering wheel, cruise control, cloth upholstery, front bucket seats, center console, cupholders, split folding rear seat, power windows, power door locks, AM/FM/CD player, tachometer, variable intermittent wipers, auxiliary power outlets, rear defogger, visor mirrors, power decklid release, automatic headlights, floormats, theft-deterrent system, dual outside mirrors, 215/60R15 tires, wheel covers.

GL1 adds: variable-assist power steering, power mirrors, remote keyless entry, driver seat w/power height adjustment and manual lumbar support, map lights, 215/60R15 tires.

GL2 adds: leather-wrapped steering wheel, alloy wheels, rear spoiler, fog lights, performance sport suspension, 225/50VR16 tires.

GLS adds: 3.4-liter V6 engine, leather upholstery, 6-way power driver seat,

Specifications begin on page 535.

OLDSMOBILE

AM/FM/cassette/CD player, 225/50SR16 tires, polished alloy wheels, Deletes: performance sport suspension, rear spoiler (sedan).

OPTIONAL EQUIPMENT:	Retail Price	Dealer Invoice
Major Packages		
Feature Pkg., GL1	$815	$725
Manufacturer's discount price	*515*	*458*
Leather-wrapped steering wheel, fog lights, alloy wheels.		
Sun and Sound Pkg., GL1, GL2	1100	979
Manufacturer's discount price	*845*	*752*
Power sunroof, AM/FM/cassette/CD player.		
Performance Suspension Pkg., GLS	250	223
Performance sport suspension, 225/50VR16 tires.		
Powertrains		
3.4-liter V6 engine, GL1, GL2	655	583
NA w/manual transmission.		
5-speed manual transmission, GX, GL2 (credit)	(785)	(699)
Requires 2.4-liter engine.		
Comfort and Convenience		
Power sunroof, GLS	700	623
6-way power driver seat, GL1, GL2	305	271
Appearance and Miscellaneous		
Rear spoiler, GL1, GLS sedan	225	200

OLDSMOBILE AURORA

Oldsmobile Aurora

Front-wheel-drive near-luxury car; similar to Buick LeSabre and Pontiac Bonneville

Base price range: $30,469-$34,644. Built in USA. **Also consider:** Acura TL, Buick Park Avenue, Lexus ES 300, Lincoln LS

Prices are accurate at time of publication; subject to manufacturer's change.

OLDSMOBILE

FOR • Acceleration (V8) • Passenger room **AGAINST** • Rear visibility • Climate controls

Aurora was redesigned for a spring 2000 debut as an '01 model, and this fall, Oldsmobile's flagship gains a standard automatic load-leveling suspension. Aurora is smaller than the 1995-99 first-generation design in most dimensions, and shares its basic platform with the Pontiac Bonneville and Buick LeSabre.

V6 and V8 engines are offered. The only transmission is a 4-speed automatic; rivals such as the Lincoln LS and Acura TL offer a 5-speed automatic. Aurora seats five, has standard front side airbags, antilock 4-wheel disc brakes, automatic climate control, leather upholstery, and wood interior trim. V8 versions have 17-inch wheels in place of the V6's 16s and include traction control and Oldsmobile's antiskid Precision Control System, both of which are options with the V6. This fall, General Motors' OnStar system is standard on all Auroras; it was previously unavailable with the V6.

PERFORMANCE Aurora is a credible attempt at an import-flavored near-luxury car, but its nose-heavy front-wheel-drive configuration keeps it from being as athletic as most European sport sedans. Our main dynamic gripe concerns overly firm suspension settings that upset body control on rough pavement, resulting in an unsettled, stiff-kneed ride—not unlike the Cadillac Seville STS. That apart, the suspension copes comfortably with most surfaces, and the steering provides good feedback.

In acceleration, the V6 proves a pleasant surprise, feeling nearly as strong as the V8 from a stop and in highway passing situations. The V8 has the edge in 30-55-mph passing response. The automatic transmissions are different for each engine, but both are smooth and alert. In our tests, a V6 Aurora averaged 21 mpg and a V8 just 14.1. Olds recommends 89-octane fuel for both engines.

The stiff structure helps keep wind and tire noise low, and Aurora's engines are fairly subdued even when pushed, though they don't sound as classy as the best import brands. Braking is strong and drama-free, although some Auroras we tested had an overly firm brake pedal that was difficult to modulate.

ACCOMMODATIONS Despite its trimmer exterior dimensions, Aurora for '01 is roomier inside than the original version. Six-footers get plenty of knee clearance in front or back, and have more than adequate head room even with the intrusion of the sunroof housing. There are enough adjustments for any driver to get comfortably situated, although the front lumbar support feels too prominent to some testers. Back-seat comfort is subpar, the cushion being too small and too soft to provide much support. Entry/exit poses no problems.

The dashboard layout generally works well, although the audio unit is

Specifications begin on page 535.

OLDSMOBILE

low in the center of the dashboard and requires a long look away from the road to adjust; redundant steering-wheel audio buttons help. Some testers also would like simpler climate controls. Aurora's transmission gear selector has a notched gate that encourages do-it-yourself shifting, though it's not as precise as the separate shift gate on such rivals as the TL and LS. Visibility directly astern is spoiled by the high tail and a bulky center stoplamp. The trunk is generous, with a large opening and low liftover, but the lid hinges dip into the cargo area. Padded interior surfaces abound, and real wood is a genuine luxury, but these upscale cues were mitigated by creaking dashboard panels on most of the Auroras we tested.

VALUE Few other sedans in this class offer a V8, but we still doubt Aurora can tempt Lexus or BMW owners. Nonetheless, this is a pleasant, slightly sporty all-rounder that should appeal to value-minded near-luxury buyers.

ENGINES

	dohc V6	dohc V8
Size, liters/cu. in.	3.5/212	4.0/244
Horsepower @ rpm	215 @ 5600	250 @ 5600
Torque (lb-ft) @ rpm	230 @ 4400	260 @ 4400
Availability	S[1]	S[2]
EPA city/highway mpg		
4-speed OD automatic	19/27	17/25

1. V6. 2. V8.

PRICES

Oldsmobile Aurora	Retail Price	Dealer Invoice
V6 4-door sedan	$30469	$27879
V8 4-door sedan	34644	31699
Destination charge	670	670

STANDARD EQUIPMENT:

V6: 3.5-liter dohc V6 engine, 4-speed automatic transmission, dual front airbags, front side-impact airbags, antilock 4-wheel disc brakes, daytime running lights, air conditioning w/automatic climate control, interior air filter, magnetic variable-assist power steering, tilt leather-wrapped steering wheel, steering wheel radio and climate controls, cruise control, OnStar System w/one year service (roadside assistance, emergency services; other services available), leather upholstery, front bucket seats, 8-way power driver seat w/power lumbar adjustment, center console, cupholders, rear seat trunk pass-through, wood interior trim, heated power mirrors, power windows, power door locks, remote keyless entry, AM/FM/cassette/CD player, digital clock, tachometer, tire inflation monitor, trip computer, illuminated visor mirrors, outside temperature indicator, overhead console, map lights, rear

Prices are accurate at time of publication; subject to manufacturer's change.

OLDSMOBILE

defogger, variable intermittent wipers, power remote decklid and fuel door release, auxiliary power outlets, automatic headlights, floormats, front and rear fog lights, theft-deterrent system, automatic load-leveling suspension, 225/60HR16 tires, alloy wheels.

V8 adds: 4.0-liter dohc V8 engine, traction control, antiskid system, dual-zone automatic climate control, 8-way power passenger seat, memory system including driver seat and outside mirrors, automatic day/night rearview mirror, compass, rain-sensing automatic wipers, universal garage door opener, 235/55HR17 tires.

OPTIONAL EQUIPMENT:

	Retail Price	Dealer Invoice
Major Packages		
All Weather Pkg., V6	$575	$512
Traction control, antiskid system. Requires Passenger Comfort Pkg.		
Passenger Comfort Pkg., V6	440	392
Dual-zone automatic air conditioning, rear seat ducts, 8-way power passenger seat, rear storage armrest, additional cupholders.		
Convenience Pkg., V6	565	503
Memory system including driver seat and outside mirror memory, automatic day/night rearview mirror, compass, rain-sensing automatic wipers, universal garage door opener.		
Comfort and Convenience		
Power sunroof	1095	975
Bose sound system	500	445
12-disc CD changer	460	409
Heated front seats	345	307
Appearance and Miscellaneous		
Gold Pkg.	175	156
Chrome alloy wheels	800	712

2002 OLDSMOBILE BRAVADA

4-wheel-drive midsize sport-utility vehicle; similar to Chevrolet Trialblazer and GMC Envoy

Base price range: NA. Built in USA. **Also consider:** Acura MDX, Dodge Durango, Ford Explorer, Mercury Mountaineer

Oldsmobile began selling the first of General Motors' redesigned midsize sport-utility vehicles in January as a 2002 model. The third-generation Bravada remains a 4-door 5-passenger wagon, but has a larger, new body-on-frame design and offers rear-wheel drive for the first time in addition to Oldsmobile's SmartTrak permanently engaged 4-wheel drive. Like the related Chevrolet TrailBlazer and GMC's similarly revamped 2002 Envoy, Bravada rides a 6-inch longer wheelbase than

Specifications begin on page 535.

OLDSMOBILE

2002 Oldsmobile Bravada

before and is some 5 inches longer overall, 5 inches wider, and about 5 inches taller. Curb weight increases about 350 pounds. Olds lists increased passenger space in most dimensions, plus more cargo volume. Styling is revised and more distinct from Chevy and GMC; the only shared body panels are the roof, front doors, and tailgate.

Like its sibling models, the '02 Bravada carries a new 4.2-liter inline 6-cylinder engine with dual overhead camshafts. It makes 80 more horsepower than the previous overhead-valve 4.3 V6, but it, too, runs on regular fuel. A 4-speed automatic remains the only transmission. The 2WD model includes traction control, and Bravada remains unique among the GM SUVs with permanent 4WD, though it lacks low-range gearing like the Autotrac system offered by Chevy and GMC.

All three brands retain a solid rear axle, but exclusive to Bravada is a new rear suspension with air springs instead of the coils used by Chevy/GMC. Olds claims this and other alterations improve both on-road ride quality and off-road handling compared to previous Bravadas. Other changes include larger antilock 4-wheel disc brakes and standard 17-inch wheels to replace 15s. Front side airbags are a new standard feature shared with Chevy and GMC, with head/chest protection for the driver, chest only for the passenger. Also new is dual-stage deployment for the dashboard airbags, which inflate at one of two force levels based on sensor input on crash severity and occupant size.

As GM's premium midsize SUV, Bravada comes with the most standard comfort and convenience features. Full details weren't available for this report, but the list includes heated door mirrors, 8-way power front seats, CD/cassette audio with steering-wheel controls and separate rear-seat functions, and leather and wood interior trim. GM's OnStar communications/assistance system becomes standard (as on Envoy), and options include front-seat heating and memory.

Unlike Chevy and GMC, Olds will apparently not offer an extended-length 7-passenger model for 2003 or later. We have not yet driven the new Bravada and thus cannot provide ratings or an evaluation.

Prices are accurate at time of publication; subject to manufacturer's change.

CONSUMER GUIDE

OLDSMOBILE

ENGINES

	dohc I6
Size, liters/cu. in.	4.2/256
Horsepower @ rpm	270 @ 6000
Torque (lb-ft) @ rpm	275 @ 3600
Availability	S

EPA city/highway mpg
4-speed OD automatic 16/21

Prices unavailable at time of publication.

OLDSMOBILE INTRIGUE

CG RECOMMENDED AUTO

Oldsmobile Intrigue

Front-wheel-drive midsize car; similar to Buick Regal and Century, Chevrolet Impala, and Pontiac Grand Prix

Base price range: $22,395-$26,515. Built in USA.   **Also consider:** Honda Accord, Nissan Maxima, Toyota Camry

FOR • Acceleration • Passenger and cargo room • Ride • Steering/handling   **AGAINST** • Climate controls

The lowest-priced version of Oldsmobile's import-flavored midsize loses its standard traction control for '01, but all Intrigues gain new standard automatic headlights and several new option packages. GX, GL, and top-line GLS models continue. All have a twincam 3.5-liter V6, automatic transmission, and antilock 4-wheel disc brakes. Traction control is standard on GL and GLS, but for '01 it's optional instead of standard on the GX, where it becomes part of the new Driver Control option package, which also includes a power driver seat and CD player. Optional on all Intrigues is Oldsmobile's Precision Control antiskid system, which is designed to selectively brake individual wheels to fight skids in turns. For '01, a new Premium Leather package is available on the GL. It includes leather upholstery, power passenger seat, and heated front seats. The GLS can be equipped with a new Precision Sport package, which incor-

Specifications begin on page 535.

OLDSMOBILE

porates the Precision Control antiskid system, a power sunroof, rear spoiler, and chrome alloy wheels. Intrigue is built from the same basic design as the Buick Regal and Pontiac Grand Prix.

EVALUATION The new Precision Control antiskid system enhances an already capable performer. Intrigue's twincam V6 doesn't deliver as much off-the-line snap as the older 3.8 in its corporate siblings, but it's a smoother, quieter engine that provides fine highway passing response and complements a well-behaved transmission. In tests we averaged 17.7-19.5 mpg on regular gas; rivals Honda Accord and Toyota Camry offer twincam V6s that make less horsepower, and Toyota recommends 91 octane premium for the Camry's. A solid structure and taut suspension provide a stable ride and capable handling, but the speed-sensitive steering feels artificially heavy off-center. Stopping power is strong, although brake-pedal feel is numb. Wind noise is generally well-muffled, but tires and suspension thump over sharp bumps and ridges. Intrigue's front bucket seats are firm and supportive, despite an unusually prominent lumbar bolster. Head room is good all around, and back-seat leg space is good with the front seats moved anywhere short of fully aft. Entry/exit is easy. The dashboard is modern and attractive, but the automatic climate control standard on GL and GLS models suffers from poorly marked, low-mounted controls that are difficult to use while driving. This system also has trouble defogging the windows in some chilly, damp conditions. Thoughtful touches include dual cupholders front and rear, and trunk-lid hinges that don't rob space or scuff luggage. Interior materials are impressive for the price. Intrigue feels more grown up than Grand Prix, more sophisticated than Regal. It's a smart blend of features and performance at prices that generally undercut competing import brands, and with sales slipping, discounts are probably available.

ENGINES

	dohc V6
Size, liters/cu. in.	3.5/211
Horsepower @ rpm	215 @ 5600
Torque (lb-ft) @ rpm	230 @ 4400
Availability	S

EPA city/highway mpg	
4-speed OD automatic	19/28

PRICES

Oldsmobile Intrigue	Retail Price	Dealer Invoice
GX 4-door sedan	$22395	$20491
GL 4-door sedan	24150	22097
GLS 4-door sedan	26515	24261
Destination charge	610	610

Prices are accurate at time of publication; subject to manufacturer's change.

OLDSMOBILE

STANDARD EQUIPMENT:

GX: 3.5-liter dohc V6 engine, 4-speed automatic transmission, antilock 4-wheel disc brakes, dual front airbags, daytime running lamps, variable-assist power steering, tilt steering wheel, cruise control, air conditioning, interior air filter, cloth upholstery, front bucket seats, center console, cupholders, power mirrors, power windows, power door locks, AM/FM/cassette, digital clock, tachometer, variable intermittent wipers, rear defogger, remote trunk and fuel door release, visor mirrors, map lights, automatic headlights, floormats, theft-deterrent system, cornering lights, 225/60R16 tires, alloy wheels.

GL adds: traction control, remote keyless entry, dual-zone automatic climate control, outside temperature indicator, 6-way power driver seat, split-folding rear seat, leather-wrapped steering wheel/armrest/shifter, AM/FM/cassette/CD player, 6-speaker sound system, steering-wheel radio controls, illuminated visor mirrors, fog lights.

GLS adds: OnStar System w/one year service (roadside assistance, emergency services; other services available), leather upholstery, heated front seats, 6-way power passenger seat, automatic day/night rearview mirror, compass.

OPTIONAL EQUIPMENT:

Major Packages

	Retail Price	Dealer Invoice
Driver Control Pkg., GX	$990	$881
Manufacturer's discount price	590	525

Traction control, remote keyless entry, AM/FM/cassette/CD player, 6-speaker sound system, 6-way power driver seat, leather-wrapped steering wheel, armrest, and shifter.

Premium Leather Pkg., GL	1595	1420
Manufacturer's discount price	995	886

Leather upholstery, 6-way power passenger seat, heated front seats.

Precision Control System, GX, GL	595	530

Antiskid system, upgraded power steering, performance axle ratio, 225/60HR16 performance tires. GX requires Driver Control Pkg.

Precision Sport Pkg., GLS	2265	2016
Manufacturer's discount price	1465	1304

Precision Control System plus power sunroof, rear spoiler, chrome alloy wheels.

Comfort and Convenience

Power Sunroof	750	668
Bose cassette/CD player, GL, GLS	500	445

Includes eight speakers, automatic tone control, amplifier.

Split folding rear seat, GX	150	134

Appearance and Miscellaneous

Rear spoiler, GX, GL	225	200
Chrome alloy wheels, GL	695	619

Specifications begin on page 535.

OLDSMOBILE SILHOUETTE

Oldsmobile Silhouette

Front-wheel-drive minivan; similar to Pontiac Montana and Chevrolet Venture

Base price range: $26,290-$33,225. Built in USA. **Also consider:** Chrysler Town & Country and Voyager, Dodge Caravan, Honda Odyssey, Toyota Sienna

FOR • Ride • Passenger and cargo room   **AGAINST** • Fuel economy

Oldsmobile's upscale version of the Chevrolet Venture and Pontiac Montana minivans counts a stowable third-row seat and a revised video system among its additions for 2001.

While its General Motors siblings offer regular- and extended-length models, Silhouette comes only in the extended body. It's available in GL, GLS, and top-line Premiere trim levels. All have dual sliding side doors. A passenger-side power door is standard on GLS and Premiere, optional on GL. Due later in the model year is an optional driver-side power door for the Premiere. (Montana already offers this option.)

Also new for '01 is a standard load levelling rear suspension. Standard on Premiere, optional on the other models, is rear parking assist that beeps to warn of objects behind the vehicle when backing up. The stowable third-row seat option due later in the model year comes with a rear floor-mounted covered storage tray. The video system is exclusive to Premier in the Silhouette line and this year replaces a 5.6-inch screen with a 6.8-inch screen and adds cordless headphones.

GLS and Premier gain standard 16-inch wheels and tires for '01 (versus 15s), and an optional 6-disc in-dashboard CD player. An universal garage-door opener is now available. Newly standard are second-row lower anchors for rear child seats, dashboard-mounted cupholders, remote keyless entry, CD player, load-leveling suspension, and GM's OnStar assistance system.

All Silhouettes have two front-row bucket seats and two second-row captain's chairs. The third row can be fitted with 3-passenger bench, the

Prices are accurate at time of publication; subject to manufacturer's change.

OLDSMOBILE

new stowable bench, or a pair of captain's chairs. The last is a Silhouette exclusive not offered by other GM vans, as is a memory system for the power driver's seat.

The sole powertrain is a 3.4-liter V6 and automatic transmission. Antilock brakes and front side airbags are standard; traction control is standard on all but the GL, where it is optional. Silhouette's performance and accommodations are similar to those of like-equipped Ventures.

The Chevrolet Venture report includes an evaluation of the Silhouette.

ENGINES

	ohv V6
Size, liters/cu. in.	3.4/207
Horsepower @ rpm	185 @ 5200
Torque (lb-ft) @ rpm	210 @ 4000
Availability	S

EPA city/highway mpg

4-speed OD automatic	19/26

PRICES

Oldsmobile Silhouette	Retail Price	Dealer Invoice
GL 4-door van	$26290	$23792
GLS 4-door van	30425	27535
Premiere Edition 4-door van	33225	30069
Destination charge	630	630

STANDARD EQUIPMENT:

GL: 3.4-liter V6 engine, 4-speed automatic transmission, dual front airbags, front side-impact airbags, antilock brakes, daytime running lights, front air conditioning, interior air filter, power steering, tilt steering wheel, cruise control, OnStar System w/one year service (roadside assistance, emergency services; other services available), cloth upholplstery, front bucket seats, center console, cupholders, second-row captain chairs, third-row split-folding bench seat, overhead console, map lights, heated power mirrors, power windows, power door locks, remote keyless entry, AM/FM/CD player, digital clock, tachometer, intermittent wipers, rear defogger, rear wiper/washer, automatic headlights, illuminated visor mirrors, auxiliary power outlets, floormats, theft-deterrent system, rear privacy glass, fog lights, roof rack, air inflation kit, load-leveling suspension, 215/70R15 tires, wheel covers.

GLS adds: traction control, leather upholstery, 8-way power front seats, third row stowable bench seat, power sliding passenger-side door, overhead storage console (includes compass, outside temperature indicator, driver information center), rear air conditioning and heater, AM/FM/cassette/CD player, leather-wrapped steering wheel w/radio controls, rear-seat radio controls, headphones, universal garage door opener, 225/60R16 tires, alloy wheels.

Premiere Edition adds: rear parking assist, LCD color screen/videocassette

Specifications begin on page 535.

OLDSMOBILE • PONTIAC

player, input jacks for video games or video camera, heated front seats, driver seat memory.

OPTIONAL EQUIPMENT:	Retail Price	Dealer Invoice
Major Packages		
Towing Pkg., GL, GLS	$370	$318
Premiere	100	86
Engine-oil cooler, heavy-duty alternator and radiator, heavy-duty flasher, 5-lead wiring harness.		
Powertrains		
Traction control, GL	195	168
Safety Features		
Rear parking assist, GL, GLS	150	129
GL requires power passenger-side door, rear air conditioning, rear radio controls.		
Comfort and Convenience		
Power sliding passenger-side door, GL	450	387
Power sliding driver-side door, Premiere	—	—
Rear air conditioning, GL	450	387
Includes rear heater. Requires rear radio controls.		
Heated front seats, GLS	195	168
Third row captain chairs, GLS, Premiere	60	52
AM/FM/cassette/CD player, GL	100	86
AM/FM w/in-dash 6-disc CD changer, GLS, Premiere	295	254
Rear radio controls, GL	125	108
Requires rear air conditioning.		
Drivers information center, GL	175	151
Includes compass, outside temperature indicator, driver information center.		
Alloy wheels, GL	295	254
Chrome alloy wheels, GLS, Premiere	695	598

PONTIAC AZTEK

Front-wheel-drive midsize sport-utility vehicle

Base price range: $21,445-$24,445. Built in Mexico. **Also consider:** Chrysler PT Cruiser, Ford Escape, Honda CR-V, Mazda Tribute, Subaru Forester

FOR • Passenger and cargo room • Interior storage space
AGAINST • Acceleration • Noise • Handling/roadholding

Aimed at young, sports-minded buyers, Pontiac's new car/SUV crossover went on sale this past summer in base and better-equipped GT models with front-wheel drive. Aztek is loosely based on Pontiac's

Prices are accurate at time of publication; subject to manufacturer's change.

PONTIAC

Pontiac Aztek GT

Montana minivan, with the same 3.4-liter V6 and mandatory automatic transmission, but with four conventional side doors and a hatchback-type glass liftgate in combination with a drop-down tailgate. Front side airbags and antilock brakes are standard. Due in January is an available 4-wheel-drive system that can distribute power to the four wheels based upon available traction. It will have 4-wheel disc brakes in place of a disc/drum setup, but is not intended for off-road use and won't have low-range gearing. Aztek's maximum towing capacity is 3500 pounds, same as Montana. Ground clearance is 6.7 inches.

Aztek is larger than the popular Lexus RX 300, another car-based crossover. Its wheelbase is 5.5 inches longer and it's 2 inches longer overall. Aztek is slightly taller and wider, with 1.5 inches more rear leg room and 93.5 cubic feet of storage with the rear seats removed; the Lexus has 75 cubic feet of cargo space.

Standard equipment includes air conditioning, tilt steering wheel, and power windows/locks/mirrors. The GT adds traction control, 16-inch wheels and tires in place of 15s, and a removable console bin that's a combination cooler and CD case. Options include power sunroof and a slide-out cargo-floor section with storage bins and roll-away wheels. Exclusive GT options include heated leather front seats, two rear captain's chairs in lieu of the standard 3-person bench, a head-up instrument display, and GM's OnStar assistance system. Recreational accessories available through dealers include washable seatcovers and a camping package with clip-on tent and fitted air mattress. Buick will offer its own version of the Aztek as the 2002 Rendezvous, which will be longer and feature three rows of seats.

PERFORMANCE It may not look like a minivan, but Aztek mostly drives like one, which means it's actually more pleasant than most any SUV.

GM's 3.4-liter V6 works well here, delivering smooth acceleration and good midrange response, though there's no surplus of either. We haven't had an opportunity to measure fuel economy with a 4WD Aztek, but the 2WD GT we tested averaged 18.7 mpg, which would please any

Specifications begin on page 535.

PONTIAC

midsize SUV owner.

Aztek isn't the ponderous-handling vehicle it might appear. Again, behavior mirrors that of a GM minivan, which means nicely weighted steering and consistent tracking though turns. Grip is good, but body lean is pronounced, and stability in crosswinds is heavily compromised. Mushy-feeling brakes reduce confidence, though routine stopping power seems more than adequate. Aztek's ride is generally absorbent and well controlled, with better bump absorption than virtually any midsize SUV. On the downside, some passengers complained of annoying side-to-side body motions on uneven pavement. Relatively low noise levels from engine, wind, and road are other high points. Few true SUVs are this quiet.

ACCOMMODATIONS Aztek is usefully roomy, with plentiful head clearance and enough back-seat knee, leg, and foot space to suit 6-footers. Front seats are comfortable, though taller drivers may wish for more rearward travel to get further back from the tilt steering wheel. And the rear bench itself is more springy foam than supportive padding. Step-in is minivan-low, making entry/exit easy to the front. Rear seaters must twist their feet to get in or out, however, and the swing-open back doors are very large. (Pontiac could have achieved some meaningful innovation had it made Aztek the only SUV with minivan-type sliding side doors.)

Gauges and generously sized controls are functional, but exaggerated shapes give the dashboard a cartoonish appearance. Thick side roof pillars interfere with visibility over the shoulder, and the driver can't easily see the front body corners in parking maneuvers. The bar separating the liftgate's two glass elements looks strange in the rearview mirror but doesn't interfere with the view aft. However, a rear wiper isn't available; further road tests will determine how rear visibility holds up against coatings of dust, snow, or salt spray.

Aztek shines for interior storage and versatility. Each door has a large map pocket with twin bottle holders, the rear bench is easily removed in two 45-pound sections, and the available sliding rear storage tray is clever and useful. Pontiac says Aztek will carry a 4x8 plywood sheet with the tailgate lowered. However, the large glass liftgate is heavy to open and, lacking a pull-down handle, unnecessarily cumbersome to close. The tailgate doesn't open flat. And there's no exterior liftgate or tailgate latch, so you have to use the key, keyfob, or dashboard release button each time you want access to the cargo area. A compact-spare tire is carried in a wind-down underbody cradle.

Cabin trim is a deliberate mish-mash of textures and hues, and most molded cabin plastics come across as low-buck; so does the cloth upholstery. The numerous interior-panel rattles in some early-production Azteks we tested were not present in later versions we evaluated.

VALUE Aztek is arguably the most comfortable sport-utiilty wagon go-

Prices are accurate at time of publication; subject to manufacturer's change.

PONTIAC

ing, but it may be too oddly styled to attract the very buyers who would be happy with an SUV that doesn't drive like a truck. It's packed with features designed for active/sporty types, but those very people demand precision gear—and Aztek's overall fit and materials are anything but. Still, Pontiac thinks there are about 60,000 folks per year looking for a vehicle that is neither car, minivan, nor SUV despite possessing elements of all three.

ENGINES

	ohv V6
Size, liters/cu. in.	3.4/207
Horsepower @ rpm	185 @ 5200
Torque (lb-ft) @ rpm	210 @ 4000
Availability	S

EPA city/highway mpg
4-speed OD automatic	19/26

PRICES

Pontiac Aztek	Retail Price	Dealer Invoice
Base 4-door hatchback	$21445	$19622
GT 4-door hatchback	24445	22367
Destination charge	550	550

STANDARD EQUIPMENT:

Base: 3.4-liter V6 engine, 4-speed automatic transmission, dual front airbags, front side-impact airbags, antilock brakes, daytime running lights, front air conditioning, power steering, tilt steering wheel, cloth upholstery, front bucket seats, center console, cupholders, split folding rear seat, power mirrors, power windows, power door locks, AM/FM/cassette, digital clock, tachometer, auxiliary power outlets, intermittent wipers, rear defogger, power decklid release, automatic headlights, cargo cover, floormats, theft-deterrent system, fog lights, 215/70R15 tires, wheel covers.

GT adds: traction control, leather-wrapped steering wheel w/radio controls, cruise control, manual dual-zone climate controls, remote keyless entry, front seat lumbar adjustment, removable console cooler, AM/FM/CD player, overhead console, illuminated visor mirrors, privacy glass, roof rack, 215/65R16 tires, alloy wheels.

OPTIONAL EQUIPMENT:
Major Packages

Option Group 1SB, Base	1040	926

Remote keyless entry, AM/FM/CD player, cruise control, privacy glass, roof rack.

Option Group 1SC, Base	2050	1825

Option Group 1SB plus traction control, 6-way power driver seat, AM/FM/cassette/CD player, sliding rear cargo tray.

Specifications begin on page 535.

PONTIAC

	Retail Price	Dealer Invoice
Option Group 1SB, GT	$720	$641

Head-up instrument display, 6-way power driver seat, sliding rear cargo tray, theft-deterrent system w/alarm.

Option Group 1SC, GT	2415	2149

Option Group 1SB plus OnStar System (Global Positioning System, roadside assistance, emergency services), leather front seats, 215/70R16 puncture sealant tires.

Trailer Pkg.	365	325

Heavy-duty engine oil cooler and alternator, load-leveling rear suspension. Requires Option Group.

Comfort and Convenience

Power sunroof, Base	650	579
GT	535	476
GT w/Group 1SC	140	125

Requires AM/FM/cassette/CD player or 6-disc CD changer. Base requires option group. GT w/Option Group 1SC deletes OnStar System.

AM/FM/cassette/CD player, Base	325	289
GT	425	378

Base requires Option Group 1SB. Includes cargo area speakers. GT without power sunroof includes rear radio controls.

In-dash 6-disc CD changer, Base w/Group 1SB	620	552
Base/GT w/Group 1SC	295	263
GT	720	641

Base requires option group. GT without sunroof includes rear radio controls.

Second row captain chairs, GT	540	481

Includes heated front seats. Requires Option Group 1SC.

Heated front seats, GT	245	218
Smoker Pkg.	15	13

PONTIAC BONNEVILLE

Front-wheel-drive full-size car; similar to Buick LeSabre and Oldsmobile Aurora

Base price range: $25,075-$32,415. Built in USA. **Also consider:** Dodge Intrepid, Toyota Avalon

FOR • Acceleration • Passenger and cargo room • Ride/handling
AGAINST • Rear-seat comfort • Fuel economy

After being redesigned last year, Pontiac's full-size sedan offers wider availability of several features for 2001 and reintroduces OnStar after a one-year absence.

SE, SLE, and SSEi models continue. All come with front bucket seats,

Prices are accurate at time of publication; subject to manufacturer's change.

PONTIAC

Bonneville SE

but the SE offers an optional bench for 6-passenger capacity. The only engine is a 3.8-liter V6. SE and SLE models have 205 horsepower, the supercharged SSEi 240. The only transmission is a 4-speed automatic. Front side airbags are standard, as are antilock 4-wheel disc brakes and a tire-pressure monitor, the last a new addition to the SE. Traction control is standard on SSEi, newly standard on SLE, and optional on SE.

General Motor's StabiliTrak antiskid system is standard on the SSEi. It's designed to selectively brake the front wheels to counteract skids in turns. SSEi models also come with GM's EyeCue head-up display, which projects main instrument readings onto the windshield. GM's OnStar assistance system, which wasn't offered for 2000, is now standard on SLE and SSEi, optional on SE. Also, heated seats for '01 are optional on all Bonnevilles, not just the SSEi.

PERFORMANCE All Bonnevilles have good acceleration. SE and SLE models feel strong throughout the speed range, and the supercharged SSEi has outstanding power—0-60 mph in 7 seconds, says Pontiac. With either engine, the transmission changes gears smoothly and downshifts quickly for passing. Our test SE averaged 20.6 mpg, good for a big sedan. The SSEi requires premium fuel and averaged 15.7 mpg in our tests.

SEs ride a bit more softly than the sportier SLE and SSEi, and tend to float more over high-speed dips, but all are comfortable enough on bumpy pavement. We like the standard load-leveling rear suspension.

The SSEi we tested suffered annoying torque steer (pulling to one side in hard acceleration), but handling is generally balanced and composed on any model. SLE and SSEi feel sharpest, thanks in part to their lower-profile 17-inch wheels and tires (SEs wear 16s). Though StabiliTrak can get confused by rapid sawing of the steering wheel, it helps the SSEi stay on course in emergency maneuvers. Stopping power with the 4-wheel antilock disc brakes feels strong and sure, though pedal modulation is not uniform in hard stops. Engines are smooth, but highway wind rush and noises from suspension and tires over coarse surfaces don't bespeak top-drawer engineering.

Specifications begin on page 535.

PONTIAC

ACCOMMODATIONS Like its exterior, Bonneville's interior takes an "expressive" design approach. There's plenty of room for four adults, though rear headroom might be tight for taller passengers. The rear seatback's protruding center section discourages 3-across seating, and the entire cushion is too soft and poorly shaped to provide comfortable support. Overall, there's not much more usable room than in Pontiac's midsize Grand Prix.

Controls for audio and climate systems are easy to reach and decipher. Two-tone surfaces enhance the dashboard's appearance, but its plastic panels feel low-budget and the overall look is cluttered with numerous curved cut lines and eight prominent air vents.

Front-seat comfort is generally good, helped by safety belts integrated into the seats. The SSEi's leather-covered buckets are too hard and not as supportive as they should be; but at least their 12-way power adjustment includes memory. Entry/exit is easy through generous door openings, but the cloth upholstery in the SE and SLE is so grippy that it can hinder getting out of the seats. There are numerous interior storage cubbies, although the front cupholders won't hold large beverages. The rear seat has a fold-down armrest and a trunk pass-through. The trunk is large, but the lid's hinges dip into the load area.

VALUE At under $26,000 to start, and SE is a good big-car value and accounts for 65 percent of Bonneville sales. We like supercharged power, but a loaded SSEi can top $34,000—well into the near-luxury realm, where most cars have more panache and refinement.

ENGINES

	ohv V6	Supercharged ohv V6
Size, liters/cu. in.	3.8/231	3.8/231
Horsepower @ rpm	205 @ 5200	240 @ 5200
Torque (lb-ft) @ rpm	230 @ 4000	280 @ 3600
Availability	S[1]	S[2]
EPA city/highway mpg		
4-speed OD automatic	19/30	17/28

1. SE, SLE. 2. SSEi.

PRICES

Pontiac Bonneville	Retail Price	Dealer Invoice
SE 4-door sedan	$25075	$22944
SLE 4-door sedan	28045	25661
SSEi 4-door sedan	32415	29660
Destination charge	655	655

STANDARD EQUIPMENT:

SE: 3.8-liter V6 engine, 4-speed automatic transmission, dual front airbags, front side-impact airbags, antilock 4-wheel disc brakes, daytime running lights, tire pressure monitor, air conditioning, power steering, tilt steering

Prices are accurate at time of publication; subject to manufacturer's change.

PONTIAC

wheel, cruise control, cloth upholstery, front bucket seats, 6-way power driver seat, center console, cupholders, rear seat trunk pass-through, power mirrors, power windows, power door locks, remote keyless entry, AM/FM/cassette, digital clock, tachometer, overhead console, map lights, intermittent wipers, illuminated visor mirrors, rear defogger, automatic headlights, floormats, theft-deterrent system, rear spoiler, fog lights, load-leveling suspension, full-size spare tire, 225/60R16 tires, alloy wheels.

SLE adds: traction control, OnStar System w/one year service (roadside assistance, emergency services; other services available), variable-assist power steering, leather-wrapped steering wheel w/radio controls, dual-zone automatic climate control, compass, outside temperature indicator, remote decklid release, performance suspension, 235/55R17 tires.

SSEi adds: 3.8-liter V6 supercharged engine, antiskid system, leather upholstery, articulating 12-way power front seats w/memory, head-up instrument display, AM/FM/cassette/CD player w/Bose sound system, automatic day/night rearview mirror, universal garage door opener, memory mirrors w/park-assist passenger-side mirror.

OPTIONAL EQUIPMENT:	Retail Price	Dealer Invoice
Major Packages		
Option Group 1SC, SE	$1840	$1638
OnStar System w/one year service (roadside assistance, emergency services; other services available), traction control, performance axle ratio, leather upholstery, leather-wrapped steering wheel w/radio controls, dual-zone automatic climate control.		
Seat and Heat Pkg., SE, SLE	530	472
Manufacturer's discount price	330	294
Heated front seats, 6-way power passenger seat. NA w/front split bench seat.		
Powertrains		
Traction control, SE	175	156
Comfort and Convenience		
Power sunroof	1080	961
SE and SLE include universal garage door opener.		
Leather upholstery, SE, SLE	850	757
Front split bench seat, SE	150	134
Heated front seats, SSEi	225	200
AM/FM/CD player, SE, SLE	100	89
AM/FM/cassette/CD player, SE, SLE	200	178
12-disc CD changer	595	530
SE requires Option Group.		
Leather-wrapped steering wheel w/radio controls, SE	175	156
Universal garage door opener, SE, SLE	100	89
SE requires Option Group.		
Chrome alloy wheels, SLE, SSEi	595	530

Specifications begin on page 535.

PONTIAC

PONTIAC FIREBIRD

CG RECOMMENDED AUTO

Pontiac Firebird 2-door convertible

Rear-wheel-drive sports coupe; similar to Chevrolet Camaro

Base price range: $18,725-$31,085. Built in Canada. **Also consider:** Ford Mustang, Mitsubishi Eclipse, Toyota Celica

FOR • Acceleration • Handling **AGAINST** • Fuel economy (V8 models) • Ride (V8 models) • Rear-seat room • Rear visibility • Wet-weather traction (without traction control) • Entry/exit

Pontiac's performance leader carries on into 2001 with stronger V8 engines and minor suspension revisions. Firebird offers hatchback coupes in base, Formula, and Trans Am trim, plus base and Trans Am convertibles with standard power top and glass rear window. All are similar to comparable Chevrolet Camaros, though Firebirds sport distinct styling. Reports have General Motors retiring Firebird and Camaro after the 2002 model year due to steadily declining sales.

A 3.8-liter V6 powers base models. Formulas and Trans Ams have a Corvette-derived 5.7-liter V8 that gains 5 horsepower this year to 310. The WS6 Ram Air option, no longer available on Formula, boosts Trans Am's horsepower by 15 and includes a functional hood scoop. Optional for Formula and Trans Am is an SLP Firehawk package that includes a 330-hp V8 beneath a special hood, upgraded suspension, unique trim, and 17-inch wheels. V6 models have a 5-speed manual transmission or optional automatic. V8s get the automatic or a 6-speed manual at no extra charge; a Hurst-brand shifter is a stand-alone option with the 6-speed. Antilock 4-wheel disc brakes are standard, traction control is optional. All models get revised shock absorbers for 2001 aimed at improving ride quality. Firebird's performance and accommodations are similar to those of like-equipped Camaros.

The Chevrolet Camaro report includes an evaluation of the Firebird.

Prices are accurate at time of publication; subject to manufacturer's change.

PONTIAC

ENGINES

	ohv V6	ohv V8	ohv V8
Size, liters/cu. in.	3.8/231	5.7/346	5.7/346
Horsepower @ rpm	200 @ 5200	310 @ 5200	325 @ 5200
Torque (lb-ft) @ rpm	225 @ 4000	340 @ 4000	350 @ 4400
Availability	S[1]	S[2]	O[3]
EPA city/highway mpg			
5-speed OD manual	19/26		
6-speed OD manual		19/28	18/26
4-speed OD automatic	19/26	18/26	19/28

1. Base. 2. Formula, Trans Am. 3. Trans Am.

PRICES

Pontiac Firebird	Retail Price	Dealer Invoice
Base 2-door hatchback	$18725	$17133
Base 2-door convertible	25345	23191
Formula 2-door hatchback	23905	21873
Trans Am 2-door hatchback	27015	24719
Trans Am 2-door convertible	31085	28443
Destination charge	575	575

STANDARD EQUIPMENT:

Base hatchback: 3.8-liter V6 engine, 5-speed manual transmission, dual front airbags, antilock 4-wheel disc brakes, daytime running lights, air conditioning, power steering, tilt steering wheel, cruise control, cloth upholstery, front bucket seats, folding rear seat, center console, cupholders, AM/FM/CD player, digital clock, tachometer, intermittent wipers, map lights, auxiliary power outlet, visor mirrors, remote hatch release, rear defogger, automatic headlights, floormats, left remote and right manual mirrors, theft-deterrent system, fog lights, rear spoiler, 215/60R16 tires, alloy wheels.

Base convertible adds: power mirrors, power windows, power door locks, remote keyless entry, leather-wrapped steering wheel w/radio controls, leather-wrapped shifter and handbrake, 6-way power driver seat, Monsoon sound system, power antenna, rear decklid release, power convertible top, theft-deterrent system w/alarm.

Formula adds to Base hatchback: 5.7-liter V8 310-horsepower engine, 4-speed automatic transmission, limited-slip differential, power mirrors, power windows, power door locks, leather-wrapped steering wheel w/radio controls, leather-wrapped shifter and parking brake, Monsoon sound system, power antenna, performance suspension, 245/50ZR16 tires.

Trans Am hatchback adds to Formula: 6-way power driver seat, leather upholstery, remote keyless entry, removable hatch roof, theft-deterrent system w/alarm.

Trans Am convertible adds: power convertible top, rear decklid release, deletes removable hatch roof.

Specifications begin on page 535.

PONTIAC

OPTIONAL EQUIPMENT:
Major Packages

	Retail Price	Dealer Invoice
Option Group 1SB, Base hatchback	$1510	$1344

4-speed automatic transmission, power mirrors, power windows, power door locks, power antenna.

Option Group 1SC, Base hatchback	2450	2181

Group 1SB plus Monsoon sound system, leather-wrapped steering wheel w/radio controls, 6-way power driver seat, remote keyless entry, theft-deterrent system w/alarm.

Option Group 1SB, Formula	1505	1339

Removable hatch roof, 6-way power driver seat, remote keyless entry, power antenna, theft-deterrent system w/alarm.

3800 Performance Pkg., Base	490	436

Limited-slip differential, faster ratio steering gear, dual exhaust, 3.42 rear axle ratio (with automatic transmission), 235/55R16 tires.

SLP Firehawk Pkg., Formula, Trans Am	3999	3439

Forced-air induction system, hood-mounted heat extractors, special hood w/scoops, 330-horsepower engine, special key fobs and dash plaque, upgraded suspension, 275/40ZR17 tires, painted alloy wheels.

WS6 Ram Air Performance and Handling Pkg., Trans Am	3150	2804

Ram air induction system, functional hood scoops, 325-horsepower engine, upgraded suspension, power steering fluid cooler, bright exhaust outlets, 275/40ZR17 tires, high-polished alloy wheels.

Sport Appearance Pkg., Base	1040	926

Specific Aero Appearance Pkg., dual exhaust. Requires automatic transmission. Hatchback requires option group. Convertible requires 235/55R16 tires.

Security Pkg., Base hatchback, Formula	240	214

Remote keyless entry, theft-deterrent system w/alarm. Base requires Group 1SB.

Powertrains

5-speed manual transmission, Base hatchback, (credit)	(815)	(725)
Requires option group.		
6-speed manual transmission, Formula, Trans Am	NC	NC
Hurst shifter, Formula, Trans Am	325	289
Requires 6-speed manual transmission.		
4-speed automatic transmission, Base	815	725
Traction control, Base	250	223
Formula, Trans Am	450	401
Rear performance axle, Formula, Trans Am	300	267
Includes 3.23 axle ratio, performance tires.		

Comfort and Convenience

Monsoon AM/FM/cassette, Base hatchback w/Group 1SB	330	294

Prices are accurate at time of publication; subject to manufacturer's change.

PONTIAC

	Retail Price	Dealer Invoice
Base hatchback w/Group 1SC, Base convertible, Formula, Trans Am (credit)	($100)	($89)

Base hatchback includes leather-wrapped steering wheel with radio controls.

Monsoon sound system, Base hatchback w/Group 1SB	430	383

Includes leather-wrapped steering with radio controls.

12-disc CD changer	595	530

Base requires Group 1SC.

Leather upholstery, Base, Formula	575	512

Base hatchback requires Group 1SC. Formula requires Group 1SB.

Articulating bucket seats, Trans Am	185	165
6-way power driver seat, Base hatchback, Formula	270	240

Appearance and Miscellaneous

Removable locking hatch roof, Base hatchback, Formula	995	886

Includes sunshades, lock, and stowage.

235/55R16 tires, Base	135	120
Chromed alloy wheels	595	530

Base hatchback and Formula require option group. NA with Ram Air Performance and Handling Pkg.

PONTIAC GRAND AM

Pontiac Grand Am SE 4-door sedan

Front-wheel-drive compact car; similar to Oldsmobile Alero

Base price range: $16,140-$21,805. Built in USA. **Also consider:** Mazda 626, Mitsubishi Galant, Nissan Altima

FOR • Acceleration (V6) • Steering/handling **AGAINST** • Engine noise (4-cylinder) • Ride • Radio controls • Rear-seat entry/exit (2-door)

Upgraded sound systems, lower anchors for rear child seats, and restyled wheels head the short list of changes to Pontiac's sales champ

Specifications begin on page 535.

PONTIAC

and America's best-selling compact car.

Coupes and sedans are offered in ascending levels of trim called SE, SE1, GT, and GT1. The mid-line SE2 has been dropped for 2001. SE and SE1 come with a 150-horsepower 4-cylinder engine; a 170-hp V6 is optional on SE1. GT and GT1 come with a 175-hp version of the V6. The 4-cylinder teams with a standard Getrag 5-speed manual transmission, while the V6 comes only with a 4-speed automatic that's optional with the four. Antilock brakes and traction control are standard for all models. Grand Am is the only car in Pontiac's line to offer the rear-seat lower child-seat anchors that will become mandatory in the 2003 model year.

For '01, revised audio systems offer additional features and include an 8-speaker Monsoon sound system with AM/FM/CD/cassette and 7-band equalizer. Oldsmobile's Alero shares the Grand Am's chassis and powertrains, but targets a slightly more upscale, import-oriented clientele.

PERFORMANCE Grand Am isn't underpowered, but it looks faster than it is. The 4-cylinder has adequate spunk and should average at least 20 mpg, though it shakes at idle and groans under hard throttle. The V6 is quieter, smoother, quicker around town, and returned 19.4-21.5 mpg in our tests. The manual transmission gives 4-cylinder models a sportier feel, despite its somewhat notchy shift action. The well-behaved automatic downshifts quickly and rarely hunts between gears. Both engines have a sporty exhaust note that quickly grows tiresome. Wind noise isn't objectionable, but tires thrum intrusively on rough surfaces and thump loudly over tar strips.

Grand Am's ride is firm without being harsh, though it gets a bit choppy over broken pavement. Handling isn't Eurosedan precise, but turn-in is reasonably quick, there's good grip and balance in corners, and the steering is pleasantly firm. Stopping power is adequate, pedal feel is good.

ACCOMMODATIONS Grand Am is as overstyled inside as it is outside. Gauges are deeply recessed under tall twin "bonnets" and aren't very legible, while circular air vents protrude from little dashtop pods. By contrast, audio and climate controls are fairly straightforward and easy to reach. Front-seat room is sufficient, though some of our drivers find the steering wheel protrudes too far. Two adults won't mind riding in the sedan's rear seat, but coupes are much tighter in back and more difficult to enter or exit. Rear visibility isn't the best, especially with the available rear spoiler, but aft "cornering" lamps help with backing up at night. Trunks are spacious, but suffer from small openings and unusually high sills. Most interior surfaces are covered by padded vinyl and sturdy feeling plastics, but an SE sedan we tested suffered creaks in body and cabin trim.

Prices are accurate at time of publication; subject to manufacturer's change.

PONTIAC

VALUE Although less refined than some rivals, Grand Am is competent in most respects. Enjoyable road manners and competitive prices in particular make this a sporty compact worth looking at.

ENGINES

	dohc I4	ohv V6	ohv V6
Size, liters/cu. in.	2.4/146	3.4/207	3.4/207
Horsepower @ rpm	150 @ 5600	170 @ 4800	175 @ 4800
Torque (lb-ft) @ rpm	155 @ 4400	195 @ 4000	205 @ 4000
Availability	S[1]	O[2]	S[3]
EPA city/highway mpg			
5-speed OD manual	21/30		
4-speed OD automatic	21/29	21/32	21/32

1. SE, SE1. 2. SE1. 3. GT, GT1.

PRICES

Pontiac Grand Am

	Retail Price	Dealer Invoice
SE 2-door coupe	$16140	$14768
SE 4-door sedan	16440	15043
SE1 2-door coupe	17870	16351
SE1 4-door sedan	18170	16626
GT 2-door coupe	20235	18515
GT 4-door sedan	20535	18790
GT1 2-door coupe	21505	19677
GT1 4-door sedan	21805	19952
Destination charge	585	585

STANDARD EQUIPMENT:

SE: 2.4-liter dohc 4-cylinder engine, 5-speed manual transmission, traction control, dual front airbags, antilock brakes, daytime running lights, air conditioning, power steering, tilt steering wheel, cloth upholstery, front bucket seats, center console, cupholders, AM/FM/cassette, digital clock, tachometer, power door locks, remote fuel door and decklid release, variable intermittent wipers, rear defogger, automatic-off headlights, visor mirrors, floormats, dual outside mirrors, theft-deterrent system, fog lights, 215/60R15 tires, wheel covers.

SE1 adds: power mirrors, power windows, remote keyless entry, cruise control, 4-way manual driver seat w/power height adjustment, split folding rear seat, AM/FM/CD player, rear spoiler, alloy wheels.

GT adds: 3.4-liter V6 engine, 4-speed automatic transmission, 4-wheel disc brakes, variable-assist power steering, leather-wrapped steering wheel, 225/50R16 tires.

GT1 adds: 6-way power driver seat, AM/FM/cassette/CD player, Monsoon sound system, steering wheel radio controls, power sunroof.

Specifications begin on page 535.

PONTIAC

OPTIONAL EQUIPMENT:	Retail Price	Dealer Invoice

Major Packages

Solid Value Appearance Pkg., SE1	$1480	$1317
Manufacturer's discount price	855	761

Power sunroof, AM/FM/cassette/CD player, 225/50R16 tires, multi-spoke alloy wheels. NA with 3.4-liter V6 engine.

Solid Value Appearance Pkg., GT	1490	1326
Manufacturer's discount price	865	770

AM/FM/cassette/CD player, power sunroof, chrome alloy wheels.

Solid Value Appearance Pkg., GT1	1120	997
Manufacturer's discount price	800	712

Leather upholstery, chrome alloy wheels.

Powertrains

3.4-liter V6 engine, SE1	655	583

Includes variable-assist power steering. Requires 4-speed automatic transmission.

4-speed automatic transmission, SE, SE1	785	699

Comfort and Convenience

Power sunroof, SE1, GT	650	579
Leather upholstery, GT, GT1	475	423
AM/FM/CD player, SE	175	155
AM/FM/cassette/CD player, SE1	340	303
GT	195	174

Includes Monsoon sound system.

Cruise control, SE	235	209

Appearance and Miscellaneous

Alloy wheels, SE1	490	436

Includes 225/50R16 tires.

Chrome alloy wheels, GT, GT1	645	574

PONTIAC GRAND PRIX

CG RECOMMENDED AUTO

Front-wheel-drive midsize car; similar to Buick Century and Regal, Chevrolet Impala, and Oldsmobile Intrigue

Base price range: $20,300-$25,535. Built in USA. **Also consider:** Ford Taurus, Honda Accord, Nissan Maxima, Toyota Camry/Solara

FOR • Acceleration • Steering/handling **AGAINST** • Fuel economy (supercharged engine) • Rear-seat entry/exit (2-door)

Altered availability of GM's OnStar assistance system along with detail revisions inside and out head the list of 2001 changes.

Prices are accurate at time of publication; subject to manufacturer's change.

PONTIAC

Pontiac Grand Prix Special Edition 4-door sedan

Grand Prix offers base SE sedan, sportier GT coupe and sedan, and high performance GTP coupe and sedan. All have V6 engines: the SE a 175 horsepower 3.1 liter, GTs a 200-hp 3.8, GTPs a 240-hp supercharged 3.8. Automatic transmission, antilock 4-wheel disc brakes, and traction control are standard. OnStar, formerly optional on all Grand Prixs, is now standard on GTP and optional only on GT. The SE gets revised frontal styling along with standard rear spoiler and an emergency escape release inside the trunklid. Also for 2001, a dual-zone manual climate-control system is standard on GTP (replacing an automatic system), and a compass and outside temperature display are added to the automatic day/night rearview mirror that's standard on GTP, optional on GT. Grand Prix shares its platform and some running gear with the Buick Century and Regal, Oldsmobile Intrigue, and Chevrolet Impala, but only Pontiac offers a coupe body style.

PERFORMANCE Grand Prix plays its sporty role well. Acceleration is adequate with the 3.1 V6, strong with the 3.8, and muscular with the supercharged 3.8. Transmissions are admirably smooth and downshift quickly for passing. Fuel economy is so-so. A test 3.8-liter SE averaged 22.7 mpg in mostly highway driving but only 15 in urban commuting. A test GTP managed 18 mpg overall on the required premium gas.

The firm SE and GT suspensions deliver a stable, comfortable ride with little bounce over undulations. Their handling is capable, their steering firm and direct. The GTP's tauter chassis provides still sharper, flatter cornering, but also more tire thump and small-bump harshness. Braking is strong in any model, though modulation is mediocre. Wind and engine noise are low, but tire thrum frequently intrudes.

ACCOMMODATIONS Like its siblings, Grand Prix has good room for four adults, five in a pinch. Front-seat comfort is adequate, but the rear bench is low to the floor and provides little support. Doors open wide, but foot clearance through the rear doors is tight. Gauges and controls are easy to see and reach, but the overall look of the dashboard is busy and cluttered. Pontiac's EyeCue head-up display projects key instrument readings onto the windshield. Some testers find the option useful, oth-

Specifications begin on page 535.

PONTIAC

ers consider it gimmicky and switch it off.

A high parcel shelf limits vision astern for parking. The trunk is wide and has a long, flat floor, but the opening is narrow and liftover high. Grand Prixs we've tested have been impressively solid over rough roads, a feeling of substance at odds with the overuse of glossy, budget-grade plastic trim inside.

VALUE Grand Prix is a capable, sporty midsize that challenges the class leaders in overall value. Like the related Intrigue, it earns our Recommended nod, with the Pontiac feeling more the brash American in contrast to Oldsmobile's import-flavored aspirations.

ENGINES

	ohv V6	ohv V6	Supercharged ohv V6
Size, liters/cu. in.	3.1/191	3.8/231	3.8/231
Horsepower @ rpm	175 @ 5200	200 @ 5200	240 @ 5200
Torque (lb-ft) @ rpm	195 @ 4000	225 @ 4000	280 @ 3200
Availability	S[1]	S[2]	S[3]
EPA city/highway mpg			
4-speed OD automatic	20/30	20/30	18/28

1. SE. 2. GT. 3. GTP.

PRICES

Pontiac Grand Prix	Retail Price	Dealer Invoice
SE 4-door sedan	$20300	$18575
GT 2-door coupe	21865	20006
GT 4-door sedan	22015	20144
GTP 2-door coupe	25335	23182
GTP 4-door sedan	25535	23365
Destination charge	600	600

STANDARD EQUIPMENT:

SE: 3.1-liter V6 engine, 4-speed automatic transmission, enhanced traction control, antilock 4-wheel disc brakes, dual front airbags, daytime running lights, emergency inside trunk release, air conditioning, power steering, tilt steering wheel, cloth upholstery, front bucket seats, center console, cupholders, auxiliary power outlet, power mirrors, power windows, power door locks, AM/FM/cassette, digital clock, tachometer, tire inflation monitor, visor mirrors, intermittent wipers, rear defogger, map lights, automatic headlights, floormats, rear spoiler, fog lights, 205/70R15 tires, wheel covers.

GT adds to SE: 3.8-liter V6 engine, variable-assist power steering, cruise control, rear seat trunk pass-through, remote decklid release, 225/60R16 tires, alloy wheels.

GTP adds: 3.8-liter supercharged V6 240-horsepower engine, full-function traction control, OnStar System w/one year service (roadside assistance, emergency services; other services available), dual-zone manual climate

Prices are accurate at time of publication; subject to manufacturer's change.

PONTIAC

control, 6-way power driver seat w/power lumbar adjustment, remote keyless entry, head-up instrument display, AM/FM/CD player w/equalizer, leather-wrapped steering wheel w/radio controls, automatic day/night rearview mirror, compass, outside temperature indicator, illuminated visor mirrors, overhead console, trip computer, sport suspension.

OPTIONAL EQUIPMENT:
Major Packages

	Retail Price	Dealer Invoice
Option Group 1SB, SE	$1100	$979
Manufacturer's discount price	675	601

Cruise control, 6-way power driver seat, rear seat trunk pass-through, cargo net, remote decklid release, 225/60R16 tires, alloy wheels.

Option Group 1SB, GT	1190	1059
Manufacturer's discount price, GT	765	681

Leather-wrapped steering wheel w/radio controls, 6-way power driver's seat, cargo net, remote keyless entry, overhead console, theft-deterrent system w/alarm.

Option Group 1SC, GT sedan	1602	1426
GT coupe	1572	1399

Group 1SB plus OnStar System w/one year service (roadside assistance, emergency services; other services available), trip computer, automatic day/night rearview mirror, compass, outside temperature indicator, illuminated visor mirrors, rear reading lights (sedan).

Option Group 1SD, GT sedan	3012	2681
GT coupe	2982	2654

Group 1SC plus leather upholstery, heated driver seat, 4-way power lumbar support, head-up instrument display, power sunroof.

Option Group 1SB, GTP	1540	1370
Manufacturer's discount price	1115	992

Leather upholstery, power sunroof.

Premium Lighting Pkg., GT sedan	637	567
GT coupe	607	540

OnStar System w/one year service (roadside assistance, emergency services; other services available), automatic day/night rearview mirror, compass, outside temperature indicator, illuminated visor mirrors, rear reading lights (sedan).

GTX Ram Air Pkg., GTP	2499	1999

Ram air induction system, functional hood scoops, K&N air filter, 250-horsepower engine, badging, gold plated key fobs.

Special Edition Pkg., GT coupe, GTP coupe	2490	2217
Manufacturer's discount price	1995	1776

Leather upholstery, two-tone seats, dashboard and console trim plates, hood heat-vents, roof fences, bright exhaust tips, chrome alloy wheels.

Security Pkg., SE	210	187

Remote keyless entry, theft-deterrent system w/alarm.

Specifications begin on page 535.

PONTIAC

Comfort and Convenience

	Retail Price	Dealer Invoice
6-way power driver seat, GT	$270	$240
Driver seat 4-way power lumbar support, GT	100	89
Requires option group. Includes heat when ordered w/leather upholstery.		
Heated driver seat, GT, GTP	50	45
Requires leather upholstery.		
Leather upholstery, GT, GTP	495	441
GT requires option group.		
AM/FM/CD player, SE, GT	100	89
SE requires option group.		
AM/FM/CD player w/graphic equalizer, GT	125	111
Requires option group.		
Bose sound system, GT	395	352
GTP	370	329
GT requires option group, AM/FM/CD player.		
Power sunroof, GT, GTP	570	507
GT requires option group. Deletes overhead console.		
Head-up display, GT	275	245
Requires Group 1SC.		
Polished alloy wheels, GT, GTP	325	289
GT requires option group.		

PONTIAC MONTANA

Pontiac Montana

Front-wheel-drive minivan; similar to Chevrolet Venture and Oldsmobile Silhouette

Base price range: $24,180-$26,520. Built in USA. **Also consider:** Dodge Caravan, Ford Windstar, Honda Odyssey

FOR • Ride • Passenger and cargo room **AGAINST** • Fuel economy

A stowable third-row bench seat and a power left-side rear door are newly available for Pontiac's minivan. The 2001 Montana also gets a standard OnStar assistance system and a minor front and rear facelift.

Prices are accurate at time of publication; subject to manufacturer's change.

PONTIAC

Montana shares its underskin design with the Chevrolet Venture and Oldsmobile Silhouette. Like Venture, Montana offers regular- and extended-length bodies, both with dual sliding rear side doors. A power right-side sliding door is optional, and extended versions can be ordered with an optional power left-side door, as well.

Montana can accommodate six to eight passengers. Front seats are buckets, while the second row gets two or three bucket seats or twin captain's chairs. The third row can be fitted with two buckets or a folding bench seat. New for extended-length models is a stowable third-row bench that folds even with a new covered floor-mounted parcel tray at the rear of the load area. The second-row integrated child safety seat is discontinued, but outboard second-row seats now have lower anchors for rear child seats.

A 3.4-liter V6 with automatic transmission is the sole powertrain. Antilock brakes and puncture-sealing tires are standard, as are front side airbags, which this year gain head and chest protection on the driver's side. Traction control is standard on the 7-passenger regular-length, optional on the extended-length. Automatic load-leveling is optional on both 7-passenger models, where a 6-disc dashboard CD changer and Homelink universal garage-door opener are newly optional. For 2001, dashboard-mounted pop-out cupholders replace seat-mounted ones, and new standard features include GM's OnStar assistance system, remote keyless entry, and a CD player. All Montanas also wear a redesigned grille and front and rear facias.

Newly optional for the extended-length model is Ultrasonic rear parking assist, a reverse sensing system that detects obstructions behind when backing up. Also optional on the extended is MontanaVision, a rear-seat entertainment system with a dashboard-mounted VCR, which gains a larger 6.8-inch screen (versus 5.6-inch) and new cordless headphones. Montana's performance and accommodations mirror those of similarly equipped Chevrolet Ventures.

The Chevrolet Venture report includes an evaluation of the Montana.

ENGINES

	ohv V6
Size, liters/cu. in.	3.4/207
Horsepower @ rpm	185 @ 5200
Torque (lb-ft) @ rpm	210 @ 4000
Availability	S

EPA city/highway mpg
4-speed OD automatic	19/26

PRICES

Pontiac Montana

	Retail Price	Dealer Invoice
Base regular length 4-door van, 6-passenger	$24180	$21883
Base regular length 4-door van, 7-passenger	25875	23417

Specifications begin on page 535.

PONTIAC

	Retail Price	Dealer Invoice
Base extended 4-door van, 7-passenger	$26520	$24001
Destination charge	640	640

STANDARD EQUIPMENT:

Base: 3.4-liter V6 engine, 4-speed automatic transmission, traction control (regular length 7-passenger), driver- and passenger-side side airbags, front side-impact airbags, antilock brakes, daytime running lights, front air conditioning, interior air filter, OnStar System w/one year service (roadside assistance, emergency services; other services available), power steering, tilt steering wheel, cruise control, dual sliding rear doors, cloth upholstery, front bucket seats w/manual lumbar adjustment, second and third row bucket seats (regular length 6-passenger), two second row captain chairs and third row 3-passenger split folding bench seat (regular length 7-passenger, extended), cupholders, heated power mirrors, power windows, power door locks, remote keyless entry, AM/FM/CD player, digital clock, tachometer, visor mirrors, intermittent wipers, rear defogger, intermittent rear wiper/washer, auxiliary power outlets, map lights, automatic headlights, floormats, theft-deterrent system, roof rack, rear privacy glass, fog lights, 215/70R15 self-sealing white-letter tires, wheel covers.

OPTIONAL EQUIPMENT:
Major Packages

Option Pkg. 1SB,
  regular length 7-passenger 1820   1647
  Power sliding rear passenger-side door, 6-way power driver seat, leather-wrapped steering wheel w/radio control, rear radio controls and headphone jacks, driver information center, illuminated visor mirrors, universal garage door opener, Sport Performance and Handling Pkg. (saddle bag storage, sport suspension, performance tires), air inflater, load-leveling suspension, alloy wheels.

Option Pkg. 1SD, extended 1125   1018
  Traction control, power sliding rear passenger-side door, saddle bag storage, air inflater, load-leveling suspension, alloy wheels.

Option Pkg. 1SE, extended 2555   2312
  Option Pkg. 1SD plus rear air conditioning, 6-way power driver seat, leather-wrapped steering wheel w/radio controls, rear radio controls and headphone jacks, driver information center, illuminated visor mirrors, universal garage door opener, theft-deterrent system w/alarm.

Option Pkg. 1SF, extended 2910   2634
  Option Pkg. 1SE plus Sport Performance and Handling Pkg. (sport suspension, performance tires).

Option Pkg. 1SG, extended 3060   2769
  Option Pkg. 1SF plus power sliding rear driver-side door, rear parking aid.

Prices are accurate at time of publication; subject to manufacturer's change.

PONTIAC

	Retail Price	Dealer Invoice
Option Pkg. 1SH, extended	$4755	$4303

Power sliding rear passenger-side door, rear air conditioning, 6-way power driver seat, leather-wrapped steering wheel w/radio controls, rear radio controls and headphone jacks, driver information center, illuminated visor mirrors, universal garage door opener, Montana Vision Entertainment System (fold-down LCD screen, videocassette player, remote control, video game input jack, wireless headphones, videocassette storage), saddle bag storage, theft-deterrent system w/alarm, air inflater, load-leveling suspension, alloy wheels.

Option Pkg. 1SJ, extended	5355	4846

Option Pkg. 1SH plus traction control, power sliding rear driver-side door, rear parking aid, Sport Performance and Handling Pkg. (sport suspension, performance tires).

Trailer Pkg., 7-passenger	165	147

Trailer wiring harness, heavy-duty engine and transmission cooling, heavy-duty flasher. Requires option pkg.

Safety Features

Ultrasonic rear parking assist, extended	150	134

Requires Option Pkg. 1SD/E/F/H.

Comfort and Convenience

Power sliding rear driver-side rear door, extended	—	—

Requires option pkg.

Rear air conditioning, extended	450	401
6-way power driver seat, 7-passenger	270	240

Extended requires option pkg.

7-passenger quad seating, 7-passenger	—	—

Includes quad captain chairs, rear stowable rear bench seat (extended).

8-passenger seating, 7-passenger	—	—

Includes five bucket seats, rear stowable bench seat (extended).

Leather upholstery, 7-passenger	1175	1046

Includes 6-way power driver seat, leather-wrapped steering wheel w/radio controls. NA w/optional seating.

Heated front seats, 7-passenger	195	174

Requires leather upholstery. Regular 7-passenger requires Option Pkg. 1SB. Extended requires Option Pkg. 1SE/F/G/J.

AM/FM/cassette/CD player, 7-passenger	100	89

Includes rear-seat audio controls and headphone jacks.

In-dash 6-disc CD changer, 7-passenger	395	352

Requires leather-wrapped steering wheel w/radio controls, rear radio controls.

Rear radio controls, 7-passenger	125	111
Leather-wrapped steering wheel, 7-passenger	185	165

Includes radio controls.

Alloy wheels	280	249

Specifications begin on page 535.

PONTIAC

PONTIAC SUNFIRE

Pontiac Sunfire SE 4-door sedan

Front-wheel-drive subcompact car; similar to Chevrolet Cavalier
Base price range: $14,175-$16,295. Built in USA and Mexico.
Also consider: Ford Focus, Honda Civic, Toyota Corolla

FOR • Fuel economy • Acceleration (2.4-liter engine) **AGAINST** • Rear visibility • Rear-seat comfort • Interior materials • Rear-seat entry/exit (2-door)

After dropping its convertible version midway through the 2000 model year, Pontiac's smallest car enters 2001 with a higher level of standard equipment.

Sunfire shares mechanical components with the Chevrolet Cavalier but has slightly different styling. It's offered as a 4-door SE sedan and a 2-door SE and GT coupe. All Sunfires use a 4-cylinder engine. A 2.2 liter is standard on SE, a 2.4 is standard on GTs, optional on SEs. Manual transmission is standard. A 3-speed automatic transmission is optional on 2.2s, and both engines can get an extra-cost 4-speed automatic. Antilock brakes are standard. Traction control is included with the 4-speed automatic.

New standard equipment for '01 includes an emergency release inside the trunk, a cassette player, and on coupes, a rear spoiler. Sunfire's performance and accommodations mirror those of like-equipped Cavaliers.

The Chevrolet Cavalier report includes an evaluation of the Sunfire.

ENGINES

	ohv I4	dohc I4
Size, liters/cu. in.	2.2/133	2.4/146
Horsepower @ rpm	115 @ 5000	150 @ 5600
Torque (lb-ft) @ rpm	135 @ 3600	155 @ 4400
Availability	S[1]	S[2]

Prices are accurate at time of publication; subject to manufacturer's change.

PONTIAC

EPA city/highway mpg

5-speed OD manual	23/33	22/32
3-speed automatic	22/28	
4-speed OD automatic	22/30	21/29

1. SE. 2. GT; optional, SE.

PRICES

Pontiac Sunfire	Retail Price	Dealer Invoice
SE 2-door coupe	$14175	$1312
SE 4-door sedan	14430	13348
GT 2-door coupe	16295	15073
Destination charge	540	540

STANDARD EQUIPMENT:

SE: 2.2-liter 4-cylinder engine, 5-speed manual transmission, dual front airbags, antilock brakes, daytime running lights, emergency inside trunk release, air conditioning, power steering, cloth upholstery, bucket seats, center console, folding rear seat, AM/FM/cassette, digital clock, tachometer, visor mirrors, intermittent wipers, rear defogger, floormats, left remote and right manual outside mirrors, theft-deterrent system, rear spoiler (coupe), 195/70R14 tires, wheel covers.

GT adds to SE coupe: 2.4-liter dohc 4-cylinder engine, tilt leather-wrapped steering wheel, AM/FM/CD player, fog lights, sport suspension, 205/55R16 tires, alloy wheels.

OPTIONAL EQUIPMENT:
Major Packages

Option Group 1SB, SE	1115	995

Tilt steering wheel, 4-speed automatic transmission, traction control, AM/FM/CD player.

Option Group 1SC, SE coupe	1865	1660
SE sedan	1905	1695

Group 1SB plus cruise control, power door locks, remote keyless entry, variable intermittent wipers, overhead console w/storage, map lights, cargo net, theft-deterrent system w/alarm.

Sun and Sound Pkg. w/Group 1SB, SE coupe	2370	2109
Manufacturer's discount price	1845	1642

Group 1SB plus power sunroof, 195/65R15 tires.

Sun and Sound Pkg. w/Group 1SC, SE coupe	3080	2741
Manufacturer's discount price	2555	2274

Group 1SC plus power sunroof, 195/65R15 tires.

Special Edition Pkg. w/Group 1SB, SE sedan	2685	2389
Manufacturer's discount price	2105	1873

Group 1SB plus power mirrors and windows, power door locks, remote keyless entry, theft-deterrent system w/alarm, 195/65R15 tires.

Specifications begin on page 535.

PONTIAC

	Retail Price	Dealer Invoice
Special Edition Pkg. w/Group 1SC, SE sedan	$3065	$2728
Manufacturer's discount price	2485	2212
Group 1SC plus power mirrors and windows, 195/65R15 tires.		
Security Pkg., SE coupe	370	329
Power door locks, remote keyless entry, theft-deterrent system w/alarm. Requires Group 1SB.		
Option Group 1SB, GT	1480	1317
4-speed automatic transmission, traction control, cruise control, power door locks, remote keyless entry, variable intermittent wipers, theft-deterrent system w/alarm.		
Option Group 1SC, GT	2135	1900
Group 1SB plus power mirrors and windows, Monsoon sound system, over head console w/storage, cargo net.		
Sun and Storm Pkg. w/Group 1SB, GT	2770	2465
Manufacturer's discount price	2270	2020
Option Group 1SB plus power sunroof, Monsoon sound system.		
Sun and Storm Pkg. w/Group 1SC, GT	3190	2839
Manufacturer's discount price	2690	2394
Option Group 1SC plus power sunroof.		
Power Pkg., SE coupe, GT	380	338
Power mirrors and windows. SE requires Group 1SC. GT requires Group 1SB.		

Powertrains

2.4-liter dohc 4-cylinder engine, SE	450	401
Requires Group 1SC and 195/65R15 tires.		
3-speed automatic transmission, SE	700	623
SE w/Group 1SB (credit)	(110)	(98)
NA with 2.4-liter engine.		
4-speed automatic transmission, GT	810	721
Includes traction control.		
5-speed manual transmission, SE, GT	(810)	(721)
Requires Group 1SB/1SC. SE sedan requires 2.2-liter 4-cylinder engine.		

Comfort and Convenience

Cruise control, SE w/Group 1SB	235	209
AM/FM/CD player, SE	155	138
AM/FM/cassette/CD player, GT	100	89
Monsoon sound system, SE coupe, GT	195	174
Requires AM/FM/CD player or AM/FM/cassette/CD player. SE requires Group 1SB or 1SC. GT requires Group 1SB.		
Power sunroof, GT w/Group 1SB	595	530
GT w/Group 1SC	555	494
Replaces overhead console when ordered with Group 1SC.		
Alloy wheels, SE	295	263
Requires Option Group 1SC.		

Prices are accurate at time of publication; subject to manufacturer's change.

SAAB

SAAB 9-3

Saab 9-3 4-door hatchback

Front-wheel-drive near-luxury car

Base price range: $26,495-$44,995. Built in Sweden and Finland.
Also consider: Acura TL, Audi A4, BMW 3-Series, Lexus IS 300

FOR • Acceleration • Braking • Cargo room (exc. convertible)
AGAINST • Rear-seat room/comfort (convertible) • Rear visibility (convertible) • Rear-seat entry/exit (exc. 4-door)

This year's compact Saabs consist of base 2- and 4-door hatchbacks, uplevel SE 4-door and convertible, and high-performance Viggen versions of all three body styles. Last year's base ragtop is gone, but this year's SE has been re-equipped to sell for only $200 more. Engines are strictly turbocharged 4-cylinder: base 185-horsepower 2.0-liter, High Output SE with 205 hp, and 2.3-liter Viggen with 230. Viggens come only with 5-speed manual shift; other models offer optional automatic. For 2001, all 9-3s add standard traction control, which wasn't previously offered. It joins standard 4-wheel antilock disc brakes, seat-mounted front side airbags, and Saab's front Active Head Restraints that are claimed to minimize whiplash injury. Convertibles have a lined power top with glass rear window and electric defroster. Also new for 2001 is GM's OnStar satellite-based communications system as standard rather than optional. (GM owns Saab's car division.) This year's OnStar adds voice-activated Internet access, phone, and e-mail functions. OnStar service is now free for the first 12 months instead of extra. Continued from mid-2000 is free scheduled maintenance for 3 years/36,000 miles for all 9-3s, though "wear and tear" items are not covered.

EVALUATION From the responsive but calm base model to the young-colt feel of the Viggen, the 9-3s offer sporty driving in a space-efficient—though somewhat quirky—package. Our base 5-speed test car ran 0-60 mph in a quick 7.5 seconds and averaged 19.4 mpg; SE models are slightly faster, and our 4-door averaged 21.3 mpg. Alas, all engines are a bit weak below 3000 rpm, and turbo

Specifications begin on page 535.

SAAB

lag—a delay in throttle response—makes smooth driving tricky. Handling is assured, however, and the now-standard traction control corrects a competitive deficit. SEs and Viggens ride much stiffer than the notably compliant base models. Hatchbacks have fairly commodious seating for five and near-wagonlike cargo room, but convertibles seat four only and stow much less gear. Gauges and controls are well-located, but the floor-mount ignition switch is a debatable Saab tradition. Detail finish is good and materials classy, but one test convertible suffered noticeable body flex over bumps, plus a creaky top. For near-luxury Swedish-style, most buyers pick a Volvo S70 sedan or V70 wagon, leaving the 9-3 largely to Saab loyalists.

ENGINES

	Turbocharged dohc I4	Turbocharged dohc I4	Turbocharged dohc I4
Size, liters/cu. in.	2.0/121	2.0/121	2.3/140
Horsepower @ rpm	185 @ 5500	205 @ 5500	230 @ 5500
Torque (lb-ft) @ rpm	194 @ 2100	209 @ 2200	258 @ 2500
Availability	S[1]	S[2]	S[3]
EPA city/highway mpg			
5-speed OD manual	19/27	20/27	20/29
4-speed OD automatic	19/25	20/26	

1. Base; 184 lb-ft @ 1900 rpm with auto. trans. 2. SE; 184 lb-ft @ 1900 rpm with auto trans. 3. Viggen.

PRICES

Saab 9-3	Retail Price	Dealer Invoice
Base 2-door hatchback	$26495	$24905
Base 4-door hatchback	26995	25132
SE 4-door hatchback	32595	30411
SE 2-door convertible	39995	36995
Viggen 2-door hatchback	37995	34575
Viggen 4-door hatchback	37995	34575
Viggen 2-door convertible	44995	40945
Destination charge	575	575

STANDARD EQUIPMENT:

Base: 2.0-liter turbocharged dohc 4-cylinder 185-horsepower engine, 5-speed manual transmission, traction control, dual front airbags, front side-airbags, front seat active head restraints, antilock 4-wheel disc brakes, daytime running lights, air conditioning, interior air filter, OnStar System w/one year service (roadside assistance, emergency services; other services available), power steering, telescoping steering wheel, cruise control, cloth upholstery, front bucket seats, driver seat manual lumbar adjustment, split folding rear seat w/trunk pass-through, cupholders, heated power mirrors, power windows, power door locks, remote keyless entry, AM/FM/cassette/weath-

Prices are accurate at time of publication; subject to manufacturer's change.

SAAB

erband w/CD changer controls, steering-wheel radio controls, power antenna, digital clock, tachometer, trip computer, variable intermittent wipers, rear defogger, rear wiper/washer, illuminated visor mirrors, automatic-off headlights, floormats, theft-deterrent system, headlight wiper/washer, front and rear fog lights, cornering lights, rear spoiler, 195/60VR15 tires, alloy wheels.

SE convertible adds: 2.0-liter turbocharged dohc 4-cylinder 205-horsepower engine, leather upholstery, 8-way power driver seat, folding rear seat w/trunk pass-through, leather-wrapped steering wheel, wood interior trim, upgraded sound system, power convertible top, sport suspension, 205/50ZR16 tires. *Deletes*: rear wiper/washer, rear spoiler.

SE hatchback adds to Base: 2.0-liter turbocharged dohc 4-cylinder 205-horsepower engine, automatic climate control, leather upholstery, 8-way power front seats w/driver seat memory, leather-wrapped steering wheel, wood interior trim, power sunroof, upgraded sound system, 205/50ZR16 tires.

Viggen adds: 2.3-liter turbocharged dohc 4-cylinder 230-horsepower engine, special interior trim, front sport seats, folding rear seat w/trunk pass-through (convertible), aerodynamic body cladding, performance sport suspension, 215/45ZR17 tires, deletes power antenna.

OPTIONAL EQUIPMENT:

	Retail Price	Dealer Invoice
Major Packages		
Premium Pkg., SE convertible	$1495	$1286
Automatic climate control, 8-way power passenger seat, driver seat memory, rear spoiler.		
Powertrains		
4-speed automatic transmission, Base, SE	1200	1032
Comfort and Convenience		
Power sunroof, Base hatchback	1150	989
Leather upholstery, Base	1350	1161
Includes leather-wrapped steering wheel.		
Heated front seats	450	387

SAAB 9-5

Front-wheel-drive luxury car

Base price range: $33,995-$40,875. Built in Sweden. **Also consider:** Acura RL, Lincoln LS, Mercedes-Benz E-Class

FOR • Acceleration • Handling/roadholding • Passenger and cargo room • Build quality **AGAINST** • Road noise • Climate controls

The larger Saabs return as sedans and wagons in base, SE, and sporty Aero versions; the last have the most power, special lower-body skirting, and uprated suspension. All have standard antilock 4-wheel disc brakes,

Specifications begin on page 535.

SAAB

Saab 9-5 4-door sedan

traction control, front head/chest side airbags, and front head restraints that spring forward to counteract whiplash in a rear-end collision. Three turbocharged engines continue. This year's base 2.3-liter 4-cylinder gains 15 horsepower for 185 total. Aeros retain a 230-hp version, SEs a 200-hp 3.0-liter V6. Automatic transmission remains standard for SEs and optional elsewhere. General Motors owns Saab, and its OnStar communication system is now standard instead of optional; also, the system adds voice-activated Internet access, phone, and e-mail functions. Finally, all 9-5s now come with free scheduled maintenance for 3 years/36,000 miles excluding "wear and tear" items like tires.

EVALUATION These are pleasant, stable high-speed cruisers that can entertain on twisty roads. Acceleration is strong too, despite some "turbo lag" throttle-response delay. Our test 4-cylinder/automatic base sedan did 0-60 mph in 8.3 seconds and averaged 22 mpg. A V6 SE sedan ran 0-60 in 7.6 seconds and averaged 19.7. Both use regular fuel. Aeros feel tepid off the line but excel over 40 mph; our automatic Aero sedan averaged 19.1 mpg on the required premium gas. Handling is secure and predictable, though the low-profile tires standard on Aero and optional on other 9-5s have poor wet-weather traction on take-off. Braking is swift and consistent, ride absorbent, noise levels low, though tire rumble can intrude on coarse pavement. Interiors are adult-size comfortable, nicely appointed, and include Saab's trademark floor-mounted ignition switch—which takes getting used to. Sedans boast great trunk space, wagons a large luggage bay that can be enhanced by an optional rollout load floor; no third-row wagon seating, though. The automatic climate control mounts too low for convenience, but ergonomics are otherwise good. Overall, the 9-5s are impressive European cars with a personality that appeals to both individualists and anyone interested in efficient design.

ENGINES	Turbocharged dohc I4	Turbocharged dohc V6	Turbocharged dohc I4
Size, liters/cu. in.	2.3/140	3.0/180	2.3/140
Horsepower @ rpm	185 @ 5500	200 @ 5000	230 @ 5500

Prices are accurate at time of publication; subject to manufacturer's change.

SAAB

	Turbocharged dohc I4	Turbocharged dohc V6	Turbocharged dohc I4
Torque (lb-ft) @ rpm	207 @ 1800	229 @ 2500	258 @ 1900
Availability	S[1]	S[2]	S[3]
EPA city/highway mpg			
5-speed OD manual	21/29		20/28
4-speed OD automatic	19/27	18/26	18/24

1. Base. 2. SE. 3. Aero: 243 lb-ft @ 1900 rpm with auto. trans.

PRICES

Saab 9-5

	Retail Price	Dealer Invoice
Base 4-door sedan	$33995	$31615
Base 4-door wagon	34695	32266
SE 4-door sedan	38650	35751
SE 4-door wagon	39350	36399
Aero 4-door sedan	40175	37162
Aero 4-door wagon	40875	37809
Destination charge	575	575

STANDARD EQUIPMENT:

Base: 2.3-liter turbocharged dohc 4-cylinder 185-horsepower engine, 5-speed manual transmission, traction control, dual front airbags, front side-airbags, front seat active head restraints, antilock 4-wheel disc brakes, daytime running lights, air conditioning w/dual-zone automatic climate control, interior air filter, OnStar System w/one year service (roadside assistance, emergency services; other services available), power steering, tilt/telescoping leather-wrapped steering wheel, cruise control, cloth upholstery, 8-way power front bucket seats, center console, cupholders, split folding rear seat w/trunk pass-through, wood interior trim, heated power mirrors, power windows, power door locks, remote keyless entry, AM/FM/cassette/CD player, steering-wheel radio controls, digital clock, tachometer, trip computer, power sunroof, glove box refrigerator, illuminated visor mirrors, variable-intermittent wipers, rear defogger, remote decklid/fuel door release, automatic-off headlights, parcel shelf/cargo cover (wagon), floormats, theft-deterrent system, roof rails (wagon), front and rear fog lights, headlight wiper/washer, cornering lights, 215/55R16 tires, alloy wheels.

SE adds to Base: 3.0-liter turbocharged dohc V6 engine, 4-speed automatic transmission, leather upholstery, memory driver seat and mirrors, tilt-down passenger-side mirror, Harman/Kardon sound system, automatic day/night rearview mirror.

Aero adds: 2.3-liter turbocharged dohc 4-cylinder 230-horsepower

SAAB • SATURN

engine, 5-speed manual transmission, bodyside cladding, sport suspension, 225/45ZR17 tires.

OPTIONAL EQUIPMENT:	Retail Price	Dealer Invoice

Major Packages
Premium Pkg., Base $1995 $1716
  Leather upholstery, driver seat memory, Harman/Kardon sound system.

Powertrains
4-speed automatic transmission, Base, Aero.......... 1200 1032

Comfort and Convenience
Power-ventilated front seats..................................... 995 856
  Base requires Premium Pkg.
Heated front
  and rear seats.. 595 512

Appearance and Miscellaneous
Wheel and Tire Pkg.,
  Base, SE.. 1650 1370
  One-piece alloy wheels, 225/45ZR17 tires.
Wheel upgrade, Aero 1650 1370
  Two-piece alloy wheels.

SATURN L-SERIES

Saturn L300 4-door sedan

Front-wheel-drive midsize car

Base price range: $14,495-$21,360. Built in USA. **Also consider:** Honda Accord, Toyota Camry, Volkswagen Passat

FOR • Acceleration (V6 models) • Steering/handling **AGAINST** • Rear-seat comfort

Optional side curtain airbags are the main addition to Saturn's midsize sedan and wagon for 2001. The L-Series is based on the German Opel

Prices are accurate at time of publication; subject to manufacturer's change.

SATURN

Vectra (Saturn and Opel are part of General Motors) and uses Saturn's dent- and rust-resistant polymer panels for front fenders, doors, and bumper fascias; other body parts are steel.

LS, LS1, and LS2 sedans essentially continue, but for '01 they're renamed L100, L200, and L300 respectively. LW1 and LW2 wagons likewise change to LW200 and LW300. The 100 and 200 models have a 4-cylinder engine. The 300s use a V6 shared with the Saab 9-5, but without Saab's turbocharger (Saab also is a General Motors holding). The 4-cylinder teams with manual transmission or extra-cost automatic; the V6 has automatic only.

Four-wheel disc brakes are standard on 300s. Antilock brakes are optional on all models and include traction control. The curtain airbags are designed to drop down and inflate from above the front and rear side windows to provide head protection in side impacts. They're optional on all L-Series models. Lower-body side airbags are not offered.

PERFORMANCE The L-Series is a reasonably accomplished performer distinguished by fine handling. Suspension tuning copied from Opel pays off in impressive high-speed stability and confident cornering. Steering is linear and communicative, although it feels heavy at low speeds and, in the 4-cylinder/manual we tested, light at high speeds. Wagons and sedans handle nearly identically, although wagons ride marginally stiffer and neither absorbs bumps as well as Toyota's Camry. In short, L-Series buyers get a firm Eurostyle ride in exchange for sporty road manners. The basic Opel braking system brings impressive stopping power and pedal feel.

As for acceleration, Saturn pegs the automatic-transmission L200 at 9.8 seconds 0-60 mph, the V6/automatic L300 at 8.2. That's roughly a second behind our test Accords, but in practice, both L-Series powertrains are up to most tasks. Some early V6 models we tested exhibited poor throttle response off the line and suffered slow downshifts in passing situations. Others felt spry, with automatics that furnished alert downshifts even in hilly terrain. The 5-speed adds a sporty flair, but provides no great leap in performance. A V6/automatic sedan averaged 19 mpg in our tests, a 4-cylinder/automatic wagon returned an impressive 26.6 mpg. Noise isolation is as good as most competitors, but no L-Series model is as quiet as a Camry.

ACCOMMODATIONS Four adults get as much room as in an Accord or Camry, although the L-Series doesn't match their interior refinement. The available leather-upholstered buckets come with seat heaters, but the cloth seats are more supportive. Rear head and leg room is ample, but the rear cushion is soft and low to the floor, and the small fold-down armrest is useless.

Instrumentation is large and clear, but the cowl is rather tall, and vision directly aft is pinched by the high deck. There's independent control of air conditioning in any vent mode, but the crude fan-speed switch is in

Specifications begin on page 535.

SATURN

contrast to smooth rotary temperature and air-flow dials. Illuminated power-window switches are in the center console. So is the gear-position readout for the automatic transmission; unfortunately, it washes out in direct sunlight, and there's no redundant indicator in the instrument cluster. The sedan's large, accessible trunk is a competitive advantage, as is the availability of the wagon, a body style few rivals offer.

Our test cars were rattle-free, but L-Series interiors have a discount-bin feel in their details typified by the turn-signal lever's brittle movement, door handles of uninviting plated plastic, and small, plasticky audio controls.

VALUE Although not a class-leader in any respect, the L-Series is a decent midsize car, offering good value. Base prices are well below comparable Accords and Camrys, but Saturn's no-haggle, full-sticker-price policy doesn't allow negotiating. However, the L-series has been a slower seller than Saturn hoped, so special leasing and financing rates may be available.

ENGINES

	dohc I4	dohc V6
Size, liters/cu. in.	2.2/134	3.0/183
Horsepower @ rpm	135 @ 5200	182 @ 5600
Torque (lb-ft) @ rpm	142 @ 4400	190 @ 3600
Availability	S[1]	S[2]
EPA city/highway mpg		
5-speed OD manual	25/33	
4-speed OD automatic	24/33	20/26

1. L100, L200, LW200. 2. L300, LW300.

PRICES

Saturn L-Series	Retail Price	Dealer Invoice
L-100 4-door sedan, 5-speed	$14495	$12901
L-100 4-door sedan, automatic	15355	13666
L-200 4-door sedan, 5-speed	16750	14908
L-200 4-door sedan, automatic	17610	15673
LW-200 4-door wagon, automatic	18835	16763
L-300 4-door sedan, automatic	19495	17350
LW-300 4-door wagon, automatic	21360	19010
Destination charge	500	500

STANDARD EQUIPMENT:

L-100: 2.2-liter dohc 4-cylinder engine, 5-speed manual or 4-speed automatic transmission, dual front airbags, daytime running lights, air conditioning, power steering, tilt steering wheel, cloth upholstery, front bucket seats, center console, cupholders, split folding rear seat, power mirrors, AM/FM radio, digital clock, rear defogger, auxiliary power outlets, remote decklid release, variable intermittent wipers, 195/65R15 tires.

Prices are accurate at time of publication; subject to manufacturer's change.

SATURN

L-200/LW-200 adds: heated power mirrors, power windows, power door locks, remote keyless entry, cruise control, AM/FM/CD player, height-adjustable driver seat, visor mirrors, rear wiper/washer (wagon), cargo cover (wagon), theft-deterrent system, roof rails (wagon).

L-300/L-300 adds: 3.0-liter dohc V6 engine, 4-speed automatic transmission, 4-wheel disc brakes, leather-wrapped steering wheel, AM/FM/cassette/CD player, floormats, fog lights, sport suspension, 205/65R15 tires, alloy wheels.

OPTIONAL EQUIPMENT:

	Retail Price	Dealer Invoice
Safety Features		
Front and rear side head-protection system	$395	$352
Antilock brakes w/traction control	595	530
Comfort and Convenience		
Power sunroof, L-200/L-300 sedan	725	645
6-way power driver seat, L-200, LW-200, L-300, LW-300	325	289
Leather upholstery, L-200, LW-200, L-300, LW-300	1295	1153
Includes heated front seats, leather-wrapped steering wheel. Requires power driver seat.		
AM/FM/CD player, L-100	290	258
AM/FM/cassette/CD player, L-100	510	454
L-200, LW-200	220	196
Advanced Audio System, L-200, LW-200, L-300, LW-300	220	196
Includes premium speakers, amplifier, subwoofer. L-200/LW-200 require AM/FM/cassette/CD player.		
Appearance and Miscellaneous		
Rear spoiler, L-100/L-200 sedan	250	223
Fog lights, L-200, LW-200	225	200
Alloy wheels, L-200, LW-200	350	312

SATURN S-SERIES

Front-wheel-drive subcompact car

Base price range: $10,570-$16,505. Built in USA. **Also consider:** Ford Focus, Honda Civic, Mazda Protege

FOR • Cargo room (wagon) • Fuel economy • Acceleration (SC2, SL2, SW2) **AGAINST** • Acceleration (SL, SL1, SC1) • Rear-seat room • Brake performance • Rear-seat entry/exit (2-door)

Saturn's 2001 S-series coupes arrived in the spring of 2000 with updated styling. They retained their unique 3-door design that incorporates a small rear-hinged left-side back door. Sedans and wagons followed in the fall, bringing few major changes save for side curtain airbags that are now optional on all Saturns. However, the base SL sedan added some

SATURN

Saturn SL2

new standard features, including body-colored bumpers (formerly black), right-side rearview mirror, and power steering. All keep Saturn's dent- and rust-resistant plastic front and side body panels.

Sedans continue in SL, SL1, and SL2 form, coupes in SC1 and SC2 models. The wagon comes in SW2 trim only. SL and "1" models retain a 100-horsepower 1.9-liter overhead-cam 4-cylinder, the "2" versions a 124-hp twincam variant of that engine. Manual transmission is standard. An extra-cost 4-speed automatic is available on all but the SL. Antilock brakes are optional and include traction control. The newly optional side curtain airbags are designed to drop down from above the windows to provide head protection to front and rear passengers in side impacts.

PERFORMANCE Neither engine is a model of refinement, but they're getting better; the twincam engine on "2" versions feels coarse and buzzy only at maximum rpm. Acceleration with the twincam remains slightly better than the class norm, at about 8.7 seconds 0-60 mph in our tests. The 5-speed SL2 we tested averaged 22.4 mpg.

SL, SL1, and SC1 furnish adequate acceleration with manual transmission, but keeping up with traffic in automatic versions often requires flooring the throttle. Our 5-speed SL1 test car averaged a commendable 28.9 mpg. With any model, the automatic transmission tends to change gears frequently, which can help performance but makes for a jerky ride.

The "2" models lean least in turns, but all these Saturns corner with pleasing quickness and control. Their suspension absorbs minor bumps well, but rough roads cause abrupt, even harsh reactions. Simulated panic stops tended to prematurely lock the front wheels of non-ABS test models, while ABS models groaned loudly and swerved mildly from side to side.

ACCOMMODATIONS Interiors are simple and well laid out. Gauges are easy to read, smooth-working dials adjust the climate controls, and radio buttons are close to the driver. Welcome surprises include an adjustable center armrest on "2" versions, and, on all models, beverage holders in the front-door map pockets. Interior materials are nothing special, but don't look cheap. Overall visibility is good in any body style,

Prices are accurate at time of publication; subject to manufacturer's change.

SATURN

though the tail is too high in sedans and coupes to easily see straight back.

Front leg room is adequate for those over 6 feet. Rear-seat space doesn't match that of the new subcompact champ, the Ford Focus, but grownups get sufficient knee room as long as the front seats are well forward. S-Series wagons provide lots of head clearance even for tall folk; sedans are a tighter fit. Coupes are tighter in back than sedans and wagons but aren't as confining as some other 2-door subcompacts.

Trunk space is adequate in coupes and sedans, and the split rear seatback folds. Few rivals offer a wagon body style, but most that do have more space than the SW2.

VALUE This General Motors division won its following selling reliable small cars with a one-price strategy. The S-Series is showing its age, but its dent- and rust-resistant composite body panels help it keep that "new" look longer, and resale values remain strong.

ENGINES

	ohc I4	dohc I4
Size, liters/cu. in.	1.9/116	1.9/116
Horsepower @ rpm	100 @ 5000	124 @ 5600
Torque (lb-ft) @ rpm	114 @ 2400	122 @ 4800
Availability	S[1]	S[2]
EPA city/highway mpg		
5-speed OD manual	29/40	27/38
4-speed OD automatic	27/38	25/36

1. SL, SL1, SW1, SC1. 2. SC2, SL2, SW2.

PRICES

Saturn S-Series	Retail Price	Dealer Invoice
SL 4-door sedan, 5-speed	$10570	$9619
SL1 4-door sedan, 5-speed	11485	9992
SL1 4-door sedan, automatic	12345	10740
SC1 3-door coupe, 5-speed	12535	10905
SC1 3-door coupe, automatic	13395	11654
SL2 4-door sedan, 5-speed	12895	11219
SL2 4-door sedan, automatic	13755	11961
SW2 4-door wagon, 5-speed	14290	12432
SW2 4-door wagon, automatic	15150	13181
SC2 3-door coupe, 5-speed	15645	13611
SC2 3-door coupe, automatic	16505	14359
Destination charge	465	465

STANDARD EQUIPMENT:

SL: 1.9-liter 4-cylinder engine, 5-speed manual transmission, dual front airbags, daytime running lights, power steering, cloth upholstery, front bucket seats, center console, cupholders, split folding rear seat, AM/FM radio, digital clock, tachometer, rear defogger, intermittent wipers, passenger-side

Specifications begin on page 535.

SATURN

visor mirror, remote fuel door and decklid release, theft-deterrent system, dual outside mirrors, 185/65R14 tires, wheel covers.

SL1 adds: 5-speed manual or 4-speed automatic transmission, auxiliary power outlet, 185/65R15 tires.

SC1 adds: tilt steering wheel, driver-side rear door, AM/FM/CD player, rear console, rear spoiler.

SL2 adds to SL1: 1.9-liter dohc 4-cylinder engine, air conditioning, variable-assist power steering, tilt steering wheel, driver-seat height and lumbar adjustment, sport suspension.

SW2 adds: rear wiper/washer, cargo cover, remote liftgate release.

SC2 adds to SC1: cruise control, leather-wrapped steering wheel, power mirrors, power windows, power door locks, remote keyless entry, fog lights, 195/60R15 tires.

OPTIONAL EQUIPMENT:

	Retail Price	Dealer Invoice
Major Packages		
Option Pkg. 1, SL1	$1955	$1701
SC1	1830	1592
Air conditioning, cruise control, power mirrors, power windows and door locks, remote keyless entry, power decklid release, theft-deterrent system w/alarm.		
Option Pkg. 2, SL2, SW2	995	866
Cruise control, power mirrors, power windows and door locks, remote keyless entry, theft-deterrent system w/alarm, power decklid release.		
Yellow Coupe Pkg., SC2	250	218
Yellow exterior color, black and chrome emblems. Requires alloy wheels.		
Safety Features		
Antilock brakes, SL	495	450
SL1, SC1, SL2, SC2, SW2	495	431
Includes traction control.		
Front and rear side head-protection system, SL	325	296
SL1, SC1, SL2, SW2, SC2	325	283
Comfort and Convenience		
Air conditioning, SL	960	874
SL1, SC1	960	835
Power sunroof, SL1, SC1, SL2, SC2	725	631
AM/FM/cassette, SL	420	382
SL1, SL2, SW2	390	339
SC1, SC2	100	87
Includes automatic tone control, premium speakers.		
AM/FM/CD player, SL	320	291
SL1, SL2, SW2	290	252
Includes premium speakers.		
AM/FM/cassette/CD player, SL	540	491

Prices are accurate at time of publication; subject to manufacturer's change.

SATURN • SUBARU

	Retail Price	Dealer Invoice
SL1, SL2, SW2	$510	$444
SC1, SC2	220	191
Includes automatic tone control, premium speakers.		
Remote keyless entry, SL1, SL2, SW2	370	322
Includes power door locks, theft-deterrent system w/alarm, power declid release.		
Leather upholstery, SL2, SC2, SW2	700	609
Includes leather-wrapped steering wheel. SL2, SW2 require Option Pkg. 2.		

Appearance and Miscellaneous

Alloy wheels, SC1	450	392
SL2, SW2, SC2	350	305
SC1 includes 195/60R15 tires.		

SUBARU FORESTER

Subaru Forester S

4-wheel-drive compact sport-utility vehicle; similar to Subaru Impreza

Base price range: $20,295-$23,895. Built in Japan. **Also consider:** Ford Escape, Honda CR-V, Toyota RAV4

FOR • Visibility • Maneuverability • Cargo room **AGAINST** • Instruments/controls • Rear-seat room

This 4-door "crossover" wagon got a minor facelift for an early 2001-model debut last spring. Forester uses the same platform as Subaru's subcompact Impreza station wagon, but has a taller body with different, SUV-flavored styling. Cargo room shrinks by 1.5 cubic feet and curb weight is up slightly for '01, but other measurements are unaffected. A restyled nose includes a new chrome grille and reshaped headlights; a revised bumper and taillamps freshen rear-end appearance.

Base L and uplevel S models continue. A new S Premium Package replaces the regular two-toning with a monochromatic look and includes front side airbags, a first for this Subaru. Continuing as the sole engine

Specifications begin on page 535.

SUBARU

is a 2.5-liter horizontally opposed 4-cylinder linked to manual or optional automatic transmissions. Standard on all Subarus is a permanently engaged 4-wheel-drive system designed to sense wheel slip and automatically send power to the wheels with best traction. Antilock brakes are standard, but the S has 4-wheel discs (versus rear drums), plus 16-inch alloy wheels instead of 15-inch steel rims. The L picks up standard intermittent wipers for '01; the S adds keyless remote entry and a 6-disc in-dash CD player.

PERFORMANCE We haven't yet driven an '01 Forester, but it shouldn't differ much from earlier models, as the latest update is mostly cosmetic. This Subaru nicely combines carlike ride and handling with the foul-weather grip and security of AWD, but it isn't quite as comfortable or refined as a conventional wagon and lacks the off-road ability and toughness of a truck-based SUV. A 2000 test model with automatic transmission did 0-60 mph in 9.3 seconds and averaged 22.1 mpg in our tests. Both figures are typical of car-based SUVs like the Honda CR-V, though fuel economy is much better than any midsize SUV can muster. Forester suffers more wind noise and a stiffer ride than the average small car, but it's quieter and less bouncy than a real SUV, not to mention being far more agile and stable through tight turns.

ACCOMMODATIONS Forester isn't that tall, but it does have a higher driving position than most cars. Add in large windows and you have outstanding all-around visibility. The "tall-boy" body also means generous head room, but a subcompact-class wheelbase limits knee clearance and foot space in back. Also, the cabin is too narrow for three adults not to feel squeezed. There's no step-up to speak of, but narrow rear-door bottoms hinder entry/exit a bit. Split rear seatbacks tilt aft for reclined seating or fold down to extend the cargo floor. The load deck itself is conveniently low, the tailgate opening swallows most large items, and packing space is a match for that of some midsize SUVs.

VALUE The most carlike of the car-based quasi-SUVs, Forester's blend of performance, comfort, utility, and value is worthy of a Recommended tag in this class. Competition is heating up fast, though, so also check out our Also Consider picks.

ENGINES

	ohc H4
Size, liters/cu. in.	2.5/150
Horsepower @ rpm	165 @ 5600
Torque (lb-ft) @ rpm	166 @ 4000
Availability	S
EPA city/highway mpg	
5-speed OD manual	22/27
4-speed OD automatic	22/26

Prices are accurate at time of publication; subject to manufacturer's change.

SUBARU
PRICES

Subaru Forester

	Retail Price	Dealer Invoice
L 4-door wagon	$20295	$18504
S 4-door wagon	22895	20776
S w/Premium Pkg. 4-door wagon	23895	21672
Destination charge	495	495

Prices are for vehicles distributed by Subaru of America. Prices may vary in areas served by independent distributors.

STANDARD EQUIPMENT:

L: 2.5-liter 4-cylinder engine, 5-speed manual transmission, permanent all-wheel drive, dual front airbags, antilock brakes, air conditioning, variable-assist power steering, tilt steering wheel, cruise control, cloth upholstery, front bucket seats, height-adjustable driver seat, split folding rear seat, cupholders, power mirrors, power windows, power door locks, AM/FM/cassette, digital clock, tachometer, outside temperature indicator, overhead storage console, map lights, intermittent wipers, rear defogger, rear wiper/washer, auxiliary power outlet, automatic-off headlights, floormats, fog lights, roof rack, full-size spare tire, 205/70R15 white-letter tires.

S adds: limited-slip differential, antilock 4-wheel disc brakes, heated power mirrors, remote keyless entry, 6-disc CD changer, leather-wrapped steering wheel, heated windshield deicer, visor mirrors, 215/60R16 white-letter tires, alloy wheels.

S w/Premium Pkg. adds: front side-impact airbags, power sunroof.

OPTIONAL EQUIPMENT:
Major Packages

Feature Group 1, L	521	340
Manufacturer's discount price	521	323
Remote keyless entry, cargo cover, theft deterrent system, tail pipe cover.		
Feature Group 2, L	336	220
Manufacturer's discount price	336	209
Remote keyless entry, cargo cover, tail pipe cover.		
Feature Group 3, S, S w/Premium	529	345
Manufacturer's discount price	529	328
Automatic day/night rearview mirror, compass, cargo cover, theft deterrent system, tail pipe cover.		
Feature Group 4	191	125
Manufacturer's discount price	191	118
Interior air filter, cargo net, armrest extension.		
Premium Sound Group 1, L	911	628
Manufacturer's discount price	695	525
CD player, upgraded sound system.		

Specifications begin on page 535.

SUBARU

	Retail Price	Dealer Invoice
Premium Sound Pkg. 2, L	$1075	$751
Manufacturer's discount price	795	600
In-dash 6-disc CD changer, upgraded sound system.		
Premium Sound Pkg. 3, S, S w/ Premium	555	361
Manufacturer's discount price	395	300
Upgraded sound system.		
Interior Upgrade Group	529	345
Manufacturer's discount price	529	327
Automatic day/night rearview mirror, compass, woodgrain shift knob, armrest extension, cargo net.		
Security Group, L	360	234
Manufacturer's discount price	360	222
Remote keyless entry, theft-deterrent system.		
Protection Group	654	454
Manufacturer's discount price	654	425
Brush guard, hood deflector, differential protector, rear dust deflector.		
Appearance Group	484	315
Manufacturer's discount price	484	299
Fender flares, rear spoiler.		

Powertrains
4-speed automatic ransmission	800	719

Comfort and Convenience
Leather upholstery, L, S	1295	975

Post production options also available.

SUBARU IMPREZA

Subaru Impreza 4-door sedan

All-wheel-drive subcompact car
Base price range: $15,995-$19,495. Built in Japan. **Also con-**

Prices are accurate at time of publication; subject to manufacturer's change.

SUBARU

sider: Ford Focus, Honda Civic, Volkswagen Jetta/Golf

FOR • All-wheel drive • Cargo room (wagons) • Maneuverability
AGAINST • Rear-seat room • Engine noise • Rear-seat entry/exit

Impreza goes unchanged into a shortened 2001 model year as Subaru prepares to introduce its 2002 successor this spring. Impreza is the only subcompact car with standard all-wheel drive. It comes in workaday L coupe, sedan, and wagon; racy 2.5 RS coupe and 2.5 RS sedan; and sport-utility-inspired Outback Sport wagon with raised roofline and extra ground clearance. All have manual or optional automatic transmission and horizontally opposed 4-cylinder engines. L models and the Outback use a 2.2-liter. The 2.5 RS models get the 2.5 liter used in Subaru's larger Forester, Legacy, and Outback models. Antilock brakes are standard for Outbacks and 2.5 RSs, but aren't available on L models. The restyled, redesigned '02 Impreza line will not include a coupe body style, but will introduce to America the high-performance WRX sedan and wagon, which make about 250 horsepower from their turbocharged 4-cylinder engine.

EVALUATION Handy size and a balanced chassis make Impreza 2.5 RS models reasonably fun to drive in good weather, and the AWD makes all models reassuring in snow or rain. But take away the AWD and you have rather ordinary small cars, with tight interiors, a slightly choppy ride, and fairly gruff and growly engines. The 2.2-liter engine provides adequate acceleration, and the 2.5 makes for spritely performance, but both are rather loud and intrusive in hard use. Generally good workmanship is let down by tinny door closings and some cheap-feeling interior details. Still, if you're among those for whom AWD is a big plus, the smallest Subarus make sense as affordable all-weather transport.

ENGINES

	ohc H4	ohc H4
Size, liters/cu. in.	2.2/135	2.5/150
Horsepower @ rpm	142 @ 5600	165 @ 5600
Torque (lb-ft) @ rpm	149 @ 3600	166 @ 4000
Availability	S[1]	S[2]
EPA city/highway mpg		
5-speed OD manual	23/29	21/28
4-speed OD automatic	23/29	23/28

1. L, Outback Sport. 2. 2.5 RS.

PRICES

Subaru Impreza

	Retail Price	Dealer Invoice
L 2-door coupe	$15995	$14695
L 4-door sedan	15995	14695
L 4-door wagon	16395	15057
Outback Sport 4-door wagon	18195	16683

Specifications begin on page 535.

SUBARU

	Retail Price	Dealer Invoice
2.5 RS 2-door coupe	$19495	$17868
2.5 RS 4-door sedan	19495	17868
Destination charge	495	495

Prices are for vehicles distributed by Subaru of America. Prices may vary in areas served by independent distributors.

STANDARD EQUIPMENT:

L: 2.2-liter 4-cylinder engine, 5-speed manual transmission, permanent all-wheel drive, dual front airbags, air conditioning, variable-assist power steering, tilt steering wheel, cloth upholstery, reclining front bucket seats, split folding rear seat (wagon), front storage console, cupholder, power mirrors, power windows, power door locks, AM/FM/cassette, digital clock, tachometer, intermittent wipers, rear defogger, remote decklid release (sedan and coupe), auxiliary power outlet, cargo cover (wagon), rear wiper/washer (wagon), automatic-off headlights, passenger-side visor mirror, map lights, rear spoiler (coupe), 195/60HR15 tires, wheel covers.

Outback Sport adds to L wagon: antilock brakes, cruise control, cargo tray, raised heavy-duty suspension, roof rack, 2-tone paint, 205/60S15 white-letter tires.

2.5RS adds: 2.5-liter 4-cylinder engine, limited-slip differential, antilock 4-wheel disc brakes, leather-wrapped steering wheel, cruise control, AM/FM/cassette/CD player, power sunroof, floormats, rear spoiler, fog lights, sport suspension, 205/55VR16 tires, alloy wheels.

OPTIONAL EQUIPMENT:
Major Packages

Popular Equipment Group 1, L wagon	—	288
Manufacturer's discount price	443	271
Floormats, roof rack, mud guards, tail pipe cover.		
Popular Equipment Group 2, L	—	126
Manufacturer's discount price	194	119
Floormats, mud guards, tail pipe cover.		
Premium Sound Pkg. 1, wagons	922	635
Manufacturer's discount price	695	525
AM/FM/cassette/CD player, upgraded speakers, tweeter, subwoofer, amplifier.		
Premium Sound Pkg. 2, L sedan/coupe	819	568
Manufacturer's discount price	625	470
AM/FM/cassette/CD player, upgraded speakers, tweeter, subwoofer, amplifier.		
Premium Sound Pkg. 3, RS	463	301
Manufacturer's discount price	335	250
Upgraded speakers, tweeter, subwoofer, amplifier.		

Prices are accurate at time of publication; subject to manufacturer's change.

SUBARU

	Retail Price	Dealer Invoice
Security Pkg. 1	—	$242
Manufacturer's discount price	370	229
Remote keyless entry, security upgrade kit.		

Powertrains
4-speed automatic transmission	800	725

Comfort and Convenience
AM/FM/Cassette/CD player, L, Outback Sport	356	267
Gauge pack, L	375	281
Compass, altimeter, barometer, outside temperature indicator.		

Appearance and Miscellaneous
Fog lights, L, Outback Sport	237	154
Roof rack, L wagon	249	162
Alloy wheels, L, Outback Sport	525	394

Post production options also available.

SUBARU LEGACY

Subaru Legacy 4-door sedan

All-wheel-drive compact car; similar to Subaru Outback
Base price range: $19,295-$24,395. Built in USA. **Also consider:** Mazda 626, Mitsubishi Galant, Volkswagen Passat

FOR • Cargo room (wagon) • All-wheel drive **AGAINST**
• Automatic transmission performance • Seat comfort

Subaru's compact sedan and wagon line for 2001 loses its budget-priced model, but the remaining Legacys gain standard equipment. Last year's base Brighton wagon is dropped, leaving L and GT sedans and wagons, and a GT Limited sedan. The popular Legacy-based Outback models are a seperate series, but share the Legacy's basic design. All Legacys use a 2.5-liter horizontally opposed 4-cylinder engine. (Outback

Specifications begin on page 535.

SUBARU

for '01 offers a 6-cylinder engine that isn't available in the Legacy line.) Manual or optional automatic transmissions team with Subaru's permanent all-wheel drive. All Legacys come with dual airbags and antilock brakes; the GT Limited sedan adds standard front side airbags, the only model where they're available. New linewide standard equipment for '01 includes an outside air temperature guage, variable-assist power steering, and automatic-off headlights.

EVALUATION Legacy's 4-cylinder engine is adequate for the job, but no more. The automatic transmission is fairly smooth, but exhibits early upshifts and a reluctance to downshift. Manual shift action is good but not great. Fuel economy is likable. In our tests, one manual GT Limited sedan returned 22.5 mpg, another 25.4; an automatic Outback averaged 24.3 mpg on a long highway trip. L models favor ride comfort over handling agility. Firmer suspension and larger tires give GTs a much sportier driving feel in exchange for sharp reactions over bumps. Brakes don't feel especially strong but provide short, drama-free stops. Wind noise is reasonably low, but tire drone is marked on coarse pavement and the growly, coarse-sounding engine is never really quiet. Legacy cabins are fairly roomy and nicely trimmed. Front seats are comfortable for most people, the basic driving position is excellent, and controls are mostly handy and guess-free. Outward visibility is good in either body style. Room in back is tight only if the front seats are fully aft. Entry/exit poses no serious problems. Sedans have a usefully shaped trunk; wagons provide good load space for the compact class, and it can be expanded with the split-folding rear seats. Legacy isn't the best compact-car choice unless you simply must have all-wheel drive.

ENGINES

	ohc H4
Size, liters/cu. in.	2.5/150
Horsepower @ rpm	165 @ 5600
Torque (lb-ft) @ rpm	166 @ 4000
Availability	S

EPA city/highway mpg
5-speed OD manual	21/28
4-speed OD automatic	22/27

PRICES

Subaru Legacy	Retail Price	Dealer Invoice
L 4-door sedan	$19295	$17560
L 4-door wagon	19995	18187
GT 4-door sedan	22895	20770
GT 4-door wagon	23795	21577
GT Limited 4-door sedan	24395	22109
Destination charge	495	495

Prices are accurate at time of publication; subject to manufacturer's change.

SUBARU

Prices are for vehicles distributed by Subaru of America. Prices may vary in areas served by independent distributors.

STANDARD EQUIPMENT:

L: 2.5-liter 4-cylinder engine, 5-speed manual transmission, permanent all-wheel drive, dual front airbags, antilock 4-wheel disc brakes, daytime running lights, air conditioning, variable-assist power steering, tilt steering wheel, cruise control, cloth upholstery, front bucket seats, cupholders, rear seat trunk pass-through (sedan), split folding rear seat (wagon), power mirrors, power windows, power door locks, AM/FM/cassette, digital clock, tachometer, outside temperature indicator, intermittent wipers, rear defogger, intermittent rear wiper/washer (wagon), auxiliary power outlets, map lights, cargo cover (wagon), automatic-off headlights, roof rails (wagon), 205/60R15 tires, wheel covers.

GT adds: limited-slip differential, single power sunroof (sedan), dual power sunroofs (wagon), 6-way power driver seat, remote keyless entry, leather-wrapped steering wheel, variable intermittent wipers, illuminated visor mirrors, fog lights, sport suspension, 205/55R16 tires, alloy wheels.

GT Limited adds: front side-impact airbags, leather upholstery, AM/FM/weatherband/cassette/CD player.

OPTIONAL EQUIPMENT:
Major Packages

	Retail Price	Dealer Invoice
Popular Equipment Group 1, L wagon	—	$213
Manufacturer's discount price	336	193
Roof rack, floormats, mud guards.		
Popular Equipment Group 2, L sedan	—	107
Manufacturer's discount price	164	97
Floor mats, mud guards.		
Popular Equipment Group 3, L/GT wagon	—	154
Manufacturer's discount price	246	144
Roof rack, floormats.		
Popular Equipment Group 4, L	—	173
Manufacturer's discount price	305	160
Automatic day/night rearview mirror, illuminated visor mirrors.		
Popular Equipment Group 6, GT, GT Limited	—	243
Manufacturer's discount price	373	229
Automatic day/night rearview mirror, Security System Upgrade Kit.		
Premium Sound Pkg. 1A, L	934	644
Manufacturer's discount price	695	525
CD player, upgraded speakers, subwoofer, amplifier, tweeter.		
Premium Sound Pkg. 1B, GT	905	624
Manufacturer's discount price	695	525
CD player, upgraded speakers, subwoofer, amplifier, tweeter.		
Premium Sound Pkg. 2, GT	1093	763

Specifications begin on page 535.

SUBARU

	Retail Price	Dealer Invoice
Manufacturer's discount price	$795	$600
In-dash 6-disc CD changer, upgraded speakers, tweeter kit, subwoofer, amplifier.		
Premium Sound Pkg. 3, GT Limited	770	553
Manufacturer's discount price	635	475
In-dash 6-disc CD changer, subwoofer, amplifier.		
Rough Road Group, wagons	—	161
Manufacturer's discount price	259	145
Acrylic hood deflector, rear window dust deflector, rear differential protector.		
Security Group, L	—	238
Manufacturer's discount price	365	222
Remote keyless entry, Security System Upgrade Kit.		

Powertrains
4-speed automatic transmission	800	722

Comfort and Convenience
CD player, L, GT	361	271
In-dash 6-disc CD changer, GT, GT Limited	520	390
Remote keyless entry, L	175	114
Automatic day/night rearview mirror	183	119
Includes compass.		

Appearance and Miscellaneous
Rear spoiler, sedans	325	212
Fog lights, L	259	168
Roof rack, wagons	172	106
Alloy wheels, L	525	394

Post production options also available.

SUBARU OUTBACK

All-wheel-drive compact car; similar to Subaru Legacy

Base price range: $22,895-$31,895. Built in USA. **Also consider:** Audi A4, Saturn L-Series, Volkswagen Passat

FOR • All-wheel drive • Cargo room **AGAINST** • Automatic transmission performance

Addition of an antiskid system and new upscale 6-cylinder models is the top 2001 news for Subaru's sport-utility-flavored, Legacy-based compacts. New to the Outback line are the VDC (Vehicle Dynamics Control) model and the L.L. Bean Edition. Both are powered by a new 3.0-liter horizontally opposed 6-cylinder engine and automatic transmission, and have standard automatic climate control, wood-trimmed steering wheel, and distinct alloy wheels. The VDC model has Subaru's first

Prices are accurate at time of publication; subject to manufacturer's change.

SUBARU

Subaru Outback 4-door wagon

antiskid system along with new Variable Torque Distribution 4-wheel drive that differs from other Subaru systems in being able to vary the amount of power sent to each wheel. The L.L. Bean Edition has a self-dimming rearview mirror with compass, an air filtration system (both optional on other Outbacks), and special L.L. Bean trim.

The rest of the Outback line continues in base and Limited wagons and a slower-selling Limited sedan, all powered by a 2.5-liter horizontally opposed 4-cylinder engine. Wagons come with manual or optional automatic transmission, the sedan with automatic only. Permanently engaged all-wheel drive is standard, but it lacks low-range gearing. For 2001, all Outbacks get a limited-slip rear differential, ambient temperature gauge, dual illuminated vanity mirrors, and front seatback net pockets. Antilock 4-wheel disc brakes are standard on all Outbacks, and all but the base have front side airbags. An integrated rear child seat is optional for the base wagon.

PERFORMANCE Outback is a compact car dressed as an SUV. It's not intended for serious off-roading despite the standard all-wheel drive and high-rider stance. The upside is a better-controlled ride than any truck-based SUV, though Outback isn't quite as comfortable as most cars. It stops shorter and handles better than typical SUVs, but cornering lean makes it feel slightly clumsy by car standards. Like Legacys, Outbacks are noisier than most compact cars and even some SUVs. Tire roar intrudes on coarse pavement, and the wagon's roof rack howls at speed.

Acceleration with the 4-cylinder is sluggish, and the gruff engine has a slight throbbiness that gets through to your feet and seat. Aggravating matters, the automatic transmission tends to upshift too soon in town and is reluctant to downshift for passing. Acceleration is better with manual—on a par with most 4-cylinder compact cars. Fuel economy exceeds the SUV norm. Our extended-use-test 5-speed Limited wagon is averaging 21.7 mpg over its

Specifications begin on page 535.

SUBARU

first 14,181 miles on 87-octane regular-grade gas. Another test example managed 24.3 on a long highway trip. Our extended-use car has been mechanically trouble-free.

Preview drives in the 2001 VDC reveal the new 6-cylinder engine to be noticeably more powerful than the four. It does 0-60 mph in 8.5 seconds, to 10.5 for the four, says Subaru. The six is also substantially smoother, with no hint of the throbbing that afflicts the four. We had no opportunity to measure fuel economy with the six, but Subaru recommends more-expensive 91 octane for best performance. We also had no opportunity to give the VDC antiskid feature a thorough workout, but initial impressions are that it works at least as well as other such systems, helping the vehicle remain on course during emergency maneuvers.

ACCOMMODATIONS Outback's driving stance isn't SUV-lofty but provides a fine view down the road. Thin roof pillars and large windows help visibility to other quarters, though the three rear shoulder belts can be minor obstructions. Audio and climate controls are within easy driver reach, but a few audio buttons are too small to easily operate while driving except on the VDC's McIntosh system, which has large controls.

Front occupants get good room, though lanky drivers may wish for more rearward seat travel. Rear passengers enjoy ample head room, especially in the raised-roof wagon, but aft leg space is tight unless the front seats are pushed up some. And there's not enough width for uncrowded 3-across adult seating. Wider rear door bottoms would make entry/exit easier.

Wagons have spacious cargo capacity and a wide, flat load deck. Sedans have a usefully shaped trunk, but also intrusive trunklid hinges and just a rear-seat pass-through instead of the wagon's more versatile 60/40 split-fold seatbacks.

VALUE An Outback wagon is a fine choice for those who want SUV looks and all-wheel-drive traction without the thirst and clumsiness of a larger vehicle or truck-based wagon. The new 6-cylinder models answer our complaints about the 4-cylinder engine's throbbiness and lack of power, but come with a hefty price premium.

ENGINES

	ohc H4	dohc H6
Size, liters/cu. in.	2.5/150	3.0/183
Horsepower @ rpm	165 @ 5600	212 @ 6000
Torque (lb-ft) @ rpm	166 @ 4000	210 @ 4400
Availability	S[1]	S[2] |//
EPA city/highway mpg		
5-speed OD manual	21/28	
4-speed OD automatic	22/27	20/27

1. Base, Limited. 2. L.L. Bean, VDC.

Prices are accurate at time of publication; subject to manufacturer's change.

SUBARU
PRICES

Subaru Outback	Retail Price	Dealer Invoice
Base 4-door wagon	$22895	$20767
Limited 4-door sedan	25995	23550
Limited 4-door wagon	26295	23815
L.L.Bean Edition 4-door wagon	29495	26687
VDC 4-door wagon	31895	28839
Destination charge	495	495

Prices are for vehicles distributed by Subaru of America. Prices may vary in areas served by independent distributors.

STANDARD EQUIPMENT:

Base: 2.5-liter 4-cylinder engine, 5-speed manual transmission, permanent all-wheel drive, limited-slip differential, dual front airbags, antilock 4 wheel disc brakes, daytime running lights, air conditioning, variable-assist power steering, tilt steering wheel, cruise control, cloth upholstery, front bucket seats, 6-way power driver seat, split folding rear seat, power mirrors, power windows, power door locks, remote keyless entry, AM/FM/weatherband/cassette, digital clock, tachometer, outside temperature indicator, overhead console, map lights, illuminated visor mirrors, variable intermittent wipers, auxiliary power outlets, rear defogger, intermittent rear wiper/washer, cargo cover, automatic-off headlights, floormats, trailer wiring harness, fog lights, roof rack, 225/60R16 white-letter tires, alloy wheels.

Limited adds: 4-speed automatic transmission (sedan), front side-impact airbags, dual power sunroofs (wagon), single power sunroof (sedan), leather upholstery, heated front seats, 6-way power driver seat, leather-wrapped steering wheel, heated power mirrors, AM/FM/weatherband/cassette/CD player, variable intermittent wipers w/de-icer, rear seat trunk pass-through (sedan), Deletes: split folding rear seat (sedan).

L.L.Bean Edition adds: 3.0-liter dohc six-cylinder engine, 4-speed automatic transmission, two-tone leather upholstery, 8-way power driver seat, wood/leather-wrapped steering wheel, automatic climate control, interior air filter, automatic day/night rearview mirror, compass, theft-deterrent system.

VDC adds: traction control, antiskid system, single-tone leather upholstery, McIntosh sound system, Deletes: interior air filter, automatic day/night rearview mirror, theft-deterrent system.

OPTIONAL EQUIPMENT:
Major Packages

Popular Equipment Group 6, Base, Limited, VDC	—	243
Manufacturer's discount price	373	229
Automatic day/night rearview mirror, Security System Upgrade Kit.		
All-Weather Pkg., Base	500	452
Heated front seats and mirrors, front windshield wiper de-icer.		

Specifications begin on page 535.

SUBARU • SUZUKI

	Retail Price	Dealer Invoice
Rough Road Group, wagons	—	$161
Manufacturer's discount price	259	145
Acrylic hood protector, rear differential protector, rear window dust deflector.		
Premium Sound Pkg. 1B, Base	934	644
Manufacturer's discount price	695	525
CD player, upgraded speakers, tweeter, subwoofer, amplifier.		
Premium Sound Pkg. 2, Base	823	763
Manufacturer's discount price	795	600
In-dash 6-disc CD changer, upgraded speakers, tweeter, subwoofer, amplifier.		
Premium Sound Pkg. 3, Limited, L.L.Bean	787	564
Manufacturer's discount price	635	475
In-dash 6-disc CD changer, subwoofer, amplifier.		

Powertrains
4-speed automatic transmission, Base, Limited wagon	800	722

Safety Features
Integrated child seat, Base	200	180

Comfort and Convenience
CD player, Base	361	271
In-dash 6-disc CD changer, Base, Limited, L.L.Bean	520	390
Automatic day/night rearview mirror, Base, Limited, VDC	183	119
Interior air filter, Base, Limited, VDC	62	41

Appearance and Miscellaneous
Rear spoiler, wagons	295	192
Security System Upgrade Kit, Base, Limited, VDC	190	124
Hitch	295	192

NA Limited sedan.

Post production options also available.

SUZUKI ESTEEM/SWIFT
Front-wheel-drive subcompact car

Base price range: NA. Built in Japan and Canada. **Also consider:** Ford Focus, Honda Civic, Toyota Echo

FOR • Fuel economy • Cargo room (wagon) • Maneuverability
AGAINST • Rear visibility • Noise • Ride • Rear-seat room (Swift) • Build quality (Swift) • Rear-seat entry/exit (Swift)

Esteem is Suzuki's 4-door sedan and wagon, Swift its 2-door hatchback. Both are front-wheel-drive subcompacts but Esteem rides a longer wheelbase and has a larger engine and outsells Swift 5-1. Esteem is

Prices are accurate at time of publication; subject to manufacturer's change.

SUZUKI

Suzuki Esteem 4-door wagon

built in Japan. It returns in GL and GLX models, as well as the GLX Plus, which is the only model with antilock brakes. New for 2000 is a GL Sport 4-door, which includes fog lamps and a rear spoiler. Esteems use a 1.8-liter 4-cylinder engine. Manual transmission is standard on all but the GLX Plus models. They come with a 4-speed automatic that's optional on other Esteems. Swift is built in Canada at a General Motors-Suzuki plant alongside the similar Chevrolet Metro, which is mostly a fleet vehicle. It uses a 1.3-liter 4-cylinder engine and manual or optional 3-speed automatic transmission. For 2000, the base Swift is renamed the GA, and a GL model with standard air conditioning and AM/FM cassette is added. Antilock brakes are unavailable on the Swift.

EVALUATION Compact dimensions give all these Suzukis nimble moves around town, but their skinny tires surrender grip easily in aggressive cornering. Esteem and Swift ride rougher than most competitors, and are noisy on the highway. Esteem has room for four adults, as long as those in back aren't over about 5-10, but the rear seat is thinly padded and the small rear doors hard to squeeze through. Swift is tighter still. Even if fuel economy and low price are your primary concerns, neither of these Suzukis strikes us as a great bargain. We'd look first at a larger, late-model used car.

ENGINES

	ohc I4	dohc I4
Size, liters/cu. in.	1.3/79	1.8/112
Horsepower @ rpm	79 @ 6000	122 @ 6300
Torque (lb-ft) @ rpm	75 @ 3000	117 @ 3500
Availability	S[1]	S[2]
EPA city/highway mpg		
5-speed OD manual	39/43	28/35
3-speed automatic	30/34	
4-speed OD automatic		26/33

1. Swift. 2. Esteem.

2001 prices unavailable at time of publication.

Specifications begin on page 535.

SUZUKI

PRICES

2000 Suzuki Esteem/Swift	Retail Price	Dealer Invoice
Swift GA 2-door hatchback, 5-speed	$9099	$8553
Swift GA 2-door hatchback, automatic	9749	9164
Swift GL 2-door hatchback, 5-speed	10099	9493
Swift GL 2-door hatchback, automatic	10749	10104
Esteem GL 4-door sedan, 5-speed	12899	12383
Esteem GL 4-door sedan, automatic	13899	13343
Esteem GL 4-door wagon, 5-speed	13399	12863
Esteem GL 4-door wagon, automatic	14399	13823
Esteem GLX 4-door sedan, 5-speed	13899	13343
Esteem GLX 4-door sedan, automatic	14899	14303
Esteem GLX 4-door wagon, 5-speed	14399	13823
Esteem GLX 4-door wagon, automatic	15399	14783
Esteem GLX Sport 4-door sedan, 5-speed	14499	13767
Esteem GLX Sport 4-door sedan, automatic	15499	14727
Esteem GLX Plus 4-door sedan, automatic	15699	15071
Esteem GLX Plus 4-door wagon, automatic	16399	15743
Destination charge: Swift	400	400
Destination charge: Esteem	450	450

STANDARD EQUIPMENT:

Swift GA: 1.3-liter 4-cylinder engine, 5-speed manual or 3-speed automatic transmission, dual front airbags, daytime running lights, cloth reclining front bucket seats, folding rear seat, front console, intermittent wipers, rear defogger, cargo cover, dual outside mirrors, 155/80R13 tires, wheel covers.

Swift GL adds: air conditioning, AM/FM/cassette.

Esteem GL adds: 1.8-liter 4-cylinder engine, 5-speed manual or 4-speed automatic transmission, power steering, cupholders, tachometer, variable intermittent wipers, split folding rear seat, rear wiper/washer (wagon), remote fuel-door and decklid releases, cargo cover (wagon), roof rails (wagon), 185/60R14 tires.

Esteem GLX adds: power mirrors, power windows, power door locks, remote keyless entry, passenger-side visor mirror, theft-deterrent system, rear spoiler (wagon), 195/55R15 tires, alloy wheels.

Esteem GLX Sport adds: fog lights, rear spoiler.

Esteem GLX Plus adds to Esteem GLX: 4-speed automatic transmission, antilock brakes, cruise control, power sunroof (wagon).

OPTIONAL EQUIPMENT:
Appearance and Miscellaneous

Two-tone paint, GLX Plus wagon	200	178

Other options are available as dealer-installed accessories.

Prices are accurate at time of publication; subject to manufacturer's change.

CONSUMER GUIDE

SUZUKI

SUZUKI VITARA

Suzuki Vitara 4-door wagon

Rear- or 4-wheel-drive compact sport-utility vehicle

Base price range: NA. Built in Japan.   **Also consider:** Honda CR-V, Subaru Forester, Toyota RAV4

FOR • Maneuverability • Cargo room   **AGAINST** • Rear-seat room • Rear visibility • Acceleration • Rear-seat entry/exit (Convertible)

A new top-line model is the primary change for 2000 to Suzuki's compact sport-utility vehicle. Regular Vitaras have 4-cylinder engines and come as 4-door wagons or as 2-door convertibles. The convertibles have a shorter wheelbase than the wagons and put a folding soft top over their rear seats. Grand Vitaras are V6 wagons with beefed-up body addenda and extra standard features; they outsell regular Vitaras at least 3-1. Both body styles use body-on-frame construction. Chevrolet Trackers share Vitara's basic design and are built by Suzuki, but don't have a Grand Vitara counterpart and won't offer the V6 until the 2001 model year. JS- and JX-model convertibles have 97 horsepower. JLS and JLX convertibles and all Vitara wagons have 127 hp. Grand Vitaras have 155 hp. This year's new top-line Grand Vitara Limited comes with exclusive leather upholstery, deep-tint glass, and fog lights. All models offer rear- or part-time 4-wheel drive; the latter, denoted by "X" in the model name, includes low-range gearing but is not for use on dry pavement. Antilock brakes are standard on the Grand Vitara JLS Plus, JLX Plus, and Limited, but are unavailable on other models.

EVALUATION Four-cylinder Vitaras are slow, thrashy devices. The V6 Grands are little quieter or quicker—a lazy 11.5 seconds to 60 mph by our stopwatch—though automatic 4x4s average between 17.9 and 20.7 mpg in our tests, slightly worse than the 4-cylinder Honda CR-V but better than larger 6-cylinder 4x4s. The ride is uncomfortably choppy on all but smooth surfaces. Hard cornering brings marked body lean and only moderate grip, though handling is predictable within its modest limits. Vitara's 4WD is less convenient than the permanently engaged systems

Specifications begin on page 535.

SUZUKI

of the rival CR-V, Toyota RAV4, and Subaru Forester, but they lack the Suzuki's 4-Low range for off-road work. High wind and road noise combine with mediocre seats and a smallish cabin for tiring long-distance travel. Vitara is also shy on cargo room, and the one-piece rear door on both body styles opens right, blocking curbside loading. In all, these Suzukis (and Chevy's similar Trackers) are compact-SUV also-rans whose only strong suit is somewhat better off-road ability than the car-based competition.

ENGINES

	ohc I4	dohc I4	dohc V6
Size, liters/cu. in.	1.6/97	2.0/122	2.5/152
Horsepower @ rpm	97 @ 5200	127 @ 6000	155 @ 6500
Torque (lb-ft) @ rpm	103 @ 4000	134 @ 3000	160 @ 4000
Availability	S[1]	S[2]	S[3]
EPA city/highway mpg			
5-speed OD manual	25/28[4]	22/24	19/22[6]
4-speed OD automatic	25/27[5]	23/25	19/21[7]

1. JS and JX conv. 2. Vitara JLS and JLX conv., Vitara 4-door. 3. Grand Vitara. 4. 25/27 w/4WD. 5. 24/27 w/4WD. 6. 19/21 w/4WD. 7. 18/20 w/4WD.

2001 prices unavailable at time of publication.

PRICES

2000 Suzuki Vitara	Retail Price	Dealer Invoice
JS 2WD 2-door convertible, 5-speed	$13499	$12959
JS 2WD 2-door convertible, automatic	14499	13919
JLS 2WD 2-door convertible, 5-speed	14999	14399
JLS 2WD 2-door convertible, automatic	15999	15359
JX 4WD 2-door convertible, 5-speed	15299	14381
JX 4WD 2-door convertible, automatic	16299	15321
JLX 4WD 2-door convertible, 5-speed	16799	15791
JLX 4WD 2-door convertible, automatic	17799	16731
JS 2WD 4-door wagon, 5-speed	15499	14569
JS 2WD 4-door wagon, automatic	16499	15509
JLS 2WD 4-door wagon, 5-speed	16299	15321
JLS 2WD 4-door wagon, automatic	17299	16261
JLS 2WD 4-door wagon w/alloy wheels, 5-speed	16699	15697
JLS 2WD 4-door wagon w/alloy wheels, automatic	17699	16637
JX 4WD 4-door wagon, 5-speed	17099	15731
JX 4WD 4-door wagon, automatic	18099	16651
JLX 4WD 4-door wagon, 5-speed	17899	16467
JLX 4WD 4-door wagon, automatic	18899	17387
JLX 4WD 4-door wagon w/alloy wheels, 5-speed	18299	16835
JLX 4WD 4-door wagon w/alloy wheels, automatic	19299	17755
Grand JLS 2WD 4-door wagon, 5-speed	18299	16835
Grand JLS 2WD 4-door wagon, automatic	19299	17755

Prices are accurate at time of publication; subject to manufacturer's change.

SUZUKI

	Retail Price	Dealer Invoice
Grand JLS Plus 2WD 4-door wagon, 5-speed	$19499	$17939
Grand JLS Plus 2WD 4-door wagon, automatic	20499	18859
Grand JLX 4WD 4-door wagon, 5-speed	19299	17755
Grand JLX 4WD 4-door wagon, automatic	20299	18675
Grand JLX Plus 4WD 4-door wagon, 5-speed	20499	18859
Grand JLX Plus 4WD 4-door wagon, automatic	21499	19779
Grand Limited 2WD 4-door wagon, automatic	21699	19963
Grand Limited 4WD 4-door wagon, automatic	22699	20883
Destination charge: convertibles	440	440
Destination charge: wagons	450	450

STANDARD EQUIPMENT:

JS/JX convertible: 1.6-liter 4-cylinder engine, 5-speed manual or 4-speed automatic transmission, dual front airbags, daytime running lights, power steering, tilt steering wheel, cloth/vinyl upholstery, front bucket seats, center console, cupholders, split folding rear seat, AM/FM/cassette, tachometer, passenger-side visor mirror, variable intermittent wipers, automatic headlights, folding convertible top, full-size spare tire, 195/75R15 tires. **4WD** models add: part-time 4-wheel drive, 2-speed transfer case, 205/75R15 tires.

JLS/JLX convertible adds: 2.0-liter dohc 4-cylinder engine, air conditioning, power mirrors, power windows, power door locks, cloth upholstery, map lights, 215/65R16 tires. **4WD** models add: part-time 4-wheel drive, 2-speed transfer case.

JS/JX wagon adds to JS/JX convertible: 2.0-liter dohc 4-cylinder engine, cloth upholstery, map lights, auxiliary power outlet, rear defogger, cargo cover, rear wiper/washer, roof rails, 215/65R16 tires, deletes folding convertible top. **4WD** models add: part-time 4-wheel drive, 2-speed transfer case.

JLS/JLX adds: air conditioning, cruise control, power mirrors, power windows, power door locks, remote keyless entry, steel or alloy wheels. **4WD** models add: part-time 4-wheel drive, 2-speed transfer case.

Grand JS/JLX adds: 2.5-liter dohc V6 engine, 235/60R16 tires, deletes alloy wheels. **4WD** models add: part-time 4-wheel drive, 2-speed transfer case.

Grand JLS Plus/JLX Plus adds: antilock brakes, CD changer, alloy wheels. **4WD** model adds: part-time 4-wheel drive, 2-speed transfer case.

Grand Limited adds: 4-speed automatic transmission, leather upholstery, deep-tinted glass, fog lights. **4WD** model adds: part-time 4-wheel drive, 2-speed transfer case.

Options are available as dealer-installed accessories.

Specifications begin on page 535.

TOYOTA

TOYOTA 4RUNNER

Toyota 4Runner

Rear- or 4-wheel-drive midsize sport-utility vehicle
Base price range: $26,355-$37,605. Built in Japan. **Also consider:** Acura MDX, Ford Explorer, Lexus RX 300, Mercedes-Benz M-Class

FOR • Cargo room • Build quality • Exterior finish • Interior materials
AGAINST • Entry/exit • Fuel economy

Toyota's midsize SUV loses its base 4-cylinder models and manual transmission for 2001, but 4-wheel-drive models now have full-time 4WD and all models get an antiskid/traction control system.

The 4Runner line slims to SR5 and uplevel Limited wagons with rear drive or 4WD. Both have a 3.4-liter V6, standard automatic transmission, and antilock brakes. Newly standard is Toyota's Vehicle Skid Control antiskid system with integrated traction control. Last year's part-time 4WD is dropped for SR5 4x4s. They adopt Limited's full-time 4WD that can be left engaged on dry pavement. This setup uses Toyota's One-Touch Hi-4 system that engages 4WD via a selector switch on the transfer case lever rather than by shifting the lever itself. The previously available locking rear differential is shelved along with manual transmission.

In other changes, all models wear a revised grille and taillamps, and the Limited adds standard heated front seats, Homelink remote door opener, and an optional in-dash CD changer. The SR5's available Sport Package returns with metal-look interior trim, plus body-colored bumpers and fender flares, hood scoop, foglights, larger brakes, and 16-inch wheels. The Limited retains wood cabin trim, but comes with the Sport Package exterior features, plus automatic climate control and leather upholstery.

PERFORMANCE The 4-cylinder engine was always a bit weak for the 4Runner, and it won't be missed. As for the V6, it delivers snappy takeoffs and good low-speed punch, though highway passing power is unexceptional in the heavier 4x4s with three or more people and their lug-

Prices are accurate at time of publication; subject to manufacturer's change.
CONSUMER GUIDE

TOYOTA

gage aboard. Like the V6, the automatic transmission is a smooth operator and responsive to your right foot. Fuel economy is class typical. Our test Limited averaged 17.2 mpg with lots of highway miles.

Engine and tire noise are well muffled, leaving wind rush as the main disturber of the peace in this tall, boxy vehicle. 4Runner is engineered like a truck, so although its ride isn't bouncy stiff, it's not carlike either, especially on 4x4s. Steering is quick and precise for an SUV, and this Toyota feels more stable in tight turns than some rivals. Simulated panic stops are safe and undramatic with ABS. Three cheers for the newly standard antiskid/traction system, which should provide an extra margin of safety in foul-weather driving.

ACCOMMODATIONS A tall build and big tires give 4Runner a loft step-in that's especially difficult for shorter people. Once aboard, there's room enough for four adults, plus better-than-average comfort for a middle-rear passenger. Cargo space is generous even without folding the split rear seat, and the full-size spare mounts out of the way beneath the rear floor. The power tailgate window is an SUV exclusive, but a little less convenient than simple flip-up glass. A no-nonsense dashboard design and fine visibility ease driving, but the pop-out dual cupholders block the climate controls. Like most Toyotas, 4Runners we've tested have been impressively solid and trouble-free.

VALUE 4Runner is among the pricier midsize SUVs, but a test drive might convince you that its top-notch quality, V6 refinement, and high resale value are worth its extra cost. This year's newly standard full-time 4WD and antiskid/traction control further enhances the appeal of this Recommended pick.

ENGINES

	dohc V6
Size, liters/cu. in.	3.4/207
Horsepower @ rpm	183 @ 4800
Torque (lb-ft) @ rpm	217 @ 3600
Availability	S

EPA city/highway mpg
4-speed OD automatic	17/20

PRICES

Toyota 4Runner	Retail Price	Dealer Invoice
SR5 2WD 4-door wagon	$26355	$23456
SR5 4WD 4-door wagon	28895	24716
Limited 2WD 4-door wagon	34955	31110
Limited 4WD 4-door wagon	37605	33468
Destination charge	480	480

Specifications begin on page 535.

TOYOTA

Prices are for vehicles distributed by Toyota Motor Sales, U.S.A., Inc. The dealer invoice and destination charge may be higher in areas served by independent distributors.

STANDARD EQUIPMENT:

SR5: 3.4-liter dohc V6 engine, 4-speed automatic transmission, traction control, dual front airbags, antilock brakes, antiskid system, daytime running lights, variable-assist power steering, tilt steering wheel, cruise control, cloth upholstery, front bucket seats, center console, cupholders, split folding rear seat, heated power mirrors, power door locks, power tailgate window, AM/FM/cassette/CD player, digital clock, tachometer, variable intermittent wipers, passenger-side visor mirror, map lights, auxiliary power outlets, rear defogger, intermittent rear wiper/washer, remote fuel-door/tailgate release, automatic-off headlights, rear privacy glass, full-size spare tire, 225/75R15 tires. **4WD** models add: full-time 4-wheel drive, 2-speed transfer case, skid plates.

Limited adds: air conditioning w/automatic climate control, leather-wrapped steering wheel, leather upholstery, heated power front seats, wood interior trim, power windows, remote keyless entry, power antenna, universal garage door opener, driver-side visor mirror, illuminated passenger-side visor mirror, cargo cover, floormats, theft-deterrent system, fog lights, fender flares, running boards, 265/70R16 tires, alloy wheels. **4WD** adds: full-time 4-wheel drive, 2-speed transfer case, skid plates.

OPTIONAL EQUIPMENT:
Major Packages

	Retail Price	Dealer Invoice
Upgrade Value Pkg. 1, SR5	$2180	$1744
Manufacturer's discount price	980	882

Air conditioning, power windows and door locks, remote keyless entry, upgraded sound system, power antenna, cargo cover, floormats. Manufacturer's discount price may not be available in areas served by independent distributors.

Upgrade Value Pkg. 2, 2WD SR5	2960	2368
Manufacturer's discount price	1760	1584

Value Pkg. 1 plus leather-wrapped steering wheel and shift knob, manual 6-way front sport bucket seats w/4-way adjustable headrests, cloth door trim panels, alloy wheels. NA w/Leather Pkg., Sport Pkg., chrome wheel lip moldings, fender flares. Manufacturer's discount price may not be available in areas served by independent distributors.

Upgrade Value Pkg. 3, SR5	3435	2748
Manufacturer's discount price	2235	2011

Upgrade Value Pkg. 2 plus 4.10 axle ratio, heavy-duty brakes, 265/70R16 mud/snow tires. Requires fender flares or chrome wheel lip moldings. NA w/Sport Pkg., Leather Pkg. Manufacturer's discount price may not be available in areas served by independent distributors.

Prices are accurate at time of publication; subject to manufacturer's change.

TOYOTA

	Retail Price	Dealer Invoice
Sport Pkg., SR5	$1700	$1360

Leather-wrapped steering wheel and shift knob, manual 6-way front sport seats w/4-way adjustable headrests, metallic instrument panel, cloth door trim panels, fog lights, hood scoop, color-keyed bumpers and grille, fender flares, 4.10 axle ratio, heavy-duty brakes, 265/70R16 tires, alloy wheels. Requires Upgrade Pkg. 1. NA w/chrome wheel lip moldings, fender flares.

Leather Pkg., SR5	1250	1000

Leather upholstery, manual 6-way front sport seats w/4-way adjustable headrests, leather-wrapped steering wheel and shift knob.

Convenience Pkg.	810	523

Cargo mat, roof rack, rear wind deflector, towing receiver hitch.

Comfort and Convenience

Rear heater	170	136

Includes rear storage console w/cupholders.

Power sunroof	815	652
AM/FM/cassette w/in-dash 6-disc CD changer, Limited	200	150
6-disc CD changer	550	385
Deluxe Security System, SR5	439	275

Includes remote keyless entry, theft-deterrent system. Requires Upgrade Pkg.

Appearance and Miscellaneous

Fog lights, SR5	269	180
Roof rack	275	165
Running boards, SR5	649	389

Requires fender flares or Sport Pkg.

Fender flares, SR5	230	184

Requires alloy wheels AL or Upgrade Value Pkg. 3.

Special Purpose, Wheels and Tires

Towing hitch receiver	339	239
Alloy wheels AY, 2WD SR5	365	292
Alloy wheels AL, SR5	840	672

Includes 265/70R16 mud/snow tires, heavy-duty brakes, 4.10 axle ratio. Requires fender flares or chrome wheel lip moldings.

Post production options also available.

TOYOTA AVALON

CG RECOMMENDED AUTO

Front-wheel-drive full-size car
Base price range: $25,845-$30,405. Built in USA.
Also consider: Buick LeSabre, Dodge Intrepid, Pontiac Bonneville

Specifications begin on page 535.

TOYOTA

Toyota Avalon

FOR • Build quality • Acceleration • Automatic transmission performance • Quietness • Passenger room • Ride/handling **AGAINST** • Brake-pedal feel

America's only import-brand full-size sedan is unchanged for 2001 following its full redesign last year. Avalon continues in XL and better-equipped XLS models, both with a 3.0-liter V6, automatic transmission, antilock 4-wheel disc brakes, front side airbags, and a choice of front bucket seats or a split front bench. Optional for XLS is an antiskid system similar to that offered by Toyota's premium Lexus brand. It's designed to activate individual brakes as needed to counteract skids in turns, and incorporates traction control as well as a Brake Assist feature that automatically applies full braking force in emergency stops. Also available are leather upholstery, power seats with memory, power moonroof, and a 115-volt AC outlet for household-type plugs.

PERFORMANCE Improved quietness was a major goal for Avalon's redesign, and Toyota achieved that and more. Except for some mild tire rumble over very coarse pavement, this is one hushed car. Even pedal-to-metal acceleration produces only a distant, rich-sounding engine note. Acceleration itself is strong enough for most anys situation. Our test car did 0-60 mph in 8.3 seconds, which is about mid-pack for the full-size class, though the 21 mpg it averaged is better than we get with most like-sized sedans. Toyota recommends 91-octane fuel. The automatic transmission is responsive and glassy smooth.

Ride is comfortable, almost plush, and though Avalon is no sports sedan, it hustles well along twisty roads, abetted by firm, communicative steering. Body roll is noticed in hard cornering, but it's not alarming. The main chinks in the dynamic armor are a bit more body drumming than we expected over rough patches, and slightly unprogressive pedal action in routine braking.

ACCOMMODATIONS The original Avalon was pretty roomy, but the latest edition has a truly spacious interior. Even 6-footers ride in tandem with plenty of leg-stretch for both. Seats are set comfortably off the floor,

Prices are accurate at time of publication; subject to manufacturer's change.

CONSUMER GUIDE

TOYOTA

yet all-around head room is fine even beneath the available moonroof. Width is adequate for three adults front and back, though middle riders must straddle a floor hump and won't have much foot room. Rear entry/exit isn't barn-door easy but is far from difficult, and all seats are comfortably supportive. Luggage space is ample, though not best in class.

Avalon's dashboard resembles some GM designs of yore, but it works far better, though the steering-wheel rim can obscure the tops of the main gauges. Climate and audio controls couldn't be better, and there's plenty of convenient small-items stowage, including a glovebox that could swallow a half-dozen Big Macs. Drivers have good visibility despite hard-to-see rear body corners, and door mirrors are usefully large.

VALUE Toyota won't say this, but the latest Avalon is almost a Lexus: roomy, quiet, smooth-riding, and quite roadable for a family-oriented sedan. In fact, we think Avalon is the next best thing to the Best Buy near-luxury Lexus ES 300, and it's more affordable to boot.

ENGINES

	dohc V6
Size, liters/cu. in.	3.0/181
Horsepower @ rpm	210 @ 5800
Torque (lb-ft) @ rpm	220 @ 4400
Availability	S

EPA city/highway mpg
4-speed OD automatic	21/29

PRICES

Toyota Avalon	Retail Price	Dealer Invoice
XL 4-door sedan, front bucket seats	$25845	$22626
XL 4-door sedan, front bench seat	26665	23344
XLS 4-door sedan, front bucket seats	30405	26305
XLS 4-door sedan, front bench seat	30305	26219
Destination charge	455	455

Prices are for vehicles distributed by Toyota Motor Sales, U.S.A., Inc. The dealer invoice and destination charge may be higher in areas served by independent distributors.

STANDARD EQUIPMENT:

XL: 3.0-liter dohc V6 engine, 4-speed automatic transmission, dual front airbags, front side-impact airbags, antilock 4-wheel disc brakes, daytime running lights, air conditioning w/dual-zone manual control, variable-assist power steering, tilt steering wheel, cruise control, cloth upholstery, manual front bucket seats w/center console or power split bench seat, cupholders, rear seat trunk pass-through, overhead console, power mirrors, power win-

Specifications begin on page 535.

TOYOTA

dows, power door locks, AM/FM/cassette/CD player, digital clock, tachometer, outside temperature indicator, rear defogger, auxiliary power outlet, illuminated visor mirrors, variable intermittent wipers, remote fuel door and decklid releases, automatic headlights, full-size spare tire, 205/65R15 tires, wheel covers.

XLS adds: dual-zone automatic climate control, interior air filter, leather-wrapped steering wheel, power front seats, heated power mirrors, JBL sound system, remote keyless entry, trip computer, compass, automatic day/night rearview mirror, universal garage door opener, theft-deterrent system, fog lights, alloy wheels.

OPTIONAL EQUIPMENT:

	Retail Price	Dealer Invoice

Major Packages

	Retail Price	Dealer Invoice
Pkg. 1, XL w/bucket seats	$1035	$828
Power front seats, remote keyless entry.		
Pkg. 2, XL w/bucket seats	1420	1136
Power front seats, remote keyless entry, 205/65HR15 tires, alloy wheels.		
Pkg. 3, XL w/bucket seats	2590	2072
XL w/bench seat	670	536
Pkg. 2 plus leather upholstery, leather-wrapped steering wheel and shift knob.		
Pkg. 4, XL w/bench seat	1820	1456
Leather upholstery, leather-wrapped steering wheel and shift knob, remote keyless entry, 205/65HR16 tires, alloy wheels.		
Pkg. 5, XLS	1375	1100
Leather upholstery, memory for driver seat and mirrors, AC outlet, 205/60R16 tires.		
Pkg. 6, XLS	1625	1288
Pkg. 5 plus in-dash 6-disc CD changer.		
Pkg. 7, XLS	1940	1540
Pkg. 6 plus heated front seats.		
Pkg. 8, XLS	330	252
In-dash 6-disc CD changer, 205/60R16 tires.		

Safety Features

	Retail Price	Dealer Invoice
Antiskid system, XLS	850	680
Includes traction control and brake assist.		

Comfort and Convenience

	Retail Price	Dealer Invoice
Power sunroof	910	728
JBL sound system, XL	360	270
Security System, XL	249	155
Includes remote keyless entry and theft-deterrent system.		

Post production options also available.

Prices are accurate at time of publication; subject to manufacturer's change.

TOYOTA

TOYOTA CAMRY/SOLARA

Toyota Camry 4-door sedan

Front-wheel-drive midsize car

Base price range: $17,675-$30,515. Built in USA, Japan, and Canada. **Also consider:** Chrysler Sebring, Ford Taurus, Honda Accord, Nissan Maxima

FOR • Acceleration (V6) • Ride • Quietness • Build quality • Exterior finish **AGAINST** • Rear visibility • Steering feel • Rear-seat entry/exit (Solara)

A special equipment package for midlevel Camrys is the main 2001 change to Toyota's most popular sedans and their 2-door Solara spin-offs. A perennial U.S. sales leader, Camry comes in CE, LE, and top-shelf XLE sedans. All have standard 4-cylinder power; a V6 is available for LE and XLE. CEs and LEs offer manual or optional automatic transmission; XLEs are automatic only.

For 2001, a new Gallery Series package dresses up LE models with 2-tone paint and cloth interior, leather-wrapped steering wheel and shift knob, and assorted other trim items. And CE models replace standard 14-inch wheels and a compact spare tire with 15-inch wheels and a full-size spare.

Unchanged for '01 are the Solara coupe and convertible, which share the sedan platform and are marketed as Camrys but have unique styling and chassis tuning. Coupes come in 4-cylinder and V6 SE trim with manual or automatic transmission and in upscale V6 SLE form with standard automatic. Convertibles offer the same model choices, but no manual shift. They have a standard power top with glass rear window.

Front side airbags are optional for both Camrys and Solaras. Antilock brakes are available on 4-cylinder models and standard on V6s. ABS-equipped models replace rear drum brakes with discs.

PERFORMANCE Camry and Solara share chassis and powertrains with the posh Lexus ES 300 sedan, so they're smooth, polished performers, though a bit dull dynamically. Strong points include a supple,

Specifications begin on page 535.

TOYOTA

absorbent ride, outstanding quietness, and strong acceleration with V6 (under 8 seconds 0-60 mph in the coupe and sedan), plus low tire and wind noise. The 4-cylinder engine is also quite refined and decently peppy, if noticeably less muscular than the V6, especially with automatic transmission. A 4-cylinder Camry averaged 22.5 mpg in testing that included lots of urban driving. Our recent V6 test models have averaged in the low-20s; a manual V6 Solara, for example, returned 23 mpg. The V6 requires premium fuel. Solara convertibles weigh about 200 pounds more than the coupes, and we timed a 4-cylinder convertible at a leisurely 11 seconds 0-60 mph. The added weight comes largely from additional structural reinforcements, though as with most 4-seat convertibles, Solara quivers and flexes over bumps.

Though safe, predictable, and pleasant to drive, none of these Toyotas is truly sporty. Steering is quick and precise, but also a bit over-assisted and numb. Even the more firmly damped Solaras tend to "float" over dips and swells. There's also marked body lean in hard, tight turns, though it's far from alarming. Braking is strong, consistent, and easily modulated.

ACCOMMODATIONS All these cars boast attractive cabins that easily carry four adults; insufficient rear shoulder width makes a fifth passenger feel cramped, especially in Solaras. Entry/exit is easy in Camrys and not too bad in the 2-doors, though Solaras suffer from low, narrowish rear passageways, no slide-forward feature on the driver's seat, and cumbersome front seat latches and belts. Cargo space is competitive, but Solara trunk openings is fairly high and not that large. The convertible's trunk is smaller than the coupe's, but still of useful size. Coupes and sedans have split-fold rear seatbacks with in-trunk security locks.

Drivers get a good range of seat/steering wheel adjustments and well-placed gauges and controls. Coupes and sedans afford generally clear outward vision, although both have nagging over-the-shoulder blind spots. Typical of ragtops, the convertible has mediocre rear visibility due to the top's thick rear "corners" and fairly slim back window. Build quality is excellent regardless of model, though interior decor can be drab, even on the pricey convertibles.

VALUE Camry and Solara are exceptionally well done mainstream midsize cars with the attractions of Toyota reliability and high resale value. We might wish for more personality and lower prices, but these cars are hard to fault and tough to beat. Convertibles are highly refined and exude typical Toyota quality, but they're not inexpensive.

ENGINES

	dohc I4	dohc I4	dohc V6	dohc V6
Size, liters/cu. in.	2.2/132	2.2/132	3.0/183	3.0/183
Horsepower @ rpm	136 @ 5200	138 @ 5200	194 @ 5200	200 @ 5200

Prices are accurate at time of publication; subject to manufacturer's change.

TOYOTA

	dohc I4	dohc I4	dohc V6	dohc V6
Torque (lb-ft) @ rpm	147 @ 4400	147 @ 4400	209 @ 4400	214 @ 4400
Availability	S[1]	S[2]	S[3]	S[4]
EPA city/highway mpg				
5-speed OD manual	23/32	23/32	21/28	21/28
4-speed OD automatic	23/30	23/30	20/28	20/28[5]

1. Camry. 2. Solara. 3. Camry V6. 4. Solara V6. 5. Solara conv. 19/26.

PRICES

Toyota Camry/Solara

	Retail Price	Dealer Invoice
Camry CE 4-cylinder 4-door sedan, 5-speed	$17675	$15657
Camry CE 4-cylinder 4-door sedan, automatic	18745	16364
Camry LE 4-cylinder 4-door sedan, automatic	20415	17873
Camry LE V6 4-door sedan, 5-speed	22385	19597
Camry LE V6 4-door sedan, automatic	23185	20298
Camry XLE 4-cylinder 4-door sedan, automatic	24095	21094
Camry XLE V6 4-door sedan, automatic	26225	22958
Solara SE 4-cylinder 2-door coupe, 5-speed	18965	16779
Solara SE 4-cylinder 2-door coupe, automatic	19765	17506
Solara SE 4-cylinder 2-door conv., automatic	25095	22228
Solara SE V6 2-door coupe, 5-speed	21675	19199
Solara SE V6 2-door coupe, automatic	22475	19908
Solara SE V6 2-door convertible, automatic	28035	24833
Solara SLE 2-door coupe, automatic	25165	22401
Solara SLE 2-door convertible, automatic	30515	27029
Destination charge	455	455

Prices are for vehicles distributed by Toyota Motor Sales, U.S.A., Inc. The dealer invoice and destination charge may be higher in areas served by independent distributors.

STANDARD EQUIPMENT:

Camry CE: 2.2-liter dohc 4-cylinder, 5-speed manual or 4-speed automatic transmission, dual front airbags, variable-assist power steering, tilt steering column, cloth upholstery, front bucket seats, center console, cupholders, split folding rear seat, tachometer, AM/FM/cassette/CD player, digital clock, intermittent wipers, remote fuel-door and trunk releases, rear defogger, auxiliary power outlet, automatic-off headlights, dual remote outside mirrors, full-size spare tire, 205/65R15 tires, wheel covers.

Camry LE adds: 2.2-liter dohc 4-cylinder or 3.0-liter dohc V6 engine, antilock 4-wheel disc brakes (V6), daytime running lights (V6), air conditioning, cruise control, height-adjustable driver seat, power mirrors, power windows, power door locks, variable intermittent wipers, automatic headlights.

Camry XLE adds: 4-speed automatic transmission, antilock brakes, 4-wheel

Specifications begin on page 535.

TOYOTA

disc brakes (V6), daytime running lights, power front seats w/driver-seat manual lumbar support, remote keyless entry, automatic climate control, JBL sound system, illuminated visor mirrors, leather-wrapped steering wheel, theft-deterrent system, 205/60R16 tires (V6), alloy wheels.

Solara SE adds to Camry LE: daytime running lights, illuminated visor mirrors, overhead console, power convertible top (convertible), automatic headlights, rear spoiler (convertible), fog lights.

Solara SLE adds: 3.0-liter dohc V6 engine, 4-speed automatic transmission, antilock 4-wheel disc brakes, automatic climate control, leather-wrapped steering wheel, leather upholstery, 8-way power driver seat, remote keyless entry, heated power mirrors, JBL sound system, automatic day/night mirror, universal garage door opener, outside temperature indicator, theft-deterrent system, rear spoiler, 205/60R16 tires, alloy wheels.

OPTIONAL EQUIPMENT:
Major Packages

	Retail Price	Dealer Invoice
Value Pkg. 1, CE	$1778	—
Manufacturer's discount price	778	700

Air conditioning, power mirrors and door locks, power windows, variable intermittent wipers, floormats.

Value Pkg. 4, LE 4-cylinder	632	—
Manufacturer's discount price	NC	NC

Remote keyless entry, power driver seat, floormats.

Value Pkg. 3, LE 4-cylinder	1042	—
Manufacturer's discount price	410	369

Antilock brakes, daytime running lights, remote keyless entry, power driver seat, JBL sound system, floormats.

GZ Gallery Series, LE 4-cylinder	782	704

Remote keyless entry, power driver seat, leather-wrapped steering wheel and shift knob, two-tone seats, unique floormats, carbon fiber interior trim, chrome exhaust tips. Requires full wheel covers or alloy wheels.

GX Gallery Series, LE 4-cylinder	1192	1073
LE V6 automatic	972	875

GZ Gallery Series plus antilock brakes, JBL sound system, daytime running lights. Requires full wheel covers or alloy wheels.

Value Pkg. 3, LE V6	822	—
Manufacturer's discount price	190	172

Antilock brakes, daytime running lights, remote keyless entry, power driver seat, JBL sound system, floormats.

Value Pkg. 5, LE V6	1290	1052

Value Pkg. 3 plus leather upholstery, leather-wrapped steering wheel and shift knob.

Value Pkg. 2, XLE	2606	—
Manufacturer's discount price,		
XLE 4-cylinder	1606	1445

Prices are accurate at time of publication; subject to manufacturer's change.

TOYOTA

	Retail Price	Dealer Invoice
XLE V6	$1106	$995

Front side-impact airbags, leather upholstery, power sunroof, JBL AM/FM/cassette w/in-dash 6-disc CD changer, map lights, floormats.

Upgrade Pkg. 1, SE coupe	692	623
SE convertible	935	732

Remote keyless entry, JBL sound system, floormats, mud guards, alloy wheels.

VH Sport Trim Pkg., SE 4-cylinder coupe	927	834
SE V6 5-speed coupe	1117	1005
SE V6 automatic coupe	1177	1059

Upgrade Pkg. 1 plus rear spoiler, leather-wrapped steering wheel.

VL Sport Trim Pkg. w/Leather, SE V6 5-speed coupe	2532	2137
SE V6 automatic coupe	2592	2191

VH Sport Trim Pkg. plus leather upholstery, power driver seat.

SW Grade Pkg., SE 4-cylinder 5-speed coupe	575	460
SE 4-cylinder automatic coupe	635	508

Leather-wrapped steering wheel, mud guards, alloy wheels.

Upgrade Pkg. 2, SE V6 convertible	1190	936

Remote keyless entry, leather-wrapped steering wheel, 8-way power driver seat, JBL sound system, floormats, 205/65R16 tires, alloy wheels.

Powertrains

Traction control, LE V6 automatic, XLE V6, SLE	300	240

Safety Features

Antilock brakes, CE, SE 4-cylinder	610	521

Camry includes daytime running lights.

Front side-impact airbags	250	215

CE requires Value Pkg. 1.

Comfort and Convenience

Cruise control, CE	250	200
Power sunroof, LE	1000	800
SE coupe, SLE	900	720
JBL sound system, LE	290	218
JBL AM/FM/cassette w/in-dash 6-disc CD changer, SLE	200	150
6-disc CD changer, Camry	550	385
Security System, CE, LE, SE	439	275

Remote keyless entry, theft-deterrent system.

Appearance and Miscellaneous

Fog lights, Camry	399	249
Rear spoiler, Camry	539	329
SE 4-cylinder coupe	435	348
Full wheel covers, LE	120	96

Requires Gallery Series.

TOYOTA

	Retail Price	Dealer Invoice
Alloy wheels, LE	$385	$308
CE, LE	592	440

Requires Gallery Series.

Post production options also available.

TOYOTA CELICA

Toyota Celica GT-S

Front-wheel-drive sports coupe

Base price range: $16,985-$22,155. Built in Japan. **Also consider:** Acura Integra, Honda Prelude, Mitsubishi Eclipse, Volkswagen New Beetle

FOR • Acceleration (GT-S 6-speed) • Handling/roadholding
AGAINST • Acceleration (GT with automatic) • Noise • Passenger room • Entry/exit

Toyota's sporty coupe was redesigned for 2000 and is unchanged for 2001. Celica is a 2-door hatchback with a 4-cylinder engine. The GT model has 140 horsepower, the sportier GT-S has 180. The GT comes with 5-speed manual transmission, the GT-S a 6-speed gearbox. Automatic is extra cost for both, with the GT-S providing manual gear selection via four steering-wheel buttons. Also optional for both Celicas are antilock brakes, front side airbags, and power sunroof.

Additional standard features include air conditioning, tilt steering wheel, and CD stereo. Sixteen-inch wheels are optional in place of 15s for the GT-S, which upgrades standard GT features with alloy wheels instead of steel rims, rear disc brakes instead of drums, power windows/door locks, leather-rim steering wheel, foglights, rear spoiler, and aluminum-trimmed foot pedals.

PERFORMANCE Toyota says the new Celicas have small engines to minimize weight. That pays off in agile handling and grippy cornering, abetted by sharp, responsive steering. Trouble is, the engines must rev like mad to produce good acceleration. That requires a heavy throttle

Prices are accurate at time of publication; subject to manufacturer's change.

TOYOTA

foot with automatic transmission, or lots of manual shifting—a pleasant task with the short-throw gearbox. Not surprisingly, the 6-speed GT-S is the liveliest Celica, though the automatic GT has adequate power except on long upgrades, where it tends to lose momentum. Still, the engines' high-rpm nature makes Celica noisy and thus wearing on a long trip—and the noise isn't that pleasant. There's also excessive tire roar.

In our tests, a manual GT-S averaged 24.2 mpg in mixed city/highway work. An automatic GT returned 30.3 mpg with help from a long highway trip. Even at that, the fuel tank gives a safe range of only about 300 miles. And the GT-S requires premium fuel.

As expected of sporty cars, Celica's firm ride is choppy on most surfaces, though this is more annoying than uncomfortable. Routine stopping ability is fine with the antilock brakes on our two test Celicas, but we think ABS should be standard on cars like this, not optional.

ACCOMMODATIONS Racecar-inspired styling helps keep cabin space to a premium. Even moderately tall front occupants have limited head and leg room—enough to cramp some drivers at the wheel. The back seat is the usual sporty-car torture chamber for adults, and entry/exit is crouch-and-crawl even in front. Happily, the front buckets provide excellent lumbar, shoulder, and lateral bolstering, though thigh support is subpar.

Drivers sit racecar low yet have a good view forward. Over-the-shoulder visibility is restricted by the roof styling, and, annoyingly, the rear spoiler partly hides following traffic. Controls are mostly simple and handy, and great shifter/wheel/pedal spacing enhances the sporty driving ambience. Gauges are legible, but the tachometer is not in the driver's direct line of sight, and warning lights are scattered around the instrument cluster. Interior materials mix some nicely textured surfaces with disappointingly thin plastic panels. Cabin stowage and cargo space are so-so, but your back should appreciate the reasonably low hatch opening.

VALUE Celicas have an edgy personality that appeals to young hotbloods. But they're tiresomely noisy and lack the low-end torque needed for decent scoot with the automatic transmission that even sporty coupe buyers often choose. Mitsubishi's Eclipse plays to more mature audiences with larger, quieter engines, including a V6. But Celica's adventurous styling and Toyota's reputation for reliability make this a sound sporty coupe value now and at resale time.

ENGINES

	dohc I4	dohc I4
Size, liters/cu. in.	1.8/109	1.8/110
Horsepower @ rpm	140 @ 6400	180 @ 7600
Torque (lb-ft) @ rpm	125 @ 6400	133 @ 6800
Availability	S[1]	S[2]

Specifications begin on page 535.

TOYOTA

EPA city/highway mpg

5-speed OD manual	31/43	
6-speed OD manual		27/42
4-speed OD automatic	31/49	28/39

1. GT. 2. GT-S.

2001 prices unavailable at time of publication.

PRICES

2000 Toyota Celica	Retail Price	Dealer Invoice
GT 2-door hatchback, 5-speed	$16875	$15033
GT 2-door hatchback, automatic	17675	15746
GT-S 2-door hatchback, 6-speed	21345	18907
GT-S 2-door hatchback, automatic	22045	19527
Destination charge	455	455

Prices are for vehicles distributed by Toyota Motor Sales, U.S.A., Inc. The dealer invoice and destination charge may be higher in areas served by independent distributors.

STANDARD EQUIPMENT:

GT: 1.8-liter dohc 4-cylinder 140-horsepower engine, 5-speed manual or 4-speed automatic transmission, dual front airbags, daytime running lights, air conditioning, variable-assist power steering, tilt steering wheel, cloth upholstery, front bucket seats, center console, cupholders, split folding rear seat, power mirrors, AM/FM/cassette/CD player, digital clock, tachometer, map lights, rear defogger, variable-intermittent wipers, visor mirrors, remote fuel door release, automatic headlights, 195/60R15 tires, wheel covers.

GT-S adds: 1.8-liter dohc 4-cylinder 180-horsepower engine, 6-speed manual or 4-speed automatic transmission w/manual-shift capability, 4-wheel disc brakes, leather-wrapped steering wheel, cruise control, power windows, power door locks, upgraded sound system, intermittent rear wiper/washer, fog lights, 205/55ZR15 tires, alloy wheels.

OPTIONAL EQUIPMENT:

Major Packages

Upgrade Pkg., GT	820	656
Cruise control, power windows and door locks.		
All Weather Guard Pkg., GT	270	223
Intermittent rear wiper/washer, heavy-duty battery and starter.		

Safety Features

Antilock brakes	550	473
Front side-impact airbags	250	215

Prices are accurate at time of publication; subject to manufacturer's change.

CONSUMER GUIDE

TOYOTA

Comfort and Convenience

	Retail Price	Dealer Invoice
Power sunroof	$880	$704
GT requires Upgrade Pkg.		
Leather upholstery, GT-S	620	496
Requires power sunroof.		
Premium sound system, GT	330	248
6-disc CD changer	550	385
Security System	439	275
Remote keyless entry, theft-deterrent system. GT requires Upgrade Pkg.		

Appearance and Miscellaneous

Rear spoiler, GT	540	432
GT-S	435	348
GT includes fog lights.		
Alloy wheels, GT	385	308

Post production options also available.

TOYOTA COROLLA

Toyota Corolla

Front-wheel-drive subcompact car; similar to Chevrolet Prizm

Base price range: $12,568-$14,198. Built in USA and Canada.
Also consider: Ford Focus, Honda Civic, Mazda Protege

FOR • Fuel economy • Build quality • Exterior finish **AGAINST** • Rear-seat room

A facelifted Corolla bowed this spring as an early 2001 model with new front and rear facias and a juggled lineup. The VE badge is discontinued, with the former mid-level CE taking its place as the base model. In the process, the CE loses such standard features as tilt steering wheel, cassette player, rear defogger, and split/fold rear seat. LE remains the top-line model, but it's decontented to the level of the old CE, with formerly standard features such as air conditioning and power

Specifications begin on page 535.

TOYOTA

windows/locks relegated to option packages. New to the line is a sport-oriented S model, equipped with color-keyed trim, fog lights, slightly wider tires, and tachometer.

All Corollas use a 1.8-liter 4-cylinder engine and manual or optional automatic transmission. Antilock brakes and front side airbags are optional. Corolla's design and powertrain originate with Toyota but are shared with the Chevrolet Prizm. Both vehicles are built at a General Motors-Toyota plant in California. (Some Corollas are also built in Canada.)

PERFORMANCE Corolla and Prizm are showing their age, but remain fine small cars. Manual-shift models feel frisky and average close to 30 mpg. Automatic versions returned 26.5-29.3 mpg in our tests, and although they felt sleepy off the line, we timed one at a respectable 9.7 seconds 0-60 mph. The air conditioning saps some pep with either transmission, however.

The suspension on these cars favors ride comfort over handling. Bumps are absorbed well, and straight-line stability is good, but body roll is the rule in hard cornering.

Corollas seem to be insulated better than Prizms against road and wind noise, but both are quieter than the subcompact-car norm. Engine thrash that's audible near full throttle goes away in moderate-speed cruising. The optional antilock brakes provide strong stopping power, though recent test Prizms suffered mushy brake-pedal feel.

ACCOMMODATIONS These cars reveal their 1993-vintage design with a rear seat that's very tight for adults, with notably little toe and leg room. The more-modern, upright styling of the new Ford Focus and Toyota's own Echo provide far roomier accommodations. At least the Corolla/Prizm rear doors are wide enough at the bottom for acceptable entry/exit by average-sized folks. Front seats are comfortable and spacious enough, and a low cowl and beltline make for great outward visibility. It's a slight stretch to radio and climate controls, but they're simple to use and clearly marked. The trunk is usefully sized, but the lid hinges dip into the load space, and base models don't offer the convenience of a split folding rear seatback. Corolla and Prizm are well built and have sturdy-feeling cabin materials. However, we've noticed irregular exterior panel gaps and minor steering-column rattles in recent examples of both versions.

VALUE They're not the newest or least expensive subcompacts around, but both Corolla and Prizm are solid, safe choices that benefit from Toyota's great reliability record. Note that Corolla handily outsells its Chevy cousin and, being a Toyota, commands higher resale values.

ENGINES

	dohc I4
Size, liters/cu. in.	1.8/110
Horsepower @ rpm	125 @ 5600

Prices are accurate at time of publication; subject to manufacturer's change.

TOYOTA

	dohc I4
Torque (lb-ft) @ rpm	122 @ 4400
Availability	S

EPA city/highway mpg
5-speed OD manual	31/38
3-speed automatic	28/33
4-speed OD automatic	28/36

PRICES

Toyota Corolla

	Retail Price	Dealer Invoice
CE 4-door sedan, 5-speed	$12568	$11456
CE 4-door sedan, automatic	12983	11833
S 4-door sedan, 5-speed	12793	11332
S 4-door sedan, automatic	13608	12054
LE 4-door sedan, 5-speed	13383	11854
LE 4-door sedan, automatic	14198	12576
Destination charge	455	455

Prices are for vehicles distributed by Toyota Motor Sales, U.S.A., Inc. The dealer invoice and destination charge may be higher in areas served by independent distributors.

STANDARD EQUIPMENT:

CE: 1.8-liter dohc 4-cylinder engine, 5-speed manual or 3-speed automatic transmission, dual front airbags, daytime running lights, power steering, cloth upholstery, front bucket seats, center console, cupholders, AM/FM radio, tachometer (5-speed), outside temperature indicator (5-speed), visor mirrors, intermittent wipers, automatic headlights, remote decklid and fuel door release, dual outside mirrors, 175/65R14 tires.

S adds: 5-speed manual or 4-speed automatic transmission, tachometer, variable intermittent wipers, outside temperature display, fog lights, 185/65R14 tires, wheel covers.

LE adds: tilt steering wheel, AM/FM/cassette, digital clock, map lights, rear defogger, split folding rear seat.

OPTIONAL EQUIPMENT:
Major Packages

Extra Value Pkg. 1, CE	730	658
Air conditioning, AM/FM/cassette, digital clock.		
Extra Value Pkg. 1, S	1095	986
Air conditioning, power windows and door locks, digital clock.		
Extra Value Pkg. 2, S	1235	1112
Extra Value Pkg. 1 plus color-keyed mirrors.		
Extra Value Pkg. 1, LE	1025	923
Air conditioning, power windows and door locks.		

Specifications begin on page 535.

TOYOTA

	Retail Price	Dealer Invoice
Extra Value Pkg. 2, LE	$1165	$1049
Extra Value Pkg. 1 plus color-keyed mirrors.		
Appearance Pkg., CE	160	128
Bodyside moldings, wheel covers.		
Convenience Pkg., S	430	354
Tilt steering wheel, cruise control.		
All-Weather Guard Pkg., CE, S	70	59
Heavy-duty heater and rear heater ducts, heavy-duty starter. NA with rear defogger.		

Safety Features
Antilock brakes, S, LE	550	473
Front side-impact airbags	250	215

Comfort and Convenience
Power sunroof, LE	735	588
S	715	572
Rear defogger, CE, S	205	164
Cruise control, LE	250	200
Power door locks, CE	270	216
AM/FM/cassette, S	210	158
AM/FM/CD player, S	335	235
LE	100	75
Alloy wheels, S, LE	365	292

Post production options also available.

TOYOTA ECHO

Toyota Echo 4-door sedan

Front-wheel-drive subcompact car

Base price range: $9,995-$11,325. Built in Japan. **Also consider:** Dodge/Plymouth Neon, Ford Focus, Honda Civic, Mazda Protege, Mitsubishi Mirage

FOR • Fuel economy • Maneuverability **AGAINST** • Acceleration

Prices are accurate at time of publication; subject to manufacturer's change.

TOYOTA

(automatic transmission) • Rear-seat entry/exit (2-door)

New for 2000, Toyota's latest entry-level small car is unchanged for its second season apart from one new exterior color. Echo is priced well below Toyota's larger Corolla subcompact, yet offers similar interior space within a shorter, taller body. Buyers have a choice of 2- and 4-door sedans, both with a 1.5-liter 4-cylinder engine. Echo's available automatic transmission features Toyota's "uphill shift logic" that's claimed to minimize "hunting" between gears on long or steep upgrades. Options include anti-lock brakes, air conditioning, power door locks (but not mirrors), and split-fold rear seat. A tilt steering wheel is standard, but power steering is optional. Echo is among the few vehicles that does not offer power windows.

PERFORMANCE Low weight and a phone-booth body give Echo a different driving feel than most other subcompacts. Handling is front-drive predictable, but cornering gets a tad tippy if you rush, aggravated by skinny tires that don't furnish much grip and tend to follow longitudinal grooves too easily. The bluff-sided styling and low weight combine to make Echo rather sensitive to crosswinds; that demands a steady hand on the helm, yet steering feel is slightly dull. By contrast, close-quarters maneuvering is a snap, aided by a tight turning radius, and ride is better than the small-car norm, though there's some jiggle on washboard freeways.

Though the engine is no powerhouse, curb weights are only around 2000 pounds—among the lightest in the class—so Echo is almost brisk with manual shift and decent with automatic. A test automatic 4-door clocked 9.8 seconds 0-60 mph. The automatic itself is generally smooth and responsive, though it sometimes hesitates a second or two when asked to downshift in the 35-55-mph range. Echo's lofty EPA ratings are confirmed by our 31-mpg average in hard driving that included gas-eating performance tests.

Noise levels are nothing special, though cross-country drives shouldn't be tiring. The main offender is marked exhaust boom near maximum rpm. Our test car lacked ABS but resisted wheel locking quite well, making short, stable simulated panic stops.

ACCOMMODATIONS Despite its external size, Echo is among the roomier subcompacts. The tall cabin is too narrow to fit three adults in back without squeezing, but rear foot room is good, all-around head room generous. Seats are comfortable if rather flat, and their high positioning allows legs to rest comfortably. Rear entry/exit isn't that easy on the 2-door despite a standard slide-forward right front seat, and narrow rear-door bottoms are a minor nuisance on the 4-door. The high-set steering wheel has a slight horizontal rake that may take getting used to, yet lanky drivers must sit with splayed knees because the front seats could use more rearward travel. Visibility is very good.

Though it seems a style gimmick, the central gauge pod atop the dash is angled toward the driver and quite legible, though it may be too

Specifications begin on page 535.

TOYOTA

distant for some eyes. Other driving controls are simple and handy. The audio unit is flanked by open bins that hold 8-10 CDs each, and the cabin has plenty of other stash spaces. The trunk is spacious for the tidy exterior package, but the short tail leaves little fore-aft length without the optional split-fold rear seat. Typical of Toyotas, Echoes we've tested have been solid and well finished. Interior materials are attractive, but still entry-level in look and feel.

VALUE This is a pleasant, efficient car with keen pricing and Toyota's strong reputation for quality and reliability. Sales have been tepid for such an affordable car, however, so discounts should be available.

ENGINES

	dohc I4
Size, liters/cu. in.	1.5/91
Horsepower @ rpm	108 @ 6000
Torque (lb-ft) @ rpm	105 @ 4200
Availability	S
EPA city/highway mpg	
5-speed OD manual	34/41
4-speed OD automatic	32/39

PRICES

Toyota Echo	Retail Price	Dealer Invoice
Base 2-door coupe, 5-speed	$9995	$9395
Base 2-door coupe, automatic	10795	10147
Base 4-door sedan, 5-speed	10525	9894
Base 4-door sedan, automatic	11325	10646
Destination charge	455	455

Prices are for vehicles distributed by Toyota Motor Sales, U.S.A., Inc. The dealer invoice and destination charge may be higher in areas served by independent distributors.

STANDARD EQUIPMENT:

Base: 1.5-liter dohc 4-cylinder engine, 5-speed manual or 4-speed automatic transmission, dual front airbags, tilt steering wheel, cloth upholstery, front bucket seats, center console, cupholders, AM/FM radio, driver-side visor mirror, dual outside mirrors, 175/65R14 tires, wheel covers.

OPTIONAL EQUIPMENT:
Major Packages

Upgrade Pkg. 1	1020	832

Power steering, intermittent wipers, split folding rear seat, digital clock, remote control outside mirrors, bodyside cladding.

Prices are accurate at time of publication; subject to manufacturer's change.

TOYOTA

	Retail Price	Dealer Invoice
Upgrade Pkg. 2, coupe	$1420	$1123
sedan	1465	1159

Air conditioning, power door locks, AM/FM/cassette/CD player. Requires Upgrade Pkg. 1.

All Weather Pkg.	275	220

Rear defogger, heavy-duty battery, rear seat heater ducts. Requires Upgrade Pkg. 1.

Safety Features

Antilock brakes	590	505

Includes daytime running lights. Requires Upgrade Pkg. 2 or All Weather Pkg.

Front side-airbags	250	215

Comfort and Convenience

Power steering	270	231
Air conditioning	925	740
AM/FM/cassette	170	128
AM/FM/cassette/CD player	270	203
In-dash 6-disc CD changer	589	414

NA w/Upgrade Pkg. 2 or AM/FM/cassette/CD player.

Power door locks, coupe	225	180
sedan	270	216

Requires Upgrade Pkg. 1.

Security System	439	275

Remote keyless entry, theft-deterrent system. Requires power door locks or Upgrade Pkg. 2.

Split folding rear seat	165	132

Appearance and Miscellaneous

Alloy wheels	499	375

TOYOTA HIGHLANDER

Front- or all-wheel-drive midsize sport-utility vehicle; similar to Lexus RX 300

Base price range: NA. Built in Japan. **Also consider:** Acura MDX, Lexus RX 300, Mercedes-Benz M-Class

Arriving in early 2001 as the fifth sport-utility vehicle under the Toyota brand, Highlander is an under-skin sibling to the popular car-based Lexus RX 300. Both are built in Japan on the Toyota Camry/Lexus ES 300 sedan platform, but Highlander wears more traditional wagon styling than the RX and strides a 4-inch longer wheelbase, with most of that going to extra cargo room. Highlander is a 5-seater; no third seating row is available.

Specifications begin on page 535.

TOYOTA

Toyota Highlander

Toyota sees Highlander as a midsize SUV for buyers interested more in on-road comfort, refinement and performance than off-road ability and a truck-tough image; those buyers will continue to be served by the truck-like 4Runner. The unibody Highlander is slightly longer than the body-on-frame 4Runner, but stands about a half-inch lower and 5 inches wider.

Highlander is offered with 4-cylinder and V6 power and a choice of front-wheel drive or permanent 4-wheel drive. The 4-cylinder is a version of the 2.7-liter engine used in Toyota's Tacoma compact pickups; the V6 is the company's familiar 3.0-liter that powers the RX 300. Both are dual-overhead-camshaft designs with four valves per cylinder and will be offered only with a 4-speed automatic transmission. The V6 4WD version is expected to be the best-selling Highlander model. An upgrade Limited Package is available, and leather upholstery is an option on V6 versions.

Pricing was not available for this report, but Toyota hopes to start the 4-cylinder model in the mid-$20,000 area, which suggests the V6 4WD will go for around $30,000. Projected sales are 50,000 in calendar '01 and 75,000 a year thereafter. We haven't yet driven the Highlander and thus cannot provide ratings or an evaluation.

ENGINES

	dohc I4	dohc V6
Size, liters/cu. in.	2.7/164	3.0/183
Horsepower @ rpm	150 @ 4800	220 @ 5800
Torque (lb-ft) @ rpm	177 @ 4000	222 @ 4400
Availability	S	S

EPA city/highway mpg

4-speed OD automatic	19/24	18/22

Prices unavailable at time of publication.

TOYOTA LAND CRUISER
4-wheel-drive full-size sport-utility vehicle; similar to Lexus LX 470

Base price: $52,895. Built in Japan. **Also consider:** Chevrolet Tahoe

Prices are accurate at time of publication; subject to manufacturer's change.

TOYOTA

Toyota Land Cruiser

and Suburban, Ford Expedition, GMC Yukon/Denali

FOR • Passenger and cargo room • Acceleration • Ride • Quietness • Build quality **AGAINST** • Fuel economy • Entry/exit

An optional navigation system is the main addition to this full-size SUV for 2001. Land Cruiser shares its design with the upscale Lexus LX 470 version sold by Toyota's luxury division. They use the same V8 engine, automatic transmission, and permanent 4-wheel drive with low-range gearing and manual locking center differential. They also come with a traction control/antiskid system and 4-wheel antilock disc brakes. Maximum trailering weight is 6500 pounds. Power sunroof, leather upholstery, and rear air conditioning are also standard for the Cruiser, which comes with seating for five and offers an extra-cost 3-person third-row bench seat.

For 2001, Land Cruiser mimics the LX 470 with a newly optional navigation system featuring an in-dash screen with map display via digital video disc (DVD). Available with that is a 6-disc CD changer that can also display DVD video on the navigation screen, though only with the transmission in Park. An auto-dimming inside mirror is newly standard, and includes a digital compass on models without the navigation system.

The Japanese-built Land Cruiser gets some in-house competition in the 2001 Sequoia, a somewhat larger but lower-priced SUV based on Toyota's Tundra pickup and built alongside it in Indiana. Sequoia also uses the Cruiser's V8 and automatic transmission, but offers a 2-wheel drive model and standard window-curtain side airbags that are not available on the Land Cruiser.

PERFORMANCE Though too large and tall to drive like cars, these SUVs are among the most refined in the full-size class. Fast turns induce predictable body lean and a slight tipsy feel, but the always-on 4WD keeps grip secure, while the independent front suspension contributes to Land Cruiser's surprisingly absorbent on-road ride. The Lexus includes driver-selected shock-absorber firmness via a console switch. We found it does little for handling and makes for a slightly wallowy ride in soft mode; the firmer settings just cause jitters over closely spaced

Specifications begin on page 535.

TOYOTA

bumps. With luxury-grade sound deadening and silken engines, both models are quieter than many passenger sedans, not to mention most all other truck-type SUVs. Still, some wind noise is noticed at highway speeds, inevitable with such blocky styling. The standard antilock brakes make simulated panic stops stable and relatively short for heavyweight SUVs.

Despite that bulk, the 4.7-liter V8 delivers 0-60 mph in a brisk 9 seconds by our stopwatch. The transmission helps performance anywhere with prompt, smooth shifts up and down. Mileage is mediocre. Though an LX 470 gave us 15.4 mpg with lots of highway driving, the 13.6 mpg of our latest Land Cruiser is a more realistic overall average—and premium fuel is mandatory.

ACCOMMODATIONS Both these rigs have plenty of head room, plus good leg room and enough cabin width for comfortable three-adult seating on the second-row bench. The available third-row seat is cramped and inaccessible for all but children. Middle-row entry/exit is no picnic either, thanks to a tall step-up and narrow door bottoms. That high stance givesdrivers a commanding view, though headrests clutter things to the rear.

Lanky drivers enjoy generous rearward seat travel, and few vehicles of any type are more comfortable in front. The user-friendly dashboard, common to both versions, features simple rotary climate controls, though a few other switches aren't so easy to see. We have not tested the newly available navigation system and can't comment on its operation or how it integrates with the standard dashboard.

There's only grocery-bag space behind the third seat, but that folds up or removes fairly easily for generous cargo room. The drop-down tailgate means a long stretch to your cargo, though a plastic filler panel between the gate and load floor makes sliding heavy items a little easier.

VALUE Land Cruiser isn't cheap, and the Lexus costs even more. Superior customer service and a longer warranty are the LX 470's only tangible advantages over the Toyota. While some SUVs offer more metal for less money, these two are highly capable off-road, as quick and comfortable as any rival on-road, and built better than most. Land Cruiser gets our Recommended nod as a better value than the LX 470 in a high-end SUV.

ENGINES

	dohc V8
Size, liters/cu. in.	4.7/285
Horsepower @ rpm	230 @ 4800
Torque (lb-ft) @ rpm	320 @ 3400
Availability	S
EPA city/highway mpg	
4-speed OD automatic	13/16

Prices are accurate at time of publication; subject to manufacturer's change.

TOYOTA

PRICES

Toyota Land Cruiser	Retail Price	Dealer Invoice
Base 4-door 4WD wagon	$52895	$46282
Destination charge	480	480

Prices are for vehicles distributed by Toyota Motor Sales, U.S.A., Inc. The dealer invoice and destination charge may be higher in areas served by independent distributors.

STANDARD EQUIPMENT:

Base: 4.7-liter dohc V8 engine, 4-speed automatic transmission, full-time 4-wheel drive, 2-speed transfer case, locking rear differential, traction control, dual front airbags, antilock 4-wheel disc brakes, antiskid system, daytime running lights, air conditioning w/automatic climate control, interior air filter, rear heater, power steering, tilt leather-wrapped steering wheel, cruise control, leather upholstery, heated front bucket seats w/power lumbar support, 10-way power driver seat, 8-way power passenger seat, center console, overhead console, cupholders, split folding rear seat, heated power mirrors, power windows, power door locks, remote keyless entry, JBL AM/FM/cassette w/in-dash 6-disc CD changer, power antenna, digital clock, tachometer, power sunroof, illuminated visor mirrors, variable intermittent wipers, automatic day/night rearview mirror, compass, outside temperature indicator, rear defogger, rear variable-intermittent wiper/washer, automatic headlights, auxiliary power outlets, remote fuel-door release, theft-deterrent system, fog lights, rear privacy glass, front and rear tow hooks, skid plates, full-size spare tire, 275/70R16 tires, alloy wheels.

OPTIONAL EQUIPMENT:
Major Packages

C7 Convenience Pkg.	1780	1184

Running boards, roof rack, rear wind deflector, towing hitch receiver.

C9 Convenience Pkg.	2329	1527

C7 Convenience Pkg. plus burlwood dashboard trim.

Third Seat Pkg.	2265	1854

Leather split folding and reclining third row seat, additional cupholders, power swing-out rear quarter windows, rear air conditioning w/independent automatic climate control.

Comfort and Convenience

Navigation system	3000	2550

Included DVD player.

TOYOTA PRIUS

Front-wheel-drive subcompact car

Base price: $19,995. Built in Japan. **Also consider:** Ford Focus, Honda Civic, Honda Insight

Specifications begin on page 535.

TOYOTA

Toyota Prius

FOR • Fuel economy • Maneuverability **AGAINST** • Low-speed acceleration • Rear visibility

The second gas/electric hybrid vehicle to be sold in America arrives after three years on the Japanese market and a year behind Honda's similarly powered Insight 2-seat hatchback coupe. Prius is a 5-passenger 4-door sedan with a 1.5-liter 4-cylinder gasoline engine working in tandem with an electric motor. Its CVT transmission functions much like a regular automatic transmission, though it does not have a set number of gear ratios. Prius's drivetrain can employ its twin power sources in any combination depending on driving demands. No external charging is required; Prius in effect recharges it batteries as it drives. Prius moves away from a stop on electric power, then kicks in the gas engine. During coasting or braking, the gas engine will shut down automatically to conserve gas. Coasting and braking energy is harnessed by the electric motor, which generates power to recharge nickel-metal-hydride batteries mounted behind the rear seat. Toyota warrants the powertrain, including battery pack, for 8 years/100,000 miles. Antilock brakes, air conditioning, cassette stereo, and power windows/locks/mirrors are standard.

EVALUATION Prius disguises its hybrid powertrain well, acting much like any gasoline subcompact car and, in fact, delivering better highway throttle response than most. But it does have quirks. Transitions between power sources are nearly seamless, but there's a slight nudge when the engine cuts in or out. And we experienced an occasional power sag as the motor switched in and out of regenerating mode during low-speed braking. We clocked Prius at 12.3 seconds 0-60 mph, a full second behind our test Insight. But the Toyota doesn't feel sluggish around town and is surprisingly lively in the 55-70 mph range. A Prius tested in the Midwest averaged 44.1 mpg, one tested in hillier California averaged 38.3. Our test Insight averaged 57.3 mpg. Prius' tall body is subject to wavering in crosswinds but does offer lots of interior room. Gauges are center-mounted on the dashboard and include a video-type screen capable of displaying a running illustration of which power or recharging

Prices are accurate at time of publication; subject to manufacturer's change.

TOYOTA

mode is in use. Compared to Insight, Prius is a more practical and pleasant proposition for daily transportation, offering superior refinement, automatic transmission driving ease, and a more usable interior package. Both these hybrids are ultra-clean and fuel-efficient, and they cost about the same. But they're also rather costly for what are essentially high-tech alternatives to orthodox subcompacts.

ENGINES

	dohc I4/ electric
Size, liters/cu. in.	1.5/91
Horsepower @ rpm	70 @ 4500
Torque (lb-ft) @ rpm	82 @ 4200
Availability	S[1]
EPA city/highway mpg	
CVT/automatic	52/45

1. Gas engine; electric motor has 44 hp @ 1040 rpm and 258 lb-ft @ 0-400 rpm.

PRICES

Toyota Prius	Retail Price	Dealer Invoice
Base 4-door sedan	$19995	$18534
Destination charge	455	455

Prices are for vehicles distributed by Toyota Motor Sales, U.S.A., Inc. The dealer invoice and destination charge may be higher in areas served by independent distributors. Some option prices not available at time of publication.

STANDARD EQUIPMENT:

Base: 1.5-liter dohc 4-cylinder engine, electric drive motor, continuously-variable transmission, dual front airbags, antilock brakes, daytime running lights, air conditioning w/automatic climate control, power steering, tilt steering wheel, cloth upholstery, front bucket seats, center console, cupholders, heated power mirrors, power windows, power door locks, remote keyless entry, AM/FM/cassette, variable intermittent wipers, rear defogger, visor mirrors, auxiliary power outlet, theft-deterrent system, rear spoiler, 175/65R14 tires, alloy wheels.

OPTIONAL EQUIPMENT:

Safety Features

Front side-impact airbags	—	—

Comfort and Convenience

Cruise control	—	—
Navigation system	—	—
CD player	335	235
In-dash 6-disc CD player	550	385

Post production options also available.

Specifications begin on page 535.

TOYOTA RAV4

Toyota RAV4

Front- or all-wheel-drive compact sport-utility vehicle
Base price range: $16,215-$18,665. Built in Japan. **Also consider:** Ford Escape, Honda CR-V, Subaru Forester

FOR • Ride/handling • Maneuverability • Instruments/controls • Visibility • Build quality **AGAINST** • Acceleration • Engine noise • Rear-seat room

Toyota's compact sport-utility vehicle is redesigned for 2001 with a huskier look, more horsepower, a roomier interior than the original 1996-2000 RAV4—and a base price cut by some $680. Outside, the '01 is about 4 inches longer in wheelbase, 1.3 inches longer overall, and 2.4 inches wider. Toyota claims improved rigidity for the 4-door wagon unibody, which in turn has allowed the suspension to be retuned for a more compliant ride.

Inside, the '01 RAV4 claims nearly 3 inches more leg room in front, but 0.6-inch less in back. Rear head room diminishes by the same amount, but there's an inch more front head room. Cargo volume behind the rear seat increases 2.4 cubic feet; maximum volume is up 10.4 cubic feet. The back seat itself is a removable 50/50 bench that can also be slid forward or folded up in sections for extra space; it has reclining backrests too.

A 2.0-liter 4-cylinder remains the only engine, but the '01 unit is a new all-aluminum design with Toyota's VVT-i variable-valve-timing system. Against the previous iron-block/aluminum-head engine, the '01 version delivers 21 more horsepower, 10 extra pound-feet of torque, and lower emissions, RAV4 newly classed as a Low-Emissions Vehicle (LEV) in California and several Northeastern states. Like the original RAV, the '01 offers front-wheel drive or permanent 4-wheel drive and a choice of manual or optional automatic transmissions.

Other standard features include 4-wheel antilock brakes, air conditioning, cruise control, power moonroof, rear privacy glass, and aluminum wheels. Options include an "L" package with power door locks, heat-

Prices are accurate at time of publication; subject to manufacturer's change.

TOYOTA

ed door mirrors, 6-speaker CD/cassette audio, a hard cover for the outside-mount spare tire (versus flexible vinyl), foglamps, and various body features keyed to paint color. Leather upholstery is available separately.

Full prices were unavailable in time for this report, but Toyota says the base, 2WD manual-transmission RAV4 will start at $16,215, and the 4WD automatic at $18,665.

PERFORMANCE Toyota's redesign polishes RAV4 performance without really improving it. Our test 5-speed 4WD ran 0-60 mph in 9.6 seconds with just a driver aboard. That's about par with a comparably equipped 4-cylinder Honda CR-V but a few ticks adrift of our V6/automatic Ford Escape (9.0). We'd guess the automatic-equipped Toyota would need 10.5 seconds for the benchmark sprint. The new engine is a bit smoother and quieter than the previous 2.0-liter, but feels little stronger for mid-range passing or carrying a passenger/cargo load of any size. Fuel economy reflects this SUV's still-underpowered nature, our tester averaging an unimpressive 21.3 mpg versus the 22.5 we got in similar hard driving with a 4WD manual CR-V.

Like its predecessor, the '01 RAV4 is pleasantly carlike to drive. It bounds a bit over big moguls and feels agitated over some washboard surfaces, but the ride is never uncomfortable, just ordinary. Maneuverability is a plus, reflecting the compact exterior and aided by quick steering with very good feel for a truck. Hard cornering induces fair body lean, yet the RAV doesn't suffer the tippy feel that still plagues many SUVs, and it's easy, almost fun to drive on twisty roads. Our test model made literal short work of our simulated emergency stops, but mild wander occurred most every time, though it was easily corrected, and nosedive was on the heavy side of moderate.

Refinement is acceptable but nothing special. The new engine suffers the same boominess at high rpm than afflicted the old 2.0-liter, though it's pretty relaxed in gentle cruising—enough that tire whine is noticed. Wind noise wasn't a factor on our calm test day, but could be in gusty weather.

ACCOMMODATIONS The new RAV offers about the same passenger package as previous models, which means good room fore but a knees-up posture for adults behind a tall front occupant. Rear toe space is meager, and the cabin is too narrow for three adults to ride in back without crowding. All-around head clearance is ample, however, reflecting the tall wagon styling that also allows a comfortably upright driving stance. Outward vision is fine even aft, as the outside spare mounts low enough not to interfere. Taller drivers might wish for more rearward seat travel to get further back from the steering wheel, but no one will have trouble with the conveniently low step-in height.

Gauges and controls are typical Toyota and thus simple and convenient, but the new RAV4 shows almost Audi-like interior design flair, with

Specifications begin on page 535.

TOYOTA

a nice mix of textures and shades, classy low-grain dashboard and door plastic, and legible instruments with an attractive semi-retro look. More debateable are the faux-metal accents around the shifter and central dashboard air vents, but we love the front cupholders, which have solid floors and strong ratcheting brackets to secure most any size drink. Equally neat is the CD/cassette radio, which has a good old-fashioned tuning knob and sits high and handy above simple dial-type climate controls.

Utility is another plus. Though it's nothing special for comfort, the split rear bench folds up or removes easily for extra cargo space, and there's enough room behind it for at least a dozen large plastic bags, which can be secured from spilling on four fold-down hooks on the seatback's rear face. A bevy of bins, slots and netted pockets provides ample small-items storage. Our test car lacked a cargo cover, though, and we find the swing-out tail door a bit clumsy.

VALUE It's a little more grown up and sophisticated now, but the RAV4 is still best regarded as a pleasant suburban errand-runner rather than serious people-mover or off-road escape vehicle. And really, that's no bad thing. Though most rivals offer more room and stronger performance, none can beat Toyota's reputation for quality, durability, and high resale value, all of which make the RAV4 a must-see among baby SUVs.

ENGINES

	dohc I4
Size, liters/cu. in.	2.0/122
Horsepower @ rpm	148 @ 6000
Torque (lb-ft) @ rpm	142 @ 4000
Availability	S
EPA city/highway mpg	
5-speed OD manual	25/31[1]
4-speed OD automatic	24/29[2]

1. 22/27 w/4WD. 2. 23/27 w/4WD.

2001 prices unavailable at time of publication.

TOYOTA SEQUOIA
4-wheel-drive full-size sport-utility vehicle

Base price range: $30,815-$42,275. Built in USA. **Also consider:** Chevrolet Tahoe and Suburban, Ford Expedition, GMC Yukon/Denali

Sequoia bows for 2001 as Toyota's second full-size sport-utility vehicle. The American-built 8-passenger wagon is larger than the Japanese-made Land Cruiser and will be priced below that luxury SUV, though pricing wasn't available for this report. The new 4-door wagon is based on Toyota's full-size Tundra pickup truck and is close to Ford Expedition size. Sequoia comes with rear-wheel drive or a

Prices are accurate at time of publication; subject to manufacturer's change.

TOYOTA

Toyota Sequoia

4-wheel-drive system that isn't for use on dry pavement but does have low-range gearing. A 4.7-liter V8, automatic transmission, and an antiskid system are standard. SR5 models come with 16-inch tires, with 17s standard for Limiteds and available for SR5s. Sequoia's one-piece rear liftgate features a power-retracting window, like the Toyota 4Runner. Window-curtain side airbags are optional in concert with front side airbags. Standard on Sequoia Limiteds and optional on SR5s are a power driver's seat, rear heating/air conditioning with second-row controls, leather upholstery, alloy wheels, premium 10-speaker JBL cassette stereo with in-dash CD changer, roof rack, and a towing package with hitch and wire harness. Maximum tow ratings are 6500 pounds on 4x2s, 6200 on 4x4s.

EVALUATION Sequoia is mechanically refined for a big truck and our test 4x4 Limited clocked 0-60 mph in 9.5 seconds, more than class-competitive. Still, considerable bulk and mass mean only adequate midrange passing power. Our test Limited averaged 15.9 mpg overall, but just 12.4 in the city; it uses regular-grade fuel. Ride and handling have the sluggish, ponderous feel found in most full-size trucks. Small imperfections register with surprising clarity, though the suspension copes well with really rough stuff. Hard cornering feels stable for a big SUV, but Sequoia is a chore on twisty roads or to parallel park. Sequoia tops a high-riding chassis with a fairly low-roof cabin, so getting in requires a big step up—even 6-footers might need to use the Limited's running boards—and all-around head room is adequate rather than generous. But leg room is bountiful in the notably comfortable first- and second- row seats. The third-row best suits pre-teens. Drivers sit big-rig high and enjoy commanding views. Gauges and controls are simple, large, and handy. Only the third-row seats remove. Each half weighs a manageable 50 pounds, but they're awkward to take out or replace. Cargo space is generous with those seats removed and the middle seat folded up, but there's not that much room behind the third seat for a vehicle this large— enough for maybe three medium suitcases or 10 large grocery bags.

Specifications begin on page 535.

TOYOTA

It suffers all the usual big-SUV vices, Sequoia compensates with near luxury-car quietness and engine refinement, many thoughtful features, and solid craftsmanship, plus class-competitive passenger room. Also in its favor are Toyota's strong resale values and enviable reliability/durability record.

ENGINES

	dohc V8
Size, liters/cu. in.	4.7/285
Horsepower @ rpm	240 @ 4800
Torque (lb-ft) @ rpm	315 @ 3400
Availability	S

EPA city/highway mpg

4-speed OD automatic	14/18[1]

1. 14/17 w/4WD.

Full prices unavailable at time of publication.

TOYOTA SIENNA

CG RECOMMENDED AUTO

Toyota Sienna

Front-wheel-drive minivan

Base price range: $23,905-$28,436. Built in USA. **Also consider:** Dodge Caravan, Ford Windstar, Honda Odyssey

FOR • Passenger and cargo room • Build quality • Exterior finish
AGAINST • Fuel economy • Radio placement

More power, a mild facelift, and new features—including available front side airbags and antiskid and video entertainment systems—highlight a busy 2001 for Toyota's Kentucky-built minivan.

Sienna continues in a single body length but loses its base 3-door CE model. That leaves CE, LE, and top-shelf XLE versions with dual sliding side doors. A power right-side slider is optional for LE and XLE models. Dual power sliding side doors are newly available for XLE. A 3.0-liter V6 is the only engine, and it gains 16 horsepower for '01. Automatic transmission, antilock brakes, and low-tire-pressure warning system are standard.

Besides a freshened exterior, all 2001 Siennas get a revamped dash-

Prices are accurate at time of publication; subject to manufacturer's change.

TOYOTA

board and, as a new option, front side airbags. In addition, the third-row bench seat is now split 50/50. In the second-row, CE and LE come with a 2-place bench seat. Twin buckets are standard for XLE and available for LE.

Also new for 2001 is this minivan's first rear-seat video entertainment option, as well as its available first antiskid system. New for XLE models is standard automatic climate control and an optional in-dash CD changer.

PERFORMANCE We haven't yet driven an '01 Sienna, but this year's added power and torque will be appreciated when running with heavier loads. Our last test model ran 0-60 mph in a brisk 8.9 seconds, but that was with just the driver aboard; extra weight bogged it down noticeably. Despite its extra muscle, the '01 should average close to the 19.4 mpg we got with our extended-use Sienna over 9100 miles, much of which was highway driving. Note that the 2001 EPA city rating is unchanged at 19 mpg, but the highway estimate rises by one mpg, to 25. Premium fuel is still required for best performance, though.

Toyota's 3.0-liter V6 is a model of refinement, complemented by a smooth, prompt automatic transmission. Ride and handling are equally pleasant. Sienna takes bumps with little impact harshness, and shows only moderate minivan cornering lean, though with some front-end plowing. Hard takeoffs induce mild steering-wheel tug that highlights the lack of traction control, even as an option; that's a drawback in the snowbelt. Braking is swift and stable. Noise levels are subdued.

Our extended-use LE was trouble-free mechanically, but suffered an instrument-panel rattle that was cured by a trip to the dealer. Another test Sienna suffered an irritating rattle from the mid-seat area.

ACCOMMODATIONS Sienna's well-designed cabin has a low floor for super-easy entry/exit. The driving position is commanding, though the middle roof pillars and rear headrests impede driver vision somewhat. Some on our staff find the cloth front seats too soft for long-distance comfort, but adults get plenty of room anywhere. However, 2nd-row occupants lose valuable leg space with the seats ahead pushed back. Likewise the 3rd row. A column-mount transmission lever allows convenient front-to-rear walk-through.

Most controls are convenient, but the radio is mounted too low for easy operation while driving, though steering-wheel controls are available. Power rear-quarter windows are optional but can't be operated individually, which slightly limits their usefulness. Bins and drink holders of various sizes make for fine interior storage. There's room for a double row of grocery bags behind the third seat, which tumble-folds for more space. Removing the heavy middle or rear seats is a 2-person job.

Specifications begin on page 535.

TOYOTA

VALUE Sienna already did everything required of a minivan while delivering better-than-expected economy and performance. The stronger '01 should be even better suited for family travel and hauling tasks. The desirable LE and XLE models are a bit pricey and become downright expensive when you start adding options, but that's offset by Toyota's typically high resale values and outstanding reliability/durability record.

ENGINES

	dohc V6
Size, liters/cu. in.	3.0/183
Horsepower @ rpm	210 @ 5800
Torque (lb-ft) @ rpm	220 @ 4400
Availability	S
EPA city/highway mpg	
4-speed OD automatic	19/25

PRICES

Toyota Sienna	Retail Price	Dealer Invoice
CE 4-door van	$23905	$21174
LE 4-door van	25755	22547
XLE 4-door van	28436	24895
Destination charge	480	480

Prices are for vehicles distributed by Toyota Motor Sales, U.S.A., Inc. The dealer invoice and destination charge may be higher in areas served by independent distributors.

STANDARD EQUIPMENT:

CE: 3.0-liter dohc V6 engine, 4-speed automatic transmission, dual front airbags, antilock brakes, low-tire-pressure-warning system, daytime running lights, front and rear air conditioning, variable-assist power steering, tilt steering wheel w/radio controls, cloth upholstery, front captain chairs, center console, cupholders, overhead console, 2-passenger second-row seat, 3-passenger split-folding third row seat, AM/FM/cassette/CD player, digital clock, visor mirrors, auxiliary power outlets, variable intermittent wipers, rear defogger, rear intermittent wiper/washer, automatic-off headlights, dual outside mirrors, 205/70R15 tires, wheel covers.

LE adds: power mirrors, power windows, power door locks, cruise control, tachometer, illuminated visor mirrors, rear privacy glass, full-size spare tire.

XLE adds: power driver seat, automatic climate control, heated power mirrors, JBL sound system, quad captain's chairs, leather-wrapped steering wheel, remote keyless entry, universal garage door opener, floormats, roof rack, theft-deterrent system, fog lights, 215/65R15 tires, alloy wheels.

Prices are accurate at time of publication; subject to manufacturer's change.

TOYOTA

OPTIONAL EQUIPMENT:

	Retail Price	Dealer Invoice
Major Packages		
Extra Value Pkg., CE 4-door	$697	$627
Cruise control, heated power mirrors, power windows and door locks, rear defogger, floormats, rear privacy glass, full-size spare tire.		
Extra Value Pkg., LE	302	272
Heated power mirrors, remote keyless entry, quad captain chairs, floormats, roof rack.		
Upgrade Pkg. 1, LE	805	624
JBL sound system, power passenger-side rear door, rear privacy glass. Requires Extra Value Pkg.		
Upgrade Pkg. 2, LE	1280	1004
Upgrade Pkg. 1 plus alloy wheels. Requires Extra Value Pkg.		
Upgrade Pkg. 1, XLE	1610	1278
Leather upholstery, in-dash 6-disc CD changer.		
Upgrade Pkg. 2, XLE	1275	1020
Power sunroof, power passenger-side rear door.		
Upgrade Pkg. 3, XLE	1675	1340
Upgrade Pkg. 2 plus power driver-side rear door.		
Luxury Pkg., XLE	3285	2618
Upgrade Pkg. 1 plus power driver-side rear door.		
Towing Pkg.	160	128
CE requires full-size spare tire.		
Safety Features		
Front side-impact airbags	250	215
Antiskid system	550	440
CE requires Extra Value Pkg.		
Comfort and Convenience		
Video Entertainment Syatem	1795	1495
Power passenger-side rear door, XLE	395	316
Heated front seats, XLE	440	352
Requires Luxury Pkg. or Upgrade Pkg. 2.		
Automatic day/night rearview mirror	275	190
Remote keyless entry, CE	220	176
Requires Extra Value Pkg.		
Security System, CE, LE	439	275
Remote keyless entry, theft-deterrent system. CE requires Extra Value Pkg.		
Appearance and Miscellaneous		
Running Boards, CE, LE	480	290
XLE	595	365
Chrome alloy wheels, CE, LE	1399	1050

Post production options also available.

Specifications begin on page 535.

506   CONSUMER GUIDE

VOLKSWAGEN CABRIO

Volkswagen Cabrio GLS

Front-wheel-drive sports coupe

Base price range: $19,600-$23,175. Built in Mexico. **Also consider:** Chrysler Sebring, Ford Mustang, Mitsubishi Eclipse

FOR • Steering/handling **AGAINST** • Cargo room • Rear visibility • Rear-seat entry/exit

Still based on the 1994-98 Golf/Jetta platform, VW's convertible adds a plush GLX version for 2001, and shuffles equipment on base GL and midrange GLS models. All Cabrios come with VW's familiar 2.0-liter 4-cylinder engine with 5-speed manual or extra cost 4-speed automatic transmission. Antilock brakes, front side airbags, and air conditioning are standard. All models also have a glass rear window with electric defroster. This year's GL gets a price reduction, but makes do with manual windows and mirrors and a vinyl manual-folding top. GLS also gets a price cut, but loses its standard leather upholstery, heated front seats, and power-operated top to the GLX. GLS retains standard power windows, heated mirrors, cruise control, and cloth roof. The new GLX includes a power top, along with leather seating and alloy wheels. All Cabrios have a fixed bar over the interior designed to enhance structural rigidity and provide some protection in a rollover accident.

EVALUATION Cabrios have decent pep with manual shift but struggle some with the optional automatic. Despite noticeable body lean in turns, handling is sporty and the ride absorbent, the latter aided by a structure that's stiffer than that of many convertibles. Drivers enjoy a high, comfortable driving position, but the rear seat is only wide enough for two, leg room disappears if the front seats are pushed back, and passengers have to duck under the roll bar to get in or out. Visibility suffers from wide rear "pillars" with the top up, and a tall top stack with it down. Cabrio is a solid convertible with good road manners, but it's pricey considering its modest interior package and on-road abilities.

Prices are accurate at time of publication; subject to manufacturer's change.

VOLKSWAGEN

ENGINES

	ohc I4
Size, liters/cu. in.	2.0/121
Horsepower @ rpm	115 @ 5400
Torque (lb-ft) @ rpm	122 @ 3200
Availability	S

EPA city/highway mpg
5-speed OD manual	24/31
4-speed OD automatic	22/28

PRICES

Volkswagen Cabrio	Retail Price	Dealer Invoice
GL 2-door convertible, 5-speed	$19600	$17974
GL 2-door convertible, automatic	20475	18811
GLS 2-door convertible, 5-speed	20600	18856
GLS 2-door convertible, automatic	21475	19720
GLX 2-door convertible, 5-speed	22300	20400
GLX 2-door convertible, automatic	23175	21264
Destination charge	525	525

STANDARD EQUIPMENT:

GL: 2.0-liter 4-cylinder engine, 5-speed manual or 4-speed automatic transmission, dual front airbags, front side-impact airbags, antilock 4-wheel disc brakes, integral roll bar, daytime running lights, emergency inside trunk release, air conditioning, interior air filter, power steering, tilt leather-wrapped steering wheel, cloth upholstery, front bucket seats w/height adjustment, center console, cupholders, folding rear seat, heated manual mirrors, power door locks, remote keyless entry, AM/FM/cassette w/CD changer controls, digital clock, tachometer, rear defogger, intermittent wipers, heated washer nozzles, illuminated visor mirrors, auxiliary power outlet, remote decklid release, floormats, manual folding top, theft-deterrent system, 195/60HR14 tires, wheel covers.

GLS adds: cruise control, heated power mirrors, power windows.

GLX adds: leather upholstery, heated front seats, power folding top, fog lights, alloy wheels.

OPTIONAL EQUIPMENT:

Powertrains

California and Northeast emissions	100	99

Required on cars purchased in Calif., N.H., N.Y., Mass., Conn., R.I., Pa., N.J., Del., Md., Va., Vt., and Washington, D.C.

VOLKSWAGEN

VOLKSWAGEN JETTA/GOLF

Volkswagen Jetta GLS

Front-wheel-drive subcompact car

Base price range: $14,900-$25,175. Built in Mexico. **Also consider:** Ford Focus, Honda Civic, Mazda Protege

FOR • Cargo room (Golf) • Acceleration (V6) • Build quality • Fuel economy (exc. V6) • Quietness • Ride/handling • Visibility • Interior materials **AGAINST** • Acceleration (2.0 4-cylinder automatic) • Automatic transmission performance • Rear-seat entry/exit (Golf)

Midyear introduction of a Jetta wagon and curtain side airbags are the big changes for Volkswagen's 2001 subcompact line. Meanwhile, a new sport suspension option and available 17-inch wheels and tires are added to start the '01 model year.

Jetta is a 4-door sedan offered in GL, GLS, and GLX trim. It far outsells the Golf, which is a hatchback offered in GLS 4-door form and in GL and sporty GTI 2-door form. Front side airbags and antilock 4-wheel-disc brakes are standard across the board.

All GL and GLS models come with a 2.0-liter 4-cylinder gas engine. A turbocharged 1.8-liter four is available on GLS versions and is standard on the base GTI. GL TDI and GLS TDI use a turbocharged diesel four, but are not sold in California or New York due to emissions regulations. A V6 is available for the Jetta GLS and is standard in the Jetta GLX and Golf GTI VR6. Manual transmission is standard on all Golfs and Jettas and an automatic is available on all but the GTI VR6.

The Jetta wagon is expected to go on sale late next spring offering 4-cylinder and V6 power, though VW hadn't nailed down trim levels or pricing in time for this report. VW says curtain side airbags will be added sometime during the model year.

In other changes, the GTI VR6 and Jetta GLX get standard leather upholstery. A firmer sport suspension (similar to that on Golf GTI models) is a new option for Golf GLS 1.8T and Jetta GLX; the GLX can also get this suspension with new 17-inch alloy wheels. The 17s are a new option for the GTI VR6. The sport suspension and 17s are included in a new Sport Luxury option package for Jetta GLS 1.8T and VR6 models. Golf GTIs and Jetta GLS and GLX models can now be ordered with

Prices are accurate at time of publication; subject to manufacturer's change.

CONSUMER GUIDE

VOLKSWAGEN

steering-wheel audio controls; the controls are newly standard on the GTI VR6. Finally, all Golfs and Jettas get revamped cupholders, and most receive revised seat fabrics.

PERFORMANCE Every Jetta and Golf has sporty road manners. Ride is firm but comfortable, cornering stable, steering linear with fine on-center feel, braking terrific. GTI and V6 models handle best with only a modest sacrifice in ride comfort, though they have more body lean than expected for sporty small cars. We have not yet tested the new sport suspension or the 17-inch wheels and tires. Noise levels are among the lowest in this class. All engines are quiet, though the diesel is somewhat noisier at highway speeds.

The base 4-cylinder gas engine furnishes only modest acceleration with automatic transmission. Even with manual, our test Jetta GL took a lengthy 10.8 seconds 0-60 mph, though a slight shortage of passing power is its most noticeable deficit. V6 models have authoritative acceleration and spirited passing response—a test 5-speed GTI VR6 took just 7.6 seconds to 60—though their automatic is reluctant to downshift at moderate speeds. The turbo gas four might be the best all-around engine choice. Even with automatic, a test Jetta 1.8T did 0-60 in a creditable 8.9 seconds, helped by minimal turbo lag. The 1.8Ts also cost less than V6 models, though all demand premium fuel and there's little difference in fuel economy.

Our test V6s averaged 23.5 mpg with manual transmission and 18.6-21.6 with automatic. A 5-speed Jetta 1.8T averaged 26.1 mpg overall, with a low of 18.7 in city driving. A test automatic 1.8T Jetta averaged 21.3. A 5-speed Golf GL returned 25 mpg.

TDI models are surprisingly spritely around town and get terrific mileage; a test 5-speed TDI Golf averaged 41.5 mpg. Only the hybrid-power Honda Insight and Toyota Prius have averaged more in our tests.

ACCOMMODATIONS These cars impress with high-class interior materials and workmanship, plus exceptional front head and leg room. Rear seats are typically subcompact tight, with modest leg room that shrinks quickly as the front seats move back, though Golfs feel more spacious in back than Jettas, thanks to their straight-back roofline. No model has sufficient rear width for three adults.

All seats are comfortably firm, and the height-adjustable front buckets are supportive on long trips. A standard tilt/telescopic steering wheel—unusual for this class—helps tailor the driving position. Gauges and switches are simple, logically arranged, and nicely backlit, but low-mounted audio and climate controls can be tricky to adjust while driving.

Helped by smartly designed tip-slide front seats, rear access in 2-door Golfs is far easier than in most coupes. Narrow rear doors make entry/exit a squeeze in Jettas and 4-door Golfs. Interior storage is plentiful. Jettas have large trunks and Golfs boast hatchback versatility. All come with folding rear seatbacks.

Specifications begin on page 535.

VOLKSWAGEN

VALUE Jetta and Golf are at the top of the subcompact price heap, but even base versions are loaded with standard features, no competitor offers a V6 engine, and few provide as much driving satisfaction. Solid build quality and fine warranty coverage are other pluses that earn these VWs our Recommended label.

ENGINES

	ohc I4	Turbocharged dohc I4	ohc V6	Turbodiesel ohc I4
Size, liters/cu. in.	2.0/121	1.8/109	2.8/170	1.9/116
Horsepower @ rpm	115 @ 5200	150 @ 5700	174 @ 5800	90 @ 3750
Torque (lb-ft) @ rpm	122 @ 2600	155 @ 1750	181 @ 3200	155 @ 1900
Availability	S[1]	S[2]	S[3]	S[4]
EPA city/highway mpg				
5-speed OD manual	24/31	24/31	20/28	42/49
4-speed OD automatic	22/28	22/28	19/26	34/45

1. Jetta GL and GLS, Golf GL and GLS. 2. Jetta GLS 1.8T, Golf GLS 1.8T and GTI. 3. Jetta GLS VR6 and GLX, Golf GTI VR6. 4. TDI.

PRICES

Volkswagen Jetta/Golf	Retail Price	Dealer Invoice
Golf GL 2-door hatchback, 5-speed	$14900	$13904
Golf GL 2-door hatchback, automatic	15775	14768
Golf GL TDI 2-door hatchback, 5-speed	16195	15101
Golf GL TDI 2-door hatchback, automatic	17070	15965
Golf GLS 4-door hatchback, 5-speed	16350	15244
Golf GLS 4-door hatchback, automatic	17255	16108
Golf GLS TDI 4-door hatchback, 5-speed	17400	16214
Golf GLS TDI 4-door hatchback, automatic	18275	17078
Golf GLS 1.8T 4-door hatchback, 5-speed	17900	16675
Golf GLS 1.8T 4-door hatchback, automatic	18775	17539
Golf GTI 2-door hatchback, 5-speed	19275	17554
Golf GTI 2-door hatchback, automatic	20150	18418
Golf GTI VR6 2-door hatchback, 5-speed	22900	20829
Jetta GL 4-door sedan, 5-speed	16700	15228
Jetta GL 4-door sedan, automatic	17575	16092
Jetta GL TDI 4-door sedan, 5-speed	17995	16764
Jetta GL TDI 4-door sedan, automatic	19180	17913
Jetta GLS 4-door sedan, 5-speed	17650	16087
Jetta GLS 4-door sedan, automatic	18525	16951
Jetta GLS TDI 4-door sedan, 5-speed	18700	17414
Jetta GLS TDI 4-door sedan, automatic	19885	18565
Jetta GLS 1.8T 4-door sedan, 5-speed	19200	17486
Jetta GLS 1.8T 4-door sedan, automatic	20075	18350
Jetta GLS VR6 4-door sedan, 5-speed	19950	18164
Jetta GLS VR6 4-door sedan, automatic	20825	19028

Prices are accurate at time of publication; subject to manufacturer's change.

CONSUMER GUIDE

VOLKSWAGEN

	Retail Price	Dealer Invoice
Jetta GLX 4-door sedan, 5-speed	$24300	$22094
Jetta GLX 4-door sedan, automatic	25175	22958
Destination charge	525	525

TDI models not available in California, New York.

STANDARD EQUIPMENT:

Golf/Jetta GL: 2.0-liter 4-cylinder engine, 5-speed manual or 4-speed automatic transmission, dual front airbags, front side-impact airbags, antilock 4-wheel disc brakes, daytime running lights, emergency inside trunk release, air conditioning, interior air filter, power steering, tilt/telescoping steering wheel, automatic day/night mirror, cloth upholstery, height-adjustable front bucket seats, center console, cupholders, split folding rear seat, heated manual mirrors, power door locks, remote keyless entry, AM/FM/cassette w/CD changer controls, digital clock, tachometer, map lights, variable intermittent wipers, illuminated visor mirrors, rear defogger, intermittent rear wiper/washer (Golf), remote decklid/hatchback and fuel door releases, cargo cover (Golf), auxiliary power outlets, floormats, theft-deterrent system, full-size spare tire, 195/65HR15 tires, wheel covers.

Golf/Jetta GLS add: cruise control, upgraded interior trim, heated power mirrors, power windows.

Golf/Jetta GL/GLS TDI add to Golf/Jetta GL or GLS: 1.9-liter turbodiesel 4-cylinder engine, cruise control, alloy wheels (GLS TDI automatic).

Golf/Jetta GLS 1.8T adds to Golf/Jetta GLS: 1.8-liter dohc 4-cylinder turbocharged engine, traction control.

Golf GTI adds: power sunroof, front sport seats, fog lights, sport suspension, alloy wheels.

Golf GTI VR6 adds: 2.8-liter dohc V6 engine, 5-speed manual transmission, leather upholstery, heated front seats, leather-wrapped steering wheel w/radio controls, wood interior trim, automatic climate control, Monsoon sound system, trip computer, automatic day/night rearview mirror, rain-sensing wipers, heated washer nozzles, 205/55HR16 tires.

Jetta GLS VR6 adds to Jetta GLS: 2.8-liter dohc V6 engine, traction control, sport suspension.

Jetta GLX adds: 2.8-liter dohc V6 engine, leather upholstery, heated 8-way power front seats w/driver seat memory, leather-wrapped steering wheel, wood interior trim, automatic climate control, power sunroof, Monsoon Sound System, trip computer, rain-sensing wipers, heated washer nozzles, rear window sunshade, fog lights, 205/55HR16 tires, alloy wheels.

Specifications begin on page 535.

VOLKSWAGEN

OPTIONAL EQUIPMENT:
Major Packages

	Retail Price	Dealer Invoice
Luxury Pkg., Golf/Jetta GLS, GLS TDI, GLS 1.8T	$1225	$1082
Jetta GLS V6	1425	1258

Power sunroof, 205/55HR16 tires (GLS V6), alloy wheels. NA Jetta GLS TDI automatic.

Sport Luxury Pkg., Jetta GLS 1.8T, GLS V6	2025	1788

Power sunroof, sport suspension, 225/45R17 tires, alloy wheels.

Leather Pkg., GTI	1050	929
Jetta GLS, Jetta GLS TDI, Jetta GLS 1.8T, Jetta GLS V6	900	796

Leather upholstery, heated front seats and washer nozzles, leather-wrapped steering wheel and shifter, steering wheel mounted cruise and radio controls (GTI). Jetta requires Luxury Pkg. or Sport Luxury Pkg. except GLS TDI automatic which requires power sunroof.

Cold Weather Pkg.	150	133

Heated front seats, heated washer jets. NA GL, GL TDI. Std. GTI VR6, GLX.

Powertrains

California and Northeast emissions	100	99

Required on gasoline engine cars purchased in Calif., N.H., N.Y., Mass., Conn., R.I., Pa., N.J., Del., Md., Va., Vt., and Washington, D.C.

Comfort and Convenience

Power sunroof, Jetta GLS TDI automatic	915	808
Monsoon Sound System	325	287

NA GL. Std. GTI VR6, GLX.

Multifunction steering wheel, Jetta GLS/GLX	—	—

Includes cruise and radio controls.

Appearance and Miscellaneous

Sport suspension, Golf GLS 1.8T, Jetta GLX	200	177
Sport suspension w/17-in. alloy wheels, Jetta GLX	600	530

Includes 225/45R17 tires.

17-inch alloy wheels, GTI VR6	400	353
GTI	600	530

Includes 225/45R17 tires.

VOLKSWAGEN NEW BEETLE

CG BEST BUY AUTO

Front-wheel-drive sports coupe
Base price range: $15,900-$22,050. Built in Mexico.
Also consider: Ford Focus ZX3, Honda Prelude, Toyota Celica

FOR • Handling/roadholding • Fuel economy • Build quality • Exterior finish • Interior materials **AGAINST** • Rear-seat head

Prices are accurate at time of publication; subject to manufacturer's change.

VOLKSWAGEN

Volkswagen New Beetle 1.8T

room • Visibility • Rear-seat entry/exit

Available 17-inch wheels and tires highlight 2001 additions to this popular retro-style hatchback. The New Beetle is based on the chassis and running gear of VW's Jetta/Golf models.

All New Beetles have a 4-cylinder engine. GL and GLS models have 115 horsepower. The GLS Turbo and GLX add a turbocharger for 150 hp. The GLS TDI uses a 90-hp turbodiesel, but is not sold in New York or California because of emissions regulations. Manual transmission is standard and automatic is available at extra cost on all. All New Beetles come with front side airbags, antilock 4-wheel disc brakes, tilt/telescopic steering wheel, and 16-inch wheels and tires.

For '01, 17-inch alloy wheels are a stand-alone option for GLX models and included in a new Sport Luxury package for GLS Turbos; that package also contains a sunroof. GLX standard equipment expands this year to include a self-dimming inside mirror, rain-sensing windshield wipers, and high-power Monsoon sound system. All models also receive larger door mirrors and redesigned cupholders.

PERFORMANCE New Beetles are as much fun to drive as their whimsical styling implies. The smooth-running base gas engine feels peppy off-the-line with manual shift, but is short on power above 60 mph with either gearbox. The turbodiesel has no problem keeping up with traffic, but its passing power doesn't match that of the base gas engine, and it suffers more vibration and noise. The turbo gas four feels sleepy below 3000 rpm, but accelerates strongly above that; VW says 0-60-mph in 8 seconds. In our tests, base models averaged 26.4 mpg with manual transmission and 21.1 with automatic, an automatic GLS Turbo got 22.7, and a manual-shift diesel averaged 42.1.

All models have a firm-riding chassis but comfortably soak up most bumps, helped by standard 16-inch wheels, large for this class. Steering and handling are a notch above the class norm, too, though we haven't yet tested a New Beetle with the 17-inch wheels. Braking is strong and sure. Above 70 mph, passengers must raise their voic-

Specifications begin on page 535.

VOLKSWAGEN

es above the engine noise, though automatic models are geared for lower rpm at highway speeds and so are somewhat quieter.

ACCOMMODATIONS The interior brims with high-grade materials and classy, imaginative design. Gauges and controls are attractive and functional, though the audio unit is a bit unorthodox, and awkward wrist-twists are needed to operate the power window and mirror switches mounted flat on the door panels.

Front seats are comfortable and supportive, and few cars offer as much front head and leg room. Its a different story in back, where leg room is tight with the front seats moved more than halfway aft, and anyone over 5-foot-6 finds their head up against the inner hatch lid. Doors open wide and both front seatbacks tip far forward, so rear entry/exit is better than in most small coupes.

The front roof pillars have thick bases and the outside mirrors are mounted unusually high, cutting the driver's vision of some traffic. Interior storage space is skimpy and luggage room under the rear hatch is modest, but the rear seats fold nearly flat to expand the cargo area. Paint quality and fit-and-finish are excellent, bodies solid and rattle-free.

VALUE The New Beetle's emotional appeal and dynamic ability compensate for the shortcomings of its retro styling, and this is actually quite a practical car as sports coupes go. It's a good value besides.

ENGINES

	ohc I4	Turbodiesel ohc I4	Turbocharged dohc I4
Size, liters/cu. in.	2.0/121	1.9/116	1.8/109
Horsepower @ rpm	115 @ 5200	90 @ 3750	150 @ 5700
Torque (lb-ft) @ rpm	122 @ 2600	155 @ 1900	155 @ 1750
Availability	S[1]	S[2]	S[3]
EPA city/highway mpg			
5-speed OD manual	24/31	42/49	25/31
4-speed OD automatic	22/28	34/45	22/27

1. GL, GLS. 2. GLS TDI. 3. GLS Turbo, GLX.

PRICES

Volkswagen New Beetle

	Retail Price	Dealer Invoice
GL 2-door hatchback, 5-speed	$15900	$15151
GL 2-door hatchback, automatic	16775	16015
GLS 2-door hatchback, 5-speed	16850	15706
GLS 2-door hatchback, automatic	17725	16570
GLS TDI 2-door hatchback, 5-speed	17900	16675
GLS TDI 2-door hatchback, automatic	18775	17539
GLS Turbo 2-door hatchback, 5-speed	19000	17691
GLS Turbo 2-door hatchback, automatic	19875	18555
GLX 2-door hatchback, 5-speed	21175	19700
GLX 2-door hatchback, automatic	22050	20564

Prices are accurate at time of publication; subject to manufacturer's change.

VOLKSWAGEN

	Retail Price	Dealer Invoice
Destination charge	$525	$525

GLS TDI not available in California, New York.

STANDARD EQUIPMENT:

GL: 2.0-liter 4-cylinder engine, 5-speed manual or 4-speed automatic transmission, dual front airbags, front side-impact airbags, antilock 4-wheel disc brakes, daytime running lights, air conditioning, interior air filter, power steering, tilt and telescoping steering wheel, cloth upholstery, front bucket seats w/height adjustment, center console, cupholders, folding rear seat, heated power mirrors, power door locks, remote keyless entry, AM/FM/cassette w/CD changer controls, digital clock, tachometer, illuminated visor mirrors, rear defogger, remote fuel door and hatchback releases, variable intermittent wipers, auxiliary power outlets, cargo cover, floormats, theft-deterrent system, full-size spare tire, 205/55R16 tires, wheel covers.

GLS adds: cruise control, power windows, fog lights.

GLS TDI adds: 1.9-liter 4-cylinder turbodiesel engine.

GLS Turbo adds to GLS: 1.8-liter dohc turbocharged 4-cylinder engine, traction control, rear spoiler.

GLX adds: leather upholstery, heated front seats, leather-wrapped steering wheel, power sunroof, Monsoon sound system, automatic day/night rearview mirror, rain-sensing wipers, heated windshield washer nozzles, alloy wheels.

OPTIONAL EQUIPMENT:

Major Packages

Luxury Pkg., GLS, GLS TDI, GLS Turbo	1225	1082
Alloy wheels, power sunroof.		
Sport Luxury Pkg., GLS, GLS Turbo	1625	1435
Power sunroof, 225/45R17 tires, alloy wheels.		
Leather Pkg., GLS, GLS TDI, GLS Turbo	900	796
Partial leather upholstery, heated front seats, leather-wrapped steering wheel, heated windshield washer nozzles. Requires Luxury Pkg.		
Cold Weather Pkg., GLS, GLS TDI, GLS Turbo	150	133
Heated front seats, heated washer jets.		

Powertrains

California and Northeast emissions	100	99
Required on gasoline engine cars purchased in Calif., N.H., N.Y., Mass., Conn., R.I., Pa., N.J., Del., Md., Va., Vt., and Washington, D.C.		

Appearance and Miscellaneous

17-inch alloy wheels, GLX	400	353
Include 225/45R17 tires.		

Specifications begin on page 535.

VOLKSWAGEN

VOLKSWAGEN PASSAT

Volkswagen Passat GLX 4-Motion

Front-wheel-drive compact car
Base price range: $21,450-$31,835. Built in Germany. **Also consider:** Chrysler PT Cruiser, Mazda 626, Mitsubishi Galant

FOR • Ride • Passenger and cargo room • Build quality • Exterior finish • Interior materials **AGAINST** • Acceleration (GLS 1.8T w/automatic) • Tire noise

Introduction of standard head-protecting window-curtain side airbags later in the model year is the big news in 2001 for Volkswagen's biggest car.

Passat shares its basic structure and some components with the larger, costlier A6 models from VW-owned Audi. Passat comes as a 4-door sedan and wagon with front-wheel drive or VW's 4Motion all-wheel drive. All Passats come with antilock 4-wheel disc brakes, front side airbags, and traction control.

A 4-cylinder turbocharged engine is standard on GLS Passats, while a V6 powers the GLS V6 and GLX models. Both come with manual transmission or extra-cost 5-speed automatic with separate manual shift gate. 4Motion is available only on automatic-equipped GLXs. It normally maintains a 50/50 front/rear power split but can sense tire slip and redistribute up to 75 percent power to either axle to restore traction. GLX models have 16-inch wheels and tires, to the GLSs' 15s, plus standard leather upholstery and wood interior trim.

VW says curtain side airbags will be phased in during the 2001 model year. Also for '01, steering-wheel controls for audio and cruise functions are a new standard feature for GLXs and an option for GLS models.

PERFORMANCE Passat has crisp handling, responsive steering, arrow-true highway stability, and a suspension that smothers all but the worst bumps. A solid structure adds to the sense of comfort. Braking is swift and undramatic.

The turbo 4-cylinder is quiet enough and generally free of turbo hesitation, but with automatic transmission, it doesn't deliver quick getaways

Prices are accurate at time of publication; subject to manufacturer's change.
CONSUMER GUIDE

VOLKSWAGEN

or fuss-free passing. The automatic's manual-shift capability helps some, but the 4-cylinder models feel transformed with the real manual transmission, being lively, eager, and genuinely sporty. The smooth-running V6 provides more power at all speeds and is the engine we strongly recommend if you want automatic transmission. The new 4Motion system is transparent in operation but provides unerring grip. An automatic 4-cylinder sedan averaged 22.2 mpg in our tests, while our 4Motion sedan and wagon averaged 18.2. VW recommends premium fuel for both engines. These are pleasantly quiet cars, with low wind rush at highway speeds and tire noise noticed only over coarse surfaces.

ACCOMMODATIONS Passat beats most compacts for space and comfort; even three adults in the back seat isn't a problem on short hops. Six-footers have only about a half-inch head clearance beneath the available moonroof, but leg room is plentiful at all outboard positions. A comfortably tall driving stance is easily tailored with help from a standard tilt/telescopic steering wheel. The dashboard combines readable gauges and simple controls that move with a pleasing smoothness. Materials and workmanship rival those of more-expensive cars, and GLXs have real wood trim. Entry/exit is easy all around. The sedan has a huge trunk, the wagon a cavernous cargo bay, and both have standard split/folding rear seats. Visibility is fine except to the rear, where the styling hides the car's exterior corners.

VALUE Four-cylinder/automatic transmission Passats have barely acceptable acceleration for modern family cars, so try the different powertrain combinations to see which fits your needs. Otherwise, the sporty, spacious, solid Passat is strong on features per dollar, powertrain warranty, and European personality.

ENGINES

	Turbocharged dohc I4	dohc V6
Size, liters/cu. in.	1.8/109	2.8/169
Horsepower @ rpm	150 @ 5700	190 @ 6000
Torque (lb-ft) @ rpm	155 @ 1750	206 @ 3200
Availability	S[1]	S[2]
EPA city/highway mpg		
5-speed OD manual	24/31	20/29
5-speed OD automatic	20/29	18/26

1. GLS. 2. GLS V6, GLX.

PRICES

Volkswagen Passat	Retail Price	Dealer Invoice
GLS 4-door sedan, 5-speed	$21450	$19519
GLS 4-door sedan, automatic	22525	20592
GLS 4-door wagon, 5-speed	22250	20242
GLS 4-door wagon, automatic	23325	21315

Specifications begin on page 535.

VOLKSWAGEN

	Retail Price	Dealer Invoice
GLS V6 4-door sedan, 5-speed	$24050	$21868
GLS V6 4-door sedan, automatic	25125	22941
GLS V6 4-door wagon, 5-speed	24850	22591
GLS V6 4-door wagon, automatic	25925	23664
GLS V6 4Motion 4-door sedan, automatic	26875	24770
GLS V6 4Motion 4-door wagon, automatic	27675	25493
GLX 4-door sedan, 5-speed	28210	25626
GLX 4-door sedan, automatic	29285	26699
GLX 4-door wagon, 5-speed	29010	26348
GLX 4-door wagon, automatic	30085	27421
GLX 4Motion 4-door sedan, automatic	31035	25528
GLX 4Motion 4-door wagon, automatic	31835	29250
Destination charge	525	525

STANDARD EQUIPMENT:

GLS: 1.8-liter dohc 4-cylinder turbocharged engine, 5-speed manual or 5-speed automatic transmission w/manual-shift capability, traction control, dual front airbags, front side-impact airbags, antilock 4-wheel disc brakes, daytime running lights, air conditioning, interior air filter, power steering, tilt/telescoping steering wheel, cruise control, cloth upholstery, height-adjustable front bucket seats w/lumbar adjustment, center console, cupholders, split folding rear seat, heated power mirrors, power windows, power door locks, remote keyless entry, map lights, trip computer, outside temperature indicator, AM/FM/cassette w/CD controls, digital clock, tachometer, rear defogger, remote fuel door/decklid release, variable intermittent wipers, auxiliary power outlet, illuminated visor mirrors, cargo cover (wagon), intermittent rear wiper/washer (wagon), floormats, theft-deterrent system, fog lights, full-size spare tire, 195/65HR15 tires, wheel covers.

GLS V6 adds: 2.8-liter dohc V6 engine, full-time 4-wheel drive (4Motion).

GLX adds: leather upholstery, heated 8-way power front seats w/driver seat memory, leather-wrapped steering wheel w/steering wheel radio controls, wood interior trim, automatic climate control, passenger-side mirror tilt-down parking aid, power sunroof, AM/FM/cassette/CD player, Monsoon sound system, automatic day/night rearview mirror, rear window sun shade (sedan), rain-sensing wipers, heated windshield washer nozzles, 205/55R16 tires, alloy wheels.

OPTIONAL EQUIPMENT:
Major Packages

Leather Pkg., GLS, GLS V6	1500	1325

Leather upholstery, heated front seats and windshield washer nozzles, leather-wrapped steering wheel w/radio controls.

Prices are accurate at time of publication; subject to manufacturer's change.

VOLKSWAGEN • VOLVO

	Retail Price	Dealer Invoice
Luxury Pkg., GLS/GLS V6 sedan	$1550	$1369
GLS/GLS V6 wagon	1435	1267
Power sunroof, rear sunshade (sedan), alloy wheels.		
Cold Weather Pkg., GLS, GLS V6	325	287
Heated front seats and windshield washer nozzles.		

Comfort and Convenience

Monsoon sound system, GLS, GLS V6	325	287

VOLVO 40 SERIES

Volvo S40

Front-wheel-drive near-luxury car

Base price range: NA. Built in the Netherlands. **Also consider:** Acura TL, Audi A4, Infiniti I30, Lexus ES 300

FOR • Ride • Steering/handling • Brake performance • Cargo room (wagon) **AGAINST** • Rear-seat room

Introduced to America only last year, Volvo's Dutch-built compact sedans and wagons get a thorough makeover for 2001. Freshened styling, a bit more power, a new transmission, and standard window-curtain side airbags headline the changes.

The S40 sedan and V40 wagon return with a turbocharged 4-cylinder engine that gains 5 horsepower. Automatic transmission remains mandatory, but is now a 5-speed unit instead of a 4-speed. The new curtain side airbags supplement carryover standard front side airbags, antilock 4-wheel disc brakes, and anti-whiplash front-seat head restraints. Also new is a sensor system designed to trigger the dashboard airbags to deploy with full or reduced force according to crash severity and whether occupants are buckled up.

Additionally, both models get a mild exterior facelift on a nominal half-inch longer wheelbase, plus subtly reshaped fenders, a new front bumper with integrated spoiler, and revised front suspension. Interiors

Specifications begin on page 535.

VOLVO

are spruced up with recontoured seats, upgraded trim, rear child-seat anchors, and power window/mirror switches moved from the center console to the driver's door. Heated front seats continue in an optional Cold Weather package, but now have dual instead of single warmth levels. Other returning options include traction control, leather upholstery, sunroof, and integrated dual rear child booster seats. The wagon continues with a standard split-fold rear seat, the sedan a trunk pass-through.

PERFORMANCE Most class rivals have V6s and are a bit quicker and more refined than the 40 series. Nevertheless, Volvo's turbo-4 provides brisk takeoffs and good midrange punch. Aided by optional traction control, our V40 took 8.3 seconds 0-60 mph in last year's test. We haven't yet driven an '01, but Volvo claims the revised engine and new 5-speed automatic would improve our time by about 0.2-second. That would be nice, but we'd like this year's powertrain to eliminate the hesitation in full-throttle kickdown shifts from midrange speeds that annoyed us last year in both S40 and V40. Those test cars averaged 21 mpg, only fair for their weight and power. Premium fuel is required, but Volvo also promises slightly better economy for '01.

Despite a relatively short wheelbase, the 40 series has a supple, comfortable ride that may be its most impressive dynamic feature. Sharp bumps do register, especially in the wagon, but the suspension copes well with large ruts and humps, albeit with occasional "float." Handling and roadholding are good, and even the wagon corners with predictable front-drive grip and moderate body lean. Precise steering and powerful brakes also enhance driver confidence, but our test wagon's tail tended to drift slightly left in simulated panic stops, which weren't super-short. Road and wind noise are well managed. The engine is quiet in top-gear cruising, but hard acceleration induces unwanted exhaust boom and intake growl.

ACCOMMODATIONS Typical of Volvos, the 40 series boasts comfortably supportive seating front and rear, plus ample space forward. In back, however, leg and foot room are almost subcompact-class, and head room is tight for those over 5-foot-7. Moving the front seats more than halfway aft also complicates entry/exit, as do narrowish rear doors that should open wider.

Most drivers can get comfortably situated, helped by a standard tilt steering wheel and available power driver's seat, but visibility is slightly hindered by the rear headrests. Gauges are clear, a useful and user-friendly trip computer is available, and this year's relocated power window/mirror switches are a plus for convenience. Interior storage remains only average, though. The sedan's roomy trunk has a usefully low liftover, but also a small opening that prevents loading bulky objects. The wagon's load deck is fairly wide but not that long, and an oddly short cargo cover leaves much of your stuff exposed.

Though not built in Sweden, the 40 series has the generally solid dri-

VOLVO

ving feel associated with other Volvos, but not necessarily the same quality of interior materials or detail workmanship.

VALUE The 40 series offers Volvo virtues—and a few vices—in a smaller package. Base prices are competitive, with window-curtain airbags a laudable safety addition for 2001. But adding a few options can lift prices to near luxury-class levels, so outright value is not strong. We'd choose an Acura TL or Infiniti I30, both of which are roomier, quicker, more refined, and cost about the same comparably equipped.

ENGINES

	Turbocharged dohc I4
Size, liters/cu. in.	1.9/116
Horsepower @ rpm	165 @ 5100
Torque (lb-ft) @ rpm	175 @ 1800
Availability	S
EPA city/highway mpg	
5-speed OD automatic	22/32

2001 prices unavailable at time of publication.

PRICES

2000 Volvo 40 series	Retail Price	Dealer Invoice
S40 4-door sedan	$23400	$21794
V40 4-door wagon	24400	22804
Destination charge	575	575

STANDARD EQUIPMENT:

Base: 1.9-liter dohc turbocharged 4-cylinder engine, 4-speed automatic transmission, dual front airbags, front side-impact airbags, front seat active head restraints, antilock 4-wheel disc brakes, daytime running lights, air conditioning w/automatic climate control, interior air filter, variable-assist power steering, tilt steering wheel, cruise control, cloth upholstery, front bucket seats, center console, split folding rear seat, rear seat trunk pass-through (sedan), cupholders, heated power mirrors, power windows, power door locks, remote keyless entry, AM/FM/cassette w/CD changer controls, power antenna (sedan), digital clock, outside temperature display, tachometer, variable intermittent wipers, rear defogger, rear wiper/washer (wagon), map lights, illuminated visor mirrors, cargo cover (wagon), floormats, theft-deterrent system, tool kit, rear fog lights, 195/60VR15 tires, alloy wheels.

OPTIONAL EQUIPMENT:
Major Packages

Sport Pkg.	750	639
Manufacturer's discount price	550	470

Leather-wrapped steering wheel, front fog lights, rear spoiler.

Specifications begin on page 535.

VOLVO

	Retail Price	Dealer Invoice
Touring Pkg.	$1735	$1478
Manufacturer's discount price	1500	1275

Leather-wrapped steering wheel, 8-way power driver seat, AM/FM/cassette/CD changer, premium speakers, trip computer.

Sport Plus Pkg.	2335	1989
Manufacturer's discount price	1900	1615

Sport Pkg. plus Touring Pkg.

Sunroof Pkg.	2585	2198
Manufacturer's discount price	2200	1870

Power sunroof, leather upholstery, simulated-wood dashboard trim and shift knob.

Cold Weather Pkg.	950	808
Manufacturer's discount price	850	725

Traction control, heated front seats, headlight wiper/washer.

Safety Features

Dual child booster seats	300	255

Comfort and Convenience

Leather upholstery	1200	1020
Power driver seat	450	385
Audio Pkg.	800	680

AM/FM/cassette/CD player, premium speakers.

VOLVO C70

Volvo C70 convertible

Front-wheel-drive near-luxury car

Base price range: $34,500-$45,500. Built in Sweden. **Also consider:** Acura CL, BMW 3-Series, Mercedes-Benz CLK

FOR • Instruments/controls • Acceleration • Steering/handling
AGAINST • Road noise • Rear-seat entry/exit • Ride

Volvo's coupe and convertible carry into 2001 with a revised lineup and

Prices are accurate at time of publication; subject to manufacturer's change.

VOLVO

an uncertain future. These front-drive cars offer a choice of turbocharged inline 5-cylinder engines: a 2.4-liter or a more powerful 2.3. Convertibles offer both engines. The coupe is no longer available with the 2.4. Despite the more-powerful engine, the 2.3 coupe's base price is $4500 below that of last year's 2.4 coupe, though a power sunroof, leather upholstery, and 3-disc CD changer are now optional instead of standard. The 2.3 coupe and convertible come with manual transmission or extra-cost automatic, which this year has five speeds instead of four. The 2.4 convertible is automatic only. Convertibles have a standard power top with heated glass rear window. All C70s come with antilock 4-wheel disc brakes, front side airbags, and Volvo's WHIPS front seats designed to absorb rear-end impacts and minimize whiplash injury. Industry sources speculate the slow-selling C70 may soon be dropped now that its companion sedans and wagons have been redesigned as this year's new S60 and V70, respectively.

EVALUATION Any C70 has good power for most any need, but the 2.4-liter base engine has a more progressive power delivery and reduced turbo throttle lag versus the high-strung 2.3. Unfortunately, both suffer frustrating throttle delay, and neither is as smooth or quiet as the V6s used by most rivals. Both engines average about 20 mph overall in our tests. Braking is strong and sure, handling capable but not top of the class. Ride is choppy with the standard 16-inch wheels, jarring with the optional 17s. Patchy pavement also induces body drumming, giving these Volvos a relatively crude driving feel. C70s are "practical" sporty 2-doors, though the back seat is as tight as any rival's and rear entry/exit is cumbersome. Front cabin space is good, the dashboard user-friendly, and visibility no problem except top-up in the convertible. Trunk space is limited, but adequate for a weekend's soft luggage. A basic design dating to 1993 and steep prices are the C70 line's main minuses. An Acura CL or BMW 3-Series coupe or convertible is a better overall value.

ENGINES

	Turbocharged dohc I5	Turbocharged dohc I5
Size, liters/cu. in.	2.4/149	2.3/141
Horsepower @ rpm	190 @ 5100	236 @ 5100
Torque (lb-ft) @ rpm	199 @ 1800	244 @ 2100
Availability	S[1]	S[2]
EPA city/highway mpg		
5-speed OD manual		21/28
5-speed OD automatic	21/28	20/27

1. C70 2.4. 2. C70 2.3.

PRICES

Volvo C70	Retail Price	Dealer Invoice
2.4-liter 2-door convertible	$43500	$40890
2.3-liter 2-door coupe	34500	32430

Specifications begin on page 535.

VOLVO

	Retail Price	Dealer Invoice
2.3-liter 2-door convertible	$45500	$42770
Destination charge	575	575

STANDARD EQUIPMENT:

2.4-liter: 2.4-liter dohc turbocharged 5-cylinder 190-horsepower engine, 5-speed automatic transmission, dual front airbags, front side-impact airbags, front seat active head restraints, rollover protection system (convertible), antilock 4-wheel disc brakes, daytime running lights, air conditioning w/dual-zone automatic climate control, interior air filter, variable-assist power steering, tilt/telescoping leather-wrapped steering wheel, cruise control, leather upholstery, 8-way power front bucket seats w/driver seat memory, center console, cupholders, heated power mirrors, power windows, power door locks, remote keyless entry, AM/FM/cassette/CD player, digital clock, tachometer, rear defogger, illuminated visor mirrors, intermittent wipers, map lights, power convertible top, floormats, theft-deterrent system, front and rear fog lights, headlight wiper/washer, 205/55VR16 tires, alloy wheels.

2.3-liter coupe adds: 2.3-liter dohc turbocharged 5-cylinder 236-horsepower engine, 5-speed manual transmission, cloth and leather upholstery, universal garage door opener, 225/50VR16 tires.

2.3-liter convertible adds: leather upholstery, automatic day/night rearview mirror, AM/FM/cassette w/in-dash 3-disc CD changer, trip computer, outside temperature indicator, Deletes: universal garage door opener.

OPTIONAL EQUIPMENT:
Major Packages

Touring Pkg., 2.4-liter	585	496
Manufacturer's discount price	400	340

Trip computer, automatic day/night rearview mirror, simulated wood interior trim.

Grand Touring Pkg., 2.3-liter coupe	2985	2536
Manufacturer's discount price	2200	1870

Power sunroof, leather upholstery, trip computer, outside temperature indicator, automatic day/night rearview mirror, simulated wood trim.

Cold Weather Pkg.	800	679
Manufacturer's discount price	650	552

Traction control, heated front seats.

Powertrains

5-speed automatic transmission, 2.3-liter	1000	1000

Comfort and Convenience

Power sunroof, 2.3-liter coupe	1200	1020
Leather upholstery, 2.3-liter coupe	1200	1020

Prices are accurate at time of publication; subject to manufacturer's change.

CONSUMER GUIDE

VOLVO

	Retail Price	Dealer Invoice
AM/FM/cassette w/in-dash 3-disc CD changer, 2.4-liter, 2.3-liter coupe	$1200	$1020
Includes Dolby Prologic Surround Sound System.		
Dolby Prologic Surround Sound System, 2.3-liter convertible	600	510

Appearance and Miscellaneous

Canisto alloy wheels	400	340
Includes 225/45ZR17 tires.		
Propus alloy wheels	1500	1275
Includes 225/45ZR17 tires.		

VOLVO S60

Volvo S60

Front-wheel-drive near-luxury car; similar to Volvo V70

Base price range: NA. Built in Sweden. **Also consider:** Acura TL, Audi A6, Infiniti I30, Lexus ES 300

Following last spring's debut of redesigned V70 wagons, Volvo's mid-range sedans get a similar makeover for 2001. Badged S60, the 2001 models replace the S70 design that originated in 1993 with the 850 series. The V70 line includes the all-wheel-drive Cross Country model, but S60s are front-drive only, though they share with the wagons the same three engines, basic structure, and many features. Among standard features are antilock 4-wheel disc brakes, front side airbags, side-window curtain airbags, and Volvo's anti-whiplash front-seat backrests and head restraints.

S60 bows in three models, all with inline 5-cylinder engines. The base version carries a 2.4-liter with 168 horsepower, the 2.4T a turbocharged 197-hp version, and the performance-oriented T5 a turbo 2.3-liter with 247 hp. Base and T5 come with 5-speed manual transmission or optional 5-speed automatic. The automatic is mandatory for the 2.4T and, except on the base model, includes Volvo's Geartronic manual shift feature.

Specifications begin on page 535.

VOLVO

Compared to the S70s they replace, the S60s are 2 inches longer in wheelbase, but nearly 6 inches shorter overall, an inch taller, and nearly 2 inches wider. Styling is visibly sleeker, similar to that of Volvo's flagship S80 sedan. Base-model curb weight is up about 100 pounds. Trunk capacity shrinks by 1.2 cubic feet, but Volvo claims slightly more interior space. Base models retain standard 15-inch wheels and tires. The T5 has standard 17-inchers that are available for the 2.4T in lieu of 16s.

Though full details weren't available for this report, the S60 option list will include a sport suspension for the T5, a satellite-linked navigation system with pop-up dashboard screen as in the V70/S80, and Volvo's On-Call Plus assistance system similar to General Motors' OnStar. Also available are two traction-control/antiskid systems. The basic setup, called Stability Traction Control (STC), is standard for T5 and optional for other S60s; it throttles back power or brakes the front wheels to maintain traction and minimize skidding. Available for T5 and 2.4T is a more sophisticated Dynamic STC that adds selective braking at all four wheels to minimize skidding.

Full pricing also wasn't available for this report, but Volvo says the base S60 will start at $27,075 including destination charge. That's $1000 below last year's base S70. We have not tested the S60 and cannot provide ratings or an evaluation.

ENGINES	dohc I5	Turbocharged dohc I5	Turbocharged dohc I5
Size, liters/cu. in.	2.4/149	2.4/149	2.3/141
Horsepower @ rpm	168 @ 5900	197 @ 6000	247 @ 5200
Torque (lb-ft) @ rpm	170 @ 4500	210 @ 1800	243 @ 2400
Availability	S[1]	S[2]	S[3]
EPA city/highway mpg			
5-speed OD manual	21/28		21/28
5-speed OD automatic	21/28	21/28	20/27

1. Base. 2. 2.4T. 3. T5.

2001 prices unavailable at time of publication.

VOLVO S80

Front-wheel-drive luxury car

Base price range: NA. Built in Sweden. **Also consider:** Acura RL, Lexus GS 300/430, Mercedes-Benz E-Class

FOR • Acceleration (T6) • Passenger and cargo room • Build quality
AGAINST • Radio and navigation system controls • Rear visibility

For 2001, the flagship Volvo comes in entry-level 2.9, twin-turbocharged 2.8-liter T6, and new T6 Executive models. All have inline 6-cylinder engines, 4-speed automatic transmission (with manual shift gate on T6s), antilock 4-wheel disc brakes, traction control, front

Prices are accurate at time of publication; subject to manufacturer's change.

VOLVO

Volvo S80 T6

and window-curtain side airbags, seatbelt pretensioners for all passengers, and anti-whiplash front seatbacks and headrests. For 2001, a new front-seat sensor system triggers the dashboard airbags at reduced force depending on crash severity and whether occupants are buckled up. Again available for all models are antiskid system, 17-inch wheels (versus 16s), and a satellite-linked navigation system. Like T6s, the 2.9 now comes with leather upholstery, memory power mirrors, and Homelink remote door opener. The new Executive offers 2 inches more rear leg room via a repositioned rear seat with standard heating. It also comes with slightly wider rear doors, power rear-window sunshade, and a rear DVD audio/video system with a central screen and remote control. The DVD system is newly standard for the regular T6 as well, optional for the 2.9; ditto a rear cooler that can hold eight 12-ounce cans. Also standard for Executive and optional for other S80s is a wireless fax/copier for vehicles equipped with cell phone. Finally, the S80's optional security package adds an Air Quality System with ventilation multi-filter; this senses the contents of incoming air and automatically activates the filter and recirculation mode when exhaust pollutants from surrounding traffic reach unhealthful levels.

EVALUATION The base S80 has only adequate power, but the turbocharged T6, new Executive included, is quick by most any standard. Fuel economy is good: our test 2.9 averaged 19.2 mpg, a T6 20.7. Both have sure-footed handling, but some testers judge the steering numb and overassisted. The 2.9 easily absorbs bumps that register more in the tauter T6. Stopping power is strong, but one 2.9 test model had dull pedal action. Doors open wide for easy entry/exit, and there's generous room front and rear. The dashboard layout is clean and modern, but the radio uses a dial instead of buttons for station presets, which takes some learning. When activated, the optional navigation system's map screen rises from the middle center of the dashboard. It's at eye level, and its controls are on the steering wheel, not the dashboard. Like many such systems, this one requires study and patience to operate. A large trunk is tem-

VOLVO

pered by a small opening. The S80 packs lots of safety and convenience features into a stylish, functional sedan. All models are competitively priced, but we believe the quick T6 is worth the extra money. The new Executive pampers rear-seaters like a Lexus LS 430, but base-prices a whopping $7700 less.

ENGINES

	dohc I6	Turbocharged dohc I6
Size, liters/cu. in.	2.9/178	2.8/170
Horsepower @ rpm	197 @ 6000	268 @ 5400
Torque (lb-ft) @ rpm	207 @ 4200	280 @ 2100
Availability	S[1]	S[2]
EPA city/highway mpg		
4-speed OD automatic	19/27	19/26

1. S80 2.9. 2. S80 T6, Executive.

2001 prices unavailable at time of publication.

PRICES

2000 Volvo S80	Retail Price	Dealer Invoice
2.9 4-door sedan	$36000	$33060
T6 4-door sedan	40500	37105
Destination charge	575	575

STANDARD EQUIPMENT:

2.9: 2.9-liter dohc 6-cylinder engine, 4-speed automatic transmission, traction control, dual front airbags, front side-impact airbags, front and rear side head protection, front seat active head restraints, antilock 4-wheel disc brakes, daytime running lights, dual-zone automatic air conditioning, power steering, tilt/telescoping leather-wrapped steering wheel, cruise control, cloth upholstery, 8-way power front bucket seats w/driver seat memory, center console, split folding rear seat, cupholders, auxiliary power outlets, heated power mirrors, power windows, power door locks, remote keyless entry, AM/FM/cassette/CD player, steering-wheel-mounted radio and climate controls, tachometer, trip computer, intermittent wipers, illuminated visor mirrors, cargo net, floormats, theft-deterrent system, 215/55R16 tires, alloy wheels.

T6 adds: 2.8-liter dohc turbocharged 6-cylinder engine, 4-speed automatic transmission w/manual-shift capability, variable-assist power steering, heated front seats, heated headlight wipers/washers, premium speakers, wood interior trim, automatic day/night rearview mirror, fog lights, 225/55R16 tires.

OPTIONAL EQUIPMENT:
Major Packages

Special Value Pkg., 2.9	2400	1920
Manufacturer's discount price	1200	960
Power sunroof, leather upholstery.		

Prices are accurate at time of publication; subject to manufacturer's change.

VOLVO

	Retail Price	Dealer Invoice
Warm Weather Pkg.	$700	$560
Manufacturer's discount price	500	400
Infrared reflective windshield, rear and side curtains.		
Cold Weather Package, 2.9	450	360
Heated front seats, heated headlight wipers/washers.		
Ultra Security System	635	508
Manufacturer's discount price	600	480
Movement sensors, incline sensor, laminated security side glass, universal garage door opener.		

Powertrains
Dynamic Stability Traction Control	1100	880
Includes antiskid system.		

Comfort and Convenience
Navigation System	2500	2140
4-disc CD changer	1000	800
Deletes cassette player.		

Appearance and Miscellaneous
Special alloy wheels, 2.9	500	400
T6	400	320
Includes variable-assist power steering (2.9), 225/50R17 tires.		

VOLVO V70

Volvo V70

Front- or all-wheel-drive near-luxury car

Base price range: $29,400-$34,900. Built in Sweden. **Also consider:** Audi A6/allroad quattro, BMW 3-Series, Saab 9-5

FOR • Acceleration (T5) • Brake performance • Instruments/controls • Cargo room • Interior materials **AGAINST** • Fuel economy

Specifications begin on page 535.

VOLVO

(T5) • Low-speed acceleration (T5) • Ride comfort (T5) • Navigation system controls

These wagons are Volvo's best-selling cars. They're redesigned for 2001 on a slightly slimmed-down version of the company's large S80 sedan platform. Compared to their predecessors they're 1.7 inches wider and 2.4 inches taller on a 3.6-inch longer wheelbase, with nearly an inch more rear head room and 1.2 inches more front leg room.

All models have a 5-cylinder engine. The base V70 2.4 has a 168-horsepower 2.4 liter, the 2.4T a 197-hp turbocharged version of that engine. The high-performance T5 has a 242-hp turbo 2.3 liter. These models have front-wheel drive. The 2.4 and T5 get manual transmission or a 5-speed automatic, the 2.4T is automatic only. The automatic has a separate gate for shifting. Traction control is standard on T5s, optional on the 2.4 models. An antiskid system is also optional on 2.4T and T5.

The SUV-flavored V70 XC, or Cross Country, has all-wheel drive, the turbo 2.4, and automatic transmission. The XC has 2 inches more ground clearance than other V70s, plus unique lower body cladding and different front styling and interior trim.

All V70s come with antilock 4-wheel disc brakes, front head/chest side airbags, curtain window airbags, and Volvo's WHIPS front seats designed to minimize whiplash injury in a rear-end collision. A rear-facing third row seat is part of a Versatility Package that also includes a cargo cover, cargo net, and additional power outlet. A satellite navigation system also is optional.

PERFORMANCE As a wagon for everyday use, the 2.4T makes a good choice, while the XC is a sensible SUV alternative. The base 2.4 could use more power, and the T5 tends to ride too stiffly for the unexceptional handling it provides.

With the turbo models, acceleration is good once the turbo has an opportunity to deliver its boost. Our test T5 did 0-60 mph in a respectable 8 seconds, and Volvo says the XC does it in 8.4. But occasional turbo lag can be frustrating in fast-paced city/suburban driving; using the automatic transmission's manual-shift feature mitigates the lag somewhat. All engines are generally smooth, despite the high-rpm growl of Volvo's 5-cylinder. For all these engines, Volvo recommends 91-octane fuel or higher. The T5 averaged 16.5 mpg in our tests, the XC 18.7.

Road manners are responsive but unremarkable, with the 2.4T providing the best ride/handling balance. All models have good grip and steering that's satisfyingly weighty and precise. With 8.2 inches of ground clearance, the XC has more body lean in turns than the other V70s, but it's not excessive and certainly less than any true SUV. And its all-wheel drive goes unnoticed until it's needed to supply traction.

XC and the 2.4 models allow most pavement features to be felt, but only large, sharp bumps register harshly. And you'll notice a bit of high-speed wavy-road float in the XC. T5s have a firmed-up suspension and,

Prices are accurate at time of publication; subject to manufacturer's change.

CONSUMER GUIDE

VOLVO

combined with the optional 17-inch wheels and tires, have a busy, thumpy ride on surface imperfections. The XC and T5 also have noticeable tire drone on most all surfaces. By contrast, braking is terrific: short, stable and free of nose dive in our simulated 60-mph panic stops.

ACCOMMODATIONS The new V70 actually started out as a "V80," so it looks and feels much like Volvo's S80 flagship sedan inside. This means handsome furnishings, a relatively high driving stance, convenient and mostly intuitive gauges and switches, and ample room in cushy front bucket seats. Both seats have lumbar adjustment, but the handwheel controls are squeezed inconveniently close to the center console. Some testers also find the brake pedal too close to the accelerator for comfort. On the downside, Volvo's navigation system uses a small screen that rises from the dashtop, where it's hard to read in some light conditions, and the three operating switches on the back of the steering wheel aren't easy to use by feel alone.

Visibility is generally good, though the rear headrests interfere some over-the-shoulder, and the bulky front headrests can make front passengers feel isolated from those in back despite a high-set rear seat. Back-seaters get decent foot room and 6-footer head clearance, but the cushion is too short for best thigh support and there's insufficient width for three grownups not to feel squeezed.

With the optional Versatility Package, the rear cargo floorboard lifts to form a self-supporting barrier that keeps paper grocery bags in place with the tailgate closed. The gate itself opens easily onto a large aperture. The spare tire is located in an underfloor well, however, and some audio systems come with a big subwoofer that bolts in above and must be unplugged and partly removed before you can get at the spare.

VALUE Roomy, contemporary, solid, and versatile, Volvo's latest wagons are its best yet. Volvo expects the XC to account for about half of V70 sales, and indeed, this model furnishes all-weather security in a package that delivers some SUV flavor without most of the SUV compromises. Among the other V70s, we'd avoid the stiff-riding T5 and focus on the pleasant, liveable 2.4 models.

ENGINES	dohc I5	Turbocharged dohc I5	Turbocharged dohc I5
Size, liters/cu. in.	2.4/149	2.4/149	2.3/141
Horsepower @ rpm	168 @ 5900	197 @ 6000	242 @ 5200
Torque (lb-ft) @ rpm	170 @ 4500	210 @ 1800	243 @ 2400
Availability	S[1]	S[2]	S[3]
EPA city/highway mpg			
5-speed OD manual	21/28		21/28
5-speed OD automatic	21/28	20/27[4]	20/26

1. 2.4. 2. 2.4T, XC. 3. T5. 4. 18/25 w/4WD; 18/22 w/XC.

Specifications begin on page 535.

VOLVO

PRICES

Volvo V70	Retail Price	Dealer Invoice
2.4 4-door wagon	$29400	$27636
2.4T 4-door wagon	32400	30456
T5 4-door wagon	33400	31396
XC 4-door wagon	34900	32806
Destination charge	575	575

STANDARD EQUIPMENT:

2.4: 2.4-liter dohc 5-cylinder engine, 5-speed manual transmission, driver- and passenger-side airbags, front side-impact airbags, front and rear side head-protection system, front seat active head restraints, antilock 4-wheel disc brakes, air conditioning, interior air filter, power steering, tilt/telescoping steering wheel, cruise control, cloth upholstery, 8-way manual front bucket seats, center console, cupholders, split folding rear seat w/cargo pass-through, heated power mirrors, power windows, power door locks, remote keyless entry, AM/FM/cassette w/CD changer controls, digital clock, tachometer, outside temperature indicator, intermittent wipers, auxiliary power outlets, illuminated visor mirrors, rear defogger, intermittent rear wiper/washer, remote fuel door/tailgate release, map lights, floormats, theft-deterrent system, rear fog lights, 195/65HR15 tires, alloy wheels.

2.4T adds: 2.4-liter dohc turbocharged 5-cylinder 197-horsepower engine, 5-speed automatic transmission, dual-zone automatic climate control, 8-way power driver seat, memory system for driver seat and mirrors, steering wheel radio controls, 205/55HR16 tires

T5 adds: 2.3-liter dohc turbocharged 5-cylinder 247-horsepower engine, 5-speed manual transmission, traction control, 8-way power passenger seat, AM/FM/cassette w/3-disc CD changer, trip computer, automatic day/night rearview mirror, universal garage door opener, front fog lights, 215/55HR16 tires.

XC adds to 2.4T: permanent all-wheel drive, 5-speed automatic transmission w/manual-shift capability, traction control, roof rails, raised ride height, 215/65HR16 tires.

OPTIONAL EQUIPMENT:
Major Packages

Touring Pkg., 2.4, 2.4T, XC	1410	1197
Manufacturer's discount price	1250	1062

8-way power driver seat (2.4), 8-way power passenger seat (2.4T, XC), AM/FM/cassette/CD player, trip computer, universal garage door opener, automatic day/night rearview mirror.

Leather Pkg., 2.4, 2.4T	1665	1415
Manufacturer's discount price	1200	1020

Leather upholstery, leather-wrapped steering wheel and shift knob, wood-grain interior trim.

Prices are accurate at time of publication; subject to manufacturer's change.

VOLVO

	Retail Price	Dealer Invoice
Leather Pkg., T5, XC	$1765	$1500
Manufacturer's discount price	1300	1105
Leather upholstery, leather-wrapped steering wheel and shift knob, wood-grain interior trim.		
Versatility Pkg.	675	573
Manufacturer's discount price	350	297
Grocery bag holder, cargo cover, cargo net, additional power outlet. NA with active subwoofer system.		
Versatility Pkg. w/third row seat	1650	1402
Manufacturer's discount price	1150	977
Rear-facing third row seat, additional power outlet, cargo cover, cargo net. NA with subwoofer system.		
Security Pkg.	635	539
Manufacturer's discount price	500	425
Mass movement sensor, level sensor, laminated security windows.		
Cold Weather Pkg.	450	382
Heated front seats and headlight washers.		
Cold Weather/STC Pkg., 2.4, 2.4T	1000	849
Manufacturer's discount price	850	722
Cold Weather Pkg. plus antiskid system and traction control.		

Powertrains

5-speed automatic w/manual-shift capability, 2.4, T5	1000	1000
Traction control, 2.4, 2.4T	550	467

Safety Features

Dynamic antiskid system, 2.4T	1250	1062
T5	1100	935
2.4T includes traction control.		
Integrated child seat	300	255

Comfort and Convenience

Navigation system	2500	2125
Includes CD map and one update.		
Power sunroof	1200	1020
AM/FM w/in-dash 4-disc CD changer	1000	850
Includes premium sound system. 2.4T requires Touring Pkg.		
Active subwoofer system	350	297
Includes 150 watt amplifier. 2.4, 2.4T, XC require Touring Pkg.		

Appearance and Miscellaneous

Metis alloy wheels, 2.4T	250	212
Amalthea alloy wheels, 2.4T, T5	500	425
Includes 235/45HR17 tires.		

Specifications begin on page 535.

SPECIFICATIONS

Dimensions and capacities are supplied by the vehicle manufacturers. **Body types:** 2-door coupe or 4-door sedan = a standard-body car with a separate trunk; hatchback = car with a rear liftgate; wagon = car w/ standard roofline with an enclosed cargo bay; regular-cab pickup truck = standard-length cab with room for one row of front seats; extended-cab pickup truck = lengthened cab with seating positions behind the front seats; crew-cab pickup truck = lengthened cab with two forward-opening rear doors. **Wheelbase:** distance between the front and rear wheels. **Curb weight:** weight of base models, not including optional equipment.

Weight listed for sport-utility vehicles is for the 4-wheel-drive version. **Height:** overall height of base models, not including optional equipment (on sport-utility vehicles, this is the overall height of the 4-wheel drive model). **Cargo volume** (does not apply to pickup trucks): coupes and sedans = maximum volume of the trunk; hatchbacks and station wagons = maximum volume with the rear seat folded; minivans and sport-utility vehicles = maximum volume with all rear seats folded or removed, when possible. **Standard payload** (applies to pickup trucks): maximum weight the base-model can carry, including passengers.

SUBCOMPACT CARS	Wheelbase, in.	Overall length, in.	Overall width, in.	Overall height, in.	Curb weight, lbs.	Cargo volume, cu. ft.	Fuel capacity, gals.	Seating capacity	Front head room, in.	Max. front leg room, in.	Rear head room, in.	Min. rear leg room, in.
Chevrolet Cavalier 2-door coupe	104.1	180.9	68.7	53.0	2617	13.2	15.0	5	37.6	41.9	36.6	32.7
Chevrolet Cavalier 4-door sedan	104.1	180.9	67.9	54.7	2676	13.6	15.0	5	38.9	41.9	37.2	34.4
Chevrolet Prizm 4-door sedan	97.1	174.2	66.7	53.7	2403	12.1	13.2	5	39.3	42.5	36.9	33.2
Dodge/Plymouth Neon 4-door sedan	105.0	174.4	67.4	56.0	2559	13.1	12.5	5	38.4	42.4	36.7	34.8
Ford Focus 2-door hatchback	103.0	168.1	66.9	56.3	2551	18.6	13.2	5	39.3	43.1	38.7	37.6
Ford Focus 4-door sedan	103.0	174.9	66.9	56.3	2564	12.9	13.2	5	39.3	43.1	38.5	37.6
Ford Focus 4-door wagon	103.0	178.2	66.9	53.9	2717	55.3	13.2	5	39.3	43.1	40.0	37.6
Honda Civic 2-door coupe	103.1	174.7	66.7	55.1	2405	12.9	13.2	5	39.0	42.5	35.4	32.8
Honda Civic 4-door sedan	103.1	174.6	67.5	56.7	2421	12.9	13.2	5	39.8	42.2	37.2	36.0
Honda Insight 2-door hatchback	94.5	155.1	66.7	53.3	1856	NA	10.6	2	38.8	42.9	—	—
Hyundai Accent 2-door hatchback	96.1	166.7	65.7	54.9	2255	16.9	11.9	5	38.9	42.6	38.0	32.8
Hyundai Accent 4-door sedan	96.1	166.7	65.7	54.9	2290	11.8	11.9	5	38.9	42.6	38.0	32.8
Hyundai Elantra 4-door sedan	102.7	177.1	67.7	56.1	2635	11.0	14.5	5	39.6	43.2	38.0	35.0
Kia Rio 4-door sedan	94.9	165.9	65.9	56.7	2242	9.2	11.9	5	39.4	42.8	37.6	32.7
Kia Sephia 4-door sedan	100.8	174.4	66.9	55.5	2478	10.4	13.2	5	39.6	43.3	37.7	34.4
Kia Spectra 4-door hatchback	100.8	176.2	66.9	55.5	2560	11.6	13.2	5	39.6	43.1	36.6	34.4
Mazda Protege 4-door sedan	102.8	174.0	67.1	55.5	2434	12.9	13.2	5	39.3	42.2	37.4	35.4
Nissan Sentra 4-door sedan	99.8	177.5	67.3	55.5	2548	11.6	13.2	5	39.9	41.6	37.0	33.7
Pontiac Sunfire 2-door coupe	104.1	182.0	68.4	53.0	2606	12.4	15.0	5	37.6	42.1	36.6	32.6
Pontiac Sunfire 4-door sedan	104.1	181.8	67.9	54.7	2644	13.1	15.0	5	38.9	42.1	37.2	34.3
Saturn S-Series 3-door coupe	102.4	180.5	68.2	53.0	2367	11.4	12.1	4	38.6	42.6	35.8	31.0

CONSUMER GUIDE™ 535

SPECIFICATIONS

SUBCOMPACT CARS CONTINUED

	Wheelbase, in.	Overall length, in.	Overall width, in.	Overall height, in.	Curb weight, lbs.	Cargo volume, cu. ft.	Fuel capacity, gals.	Seating capacity	Front head room, in.	Max. front leg room, in.	Rear head room, in.	Min. rear leg room, in.
Saturn S-Series 4-door sedan	102.4	178.1	66.4	55.0	2331	12.1	12.1	5	39.3	42.5	38.0	32.8
Saturn S-Series 4-door wagon	102.4	178.1	66.4	55.6	2452	58.2	12.1	5	39.3	42.5	39.2	30.7
Subaru Impreza 2-door coupe	99.2	172.2	67.1	55.5	2820	11.1	13.2	5	39.2	43.1	36.7	32.5
Subaru Impreza 4-door sedan	99.2	172.2	67.1	55.5	2730	11.1	13.2	5	39.2	43.1	36.7	32.5
Subaru Impreza 4-door wagon	99.2	172.2	67.1	55.5	2835	62.1	13.2	5	39.2	43.1	37.4	32.4
Subaru Impreza Outback 4-door sedan	99.2	172.2	67.1	60.0	2860	62.1	13.2	5	39.2	43.1	37.4	32.4
Suzuki Esteem 4-door hatchback	93.1	149.4	62.6	54.7	1895	8.4	10.3	4	39.1	42.5	36.0	32.2
Suzuki Esteem 4-door wagon	97.6	166.3	66.1	53.9	2271	10.3	12.7	5	39.1	42.5	37.3	32.3
Suzuki Swift 2-door hatchback	97.0	172.2	66.5	55.9	2403	61.0	12.7	5	38.8	42.3	38.0	34.1
Toyota Corolla 4-door sedan	97.0	174.0	66.7	54.5	2403	12.1	13.2	5	39.3	42.5	36.9	33.2
Toyota Echo 2-door coupe	93.4	163.3	65.4	59.1	2020	13.6	11.9	5	39.9	41.1	37.6	35.2
Toyota Echo 4-door sedan	93.4	163.3	65.4	59.1	2030	13.6	11.9	5	39.9	41.1	37.6	35.2
Toyota Prius 4-door sedan	100.4	169.6	66.7	57.6	2765	11.8	11.9	5	38.8	41.2	37.1	35.4
Volkswagen Golf 2-door hatchback	98.9	163.3	68.3	56.7	2767	41.8	14.5	5	38.6	41.5	37.4	33.5
Volkswagen Golf 4-door hatchback	98.9	163.3	68.3	56.7	2864	41.8	14.6	5	38.5	41.3	37.7	33.3
Volkswagen Jetta 4-door sedan	98.9	172.3	68.3	56.9	2884	13.0	14.5	5	38.6	41.5	36.9	33.3

COMPACT CARS

	Wheelbase, in.	Overall length, in.	Overall width, in.	Overall height, in.	Curb weight, lbs.	Cargo volume, cu. ft.	Fuel capacity, gals.	Seating capacity	Front head room, in.	Max. front leg room, in.	Rear head room, in.	Min. rear leg room, in.
Chrysler PT Cruiser 4-door wagon	103.0	168.8	67.1	63.0	3123	64.2	15.0	5	40.4	40.6	39.6	40.8
Hyundai Sonata 4-door sedan	106.3	185.4	71.6	55.5	3072	13.0	17.2	5	39.3	43.3	37.6	36.2
Mazda 626 4-door sedan	105.1	187.4	69.3	55.1	2864	14.2	16.9	5	39.2	43.6	37.0	34.6
Mitsubishi Galant 4-door sedan	103.7	187.8	68.5	55.7	2835	14.0	16.3	5	39.9	43.5	37.7	36.3
Nissan Altima 4-door sedan	103.1	185.8	69.1	55.9	2851	13.8	15.9	5	39.4	42.0	37.7	33.9
Oldsmobile Alero 2-door coupe	107.0	186.7	70.1	54.5	2973	14.6	14.3	5	38.4	42.2	36.5	35.5
Oldsmobile Alero 4-door sedan	107.0	186.7	70.1	54.5	3026	14.6	14.3	5	38.4	42.2	37.0	35.5
Pontiac Grand Am 2-door coupe	107.0	186.3	70.4	55.1	3066	14.6	14.3	5	38.3	42.1	37.2	35.5
Pontiac Grand Am 4-door sedan	107.0	186.3	70.4	55.1	3116	14.6	14.3	5	38.3	42.1	37.6	35.5
Subaru Legacy 4-door sedan	104.3	184.4	68.7	55.7	3245	12.4	16.9	5	38.1	43.3	36.6	34.2

SPECIFICATIONS

Subaru Outback 4-door sedan	104.3	184.4	68.7	58.3	3485	12.4	16.9	5	38.1	43.3	36.6	34.2
Subaru Outback 4-door wagon	104.3	187.4	68.7	63.3	3415	68.6	16.9	5	38.5	43.3	37.2	34.3
Volkswagen Passat 4-door sedan	106.4	184.1	68.5	57.6	3043	15.0	16.4	5	39.7	41.5	37.8	35.3
Volkswagen Passat 4-door wagon	106.4	183.8	68.5	59.0	3136	78.7	16.4	5	39.7	41.5	37.8	35.3

MIDSIZE CARS

Buick Century 4-door sedan	109.0	194.6	72.7	56.6	3368	16.7	17.5	6	39.4	42.4	37.4	36.9
Buick Regal 4-door sedan	109.0	196.2	72.7	56.6	3438	16.7	17.5	5	39.4	42.4	37.4	36.9
Chevrolet Impala 4-door sedan	110.5	200.0	73.0	57.5	3389	18.6	17.0	6	39.2	42.2	36.8	38.4
Chevrolet Malibu 4-door sedan	107.0	190.4	69.4	56.7	3051	17.1	14.3	6	39.4	41.9	37.6	38.0
Chevrolet Monte Carlo 2-door coupe	110.5	197.9	72.3	55.2	3340	15.8	17.0	5	38.1	42.4	36.5	35.8
Chrysler Sebring 2-door coupe	103.7	190.2	70.3	53.7	3100	16.3	16.3	5	38.5	42.3	36.0	34.0
Chrysler Sebring 2-door convertible	106.0	193.7	69.4	55.0	3489	11.3	NA	6	NA	NA	NA	NA
Chrysler Sebring 4-door sedan	108.0	190.7	70.6	54.9	3250	16.0	16.3	5	37.3	42.3	35.8	38.1
Dodge Stratus 2-door coupe	103.7	190.2	70.3	53.7	3012	16.3	16.3	5	38.5	42.3	36.0	34.0
Dodge Stratus 4-door sedan	108.0	191.2	70.6	54.9	3226	16.0	16.3	5	37.6	42.3	35.8	38.1
Ford Taurus 4-door sedan	108.5	197.6	73.0	56.1	3333	17.0	18.0	6	40.0	42.2	38.1	38.9
Ford Taurus 4-door wagon	108.5	197.7	73.0	57.8	3516	81.3	18.0	8	39.4	42.2	38.9	38.5
Honda Accord 2-door coupe	105.1	186.8	70.3	54.9	2967	13.6	17.1	5	39.7	42.6	36.5	32.4
Honda Accord 4-door sedan	106.9	189.4	70.3	56.9	2943	14.1	17.1	5	40.0	42.1	37.6	37.9
Hyundai XG300 4-door sedan	108.3	191.5	71.9	55.9	3604	14.5	18.5	5	39.7	43.4	38.0	37.2
Mercury Sable 4-door sedan	108.5	199.8	73.0	55.5	3379	16.0	18.0	6	39.8	42.2	38.7	38.9
Mercury Sable 4-door wagon	108.5	197.8	73.0	57.8	354	81.2	16.0	6	39.4	42.2	38.7	38.5
Nissan Maxima 4-door sedan	108.3	190.5	70.3	56.5	3186	15.1	18.5	5	40.4	44.8	37.2	35.4
Oldsmobile Intrigue 4-door sedan	109.0	195.9	73.6	56.6	3434	16.4	17.0	5	39.3	42.4	37.4	36.2
Pontiac Grand Prix 2-door coupe	110.5	196.5	72.7	54.7	3396	16.0	17.0	5	38.3	42.4	36.5	36.1
Pontiac Grand Prix 4-door sedan	110.5	196.5	72.7	54.7	3414	16.0	17.0	6	38.3	42.4	36.7	35.8
Saturn L-Series 4-door sedan	106.5	190.4	68.5	56.4	2944	17.5	15.7	5	39.3	42.3	38.0	34.4
Saturn L-Series 4-door wagon	106.5	190.4	68.5	57.3	3081	79.0	15.7	5	39.3	42.3	39.6	35.4
Toyota Camry 4-door sedan	105.2	188.5	70.1	55.4	2998	14.1	18.5	5	38.6	43.5	37.6	35.5

CONSUMER GUIDE™ 537

SPECIFICATIONS

MIDSIZE CARS CONTINUED	Wheelbase, in.	Overall length, in.	Overall width, in.	Overall height, in.	Curb weight, lbs.	Cargo volume, cu. ft.	Fuel capacity, gal.	Seating capacity	Front head room, in.	Max. front leg room, in.	Rear head room, in.	Min. rear leg room, in.
Toyota Solara 2-door convertible	105.1	190.0	71.1	55.5	3437	8.8	18.5	4	38.8	43.3	37.7	35.3
Toyota Solara 2-door coupe	105.1	190.0	71.1	55.1	3120	13.8	18.5	5	38.3	43.3	36.3	35.2

FULL-SIZE CARS

	Wheelbase, in.	Overall length, in.	Overall width, in.	Overall height, in.	Curb weight, lbs.	Cargo volume, cu. ft.	Fuel capacity, gal.	Seating capacity	Front head room, in.	Max. front leg room, in.	Rear head room, in.	Min. rear leg room, in.
Buick LeSabre 4-door sedan	112.2	200.0	73.5	57.0	3567	18.0	18.5	6	38.8	42.4	37.8	39.9
Chrysler Concorde 4-door sedan	113.0	209.1	74.6	55.9	3488	18.7	17.0	6	38.3	42.2	37.2	41.6
Dodge Intrepid 4-door sedan	113.0	203.7	74.7	55.9	3471	18.4	17.0	6	38.3	42.2	37.4	39.1
Ford Crown Victoria 4-door sedan	114.7	212.0	78.2	56.8	3917	20.6	19.0	6	39.4	42.5	38.0	39.6
Mercury Grand Marquis 4-door sedan	114.7	211.9	78.2	56.8	3958	20.6	19.0	6	39.4	42.5	38.1	38.4
Pontiac Bonneville 4-door sedan	112.2	202.6	74.2	56.6	3590	18.0	18.5	6	38.7	42.6	37.3	38.0
Toyota Avalon 4-door sedan	107.1	191.9	71.7	57.7	3330	15.9	18.5	6	38.7	41.7	37.9	40.1

NEAR-LUXURY CARS

	Wheelbase, in.	Overall length, in.	Overall width, in.	Overall height, in.	Curb weight, lbs.	Cargo volume, cu. ft.	Fuel capacity, gal.	Seating capacity	Front head room, in.	Max. front leg room, in.	Rear head room, in.	Min. rear leg room, in.
Acura CL 2-door coupe	106.9	192.0	70.6	55.5	3470	13.6	17.2	4	37.5	42.4	36.7	33.0
Acura TL 4-door sedan	108.1	192.9	70.3	56.1	3483	14.3	17.2	5	39.9	42.4	36.8	35.0
Audi A4 4-door sedan	103.0	178.0	68.2	55.8	3164	13.7	16.4	5	38.2	41.3	36.9	33.4
Audi A4 4-door wagon	102.6	176.7	68.2	56.7	3351	63.7	15.9	5	38.2	41.3	37.8	33.4
Audi A6 4-door sedan	108.1	192.0	71.3	57.2	3759	17.2	18.5	5	39.3	41.3	37.9	37.3
Audi A6 4-door wagon	108.6	192.0	71.3	58.2	3947	73.2	18.5	5	39.3	41.3	38.7	37.3
Audi allroad quattro 4-door wagon	108.5	189.4	76.1	59.1	4167	73.2	18.5	5	39.3	41.3	38.7	37.3
BMW 3-Series 2-door coupe	107.3	176.7	69.2	53.5	3020	9.5	16.6	4	37.5	41.7	36.5	33.2
BMW 3-Series 4-door sedan	107.3	176.0	68.5	55.7	3153	10.7	16.6	5	38.4	41.4	37.5	34.6
BMW 3-Series 2-door convertible	107.3	176.7	69.2	54.0	3560	7.7	16.6	4	38.3	41.7	36.9	32.0
BMW 3-Series 4-door wagon	107.3	176.0	68.5	55.5	3351	25.7	16.6	5	38.4	41.4	37.7	34.0
Buick Park Avenue 4-door sedan	113.8	206.8	74.7	57.4	3778	17.2	18.5	6	39.8	42.4	38.0	41.4
Cadillac Catera 4-door sedan	107.5	192.2	70.3	56.4	3815	14.5	16.0	5	38.7	42.2	38.4	37.5
Chrysler 300M 4-door sedan	113.0	197.8	74.4	56.0	3591	16.8	17	5	38.3	42.2	37.7	39.1

538   CONSUMER GUIDE™

SPECIFICATIONS

Chrysler LHS 4-door sedan	113.0	207.7	74.4	56.0	3573	18.7	17	5	38.3	42.2	37.2	41.6
Infiniti G20 4-door sedan	102.4	177.5	66.7	55.1	2923	13.5	15.9	5	39.2	41.5	36.8	34.6
Infiniti I30 4-door sedan	108.3	193.7	70.2	56.5	3342	14.9	18.5	5	40.5	43.9	37.4	36.2
Lexus ES 300 4-door sedan	105.1	190.2	70.5	54.9	3373	13.0	18.5	5	38.0	43.5	36.2	34.4
Lexus IS 300 4-door sedan	105.1	176.6	67.7	55.5	3270	10.1	17.5	5	39.1	42.7	37.8	30.2
Lincoln LS 4-door sedan	114.5	193.9	73.2	56.1	3593	13.5	18.0	5	40.4	42.8	37.5	37.4
Mazda Millenia 4-door sedan	108.3	191.6	69.7	54.9	3358	13.0	18.0	5	37.9	43.3	36.5	34.1
Mercedes-Benz C-Class 4-door sedan	106.9	178.3	68.0	55.2	3360	12.0	16.2	5	37.1	41.7	37.3	33.0
Mitsubishi Diamante 4-door sedan	107.1	194.1	70.3	53.9	3440	14.2	19.0	5	39.4	43.6	37.5	36.6
Oldsmobile Aurora 4-door sedan	112.2	199.3	72.9	56.7	3627	14.9	18.5	5	38.6	42.5	37.7	38.0
Saab 9-3 2-door hatchback	102.6	182.3	67.4	56.2	2980	46.0	17.0	5	39.3	42.3	37.9	34.1
Saab 9-3 4-door hatchback	102.6	182.3	67.4	56.2	3020	46.0	17.0	5	39.3	42.3	37.9	34.1
Saab 9-3 2-door convertible	102.6	182.3	67.4	56.0	3200	12.5	17.0	4	38.9	42.3	37.9	33.0
Volvo 40 series 4-door sedan	100.9	176.4	67.7	55.5	2990	13.2	15.8	5	38.7	41.4	37.2	32.7
Volvo 40 series 4-door wagon	100.9	176.4	67.7	55.5	3040	61.3	15.8	5	38.7	41.4	38.3	32.7
Volvo C70 2-door coupe	104.9	185.7	71.5	55.7	3365	13.1	17.9	4	37.4	41.3	36.6	34.6
Volvo C70 2-door convertible	104.9	185.7	71.5	56.3	3601	7.9	17.9	4	39.0	41.3	36.6	34.6
Volvo S60 4-door sedan	106.9	180.2	71.9	56.2	3146	13.9	21.1	5	38.9	42.6	37.9	33.3
Volvo V70 4-door wagon	108.5	185.4	71.0	58.6	3366	72.8	21.1	5	39.3	42.6	38.9	35.2

LUXURY CARS

Acura RL 4-door sedan	114.6	196.6	71.4	56.5	3858	14.0	18.0	5	38.8	42.1	36.8	35.4
BMW 5-Series 4-door sedan	111.4	188.0	70.9	56.5	3495	11.1	18.5	5	38.7	41.7	37.8	34.2
BMW 5-Series 4-door wagon	111.4	189.2	70.9	56.7	3726	65.2	18.5	5	38.7	41.7	38.5	34.2
BMW 7-Series 4-door sedan	115.4	196.2	73.3	56.5	4255	13.0	22.5	5	37.7	41.9	37.9	36.7
BMW 7-Series 4-door sedan	120.9	201.7	73.3	56.1	4288	13.0	25.1	5	37.7	41.9	38.1	41.9
Cadillac DeVille 4-door sedan	115.3	207.0	74.4	56.7	4049	19.1	18.5	6	39.1	42.4	38.3	43.2
Cadillac Eldorado 2-door coupe	108.0	200.6	75.5	53.6	3814	15.3	19.0	5	37.8	42.6	38.3	35.5
Cadillac Seville 4-door sedan	112.2	201.0	75.0	55.7	3970	15.7	18.5	5	38.2	42.5	38.0	38.2
Jaguar S-Type 4-door sedan	114.5	191.3	71.6	55.7	3816	13.1	18.4	5	38.6	43.1	36.4	37.7
Jaguar XJ Sedan 4-door sedan	113.0	197.8	70.8	52.7	3946	12.7	23.1	5	37.2	41.2	36.3	34.3

CONSUMER GUIDE™ 539

SPECIFICATIONS

LUXURY CARS CONTINUED

	Wheelbase, in.	Overall length, in.	Overall width, in.	Overall height, in.	Curb weight, lbs.	Cargo volume, cu. ft.	Fuel capacity, gals.	Seating capacity	Front head room, in.	Max. front leg room, in.	Rear head room, in.	Min. rear leg room, in.
Jaguar XJ Sedan 4-door sedan	117.9	202.7	70.8	53.2	3988	12.7	23.1	5	37.2	41.2	36.9	39.2
Jaguar XK8 2-door coupe	101.9	187.4	72.0	50.5	3726	11.1	19.9	4	37.0	43.0	33.3	NA
Jaguar XK8 2-door convertible	101.9	187.4	72.0	51.0	3962	9.5	19.8	4	37.0	43.0	33.2	NA
Lexus GS 300/430 4-door sedan	110.2	189.2	70.9	56.7	3638	14.8	19.8	5	39.0	44.5	37.4	34.3
Lexus LS 430 4-door sedan	115.2	196.7	72.0	58.7	3955	20.2	22.2	5	39.6	44.0	38.0	37.6
Lincoln Continental 4-door sedan	109.0	208.5	73.6	56.0	3848	18.4	20.0	6	38.9	41.9	38.0	38.0
Lincoln Town Car 4-door sedan	117.7	215.3	78.2	58.0	4047	21.0	19.0	6	39.3	42.6	37.6	41.1
Lincoln Town Car 4-door sedan	123.7	221.3	78.2	58.0	4215	20.6	19.0	6	39.3	42.6	37.6	47.1
Mercedes-Benz CL-Class 2-door coupe	113.6	196.6	73.1	55.0	4115	12.3	23.3	4	36.9	41.7	36.8	30.8
Mercedes-Benz CLK-Class 2-door coupe	105.9	180.2	67.8	54.0	3213	11.0	16.4	4	36.9	41.9	35.8	31.2
Mercedes-Benz CLK-Class 2-door conv.	105.9	180.2	67.8	54.3	3566	9.4	16.4	4	37.5	41.9	36.5	27.4
Mercedes-Benz E-Class 4-door sedan	111.5	189.4	70.8	56.7	3491	15.3	21.1	5	37.6	41.3	37.2	36.1
Mercedes-Benz E-Class 4-door wagon	111.5	190.4	70.8	59.3	3739	95.0	18.5	7	38.6	41.3	37.0	36.1
Mercedes-Benz S-Class 4-door sedan	121.5	203.1	73.1	56.9	4133	15.4	23.2	5	37.6	41.3	38.4	40.3
Saab 9-5 4-door sedan	106.4	189.2	70.5	57.0	3470	15.9	18.5	5	38.7	42.4	37.6	36.6
Saab 9-5 4-door wagon	106.4	189.3	70.5	58.9	3620	73.0	18.5	5	38.7	42.4	38.2	36.6
Volvo S80 4-door sedan	109.9	189.8	72.1	57.2	3602	14.2	21.1	5	38.9	42.2	37.6	35.9

SPORTS COUPES

	Wheelbase, in.	Overall length, in.	Overall width, in.	Overall height, in.	Curb weight, lbs.	Cargo volume, cu. ft.	Fuel capacity, gals.	Seating capacity	Front head room, in.	Max. front leg room, in.	Rear head room, in.	Min. rear leg room, in.
Acura Integra 2-door hatchback	101.2	172.4	67.3	52.6	2643	13.3	13.2	4	38.6	42.7	35.0	28.1
Acura Integra 4-door sedan	103.1	178.1	67.3	53.9	2703	11.0	13.2	5	38.9	42.2	36.0	32.7
Chevrolet Camaro 2-door hatchback	101.1	193.5	74.1	51.2	3306	12.9	16.8	4	37.2	42.9	35.2	26.8
Chevrolet Camaro 2-door convertible	101.1	193.5	74.1	51.8	3500	7.6	16.8	4	38.7	42.9	39.4	26.8
Ford Mustang 2-door coupe	101.3	183.2	73.1	53.1	3114	10.9	15.7	4	38.1	42.6	35.5	29.9
Ford Mustang 2-door convertible	101.3	183.2	73.1	53.2	3254	7.7	15.7	4	38.1	42.6	35.8	29.9
Ford ZX2 2-door coupe	98.4	175.2	67.4	52.3	2478	11.8	12.8	4	38.0	42.5	35.1	33.4
Honda Prelude 2-door coupe	101.8	178.0	69.0	51.8	2954	8.7	15.9	5	37.9	43.0	35.3	28.1

SPECIFICATIONS

Hyundai Tiburon 2-door hatchback	97.4	170.9	68.1	51.7	2633	12.8	14.5	4	38.0	43.1	29.9
Mercury Cougar 2-door hatchback	106.4	185.0	69.6	52.2	3013	24.0	15.5	4	37.8	42.6	33.2
Mitsubishi Eclipse 2-door hatchback	100.8	175.4	68.9	51.6	2822	16.9	16.4	4	37.9	42.3	30.0
Mitsubishi Eclipse 2-door convertible	100.8	175.4	68.9	52.8	3042	7.2	16.4	4	39.4	42.3	29.4
Pontiac Firebird 2-door hatchback	101.1	193.3	74.4	51.2	3323	33.7	16.8	4	37.2	43.0	35.2
Pontiac Firebird 2-door convertible	101.1	193.3	74.4	51.8	3402	12.9	16.8	4	38.7	43.0	39.4
Toyota Celica 2-door hatchback	102.3	170.4	68.3	51.4	2425	16.9	14.5	4	38.4	44.0	28.8
Volkswagen Cabrio 2-door convertible	97.4	160.4	66.7	56.0	2831	8.0	13.7	4	38.7	42.3	27.0
Volkswagen New Beetle 2-door hatchback	98.9	161.1	67.9	59.5	2769	12.0	14.5	4	41.3	39.4	33.5

SPORTS & GT CARS

BMW Z3 Series 2-door convertible	96.3	158.5	66.6	50.7	2701	5.0	13.5	2	37.6	41.8	—
BMW Z3 Series 2-door hatchback	96.3	158.5	68.5	51.4	2943	9.0	13.5	2	36.7	41.8	—
Chevrolet Corvette 2-door hatchback	104.5	179.7	73.6	47.7	3212	24.8	18.5	2	37.9	42.7	—
Chevrolet Corvette 2-door coupe	104.5	179.7	73.6	47.7	3130	13.3	18.5	2	37.8	42.7	—
Chevrolet Corvette 2-door convertible	104.5	179.7	73.6	47.8	3207	13.9	18.5	2	37.9	42.7	—
Mazda Miata 2-door convertible	89.2	155.7	66.0	48.3	2387	5.1	12.7	2	37.1	42.7	—

MINIVANS

Chevrolet Astro 3-door van	111.2	189.8	77.5	74.9	4323	170.4	27.0	8	39.2	41.6	36.5
Chevrolet Venture 4-door van	112.0	186.9	72.0	67.4	3699	119.8	20.0	7	39.9	39.9	36.9
Chevrolet Venture 4-door van	120.0	200.9	72.0	68.1	3838	140.7	25.0	8	39.9	39.9	39.0
Chrysler Town & Country 4-door van	119.3	200.5	78.6	68.9	4087	146.9	20.0	7	39.6	40.6	39.7
Chrysler Voyager 4-door van	113.3	189.1	78.6	68.9	3920	127.5	20.0	7	39.8	40.6	36.6
Dodge Caravan 4-door van	113.3	189.1	78.6	68.9	3920	127.4	20.0	7	39.8	40.6	36.6
Dodge Caravan 4-door van	119.3	200.5	78.6	68.9	4090	146.9	20.0	7	39.6	40.6	39.7
Ford Windstar 3-door van	120.7	202.8	76.6	66.1	3890	139.0	26.0	7	39.3	40.7	38.6

SPECIFICATIONS

MINIVANS CONTINUED

	Wheelbase, in.	Overall length, in.	Overall width, in.	Overall height, in.	Curb weight, lbs.	Cargo volume, cu. ft.	Fuel capacity, gals.	Seating capacity	Front head room, in.	Max. front leg room, in.	Rear head room, in.	Min. rear leg room, in.
GMC Safari 3-door van	111.2	189.8	77.5	74.9	4323	170.4	27.0	8	39.2	41.6	37.9	36.5
Honda Odyssey 4-door van	118.1	201.2	76.3	68.5	4248	146.1	20.0	7	41.2	41.0	40.0	40.0
Mazda MPV 4-door van	111.8	187.0	72.1	68.7	3657	127.0	18.5	7	41.0	40.8	39.3	37.0
Mercury Villager 4-door van	112.2	194.9	74.9	70.1	3997	127.6	20.0	7	39.7	39.9	40.1	36.4
Nissan Quest 4-door van	112.2	194.6	74.9	64.2	3915	135.6	20.0	7	39.7	39.9	39.9	36.4
Oldsmobile Silhouette 4-door van	120.0	201.4	72.2	68.1	3948	141.9	25.0	7	39.9	39.9	39.3	39.0
Pontiac Montana 4-door van	112.0	187.3	72.0	67.4	3803	119.8	20.0	8	39.9	39.9	38.9	36.9
Pontiac Montana 4-door van	121.0	200.9	72.0	68.2	3942	140.7	25.0	8	39.9	39.9	39.3	39.0
Toyota Sienna 4-door van	114.2	193.5	73.4	67.3	3881	143.0	21.0	7	40.6	41.9	40.7	36.5

COMPACT SPORT-UTILITY VEHICLES

	Wheelbase, in.	Overall length, in.	Overall width, in.	Overall height, in.	Curb weight, lbs.	Cargo volume, cu. ft.	Fuel capacity, gals.	Seating capacity	Front head room, in.	Max. front leg room, in.	Rear head room, in.	Min. rear leg room, in.
Chevrolet Tracker 2-door convertible	86.6	151.8	67.3	66.5	2811	33.7	14.8	4	40.9	41.4	39.5	35.9
Chevrolet Tracker 4-door wagon	97.6	162.8	67.3	66.3	2987	44.7	17.4	5	39.9	41.4	39.6	35.9
Ford Escape 4-door wagon	103.1	173.0	70.1	67.0	3238	63.3	15.3	5	40.4	41.6	39.2	36.4
Honda CR-V 4-door wagon	103.2	177.6	68.9	65.9	3126	67.2	15.3	5	40.5	41.5	39.2	36.7
Hyundai Santa Fe 4-door wagon	103.1	177.2	72.6	65.9	3455	100.7	17.2	5	39.6	41.6	39.2	36.8
Isuzu Rodeo Sport 2-door convertible	96.9	168.0	71.4	67.0	3329	62.4	17.7	5	38.9	42.1	37.3	33.3
Jeep Wrangler 2-door convertible	93.4	155.4	66.7	71.1	3105	55.2	19.0	4	42.3	41.1	40.6	34.9
Kia Sportage 2-door convertible	92.9	156.4	68.1	65.0	3230	39.4	14.0	4	39.6	41.3	38.2	31.0
Kia Sportage 4-door wagon	104.3	170.3	68.1	65.0	3352	55.4	15.8	5	39.6	44.5	37.8	31.1
Mazda Tribute 4-door wagon	103.1	173.0	71.9	69.9	3245	63.9	16.4	5	40.3	41.7	38.9	36.9
Subaru Forester 4-door wagon	99.4	175.6	68.3	65.0	3140	63.1	15.9	5	40.2	43.0	39.6	33.4
Suzuki Vitara 2-door convertible	86.6	152.0	67.3	66.8	2778	33.7	14.8	5	40.9	41.4	39.5	30.5
Suzuki Vitara 4-door wagon	97.6	164.6	70.1	67.8	3197	44.7	16.8	5	39.9	41.4	39.6	30.5
Toyota RAV4 4-door wagon	98.0	165.1	68.3	65.3	2877	68.3	14.7	5	41.3	42.4	38.4	32.6

SPECIFICATIONS

MIDSIZE SPORT-UTILITY VEHICLES

Acura MDX 4-door wagon	106.3	188.5	76.3	68.7	4328	81.5	19.2	7	38.7	41.5	39.0	37.8
BMW X5 4-door wagon	111.0	183.7	73.7	67.2	4519	54.4	24.3	5	39.9	39.3	38.5	35.4
Chevrolet Blazer 2-door wagon	100.5	177.3	67.8	64.7	3848	NA	19.0	4	39.6	42.4	38.2	35.6
Chevrolet Blazer 4-door wagon	107.0	183.3	67.8	64.6	4049	67.8	18.0	6	39.6	42.4	38.2	36.3
Dodge Durango 4-door wagon	115.9	193.3	71.5	71.0	4408	88.0	25.0	8	39.8	41.9	40.4	37.3
Ford Explorer 2-door wagon	101.8	180.4	70.2	68.2	3962	71.4	17.5	4	39.4	42.4	39.1	36.6
Ford Explorer 4-door wagon	111.6	190.7	70.2	67.5	4045	79.8	21.0	6	39.9	42.4	39.3	36.8
Ford Explorer crew cab	125.9	205.9	71.8	70.1	4323	—	—	5	39.4	42.4	38.9	37.8
2002 Ford Explorer 4-door wagon	113.7	189.5	72.1	71.9	4334	88.0	20.5	5	39.9	43.9	38.9	37.2
GMC Envoy 4-door wagon	113.0	191.5	72.0	69.8	4442	80.5	22.5	5	39.9	43.1	38.9	38.3
Honda Passport 4-door wagon	106.4	178.2	70.4	68.6	3774	81.1	18.7	5	40.3	42.1	38.3	35.0
Infiniti QX4 4-door wagon	106.3	183.1	72.4	70.7	4352	85.5	21.1	5	38.9	41.7	37.5	31.8
Isuzu Rodeo 4-door wagon	106.4	176.7	70.4	68.8	3651	81.1	21.1	5	39.5	42.1	38.3	35.0
Jeep Cherokee 2-door wagon	101.4	167.5	69.4	64.0	3181	66.0	20.0	5	38.9	41.4	38.0	35.0
Jeep Cherokee 4-door wagon	101.4	167.5	69.4	64.0	3226	66.0	20.0	5	37.7	41.4	38.0	35.0
Jeep Grand Cherokee 4-door wagon	105.9	181.5	72.3	69.4	3972	72.3	20.5	5	37.8	41.4	39.5	35.3
Land Rover Discovery 4-door wagon	100.0	185.2	74.4	76.4	4576	63.3	24.6	7	39.7	41.4	39.5	35.8
Lexus RX 300 4-door wagon	103.0	180.3	71.5	65.7	3924	75.0	19.8	5	40.4	42.3	40.1	37.3
Jeep Cherokee 2-door wagon	101.4	167.5	69.4	64.0	3181	66.0	20.0	5	39.5	40.7	39.2	36.4
Mercedes-Benz M-Class 4-door wagon	111.0	180.6	72.2	69.9	4586	81.2	19.0	5	39.8	40.3	39.7	38.0
Mercury Mountaineer 4-door wagon	111.6	190.7	70.2	70.5	4045	79.1	21.0	5	39.9	42.4	39.3	35.8
2002 Mercury Mountaineer 4-door wagon	113.7	190.7	72.1	71.1	4410	88.0	22.5	7	39.1	38.9	43.9	37.2
Mitsubishi Montero Sport 4-door wagon	107.3	178.3	66.7	65.6	3980	79.3	19.5	5	38.9	42.8	37.3	33.5
Nissan Pathfinder 4-door wagon	106.3	182.7	69.7	67.9	4131	85.3	21.1	5	39.5	41.7	37.5	31.8
Nissan Xterra 4-door wagon	104.3	178.0	70.4	69.4	3668	65.6	19.4	5	38.6	41.4	37.5	32.8
2002 Oldsmobile Bravada 4-door wagon	113.0	190.0	72.0	70.0	4000	80.5	18.7	5	40.3	43.1	39.8	38.3
Pontiac Aztek 4-door wagon	108.3	182.1	73.7	66.7	3778	93.5	18.5	5	39.7	40.5	39.1	38.0
Toyota 4Runner 4-door wagon	105.3	183.3	66.5	67.5	3725	79.8	18.5	5	39.3	42.6	38.7	34.9

CONSUMER GUIDE™ 543

SPECIFICATIONS

MIDSIZE SPORT-UTILITY VEHICLES CONTINUED	Wheelbase, in.	Overall length, in.	Overall width, in.	Overall height, in.	Curb weight, lbs.	Cargo volume, cu. ft.	Fuel capacity, gals.	Seating capacity	Front head room, in.	Max. front leg room, in.	Rear head room, in.	Min. rear leg room, in.
Toyota Highlander 4-door wagon	106.9	184.4	71.5	66.1	3715	NA	19.8	5	40.0	40.7	40.0	36.4

FULL-SIZE SPORT-UTILITY VEHICLES

	Wheelbase, in.	Overall length, in.	Overall width, in.	Overall height, in.	Curb weight, lbs.	Cargo volume, cu. ft.	Fuel capacity, gals.	Seating capacity	Front head room, in.	Max. front leg room, in.	Rear head room, in.	Min. rear leg room, in.
Cadillac Escalade	116.0	198.9	78.9	74.2	5809	138.4	26.0	7	40.7	41.3	39.0	39.1
Chevrolet Tahoe 4-door wagon	116.0	198.9	78.9	76.3	5050	104.6	26.0	9	40.7	41.3	39.4	38.6
Chevrolet Suburban 4-door wagon	130.0	219.3	78.8	75.4	5123	138.4	33.0	9	40.7	41.3	39.0	39.1
Ford Excursion 4-door wagon	137.1	226.7	79.9	80.2	7087	146.4	44.0	9	41.0	42.3	41.1	40.5
Ford Expedition 4-door wagon	119.1	204.6	78.6	76.6	5345	110.7	26.0	9	39.8	40.9	39.8	38.9
GMC Yukon/Denali 4-door wagon	116.0	198.8	78.8	76.5	5113	104.6	26.0	9	40.7	41.3	39.4	38.6
GMC Yukon XL/Denali XL 4-door wagon	130.0	219.3	78.9	75.7	5219	131.6	32.5	9	40.7	41.3	39.4	38.6
Isuzu Trooper 4-door wagon	108.7	187.8	69.5	72.2	4455	90.2	22.5	5	39.8	40.8	39.8	39.1
Land Rover Range Rover 4-door wagon	108.1	185.5	74.4	71.6	4960	58.0	24.6	5	38.1	42.6	38.2	36.5
Lexus LX 470 4-door wagon	112.2	192.5	76.4	72.8	5401	90.4	25.4	8	40.0	42.3	39.4	34.3
Lincoln Navigator 4-door wagon	119.0	204.8	79.9	76.7	5746	109.9	30.0	8	39.8	42.8	39.8	39.7
Mitsubishi Montero 4-door wagon	109.5	188.9	73.9	73.1	4540	82.0	23.8	7	41.4	42.7	40.2	37.6
Toyota Land Cruiser 4-door wagon	112.2	192.5	76.4	73.2	5115	90.8	25.4	8	40.6	42.3	39.8	34.3
Toyota Sequoia 4-door wagon	118.1	203.9	78.0	74.0	5270	128.1	21.7	8	41.1	41.6	40.6	38.4